MW00681879

Policing the Banks

Accountability Mechanisms for the Financial Sector

MAARTJE VAN PUTTEN

McGill-Queen's University Press

Montreal & Kingston · London · Ithaca

© McGill-Queen's University Press 2008
ISBN 978-0-7735-3401-8 (cloth)
ISBN 978-0-7735-3402-5 (paper)

Legal deposit third quarter 2008
Bibliothèque nationale du Québec

Printed in Canada on acid-free paper that is 100% ancient forest free
(100% post-consumer recycled), processed chlorine free.

McGill-Queen's University Press acknowledges the support of the
Canada Council for the Arts for our publishing program. We also
acknowledge the financial support of the Government of Canada through
the Book Publishing Industry Development Program (BPIDP) for our
publishing activities.

Library and Archives Canada Cataloguing in Publication

Policing the banks: accountability mechanisms for the financial sector /
Maartje van Putten.

Includes bibliographical references and index.
ISBN 978-0-7735-3401-8 (bnd)
ISBN 978-0-7735-3402-5 (pbk)

1. Banks and banking, International. 2. Investments, Foreign – Developing countries.
3. Private banks – Developing countries. 4. Social responsibility of business –
Developing countries. 5. Investments, Foreign – Social aspects. 6. Investments,
Foreign – Environmental aspects. I. Putten, Maartje van, 1951–

HG1725.P63 2008   332.1'5   C2008-902599-7

This book was typeset by Interscript in 10/12 Baskerville.

The ultimate democracy does not fear people who speak up if their lives are interrupted by the plans of authorities, whether local, national, or international, even if the planning is done with the best intentions and focuses on the good of all.

I dedicate this work to the citizens of the world who take their destiny in their own hands, who are not afraid to address their problems to the right authorities, and who demand attention for their causes using peaceful means.

Contents

Abbreviations

ADB	Asian Development Bank
AfDB	African Development Bank
BCBS	Basel Committee on Banking Supervision
BIC	Bank Information Center
BIC	Bank Inspection Committee (of the ADB)
BIS	Bank for International Settlements
BTC	Baku-Tbilisi-Ceyhan
CAO	compliance advisor ombudsman (of the IFC)
CCO	chief compliance officer
CEC	Commission for Environmental Cooperation
CEDHA	Center for Human Rights and Environment
CEE	Central Eastern Europe
CERES	Coalition for Environmentally Responsible Economies
CIEL	Center for International Environmental Law
CODE	Committee on Development Effectiveness
CRMU	Compliance Review and Mediation Unit (of the AfDB)
CRP	Compliance Review Panel
CSR	corporate social responsibility
DMC	developing member country
EA	environmental assessment
EBRD	European Bank for Reconstruction and Development
ECB	European Central Bank
ECA	export credit agency
ED	executive director
EDF	Environmental Defense Fund
EDF	European Development Fund
EIA	environmental impact assessment
EIB	European Investment Bank
EIF	European Investment Fund
EMP	environmental management plan
EP	European Parliament

EPs	Equator Principles
EPFI	Equator Principle financial institution
EPs	Equator Principles
EPs II	Equator Principles II
EU	European Union
FDI	foreign direct investment
FI	financial institution
FOMC	Federal Open Market Committee
FSF	Finance Stability Forum
GRI	Global Reporting Initiative
IADB	Inter-American Development Bank
IAM	independent accountability mechanism
IBRD	International Bank for Reconstruction and Development
ICC	International Chamber of Commerce
ICSID	International Center for Settlement of Investment Disputes
IDA	International Development Association
IEO	Independent Evaluation Office (of the IMF)
IFC	International Finance Corporation
IFI	international financial institution
ILO	International Labor Organization
IMF	International Monetary Fund
INTACH	Indian National Trust for Art and Cultural Heritage
IRM	Independent Recourse Mechanism (of EBRD)
ISO	International Standards Organization
IUCN	International Union for the Conservation of Nature
JBIC	Japan Bank for International Cooperation
MAI	Multilateral Agreement on Investment
MDB	multilateral development bank
MFI	multilateral financial institution
MIGA	Multilateral Investment Guarantee Agency
NAAEC	North American Agreement on Environmental Cooperation
NAFTA	North American Free Trade Agreement
NBA	Narmada Bachao Andolan
NC	Netherlands Committee
NCP	National Contact Point
NGO	nongovernmental organization
ODA	official development assistance
OECD	Organization for Economic Cooperation and Development
OED	Operations Evaluation Department
PAD	project appraisal document
PRSP	poverty reduction strategy paperó
SPF	special project facilitator (of the ADB)
TES	thermal electric power station
TNC	transnational corporation
UDHR	Universal Declaration of Human Rights

UN   United Nations
UNCTAD   United Nations Conference on Trade and Development
UNDP   United Nations Development Program
UNECE   United Nations Economic Commission for Europe
UNEP   United Nations Environment Programme
UNEP FI   United Nations Environment Programme Finance Initiative
WB   World Bank
WTO   World Trade Organization
WWF   World Wildlife Fund

Foreword

JAMES MACNEILL

In 1993, on the eve of its 50th anniversary (and following a period of intense pressure for reform), the World Bank established an independent Inspection Panel to receive complaints of harm from those directly affected by its projects and to report the results of its investigations directly to its Board of Governors, the bank's highest governing body, as well as to the public at large. It was an unprecedented move. Never before had an international organization given a voice to the most vulnerable of those it intended to serve, making itself *accountable* to civil society for complying, or failing to comply, with its own policies and procedures. Of course, no private bank or corporation had even contemplated doing so. Within a decade, the panel had evolved into an effective institution; it became a model for similar mechanisms in the other multilateral development banks (MDBs), and, to the surprise of many, a few private financial institutions slowly began to move in the same direction.

In *Policing the Banks*, my former colleague Maartje van Putten provides a unique, frank, and candid account of these remarkable and historic advances.

When I joined the Inspection Panel in 1997, the board had just confirmed its mandate following a review of its first two years of operation. As a result, my colleagues and I felt, as bank president Jim Wolfensohn said in welcoming me, that with our mandate now clarified, we could look forward to the future with confidence. But the struggle for a meaningful accountability mechanism had not ended with the first review; it had just begun. Within a few months, the board launched a second review, which took two years and proved highly contentious.

Accountability is fundamentally a question of power, and in giving a voice to civil society, the panel was disturbing the comfortable balance of power that had reigned so long within this historically closed institution. The panel had begun to provide those affected by bank projects with an avenue to the board, and panel members had taken very seriously their mandate to investigate management's responsibility for any alleged harm suffered. Management didn't like this and found allies in some large borrowing countries who realized that the panel process would necessarily throw light on any harm done to their citizens as a result of their own actions on a project.

During the two years of the review (near the end of which I became chairman), the panel struggled against frequent attempts to undermine this evolving but still fragile mechanism. We fought to ensure the panel's independence, the strength of our mandate, the existence of clear, transparent, fair, and usable procedures, and our continued right to investigate alleged harm to people affected by a project, whether the source of that harm was the bank or the borrowing government. We lost our battle to investigate the latter. Historically, the bank has resolved a number of intractable issues with agreement to observe certain fictions. Although the second review strengthened the panel in a number of ways, particularly the board's agreement to acquiesce to panel recommendations for investigations (provided certain criteria were met), it imposed a new fiction on the panel: namely that any harm identified by the panel should be attributed exclusively to management's failure to comply with the bank's operational policies. Patent nonsense, of course, but it meant that borrowing countries could rest easy.

As it happened, all was put to the test in the most controversial project in the bank's then fifty-six-year history. Shortly after the board approved its second clarification of the panel's mandate, we received a claim concerning the Western Poverty Reduction Project in the province of Qinghai, China, next door to Tibet. The claim was carried to us via a chain of Tibetan monks, ending in the office of the International Campaign for Tibet in Washington. A little more than a year later, on 7 July 2000, after a comprehensive investigation by the panel and several episodes of serious stress between the bank, China, its largest client, and several Western shareholders led by the United States, China withdrew the project from the bank's portfolio in a board meeting marked by high drama. During its investigation the panel was tested on several fronts. Initially, the Chinese authorities demanded the identities of the claimants; we made it clear that under our rules their identities would remain known to the panel alone. Later, they indicated they would refuse visas to any consultant or interpreter they did not approve; when we made it clear that any such refusal would abort the investigation, they backed away. At one point, pressures became so intense that, following consultation, my colleagues and I let it be known that we would resign if necessary to protect the panel's independence.

When establishing criteria for selection of panel members in 1993, the then board said that members "shall be elected on the basis of ... their integrity and their independence from Bank Management." As a result of the China investigation, I became convinced that pressures to compromise the panel's independence would always exist and that, although selection criteria (and the selection process) do matter, only the panel members themselves could guarantee the panel's independence. Without independence, as Ms van Putten says, the panel has no meaning.

During our investigations, I often felt constrained by other bank fictions, some deeply rooted in the founding Articles of Agreement. On my first day at the institution, I was told that "the bank does not engage in political activity." Having witnessed over a long career how decisions to finance hydroelectric, irrigation, and other large projects are made, and having observed how they created both losers and winners, I knew this was silly. Anyone alert and over the age of sixteen knows that structural adjustment projects, agricultural, energy, mining, and other types of projects the bank supports, have significant political implications. Yet the "we're not in politics" fiction is repeated by board members and bank officials like a mantra. As Jim Wolfenshon says in a fascinating interview with Maartje presented in appendix 3, "the suggestion that we be nonpolitical is complete nonsense." And, he adds, "If you get involved in food or education projects, or a housing project, or an environmental project, every one of those things has political implications." Throughout the interview, he is justifiably proud of several instances in which he took actions that were, he says, "political," as in the case of Chad. Yet, speaking of our China investigation later in the same interview, he declares: "you in the panel are not supposed to be involved in the political aspects." Given his earlier assertion that such projects have "political implications," it is a bit of a mystery to me how the panel might investigate such projects without appearing to be political, at least to those who don't like the results of the investigation. We did our very best to be objective and fair, but sooner or later, the bank must address this absurd fiction. In the meantime, I am sure the panel will continue to find honest and more or less "politically correct" ways to conduct its investigations and write its reports.

For over five decades, this same fiction paralyzed bank efforts to combat corruption. The bank's establishment was firm: corruption was political and, therefore, a no man's land for bank officials. It was Jim Wolfensohn who smashed the myth. He redefined corruption as an economic and social issue and in a courageous speech at the bank's 1996 annual meeting in Hong Kong, he attacked the "cancer of corruption" that was impeding the advance of developing economies. The myth in shatters, the bank was able to implement necessary measures: a 24-hour hotline, a "sanctions committee" to punish companies and individuals guilty of corruption, a Department of Institutional Integrity, and other initiatives. Today, most bank officials are proud of this breakthrough.

As the panel found, bank projects can also raise serious concerns about violations of human rights. These issues are of course political, and the bank needs a similar breakthrough on them. I was extremely frustrated by our inability to deal with them in a straightforward manner, a frustration shared by Ms van Putten from the moment she joined the panel, as she underlines throughout the book. We often cited what were clear violations of human rights in our reports but without using the term. In our China investigation, however, we deliberately broke the constraints imposed by our mandate. We described witnessing disturbing and dramatic examples of "a climate of fear" among people we interviewed, mainly Tibetans, in the proposed project area. We reported having to visit sites without prior notification, to change our itinerary without advance notice, and to break away surreptitiously from our "handlers" in the evenings in order to interview other Tibetans who were afraid to reveal their identities. Anyone following recent events can understand why. In our 1991 report on the Chad Petroleum and Pipeline Project, we included a special box highlighting our "Concern over Human Rights in Chad." We could do no less. Chad's president had arrested the individual who had submitted the claim to the panel, opposition leader Ngarlejy Yorongar. We visited him in Paris after he had been released at the insistence of Jim Wolfensohn (who threatened to otherwise cancel the project) and saw the signs of appalling torture on his body. We reported this and quoted Amnesty International to the effect that "The efforts to silence Yorongar are not an isolated incident. Chad's overall human rights record is abysmal."

There is some evidence that the bank is beginning to recognize that it should no longer hide behind its Articles of Agreement but rather accept at least a degree of accountability when its projects result in violations of human rights. But it has been moving much too slowly. Twelve years after Jim Wolfensohn found a way to address corruption, the bank should also have found a way to address human rights violations. Why not use the same device and redefine human rights as an economic and social issue? As Ms van Putten points out, human rights violations, like corruption, can affect the investment climate in a recipient country.

There are a number of other holdovers from the attitudes and culture of the mid-1940s when the Bretton Woods institutions were established. They were, for example, granted immunity and are thus protected from any legal action that individuals, corporations, or governments might wish to bring against them. Anyone harmed by the projects these institutions finance, however justified their claim, is unable to seek redress in their national courts: he or she is simply out of luck. In an era when financial institutions, including multinationals, are expected to abide by the laws of the countries in which they operate and to assume responsibility and liability for their conduct, this is no longer tenable. In time, I expect, it too will change.

The most significant changes needed, however, concern the private sector. With private flows of foreign direct investment now dwarfing official flows, private financial institutions are in a position to exercise tremendous power over the economic policies of developing countries. The projects they finance exceed by far in both number and cumulative scale those financed by the MDBs and similarly impact the livelihoods of increasing numbers of vulnerable people. At the moment, however, they are effectively accountable to no one, enjoying rights and power without responsibility. But even here, there has been some movement for change. A group of private banks has adopted what are called the Equator Principles. In doing so, they have agreed to work with the same policies or standards as the World Bank when financing projects in those countries in which the bank and other MDBs operate as well. This may be a significant step forward. It will be impossible to tell, however, without a good deal more information, as Ms van Putten explains in her excellent chapter on this development. Accountability requires a degree of transparency and information disclosure that private banks are not accustomed to providing. It also requires a mechanism, which only the participating banks themselves can establish, that can hold them accountable for compliance with the policies they have adopted.

Ms van Putten's frank account of the evolution and work of the Inspection Panel has stirred my memories of many shared adventures in various parts of the world – the night train from Calcutta to Ranchi, the protests at our public hearings in Uganda, my apartment in Foggy Bottom on 9/11, where the panel retired after the bank was evacuated and where we continued to work on an urgent report while trying to call worried family members. And many others.

This is a timely book and required reading by those involved in, or simply concerned about, the need to make international financial institutions more accountable and development assistance more responsive to the needs of the world's poor.

James MacNeill, OC
Chairman, Inspection Panel, 1/3/99 – 31/12/01
Ottawa, Ontario
May 2008

Acknowledgments

This book would not exist without Professor John Rijsman of Tilburg University in the Netherlands and Dr Mark Curtis of McGill University in Canada. While we walked through the streets of Paris, John convinced me that I should write about my experience as a member of the World Bank Inspection Panel. I am very grateful to him for having done so. I do not know anyone who can be as encouraging as John. Enormous gratitude also goes to Mark for his constant guidance. Soon after the idea was born to do this study, he offered me an office at the MacDonald Campus of McGill University where I could work in silence and experience the atmosphere of one of the world's best universities. The structure of the questionnaire discussed in chapter 7 was written out on a blackboard in that office and further discussed on the banks of the Saint Lawrence River when outside temperatures were −32°C. This work definitely came about with assistance from both Tilburg University and McGill University.

I would never have met Mark in not for Professor Michel Bouchard of the Université de Montréal, at the time director general of the Secrétariat francophone de l'Association internationale pour l'évaluation d'impacts. From Michel, I regularly received helpful guidance and suggestions along the way.

I thank Eduardo Abbott, executive secretary of the Inspection Panel, for his advice and checks on the history and procedures of the panel; my former colleague Jim MacNeill, former chairman of the panel, who always responded to my calls, even during his work in the field at the Baku-Tbilisi-Ceyhan (BTC) oil pipeline; and likewise Daniel McGlinchey, assistant to Congressman Barney Frank, for his insights into the minutes of hearings held at Capitol Hill on the making of the Inspection Panel. Johan Frijns, coordinator of BankTrack, supported me in the constant updating of the developments of the Equator Principles, as did André Abadie of ABN-AMRO Bank. The more than seventy experts who filled out the questionnaire have added great value to the study, and I am grateful to all of them, particularly Robert Goodland. A list of the experts who contributed to this study is included as appendix 4. Further thanks for all kinds of support go to Angie Nash at the library of the World Bank, Jaqueline den Otter and Marjolijn van Milligen at the World Bank, Bram Schim van der Loeff at the European Investment Bank, Tom Goossens of the Free University in Amsterdam, and Henk van Dam at the Royal Tropical Institute in Amsterdam.

Last but not least, I am most grateful to my family, the "Rutten-van Putten clan," of whom Michiel, Laurens, Swaan, Pieter, Eveline, Renske, Roos, Floris, Dana, and Sander have been "affected people" as a result of this van Putten project. I wonder whether I have been in compliance with family values over recent years.

Introduction

Pictures of demonstrations and banners in front of the World Bank head-quarters in Washington, DC, a few hundred feet from the White House, always feed into the image of the World Bank as an unassailable bastion. The institution is considered a leader in global economic affairs, and its activities have major impacts on the lives of millions of people. In this light, it was a historic moment when the bank's Board of Governors decided to establish an independent Inspection Panel to look into the allegations of people who were being harmed or could be harmed by activities financed by the institution. For the first time, an important international institution gave voice to such people, a somewhat courageous decision. After all, by establishing the panel, the bank had made itself vulnerable to critics from the outside. The decision was initiated mainly by the efforts of US nongovernmental organizations (NGOs) in cooperation with the US Congress and was welcomed by most of the bank's executive directors, who at the time wanted to have more control over management's activities.

Jim Wolfensohn, president of the World Bank until June 2005, wrote this in 1998 about the panel:

> When the Board of Directors of the World Bank created the Inspection Panel five years ago, it created an unprecedented means for increasing the transparency and accountability of the bank's operations. This was a first of its kind for an international organization – the creation of an independent mechanism to respond to claims by those whom we are most intent on helping that they have been adversely affected by the projects we finance. By giving private citizens – and especially the poor – a new means of access to the Bank, it has empowered and given voice to those we most need to hear. At the same time, it has served the Bank itself through ensuring that we really are fulfilling our mandate of improving conditions for the world's poorest people. The Inspection

Panel tells us whether we are following our own policies and procedures, which are intended to protect the interests of those affected by
our projects as well as the environment. In testament to the success
of this approach, other international financial institutions have seen its
value and have followed suit.[1]

And so it is.

This book is written with the notion that at this time someone particularly needs to describe the history of the establishment of the World Bank
Inspection Panel and the driving forces behind it, taking into account what
hindrances the panel has been confronted with regarding its mandate and
operations, how the panel became the role model for other multilateral financial institutions (MFIs), and finally, how the private financial sector today is being called upon to create similar accountability mechanisms. This
book is about the opportunities that citizens of the globe today have to express their problems and protect their rights when foreign direct investment of the financial world impacts upon their lives.

As a member of the Inspection Panel from October 1999 to the end of
September 2004, I took the opportunity to collect information and look at
the developments. When I was appointed, it was shortly after the second
revision of the resolution that had established the panel. The mandate of
the panel then became stronger just as it was being confronted with several
very complex and much-disputed World Bank projects on which it had to
conduct investigations. With the amended resolution, the panel's mandate
somewhat expanded, and this had immediate effects on the workload of
the panel. In June 2007 I was appointed one of the first three members of
the Independent Review Mechanism of the African Development Bank, an
accountability mechanism somewhat similar to the Inspection Panel. So all
the written material and the conclusions in this study have to be understood within the context of my experiences.

This work is definitely not complete and may be only the beginning of
more studies in the field of accountability mechanisms for financial institutions. Nevertheless, I regard what is written here in the first place as an
asset for officials both in management and at the executive level of the financial institutions that are involved daily with those policies and procedures of their institutions that are intended to protect the environment
and living conditions of people in the project areas. If the projects they
work on are not in compliance, then the projects may need to become
subject to an independent problem-solving mechanism or accountability
mechanism. The present work will also be useful for politicians, for officials of the member countries of the multilateral financial institutions, and
for the managers of private financial institutions. For them, it is essential to
understand the background of the developments that led to the establishment of the mechanisms and the weaknesses that still exist in mandates of

the mechanisms. Likewise, this work could be helpful for all those who seriously study the global financial arena and are concerned about the economic impacts from societal, legal, and environmental points of view. Last and certainly not least, the information contained in these pages may also help to further empower nongovernmental agencies and watchdog organizations, which are still out there working to help the vulnerable find their way through the doors of the institutions.

That most studies about accountability mechanisms, compliance mechanisms, and review panels – and more specifically the Inspection Panel – have been done by lawyers was a hindrance and challenge. So far, accountability mechanisms have been structured mostly within a rather legalistic framework. It is my impression that "accountability" and "compliance" are the words used most in a legal context. I come from another corner of the playing field, namely sociology and community work. Lawyers and social workers do not always use the same terminology or find each other on the same wavelength when formulating a problem or its solution. To me, law is the last resort when other solutions for problems cannot be found. For the same reason, it is evident that each discipline complements the other. Still, for me, understanding the rationale behind the structure of accountability mechanisms was a very legalistic activity and a matter of becoming acclimatized to the world of jurists and lawyers.

From the starting point of social science, I wanted to examine the necessity of accountability mechanisms at the present time for the international financial world and to explore what type of format and what kind of mandate they should have. That the mechanisms have existed for over ten years gives rise to the risk that the mechanisms are becoming taken for granted. It could be forgotten that an international group of activists and politicians (see chapter 3) had to struggle with a closed institution that in the beginning certainly did not want to discuss its work and results with the public. The danger of this possibility is that the original idea and meaning of the mechanism will be lost.

The main hypothesis of my work is that like multilateral financial institutions, private banks have to be accountable for the effects of their actions. At present, it is my conviction that to fulfil their goals they need to create a problem-solving mechanism (ombudsman function) and an independent accountability mechanism with a clear and transparent structure, procedures, and mandate. The methodology I have chosen is empirical and can be described as participatory observational research.

In the short history of the Inspection Panel, I want to distinguish four main (social) processes that occurred in the order below:

- A period of criticism toward the institution (World Bank) (see chapter 2)
- A demand for more control, accountability, and structure (see chapters 3 and 4)

- The establishment of the accountability mechanism and its structure and working practices (see chapters 3 and 6)
- The expectation that the present accountability mechanism provides an answer to a lack of independent and democratic control mechanisms in a globalized world (see chapter 7)

The last phase, or process, the awareness that the present accountability mechanism may provide answers to a present global demand, is where we are at present. This research is part of that process. Chapter 7 contains the outcomes of a questionnaire concerning the role and mandate of such mechanisms.

I could have chosen between several quantitative research methods, such as a questionnaire with quantitative analyses of the responses, a questionnaire with open questions, or in-depth interviews of key experts in the field. I chose to do all three. In the world of empiricism, which seeks to apply experience to a relevant domain, the most simple and natural method is to speak with the key people. I spoke with people who had a role in the inception of the mechanisms. I spoke with those who are or were members of the World Bank Inspection Panel or members of other mechanisms and their staffs and with those who are very familiar with the working of the mechanisms, inside and outside the institutions.[2] Interviews were conducted with actors from other multilateral financial institutions, from private-sector enterprises, and from NGOs. People were frank and willing to openly discuss events that led to the particular accountability mechanisms in the institutions or enterprises they represented.

The issues raised during the interviews were of a kind that the key actors and experts of accountability mechanisms would recognize. They expected questions from me showing my commitment to the subject. So far as my role as interviewer was concerned, it would have been undesirable if I had given the impression of being entirely neutral and uninvolved. Information gathered during the interviews sometimes contained sensitive material. In such a process all those willing to participate had the right to be assured that such information was to be used only for the correct analysis and interpretation of the study. The aim was to identify principles of a general nature that are relevant for the formation of any accountability mechanism. In this sense, casuistry is only a means. Some of the interviews are to be found in appendix 3 of this study. Most of those involved, with the exception of some specialists in Japan[3] Africa, and the Philippines,[4] work in Europe and North America.

All the participants whom I approached belong to the small world of specialists familiar with accountability mechanisms, being members of the Inspection Panel, staff of the MFIs and transnational corporations (TNCs), representatives of civil society organizations, or recognized experts who have worked outside these entities (e.g., consultants and academics). They all were part of the same focus group and received the same questionnaire.

At the same time, they have different backgrounds, so they can be regarded as naturally different stakeholders who are recognized as such by the stakeholders themselves and by the world community. I divided the experts into four subgroups because of their various responsibilities and constituencies.

Group 1 is formed by experts working for the multilateral financial institutions, such as a former executive director, former and current members of panels, members of the staff of panels, and a group of specialists from the legal departments of the institutions and those responsible for the implementation of the different policies, such as environmental impact assessments. In sum, they all work or have worked for an MFI and are entirely familiar with the accountability mechanisms.

What distinguishes them from the other subgroups is that they are or have been employees of the institutions themselves. Although many of them, if not all, carry a strong commitment to social causes, they tend in the first place to protect or defend the corporate body. Some of them indirectly represent governments in that they all work with or through governments.

Group 2 is formed by experts working for different transnational corporations, most of them for private banks (signatories of the Equator Principles). Just as in group 1, they tend to protect and defend the corporate organization, and they are supportive of a social mission if it exists. Their work is influenced by laws made by governments or international governing bodies, but as a result, they do not work directly with or for governments, which differentiates them from group 1.

Group 3 is formed by the so-called "users of the mechanisms": experts working for one of the nongovernmental organizations addressing an international agenda. They represent the United Nations concept of individual rights and often promote community rights for marginalized groups. To a certain extent, one can say that their mission is dependent on the work done by the MFIs and TNCs.

Group 4 is formed by experts from different parts of the world who represent the independent view on the structure and scope of the mechanisms and the institutions. This pool of experts is mainly formed of independent consultants or academics with backgrounds in the field who have sometimes served as advisors on the accountability mechanisms. They represent an independent view on the ethics, integrity, and tenor of the policies of the institutions. Their views are presumably impartial, and they are not representative of an entity with its own interests.

The value of the outcome of the study is finally that all the experts recognize and reconfirm the present need for accountability mechanisms in the financial sector.

POLICING THE BANKS

1

Globalization and the Rise
of Accountability Mechanisms

Walking into any academic bookstore is very revealing, as it shows that the fashionable subject for the academic world of today is globalization. There are good reasons for this. The modern world created by human nature and its ingenuity involves communication, transport, and endless streams of products that are made of raw materials from one continent, manufactured on another, and finally transported for use on a third. The technologies developed by humankind over the years have created dependencies in all sectors of our lives. The food we eat, the shoes we wear, the air we breathe, the papers we read, and even the messages in which we believe are dependent on factors outside our own "little" borders. Very few people on this globe are still able to control their daily lives without intrusions from outside and far away. And even those – like the Inuit in northern Canada – face changes today. If it is not global warming that rapidly alters their living conditions or the ecosystems on which they depend, it will be interference in their hunting practices by animal-welfare groups lobbying the citizens of Europe to eliminate fur exports to European markets.

Not only products but also finance flows across borders. Above all, this reality means a world with more and more porous borders where nation-states experience a decrease in their influence on the production process, labour conditions, and "rules of the game" in the economy. Who controls when nation-states lose their say? What mechanisms do we have at the present time to ensure that certain rules and standards are followed?

To understand the developments (described in chapters 2 through 5) that led to the creation of accountability mechanisms in most of the multilateral financial institutions (MFIs) and in the private financial sector, we must consider the ongoing debate on globalization's structure, or form, and its impacts both on the financial sector and on the role of governments and states. In this chapter, I first refer to those experts who comment on the loss of the nation-state as the democratic (and nondemocratic) financial controlling mechanism. This is followed by an account of the different initiatives of civil society organizations that are trying to make multilateral financial institutions, transnational corporations (TNCs), and moreover, the private banks accountable for their acts. In the endeavour to establish accountability within internationally operating institutions, many initiatives have been launched. Most of these are codes that can be adopted voluntarily. The most remarkable and latest development, the so-called Equator Principles, an initiative taken by the private sector itself, is described at the end of the present chapter and further discussed in chapter 5.

In this context the study that follows is intended to describe and critically assess accountability mechanisms of the multilateral financial institutions and similar mechanisms for the private sector. While this topic as a whole is clearly connected to globalization, my treatise is not in fact intended to address that vast subject in any substantial way. However, I wish here simply to acknowledge that globalization is indeed the soil of our times in which the seeds of accountability mechanisms have recently been sown. The purpose of this study is to examine the existing accountability mechanisms of the MFIs and other international financial institutions in order to clarify the options that exist for enhancing their functionality.

GLOBALIZATION: A CHALLENGE OR A RISK?

Whether globalization is good for humanity is a question I will not try to answer. I do not subscribe to "conspiracy theories" claiming that a group of people somewhere came together and planned to change the world in the direction it is going at present. It is more a matter that, step by step, the technological inventions of people with creative minds have created room for many to make innovative use of these inventions. That financial profits and access to control over processes have motivated people, industries, some governments, and transnational corporations to use the technologies is evident (see below). Many argue that globalization is progress, and even more seem to argue that it is not. And between them there is a whole range of those who see both opportunities and risks. Gavin Anderson states that the only point of conformity is that the term globalization is "an essentially contested concept,"[1] and he subsequently mentions three schools describing economic globalization: "the hyperglobalists, for whom the world is now a 'borderless' single market where nation-states are becoming obsolete; sceptics, who emphasise the continuing importance and power of nation-states, and who cast current economic phenomena more as 'regionalisation' or 'internationalisation'; and transformationalists, who regard globalization as the source of radical societal changes, which are circumscribing, but not eliminating, state sovereignty in an increasingly interconnected world."[2] I do not yet know where to place myself in this division: either in the first group or the last, or somewhere in between.

Those who see opportunities often point at the endless potential of our contemporary information society. Globalization in all its manifestations changes our lifestyles for the better or the worse. New technologies, and most of all the digital era, have rapidly changed the world. The developments arise so quickly that society is often not prepared to control or incorporate the outcomes. An example of the impacts on children is given by Nico van den Oudenhoven and Rekha Wazir: "It is tempting to speculate about the extent to which children incorporate virtual elements in building their own identity. In the digital world, they can change and assume diverse and contrasting identities at the click of a mouse ... There are no available guidelines as to how to respond to this wondrous new universe where boundaries recede, or disappear altogether, as soon as they are touched."[3]

In 1985, with Nicole Lucas, I published *"Made in Heaven,"* a book about the first wave of outsourcing of manual work to the so-called low-wage countries and the globalization of the labour market. The portion of jobs held by traditional workers on the factory floor dropped dramatically in the entire Western labour market. Computer-aided design and computer-aided manufacturing were introduced. The focus was mainly on the textile sector and component industry situated in the different free-trade zones, for the most part in southeast Asia. I continued my survey by writing about the first signs of outsourcing in the service sector and found in Mexico, near the US border, not only the Maquiladores producing textiles or televisions and radios for the US market but also big plants with hundreds of workers that already by then worked with data for the service sector. But in the first place I followed the more traditional industries.

From Europe I went to the Philippines to investigate the operations of western European companies, such as the Dutch-based TNC Philips, which produces computer components in Manila, and the operations of textile companies in the informal sector. As a young mother, I was shocked to see the labour conditions of mostly women producing goods for the Western markets. The clothes in our shops were perhaps made by other young mothers trying to survive on an income per day with which they could not even buy a cup of coffee in my home town of Amsterdam. Those were the days when we as young people protested about the often dangerous labour conditions of those in Asia who worked in badly constructed production halls with locked doors. When fire broke out, as happened on many occasions, hundreds died. I wanted to understand how European companies came to the decision to resettle their operations in low-wage countries. And soon after I arrived it became clear that this was a world lacking the standards of our protected world, which has strong unions and labour inspections. I wondered how it was possible that while we were used to high living standards and to the conditions under which we had once produced consumer goods, the same companies could so easily abandon these in another part of the world. I became part of the first group that ran into the phenomenon of globalization, placing it on the political agenda.

A group of well-known Dutch Social Democrats, among them Nobel Prize-winning economist Professor Jan Tinbergen, discussed the developments in the world labour market. At the time, their view was that the departure of traditional industries to the South was positive. It was supposed to bring development to the Southern Hemisphere and bring the world to a better balance. Their motto was, as I recall: "We in the West will have the service sector while the South will have the industries." They admitted that the labour conditions were bad but judged this to be a temporary problem. Finally, they believed that this was a win-win arrangement for both the South and the North. There was nothing wrong with the intentions of the Social Democrats. They made a crucial mistake only in their estimations concerning the global developments and did not have a long-term perspective on what the global labour market would look like down the road. The service sector was not exclusively for the developed countries. It also left for the low-wage countries soon after the traditional industries had departed. This I noticed during my stay at the Mexican-us border in the city of Ciudad-Juarez.

One night I was able to record some video at the plant in Mexico with a camera crew for a television documentary on globalization.[4] Around 600 workers, 80 per cent women, were inputting data from consumer rebate coupons. The coupons, cut from product packages, could be redeemed by consumers for a dollar if they sent in the coupons together with information about the products, when and where they were bought, and a bank account number. The manager, in his New York office, proudly said that the sum of the salaries he had to pay in Mexico to those working with data for marketing research was far less then salaries in the us and even less then the rent of an office in New York to house his workers. He said, "Today the computer is our office. I know exactly how much Coca-Cola or corn flakes, you name a product, the market is asking for on let us say October 7 this year in the supermarket around your corner."

The labourers I filmed at the Mexican border worked in long rows behind computers. The 800 computers were connected to 3 main computers that provided processed data to the New York office several times a day. This was long before supermarkets introduced client cards, with which they today collect the same data directly via the computerized cash register at the counter. The consumer receives a discount or air miles, and the company gets easy access to market information. The workers in Mexico are presumably no longer necessary and have long since lost their temporary jobs.

So globalization is the "buzz word" for the uncertainty or fear that many people feel about the future ahead. An impressive anti–globalization movement, and within it a diversity of visions and groups from the extreme to the scientific, has emerged. The world noticed those protesting against the negotiations of the World Trade Organization (wto) in Seattle in December 1999; against the twenty-seventh G-8 meeting in Genoa in 2001, where a demonstrator was shot dead; and more recently against the work and position of the wto in Hong Kong in 2005 during the sixth wto Ministerial Conference, where 900 demonstrators were arrested. In the 2005 annual report of the World Watch Institute, a reference is made by Michael Renner to what "opinion leaders" of the world think about the future: "June 2003 poll of 2,600 'opinion leaders' in 48 countries found a broad sense of pessimism, with at least two-thirds in every region of the world describing themselves as 'dissatisfied' with the current world situation. And in a series of World Bank-facilitated consultations involving some 20,000 poor people in 23 developing countries, a large majority said they were worse off than before, had fewer economic opportunities, and lived with greater insecurity than in the past."[5]

Without a doubt, the pessimism has resulted from the notion that we no longer control our living conditions within an orderly framework, such as that previously offered by nation-states or regional governments. Renner notes: "The challenges the world faces are compounded by weak and corrupt public institutions, the lack of recourse to justice, and unconstitutional or irregular means of political change, such as coup d'état and revolts. And they are heightened by an uneven process of globalization that draws nations and communities together in often unpredictable ways that entail risks for many and that allow extremist groups to operate more easily than in the past."[6] A Dutch judge with experience in corruption cases recently expressed his concern that the legislative authority, the national Parliament, has never looked into the convictions of fraud and corruption cases. He expressed concern about the warnings judges give in their final judgments, namely that there are few means within the law to convict those who commit financial crimes.[7] The judgments, he stated, should be read by parliamentarians so that they can change the laws. Moreover, there are very few public prosecutors and judges today who have enough experience to understand the complexity of many of these cases. The question can be raised of how far we in the so-called developed world are from weak judicial processes compared to systems such as in Cameroon (see chapter 6).

Renner finally remarks that "Awareness of the threats and challenges that cannot be resolved within the traditional framework of national security led a wide range of nongovernmental organizations, scholars and others to refine and redefine our understanding of security over the past two decades."[8] The questions today are how do we as a world society react to these developments and, more particularly, how do we control the stream of payments and investments when nation-states no longer have a say? What mechanisms do we have for exercising control? In what ways can we organize control? Are any systems or accountability mechanisms recognized and accepted by civil society and governments all over the world?

GLOBALIZATION OF THE ECONOMY

Globalization of the labour market paralleled globalization of the financial market. The latter is probably harder to follow than the former. The transfer of work to the low-wage countries and the increase in unemployment in the "developed" world was at least visible. The focus of our study in 1985 was essentially on labour conditions in the low-wage countries and rising unemployment in the developed countries and on the informal sector in both the developed countries and developing countries. We noticed globalization but still called it "mondialization" or "trans-nationalization" of the economy: "a global market came into being. With that we recognize one economic system for the entire world. We no longer can speak about the 'Rich West' and a 'Third World' with only poor people. In the informal sector of the 'West' people, and amongst them mainly women, work under 'Third World' conditions with 'Third World' earnings. In the 'Third World' live rich elites with little care for the poor in their countries."[9] I do not recall whether in the early days we discussed the role of private investors extensively. At present, one notices a repetition of this: media reporting to the public on the outsourcing of work today to China, India, or eastern Europe occurs without explanation of the driving forces behind it, other than economic reasons, such as competition on a global scale. Governments usually say there is little they can do since these are effects of a liberalized market and competition rules.

Manuel Castells does not believe in innocence and notes that "The decisive agents in setting up a new, global economy were governments, and particularly, the governments of the wealthiest countries, the G-7, and their ancillary international institutions, the International Monetary Fund, the World Bank, and the World Trade Organization. Three interrelated policies created the foundations for globalization: deregulation of domestic economic activity (starting with financial markets); liberalization of international trade and investment; and privatization of publicly controlled companies (often sold to foreign investors)."[10] Today, the capital markets are globally interdependent, says Castells. Cross-border transactions have increased phenomenally in the past two to four decades. According to Castells, between 1970 and 1996 "cross-border transactions increased by a factor of about 54 for the US, of 55 for Japan, and almost 60 for Germany."[11] He continues by pointing to the emerging markets and transition economies that became integrated "in the circuits of global capital flows" such that the "total financial flows to developing countries increased by a factor of 7 between 1960 and 1996."[12] Finally, Castells gives the following figures:

The banking industry stepped up its internationalization in the 1990s. In 1996, while investors bought stocks and bonds from emerging markets for $50 billion, banks lent in these markets $76 billion. Acquisition of overseas stocks by investors in industrialized economies increased by a factor of 197 between 1970 and 1997. In the US, overseas investment by pension funds increased from less than 1 percent of their assets in 1980 to 17 percent in 1997. In the global economy, by 1995, mutual funds, pension funds, and institutional investors in general controlled $20 trillion; that is, about ten times more than in 1980, and an amount equivalent to about two-thirds of Global GDP at that time.[13]

The figures of investment inflows from the private sector to developing countries are frequently confirmed by the media and international organizations. *World Investment Report 2005*, produced by the United Nations Conference on Trade and Development (UNCTAD), notes:

> On account of a strong increase in Foreign Direct Investment (FDI) flows to developing countries, 2004 saw a slight rebound in global FDI after three years of declining flows. At $648 billion, world FDI inflows were 2% higher in 2004 than in 2003. Inflows to developing countries surged by 40%, to $233 billion, but developed countries as a group experienced a 14% drop in their inward FDI. As a result, the share of developing countries in world FDI inflows was 36%, the highest level since 1997. Nevertheless, the United States retained its position as the number one recipient of FDI, followed by the United Kingdom and China.[14]

The "competition" between the World Bank and the private sector as investors or lenders in the world market has become a fact over recent decades. Not only is the World Bank losing clientele in the middle-income countries,[15] but it is also, in any case, in competition with private foreign direct investment. The bank notes that "In many countries the resource flows from the World Bank – and even official development assistance (ODA) flows more broadly – are not large enough for the money alone to make a major difference relative to the scale of the challenge. ODA totalled about $54 billion in 2000. This was only one-third as much as the private foreign direct investment flowing to developing countries, which in turn made up only about one-tenth of those countries' total investment of nearly $1.5 trillion."[16]

This is a visible trend that began some years ago. Does it mean the private sector will take over? The answer to this question is given by the UN World Commission on the Social Dimension of Globalization: "The governance structure of the global financial system has also been transformed. As private financial flows have come to dwarf official flows, the role and influence of private actors such as banks, hedge funds, equity funds and rating agencies has increased substantially. As a result, these private financial agencies now exert tremendous power over the economic policies of developing countries, especially the emerging market economies ... A further important source of failure in this global financial market is the absence, at that level, of effective institutions for supervising it, such as exist at the national level."[17]

The figures are impressive but the question still remains as to who is controlling the private and multilateral investments and the effects of these investments on millions of people? What supervising institutions do we have?

THE NATION-STATE AND DIMINISHING CONTROL

On 23 September 2003 Secretary General Kofi Annan said in his address to the UN General Assembly that the world had "come to a fork in the road."[18] Annan established the World Commission on the Social Dimension of Globalization, which "had to address some of the challenges facing the world as it stands at this fork."[19] The commission has further commented on its task: "As human beings it is in our power to take a correct turn, which would make the world safer, fair, ethical, inclusive and prosperous for the majority, not just for a few, within countries and between countries. It is also in our power to prevaricate, to ignore the road signs, and let the world we all share slide into further spirals of political turbulence, conflicts and wars."[20] In expressing its concerns, the commission notes that the debate on globalization is at an impasse and calls for new visions and actions. One such call refers to the accountability of public and private actors in the process: "Public and private actors at all levels with power to influence the outcomes of globalization must be democratically accountable for the policies they pursue and the actions they take." And again this commission of very senior experts also mentions the rapid integration of financial markets as "the most dramatic element of globalization over the past two decades."[21] Subsequently, the commission addresses the supervising role of national governments or states: "Although globalization has reduced the power and autonomy of States in various ways, States – particularly the powerful ones – continue to exercise important influence on global governance through their own policies and behavior and their decisions in intergovernmental agencies. It is therefore surprising that so few States subject the decisions taken by their representatives in those fora, to parliamentary or other public scrutiny."[22]

So governance of globalization is still the issue.

Thomas Friedman, in his book *The Lexus and the Olive Tree*, provides an entertaining but nevertheless serious perspective on this new state of the world:

Enter globalization. Once it became the dominant international system with the end of the Cold War, globalization put a rather different frame around geopolitics. While the globalization system does not end geopolitics, to think that it doesn't affect it in some fundamental ways is flat out stupid. To begin with, in the era of globalization there is no more chessboard, on which the entire world gets divided up into white or black squares. Since the Soviet Union has collapsed, there is no black anymore, so there is no white anymore. There are no "their guys," so there are no "our guys." Therefore, the inbuilt Cold War incentive for every regional conflict to escalate into a global conflict is gone. And so too are the resources. In the era of globalization, someone new is holding the checkbook. The Electronic Herd is the only entity now with cash to throw around. The Soviet Union doesn't exist anymore to write big checks, and the United States has put on the Golden Straitjacket and won't write big foreign aid checks anymore.

The only place a country can go to get big checks is the Electronic Herd, and the Electronic Herd doesn't play chess. It plays Monopoly. Where Intel, Cisco or Microsoft builds its next factory, or where the Fidelity global mutual fund invests its cash, is what determines who gets funded and what does not. And the bulls of the Electronic Herd do not write blank checks to win a country's love and allegiance; they write investment checks to make profits. And the Supermarkets and the Electronic Herd really don't care what color your country is outside any more. All they care about is how your country is wired inside, what level of operating systems and software it's able to run and whether your government can protect private property.[23]

Friedman, although fundamentally somewhat pessimistic and cynical in his view of globalization, still uses an interesting word: "Herd." A cowherd normally cares about his cattle, a human emotion that we probably cannot attribute to an invisible "Electronic Herd." Friedman's electronic herd is interested only in the protection of its private property. Still, Friedman describes one positive effect, namely that there is less chance that wars, financed before by superpowers, will be financed by the electronic herd: "the Herd will actually punish a country for fighting a war with its neighbors, by withdrawing the only significant source of growth capital in the world today. As such, countries have no choice but to behave in a way that is attractive to the herd or ignores the herd and pay the price of living without it."[24]

If Friedman is right, we will see fewer conflicts, which is a net gain if we forget for the moment the means in the hands of terrorist organizations. Nevertheless, we also have to understand from Friedman that the new chessboard is bringing about new international rules, enforced by – yes – the electronic herd. The question is who or what is this powerful electronic herd? Parts of the appearance of the herd in the globalized world are definitely international financial institutions and stockbrokers with their transactions, loans, and investments. Friedman describes the characteristics of the herd in the form of appropriate behaviour by those he considers the correct stakeholders – for example, US businessmen who do no business with entrepreneurs not paying tax.[25] Friedman notes: "I call the process by which the herd helps to build the foundation stones a democracy 'revolution from beyond' or 'globalution.'"[26] Groups in society, such as well-educated young professionals and nongovernmental organizations (NGOs), "might be able to import from beyond the standards and rules-based systems that they knew would never be initiated from above and could never be generated from below."[27] A subsequent question is who will govern the herd if nation-states or their democratic institutions are no longer able to do so?

Almost all presently studying globalization remark on a relation between global economic integration and the transformation of governance systems.

Saskia Sassen, although recognizing the developments of what is called "globalization" by many others, has a somewhat different view on the diminishing role of the nation-state:

> Even though transnationalism and deregulation have reduced the role of the state in the governance of economic processes, the state remains as the ultimate guarantor of the rights of capital whether national or foreign. Firms operating transnationally want to ensure the functions traditionally exercised by the state in the national realm of the economy, notably guaranteeing property rights and contracts. The state here can be conceived of as representing a technical administrative capacity which cannot be replicated at this time by any other institutional arrangement; further this is a capacity backed by military power.[28]

Fascinatingly, Sassen notes that the state is still a necessity as a tool for transnational corporations to defend their interests. But not all states are considered sufficient to play this role. Sassen states: "this guarantee of the rights of capital is embedded in a certain type of state, a certain conception of the rights of capital, and a certain type of international legal regime: it is largely the state of the most developed and most powerful countries in the world, Western notions of contract and property rights, and a new legal regime aimed at furthering economic globalization."[29] Nevertheless, Sassen notes that "Deregulation has been widely recognized as a crucial mechanism to facilitate the globalization of various markets and industries because it reduces the role of the state."[30] So certain states or roles of states should be set aside if they are a hindrance to markets and industries. Finally, Sassen says: "it is not simply a matter of a space economy extending beyond a national realm. It also has to do with the formation and legitimation of transnational legal regimes that are operative in national territories. National legal fields are becoming more internationalized in some of the major developed economies and transnational legal regimes become more important and begin to penetrate national fields hitherto closed."[31] Sassen further describes the need for new policy frameworks for governance since the powerful (financial) sectors operate in electronic spaces "not bound by conventional jurisdiction."[32]

Wolfgang Kleinwächter also refers to the old governing systems "rooted in the concept of sovereign states," which today are complemented by "an emerging new governance system, which is global by nature and includes more actors than the 180+ national governments and their intergovernmental international organizations."[33] Like many others, Kleinwächter recognizes the role of other stakeholders, such as civil society and the private sector, "that have both common and divergent interests."[34] He particularly notes that "neither stronger government regulation nor industry self-regulation offers an answer."[35] Thereupon, Kleinwächter stresses that only a new system of co-regulation provides an answer:

[A] new system of co-regulation offers the opportunity for governments, industry and the public to develop bottom-up policy and legal frameworks that would give all partners stability and flexibility. While this trilateral relationship sounds good in theory, it is much more unclear how this could work in practice. Who will define the aims, norms, principles, criteria, priorities and procedures? How will the three global players constitute themselves and agree on an interaction? Where are the checks and balances and the safeguards if something goes wrong or parties are unable to agree? Where are the risks and threats? How can such a trilateral relationship for the global information society interact with the traditional political, economic and social system of the real world, which does not disappear when the door to cyberspace opens? The present system of governance, now with nearly 200 nation-states, has functioned more or less satisfactorily over the last 200 years. But with globalization, the system based on the sovereign nation-state shows some cracks when confronted with global challenges ... New actors which create new institutions move into the new territory, filling emerging gaps regardless of whether there is a governmental order or not. National governments will not disappear during the coming century but they will become one actor among others, obliged to join into cooperative networks and consensual arrangements with other global actors and to share power with them.[36]

The view of Kleinwächter is important and relates to one of the major results of this study: the necessity of accountability mechanisms both for multilateral financial institutions and for the private sector (see chapters 4 and 5).

Also somewhat optimistic about a remaining role for the nation-state is Robert Keohane:

[A]s a reaction to global integration, nation states have established rudimentary institutions of governance, bilaterally, regionally, or globally if there are no nation states with their democratic entities that can do it? These attempts at governance, including global governance, are a natural result of increasing interdependence ... Since states do not monopolize channels of contact among societies, they cannot hope to monopolize institutions of global governance, even those that they have formally established, such as the World Bank, the International Monetary Fund and the World Trade Organization. States have a privileged position in these organizations, since they founded them, constituted their membership, monopolize voting rights, and provide continuing financial support. Except in the European Union, states also retain the legal authority to implement the decisions of international organizations in domestic law.[37]

In other words, if nation-states are losing their ability to legislate and control foreign direct investment (FDI) flows that influence the nation-states and their inhabitants, they could organize control via international institutions. An earlier attempt to control FDI via the so-called Multilateral Agreement on Investment (MAI) in the Organization for Economic Cooperation and Development (OECD) was abandoned in 1998 when a majority of the European Parliament voted against it. I also voted against it. We were strongly lobbied by NGOs and trade unions stressing that the MAI was mainly about the rights of foreign investors, not about their duties. Special concern was expressed about the position of poor nations that could not handle powerful investors taking over their entire financial systems when entering their fragile markets. In this context, the Commission on Globalization states: "Many commentators have noted that the draft articles of the MAI established a series of rights for foreign investors with no attendant responsibilities in respect of investor conduct. Two important lessons emerged. First was the need to have the relevant actors at the table so as to balance the interest of home and host countries, investors (both domestic and foreign), workers and the public. Second was the need for a transparent and open process. Its absence fuelled public suspicion and opposition to the MAI."[38]

Another remarkable observation about the rules and practices of foreign direct investment, the legal status of the contract, and threats to the protection of human rights is made by Professor Sheldon Leader:

> [T]he relationship between international investment and human rights is entering new terrain. It is beginning to move away from earlier, and starker, confrontations between human rights and business communities and is coming into a period marked by attempts by the latter to accommodate the demands of the former ... Investment law encounters human rights in a special way ... The problem here begins with a hoste state's own initiative to sign up to international standards, alongside the standards that automatically apply to it. Investment contracts can amount to attempts to turn around and contract out of those standards: not so that they would not apply to the state itself, which is not possible to achieve via such an agreement, but so that the standards would not apply to a portion of the population in their daily lives as affected by the investors' activities.[39]

Nevertheless, most of what is said about the governance of FDIs does not appear to address the effects of the investments and projects on the environment or living conditions of people in the areas concerned. This notion is expressed more strongly by the NGO community, which is asking for accountability both from the international financial institutions and from the private financial institutions.

ACCOUNTABILITY AS A CONCEPT

But what *is* accountability? To answer this question, we have to read some definitions. The mission statement of the World Bank contains the word "accountable." In the subpart "Our Principles," the bank claims that it is "Accountable for quality results."[40] The governance research indicators for 1996 to 2002 mention "Voice and Accountability" as the first indicator of the quality and transparency of a state's undertakings, followed by political stability and absence of violence, government effectiveness, regulatory quality, rule of law, and control of corruption. So the World Bank is asking the countries they support to be accountable.[41] The NGOs continually call on the World Bank to be "accountable." Accountability is today mentioned by all international institutions, governments, and private-sector entities.

In the context of this study, the following statement is remarkable: "Accountability is fundamentally a relationship of power. When accountability works, citizens are able to make demands on powerful institutions, and ensure that those demands are met."[42] Another interesting definition of "accountability" is given by the Regional Health Authorities (RHAs) of the Government of Manitoba, in Canada, which equates accountability with a commitment to "results-oriented, open government."[43] A document about the health services, called "Achieving Accountability," states: "The people of Manitoba have the right to know what health services are being delivered and what results are being achieved. This is known as accountability. The following definition of accountability is used extensively in health care literature: Accountability is the obligation to answer for a responsibility that has been conferred."[44] The unnamed writers of this document stress that the process of achieving accountability should begin with "establishing the responsibilities and expectations of the relationship."[45] The reporting phase, then, should "outline measuring outcomes, performance or progress toward meeting the defined responsibilities and expectations."[46] Finally, before the cycle starts again, the evaluation phase should involve "analyzing the information and performance reports received during the reporting phase and making decisions based on that information."[47]

It is a clear definition that quite closely coincides with my own working definition of "accountability." I would add the word "delegated" to the above definition, making it: *accountability is the obligation to answer for a responsibility that has been conferred and delegated.* Those who perform tasks in the name of an organization – which is definitely the case of officials working for governments or MFIs – have to be constantly aware that they have an obligation to society for which they will be held accountable. It is the tax money of the same society that pays for their acts and their salaries.

Richard Mulgan calls "accountability" a "chameleon-like term" commonly accepted in public administration literature, a word that a few decades ago was rarely used and interestingly does not have an equivalent in other European languages.[48] Accountability goes together with another new term, "governance." Mulgan stresses that accountability in the past had a more restrictive meaning, and he makes crystal clear the relations between the party held accountable and the party demanding accountability:

One sense of "accountability," on which all agreed, is that associated with the process of being called "to account" to some authority for one's actions. Indeed, this sense may fairly be designated the original or core sense of "accountability" because it is the sense with the longest pedigree in the relevant literature and in the understanding of practitioners. Such accountability has a number of features: it is external, in that the account is given to some other person or body outside the person or body being held accountable; it involves social interaction and exchange, in that one side, that calling for the account, seeks answers and rectification while the other side, that being held accountable, responds and accepts sanctions; it implies rights of authority, in that those calling for an account are asserting rights of superior authority over those who are accountable, including the rights to demand answers and to impose sanctions.[49]

Mulgan's description of the original concept of "core accountability" and the relations between the one held accountable and the one demanding accountability seems the most applicable to "accountability mechanisms" as discussed in this study. His definition makes accountability a matter not only for individuals but also for institutions – in this study, the MFIs or private financial institutions – which of course are comprised of individuals to be held accountable. As will become clear, the issue of accountability within the context of globalization is a complex matter. Trying to hold international organizations accountable is not a sinecure and can become a matter of international law (see chapter 6), wherein "accountability" is defined mainly in legal terminology. Mulgan further notes that "In the context of a democratic state, the key accountability relationships in this core sense are those between citizens and holders of public office and within the ranks of office holders, between elected politicians and bureaucrats."[50]

He continues by explaining that accountability has increasingly been extended beyond its core meaning of external inquiry. Today, according to Mulgan, accountability refers to individual responsibility ("professional" and "personal" accountability); it is linked to governments, which pursue the wishes or needs of their citizens; or it is applied to the public discussions between citizens on which democracies depend.[51]

Accountability has also been targeted by Henry McCandless, who writes about how we as citizens can hold our fellow citizens – such as elected representatives, senior civil servants, top military commanders, judges, governing boards, professionals, academics, and journalists – accountable in their official duties. His definition is: "Accountability means the obligation to answer for the discharge of responsibilities, through explanation to those having a significant legitimate interest in what the decision-makers intend to do. People whose responsibilities and decisions significantly affect the public cannot confine their answering to reporting only to their superiors. The answering obligation, like the answering itself, is both before and after the fact."[52] Thus, to the definition adopted by the

Government of Manitoba, McCandless adds the notion that officials should report to those who want to be informed before and after the planned activities executed on their behalf.

Compared to Mulgan's definition, the one offered by McCandless reflects a new trend in which personal responsibility has come to the fore. McCandless's work is a call for citizens to demand accountability. It is, as he says, less an indictment against authorities and more a matter of a society not proactive enough to ask for accountability. He illustrates the need for society to act by alluding to some dramatic cases in which Canadian people were victims of the work of authorities that affected the lives of thousands of people. He describes what happened step by step, what the reactions of society and governing bodies have been, and who reported to whom. For example, he refers to the 60,000 Canadians who received blood or blood products that killed them "fairly quickly, shortened their lives or gave them life sentences of reduced capacity ... Part of this Canadian disgrace is that we don't even know the total number killed or injured from HIV and hepatitis C contracted through blood transfusions."[53] Other cases he covers include an explosion in a newly opened coalmine in Nova Scotia that killed twenty-six miners and the disaster with the British car-ferry *Herald of Free Enterprise*, which left the harbour of Zeebrugge with its bow doors still open.

That many of the government bodies responsible did not directly report to the citizens is a theme throughout these stories. McCandless says:

> We like to believe, regardless of the evidence, that people in authority will do the right thing. Or, if we don't think they will, we expect that someone will deal with it. ("Authority" means elected and appointed officials and governing bodies' authority or power to make decisions that affect citizens in important ways.) ... Simply saying that authorities "must be made accountable" adds nothing. Authorities making decisions have always had the fairness obligation to publicly explain their intentions and reasoning before taking their decisions. The point is that we never made them give adequate public explanation before the fact. We have confused responsibility, the obligation to act, with accountability, the obligation to answer for responsibilities.[54]

He adds: "To install public answering to a reasonable standard, citizens must agree on what it means. At present we have a variety of notions of accountability that keep the concept unclear." For McCandless, "accountability" means: "Holding fairly to account means exacting from decision-makers the information we need to assess both the implications of their intentions and the effects of their actions; equally it means doing something sensible with answering given in good faith. Holding to account supersedes blind trust in authorities, helping us to head off decisions leading to harm and injustice."[55] However, he notices a challenge: "Answering the question 'Who is accountable to whom, for what?' clarifies responsibilities, reduces uncertainty and helps identify gaps in important responsibilities for safety and fairness. If we accept the argument that the requirement to answer influences the conduct of authorities, and that adequate public answering allows us to increase our control of what goes on, holding fairly to account will fundamentally change the relationship between citizens and people in authority."[56] Finally, McCandless states that when governments claim to produce benefit-cost assessments, what is missing is the "who?" question: "who benefits and who pays – and for how long?"[57]

Jonathan Fox speaks about political accountability and draws attention to an analytical distinction between vertical and horizontal dimensions of political accountability: "The former one refers to power relations between the state and its citizens, while the latter one refers to institutional oversight, checks and balances within the state."[58] According to Fox, the role of civil society is to "empower the state's own checks and balances."[59] Civil society should play a role directly and indirectly by strengthening institutions, electoral democracy, and independent media: checks and balances. Fox notes that "Civil society campaigns may also drive the creation of certain institutional checks and balances in the first place. However, though civil society's contribution to an accountable governance has been widely asserted, the casual mechanisms that determine the patterns of civil society influence on horizontal accountability have not been well-specified. We still lack analytical frameworks that can account for the conditions under which civil society actors manage to bolster the institutions of horizontal accountability."[60]

Again, the role of civil society is overwhelmingly recognized as the driving force behind changes to institutions. The earlier mentioned UN World Commission on the Social Dimension of Globalization notes this too: "They are actively engaged in advocacy and mobilizing public opinion. They promote transparency and democratic accountability ... Apart from a few exceptions, they have no formal representation in international organizations and global conferences. Nevertheless, their emergence has enriched the process of global governance."[61]

Indeed, the NGOs have all the right in the world to ask for accountability from the MFIs, which of course does not exclude them from being held accountable. They often express skepticism about the accountability of the MFIs. Kay Treakle, a former managing director of the Bank Information Center, a nongovernmental organization based in Washington, DC, that monitors the policies and projects of the multilateral development banks (MDBs), describes what happened with the Yacyretá case, filed for the first time at the Inspection Panel of the World Bank in September 1996.[62] The Yacyretá Hydroelectric Dam, located on the border between Argentina and Paraguay, is "one of the largest and most complex construction projects ever undertaken in Latin America."[63] Treakle describes the complexity of the project,[64] noting the implications of a dam 83 metres high and 67 kilometres long in the Parana River between the two countries, expected to generate 3,100 megawatts of electricity for Argentina, flooding over 80,000 hectares of land in Paraguay and 29,000 in Argentina and requiring the involuntary resettlement of over 50,000 urban poor in the two countries. The World Bank got involved in the project when 85 per cent of the engineering was complete.[65] In her introduction, Treakle writes: "While the Yacereta project is a colossal mistake when examined from just about any angle – financial, economic, political, social and environmental, this paper will highlight the Bank's failures to protect the environment and compensate displaced people in violation of their own policies."[66]

Treakle conscientiously describes the process that took place. In short, her text is about how, since its inception, the project "has been fraught with corruption scandals, gross mismanagement, construction delays, and cost overruns amounting to billions of dollars."[67] The regional and international NGOs opposed the project in 1992, citing the inadequacy of the environmental assessment, improper financing arrangements for the resettlement plans and environmental mitigation plans, questions about the precarious economics of the project, inclusion of the World Bank on conditionality, the lack of money for environment and resettlement activities, violation by both countries of the condition that the reservoir level be raised to 76 masl only if the required environmental mitigation and resettlement measures were completed,[68] local people still waiting for adequate and timely compensation for loss of jobs and livelihood and forced resettlement, World Bank management denying that the problems raised in the claim resulted from "any alleged Management violation of the Banks policies and procedures," the Inspection Panel's report that found "fundamental inadequacies in the Action Plan" and "criticized Bank management for failing to consult with locally affected people,"[69] numerous visits by NGOs from the region to Washington, DC, to meet with the president of the bank and with the board in order to advocate their own views, and finally, how, after many years, bank staff began listening to local leaders explaining the situation on the ground and were shocked "at the misery, poverty, hunger and complete lack of social services in the dam's area of influence in Paraguay."[70]

The process described by Treakle clearly shows how large projects, involving the lives of thousands of mainly poor people, can become a drama that many people no longer know how to turn back or to stop in order to mitigate the failures of the undertaking. Some have gained in the process and many more have lost. The description of the process could probably serve as a model for how many such projects go wrong. This case is the more painful since it was implemented under the flag of "development" and gives rise to the question of what development finally is: development for whom and at what costs? And who pays the bill?[71] Treakle also explains that some measures were taken, such as establishing information centres on both sides of the border. But she is skeptical about whether the new loan to Paraguay can "address some social impacts that aren't currently covered by previous loans."[72] She notes that "NGOs have questioned whether putting Paraguay's citizens in debt to the Bank is a reasonable way for the Bank to solve problems resulting from their own mismanagement."[73] So we are back to the issue of the accountability of officials. Concerning accountability, Treakle makes some observations:

1. Institutional accountability remains illusory. There are no incentives for Bank staff to comply with policies, or consequences if they don't. Without an Inspection Panel, the World Bank and its staff have immunity from accountability – i.e. they are protected from any legal action that might be brought by individual citizens, corporations or governments ...

2. At the level of management and the Board, the claim process is driven by politics not facts. In a recent workshop in Mexico, former Panel chair Alvaro Umana said, "The only people who have followed the Panel procedures have been the claimants and the Panel." The initial management response to the Yacyretá claim had four basic thrusts: One was to challenge the eligibility of the claimants and of the claim itself. Second, management denied that the problems resulted from policy violations. Third, they asserted that the required actions related to environment and resettlement at 76 masl had been met and that problems alleged in the claim had not occurred. Finally, management issued an Action Plan that appeared to be a response to issues raised in the claim. In other words, after having denied that there were problems, management submitted an Action Plan ostensibly to deal with them because it was politically expedient to do so ...

3. The complexity of the process requires the active involvement of an organized, international civil society ... Finally, without an organized civil society, and especially without advocates in Washington, the claimants would have been completely at the mercy of Bank Management's attempts to whitewash the Panel's report in the Paraguayan press ... The outcome of this process remains to be seen. But it implies that citizens have been able to use the Inspection Panel as a way to legitimately challenge the MDBs, EBY [Ente Binacional Yaciretá], and governments using the policy and accountability tools that the Banks themselves have made available.[74]

Finally, it is important to note that accountability is not possible without transparency. Equally, transparency is not possible without information. Sylvester Eijffinger and Petra Geraats have developed "an index of the transparency of nine central banks – the eight that matter most in foreign-exchange markets plus New Zealand's, the pioneer of central-bank clarity."[75] This index "focuses on the informativeness about each stage of the policymaking process and covers all public communication by central banks." In their conceptual framework, Eijffinger and Geraats "distinguish five aspects of transparency: political, economic, procedural, policy and operational."[76] Some of their findings are worth mentioning:

Most of the central banks in our sample provide a description of their monetary policy framework in the form of an explicit monetary policy strategy. Typically, the strategy is some form of inflation targeting, although the ECB's [European Central Bank's] "two pillar strategy" is a notable exception. Only the Bank of Japan and the Federal Reserve do not have an explicit monetary policy framework. Several central banks, in particular the Bank of Japan, the Riksbank, the Bank of England and the Federal Reserve, release a comprehensive account of policy deliberations within a reasonable amount of time (eight weeks) in the form of (non-attributed) minutes ... These central banks are also the ones that publish individual voting records ... The most transparent central banks are the Reserve Bank of New Zealand, the Swedish Riksbank and the Bank of England. The subtop is formed by the Bank of Canada, the European Central Bank and the Federal Reserve. The least transparent central banks in our sample are the Reserve Bank of Australia, the Bank of Japan and the Swiss National Bank. Although the most transparent central banks in our sample are all inflation targeters, ... inflation targeting is not a necessary condition for political transparency, as is exemplified by the European Central Bank.[77]

I could not agree more with McCandless, who states that "Holding to account supersedes blind trust in authorities, helping us to head off decisions leading to harm and injustice."[78] It is not so much a matter of distrusting individuals; it is a healthy distrust about what officials can produce once they are part of a system where pressure comes from inside and outside to decide in certain directions and where procedures that have been in place for a long time seem to be normal. In such an atmosphere, it is not very common to expose difficult questions about the effects of what is planned without the risk of being placed outside the stream of what is the ordinary. It is in this "ordinary," the stream of the daily decisions, that we can notice the danger and the failure of an institution to become alerted in time about wrong decisions, as I experienced as a member of the Inspection Panel from 1999 to 2004.

Treakle identifies the World Bank Inspection Panel, an accountability mechanism created under pressure of the international NGO community and the US Congress, as the only opportunity people have to "legitimately challenge" the activities of this powerful institution. The Inspection Panel is fully aware of its difficult task of holding the institution accountable for its activities. This is not an easy duty, as discussed in chapter 6.

Finally, as Eijffinger and Geraats indicate, some central banks publish the minutes of their meetings, "as is standard from the responsible Policy Board,"[79] and in this respect these banks are definitely trendsetters. Up to now, such transparency has been unthinkable in the case of the World Bank.

ACCOUNTABILITY, GLOBAL GOVERNANCE, AND MULTILATERAL FINANCIAL INSTITUTIONS

Former US president Bill Clinton once said that the rise of the NGO community was one of the most remarkable features of the twentieth century. In documents about globalization, the rise of NGOs is described as an effect of globalization: the new communication technologies offer them a range of tools for communication and action. According to the World Commission on Globalization, NGOs grew "from some 1,500 in the mid-1950s to about 25,000 in 2001. While the nature and frequency of contact and mode of interaction between international agencies and CSOs [civil society organizations] vary, the trend towards increased collaboration has been across the board."[80]

Globalization and accountability go together. As stated above, with globalization, control over FDIs requires new governance systems since the old model, based on the concept of the sovereign state, no longer holds. In this study accountability is considered in relation to multilateral financial institutions and the private financial sector. Accountability and MFIs is a somewhat different subject from accountability and the private financial sector, not that accountability is profoundly different in each case or should be different; it is only that the MFIs have a different starting point. MFIs operate with the tax money of millions of people from all over the globe and within the framework of public international law (see chapter 6).

Robert Keohane and Joseph Nye stress that international institutions, when asked about their own accountability, normally reply guardedly by referring only to the role they have, which is to promote international cooperation and to provide global public goods.[81] There is nothing wrong with this role, but the legitimacy or accountability of these international institutions is at stake. Citing Robert Dahl, who says that "international organizations are not and are not likely to be democratic,"[82] Keohane and Nye add that "chains of delegation [within the international organizations] are too long, there is too much secrecy, and much international organizational activity does not take place even in the shadow of elections."[83]

Remarkably, Keohane and Nye further note a difference between "accountability" and "democratic accountability": "If we focus on accountability per se, international organizations clearly have more of it than the classic realist model of inter-state relations. The head of state of a hegemonic power is accountable to no one outside of his country, while the executive heads of international organizations are accountable to states through a regularized process of election and re-election. In reality, heads of international organizations may be accountable, through a hierarchical process, to one or a few powerful states."[84] Keohane and Nye then note that this is not per se democratic, referring to the case of a former secretary general of the United Nations, Boutros Boutros-Ghali, being denied a second term due to opposition from the United States. Subsequently,

Keohane and Nye say: "Democratic accountability is more elusive. In principle ... democratic accountability could be enhanced by increasing legislative control over policy at the supranational level, either by giving national legislators a direct oversight role with respect to international institutions or by creating supranational legislators."[85] The latter conclusion is germane in the light of this study, which focuses on accountability mechanisms for the financial sector based on the history of the World Bank Inspection Panel in the first place (see chapters 3, 6, and 7).

The subject of global governance and accountability in the financial sector has finally become a subject for world leaders. On 7 July 2001 the G-8's finance ministers and Central Bank governors came together in Rome, Italy. On the agenda was the issue of "Strengthening the International Financial System and the Multilateral Development Banks."[86] In the meeting's final declaration, the following terms were adopted, among others:

1. The international financial system is central to the functioning of the global economy. It provides a framework that facilitates the exchange of goods, services and capital, and that sustains sound economic growth. A central objective for us, the Finance Ministers of G7 countries, is to foster the continuing development of the conditions necessary for financial and economic stability, which in turn are essential if the benefits of global economic integration are to be sustainable and broadly shared.

15. We reaffirm our commitment to promote the implementation and surveillance of internationally agreed codes and standards, in particular the 12 key standards identified by the Financial Stability Forum (FSF). Their implementation is in the economic interest of all countries, and ownership is an important element in this process. We welcome the contributions of the many different actors, including the IMF [International Monetary Fund], the WB [World Bank] and the FSF, in making it possible for countries to implement codes and standards and assessing their compliance. These efforts should be continued and coordination among the relevant institutions (IFIs [international financial institutions] and standard-setting bodies) strengthened to ensure that all inputs are effectively integrated.

32. The Multilateral Development Banks are an essential component of the development architecture and have an important role to play in ensuring that the benefits of increasing global prosperity are shared by all countries. In our report for the Okinawa Summit (Fukuoka Report, July 2000), we underscored the importance of strengthening the Multilateral Development Banks (MDBs) to best adapt them to the new challenges. We are committed to moving ahead with this agenda. We stressed that "accelerating poverty reduction in developing countries must be the core role of the MDBs. An increased focus on poverty reduction should underpin all aspects of the MDBs' work, including in programs of policy reform, investment projects and capacity building." We

also underscored that "economic growth is the primary determinant of country's ability to raise incomes and reduce poverty and inequality."

38. Internal Governance – Enhancing internal governance, accountability and transparency is crucial to enable the MDBs to strengthen their role in the fight against poverty and retain institutional credibility. Over the last few years, significant progress towards greater transparency and openness has been made. However, there is still scope for further improvement. To this end, we call upon the MDBs to:[87]

- Establish or improve existing mechanisms, fully independent from staff responsible for project preparation, to ensure compliance of project proposals with policies and procedures prior to submission to the Board.
- Strengthen or establish inspection mechanisms reporting directly to the Board.[88]

Four years later, in 2005, hundreds of members of parliaments from all over the world signed a petition seeking democratic oversight of the World Bank and the International Monetary Fund (IMF), as has been noted by Olivia McDonald.[89] The following examples of steps that the parliamentarians demanded clearly express the need for a process that makes the institutions more transparent, democratic, and accountable:[90]

The parliamentarians asked the international financial institutions (IFIs) to:

- Stop imposing economic policy conditions; citizens and their representatives should have the final say over economic policy choices;
- Respect national laws and constitutional provisions regarding grants and loans. If provisions for parliamentary approval exist, and a parliament either partially or fully rejects a loan, the IFIs should withdraw or renegotiate these proposals;
- Agree to minimum standards that will ensure due diligence and impartiality of World Bank and IMF staff when dealing with sovereign democracies, developing an accompanying complaints procedure to address cases where they have not been upheld;
- Help build the capacity of parliaments to play an effective role in negotiating or monitoring IFI-financed projects. This should include ... pertinent information to inform their decision making.

They asked the governments of developing countries to:

- Establish or extend provisions for parliamentary involvement and scrutiny of all external financing proposals, including grants. Such steps should ensure proposals comply with national development and poverty reduction objectives, as well as borrowing and repayment ceilings;

- Create a stronger role for parliamentarians in PRSP [poverty reduction strategy paper] formulation and monitoring, and secure parliamentary approval of PRSPs.

Finally, they asked the member states to:

- Allow parliamentary scrutiny of government policy on the IFIs, and encourage regular reporting to parliament on government's activities within these institutions ... Making available the policy positions of and statements made by executive directors at board meetings.
- Open up the selection process for executive directors, accountable to both government policy towards the institutions and the decisions of the institutions themselves, to scrutiny by relevant national bodies, such as senatorial or parliamentary sub-committees, or ombudsmen.[91]

First, it has to be said that the parliamentarians demonstrated courage by organizing themselves as a global group of elected citizens who want to have better control over international institutions. On the one hand, one could praise them for this initiative; on the other hand, one could conclude that it is their duty to control these institutions. Second, they asked for regular reporting to parliaments on policy positions and for improved availablity to parliaments of the statements of these institutions' executive directors. Here, the parliamentarians forgot to mention that they could take up part of this role by organizing subcommittees in their parliaments and ensuring regular debate with officials and their representatives involved in the work of international institutions such as the World Bank. The US Congress was able to organize hearings that finally led to the establishment of the World Bank Inspection Panel and a policy requiring much more transparency within the institution, which goes together with accountability (see chapter 3). Third, it is not clear what the group has in mind when asking for an "accompanying complaints procedure," other than the Inspection Panel. This request can be understood only if they felt that such a mechanism should also be created for the IMF (on the IMF, see chapter 4). During my time on the Inspection Panel, this group of parliamentarians never met with the panel's members.[92]

Lastly, the World Bank's former president, Paul Wolfowitz, announced to the bank's management in July 2005 that he had appointed Robert Pozen, an authority on corporate governance, to study mechanisms for ensuring transparency, accountability, and ethics. According to my information, Wolfowitz found too many separate mechanisms in various offices and departments within the World Bank. Without a doubt, the demand for accountability has given rise to many mechanisms, making clearance and restructuring necessary. Nevertheless, the Inspection Panel was created by the bank's executive directors in response to demand from elected parliamentarians (the US Congress and European Parliament to begin with). To

my knowledge, President Wolfowitz, appointed in 2005, had no intention
to downgrade the Inspection Panel, which would keep its strong position
within the bank. Wolfowitz described the panel as "Indispensable to the
work and the credibility of the World Bank ... the Panel provides accountability and transparency. The world's poorest citizens can take their concerns about Bank-funded projects to the Panel and know that their voices
will be heard ... Bank staff has the chance to address these concerns."[93]

ACCOUNTABILITY IN PRIVATE FINANCIAL SECTOR INITIATIVES

At the beginning of this chapter, I dealt with globalization and the financial market, noting the rapid and colossal growth of foreign direct investment in emerging markets. I drew attention to the diminishing power of
nation-states to control the global financial world or to hold corporations
accountable for their acts. I described what many experts say about the
non-existence of international mechanisms, structures, or legislation to
control the private financial sector. While private capital goes abroad, does
each nation-state have "its own set of regulatory mechanisms within which
the private sector must operate"?[94] A parallel track of new legislation was
not created while capital went abroad.

As figures show (see above), the private financial sector is actually taking
over the leading role of the World Bank and other MFIs. Until now, this
fact has not been recognized by many citizens groups, national parliaments, and sometimes even governments. One could compare the money
flowing into emerging markets from the MFIs to the water from a kitchen
tap and the money flowing in from the private sector to a rising river over-
flowing its banks. The water from the tap, so we are told, is controlled and
divided among the different users (developing countries) that need water,
while the river flows "naturally" down to the regions where its waters create
good profits mainly for the "happy few" (the liberalized markets). The concern here is that the system for purifying the water/money from the tap is
not necessarily used to treat the water/money from the river in order to
make it potable for all.

Fortunately, the private sector itself has become actively involved in seeking a way to address this problem. Despite the somber visions expressed by
many that the private financial sector can operate without any control, the
sector initiated (albeit under pressure from outside) "voluntary rules, standards, decision-making procedures, and accountability mechanisms for
corporations and their suppliers that cover a wide range of issues. This industry self-regulation is now a significant element of global governance."[95]
There have been a range of different initiatives. One of the first was the
Principles of Corporate Governance of the Organization for Economic
Cooperation (now the OECD), an initiative "set up in 1947 with support
from the United States and Canada to co-ordinate the Marshall Plan for

the reconstruction of Europe after World War II ... Since then, its mission has been to help governments achieve sustainable economic growth and employment and rising standards of living in member countries while maintaining financial stability, so contributing to the development of the world economy."[96]

Regarding these principles, the OECD states on its website:

> Policy makers in both developed and emerging economies face challenges in ensuring good corporate governance. The OECD Principles of Corporate Governance set out a framework for good practice which has been agreed by the governments of all 30 countries that are members of the OECD. They have been designed to assist governments and regulatory bodies in both OECD countries and elsewhere in drawing up and enforcing effective rules, regulations and codes of corporate governance. In parallel, they provide guidance for stock-exchanges, investors, companies and others that have a role in the process of developing good corporate governance.[97]

Although the original OECD Principles stem from the time of the creation of the OECD, the organization's Guidelines for Multinational Enterprises were drawn up and adopted in June 1976. In June 2000 the guidelines were revised. The principles, or guidelines, are formulated as recommendations from governments to the private sector and include ten chapters: Concepts and Principles, General Policies, Disclosure, Employment and Industrial Relations, Environment, Combating Bribery, Consumer Interests, Science and Technology, Competition, and Taxation.[98] The new guidelines include a complaint mechanism through which NGOs and even individuals, in addition to labour unions, can lodge a complaint against a multinational enterprise for violation of the guidelines. The adopted text states: "Adhering countries shall set up National Contact Points [NCPs] for undertaking promotional activities, handling inquiries and for discussions with the parties concerned on all matters covered by the Guidelines so that they can contribute to the solution of problems which may arise in this connection, taking due account of the attached Procedural Guidance. The business community, employee organisations, and other interested parties shall be informed of the availability of such facilities."[99]

Soon after the guidelines were adopted, a divergence of views arose over the role of the NCPs. Some argued that they should serve a conciliatory function, whereas others opted for a function in the arena of administrative law.[100] OECD Watch, an umbrella organization of NGOs in twenty-eight countries, noted in 2005 about the NCPs: "OECD Watch believes that the legitimate expectations of civil society groups that participated in the 2000 revision of the Guidelines have not been met as far as the implementation procedures are concerned. Five years on, there is no conclusive evidence that the Guidelines have had a positive, comprehensive impact on multinational enterprises. Furthermore, there is no evidence that the Guidelines have helped to reduce the number of conflicts between local communities, civil society groups and foreign investors."[101]

OECD Watch's concerns about the weak implementation of the guidelines and about the NCPs' differing mandates has already had some impact: the Dutch government investigated the Dutch NCP's functioning and decided to create an NCP that is independent from government. I have not otherwise studied the relatively new and remarkable guidelines of the OECD nor how the NCPs function.

In March 1989 the oil tanker Exxon Valdez lost its oil after the ship ran aground. The ship carried 1,264,155 barrels of oil, and soon 1,300 miles of shoreline were oiled.[102] As a result of this environmental tragedy, the activities and responsibilities of transnational corporations became a main focus of many citizens around the world, who also directed their attention to the management of companies themselves. In the same year a remarkable initiative was the creation of the Coalition for Environmentally Responsible Economies (CERES) in the United States. "A national network of investment funds, environmental organizations and interest groups working to advance environmental stewardship on the part of business, CERES is renowned for its unique ability to bring diverse groups together to find positive solutions for complex environmental and social challenges. For example, in May 2005 at the United Nations CERES brought together representatives of U.S. and international pension funds representing $5 trillion in capital to address the profound investment risks and emerging business opportunities driven by climate change."[103] CERES, which today exists as a coalition of eighty-five members, also developed a set of principles, "a ten-point code of corporate environmental conduct to be publicly endorsed by companies as an environmental mission statement or ethic. Imbedded in that code of conduct was the mandate to report periodically on environmental management structures and results."[104] CERES operates four programs: company programs, industry programs, investor programs, and sustainability reporting. In 1997 it was CERES that launched the Global Reporting Initiative (GRI),[105] which today is an international standard for reporting on economic, social, and environmental performance to which more than 700 companies around the world adhere. The GRI is a rather effective initiative supported not only by the private sector but also by governments.

Another related initiative that should be mentioned is the Global Compact, an initiative of former UN secretary general Kofi Annan, who launched it in July 2000. According to the UN website, the "Compact addresses environment, human rights and 'workers rights" and is a "global multi-stakeholder, multi-issue network with more than 40 regional and national sub-networks."[106] Other initiatives, to name a few that have been rather influential, include: ISO 14001 for environmental compliance;[107] the Accountability 1000 framework,[108] which defines best practices in social and ethical auditing; Social Accountability 8000, which provides a standard "to make workplaces more humane";[109] and the Clean Clothes Campaign: Model Code,[110] which is a wide network of groups in several European countries whose aim is to improve the working conditions in the garment and sportswear industries. Since the introduction of the OECD Principles, many other initiatives for the private sector have arisen, only a few of which are mentioned here. Some of the codes, standards, and principles were originally initiated by governments and civil society. Others were created by the private sector itself. Within a decade, environmentally sustainable financing has ceased to be a matter of philanthropy. The most remarkable developments for the private financial sector have been the creation of the United Nations Environment Programme Finance Initiative (UNEP FI) and the Equator Principles.

According to Ken Maguire of the UNEP FI, the concept was

> launched in 1991 when a small group of commercial banks, including Deutsche Bank, HSBC Holdings, Natwest, Royal Bank of Canada, and Westpac, joined forces with UNEP to catalyze the banking industry's awareness of the environmental agenda. In May 1992, in the run-up to the Rio Summit that year, the UNEP Statement by Banks on the Environment and Sustainable Development was announced in New York, and the Banking Initiative was formed. This Initiative, which operated under the auspices of the United Nations Environment Programme, engaged a broad range of financial institutions, including commercial banks, investment banks, venture capitalists, asset managers, and multi-lateral development banks and agencies – in a constructive dialogue about the nexus between economic development, environmental protection, and sustainable development. The Initiative promoted the integration of environmental considerations into all aspects of the financial sector's operations and services. A secondary objective of the initiative was to foster private sector investment in environmentally sound technologies and services.[111]

On the question of the UNEP FI's role toward the private financial institutions, Maguire states: "We act as a catalyst and provide our signatories with practical research, capacity building, action oriented publications, as well as hosting international conferences and events that bring together professionals from around the globe. UNEP FI provides quality support for your organization. In addition to our dedicated team, UNEP FI opens up a vast network of sustainable development contacts, information and networking services that are dedicated to helping you and your organizations make a difference."[112]

On the difference between the UNEP FI and the Equator Principles, Maguire adds: "It should be noted that the two initiatives are of a voluntary nature. In summary, the key objectives of the initiatives are: 1. UNEP Finance

Initiative is a public private partnership based on a voluntary approach
and seeking to abide by broad, aspirational statements of commitment by
member financial institutions to environmental and sustainability best practice. 2. The Equator Principles specifically addresses environmental, social
and human rights best practice approaches associated with project finance
activities of banks on projects above US$50 million."[113]

Membership in the UNEP FI is based on agreement with a series of negotiated statements that require a voluntary commitment from member companies and are aspirational in nature. The statements seek to foster
corporate support for and commitment to best-practice approaches by financial institutions regarding internal and external environmental and
sustainability opportunities and challenges. The three UNEP FI statements
that provide the basis of the initiative are: (1) the 1992 Statement of Commitment to Environment and Sustainability by Financial Institutions, (2)
the 1995 Statement of Commitment by the Insurance Sector, and (3) the
2002 Statement of Commitment by the UNEP FI to the World Summit for
Sustainable Development.

The Equator Principles relate specifically to project-finance activities
above US$50 million and are based, in part, on the International Finance
Corporation's safeguard policies for its project-finance activities.* The
Equator Principles were initiated in late 2003 by a group of four banks
working on a voluntary basis to create a globally accepted industry standard for institutions involved in project-finance activities. Support for the
Equator Principles has grown from the original four banks to fifty-one financial institutions representing more than 80 per cent of the global project-
finance market. There is no formal link between the UNEP FI and the
Equator Principles, although the two voluntary initiatives do have overlapping member banks.

How do these initiatives differ in terms of environmental and social standards for investments? Do they require any environmental impact assessments? Maguire states:

> The UNEP FI statements are broad and apply across the various sub-
> sectors of the financial services sector covering banking, insurance,
> reinsurance and asset management. The statements do not prescribe
> specific operational activity but encourage member institutions to iden-
> tify and move towards the application of best practice as it relates to envi-
> ronmental and sustainability issues. Where Environmental Impact
> Assessments (EIAs) are required as part of legal or commonly accepted
> standards in a given jurisdiction then the UNEP FI statements, founded
> as they are to foster adoption of best practice, would support EIAs where

---

* Under the Equator Principles II, adopted in 2006, the bar has been set at US$10 million;
  see chapter 5 and appendix 2.

and when appropriate for given activities by financial services companies. Project finance activities above US$50 million, as per the Equator Principles criteria, would normally require comprehensive environmental and social impact assessments as part of a best practice due diligence approach. EIA requirements vary depending upon the jurisdiction where the project is being implemented.[114]

Last but not least, the Equator Principles seem to be the most innovative and probably influential development that the financial sector has seen in years. The history of the Equator Principles and the challenges they present are described in chapter 5. The principles might prove what many today are saying about the private sector taking over the lead of governance in the world. The *Washington Post* has stated:

> Most people agree that globalization is here to stay; that it has both positive and less positive effects; and that the world lacks good institutions to ameliorate the negative ones. The 'Equator Principles,' created by the private-sector arm of the World Bank in 2003 and now embraced by 51 [61 as of September 2008] major private banks, are a rare creative effort to grapple with this deficit. The principles govern the social and environmental impact of large-scale projects such as mines or roads or dams; although their implementation remains uneven, the fact that perhaps $125 billion of the $170 billion in global project finance is supposed to respect the Equator code represents genuine progress.[115]

It is good to see more people recognizing the enormous challenge that the Equator Principles initiated when they were introduced in 2003. However, in the spirit of openness, it is time that the private financial institutions who adopted the principles provide evidence of how their operations today differ from their operations before the principles were introduced.

2

The World Bank and the History of Accountability

In 1944 at Bretton Woods,[1] the United Nations Monetary and Financial Conference established the International Bank for Reconstruction and Development (IBRD), later called, and better known as, the World Bank. At the same time, the International Monetary Fund (IMF) was created. The final declaration was a result of three weeks of consultations. Forty-four countries were represented and twenty-eight governments signed the Articles of Agreement in Washington in 1945, after which the first operations started in June 1946. The main background of the design of the institution was the need to rebuild the European economy after the Second World War.[2] Since then, it has often been suggested that the World Bank's noble aim of rebuilding Europe was also based on self-interest, as doing so would create a market for US industry, which had also suffered from a world recession before and during the war.

The start of both the World Bank and the IMF engendered controversy and debate. Most governments waited for the United States to act. President Roosevelt sent Congress the Articles of Agreement of both the IBRD/World Bank and the IMF. According to Edward Mason and Robert Asher, most of the discussion in the US Congress focused on the IMF, with the World Bank receiving little attention. Mason and Asher refer to what Allan Sproul, president of the New York Federal Reserve Bank, said in Congress after delivering a few words about the bank: "The rest of what I have to say is centered on the fund because the Bank seems to have become almost noncontroversial."[3] Mason and Asher cite another speaker in a US Senate hearing, Edward Brown, who was a member of the US delegation at Bretton Woods. Overenthusiastically, Brown said: "Now, take the United States contribution of $3 billion and take Canada's and Cuba's and the United Kingdom, the Scandinavian countries, Holland and Belgium, it is inconceivable to me that you would get a situation where even if the whole US$10 billion were guaranteed that the guarantee of the Bank would not be good."[4]

Still, some resistance is noted by Mason and Asher. They refer to members of the New York banking community who "were soon to demonstrate a different view [and] withheld their fire from the Bank for the time being and concentrated it on the Fund. The late Ansel Luxford subsequently described this as a tactical manoeuvre. They did not want to appear negative to both."5 What is clear from the history of the Word Bank and the IMF is the founding-father role played by the US Congress and US Senate and their attempts since then to control both institutions.

Since its inception, the World Bank has undergone many transformations. The institution can be described as a chameleon: new problems and demands of the world have been taken up by the bank in one way or another, depending on the era, depending on which president was in charge, and depending on the "trends of the day." The institution has outlived its initial mandate, now fulfilled, by taking up other world problems. This in itself is not necessarily a bad outcome, as the institution's experience has been valuable for addressing the increasing demands in other parts of the world. However, the bank has grown uncontrollably and now administers a multitude of tasks.

Jonathan Pincus and Jeffrey Winters state:

> From its humble beginnings as a funding agency for post-war reconstruction, the Bank transformed itself in stages into a development bank, an aid agency, an antipoverty crusader, and a leading proponent of state retrenchment under the rubric of structural adjustment. More recently, the Bank has taken on issues as diverse as post-conflict reconstruction, biodiversity, crime, governance, and public participation in development planning. Each new operational initiative has led the Bank to take on new functions: add new agencies, offices, and programs, collaborate with a wider range of institutions, and address new constituencies.
>
> Yet, like most large bureaucracies, the Bank has found it easier to expand than to retrench: archaeological remnants of previous Bank reforms are readily apparent within the Bank's labyrinthine organizational structure and its portfolio of lending operations ... Confronted with increasing demands from member countries, pressure groups, and business interests, the Bank has attempted to accommodate these demands through ever more inclusive and wide-ranging consultation mechanisms. This in turn, has led to longer lists of operational targets and development objectives, more demands, and yet more consultation. Overwhelmingly, the Bank has responded to political challenges by growing and taking more.6

Despite all the changes experienced by the World Bank, the Articles of Agreement, determined in 1945 after amendments, still remain in their basic form those of the IBRD, the main "partner" and "founder" of the World Bank Group. When conflicts arise over the role of the bank, the Articles of Agreement are the fallback position. However, those who are familiar with the bank know that the Articles of Agreement no longer fully correspond to its present operations. On this point, Pincus and Winters state: "The World Bank as we know bears little resemblance to the institution envisaged at the Bretton Woods Conference in 1944. Moreover, if the Bank did not exist, it is unlikely that a similar conference held today would design anything remotely similar to the present-day World Bank Group. Six decades of incremental change spawned an institution of immense size and complexity, driven by grandiose ambitions and operating beyond its core areas of competence."[7] Nevertheless, to understand the institution of today, one still has to study the Articles of Agreement.

ARTICLES OF AGREEMENT

In Article I, the purposes of the World Bank are proclaimed.[8] This first article is a clear message that the World Bank is a bank and will operate in the first place as a financial institution. According to the Articles of Agreement, the bank started with capital stock totalling us$10 billion.[9] Jean Hardy states that almost fifty years later, in 1993, the total callable capital[10] of the World Bank was about us$166 billion for 4,000 projects in some 100 countries.[11] In 2004 the bank provided us$20.1 billion for 245 projects,[12] and its callable capital was us$178.2 billion,[13] the same total as was reported in 2006 and 2007.[14] Hardy says: "the Bank's resources are huge. The IBRD makes loans only to creditworthy borrowers and has suffered no losses on the loans it has made. Throughout that whole time it has made a profit. A substantial part of that income goes to strengthen its reserves and to fund the International Development Association."[15]

In the remainder of Article I, which deals the purposes of the World Bank, there is little reference to a social agenda for the institution. It is significant that within a powerful economic agenda, only a few phrases give the impression of a social agenda: "peacetime needs," "the standard of living and conditions of labor," and "a smooth transition from wartime to a peacetime economy." Economists might argue that a healthy economy or economic growth will automatically create a higher standard of living, with all its positive social consequences. This might often be the case but only, it seems, if growth is embedded in social policies. That aid provided to developing nations by the International Development Association (IDA)[16] is guaranteed partly through the profits made from IBRD loans could be considered an indication of the bank's high principles; however, financing such development is a rather tall order, and as a result, the middle-income countries have also become important financers of the poorest countries of the world. The World Bank has been affected by the rapid pace of global change. In 1999 China was still treated as an IDA country and regarded as a member of the group of the poorest countries of the world. That soon changed.[17] In 2008, for the first time, China will be a donor country to the World Bank, with a contribution of us$30 million. This is not yet a large sum; however, the contribution marks a principal shift and signals a changing world. In the mean time, the United Kingdom has taken over the position of the United States as the largest funder to the IDA in the World Bank, their respective contributions being 14 per cent and 11 per cent.

Article II, which treats membership in and capital of the World Bank, is all about the organization and ownership of this capital: the pricing of shares, the division and calls of subscribed capital, the matters of payment, and so on. This study does not examine the technical financial details of the World Bank. One remark to be made is the visible dominance of the US dollar in the system, regardless of its value on the world currency market. This can be explained by the institution's history as an initiative born on US soil.

Article III treats general provisions relating to loans and guarantees. Section 1, on use of resources, states in subsection 1b: "For the purpose of facilitating the restoration and reconstruction of the economy of members whose metropolitan territories have suffered great devastation from enemy occupation or hostilities, the Bank, in determining the conditions and terms of loans made to such members, shall pay special regard to lightening the financial burden and expediting the completion of such restoration and reconstruction." Besides emphasizing again the reconstruction of the economy, it still refers to reconstruction after wartime.

WORLD BANK IMMUNITY

Article VII,[18] on status, immunities, and privileges, has other remarkable sections that need to be mentioned in the context of this work. Sections 2, 3, and 8 make the World Bank, among others, almost "untouchable." Section 2, on the status of the bank, reads:

The Bank shall possess full juridical personality, and, in particular, the capacity:
  (i)   to contract;
  (ii) to acquire and dispose of immovable and movable property;
  (iii) to institute legal proceedings.

Section 3, on the position of the bank with regard to judicial process, reads:

Actions may be brought against the Bank only in a court of competent jurisdiction in the territories of a member in which the Bank has an office, has appointed an agent for the purpose of accepting service or notice of process, or has issued or guaranteed securities. No actions shall, however, be brought by members or persons acting for or deriving claims from members. The property and assets of the Bank shall, wherever located and by whomsoever held, be immune from all forms of seizure, attachment or execution before the delivery of final judgment against the Bank.

Section 8, on the immunities and privileges of officers and employees, reads:

> All governors, executive directors, alternates, officers and employees of
> the Bank:
> (i) shall be immune from legal process with respect to acts performed
>   by them in their official capacity except when the bank waives
>   this immunity.

Thus when the institution was created, it was granted immunity from legal prosecution. It is this immunity that, down the road, caused many problems and occasioned protests by civil society. As I noted in chapter 1, this
apparent lack of formal accountability has been somewhat superseded by
the realities of globalization. The World Bank's activities are financed with
tax money, whether from the United States or other donor countries, and
much of it is European and Japanese tax money. In postmodern democratic states, the people (or their representatives) like to know what happens with the taxes they pay.

POLITICAL ACTIVITY PROHIBITED

Article IV,[19] section 10, entitled "Political Activity Prohibited," is by far the
most difficult and contradictory section given the daily operations of the
World Bank. This very small, easily overlooked section has turned out to be
a hindrance to the operations of the institution and its staff. The borrowing countries, as members of the bank,[20] do not allow any interference in
the political affairs of their nations, and only economic considerations are
expected to play a role.[21]

The prohibition against the bank's interference in national politics
seems in practice to be an impossible undertaking. A clear distinction between where the role and responsibility of management ends and that of
the borrowing country begins cannot always be made. Mason and Asher
note that "In theory the IBRD, up to the point of appraisal, acts only as an
advisor to the borrower; it then puts on the hat of a lender and disposes of
the application. Early in the history of Bank project lending this 'arm's
length' relationship in fact existed. It was asserted that if the Bank had
helped in the preparation of a project, it could not then objectively ap-
praise its own work. But this long ago gave way to a more incestuous relationship."[22] Mason and Asher put the finger on a sore spot. As a member
of the Inspection Panel, I regularly listened during investigations to staff
members explaining that there would have been no project if they had not
pulled and pushed from the beginning to the end and complained about
the many difficulties they had to overcome.

Mason and Asher quote from some internal bank documents by Warren
Baum.[23] Two of these are relevant to understanding both the procedures
and the difficult relationships involved in the management of borrowers.
Concerning the procedures to be followed, Baum writes:

There are essentially three tests involved in the identification of a project. The first is whether the sector of the economy into which the project falls, and the project itself, are of high priority for development and are so recognized in the government's development plans. The second is whether, on prima facie grounds, the project seems to be feasible; that is, whether a technical solution to the problem to which the project is addressed can be found at a cost commensurate with the benefits to be expected. And the third test is whether the government is willing to support the project by financial and other means.[24]

The second statement by Baum concerns the deep involvement of management in formulation and implementation at all stages of a project:

> Experience has demonstrated that we do not get enough good projects to appraise unless we are involved intimately in their identification and preparation. The result is that, instead of having an invisible dividing line, with identification and preparation of projects on a side and appraisal and supervision on the other, there is a continuing cycle in which the Bank is closely engaged at all stages. One of the benefits of this change of attitude is that, through better preparation, fewer projects are rejected at the appraisal stage, although the final version of the project may be quite different from its original conception.[25]

This statement shows the fiction of noninterference that already existed early in the history of the World Bank. The bank has officially declared that it will not interfere in national politics, yet in practice it does, as was evident in 1966. Others argue that there are earlier examples of political interventions. Ricardo Faini and Enzo Grilli, who examine the role of the World Bank and the International Monetary Fund in the international economic architecture, also comment on the political interventions of the institutions:

> Despite claims of "functionalism" and "content-based" decision making, which are standard regarding international financial organizations, a good part of their decisions are inevitably political, in the sense that they respond to the national interest of one or a group of shareholders, who can mass enough support from the others to carry them through or to block them. There are "historically" famous such cases, like the decision of the World Bank not to finance the Aswan Dam in Egypt in 1955 or the decision of the IMF to extend a huge loan to Mexico in 1995 (supported by a credit facility of the United States and a Bank or International Settlement loan on account of the Group of 10), that are normally categorized as political decisions. The former took place under pressure from the United States and the United Kingdom wishing to "punish" in some way President Nasser for his dealings with the Soviet Union. The second was taken, largely on behalf of the

United States (and the nine other members of the G-10), set on helping a critically important country in the Western Hemisphere.[26]

Management is fully aware of its involvement in politics, as was made
clear in a newsletter of the World Bank Group Staff Association. Not that
long after the attacks on New York and the Pentagon on 11 September
2001, bank management commented:

> Even before the September attacks, the Bank was about to be the desti-
> nation of an estimated 100,000 protesters pushing politically in one
> direction, while U.S. Treasury Secretary Paul O'Neill and some conserva-
> tive forces close to President George W. Bush appeared to be mounting
> something of a push in the other direction. The need to balance
> pressures is endemic to a global development assistance organization,
> but perhaps staff needs to be especially conscious of pressures on
> Mr. Wolfensohn and Senior Management right now. Most of the time,
> staff is highly focused, works hard, and tends to put its head down and
> dig into the immediate tasks. However, occasionally it helps to pause and
> look around at the larger and more difficult context in which the institu-
> tion and its senior management operate.[27]

This statement clearly spells out management's awareness of its position
within the institution and of the institution's position within the global
context. The statement also corresponds to my personal experiences inside the bank. Often during investigations by the Inspection Panel, management did articulate its views on the political situations in countries
being investigated as well as on the control that donor countries have over
developing nations.

According to the Staff Association, there had already been political pressure before the institution opened. There was wrangling over the location
of the bank. Some argued it should be located outside the United States –
an idea that never had a chance. The United States would never have
agreed. John Keynes,[28] one of the founding fathers of the institution, said
that it was necessary to keep the bank "clear of the politics of congress and
the nationalistic whispering gallery of the Embassies and Legations."[29] Further, according to the Staff Association: "The U.S. view prevailed on a DC
location and also on a critical decision about the executive directors:
would they be periodic visitors to the Bank, or permanent residents? Since
the voting power of the U.S. ED [executive director] was the greatest, the
White House sought maximum influence and control, wanting the EDs
right on campus. This and other details so infuriated Keynes (a towering
figure in modern economics) that he washed his hands of the new institution and went home to Britain."[30] Keynes definitely had a sharp eye. What
he was afraid of is exactly what happened. The World Bank became a political institution right away.

The Staff Association went on to say: "In dealing with the U.S. government, the new Bank had to confront not only the President but also the houses of congress, who might not agree with the administration, or even with each other. The Bank's biggest need has been for a supportive U.S. President."[31] The Staff Association cited a statement by Alex Shakow[32] to underline the influence and power of the US president: "If you put aid programs, including those for the Bank, to a vote in congress without strong presidential support, they would fail, because it requires a kind of global view to see the Bank's value."[33]

The US Congress still exerts pressure on the World Bank. The US has created, as the Staff Association refers to it, a special liaison of the bank to Capitol Hill in order to defend and control US interests.[34] The article describes many further examples of political pressure from the US Congress.[35] As I note later, in chapter 3, it was pressure from the US Congress, responding to the demand of a group of the bank's executive directors, that forced management to install the Inspection Panel.

However, not only the US put political pressure on the bank. Other donors could hold "Management's feet to fire when it suited their national interests to do so,"[36] states the Staff Association. A remarkable example drawn from the role of France is also mentioned: France actually had a World Bank staff member pulled out of the Africa Region for suggesting that it hurt Francophone African countries to keep their francs overvalued along with the French franc. The "power game" of the French is not new. My ten years as a member of the European Parliament in Strasbourg and Brussels was enough time to develop a picture of French operations in the territories that they regard as under their influence.

One can conclude that the Articles of Agreement prohibiting political activity by the World Bank are all just a sham, a fiction. In most countries, there seems to be no real hindrance of management's interference in national procedures and decisions for the bank's normal operations. The difficulties are to be found in countries with a low or bad performance in the fields of environment, good governance and corruption, social policies, transparency, democracy, and human rights.

The World Bank is the global arena of international politics. I permit myself to say that the bank, together with the IMF, is probably at least as political as any other international institution. The history of the World Trade Organization (WTO) is too short to judge whether the same is the case for that institution.

HUMAN RIGHTS AND THE WORLD BANK

In the section of Article IV that prohibits political activity, one also finds the following: "Only economic considerations shall be relevant to their [the bank's] decisions, and these considerations shall be weighed impartially in order to achieve the purposes stated in Article I." In its ten years of reporting, the Inspection Panel has noted the following internal reactions on the delicate issue of human rights: "As two legal opinions (in 1990 and 1995) by the Bank's General Counsel and senior vice-president state with respect to human rights, the prohibition of political activities in the Bank's work translates into a prohibition to interfere in the manner in which a country deals with political human rights, as long as this has no demonstrable effect on the country's economy."[37]

In countries where human rights are violated management thus argues that it cannot act or enter into discussions to prevent the violations. This is often felt to be a hypocritical and duplicitous role. On the one hand, there is interference in national economic policies and procedures, with considerable effects on the targeted countries; on the other hand, there is the official point of view that there should be no interference. Thus when there is a real need to act in the field of human rights violations, the bank is usually silent. This position has come under pressure lately, both inside and outside the bank. A strong argument against the official neutrality of the bank when human rights are threatened has been made by the 195 members of the World Bank, a large majority of whom support the Universal Declaration of Human Rights (UDHR), and many human rights principles are already embodied in the constitutions of these members, which include countries with a wide diversity of cultures and religions.[38] Other financial institutions are confronted with the same criticism about their disregard for human rights.

The bank's constant reference to the Articles of Agreement and to the notion that human rights violations can be addressed only "as long as this has no demonstrable effect on the country's economy" was regarded by the Inspection Panel as rather cynical. This was the case during the investigation in 2001 and 2002 into the Chad-Cameroon Petroleum Development and Pipeline Project, in which I took part as a member of the panel. On the bank's view regarding its policy for addressing human rights violations, the panel referred to a statement made by management in its response to the Inspection Panel's report on Chad:

> The Bank is concerned about violations of Human Rights in Chad as elsewhere while respecting the Bank's Articles of Agreement which require the Bank to focus on economic considerations and not on political or other non-economic influences as the basis for its decisions. In evaluating the economic aspects of any project, human rights issues may be relevant to the Bank's work if they may have a significant direct economic effect on the project. Having carefully considered all aspects of this issue, Management's conclusion is that the Project can achieve its developmental objectives.[39]

The panel reacted to this statement by saying: "In other words, according to the Management Response, if Human Rights issues have 'significant direct economic effects' on a Bank project, they become a matter of concern to the Bank. Otherwise they don't. In this case, management feels that the project 'can achieve its development objectives,' so human rights issues are of no *direct* concern."[40]

The Inspection Panel's influence on human rights became manifest in 2001 during the investigation of the Chad-Cameroon oil pipeline. The panel, after being confronted with clear human rights violations in Chad, acknowledged in its report that it has in fact no mandate over human rights. Nevertheless, the panel unanimously concluded after strong internal discussions to go beyond its mandate by reporting on the violations. The panel stated: "It is not within the Panel's mandate to assess the status of Governance and human rights in Chad in general or in isolation, and the Panel acknowledges that there are several institutions (including UN bodies) specifically in charge of this subject. However, the Panel felt obliged to examine whether the issue of proper governance or human rights violations in Chad were such as to impede the implementation of the project in a manner compatible with the Bank's policies."[41]

And the panel went on to state:

> As for human rights, the Panel has examined several reports addressing the situation in the country and the extensive exchange of correspondence between Bank Management and NGOs in Chad and abroad. The Panel takes note of the fact that on more than one occasion when political repression in Chad seemed severe, the Bank's President personally intervened to help free local opposition leaders, including the representative of the Requesters, Mr. Yorongar, who was reported as being subject to torture. During its visit to Chad, the Panel did not seek out two other opposition leaders in N'Djaména[42] who had been arrested. In the field, however, several local leaders and organizations mentioned to the Panel that, while at times feeling harassed by the authorities, they have expressed their opinions about the project without incurring physical violence. The Panel observes that the situation is far from ideal. It raises questions about compliance with Bank policies, in particular with those that relate to informed and open consultation, and it warrants renewed monitoring by the Bank.[43]

It is clear that the Chad report was breaking ground in the World Bank with its reference to human rights violations. For the first time, the executive directors of the board had to consider the subject, and the chairman of the panel, Eddy Ayensu, made a statement to the board.[44]

Outside the World Bank the discussion also goes on. J.G. Taillant proposes practical ways that international financial institutions (IFIs) could and should address human rights violations with so-called "right-based policies."[45] In doing so, he focuses primarily on the World Bank and the IMF. Given the history of the institutions and the history of the Universal Declaration of Human Rights, he sees a logical link between the two:

History would have it that these two institutions became two of the most important development institutions of the planet, and today, despite their very clear mandates to do otherwise, they must answer to a new set of problems and issues which are a product and concern of our time just as reconstruction was the focus of concern after World War II. Today, we assign a much broader mandate to the Bank, and the Bank itself recognizes its "primary focus to be helping the poorest people and the poorest countries." In even the most strict interpretations of its mandate, the Bank says that what it strives for today is a far stretch from its purposes as outlined in the Articles of Agreement, which makes absolutely no mention of poverty. It is important to point out that while the foundational charters of the Bank and Fund do not refer to the issues surrounding development which concerns us today, we should not think of the Bank and Fund as somehow having been created outside of the context in which they in fact came to be. The Bretton Woods agreements which gave rise to the Bank and the Fund took place more or less at the same historical moment leaders gathered to create the United Nations (UN), and gave form to the Universal Declaration of Human Rights (UDHR).[46]

It is Taillant's assumption that the global leaders at the time created the UN, the IMF, and the World Bank and operated in the same arena with the same views and targets by "paving the way towards more cohesive, collaborative and harmonic international development."[47] He underscores this view with a reference to the preamble of the UDHR, which states that "Every individual and every organ of society, keeping this declaration constantly in mind, shall strive by teaching and education to promote respect for these rights and freedoms and by progressive measures, national and international, to secure their universal and effective recognition and observance, both among the peoples of Member States themselves and among the peoples of territories under their jurisdiction."[48] No doubt, the different stakeholders who established the institutions and the UN were influenced by the same spirit of the age. And it is most likely that those creating the UN tried to keep the two institutions under their umbrella. The statement quoted by Taillant could be read as a demand for formal recognition of the UDHR by international institutions such as the IMF and the World Bank. The relationship between the institutions and the UN is evident. The World Bank's formal relationship with the UN is defined by a 1947 agreement that recognizes the bank both as an independent specialized agency of the UN and as an observer in many UN bodies, including the General Assembly.[49] Nevertheless, the main objective of the driving forces behind the World Bank and the IMF was purely economic. So long as the Articles of Agreement are not changed, and so long as the financial forces in the United States have a strong influence on the operations of the bank and on its Articles of Agreement, it is most unlikely that these articles will be changed.

Taillant adds a convincing explanation for the resistance of the World Bank and other IFIs to take up human rights by setting conditions for borrowing governments:

> Both institutions, however, have strongly resisted assuming any responsibility for the assurance of guarantee of human rights. The standard argument of the IFIs on this approach centers on the IFIs unwillingness to place conditionality on countries for not complying with human rights obligations under the treaties they have signed. They do not wish to become human rights policemen. This position is strongly echoed in the IFIs Executive Directors board rooms where countries like China, are vehemently opposed to international bodies reacting to their human rights performance. Clearly the fear of many countries like China is the potentially adverse impact to their economic trade and commerce due to trade sanctions levied under claims that they are not complying with Western-conceived views of how societies should be organized and how it should treat individuals. Human rights, in this respect is seen by many non-Western or underdeveloped nations as merely another weapon wielded by the west (namely the USA and Europe) to hinder free trade and economic progress of non-Western and/or underdeveloped societies with a legally fundamental excuse. This is also the view, for example of many Western underdeveloped countries like Argentina and Brazil, who refuse to speak of human rights in forums such as the WTO and other regional trade agreements claiming that this is just another way for the US and Europe to gain an upper hand in their trade markets.

I fully recognize this explanation by Taillant for the lack of action on human rights. There is no doubt that the World Bank and the borrowing countries fear human rights becoming part of the conditions that can be imposed on them. (I return to the subject of human rights elsewhere, notably in chapter 6.)

THE WORLD BANK AND ACCOUNTABILITY

It is the World Bank itself that correctly is asking for good governance, accountability, and transparency of governments in countries where it operates. At present, the bank has made good governance an important aim of the institution. It is clear that the bank as an institution and moreover those who work for it are not blind to the actual demands of society. Within the corridors of the bank, one can hear the same discussions as those held in the media and public forums, including the criticisms.

Among all multilateral financial institutions (MFIs), the World Bank is followed the most closely by the outside world and as a result is also heavily criticized. That other banks also have impressive portfolios, such as the European Investment Bank (EIB), raises the question of why so little attention is given to those banks by the media.[50] This is even more interesting given the strong activities of the Central Eastern Europe (CEE) Bankwatch Network. One reason for the heightened scrutiny of the World Bank is its location in Washington, DC, which is considered the centre of world politics, in contrast to the EIB's location in the somewhat dull and hidden "village" of Luxembourg, the capital of the Grand Duchy of Luxembourg, which is one of the twenty-seven independent states of the Erupean Union. A demonstration in front of the EIB's entrance will never get as much media attention as a demonstration in front of the World Bank headquarters, located 500 metres from the White House. A more important reason for the media's focus on the World Bank is that it has become an institution with operations in almost every nation of the world, which has given it an exemplary function and has required that it play a leading role. The World Bank was the first MFI to serve as "big brother" for the many other MFIs created in later years.

The point to be made here is that the bank's immunity from legal prosecution in its operations was the main trigger for nongovernmental organizations (NGOs) to ask for more accountability. Before this awareness took hold in the bank, a lot still had to happen. This is further explained in chapter 3.

POSITION OF THE EXECUTIVE DIRECTORS

Last but not least, Article V, on organization and management, is about governance of the World Bank and explains the position of the bank's executive directors, who finally decided to create the World Bank Inspection Panel in 1993.

Article V, section 1, on the structure of the bank, states: "The Bank shall have a Board of Governors,[51] Executive Directors, a President and such other officers and staff to perform such duties as the Bank may determine." Officially, all the powers of the bank reside with the Board of Governors, which has delegated most of its power to the executive directors.[52] The bank has twenty-four executive directors, of whom eight shareholders represent their own countries exclusively.[53] Five of them form the "old group" of stakeholders that, after the Second World War, created the institution: the United States, Japan, France, the United Kingdom, and Germany. These five are entitled to appoint an executive director themselves, while the rest share the remaining seats and form constituencies. How the groups are formed is not provided for in the Articles of Agreement, so the countries negotiate among themselves. So far, these negotiations seem to have taken place in the dark, as very little is known or has been written about them.

In 1946 the Board of Governors had twelve seats: five appointed by the governors of the bank for the first five countries with the largest numbers of votes (depending on the shares) and seven elected seats. At that time, the appointed seats were distributed among the United States, China, the United Kingdom, France, and India. The five seats for "appointing members" are still reserved for the five states with the most votes. An "electing member" can become an "appointing member" and vice versa. But the elected seats have expanded since 1946. In 1948 the board had fourteen seats, and in each of the following years (i.e., 1952, 1956, and 1958), the board expanded by one seat, bringing the total to eighteen. In 1964 two new seats were created, and 1980 and 1986 each saw the addition of another seat. The last expansion took place in 1992, when two seats were created, resulting in twenty-four seats. Since then, the appointed seats have been held by the United States, Japan, Germany, France, and the United Kingdom. Three states each have an elected seat of their own:[54] China, the Russian Federation, and Saudi Arabia.

Nothing is to be found in libraries, including the library of the executive directors in the World Bank, regarding how the constituencies are formed. I often hear that it is a matter of "high international politics." The only place where one might find some history of the formation is in the confidential files of the various ministries of the member states and in the files of the bank itself. What is clear is that countries have no other choice but to be part of a constituency. One story in circulation is that when Switzerland became a member of the IBRD in 1992,[55] it wanted to have a seat and was able to ensure this by inviting other member countries, all from eastern Europe, to enter the Swiss constituency. The question is whether special funding was offered.

Canada, which has more votes than China, does not have a seat for itself but has formed a constituency with many small states in the Caribbean.[56] The subject of the constituencies and the position of the executive directors on the grouping of the constituencies is further addressed later in this chapter.

Andrés Rigo Sureda, former deputy general counsel for operations of the World Bank, has noted that "The Articles of Agreement provide only general guidance on the respective roles of the President and the Executive Directors."[57] He refers to the following text from Article V: "The Executive Directors shall be responsible for the conduct of the general operations of the Bank, and for this purpose, shall exercise all the powers delegated to them by the Board of Governors."[58] This article can be interpreted in many ways. What are the general operations? And how much power is given to the directors by the Board of Governors? Rigo Sureda also refers to the relationship between the president and the directors: "The President is 'the chief of operating staff,' responsible for the conduct of 'the ordinary business of the Bank' under the 'direction' of the Executive Directors, and subject to their 'control' responsible for the organization, appointment and dismissal of the officers and staff."[59] Rigo Sureda then describes and comments on "the lack of a precise definition of the role of the President or the Executive Directors."[60] He says that this is the result of a compromise at Bretton Woods, where the institutions of the World Bank and the IMF were created.

During the negotiations, one group was of the opinion that the executive directors should be a consultative body. Another group wanted to see them play a more directing role. When the institution started, the first president was Eugene Meyer, who, according to Rigo Sureda, "spent most of his time and energy battling with the Board for leadership of the institution. Frustrated, Mr. Meyer resigned after six months. He viewed his tug of war with the much younger U.S. Executive Director as a contest with someone who was out to get his job rather than as an almost predictable result of ambiguities in the Articles of Agreement and specifically provisions in the Bretton Woods Agreements Act adopted by the U.S. Congress. New understandings would be necessary if his successor were to have power commensurate with the responsibilities of his office."[61]

PRESIDENTS OF THE BANK AND RELATIONS WITH THE EXECUTIVE DIRECTORS

Eugene Meyer's successor, John McCloy, would use this new insight to acquire power commensurate with his responsibilities by making such power a condition for accepting the position of president. I understand that what happened at the time was rather crucial. A decision about the division of responsibilities between the president and the executive directors was taken. The directors would be responsible for deciding on all matters of policy in connection with the operations of the World Bank, including the approval of loans. Management would be responsible for developing recommendations on policy matters. In other words, management had the right to develop recommendations on policy matters, whereas the board could only accept or refuse them. This arrangement was proposed by the board's Committee on Organization and approved in 1947. The division has remained in effect ever since. According to Rigo Sureda, the "longevity of this arrangement is also attributable to the nature of the Bank's business, a project finance agency funded from private capital markets with independent sources of funds to finance its budget."[62]

This relationship between the World Bank's board and management brings to mind the position of the European Parliament, which agrees or disagrees with proposals for European legislation formulated by the European Commission, without having the right to propose legislation or policies itself. If this is an apt comparison, then daily power at the bank is in the hands of management. The executive directors can agree, disapprove, or delay a decision by asking that more information be provided, studies be done, or changes be made. Although one never hears the word "amendments" in the context of World Bank decisions, a rather similar process takes place in Europe (and in other UN institutions). The directors or their staff meet and negotiate regularly on all proposals that are placed on the agenda. In the negotiations and preceding meetings, it becomes clear whether a refusal or a demand for changes will have enough votes. The division of votes among the directors is related to the number of subscribed shares in the bank's capital held by the country or countries they represent. The difference from the European Parliament is that demands by the board are hardly ever put to a vote. Before the official meeting of the board, the general intention is to come to a consensus.

Still, management's power is strong, as Mason and Asher saliently observe:

> It is in the nature of things that relations between "management" and "board" will have their ups and downs. Management's objective is inevitably to translate its plans into action and to pursue its business with as much backing and as little "interference" as possible from its board of directors. The board, if it has any conscience at all, wants to be more than a rubber stamp; at least some of its members will want to alter certain policies or get into "operational details." Customary differences in point of view are usually submerged, however, and a common front formed when the institution is subjected to "attacks from the outside."[63]

From my years at the World Bank, I fully recognize, as Mason and Asher state, that the bank's inclination to form "a common front" is simply "the nature of things." It appears to be a human reaction to defend an institution from the inside when it is attacked from the outside. This is even more the case when one is part of a governing body of such an institution as the World Bank.

Under the leadership of Eugene Black,[64] who succeeded McCloy as president in 1949, the division of powers between the executive directors and the president was further established. According to Jochen Kraske:

> McCloy, a hard and energetic worker, had little patience with the formalities represented by the Board of executive directors. Not surprisingly, by the time he left, considerable resentment had built up among the executive directors. This changed quickly when Black became the third president in 1949. He took the time to cultivate the Board members – socially to some extent, but also by being available to listen to them and by conveying a sense of appreciation. In board meetings he was able to make the executive directors feel that the ultimate authority was theirs without giving them any more power than they had previously been accorded.[65]

Black served as president of the World Bank from 1949 to 1962. About this era Kraske says:

> Black's successors would not have to create a bank as Black had done, to give substance to an idea. They would have to shake up a bank that had acquired an enviable reputation and naturally tended to value the

way things were. They would have to open the institution to meet the challenges posed by a sharp increase in Bank membership, by the emergence of a less supportive view of economic assistance among donor countries, by the new understandings of the meaning of development, and by inevitable, although gradual, generational changes in staff and management.[66]

In 1973 Mason and Asher were not afraid to describe the position of the board in a somewhat irreverent manner: "Unlike most policy boards, the Bank's executive directors are on the premises virtually all the time. Their duties include selecting the president of the Bank, interpreting the Articles of Agreement, passing on all loans and bond issues, approving the annual budget, giving general guidance on matters of policy, and serving as links with the capitals of member governments. Their jobs can be sinecures or arduous assignments, depending on their interpretation of the role and its requirements."[67] The part played by the executive directors in the selection of presidents has been minimal. Once it was conceded that the president should be a US national, the task of finding a candidate acceptable at the highest levels of the US government and in the US financial community inevitably fell upon the executive branch of the US government. Presidents McCloy, Black, and George Woods played active roles in selecting their successors. The executive directors at times have indicated unhappiness with the nominee and have privately grumbled about having had someone "forced down their throats." An opportunity to choose from a short list of nominees who were equally acceptable to the US government would have been much appreciated but was never provided. All that is written about the powers of the executive directors leads to the conclusion they are in a constant battle to acquire and maintain some control over the daily operations of the bank. Indeed, many experts describe the role of the directors as minimal, and some descriptions are somewhat a caricature.

However, in the spring of 2007 the situation changed dramatically when a majority of the executive directors no longer accepted President Paul Wolfowitz, who was appointed by US president George W. Bush, as the head of the World Bank, resulting in his resignation. President Wolfowitz had a pre-existing relationship with a bank staff member, Shaha Riza, who as a consequence of Wolfowitz's appointment and the existing internal rules of the bank, had to be relocated. Although she was sent away on secondment, her salary was still paid for by the World Bank. Wolfowitz himself was directly involved in the process of compensation for this staff member, including a salary increase that was outside the bank's internal rules. A report by the board's Ethics Committee noted the following: "By involving himself in the specific terms of Ms. Riza's external assignment, Mr. Wolfowitz acted in a manner that was inconsistent with his obligations to the Bank in two important respects. One relates to his obligation to avoid conflict of interest situations. The other relates to his obligation to act in a manner that is consistent with the Staff Rules and other obligations that pertain to staff."[68] According to the report, the salary increase was 28.2 per cent.

For the first time in the history of the World Bank, the executive directors no longer accepted a president appointed by the US government. And what is more, for the first time the European executive directors spoke with one voice. With their actions, they opened the door for structural changes in the framework of governance of the bank. The Ethics Committee report states: "At an even higher level, the issues which have been uncovered and have unfolded in the course of the last few weeks, may give rise to a careful examination of the Bank's overall governance framework, and in particular, the oversight function of the Executive Directors. In the course of this examination, consideration should be given to changes that may be required to bring the Bank's governance framework to the state of the art now existing in the twenty-first century."[69] It is a remarkable statement that could have far-reaching implications. As far as I can tell, it has been overlooked by the media, which all concentrated on Wolfowitz's "departure."

GROWTH OF THE WORLD BANK GROUP

Over the years, the World Bank's membership,[70] staff, and portfolio have grown, and so too has its visibility. During Eugene Black's tenure, a firm foundation was laid down, on which his successors built the powerful and worldwide institution of today. In 1956 Black established the International Finance Corporation (IFC) and in 1960 the International Development Association (IDA). The IFC promotes economic development through the private sector, while IDA assists the poorest countries (often identified by the bank as "IDA-Countries") by providing interest-free loans with maturities of thirty-five to forty years. Today, they are part of the World Bank Group, which consists of five closely associated agencies.[71] The oldest and largest such agency is the International Bank for Reconstruction and Development (IBRD), established in 1945, which in 2007 had 185 member countries. The International Finance Corporation (1956) has 179 members; the International Development Association (1960) has 166 members; the Multilateral Investment Guarantee Agency (MIGA; 1988) has 171 members; and the International Centre for Settlement of Investment Disputes (ICSID; 1966) has 140 member countries.[72]

In September 1952, under President Black, the first reorganization of the World Bank took place.[73] The operational activities were reorganized on a geographical, rather than functional, basis. Three regions in the Operational Department were created: Asia and the Middle East; Europe, Africa, and Australasia; and the Western Hemisphere. Other departments created were the Department of Technical Operations, the Economic Staff, the Technical Assistance Staff, and the Liaison Staff.

BANK PRESIDENTS, 1963–1986

When President Black left the World Bank, an era passed at the institution with little visible turbulence and, most of all, little growth. Between 1963 and 1986, the following three presidents took office: George Woods (1963–68), an "experienced investment banker, chairman of the first Boston Corporation,"[74] who, given his impoverished youth, was devoted to poverty alleviation and thus wanted the bank to cease "piling up its profits at an almost indecent rate"[75] and instead use its reserves to intervene earlier in the development process, who promoted the concept of aid coordination, and who wanted the economists to be given a larger and more prominent role in the bank;[76] Robert McNamara (1968–81), who enlarged the bank's lending thirteen-fold and more than tripled its staff and is seen as the president who was able to transform the bank's mission "from closing the gap between industrial and developing countries to alleviating world poverty";[77] and Alden Clausen (1981–86), who had spent his working life as Bank of America's chief and who turned out to have difficulties understanding and leading the World Bank since he lacked government (i.e., public sector) experience and knowledge of Washington circles, thus prompting him to announce his retirement at the end of his five-year term.

After Clausen, Barber Conable (1986–91) took over. He was a Republican member of the US Congress and a Washington insider who knew few people, and little about issues, outside US political circles. With little managerial experience, Conable started a painful reorganization that reduced staff numbers; according to Kraske, "In effect, everyone had to consider himself without a job, unless and until chosen for reassignment."[78] This process demoralized the bank's staff. Nevertheless, Conable was able to secure more US funding for IDA. However, what is more, during his term the so-called Brady Plan was introduced, which demanded that countries wanting debt relief accept an economic adjustment program before debt reduction could be endorsed. It was under Conable that critics targeted the bank, initiating its painful economic reform; because of the structural adjustment loans, the poorest sections of society suffered.

Conable was confronted with criticism not only on structural adjustment but also on environmental degradation. Weeks after he took office, the World Bank issued the following statement: "The Bank is deeply concerned about the destruction of tropical forests and it is intensifying efforts to effectively deal with the problem, including a shift from industrial plantations and logging to social forestry or community forestry."[79] At the end of the 1980s and the beginning of the 1990s, criticism had also started concerning the bank's involvement in the Narmada Dam project in India (see chapter 3).

In October 1990 the environment director, Kenneth Piddington, reacted to a public statement by NGOs that attributed all blame for environmental problems to the World Bank. He said that for progress to be made in this area three things must happen: "The links between development and ecological concerns must be recognized; development institutions must be more open in their procedures, especially in the way they apply environmental assessment; and NGOs must respond to governments and development institutions by clearly identifying areas where they want to be involved."[80]

At the time, criticism of the bank's involvement in the Narmada Dam project in India greatly increased. On 17 June 1991, during the last weeks that President Conable was in office, he established an independent review committee named after its chairman, Bradford Morse (see chapter 3). This was the first independent review of a bank project commissioned by the bank.[81] A few weeks later, just before Conable resigned, he said: "When I first came to the Bank, it was unnecessarily criticized for ignoring environmental issues. It is still criticized, but we are doing better. Most important, we have reaffirmed our commitment to poverty reduction. The World Bank exists for only one reason, to make people's lives better."[82] Shortly thereafter, Conable left the outcome of the Morse Commission's report to his successor, Lewis T. Preston.

INCREASE IN WORLD BANK STAFF

Mason and Asher raise another notable point related to the rapid increase in the number of staff. They posit the problem of an organization that is growing too quickly being unable to cope with such change:

> Large numbers of new personnel are difficult for a functioning organiza-
> tion to digest. And when the arrival of 'new boys' coincides with the subtle
> changes in personal relationship that always accompany the settling-in of a
> new president, morale in some quarters is bound to suffer, at least for a
> while. A US diplomat with long experience in the US government recently
> observed, not entirely facetiously, that when the staff of a public agency
> exceeds 1,000, the employees deal only with each other and stop commu-
> nicating with the rest of the world. In the history of the World Bank, the
> 1,000-employee point was reached toward the middle of the 1960s.[83]

The US diplomat's assertion is correct in the sense that it could apply to any other fast-growing institution.

Thereafter, Mason and Asher make a statement that in 1973, the year their book was published, was rather prophetic:

> While the IBRD continues to "communicate" with the outside world and
> is in many respects a more effective broker between developed and de-
> veloping countries than ever before, it is also true that the Bank group is
> by now a sizable bureaucracy, showing familiar signs of the hardening of
> the arteries that is characteristic of bureaucracies. These include extra

layers of personnel that have to be penetrated (frequently by strangers dealing with strangers), extensive concern with procedural and presentational details, difficulty in getting information promptly to those who ought to have it, and on the other hand, burying the internal messenger service under an avalanche of papers for distribution to a growing list of recipients whose status and psyche require them to receive the papers but not necessarily to read or act upon them.[84]

This statement is still valid in 2007. In the words "extensive concern with procedural and presentational details," I recognize some of the symptoms of the problems with the World Bank today.

According to Rick Scobey,[85] at the turn of the century the World Bank Group had human capital of 10,500 staff members from 195 countries, a figure that, according to the bank's website, remains almost the same in 2007. It has the largest source of capital for the developing world: almost $500 billion in loans. The IBRD is a AAA-rated financial institution and is consistently profitable. During fiscal year 2006 the IBRD's lending reached $14.1 billion for 112 new operations in 33 countries.[86] The same year, IDA approved credits totalling $9.5 billion for 167 new operations in 59 countries.[87] Also in 2006 the IFC approved financing totalling $6.7 billion for 284 projects in 66 countries,[88] while the MIGA issued guarantees for a total coverage of $1.3 billion.[89]

The figures cited by Jean Hardy concerning increases in the bank's capital, in the number of its members, and in the extent of its activities are informative:

Presently the World Bank has four main sections. The IBRD, the largest, is currently owned by the governments of 176 countries, including all 15 of the republics which formed the Eastern European block. This is a four-fold increase of membership over the 44 countries which conceived of the institution in 1944. In 1946 the Bank had an authorized capital of $10 billion, worth about 20 times as much today. In 1993 the Bank's total callable capital was almost $166 billion, though of that only $10.53 was paid in. From mid 1946 to mid 1986 the World Bank lent a total of $160 billion for 4,000 projects in some 100 countries, its lending more than doubling in the last 10 years of that time. By any reckoning the Bank's resources are huge. The IBRD makes loans only to creditworthy borrowers and has suffered no losses on the loans it has made. Throughout that whole time it has made a profit. A substantial part of that income goes to strengthen its reserves, and to fund the International Development Association (IDA), the Agency set up within the Bank in the 1960s to lend to developing countries.[90]

What is remarkable about Hardy's comments is the observation that the profits made by the IBRD are used for the security of its reserves and to fund IDA. If this is the case, the conclusion should be that the middle-income countries, the clients of the IBRD, directly influence the amount of funds available for IDA: if the middle-income countries turn to the private sector for loans, this could have implications for the poorest countries, which rely on IDA money.

Others at the bank estimate that between 10,000 and 15,000 employees work for the World Bank. The total depends on whether one includes only full-time staff or also includes temporary contractors. The World Bank, for example, relocated two-thirds of its country directors from its headquarters in Washington, DC, to the field in the mid-1990s. The percentage of staff members who work in the field has increased significantly. Today, the bank operates offices in more than 100 countries. It also has offices at the United Nations in New York, in Paris, and in Tokyo. Many of the offices in the developing countries serve as Public Information Centers.[91]

THE CHANGING ROLE OF EXECUTIVE DIRECTORS

Not surprisingly, the member countries, both borrowers and lenders, have tried to gain more influence over the institution in response to its ongoing expansion and the increasing influx of funding from the donor countries. Having an influence or a say is a complex matter of diplomacy requiring negotiations over funding and the creation of alliances between some member countries or between the constituencies on the board. In the final analysis, it is the position taken by the executive directors that matters. Simultaneously, their position today has not changed regarding the Articles of Agreement, which are still formulated as they were at the start.

Despite the "longevity" of this arrangement, the position of the executive directors has changed somewhat over time. According to Rigo Sureda, the following factors have increased the role of the executive directors as policy decision makers: "the establishment of the International Development Association (IDA) funded with grants from governments, developments in the nature of the Bank's business, the development of country assistance strategies, and internal and external concerns about the quality of Bank operations and its accountability as an institution."[92] Rigo Sureda's conclusion appears logical, correct, and relevant. Countries receiving funds shortly after the Second World War became donors themselves decades later. Many of these countries, such as France, Germany, the Netherlands, Sweden, and Italy, are at present some of those substantial founders that want to have a bigger say in the institution.

Mason and Asher come to the same conclusion that the establishment and expansion of IDA changed the position of the executive directors:

> The relationship of the president to this Board of Directors was destined to change in any event – the 1970s are not the 1950s – but the rate of change has been accelerated by the establishment and expansion of

IDA ... [U]ntil the advent of IDA, the president of the World Bank could exercise great freedom in allocating available resources because he had raised those resources in private capital markets and could raise more when more "good" projects were presented for financing. By and large, allocation was no problem. When IDA entered the picture, allocation became a problem because every IDA project that was approved reduced the balance available for commitment to other projects. The resources were contributed by governments, and governments (through their executive directors) gradually became more interested in eligibility criteria, economic performance, development strategy, and the means proposed for stimulating previously neglected sectors of the economy. The full impact of the board of directors' growing interest in development policy became most apparent only toward the end of the 1960s. For most of IDA's first decade, representatives of the treasuries, ministries of finance, and central banks of Part I countries were their principle spokesmen.[93]

IDA: A HISTORIC CHANGE

I confirm the observations of Mason, Asher, and Rigo Sureda. When a sensitive project was discussed that involved IDA money, I observed an executive director demanding more control and compliance with the policies. I heard the approximate phrase "since IDA money is involved" and such wording as "it is finally our citizens' tax money."[94]

Indeed it was, as described above, a historic change when IDA was established. President Black, according to Kraske, concluded: "There is need for new supplies and sources of international development capital, and I believe that international organization can be the practical, twentieth century way of meeting that need."[95] Kraske goes on to write: "The creation of IDA signalled the transformation of the Bank into a development institution. It was now able to assist all its members regardless of their income level and debt-servicing capacity; it was also in a position to support all the activities relevant to the long term economic advance of its members irrespective of their potential for revenue generation. To be sure, the formal integrity of the Bank as a marked-funded financing institution was preserved by incorporating IDA as a separate fund."[96]

IDA ARTICLES OF AGREEMENT

The Articles of Agreement for IDA, effective since 24 September 1960, are interesting in that they are in their fundamentals often literally copied from the IBRD Articles of Agreement. Clear differences are to be found in Article I, which treats the bank's purposes:

The purposes of the Association are to promote economic development, increase productivity and thus raise standards of living in the less-developed areas of the world included within the Association's membership, in particular by providing finance to meet their important developmental requirements on terms which are more flexible and bear less heavily on the balance of payments than those of conventional loans, thereby furthering the developmental objectives of the International Bank for Reconstruction and Development ... and supplementing its activities. The Association shall be guided in all its decisions by the provisions of this article.

The change in Article I is a logical consequence of the new approach and of the creation of a new development institution within the World Bank Group. With IDA, the bank made a real switch and turned somewhat away from being a pure financial institution or capital supplier. Still, the language used is a combined language of economists and lawyers. The question is how many experts in the fields of, for example, sociology (poverty, gender, etc.), biology (environment), health, law, and human rights (e.g., of indigenous peoples) have been involved in the establishment of IDA? Article V, on operations, states in section 1, on the use of resources and conditions of financing:

a) The Association shall provide financing to further development in the less-developed areas of the world included within the Association's membership.
b) Financing provided by the Association shall be for purposes which in the opinion of the Association are of high developmental priority in the light of the needs of the area or areas concerned and, except in special circumstances, shall be for specific projects.[97]

The phrases "less-developed areas," "high developmental priority," and "the needs of the area or areas concerned" indicate somewhat the newly created approach. Still, many of the articles are much of the same, compared to those of the IBRD. Salient is the legal division of IDA and the IBRD. Article VI, on organization and management, section 6(c), states that "Nothing in this Agreement shall make the Association liable for the acts or obligations of the Bank, or the Bank liable for the acts or obligations of the Association."

Kraske makes an even more interesting observation concerning the Articles of Agreement of the World Bank. Here it is important to be reminded again that when Kraske refers to "the Bank," he means the IBRD, the first in the World Bank Group. Kraske notes: "Amending the Articles of Agreement of the Bank to provide for the accommodation of the IDA fund could have been simple [*sic*]; but it would have been hazardous as well, for it would have provided opportunity for other amendments. Above all, the separate identity of IDA served to 'emphasize to the world, especially to the investors in Bank bonds that their interest in the Bank would not be diluted by the diversion of the funds into the softer IDA channels.'"[98] Kraske's observation shows his realistic evaluation of the situation at the time, notably his understanding of the dominant influence of the US financial sector in the bank. The abovementioned Article VI, section 6(c), about the liability of the IBRD versus that of IDA, tells its own story. IDA will not form any risk for the IBRD.

When Kraske states that it would have been "simple" to amend the Articles of Agreement, his focus is on the interests of the financial world. I find it a rather remarkable comment for a totally different reason. The creation of IDA was indeed a source of momentum to change the Articles of Agreement. One can speculate about what "would have been hazardous" in doing so. In my opinion, amendments could have cleared up the vague and problematic division of tasks between management, the president, and the executive directors. At the time, the important Group II countries that submit substantial funds to IDA (and the IBRD!) should have demanded a stronger role for the board by giving it the right to take initiative. The same is valid for the superseded division of constituencies. For certain, it was too early for European countries to form constituencies more in line with the then nascent European Community and its territory. Nevertheless, an opportunity was missed.

THE EUROPEAN UNION
AND THE WORLD BANK GROUP

There are twenty-four seats on the World Bank's board. These seats are divided among constituencies within the European Union, most of which are formed by groups of countries. Instead of one seat on the board for the entire EU, the interests of the twenty-seven EU countries are divided over all kinds of constituencies that take us back to the early days of the institution's creation and even to colonial times rather than reflecting the present-day structures in the world. Spain, together with a group of Latin American countries,[99] forms one constituency. After its independence, East Timor became a member of the same constituency as Portugal.[100] The Nordic countries of the EU have a seat that includes Norway and Iceland, which are not (yet?) part of the EU. For a long time already, the Netherlands has held a seat on the board of the World Bank, representing eleven other countries in its constituency.[101] Three countries in the latter group are EU members. Poland, a new EU member, finds itself in a constituency with eight former Soviet states, none of which is an EU country. And what about EU member Ireland, which, like Canada, is in a group with only Caribbean countries?

In the absence of a homogeneous EU constituency, the division of powers across these different groups has long made it difficult, if not almost impossible, for the EU to play a significant role in the World Bank. As described above, this changed for the first time when the Europeans collectively withdrew their support for President Wolfowitz. Yet the creation of the constituencies can be understood and explained in light of the history of the institution. At the time, a still-divided Europe was the first target of the World Bank, and no one could have foreseen such rapid economic growth of the European continent and simultaneously a European integration. This integration would never have occurred if economic growth, and the recovery from wartime, had not taken place. If one believes this correlation, then one could also argue that Europe's integration process came about partly as a result of economic support from the World Bank and the Marshall Plan.

Today, the combined payments of the twenty-seven[102] EU member states[103] are higher than the combined payments of the United States and Japan.[104] On 14 December 2007, forty-five donor countries, including new donors China, Egypt, Estonia, Latvia, and Lithuania, met in Berlin under the lead of the Portuguese EU presidency to conclude the negotiations for the so-called "fifteenth replenishment" of IDA, which establishes these members' payment commitments to the World Bank for a period of three years. According to a press release of the Portuguese presidency, the

> donor countries pledged a record of US$25,1 billion for IDA to help overcome poverty in the world's poorest countries. In total, the IDA-15 replenishment for FY [fiscal year] 2009–2011 will provide US$41,6 billion, an increase of US$9,5 billion over the previous replenishment (IDA-14), which provided US$32,1 billion. IDA's 24 donor countries reaffirmed their strong support for the institution, President Zoellick [the new president], management and the Board of Directors, and, in a very significant joint effort, were able to collectively reach a 58% share of IDA-15 total donor contributions, compared to the 55% share in IDA-14.[105]

This strong position of the EU members as a group within the bank and the appearance of new members such as China and Egypt as donors should be a reason to restructure the division of the constituencies and their voting powers. The opportunity to do so is dependent on the United States, which has the most voting power, at 16.38 per cent of the total. To veto a proposal by the Board of Governors, an executive director needs 13 per cent of the votes. It seems clear that the above-described structure has no chance of being changed in the near future, for two reasons: first, one assumes that the United States will not be prepared or willing to give up its powers on the board and within the institution; second, given the structure of the constituencies, either EU members are unwilling to cooperate with each other within the institution or they are confronted by the impracticability of doing so.

At present, EU integration has not formally taken place. In recent years there have been several attempts at cooperation. Eckhard Deutscher, the German executive director, tried to convince members of the European Parliament to ask the European Council and European Commission to study the opportunities for a much more coordinated role for the EU within the World Bank.[106] It would make a historic difference if the EU member states unanimously decided to express their will to create a constituency for the EU as one entity with one seat on the bank's board. A necessary change to the Articles of Agreement could of course be prevented by other countries with membership in the World Bank. And the opinion that the EU should not play a major role within the institution, based on geo-political rationale, cannot be ignored. However, the strongest resistance to changing the grouping of countries might come from inside the EU itself. The Netherlands, for example, as I was often told, is not in favour of changing the structure. Government officials are fully aware that a European seat on the bank's board would mean a loss of the "Dutch seat." While, under the present circumstances, the Netherlands will likely lose some influence in the international arena, including the EU,[107] and even more so after the enlargement of the EU, it can still retain its powers in the World Bank and the IMF. And what about the United Kingdom, France, or Germany? Would they be prepared to give up their own seats for the sake of the EU? There is still a long way to go before a common role can be established for European members in the World Bank and in the IMF.

VOTING POWERS

The voting power in the institutions reflects the member countries' financial power. Article V, section 3(a), of the Articles of Agreement of the IBRD is short and clear: "Each member shall have two hundred fifty votes plus one additional vote for each share of stock held." Thus the Articles of Agreement provide for so-called weighted voting. In the media this is often described as "one dollar one vote, instead of one member one vote." The comments on and criticism of the division of power by civil society organizations are understandable. If in an institution a minority group of representatives has enough shares to determine outcomes by means of a majority vote, one could question the democratic level of the institution.

However, voting almost never takes place in the institution. Before approval in the official meetings, most of the positions have already been set and decisions have been taken without a vote. This is often referred to as "nonvoting consensus." Rigo Sureda points to many publications about this phenomenon and cites two remarkable quotations. One is by J. Gold, former general counsel of the IMF,[108] who said: "The weighted voting results in an enormous difference in voting strength. One result of this is that we avoid voting. We have found that the voting strength is so disproportionate that this in itself produces resistance to voting, although it is not the only reason for that attitude."[109]

Even more striking is a comment made by the secretary general of the United Nations Conference on Trade and Development (UNCTAD) at the opening of the first session of UNCTAD in 1964: "There is obviously no immediate practical purpose in adopting recommendations by a simple majority of the developing countries but without the favorable votes of the developed countries, when the execution of those recommendations depends on their acceptance by the latter."[110] In this statement, the reality is expressed aptly. The custom in UN institutions to first try to reach consensus is, as I understand, normally the only way to go. Indeed, as stated above, it does not make sense to take a decision against the wishes of a country that will then, against its will, have to execute the decision on its own territory.

Aldo Caliari and Frank Schroeder recognize that decisions are traditionally made by consensus. Nevertheless, as they state, this "does not diminish the importance of voting power in the outcome of such decisions. In fact, during Board discussions in the IMF and the World Bank, the secretary keeps a tally of votes on particular decisions which assist the Chairman in formulating the 'sense of the meeting' and that 'sense of the meeting' simply reflects the respective voting powers of those who favor and oppose a particular outcome."[111] On the US's veto power, they say:

> The original Articles of Agreement of the IMF and the Bank ensured that only a few key decisions had to be taken by special majorities. In the case of the IMF, the US share meant that in a number of these decisions, which could only be taken with a special majority of the votes, the US would effectively have veto power. Over the years, however, the categories of decisions that require special majority have only increased and so has the number of decisions subject to US veto power.[112] Within the Bank, the decision to amend the Articles of Agreement was, in 1989, turned into a decision requiring 85% of the votes in order to preserve the US veto. These trends are the result of quid pro quo negotiations where the higher number of decisions susceptible to US veto has been the way of off-setting declines in relative US power in the organizations.[113]

This veto right can also be created by any other group that forms a block to secure the 85 per cent required. Ricardo Faini and Enzo Grilli note that a group like the UK, France, and Germany can act "in concert" to this end.

Faini and Grilli further describe political positions inside the institutions, describing them as "in many ways inevitable, given their nature, ownership structure and functions." The cases they mention are

> the decision of the World Bank not to finance the Aswan Dam in Egypt in 1995 or the decision of the IMF to extend a huge loan to Mexico in 1995 (supported by a credit facility of the United States and a Bank for International Settlements loan on account of the Group of 10), that are normally categorized as political decisions. The former instance took place under pressure from the United States and the United Kingdom,

which wished to "punish" President Nasser in some way for his dealings with the Soviet Union. The second decision was taken, largely on behalf of the United States (and the nine other members of the Group of 10), which was set on helping a critically important country in the Western Hemisphere.[114]

Faini and Grilli state that it is difficult to determine what "coalitions emerge in the governing Boards" of the World Bank and the IMF.[115] But they add: "Views are nonetheless often expressed on who holds the most influence in these institutions. Some of them are held with particular vigor. The United States, the G-7, the United States-Europe acting in concert are often identified as the critical power holders in both the World Bank and the International Monetary Fund."[116]

As a member of the Inspection Panel, I did witness one of those moments when a vote was necessary by the board of the World Bank. This was on 6 and 7 July 2000, in a final board meeting to discuss the final report of the Inspection Panel on the China Western Poverty Reduction Project.[117] This project is considered "one of the most controversial projects in the entire 54-year history of the World Bank."[118] Our rather critical report led to a disagreement and divided opinions on what should be done to improve the conditions and to mitigate the circumstances for the people involved. With this project, the custom of consensus voting was no option.

By majority vote, the board decided to ask management for further research, which could have delayed the bank's final decision on the loan by at least a year. Very sadly, the final outcome was that China decided to go ahead with the project without the World Bank.[119] This was a victory for none of us.

WORLD BANK MISSION STATEMENT

Finally, little wording, if any, can be found in the IBRD and IDA Articles of Agreement that addresses what at present is advertised as the main goal of the World Bank: poverty alleviation. The title of the World Bank's mission statement is "Our Dream Is a World Free of Poverty." Other phrases in the mission statement that greatly differ from the economic terminology in the Articles of Agreement include: "Fight poverty with passion" and "Help people help themselves."[120]

This criticism sould not be taken to imply that I do not understand the power of economic growth as an important means for poverty alleviation. I am not blind to the need to inject (soft) loans into the poorest countries of the world. I also recognize that these capital injections have to go together with market-oriented measures, such as some liberalization of the market, fighting corruption, and supporting good governance through capacity building. However, these interventions have to be combined with a just distribution of wealth. A fair distribution is the only way to fight poverty. In my opinion, the world is still far from a fair distribution. On the contrary, the gap between the rich and the poor is growing. No longer is this a "simple" gap between countries. Although one cannot ignore the differences between the poorest countries of the world and the wealthy Western countries, one also cannot ignore the existence of extremely rich individuals in the poorest countries of the world (often as a result of corruption) and the rise of poverty in the Western world.

Yet economic activities have to be embedded in national and multilateral structures that guarantee enough tax income for governing institutions to provide public services to society and for democratically elected bodies to control all activities on a national and international level. Who will contest the necessity of a strong public education system, which is the basis for any democratic society? The same is true of good transportation infrastructure and of an independent law and order system based on highly educated jurists who are not vulnerable to bribes. How many economists have referred to the correlation between investment in education and science, on the one hand, and economic growth, on the other?

INTERNAL AND EXTERNAL CRITICISM LEADING TO ESTABLISHMENT OF THE INSPECTION PANEL

As mentioned above, President Preston took office at the World Bank in 1991,[121] when the institution was already facing criticism that it ignored environmental issues. Preston wanted to review the overall efficiency of bank operations.[122] To this end, a taskforce was formed, headed by a senior manager, Willi Wapenhans. The internal report that was submitted to the executive directors in the fall of 1992 has since come to be known as the Wapenhans Report.[123] The introduction of the report states:

> As a development institution, the Bank has continuously broadened its activities. Increasingly ambitious goals and development priorities have expanded its reach in a rapidly growing membership at a time of substantial volatility in the global economy. The projects the Bank supports – as a lender of last resort – of necessity entail substantial risk taking. This calls for vigilance, realism, and constructive self-evaluation. The Bank must be no less restrained in diagnosing and seeking to remedy its own shortcomings than it is in seeking to help member countries recognize and address theirs. For only through rigorous and continuous self-assessment based on exacting standards can a large and influential institution such as the Bank maintain its effectiveness.[124]

The findings of the report, which were an important milestone in the bank's self-evaluation efforts, are presented in unmistakable terms. A few examples are:

The risks arising from weak borrower commitment receive inadequate attention, as do other risks. Inadequate attention is also given to sensitivity analyses, implementation planning (including procurement scheduling) and sustainability.[125]

Only 17 percent of staff interviewed felt that analytical work done during project preparation was sufficient to ensure the achievement of project quality. Most others (believing timely delivery is the dominant institutional value) thought that better project work would be done if annual lending contracts were to put less pressure on departments, divisions, and task managers to deliver projects on schedule.[126]

A number of current practices with respect to career development, feedback to staff, and signals from managers militate against a sharper focus on portfolio performance management. Existing incentives act as barriers to desirable changes in behavior. Practices tend to put a premium – in recruitment, in formulating work programs, and in promotions – on conceptual and planning abilities rather than on practical managerial and implementation experience. There is a widely held staff perception that exposure to appraisal and lending work ... enhances career development prospects whereas portfolio management experience does not.[127]

Noncompliance remains a serious problem, particularly in relation to financial and audit covenants. In an era of heightened concern over the importance of prudent governance, it is unacceptable that instruments of transparency and accountability are neglected.[128]

A former general counsel of the World Bank, Ibrahim Shihata, also refers to a rather striking finding of the Wapenhans Report:

One of the findings of the Task Force's report (Wapenhans Report), submitted to the Bank's Board of Executive Directors in November 1992, was that the Bank staff were often concerned about getting as many projects as possible approved under the Bank's lending program. In such an "approval culture," less attention had been given to the commitment of borrowers and their implementing agencies, or to the degree of "ownership" assumed by borrowers of the projects financed by the Bank and the policies underlying them. At the project level, the leading design problem identified was that projects had become too complex. The Task Force concluded, inter alia, that the Bank should improve the performance of its portfolio through changes in its own policies and practices.[129]

The follow-up on the Wapenhans Report came with an action program that proposed detailed steps to be taken. The introduction of this follow-up document from the bank president to the executive directors states: "This action program must be considered within the Bank's overarching objective of poverty reduction which can be achieved only by restoring or accelerating economic growth and by focusing on policies and programs that specifically benefit the poor. It is therefore critical that the linkage between the Bank's central focus on poverty reduction and the proposed heightened emphasis on implementation be fully recognized."[130] This document further proposes many major improvements in the bank's implementation performance, such as the introduction or revision of training programs, different rewards and incentive systems, a more user-friendly system to document and disseminate the bank's operational policies and procedures, and a revision of the role of field offices, among other initiatives.

In chapter G of the follow-up document, entitled "Giving Attention to Generic Factors Affecting Portfolio Performance," I found the first reference to an inspection panel in a bank document:[131] a "suggestion that the Bank consider establishing an independent operations inspection unit." I assume that this proposal was occasioned by outside pressure on the bank to establish a permanent accountability mechanism. The paragraph containing this "suggestion" reads as follows:

Inspection Function. Responding to the suggestion that the Bank considers establishing an independent operations inspection unit, a review was commissioned to take account of experience with inspection functions in selected member countries and consider whether a new inspection function was needed to augment the Bank's existing supervision, audit, and evaluation functions. A related but separate issue analyzed was whether the Bank has ready access, when necessary, to a reliable source of independent judgment about specific operations that may be facing severe implementation problems. The review concluded that the interests of the Bank would be best served by the establishment of an independent Inspection Panel. The draft report was circulated to Executive Directors in June 1993 for discussion at an informal seminar in July. It will then be revised in light of the discussion and subsequently submitted to the Board for approval.[132]

The context in which the proposal was made, namely the follow-up document on the Wapenhans Report, raises the question of who may claim to be the "founding father" of the Inspection Panel. It is obvious that the outside world, particularly the NGOs operating internationally at the time, were demanding accountability. It is undeniabe that they had a strong impact and were feeding the discussions at the bank.

Nevertheless, the forces inside the institution clearly came to the same conclusions, with Shihata being the frontrunner. In an institution of the World Bank's magnitude one can find the same commitment to evaluation and positive change that one sees coming from outside the bank. The people inside the institution are a reflection of society in general. Thus with the acceptance of the Action Plan in the summer of 1993, the first step was taken by the executive directors to create an accountability mechanism. It clearly has been the deliberate wish of the executive directors to have more authority over the extended activities of the institution.

On the basis of historical evidence, it can be concluded that the World Bank, established with the special purpose of reconstructing Europe after the Second World War, has become a different institution over time. The tasks taken on by the bank have grown rapidly, transforming the institution from a postwar reconstruction agency into a development bank. An important marker for the change was the establishment of IDA, a measure directed at the least developed countries in the world. During the past half-century, borrowing countries have become donors and demanded more influence in the institution through their executive directors. Their position was not clear at the time the institution was built. Over time, the executive directors have tried to obtain more control over the institution, in which management continues to have a powerful position. In 1947 management received the right to develop recommendations on policy matters, while the board could only accept or refuse these – an arrangement that still exists today. The part that the executive directors have played in the selection of the presidents of the bank has been minimal. All that has been written about the powers of the executive directors leads to the conclusion that they are in a constant battle to obtain and maintain some grip on the daily operations of the bank.

The World Bank's staff increased enormously during the 1950s and more so during the 1960s, while its financial portfolio grew even faster. At the same time, with all the new tasks, issues, targets, and wide-ranging development objectives that were being taken up, the bank became a complex institution. At the bank's headquarters, the Main Complex Building, one office does not necessarily know what the others do.

After all the input of management has been given, whether or not management interferes in a proposed project, it is ultimately the national, regional, or local authorities who are responsible for the correct implementation of the elements and components of the project agreed upon in the project appraisal document (PAD). Management often discovers, to its displeasure, that the reality on the ground is rather different from the conditions for implementation envisioned in the PAD. Management is hindered by the restriction that it work only on project planning, and even after consultation there are still no real tools to guarantee that at national levels implementation is done appropriately. Governments prefer to keep their sovereignty instead of being controlled by a multilateral financial institution that, in its turn, is controlled by Western governments, most dominantly the United States, followed by Europe and Japan.

The Wapenhans Report mentions in unmistakable terminology the many shortcomings of the World Bank's operations. One shortcoming is that bank staff have been more occupied with approving as many projects as possible than with giving attention to sensitivity analyses, implementation planning (including procurement scheduling), and sustainability. It is evident that publication of the internal Wapenhans Report, plus the pressure of civil society, laid the ground for the executive directors to finally create the Inspection Panel.

3

Inception of the World Bank Inspection Panel, Its Mandate, and Its Structure

The history of the World Bank Inspection Panel begins in the 1980s with the bank's involvement in the Narmada Dam Project in India, which comprised a dam and power project as well as a water delivery and drainage project. By then, the bank was already under fire for its weakness on strong environmental policies and its lack of transparency.[1] Former general counsel Ibrahim Shihata calls the Narmada Dam Project "the most important case to draw public attention to the accountability issue."[2] Shihata explains the historical involvement of the bank: "Agreements with the World Bank to partially finance both projects were signed in 1985 and became effective on January 6, 1986,[3] although the International Development Association (IDA) credit for the International Bank for Reconstruction and Development (IBRD) loan and the IDA credit for the dam project were still under disbursement when issues related to the project's implementation attracted world-wide attention."[4]

The design of this megaproject in India and the expected consequences for hundreds of thousands of people and for the environment caused international disarray. Nongovernmental organizations (NGOs) from India, the United States, and Europe sounded the alarm. Hearings were organized in the US Congress under the chairmanship of Barney Frank, and protests were expressed in the European Parliament.[5] The result was finally the creation in 1993 of the World Bank Inspection Panel,[6] the first body of this kind giving voice to private citizens in an international context. This chapter first briefly describes the events that led to the creation of the panel and the initial environmental and social policies that were adopted, followed by an account of the role of some of the bank's executive directors. Then the resolution establishing the panel is described as well as the two revisions of the resolution, which take into account the evolving role of the panel. In this latter part, certain dilemmas in the mandate are reviewed.

THE NARMADA DAM

The Sardar Sarovar Dam, also called the Narmada Valley Development Project, involves the construction of thousands of dams on the Narmada (Nermŭ'de) River, considered one of the holiest rivers in India. On this point, the Indian National Trust for Art and Cultural Heritage (INTACH), an autonomous body for the conservation of natural and cultural heritage, states:

> Ours was a country which always had a spectrum of vibrant cultures. This has been so because the land was rich. We owe the richness of our land to our rivers big and small, great and obscure. That is why in India we venerated our rivers. Narmada is one of the most sacred of our rivers flowing through the real heartland of the sub continent, far surpassing Ganga or any other river in India in antiquity. According to our beliefs she should never be fettered. We have seen the slow death of other rivers in our land. The tired exhausted land can no longer support a youthful full river. So the latter also dies prematurely. We have seen the outright murder of our rivers for short term profit. We have stone walled our rivers or put them in dungeons of concrete. Naturally then, the land and the culture dies. There is no choice. Of course one dogmatically says that the culture is advancing and is successful. One can find prosperity in the teeming, consuming and squandering urban centres and in the parasitic pollutive short lived industrial centres. But then the ultimate index of success is survival. And this demands the essential conditions for life to continue for all and forever. That is exactly what a living river symbolises.[7]

The turbulent Narmada River stretches over 1,250 kilometres, arising in Madhya Pradesh state, in central India, and flowing through Gujarat state to the Gulf of Khambat.[8] The project includes 30 major dams, 135 medium dams, and over 3,000 small dams, to be constructed over fifty years. Its centrepiece, the Sardar Sarovar Dam, was designed to stretch 4,000 feet (1,219 metres) across the river and rise to the height of a forty-five-storey building – making it the largest water development project in India and possibly the world. The multibillion-dollar venture is intended to irrigate nearly 4.8 million acres (1.9 million hectares) of farmland and bring drinking water to 30 million people living along its banks and in surrounding communities. Its construction would also uproot almost a half-million people living along its banks and in surrounding communities, many of them indigenous people known in India as the Adivasi.[9]

Over the years, protest in India grew against the project. The National Alliance of People's Movements and Narmada Bachao Andolan's (NBA's) Save Narmada Movement, both under the leadership of Medha Patkar, received international support from NGOs from Europe and the Unites States. Lori Udall, who was probably the most important supporter of the protesters in the United States, says of this period: "The grassroots movement against the Sardar Sarovar Dam in India, now known as Narmada Bachao Andolan ('Save the Narmada Movement'), is one of extraordinary vision, perseverance and vitality. It is also one of the largest, most sustained grassroots movements against a World Bank-funded project anywhere in the world."[10] The international alliance took the case to both the US Congress and the European Parliament, of which I was then a member.[11]

THE EUROPEAN PARLIAMENT AND NARMADA

On 11 July 1991 the European Parliament adopted a resolution "On the disastrous consequences of the Narmada project in India."[12] The final resolution was a joint effort of some members of Parliament (including myself).[13] During the debate in Parliament, held in the hours set aside for urgent matters (mostly human rights issues), two members joined the debate with Peter Schmidhuber, the European commissioner who was then responsible for EU budgets, the EU Cohesion Fund, and antifraud measures: Wilfried Telkämper for the Green Party and myself for the Socialist group. Here is a selection of the words from the floor:

> Van Putten: President, what is one minute[14] to talk about a project in India involving the construction of more then 3,000 dams in a vast river basin as big as the Rhine and which would stretch from Basle to the North Sea of the Dutch Coast? If this project is implemented in full, more than one million people[15] will be forced off their land and vast expanses of fertile land and forest areas will disappear under water. Our aim in this resolution is to make clear to the World Bank, which is involved in the project, that it must wait for the findings of an independent mission whose task is to investigate whether this project, which was drawn up fifteen years ago, is not completely obsolete and out of date.
>
> Telkämper: In our view, far too little attention has been paid to the social consequences of this project and the associated economic and social costs of the project yet to be calculated – and indeed cannot be properly calculated, just like the costs of German unification ...
>
> Because of protests from a range of countries and appeals from international NGOs – there is a worldwide campaign of opposition to the project – the World Bank, as one of the principal sources of finance has decided to suspend its aid and investigate the whole project further. We should support this decision by the World Bank. That is why I am calling on the Commission to consider as a matter of principle, whether the Community should go on financing major dam projects or rather wait and see how the World Bank responds.[16]

On 17 June 1991, just before the debate in the European Parliament, President Barber Conable of the World Bank commissioned an independent review panel of the ongoing implementation of the Sardar Sarovar Projects, partially financed by the World Bank. Bradford Morse, a former US congressman and former administrator of the United Nations Development Program (UNDP), was selected to head the commission, which was to study the environmental and resettlement issues associated with the project.[17] The commission was co-chaired by Thomas Berger, a Canadian judge of the Supreme Court who was instrumental in the inclusion of aboriginal rights in the new Canadian Constitution.[18] Other members of the Morse Commission were Donald Gamble, an environmental specialist, and Hugh Brody, an anthropologist.[19]

Precisely a year later the European Parliament had to discuss the Narmada Dam again after it received the report of the independent Morse Commission. By then the impression existed that the World Bank was not going to adequately react and take the recommendations made by the Morse Commission seriously (see below). A new joint resolution was adopted asking for the bank's withdrawal from the project, as concluded by the Morse Commission.[20]

The following demands were included in the resolution:

(1) Calls on the Member States to take note of the Morse Report;

(2) Thanks the members of the committee of inquiry for their thorough and conscientious work;

(3) Recommends that thorough inquiries be held as a matter of principle before construction work on mega-projects;

(4) Reiterates that projects should only be implemented on the basis of agreement with those affected;

(5) Calls on all Member States to draw the appropriate conclusions from the report of the Morse Committee and to urge their executive directors to vote against further World Bank support for the project;

(6) Points out to the Commission that the human rights of the people in the region in question are at stake and requests that it question this aspect of the dams project in the context of development cooperation relations with India;

(7) Calls on the World Bank to withdraw from the project, pay compensation to those who have suffered as a result of the Sardar Sarovar projects and write off the US$250 million spent on building the dam if it is not completed;

(8) Calls on the Japanese Government to stand by its decision, announced at the meeting of donors of the World Bank in Paris in April 1991, and to refrain from providing any further support for the execution of the project;

(9) Calls on the Indian Government and the Governments of Gujarat, Maharashtra and Madhya Pradesh to refrain from further building

on the basis of the plans hitherto and to seek and implement
viable alternative means of supplying water to areas threatened
by drought;

(10)   Instructs its President to forward this resolution to the Council,
the Commission, the governments of the Member States, the
Governments of India and Japan, the World Bank and the
Morse Committee.[21]

NARMADA INTRODUCED AT THE WORLD BANK

The "real battle" took place not in Strasbourg or Brussels but in Washington, DC. In the 1980s the problems with the Narmada project had already attracted the attention of the then Dutch executive director, Paul Arlman, who said to me in an interview about this period:

It started for me in 1988 or 1987. We received disturbing messages from the activists in India: from Mehdi Patkar. These messages were picked up by the international environmental movement in an activist format. The spokesman and organizer was Wouter Veening. Wouter, who was accompanied by five to ten people from all kinds of environmental organizations, had the idea to talk to the executive directors about those dams. Bank staff did not welcome this initiative; however, I picked it up. In this group, the Canadian and the US offices were also present, from neither office the executive director but the advisor – the French, English, and German. So the core of the EU was there. Scandinavia was also present. I chaired it; usually we met in my office, very informally. No official reports were made. Bank staff was also heard.

In a certain way, we were acting like the panel as we were having bank staff involved and were asking questions like, "What do you think about this?" and "What do you know about that?"

There it appeared, after we heard Patkar and the environmental activists' story, that bank staff partly did not know it themselves. Bank management did not appreciate our finding out about cases that had been decided upon or discussed with India. The role of the bank in India, IDA, has always been one of direct bargaining with India itself. Bank management did not attend. They preferred not to discuss it. I always, and I also found this in old notes, we always invited the Indian executive director. He never attended and also did not contact us. But he was always informed. I informed him beforehand – excellent information – when the group would meet. If there were reports made, he would receive these undoubtedly. Therefore, it had to be held in the open. However, it was simultaneously very clear that we had rather different opinions about that, and the bank could not continue in this fashion. That continued for two or three years. Then [November

1990], I passed it on to Eveline Herfkens, and she approached this from a more social angle than an environmental one.[22]

The role of Arlman and his successor, Eveline Herfkens, drew the attention of Devesh Kapur, John Lewis, and Richard Webb, who were requested by the World Bank to write its history:

> In 1988 the Dutch executive director, Paul Arlman, began to take a particular interest in Narmada and convened a small group of Part I country executive directors to follow it. Some of them met with Oxfam's John Clark and EDF's [Environmental Defense Fund's] Lori Udall, and with the NBA's Medha Patkar. After the meeting with Patkar, one executive director commented, "When I hear what NGOs say about this project and then what the operations people say, it sounds like they are talking about two different projects." In the mid-1990s, the U.S. Executive Director began to sound out the Director-General of the Bank's Operations Evaluation Department about undertaking a special review of Sardar Sarovar. There was general uneasiness about the idea all round. Then, at the end of 1990, Medha Patkar and the NBA led a "Long March" to the dam site, where they planned to stop construction by means of a sit-in. They were stopped at the Gujarat border by the police. Medha Patkar and several others began a fasting to the death. The fasting injected new urgency. What would persuade Patkar to stop? She was demanding that the whole project be comprehensively reviewed but the Bank would not agree. As she grew weaker and the Bank still said nothing, John Clark, Lori Udall, and others made desperate attempts to persuade the senior operational Vice-President, Moeen Querishi, to announce a review. He did so just in time, and in the spring of 1991, a small number of Executive Directors, led by the new Dutch Executive Director, Eveline Herfkins [sic],[23] began to consider the membership and terms of reference of an independent review panel.[24]

Kapur, Lewis, and Webb further describe the process inside and outside the bank leading to the appointment of the so-called Morse Commission, noting that "There were no precedents to draw on."[25] The India Department's environment and resettlement coordinator was given the task of organizing the Inspection Panel. He approached several prominent experts, and they all refused; the writers do not mention why. In the meantime, President Conable, nearing the end of his term, became desperate and wanted fast decisions. He then approached Bradford Morse, a former congressman and former head of the United Nations Development Program, who, we are told, was in poor health. Conable could convince him only to chair the independent review panel, "while others did the work."[26] At this stage, the environmental coordinator, Thomas Blinkhorn, began to search for someone to head up the real work. The presence of the Environmental

Defense Fund (EDF) at the bank was evident; Blinkhorn commented that they were "practically camping in the living room," noting that they were able to get so much leaked information from the bank that they were better informed than was he.[27]

Lori Udall, of the EDF, had been without doubt a leading activist in Washington campaigning against the Narmada Dam. She worked together with other lobbyists such as David Hunter,[28] Daniel Bradlow,[29] and Dana Clark.[30] I remember Lori Udall from this period when she showed up in the European Parliament to lobby those parliamentarians who were receptive to the subject. In Washington her influence was even greater. The background of Udall and her network was definitely part of the key to getting the important stakeholders to act. Udall's father had been a member of Congress, as are her brother and nephew at present. Not only that, but Kapur, Lewis, and Webb note: "Udall started a letter-writer campaign aimed at the Dutch executive director Herfkins [sic], to persuade her to push for the appointment of Thomas Berger as the principal investigator. Berger was a well-known Canadian jurist and advocate of Native American Rights. He was also a friend of Udall's uncle, former U.S. Secretary of the Interior: Stuart Udall, who had subsequently worked closely with Berger in a major legal case on Native American Rights."[31]

Herfkens supported the candidature of Thomas Berger. Then Blinkhorn interviewed Berger and recommended him to Bradford Morse. Blinkhorn knew about Berger's reputation as a defender of indigenous peoples rights, which, combined with the abundance of such peoples in the Narmada area, made it possible, we are told, for Blinkhorn "to show that the Bank was bending over backwards to be impartial."[32] Finally, President Conable and Vice President Sven Sandstrom appointed Berger.

According to Kapur, Lewis, and Webb, Udall had regular contact by phone with the core members of the review panel and met them at their hotel, where she briefed them on "how they could retain their credibility in the NGO-world, which NGOs were fighting which, which were trustworthy, who was doing what in the Bank, and what rules of operation to insist upon in regard to the Bank."[33] We are told that Berger also spent a day with Dana Clark and others at Oxfam. These meetings with Udall and Clark resulted in rules that the review panel "insisted upon as a condition of acceptance:"

1 Complete access to all project files from the bank and from the government of India, and to Indian NGOs and the Narmada Valley.
2 An extended period of time (originally seven months, extended to nine).
3 An independent budget, initially of $400,000 that grew to about $1 million. (The budget came from the president's contingency fund.)
4 Independent publication of the results, without the Bank's editorial control.
5 No post review Bank employment of panel members.

Its terms of reference were limited to resettlement and environment: its tasks being to assess the Bank's performance in these two domains in relation to the Bank's own policies and loan agreements.[34]

When comparing the above conditions with the later mandate for the Inspection Panel, established in the resolution,[35] one notes the resemblance: the preliminary work was done.

On 18 June 1992 the Morse Commission's report was issued. This report was rather critical and concluded that the bank had been seriously out of compliance with its own policies and procedures on environment and resettlement. It had failed to involve local communities in the development process and to take the complaints and problems of the affected people seriously.[36] The 363-page report further concluded that "the richest source of material about the problems with resettlement in India are in the Bank's own internal documents."[37] Finally, the Morse Commission recommended that the bank "step back" since it expected that further implementation could take place only with police force.[38] The project had already become highly sensitive. Before the bank's Board of Governors met to discuss the Morse Commission report and actions to be taken, management sent a team to India on a field mission. According to Udall, the team travelled through the villages "accompanied by over 100 police."[39] And instead of what the NGO communities and the Morse Commission expected, on 11 September 1991 management presented an Action Plan to the board, entitled "Sardar Sarovar Projects, Review of Current Status and Next Steps."[40] The plan was to go forward with the project after a six-month conditional period in order to improve the resettlements.

THE WORLD BANK LEAVING NARMADA

Just before the annual meeting of the bank in 1992, the NGO community placed full-page advertisements in the *Washington Post, New York Times,* and *Financial Times* "calling for the World Bank to immediately withdraw from Sardar Sarovar." On 21 September, as finance ministers from over 150 member countries of the World Bank were arriving in Washington, DC, for their annual meeting, the ads ran a warning that if the bank continued to fund the Narmada Dam Project after the overwhelming evidence presented by the independent review, then "NGOs and activists would put their weight behind a campaign to cut off funding to the Bank."[41] The Action Plan, according to Kapur, Lewis, and Webb, "satisfied virtually no one." The task force at the bank was "paralyzed with disagreement," the people working on the project were not allowed to reply to the Morse Report themselves, the Government of India had no "input" on the Action Plan's "Next Steps," and the vice president for South Asia signed a response to Morse and Berger "rejecting virtually all its claims."[42]

Finally, in the spring of 1993 the Board of Governors had to decide whether to continue with the project. The position of the Government of India and the Government of Gujarat was clear to all stakeholders: they would not stop building the dam while the outstanding matters were addressed. On the contrary, their attitude was, "Damn the NGOs, we are not going to submit to cry-babies, we will continue to build the dam."[43]

Inside the bank there was growing concern that the Narmada Dam was going to affect IDA, the fund for the poorest countries. Important member countries under pressure from outside activists might take measures to distance themselves from the fund. So finally the Government of India lost its interest in the World Bank's involvement in the project since only the state of Gujarat could benefit. "The project had become a cancerous tumor on the country's overall portfolio with the Bank."[44] A few days before the board meeting, the Government of India announced that it would not ask the bank for further disbursements. In other words, the bank was asked to leave.

THE UNITED STATES CONGRESS AND THE INSPECTION PANEL

Subsequent work on the Narmada Dam, a project still under construction, is not part of this study. What is important is that the Narmada Dam Project was the cause of the establishment of the Inspection Panel shortly after the bank left the project in India. According to Lori Udall, David Hunter was a "key in the design of the procedures of the Panel." Udall explains that over a three-month period she was in almost daily contact herself with the staff of Congressman Barney Frank, "either on the phone or in person about the design and procedures." She states that the first group to lobby for creation of the panel, both at the bank and on Capitol Hill, convinced Frank to "take up the issue of Appeals Mechanism (what we first called it) and Information Disclosure."[45] This group included Udall, Bruce Rich (EDF), Larry Williams (Sierra Club), Barbara Bramble (National Wildlife Federation), Jim Barnes (Friends of the Earth), and Chad Dobson (Bank Information Center).[46] John Clark of Oxfam UK was helpful "with his own Executive Director."[47]

On 5 May 1993 a first hearing was held in the US House of Representatives before the Subcommittee on International Development, Finance, Trade and Monetary Policy of the Committee on Banking, Finance and Urban Affairs, chaired by Barney Frank (Democrat).[48] First, Frank and other members of the House spoke about the tenth replenishment[49] and about the US funding of IDA. Frank opened the session by saying:

> We begin today with a set of questions that are both specific and general, the specific question being, should we replenish IDA and deal with some ancillary issues? I say "ancillary" as an unfair term, related issues, which Treasury has, I think, sensibly proposed be discussed in this

context. We also deal with a broader set of questions which is, how can we best promote economic development, reduce poverty, and promote human rights in much of the world where those are great needs? We will be looking at the structure of the existing, multilateral institutions and how we can try to get them to do better. We will be looking at the question of resources and where we will find them. One thing should be very clear. There has been a great deal of dissatisfaction with the performance of the multilateral institutions. Much of it, in my judgment, is justified. The task we have is to see if a way can be found to improve substantially the way in which these institutions function so that we do not find ourselves faced with a couple of unhappy choices, one of which would be to put money where we do not think it is doing much good, and the other would be to cut off money which would punish those who are already victimized by problems. That is the goal of this hearing.[50]

Frank concluded by asking the speakers to be very specific in the hearing and to make optimal use of their speaking time.

Other congressmen followed Frank with opening statements: Mr Doug Bereuter, Mr John J. LaFalce, Mr Alfred A. McCandless, Mr Joseph P. Kennedy, Mr Jim Nussle, Ms Maxine Waters, and Mr Bernard Sanders. Kennedy noted:

I am also concerned, as others are, about some of the issues pertaining directly to the IDA. The fact is that there are a number of concerns that we have addressed over the course of the last few years pertaining to environmental damage that has been taking place in many of the loans because of the size and scope of the projects. We have seen a distinct lack of local participation in the determination of those projects. And also we have seen many issues which you, Mr. Chairman, have spoken out on here in this country, regarding displacement of poor people as a result of the scope of many of those projects. And I think that if we hold the same standards that we hold to here in the United States, for looking out for the voiceless, that this subcommittee can do a great deal of good in terms of promoting not only the interests of economic development but doing it with some sensitivity to the local needs.[51]

Waters said:

I did not agree with some of the policies that came out of the last administration relative to the multilateral development banks, but now I see that we have some real hope with the new direction that is being fostered by this administration. I am very much concerned about development in poor countries ... I agree with Mr. Kennedy that we should be concerned about the level of expenditures on military operations, and I think that our concerns about how precious resources are being spent in some countries and our revitalized efforts to invest in real human potential will be able to make a significant difference.[52]

After the members of the House spoke, the floor was given to Lawrence Summers, under secretary for international affairs of the US Department of the Treasury. Summers first spoke about the US role in development in general and its significance for the US economy. About the US contribution to the World Bank he said:

[E]ach dollar that the United States contributes to IDA catalyzes some $6 of support for the development effort in Africa, in South Asia, and in other very poor parts of the world ... It is also a wise economic investment. Exports have been the most rapid source of growth in the US economy in recent years, and exports to less developed countries have grown twice as rapidly as exports to industrial countries. Their growth has, to a substantial extent, been fuelled by assistance that has been provided by the multilateral institutions. And the multilateral institutions have proven themselves flexible and capable of rapid response in addressing key US foreign policy objectives.[53]

On the issues of the problems with the Narmada Dam and the Wapenhans Report (see below), Summers said:

The World Bank's overdue Wapenhans Report contains a remarkably frank assessment of problems in the Bank's loan portfolio. The report represents a milestone in the history of the Bank. It calls for a clear break with the patterns of the past, and there is no question that a major cultural transformation at the Bank is required. Yesterday, the Board of Executive Directors held an informal seminar on management's response to the Wapenhans Report ... because we had made clear that the initial response was insufficiently far reaching ... in responding to concerns about the need for much more adequate supervision of Bank projects. There needs to be much more emphasis on effective implementation of Bank projects, rather than simply getting agreements on loans ... Secondly, a critical priority is transparency and openness. Poverty and environmental groups say they can't get information out of the banks. They are right. Transparency and openness will improve the operations of the banks and help them avoid costly mistakes that must be corrected at even greater expense later on. We want the banks to be accountable to the public, and we will work hard to ensure that they have a more information policy ... World Bank President Preston made clear recently that poverty reduction must be the benchmark against which the IBRD's performance as a development institution is to be judged. Our job in the US Government is to ensure that this rhetoric is translated into reality. That means no more Narmadas in the future.[54]

Summers further spoke about the new Global Environment Facility but did not yet mention an inspection function.

The Washington-based environmental NGOs testified in Congress that they would oppose U.S. contributions to the bank unless the bank could meet a series of tough new benchmarks, which included a complete revision of the bank's information policy and the creation of a citizens' appeals panel that would give directly affected people the opportunity to file complaints with an independent body.[55] The NGO representative who spoke first was Barbara Bramble, director of international programs for the National Wildlife Federation. She mentioned several measures that should be taken by the bank, including an independent appeals mechanism, and said that Udall would go into detail on this. Speaking next, Udall stated:

> We are proposing the creation of an independent appeals commission that would receive complaints from people in developing countries regarding violations of loan agreements, bank policy guidelines, and violations of international human rights law that are associated with World Bank-funded projects. The commission would be competent to recommend the suspension, modification and cancellation of a project. The key characteristics that we view this commission should have would be independence from World Bank operations, access to Bank information and Bank project files. The reports or judgments that the commission renders would be made public. The commission would have an independent budget, which would be established annually. And the other key characteristic is that no one that has worked in the Bank would be part of the commission. There has been some suggestion both by Treasury and by some people in the World Bank that there be an expansion of the Operations Evaluation Department (OED) to take over this type of monitoring. We disagree with this approach. We feel that currently the OED is not fulfilling its own mandate, which is to complete evaluations and the audits of completed projects, and also to provide feedback so they have an impact on future operations ... So we believe that it is unlikely that this type of agency that has operated in secrecy over the years would be able to fulfil the functions that we envision in this new appeals commission.[56]

Other NGO representatives spoke about the different issues concerning the World Bank and also mentioned the independent appeals mechanism. Glenn Prickett, a senior associate of the Natural Resources Defense Council, posed the question, "Who would appoint them? I don't mean specific details, but who would they be appointed by, the Bank Directors or some other body? How would we do that?"[57]

Udall then intervened and said: "The recommendation that we are making is that they be appointed by the World Bank Executive Directors and that the commission would be created by the Executive Directors. There is a section in the bylaws that would allow the Executive Directors – I believe it is section 1(b) – to create any agencies or offices anywhere in the world in order to conduct the business of the Bank."[58]

Then Frank added: "It strikes me there is an analogy, as you explain it, to the movement that we are seeing in America of the outside directors of corporations exercising more involvement vis-à-vis the officers. It is a very similar thing. You cannot be hostile or apart from the organization, but these are the oversight boards institutionalizing their oversight. I think there is a great deal to be said for it, we can direct the influence through the US Executive Director."[59]

According to Udall, testimony by the Environmental Defense Fund contained letters and statements from Indian NGOs criticizing the poor performance of the World Bank in India, one of the largest borrowers of IDA funds.[60] The EDF, together with the Center for International Environmental Law, proposed a resolution that "envisioned an independent appeals body which could accept and investigate claims, have access to all relevant Bank documents, make binding recommendations, and report to the Board of Executive Directors."[61] Other NGOs testifying on the need for an appeals body at the hearing were the National Wildlife Federation, Church World Service, and Lutheran World Relief.[62]

A year later, on 21 June 1994, another hearing was held. The resolution to establish the Inspection Panel was adopted by the bank. Nevertheless, there is still great concern about serious implementation of the measures demanded. The genuine independence of the Inspection Panel is still a subject. The subcommittee, meeting in the same room, called it "an oversight hearing on the results of the efforts of the U.S. Treasury Department and others to persuade the World Bank to make changes."[63] This time, the members of the committee expressed their views even more strongly than they had the year before. After the opening words of Chairman Frank, the floor was given to Bereuter: "Many of the difficulties that we have seen in the implementation of the World Bank efforts have, in fact, been corrected. But others are there that need to be addressed, and I do think that the U.S. Congress ... has had more impact upon reforming the multilateral development organizations, especially the World Bank, than any other entity on earth ... It has been this subcommittee that has had the major impact. So I am pleased that we are continuing that oversight role."[64]

The next speaker was Congressman John Kasich:

Mr. Chairman, many Americans have deep, misgivings about U.S. foreign aid programs. With repeated reports of corruption, waste, and mismanagement, they understand that efforts to bring relief, prosperity, and security to impoverished peoples in other countries have gone seriously wrong. For this reason, I believe that congress must move quickly to achieve meaningful reform ... The best example, of course, is the destruction of the rain forest. These have been outlined in a Time

Magazine, April 1, 1991 article. Believe it or not, the World Bank was involved in a project that ended up destroying a significant portion of the rain forest. And of course, Sardar Sarover ... The second one is forced resettlement, a situation where projects have actually been funded, where projects have started and people found themselves without any place to live, and have been placed is a situation of experiencing forced resettlement. Third, administrative costs of the Bank that were growing between 12 percent and 15 percent annually. And finally, making loans that did not meet the Bank's own standards.[65]

Kasich went on with many examples of what had gone wrong at the World Bank. He spoke about the need for timely and useful information and the need for strict environmental standards, among other things. He then referred to an earlier amendment, proposed by himself and Congressman Chris Shays, that sought to withhold funding from the World Bank: "We took this step after meeting with former Bank employees who stated that this was the only way to get the Bank's attention concerning the need to reform. The fact that I am testifying before you today seems to indicate that our action, coupled with your actions, Mr. Chairman, have moved the issue."[66] So the subject of withholding funding from the bank became an issue.

Congressman "Barney Frank's main tactic was to stall the authorization of the United States' $3.7 billion contribution until the Bank had concrete, adequate, written proposals on both reforms. High level Bank officials who worried that Frank would stall the funds indefinitely went directly to Capitol Hill to lobby Frank and others, often bypassing the U.S. Treasury, the agency that normally lobbies the U.S. Congress for U.S. contributions to the Bank."[67] Nevertheless, Congress took "the unusual step of authorizing U.S. funding to the Bank for two years only."[68] Normally, Congress authorizes IDA replenishments in three-year increments. "Congress also cut the U.S. Treasury's pledge to IDA by $200 million and the pledge to the International Bank for Reconstruction and Development (IBRD) by $15 million."[69] Udall argues that although the amounts were small, the message sent to the bank was clear. Udall demonstrates the success of the NGO community in Congress with a quotation from the congressional record:

While the conferees recognize that the World Bank has adopted procedures in these areas and recently issued a resolution on an independent Inspection Panel, the reforms as written do not adequately address the conferees concerns. Therefore, the conferees have authorized the equivalent of only two thirds of the United States three year contribution to IDA-10. It is the conferees strong believe that the World Bank needs to progress further in these areas and that additional funding in support of IDA-10 will depend on the matter in which these new procedures are implemented and where necessary, broadened.[70]

When I interviewed Frank,[71] he said about this period:

The Morse Commission on Narmada had already happened by the time
I got involved. I don't know what the timing is, but I didn't take over
here until 1993. I am pretty sure the Morse Commission was before that,
and I was not involved in the Morse Commission. But the Morse Commission was an example for us on how something like this could work.
And as I remember we were talking essentially about sort of institutionalizing that. Not having it have to be an ad hoc thing each time. So they
came to me and asked me to make the syndication. I mean the bank
needed us to "ok" the money ...
   And I did more than two hearings, I believe. I think we had several
hearings. As to the structure and mandate. I think that was kind of
frankly negotiated by the NGOs and the bank ...
   [T]he structure was that it had to be independent, and the mandate
was to be able to listen to critics of the program of a particular project
both governmental and nongovernmental from within the country independently, because one of the big things we had to resist [was that] the
bank as an institution could not and would not listen to people in a particular country other than the government. And an important part of
the Inspection Panel was precisely to give nongovernmental people, citizens or organizations, from the affected country someone to talk to.
That was explicit that the governments of the countries where the projects were happening could not veto the communications from their own
residents. In other words, before that the only people that the bank
could talk to in a country where they were planning a project were the
governments. And we said: "No you have to have citizens, not governments, to talk to the bank through the Inspection Panel."

I then asked Frank whether he had any discussion at the time with management or the president of the World Bank. His answer:

I worked very closely with ... There was a former congressman named
Matthew McHugh, a very good man. He was the assistant to the president of the bank at the time. And I talked to him, and they said to me:
"Look, you can't order us to do anything." I said: "I agree, and you can't
order me to pass the bill with the money." So it was a kind of step-by-step
operation. And in fact, at the time I said: "We are not going to vote the
whole three years. We are going to vote it one at a time." They said, "You
can't do that." I said, "Yes we can" ...
   So we did talk to them and basically make clear that yes they could
refuse to appoint the panel and make the country reports available. And
I could pop the bill. So that's the way it worked. And Treasury was reluctant. Treasury was on the same side as the bank, and they just had to
go along. Larry Summers was the guy at Treasury that we had to deal

with who came from the bank. So we just told Treasury: "It is hard ... money for the World Bank is never popular in Congress." It was hard enough for them to get the money with me supporting it. If I opposed it, they would have no chance of getting the money. That is the role of the chairman of the subcommittee.

The influence of the US Congress, more specifically the role of Congressman Barney Frank (Democrat), and the successful lobby of Lori Udall, Bruce Rich, Larry Williams, Barbara Bramble, Jim Barnes, Chad Dobson, David Hunter, and John Clark were the most important factors in the bank's creation of the Inspection Panel.[72] If "only" Europeans had been asking for such an entity, I wonder whether it would have been established. These individuals deserve credit for the establishment of a mechanism that has had much greater implications than one could have foreseen at the time.

DISCONTENT OF EXECUTIVE DIRECTORS

Criticism of the World Bank's involvement in the Narmada Dam Project arose in concurrence with internal criticism of the bank's operations in general. Inside the bank, officials could explain that the Inspection Panel emanated from a task force established by President Lewis T. Preston. The task force, chaired by a high-ranking official at the bank, Willi Wapenhans, had to examine the quality of the bank's loan portfolio. The report, since then known as the Wapenhans Report, was leaked. As described in chapter 2, the report illustrated a serious deterioration of the quality of projects, that the staff were often most concerned with getting as many projects as possible approved, and that in this "approval culture" inadequate attention had been paid to the commitment of borrowers and their implementing agencies and to the bank's supervision of project implementation.[73] An external concern was also expressed about the incompatibility of economic development and environmental sustainability, mainly in member countries with large subscriptions in the bank's capital and large subscriptions/contributions to IDA.[74] Projects other than the Narmada Dam were likewise heavily criticized, such as the Transmigration Program in Indonesia, the Polonoroeste road project in Brazil, and other dam projects, including the Arun in Nepal and the Yacyretá in Argentina.

These criticisms and the incidents of protest surrounding Narmada created a breeding ground for the development of environmental policies and procedures. Mani Muthukumara and Andres Liebenthal, of the bank's Operations Evaluation Department, clearly laid out the chronology of the evolution of the bank's Environmental Assessment Policy in an internal document. They explained that a first guideline on environmental dimensions of projects appeared in 1975 with a list of subjects to be handled cautiously in projects. They note that in 1984 the first general statement was made requiring that environmental considerations be introduced at the time of project identification and preparation.[75] The next step was in 1989, when the Operational Directive[76] (OD) on Environmental Assessment[77] (EA) was introduced, making it obligatory for management to execute an assessment for all projects that could have major impacts on the environment. Ibrahim Shihata, a former general counsel of the World Bank, noted that "a small number of ODs, because of the sensitivity or complexity of their subject matter, were discussed in draft in Board seminars before their issuance by Management. These included the ODs on environmental assessments,[78] poverty,[79] and procedures for investment operations under the GEF[80] [Global Environment Facility]."[81]

The World Bank moves slowly. Only in 1991 did the bank take the major decision to adopt a strong Operational Directive on Environmental Assessment[82] that outlined specific procedures, including categorization of the assessment to be undertaken. Two different EAs were foreseen: project-specific EAs and regional and sectoral EAs.[83] The Operational Directive on Environmental Assessment was revised once more in 1999.[84] Still valid, the 1999 policy notes:

> The Bank undertakes environmental screening of each proposed project to determine the appropriate extent and type of EA. The Bank classifies the proposed project into one of four categories, depending on the type, location, sensitivity, and scale of the project and the nature and magnitude of its potential environmental impacts.

> (a) *Category A*: A proposed project is classified as Category A if it is likely to have significant adverse environmental impacts that are sensitive, diverse, or unprecedented. These impacts may affect an area broader than the sites or facilities subject to physical works. EA for a Category A project examines the project's potential negative and positive environmental impacts, compares them with those of feasible alternatives (including the "without project" situation), and recommends any measures needed to prevent, minimize, mitigate, or compensate for adverse impacts and improve environmental performance. For a Category A project, the borrower is responsible for preparing a report, normally an EIA [environmental impact assessment] (or a suitably comprehensive regional or sectoral EA) that includes, as necessary, elements of the other instruments referred to in para. 7.

> (b) *Category B*: A proposed project is classified as Category B if its potential adverse environmental impacts on human populations or environmentally important areas – including wetlands, forests, grasslands, and other natural habitats – are less adverse than those of Category A projects. These impacts are site-specific; few if any of them are irreversible; and in most cases mitigatory measures can be designed more readily than for Category A projects. The scope of EA for a Category B project

may vary from project to project, but it is narrower than that of Category A EA. Like Category A EA, it examines the project's potential negative and positive environmental impacts and recommends any measures needed to prevent, minimize, mitigate, or compensate for adverse impacts and improve environmental performance. The findings and results of Category B EA are described in the project documentation (Project Appraisal Document and Project Information Document).

(c) *Category C*: A proposed project is classified as Category C if it is likely to have minimal or no adverse environmental impacts. Beyond screening, no further EA action is required for a Category C project.

(d) *Category FI*: A proposed project is classified as Category FI if it involves investment of Bank funds through a financial intermediary, in subprojects that may result in adverse environmental impacts.[85]

INSPECTION FUNCTION MENTIONED

In any case, a change of attitude was in the air. Shihata writes: "The creation of an operations inspection function in the World Bank came as a response to Management concerns with the efficiency of the Bank's work."[86] According to Shihata, the president's proposal to establish the inspection function mentioned two distinct but interwoven concerns. The first concern was the internal Wapenhans Report.[87] The second concern was expressed in February 1993. Four executive directors (three representing nonborrowing countries and one representing a number of borrowing countries)[88] proposed the establishment of an "independent in-house inspection for on-going projects"[89] that would undertake inspections on the request of borrowers or executive directors. There was no mention of affected parties.

Events in the outside world and the activities of both the NGO community and the US Congress rendered this proposal obsolete almost immediately. According to Shihata: "The second concern – prevalent among external parties, and reflected in the views of some Executive Directors – was that the Bank was perceived to be less accountable for its performance and less transparent in its decisions-making than it should be."[90] On 22 July 1993 the bank's Board of Governors received an Action Plan from the president containing "specific measures to be undertaken within the areas of concern mentioned in the 'Wapenhans Report.'"[91]

As Shihata notes, the president's memorandum mentioned the creation of an inspection function:

> In this respect, the plan referred to a review to be "commissioned to take account of experience with inspection functions in selected member countries," which would consider whether a new inspection function was needed to augment the Bank's existing supervision, audit, and evaluation functions. Knowing that the preparatory work for the launching

of such a function was in an advanced stage, the plan's authors high-lighted the Bank's need for access, when necessary, "to a reliable source of independent judgment about specific operations that may be facing severe implementation problems" and concluded that "the interest of the Bank would be best served by the establishment of an independent Inspection Panel."[92]

The term "Inspection Panel" caused some discussion among the executive directors and management. The word "inspection" was criticized the most and was not liked by some member countries since it has a negative conno-tation. Some said that since the panel's work would be focused on compli-ance with the bank's policies and procedures, this work could still "be construed as an infringement of the sovereignty of the borrower" if under-stood to be an "inspection." The remark was made that the terms "investi-gation" and "inspection" are used worldwide by governments and others confronting fraud and wrongdoing.

Nathan Kathigmar speculates that the accountability mechanism's name was chosen for the following reason:

The reference to "inspectors" was most probably borrowed from the us-age of that term to refer to government officials conducting planning enquiries in England and would suggest a role for the Panel analogous to that of planning inspectors. Planning inspectors regard criticism of government policy as outside their competence[93] and, likewise, the Bank Panel will only determine questions of violation of Bank policies, rather than the policies themselves. The analogy with the planning enquiry fails, however, when one realizes that a planning enquiry is held to hear objections to a planning exercise, not in violation of the law but pursu-ant to the law, whereas the Bank Panel will hear requests alleging that the Bank is in violation of the rules, the equivalent of law, that it has set for itself.

However, the fact that:

(i)   In effect, there is a dispute[94] between an affected party and the Bank;

(ii)   Bank management has to respond to the charges within a speci-fied period;[95]

(iii) The Panel conducts the investigations within the Bank as well as in the country in which the project is located, including hearing testi-monies from both sides;[96] and

(iv)   The findings of the Panel have some binding character,[97]

would signify the creation of a new international quasi-judicial organ, albeit an unconventional one, with severe limitations. Since some charges against the Bank can be very serious (corruption, bias, etc.) and the careers of Bank managers and staff could be affected by the Panel's adverse findings, the Panel would be constrained to take a strictly judicial approach, at least in some extreme cases.[98]

Nonetheless, the name "Inspection Panel" has been badly received by many and is not used by any other multilateral financial institution (MFI) that, following the World Bank, established similar accountability mechanisms.

There was much debate at the bank about the "judicial" character of the Inspection Panel. I was often told that the panel is "not a court." Once, in a lunch meeting, the panel[99] discussed its work procedures and experiences with a large group of senior management. In response, one manager asked, "So you guys are a sort of United States Supreme Court?"[100] Sometimes, the word "semi-judicial" was used. Nevertheless, the interesting matter highlighted by Kathigmar is indeed the judicial structure of the mechanism. His recognition of this feature is in line with my experience with the working methods of the panel, which are definitely based on judicial systems. The structure of the panel's reporting is clearly of a legal nature, as is the system of hearings held during investigations (or "interrogations," as some have said) inside the bank or during field visits.

Another observation about the "judicial" status of the Inspection Panel is made by Charles Chatterjee:

> The setting up of a panel for investigating allegations of the World Bank's failure or omission to comply with its policies and procedures in consequence of which a party claims to have suffered or is likely to suffer harm/injury is laudable, but the fact remains that its investigation procedure cannot be initiated unless the Board of Executive Directors recommends that the allegation should be investigated.[101] Where an investigation is allowed, it is only on the basis of the Panel's finding and the Bank management's recommendations that the Board of Executive Directors considers what action, if any, should be taken by the Bank. An allegation cannot relate to the Bank's policies and procedures, but only to its failure or omission to comply with them. The investigation procedure complies with the rules of natural justice.[102]

ADOPTION OF THE RESOLUTION

On 22 September 1993, after internal deliberations, the executive directors finally adopted two resolutions, one for the IBRD[103] and one for IDA,[104] which were combined in a single text.[105]

In the first paragraph, which speaks for itself, the establishment of "an independent Inspection Panel" is recorded. The objectives of the panel's function are not mentioned in the resolution. Nevertheless, it was generally understood and accepted that the objectives are, first, to improve quality control respecting project design, appraisal, and implementation and, second, to enhance transparency in and accountability for execution of the bank's policies and procedures.

Articles 2 to 11 of the resolution deal mostly with technical procedures regarding the necessary qualifications of new panel members, how the election of members will be handled, how to remove them from office, and the life-time ban on a member from working for the World Bank after the five-year term is over.[106] Articles 12 to 15 are about the powers of the panel.

Article 12, the heart of the resolution, explains explicitly that "an affected party" from a territory of the borrower can lodge a request – if the party "is not a single individual" but "a community of persons, such as an organization, association, society or other grouping of individuals" – and that the requesting party must demonstrate "that its rights or interests have been or are likely to be directly affected by an action or omission of the Bank as a result of a failure of the Bank to follow its operational policies and procedures with respect to design, appraisal and/or implementation of a project financed by the Bank (including situations where the Bank is alleged to have failed in its follow-up on the borrower's under loan agreements with respect to such policies and procedures) provided in all cases that such failure has had, or threatens to have, a material adverse effect." The composition of a group of individuals became a matter of interpretation in the years to follow (see below). Article 12 further mentions the executive directors's option to "at any time instruct the Panel to conduct an investigation."

Article 19 describes the structure of two procedural phases. In the first phase of twenty-one working days, the panel has to assess whether a request meets the eligibility criteria of the resolution and deliver a recommendation to the board about whether a further investigation is necessary. In the second phase, after approval by the board, an investigation can take place.

By establishing the Inspection Panel, the bank "opened its doors" to people in the countries where it fulfils its tasks. Yet Article 14 immediately sets the limitations and exclusions of the mechanism:

(a) Complaints with respect to actions which are the responsibility of other parties, such as a borrower, or potential borrower, and which do not involve any action or omission on the part of the Bank.

(b) Complaints against procurement decisions by Bank borrowers from suppliers of goods and services financed or expected to be financed by the Bank under a loan agreement, or from losing tenderers for the supply of any such goods and services, which will continue to be addressed by staff under existing procedures.

(c) Requests filed after the Closing Date of the loan financing the project with respect to which the request is filed or after the loan financing the project has been substantially disbursed. This will be deemed to be the case when at least ninety five percent of the loan proceeds have been disbursed.

(d) Requests related to a particular matter or matters over which the Panel has already made its recommendation upon having received a prior request, unless justified by new evidence or circumstances not known at the time of the prior request.

The limitations were soon criticized, mostly from outside but also from inside. The us executive director at the time I was appointed told me that from the beginning the us and some of the Nordic European countries had been in favour of a further extension of the mandate of the Inspection Panel so that if projects failed or omissions occurred on the part of the borrower, the panel would have the right to report on this as well. As has been explained, this proposal was "a station too far" and not in accordance with the Articles of Agreement.

Shihata points out another option that was discussed by the board: "During the Board discussion of the draft Resolution, some Executive Directors suggested that the International Finance Corporation (IFC) should also be included in the Panel's work."[107] The last time I met with Shihata in Washington, DC, not long before he passed away, he told me that it would have been an easy decision for the board to have included the IFC under the mandate of the Inspection Panel. This restriction did not exonerate the bank in the event that the Inspection Panel received a request concerning an IFC project. As I explain below, IFC projects that involve IDA financing can be investigated by the Inspection Panel.[108]

In 1995 a complaint regarding a full IFC project was indeed lodged with the panel, as Lori Udall explains:

The Claim catalyzed an unprecedented independent review of an International Finance Corporation (IFC) financed project.[109] The Panel sent the claim to Wolfensohn and the Board and suggested that the claim be investigated independently. Wolfensohn hired an independent review team to look at the project over an eight month period. The team found extensive violations of Bank policy. Following the partial need for the Inspection Panel's jurisdiction to extend to the IFC ultimately led to the creation of a compliance/ombudsman office which will advise senior Management on violations of IFC policies on information, and social and environment issues.[110]

As a result of this decision, the IFC is subject to a problem-solving mechanism, while IDA and the IBRD are subject to an accountability mechanism or compliance review mechanism. In chapter 7, I raise the question of whether both mechanisms should be available independently: a problem-solving mechanism for all relevant members in the World Bank Group and an accountability mechanism for the same members in the group as the last resort.

Finally, the restriction against the panel investigating a project for which
95 per cent of the loan has been disbursed is considered to be a missed
opportunity. The mandate of the accountability mechanism of the Asian
Development Bank is more extensive than this. Another restriction is on
procurement. The word "procurement," I maintain, is an instance of
veiled language. It is clear that the panel should not be involved in disputes on tenders or purchasing of goods. Nevertheless, this stipulation is
also used to restrict the panel when it is confronted with corruption. Members of the panel, so far as I am aware, are always of the opinion when confronted with corruption that it is one's duty as a responsible citizen to
report on this to the right authorities, who will have to take it up. President
Jim Wolfensohn, who placed corruption clearly on the agenda of the bank,
appointed a director for the Department of Institutional Integrity responsible for investigating internal and external corruption: Maarten de Jong.[111]
I met with him several times to discuss topics that later were formally discussed with the panel.

Articles 16 to 23 of the 1993 resolution relate to the procedures to be followed by requesters filing a claim, which "shall be in writing and shall state
all relevant facts, including, in the case of a request by an affected party, the
harm suffered by or threatened to such party or parties by the alleged action
or omission of the Bank." The articles describe the time schedule for the
chairperson of the panel to inform the executive directors, the twenty-one
working days for management to provide the panel "with evidence that it
has complied" (Art. 18), the twenty-one working days for the Panel to determine "whether the request meets the eligibility criteria" (Art. 19), the access
of the panel to "all staff who may contribute information and to all pertinent Bank records" (Art. 21), the consultation with the borrower and
executive directors before and during investigation since "Inspection in the
territory of such country shall be carried out with its prior consent" (Art. 21),
the reporting of the panel to the executive directors and the president, who
together "shall consider all relevant facts, and shall conclude with the
Panel's findings whether the Bank has complied with all relevant Bank policies and procedures" (Art. 22), and the six weeks after receiving the panel's
findings for management to "submit to the Executive Directors for their
consideration in response to such findings" (Art. 23).

Articles 24 to 28, which conclude the resolution, refer to the reports of
the panel, which, "pursuant to [Article] 22, shall be reached by consensus
and, in the absence of a consensus, the majority and minority views shall be
stated" (Art. 24). Article 25 notes that the bank will make publicly available
within two weeks of the board's consideration both the request of the
panel and its recommendation on "whether to proceed with the inspection
and the decision of the Executive Directors in this respect." Article 27
notes that the executive directors "shall review the experience of the Inspection Panel function established by this resolution after two years from
the date of the appointment of the first members of the Panel."

What is clear at this time is that the decision about whether an investigation will take place after the Inspection Panel has recommended a further investigation is still entirely in the hands of the executive directors. Article 19 notes: "The recommendation of the Panel shall be circulated to the Executive Directors for decision." This became one of the issues during the revision of the resolution in 1996 and 1999, as described below. Nevertheless, a historic decision was taken by giving a voice to the people in the areas of bank operations.

PRESIDENT WOLFENSOHN AND GENERAL COUNSEL SHIHATA

While the decision to establish the Morse Commission was taken under President Conable and the resolution establishing the Inspection Panel was adopted under President Preston, it was finally under President Wolfensohn that the earlier work of the panel was conducted. Wolfensohn, leading the process of implementation of the resolution, benefited from the legal guidance of Ibrahim Shihata, the general counsel of the World Bank. Shihata's book *The World Bank Inspection Panel: In Practice* has been an important source for many who have tried to understand the far-reaching (judicial) implications of the introduction of the Inspection Panel at the World Bank. His work forms the basis for describing and understanding the years of the resolution's implementation and the developments both of the procedures and of the mutual relations between the panel, the board, and management. That being said, the panel has not always agreed with the position taken by Shihata.

Wolfensohn undoubtedly had his difficult moments with the Inspection Panel, such as during the panel's investigations into and final reporting on the China Western Poverty Reduction Project, which has been called "one of the most controversial projects in the entire 54-year history of the World Bank."[112] Nonetheless, he believed in the mechanism and was a supporter of the panel. In the foreword to Alvaro Umaña Quesada's book *The World Bank Inspection Panel: The First Four Years, 1994–1998*, Wolfensohn states the following about the historic decision to establish the Inspection Panel:

> When the Board of Directors of the World Bank created the Inspection Panel five years ago, it created an unprecedented means for increasing the transparency and accountability of the Bank's operations. This was a first of its kind for an international organization – the creation of an independent mechanism to respond to claims by those whom we are most intent on helping that they have been adversely affected by the projects we finance ...
>
> By giving private citizens – and especially the poor – a new means of access to the Bank, it has empowered and given voice to those we most need to hear. At the same time, it has served the Bank itself

through ensuring that we really are fulfilling our mandate of improving conditions for the world's poorest people. The Inspection Panel tells us whether we are following our own policies and procedures, which are intended to protect the interests of those affected by our projects as well as the environment. In testament to the success of this approach, other international financial institutions have seen its value and have followed suit.[113]

In an interview that I conducted with Wolfensohn, after being asked whether he still believes in the function of the panel, he said:

I think it is a very good mechanism and it is an evolving mechanism. I think the principle that you could have – that interested parties can come to [the panel], have the agreements looked at it in a public way, from a group that is independent of management – is an extremely important and commendable tool. Extremely important. But if you are going to get the benefit from it, it shouldn't be just to come up with the verdict guilty or not guilty. It should be something which is a part of the process.[114]

In 1994 the following three panel members were selected and appointed: Ernst-Günter Bröder (a German national)[115] for five years, Alvaro Umaña Quesada (a Costa Rican national)[116] for four years, and Richard Bissell (a United States national)[117] for three years. According to Article 3 of the resolution, the first three members were to be appointed for five, four, and three years, while all future members are to be selected for five-year terms. The stipulation of five, four, and three years for the first three appointed members was to guarantee institutional memory. From then on, both the Inspection Panel and the bank have had to find their way with this new entity, and they will continue do so through experience still to come. Bröder acted as the first chairman of the panel.[118]

1996: FIRST CLARIFICATIONS OF THE RESOLUTION

As provided for in the resolution, the bank's experience with the inspection function was to be reviewed by the executive directors "after two years from the date of appointment of the first members of the Panel."[119] Since the first appointment of Bröder was on 1 August 1994, this review was to take place in April 1996.[120] In September 1995, after the first year of the panel's operations, a proposal was made by three executive directors to have a general discussion on the bank's initial experiences with the panel and, more specifically, on the panel's role in assessing the eligibility of a request. The chairman of the panel expressed his willingness to submit to the board a working paper on the panel. Thus on 27 November 1995, fifteen months after the panel began its operations, the chairman tabled the document "Practical Suggestions Based on Experience to Date."[121] This report not only referred to the first signals of a positive attitude among staff and managers, who had begun to take the policies and procedures of the panel more seriously, but also noted that some might become more cautious about accepting projects with a high risk. The World Bank and the panel still had to find a way to have the new compliance "organ" adopted by the institutional "body." A defensive rejection could still be expected.

In his report of November 1995 the chairman, on behalf of the panel, explained two major difficulties that had become clear. To begin with, the panel members found that it was hard to agree on the necessity of an inspection. The difference between an eligibility stage and an investigation stage appeared to be unclear. The amount of information that the board expected the panel to deliver could not be collected within the twenty-one working days stipulated in the resolution. According to the panel, the information that the board expected was "at the preliminary stage sometimes equivalent to the content of an investigation."[122] Shihata also refers to the preliminary period of twenty-one working days: "The Panel specifically added that 'extending the time period of the preliminary stage reduces the need for a formal investigation/inspection,' which can still be authorized by the Board as a last resort."[123]

In some cases the executive directors had already extended the period. The advantage of this extension was that the panel could "undertake a 'preliminary assessment' of the damages alleged by the requester (in particular when such preliminary assessment could lead to a resolution of the matter without the need for a full investigation)."[124] The advantage to the executive directors, especially those representing the Group II countries,[125] was that a preliminary assessment instead of a full investigation was perceived as "beneficial rather than an infringement of sovereignty that an 'investigation' could evoke in certain cases."[126] A prolonged debate on the matter ensued between management, the board, and the panel.

The panel also initiated discussion about who could file a request and articulated its discontent with some opinions expressed within the bank about the background of those filing a claim. As I was told, management had difficulties with parties other then the poor themselves in the project areas lodging a complaint: "Experience to date shows that directly affected parties will be left out of the process unless international NGOs or lawyers know about their situation and are interested in taking up and funding their cause."[127] Over the years, debate has continued between those defending support from international NGOs as a guarantee of access to the bank for the poor, who do not know how to work their way through complex and necessary requirements under the resolution, and those arguing that most cases, if not all, have been "instigated" not by the poor but by NGOs from Western countries "that feel locked out of the big decisions on development."[128] The latter statement is from Sebastian Mallaby, a

Washington Post columnist who wrote a book on the era of President Wolfensohn at the World Bank, probably the most mentioned, cited, and read text in World Bank circles in recent years, entitled *The World's Banker: A Story of Failed States, Financial Crises, and the Wealth and Poverty of Nations* (see chapter 8). Mallaby writes rather cynically about the NGOs:

> [S]ome NGOs cannot be placated; their whole reason for existence is to be implacable. Campaigning NGOs, as distinct from those with programs in the field, almost have to be radical; if they stop denouncing big organizations, nobody will send them cash or quote them in the newspapers. Partly for this reason, and partly out of a likable conviction that the status quo is never good enough, most NGOs do not have an off switch. You can grant their demand that you abandon structural adjustment or call in the Inspection Panel, but they will still demonstrate outside your building.[129]

Another interesting issue in the panel's 1995 report is the bank president's lack of access to the Inspection Panel.[130] The president and the panel cannot be hindered from meeting with each other, so that is not the issue here, but the report does propose giving the president an opportunity to ask the panel to act at an early stage, such as in cases of sensitive projects. This would provide flexibility and give the panel a more positive role than that of just checking on compliance with policies. It would ensure accountability *before* the bank's final approval of such projects, providing a sort of early-warning system that would mitigate against potential harm to the people in the project area. With early involvement, the panel said that it could prevent management from later being found in noncompliance. Never again have I seen this issue mentioned in panel documents.

Why the panel at the time believed that only the president could create this different type of panel involvement is not clear to me. This early proposal for discussion also does not define the president's functional capacity with respect to the panel – that is, whether he is to interact with the panel as president of the board or as president of management and staff. This "double role" could confuse the process. Nevertheless, these initial notes of the Inspection Panel contain mention of the need for a kind of problem-solving mechanism at an early stage, although not clearly formulated as such. It is all the more surprising that a problem-solving mechanism or ombudsman function has never been made effective for the IBRD and IDA in the World Bank Group.

It took the bank more than a year to finalize the first review of the resolution. An informal board meeting took place on 27 February 1996. Besides the document submitted to the board by the panel, four papers were submitted by management. According to Shihata: "These included (i) 'a non-exhaustive list of issues for discussion;'[131] (ii) a table summarizing the manner in which the requests before the Panel were handled; (iii) a list summarizing the Panel's views (expressed in a November 1995 'working

paper') and the views communicated by NGOs to Bank Management; and
(iv) a note and a table comparing the Bank's Panel with the inspection panels established by the Inter-American Development Bank (IADB) and the
Asian Development Bank (ADB) in 1994 and 1995, respectively."[132]

Prior to this meeting, the international NGO community approached the
bank with its recommendations for reform and demanded a role in the
revision. According to Shihata, reports with "detailed suggestions" were received from Oxfam International and International Rivers Network.[133]
The Policy Department of Oxfam United Kingdom in Ireland produced an
assessment of the operations of the panel. In summary, it recommended
the following:

- The procedures for inspection should be simplified so that genuinely affected groups can have easier recourse to the panel;
- All parties should have equal access and rights of participation under the
  inspection function to ensure a fair hearing;
- The panel should be given greater discretion in assessing both the eligibility of the complainant and the interpretation of the resolution;
- The panel should be encouraged to propose changes to the design and
  implementation of projects and programs and to the bank's operational
  policies and procedures;
- To ensure consistency, and in view of the expansion of the World Bank's
  loans and guarantees to the private sector, the panel's remit should en-
  compass complaints related to the operations of other bank bodies such
  as the International Finance Corporation and the Multilateral Investment Guarantee Agency;
- A single-stage review should replace the current two-stages process only
  if the complainants are guaranteed equal access and full participation;
- In exceptional circumstances, public-interest cases should be considered
  by the panel in consultation with the president.[134]

At the meeting, the board took the decision that first its Committee on
Development Effectiveness (CODE) should look into the matter in depth
and then submit "its own recommendations to the full Board."[135] In May
management sent CODE a first document on the review. Management
"noted that the Resolution did not exclude the Bank's private sector operations and agreed in principle that such operations in bank affiliates may
also be subject to inspection. Such inspection should, however, differ in
certain respects from that provided for in the Resolution."[136] It was recognized that "any inspection of private sector operations might also require
stricter safeguards with respect to disclosure of documents, shorter procedures to avoid delay, and greater attention to the requirements of domestic
law with respect to property and privacy rights."[137]

Nevertheless, according to Shihata: "Once CODE had completed its consideration of the Inspection mechanism for IFC and MIGA projects, it was

Management's intention, as declared at the time, to propose a common approach to inspection for all Bank Group private sector operations."[138] The private-sector clients were then consulted about the idea (see chapter 8).[139] Shihata writes:

> The report showed that a majority of those consulted were not in favour of an inspection function and would not, at any rate, welcome inspection under the established procedures of the existing Panel. Discussion in CODE on this point was not conclusive; Management was asked to present different options to a subsequent meeting. Consequently, IFC Management submitted to CODE a joint IFC/MIGA paper on several options, including, among many others, the possibility to extend the mandate of the Bank's Inspection Panel to IFC and MIGA, with or without modifications to meet the special requirements of private sector operations. The paper, however, emphasized the shortcomings of this option. Without prejudice to the outcome of the debate, the IFC and MIGA jointly proceeded with implementation of one of the options mentioned in the paper, namely the appointment of a compliance advisor/ombudsman.[140]

In the end, the decision was taken to appoint a compliance advisor/ombudsman with a greater problem-solving role instead of introducing a compliance review mechanism.[141] So the panel lost the possibility of having the IFC under its mandate. Still, the subject is a "bone of contention" at the bank.[142] The ombudsman function at the IFC is further discussed in chapter 4.

In October 1996 the board came to a final conclusion. Instead of approving amendments to the resolution, the board approved several clarifications. The panel was granted the opportunity to carry out "a preliminary assessment of the damage alleged by the requester" within a longer period than the twenty-one days originally stipulated. In this case, the panel had to indicate to the board "the date on which it would present its findings and recommendations as to whether a full investigation was still required."[143] If the date was later than eight weeks after receipt of management's response, the board had to give approval for the extension. Moreover, the board indicated that this preliminary stage was primarily intended to determine "whether the complaint was prima facie justified and warranted a full investigation because it was eligible under the Resolution."[144] The difference between the first eligibility phase and the second investigation phase of the assessment was made clearer. In permitting the panel alone to decide whether to undertake a preliminary assessment, the board clearly extended the panel's powers as originally specified in the resolution.[145]

The 1996 clarifications reassert that the panel is not allowed to review the bank's general compliance with its policies and procedures "but is limited to cases of alleged failure by the Bank to follow its operational policies and procedure with respect to the design, appraisal, and/or implementation of projects." The clarifications, however, do add that this function of the panel also includes "cases of alleged failure by the Bank to follow-up on the borrowers" with respect to their obligations under loan agreements.[146] Although this clarification seems to extend the scope of the panel's jurisdiction, in reality this had already been stipulated in Article 12 of the original resolution.

A third clarification concerns the disclosure of information. The board "agreed to make Management's response to the request for inspection, as well as the opinions of the General Counsel of the Bank on matters related to the Panel, available to the public promptly after the Board had discussed these documents. Both changes were requested by NGOs and welcomed by Management. The Board also shortened the period of disclosure of all documents from two weeks to three days from the date of Board decision."[147] A result of this agreement has been an unequivocal increase in the transparency of the work of the panel, more specifically an increase in the transparency of the complex and highly politicized communication between the board, the panel, and management.

A fourth clarification concerned the agreement that significant efforts should be made by management to "make the Inspection Panel better known in borrowing countries."[148]

Finally, on a proposal of management, the 1996 clarifications confirmed that the board has authority to interpret the resolution and to authorize inspections. Subsequent to this statement, in a repetition of Article 15, it is again emphasized that the panel's application of the resolution is "subject to the Board's review."[149]

What changes were not adopted? Several NGOs had asked that the Inspection Panel be given the power to come up with "recommendations." This request was denied. According to Shihata, "endowing it [the panel] with a substantive advisory function that went beyond the investigation of requests would require placing at its disposal technical and financial resources far beyond its existing facilities."[150] The board decided that recommendations were what management should deliver and that the panel should deliver findings. Nevertheless, over the years the NGO community and media, and even executive directors in their informal discussions with the panel, have taken the panel's findings as recommendations. It has all been a matter of interpretation. The demand of some NGOs "that the Board should have a separate Legal Counsel to advise on Panel matters, separate from the Bank's General Counsel, was not granted."[151] I was told that when this option was discussed by the board, Shihata said, "Well in that case that may cause me to resign." I was also told that Eveline Herfkens, the Dutch executive director, then said, "No, that is not what we want."

It became clear that the panel and management's legal department had different perceptions of the term "affected party." Under the resolution, the term is defined as "a community of persons, such as an organization, association, society or other grouping of individuals." A single individual cannot be considered an "affected party." According to internal bank documents to which I had access, the panel understood the term to mean any two or more persons and accordingly indicated this in its operational procedures. The board defined the term more precisely as "any two or more individuals with common interest or concern." This excludes complaints on behalf of the public at large (*actio popularis*).[152]

The panel expressed its concern "that if a more restrictive interpretation of the current eligibility requirements was made, access to the Panel would be limited to 'the fortunate few that can rely on the advice of international lawyers and NGOs.'"[153] This was a view also taken by the NGOs that wrote to the bank asking that access to the panel be broadened to cover "requests submitted by foreign NGOs and to local NGOs whose rights or interests had not been affected by the project, or, more generally, to claims submitted in the public interest."[154] Nevertheless, the board maintained the language of the resolution as mentioned above, "confirming an interpretation given on earlier occasions by the Board on the General Counsel's advice."[155]

About this important discussion on the mandate, Shihata writes:

> Management did not object to broadening access to any party as long as it was an "affected party," that is, a party whose rights or interests might be harmed or threatened by an alleged Bank action or omission related to a specific project. Management noted that that would not meet the broader demands of NGOs, but suggested that NGOs that were not "affected parties" might, under the Resolution, submit a request to an Executive Director. If the later was convinced of the seriousness of the request, he could forward it to the Panel if he was not satisfied with the initial Management reply. Neither CODE, nor the full Board, supported extending the inspection function beyond the scope provided for in the Resolution.[156]

In a footnote, he adds that the NGOs were mistaken in their claim that the general counsel's "advice meant that the interests of the complainants ought to be 'affected in the same way.'" And he goes on to refute their argument "that individual complainants may not meet the commonality of interest standard if affected in a different manner."[157] General Counsel Shihata was clearly upset by the allegation, saying further in the footnote: "No such requirement should be drawn, however, from the General Counsel's Legal Memorandum, the text of the Resolution, or its Board-approved interpretation."

1999: SECOND CLARIFICATIONS OF THE RESOLUTION

Despite the first clarifications, the board still experienced difficulties with the panel's mandate. A year after the first clarifications, on 13 November 1997, another informal board meeting took place for a second round of clarifications. This time it would take two years to complete the process. Many new optional procedures were proposed by both management and the panel. Listening to those who had a role early in the process and reading documents from that time have given me an impression of the difficult relationship between management and the panel.[158] One can understand the nature of this relationship. Management felt "controlled," whereas previously it had enjoyed a great deal of freedom in conducting the bank's daily operations. As well, the mostly (but not always) negative attitude toward the panel showed a lack of understanding of the richness of such mechanisms when, in fact, management should have been proud that the World Bank was the first such institution to give voice to the people concerned. Nevertheless, time is necessary to change an existing culture and to make an institution and, even more, its people accept an accountability mechanism as a natural in-house "self-healing" mechanism.

The different proposals and documents intended to better clarify the "jurisdictional" role of the panel were exchanged between management, the board, and the panel. The panel expressed its view that its role had changed, saying: "A review of past Board decisions reveals that the Panel's role in checking compliance with operational policies has been downplayed, while its role in addressing actual or potential harm to local populations and assessing remedial actions has been emphasized."[159] This view originated from "Management's practice to submit borrowers' remedial action plans before the Board meets to consider the Panel's recommendation on whether to investigate. It described that practice as having effectively pre-empted the process envisaged in the Resolution."[160]

The panel circulated two "possible courses"[161] for addressing the latter complaint. The first option, which is more consistent with the original resolution, was that management should first receive the requesters' complaint. Management could answer this either with an explanation of why there was no violation of policies or with an admission that violations had occurred and an explanation of the steps that would be taken to address these violations. If the requesters still wanted to submit a request to the panel, the panel would first have to determine whether the matter had been addressed. If so, it would recommend to the board that the panel not do further investigation. In the case of dissatisfaction with management's response to the requesters, the panel would propose a full investigation. The second option, more in line with the 1996 clarifications, was to fulfil the panel's desire that it conduct an elaborate preliminary review and so avoid a full investigation. The benefit of this option could be an early remedy, but the negative aspect was that it could be understood as undermining the panel's role.

There were legal arguments over who should report when and to which body within the bank as well as over where to place blame for the failures – on the borrowers or on management. All kinds of formulations were recorded by management in several documents.[162] This all led to a set of "tailor-made" scenarios to be chosen from when determining the nature of management's response to a request for an inspection, called the "Commentary."[163] The panel disagreed with the "Commentary's view of unbundling the issues involved and stated that under the different scenarios the Board could be confronted with two views (of Management and Panel, respectively) on how responsibilities for alleged harm should be assigned."[164]

Shihata notes a rather fundamental reason for the panel's disagreement with management's proposals: "As Management was a party to the matter in dispute and tended to assign responsibility to the borrower in previous cases, the Panel felt that it would not be fair to give it the power of making an assignment of responsibility, even if it was reflecting only Management's view and was completely subject to the Panel's evaluation."[165]

In March 1998 the board decided to establish a working group of six executive directors. In contrast to the process leading to the 1996 clarifications, the working group heard from both the panel and management but held its discussions behind closed doors. On 9 December 1998 the group's members presented a report with seventeen main recommendations,[166] summarized as follows:

1 The board should strongly reaffirm the importance of the Inspection Panel process, enhancing project quality.

2 The panel must be independent, and the integrity of the resolution must not be compromised.

3 The paragraph entitled "The Panel's Function" in the 1996 clarifications should be revised on the basis of the proposals below and modified according to the relevant procedures.

4 Except for managements' recommendations to the board after the panel completes its investigation, management should not communicate directly with the board about a request.

5 After the panel has forwarded a request to management, the latter should provide evidence: (i) that it has complied with the bank's operational policies, (ii) that there are serious failures attributable to its own actions but that it intends to comply with the policies, or (iii) that the serious failures are attributable to the borrower or to factors external to the bank, or (iv) that the serious failures are attributable both to the bank and to the borrower or external factors.

6 If management admits failures attributable exclusively or partly to the bank, it may provide, together with its response, evidence that it has since complied or taken steps to comply.

7 The panel shall determine the eligibility of a request for inspection independently of any views that may be expressed by management.

8 The panel is expected to seek the view of the bank's legal department with respect to matters relating to the bank's rights and obligations.

9 When making its recommendations, the panel should satisfy itself that all eligibility criteria provided for in the resolution have been met.

10 In the first stage of the process (before investigation), the panel may visit the project country if it believes this is necessary. However, any definite assessment of the bank's failure to respect its policies will be done after the panel has completed its investigation.

11 As to the important question of the two-stage approach, the two stages should be maintained in principle, but the board "will authorize an investigation without making a judgment on the merits of the claimant's Request and without discussion, except with respect to the technical eligibility criteria."[167]

12 The working group stressed the "non-judicial," "evaluative" nature of the panel's investigation.

13 The panel was urged to keep its profile low during investigation, "in keeping with its role as a fact-finding body on behalf of the Board."[168]

14 The panel's findings "should focus [only] on serious Bank failures to observe its operational policies and procedures with respect to project design, appraisal, and/or implementation and discuss only those material adverse effects, alleged in the Request."[169] "This is consistent with paragraph 14 (a) of the Resolution, which excludes from the Panel's purview 'complaints with respect to actions that are the responsibility of other parties, such as borrower or potential borrower and that do not involve any action or omission on the part of the Bank.'"[170]

15 In the panel's assessment of material adverse effects, it should compare the current situation with that prevailing before the bank-financed project existed. "Non-accomplishments and unfulfilled expectations that do not generate a material deterioration compared to the without-project situation should not be considered as material adverse effect"[171] – a recommendation that later became the most controversial.

16 Management should communicate to the panel the nature and outcome of consultations with affected parties, and the panel may submit to the board a report on its view of the adequacy of such consultations. The board should not ask the panel to monitor implementation of the Action Plan.[172]

17 Finally, the working group emphasized that its proposals would enhance the effectiveness of the panel only if they were adhered to "by all parties in good faith"[173] and if borrowers do not withhold their consent for the panel's field visits.

After the report was finalized by the working group, a battle began involving not only the parties concerned at the bank (i.e., the panel, the board, and management) but also the NGO community and the media. Washington-based NGOs requested that the board allow public participation in the clarifications and that it postpone the board meeting. Shihata refers to an article the following day in the *Wall Street Journal* with the heading "Effort Would Curb Watchdog of World Bank – Big Borrower Nations Seek Limit on Probing Harm to People and Ecology."[174] Emotions were running high. According to Shihata, the *Wall Street Journal* published information about restrictions of the panel that were not at all in the report.

THE PANEL'S REACTION TO RECOMMENDATIONS

In turn, the panel reacted to the recommendations of the working group with a set of comments.[175] In brief, some important reactions as they have been explained to me include:

1 The panel showed its satisfaction with the working group's reaffirmation of the resolution, with its assertion that the panel's integrity and independence be conserved, and with its emphasis on the importance of the panel's process and its contribution to improving the effectiveness of bank policies.

2 The panel referred to a publication in which former president Wolfensohn commented on the panel's establishment: "By giving private citizens – and especially the poor – a new means of access to the Bank, it has empowered and given voice to those we most need to hear."[176] The panel also cited a statement by President Preston: "the Panel provides a safety net in the exceptional cases where the bank's own high standards might not be met. In that sense, the Panel is a positive step in strengthening the links between the bank and the people affected by the operations it finances."[177] The panel recalled its purpose and mission and stressed that "the redressal of alleged harm is the most important feature of the Panel process. Requests for inspection are not based on an intellectual concern that Bank policies and procedures may have been violated. Rather, they are motivated by a keen desire that the Bank redress the adverse effects resulting from such violations."[178]

3 Rather critical notes were made on the working group's preference for "unbundling" responsibility for failures of compliance in order to distinguish between failures originating with the bank and those orginating with the borrower or other parties since the latter do not fall under the panel's mandate.[179] The panel doubted the practicability of "unbundling," noting that during implementation it would not always be possible to determine whether noncompliance had resulted from internal bank decisions and operations or from the acts of the national implementing authorities. Making this distinction is definitely one of the most difficult parts of the panel's mandate. My experience during five years on the panel was that attempts to make this distinction often took us into a "grey zone." As a result, a finding of noncompliance could often be attributed only to the absence of a justifiable level of management supervision of project implementation.

4 Based on the assumption that unbundling could take place, the working group proposed that in cases of noncompliance, management should prepare a Compliance Plan "to address its own failures, if any,"[180] and

prepare a remedial Action Plan to be agreed upon by the bank and the borrower. According to the working group's recommendation, the Compliance Plan would be management's response to the panel, while the Action Plan would stay outside the panel's scope. The panel strongly disagreed with the proposal to divide the remedial actions in this way and expressed its belief that the plan would not work in reality and would lead to lots of frustration, most of all for the requesters. Further elaborating on the Action Plan, the working group recommended that "Management should communicate to the Panel the nature and outcome of consultations with affected parties," and "the Panel may submit to the Board a report on their view of the adequacy of such consultation."[181]

5 Another concern raised by the panel was the working group's "strong recommendation" that the two stages for investigating a complaint remain and that the board authorize an investigation recommended by the panel "except with respect to the technical eligibility criteria."[182] In my experience, the meaning of "technical eligibility criteria" was not clear to the panel. A discussion about this point between the board and the panel could delay or stop the process without the panel's having properly assessed a request. Today, one could say that it was an important clarification since the board is more or less "forced" to accept a request for further investigation (the second stage). Since the 1999 clarifications, requests for further investigation have (so far) always been accepted by the board.

6 Last but not least, another very sensitive comment made by the panel concerned the working group's recommendation that the panel use the "without-project" situation for a proper comparison when assessing a project's material adverse effects. Shihata notes a basic difference between the panel's view of its role and the working group's perception of this role.[183] The panel found it difficult to define "harm" in the context of such an abstract definition. And what was to be done if a project had been under execution for some years? Besides, the panel did not have at its disposal baseline data with which to compare such abstract situations. It is worth mentioning that the Inspection Panel had in mind the so-called Yacyretá project,[184] which it reviewed (without investigation) and which had been under implementation for more then twenty years when the request for an investigation was received on 17 May 2002. Moreover, with this project the panel found it very difficult to work with data since over time "the plan, budget, and particularly the timetable envisaged within that plan have not worked as originally intended."[185] There were no reliable baseline data. It was impossible to compare the with-project and without-project situations.

As mentioned above, not only did the panel react strongly to the recommendations, but the media also published several articles, and well-known members of the US Congress wrote a joint letter to the bank's president criticizing the working group's report, whose recommendations, according to Shihata, were aligned with the concerns of the NGO community.[186] Between the lines, Shihata suggests that all the parties were influenced by each other: "Before the Board meeting with the NGOs, several inaccurate press articles reported negatively on the Working Group's report. Objections were also received from NGOs echoing previous comments made during the first review as well as the Panel's own comments on the Working Group's report."[187]

In April 1999 the board finally decided on the second clarifications. The US executive director expressed three concerns: (1) that the board remained at the centre of decision making, (2) that asking the panel to assess harm on the basis of a "without-project" standard would "probably not pass the test of reasonableness," and (3) that "the proposal for unbundling" would prove impracticable.[188]

The board overwhelmingly supported the working group's report with, according to Shihata, some "substantive changes": (1) the term "force majeure" justifying extension of the twenty-one working days within which the panel must conduct its initial investigation of a requester's complaint is now defined to mean "reasons beyond control of Management or the Panel";[189] (2) the criterion relating to the identity of the affected party now reads "any two or more persons with common interests or concerns and who are in the borrower's territory";[190] (3) the criterion relating to the assertion in the request of a serious violation resulting in material adverse effect has been reworded to clarify the intended meaning; that is, the issue that may be discussed by the board at this stage is not whether the violation took place and the harm existed or was likely to occur but only whether the request "does assert in substance" such violations and harm; (4) the "Conclusions made it clear that the Board requires that the information to be disclosed to claimants be provided *by Management* to claimants in their language";[191] and (5) the words "absolutely necessary" have been changed to "necessary" in the description of the circumstances in which the panel or management may respond to the media.

In addition to the "substantive" changes mentioned by Shihata, who (as a key player) was not necessarily neutral in what he considered "substantive," I would also like to mention several changes.

One, a provision prohibits management from communicating with the board before the panel completes its inspection "on matters associated with the request for inspection, except as provided for in the Resolution. It will thus direct its response to the request, including any steps it intends to take to address its failures, if any to the Panel." So the respective clarification limits the ability of management to communicate with the board (i.e., influence its decisions).[192] Here, I would like to note that according to what I have been told, management had made it a practice to "brief" the board without the panel's presence on ongoing requests in the context of other projects or policy papers that were before the board in order to influence its decisions.

Two, the 1999 clarifications repeat that it is for the Inspection Panel to "satisfy itself as to whether the Bank's compliance or evidence of intention to comply is adequate, and reflect this assessment in its reporting to the Board."[193] And the panel "will determine the eligibility of a request for inspection independently of any views that may be expressed by Management."[194] The repetition here emphasizes the panel's independence in coming to its decisions, a condition to be preserved.

Three, in the event that the panel recommends an investigation, the board will authorize the investigation unless the following technical eligibility criteria are not met: (1) two or more persons are the affected party, (2) the complainant asserts that a serious policy violation by the bank has or is likely to have a material adverse effect, (3) the matter has been brought to the attention of management without adequate response, (4) the complaint is not related to procurement, (5) the loan has not been closed or substantially disbursed, and (6) there has been no previous recommendation by the panel on the matter. This is an important clarification in that the board is now more or less "forced" to accept a request for investigation if recommended by the panel.

Four, the recommendation remained in the text that "for assessing material adverse effect, the without-project situation should be used as the base case for comparison." But it was noted that this requirement should "take into account what baseline information may be available." No consideration was shown for the panel's expressed problems with this "provision." In practice, this created many difficulties in the panel's daily work. Often the panel reported on a lack of baseline data. For the panel, the without-project situation is a mission impossible. In the event of a future clarification of the resolution, this recommendation should be deleted.

Five, the 1999 clarifications state that "The 'preliminary assessment' concept, as described in the October 1996 Clarification, is no longer needed."[195] Mention of this concept was thus deleted. This reversal was perhaps part of a clearer division between the eligibility phase and the investigation phase. Nevertheless, it could also be seen as limiting the panel's options during the first stage. I do not recall that this caused any limitation. The provision that an extension would be allowed in case of "force majeure" was implemented in several cases.

Six, the 1999 clarifications further state that "The panel will discuss in its written report only those material adverse effects, alleged in the request, that have totally or partially resulted from serious Bank failure of Compliance with its policies and procedures."[196] This stipulation is again a limitation of the panel's jurisdiction.

Seven, promptly making documents publicly available to claimants in their language, to the extent possible, is another important provision given the institution's aim of transparency. However, I doubt that this requirement is always met.

Eight, one can conclude that many of the demands voiced by the panel and by outside communities were not accepted by the board. The NGO community was definitely not satisfied with the revised mandate of the Inspection Panel. In 2003 a group of experts who had been following the World Bank and the Inspection Panel for years published a book on the panel's work and its impact at the bank. They express the opinion that the board excluded "an oversight role from the panel's mandate" and "failed to create an alternative way to monitor" whether projects had been brought into compliance. They note that, as a result, "local people are often denied meaningful remedies." They also criticize the board's lack of "systematic oversight" and "institutional memory," which they consider a "key weakness in the Inspection Panel process."[197]

Nine, nevertheless, in the natural process of the panel's becoming a mature mechanism, some important steps have been taken. Notably, the board has again confirmed the necessity of the Inspection Panel. When the panel recommends an investigation, the board will now authorize the investigation. After many difficult years, the panel, the board, and management have found their way in adopting the procedures and working methods of an accountability mechanism that they themselves established. Perhaps this process is finished, but it is more probable that the mechanism will be further developed. Some may still consider the panel to be an unnatural organ of the body and view it as likely to trigger some rejection symptoms. Others see it as a kind of "self-healing" mechanism or as a "learning-by-doing" system. What the mechanism finally is or should be inside the institution is the subject of this study.

4

Accountability Mechanisms in Other Multilateral Financial Institutions

Since the World Bank's adoption of a resolution establishing the Inspection Panel on 23 September 1993,[1] followed by the installation of the panel at the beginning of 1994, it is evident that the bank has provided the role model for the other multilateral financial institutions (MFIs). Many writings about the Inspection Panel have recognized its impacts on the operations of the World Bank, namely greater transparency and accountability and the granting of a voice to affected people.[2] In their rationales and objectives, the accountability mechanisms that were established afterward in the other MFIs are both similar to and different from the Inspection Panel. Nevertheless, as I described in chapter 3, the panel is still criticized for weaknesses in its mandate (see also chapters 6 and 7). Eisuke Suzuki and Suresh Nanwani, who were involved in the creation of the accountability mechanism at the Asian Development Bank (ADB), refer for example to the lack of a problem-solving mechanism at the World Bank, the lack of "oversight over the implementation of remedial measures, and the [lack of] ability to assess whether Management's proposed remedial measures satisfy the concerns of the claimants and/or bring the project into compliance."[3]

Thereupon, Suzuki and Nanwani make a rather strong general and critical observation about the working of the inspection function, which they regard as a function that has fallen into decay:

The net result of the inspection function is that the question of internal compliance or noncompliance has become the focus of the inspection process, and the real question of accountability toward people who are affected by MDBs' [multilateral development banks'] projects has become sidelined. Once the inspection function accepts the complainants' request for inspection and authorizes an inspection, the complainants themselves are left outside the system. The affected people who requested "inspection" will eventually be informed of the outcome of the inspection process only after the process is completed, with the possibility that their problem will remain unresolved.[4]

The two rightly point to a risk that the mechanism will lose its original purpose and become an inward-looking, technical mechanism whereby the
working procedures are no longer instruments used to reach a desired aim
but have become the aim itself. Still, it is not too late. Representatives of
civil society, executive members of the boards of the MFIs and MDBs, members of parliaments and Congress, and most of all, members of the mechanisms themselves could still defend the original design and meaning of
these mechanisms.

On 20 and 21 May 2004 representatives of the mechanisms of the following MFIs met at the World Bank for the first time in a closed session at
the invitation of the Inspection Panel, initiated by the chair of the panel,
Edith Brown-Weiss: the Asian Development Bank, European Bank for Reconstruction and Development (EBRD), Inter-American Development
Bank (IADB), International Finance Corporation (IFC), Japan Bank for International Cooperation (JBIC), Export Development Canada (EDC),[5] and
North American Commission on Environmental Cooperation. Thereafter,
a yearly meeting was organized: by the Asian Development Bank in Manila
(2005); by the Commission for Environmental Cooperation (CEC) – an institution "established to steward the implementation of the North American Agreement on Environmental Cooperation (NAAEC)"[6] – in Montreal
(2006); by the European Bank for Reconstruction and Development in
London (2007); and by the African Development Bank (AfDB) in Tunis
(2008). In 2007 the Inspection Panel got involved in two requests that had
also been lodged with two other accountability mechanisms. The case of
the so-called "Bujagali Dam" in Uganda was again a case for the Inspection
Panel and the first case for the newly established Independent Review
Mechanism of the African Development Bank. Furthermore, an energy
project in Albania became a case for both the Inspection Panel and the
EBRD's Independent Recourse Mechanism (see below).

In this chapter, I describe some of the different mechanisms that already
exist in the MFIs as well as the process of creating such mechanisms in the
case of banks that are just beginning to do so. I also look at the situation of
the Inter-American Development Bank, which is revising its mechanism. In
the latter case, I was asked to comment on the draft for a revised mechanism, entitled "Proposal for Enhancement to the Independent Investigation Mechanism."[7] My comment is included in this chapter. I am aware
that by the time this study is published, the IADB may have already decided
on a new mandate and formula and already installed its new compliance
review panel. To understand the different mechanisms, in 2004 and 2005 I
visited the European Investment Bank in Luxembourg, the European
Bank for Reconstruction and Development in London, the African Development Bank in Tunis, and the Inter-American Development Bank in
Washington, DC. I also had regular contact with former officials of the
Asian Development Bank. Rather new is the so-called Aarhus Convention
Compliance Committee, which can investigate projects funded by financial

institutions such as the European Investment Bank as long as they are party to the Aarhus Convention (see below).

The following coverage of different mechanisms is by no means complete. New information regularly becomes available. It may well be that an important new mechanism has been overlooked. To the best of my knowledge, I have been as complete as possible. Some mechanisms I describe in full, while others are just mentioned. The ADB accountability mechanism is described the most extensively since I consider this to be the best model at present. The first two described, the compliance advisor ombudsman of the IFC and the Independent Evaluation Office (IEO) of the International Monetary Fund (IMF), are both mechanisms of the Bretton Woods institutions (see chapter 2).

OMBUDSMAN OF THE IFC AND MIGA

In everyday business the compliance advisor ombudsman (CAO) of the IFC and the Multilateral Investment Guarantee Agency (MIGA), both of which are members of the World Bank Group, is often called the IFC ombudsman. The administrative budget of the function is shared by these two bank members. In fiscal year 2003, 80 per cent of the budget was provided by the IFC and the other 20 per cent by MIGA, for a total of US$1,866,446.[8] "In fiscal year 2007, the CAO had an administrative budget of [US]$2,618,373. The office also has an agreement with IFC and MIGA that additional funds from a CAO contingency fund will be made available, on request, in the event of an unexpected volume of complaints, a large-scale mediation effort, or other ombudsman-related activity. This contingency fund is [US]$1 million. In FY [fiscal year] 2007, the CAO did not need to draw any funds from the contingency fund."[9] In the more recent annual budget, one can notice the extension of the CAO's work load. And similar to the Inspection Panel, the CAO has been provided a significant budget, a signal that it is well embedded in the institution. The establishment of the mechanism took place in 1999, some years after the establishment of the Inspection Panel at the World Bank. The positioning of both mechanisms inside the World Bank is somewhat complex. So far, the activities of the two mechanisms have never been integrated but remain entirely separate.

According to the CAO, the office is "an independent post that reports directly to the President of the World Bank Group. The CAO reviews complaints from communities affected by development projects undertaken by the International Finance Corporation (IFC) and the Multilateral Investment Guarantee Fund (MIGA). We work to respond quickly and effectively to complaints through collaborative processes headed by our Ombudsman, or through compliance audits that ensure adherence with relevant policies."[10] Since its inception in 1999, "the CAO has handled 66 cases on 24 different IFC/MIGA projects."[11] According to the IFC's own Operational Guidelines,[12] the ombudsman has three distinct roles.

First, there is the ombudsman role:

The Ombudsman role (CAO Ombudsman): Responding to complaints by individual(s), group(s) of people, or organization(s) that are affected by IFC/MIGA projects (or projects in which those organizations play a role) and attempting to resolve fairly the issues raised, using a flexible, problem-solving approach. The focus of the CAO ombudsman role is on helping to resolve complaints, ideally by improving social and environmental outcomes on the ground.[13]

About the compliance role, the following is noted:

Compliance role (CAO Compliance): Overseeing audits of the social and environmental performance of IFC and MIGA, particularly in relation to sensitive projects, to ensure compliance with policies, guidelines, procedures, and systems.[14]

Last, there is the advisory role:

Advisory role (CAO Advisor): Providing a source of independent advice to the President of the World Bank Group and the management of IFC and MIGA. The CAO Advisor will provide advice in relation to broader environmental and social policies, guidelines, procedures, strategic issues, trends, and systemic issues. The emphasis is on improving performance systemically.[15]

It is further noted that:

The CAO Ombudsman responds directly to the concerns of individual(s), group(s) of people, or organization(s) affected by IFC or MIGA projects that lodge a complaint with the CAO (complainants). CAO activities under the CAO ombudsman role are always initiated in response to an external complaint. The CAO has established systems to protect the confidentiality of the complainant, if so requested. The principle of confidentiality applies to information provided to the CAO by any of the parties to a complaint.[16]

The CAO advisory role, unlike the CAO ombudsman and Compliance roles, is not project specific. It is aimed at improving performance systemically. The CAO will not give project-specific advice, as this could undermine the ability of the CAO to act as independent ombudsman or Compliance auditor. However, in its advisory role, the CAO can offer advice on emerging or strategic issues and trends, policies, processes, or matters of principle. Advice will often be based on the lessons learned from CAO ombudsman or Compliance activities. A request for advice can be initiated by a number of different parties.[17]

Most of the documents published by the CAO since it was established also mention that "the independence and impartiality of the CAO foster the trust and confidence of the project's sponsors, local communities, NGOs [nongovernmental organizations], and civil society in general."[18]

An important statement was made about the role of the CAO in the CAO's annual report for fiscal year 2004–05, and I tend to agree with the mentioned importance of problem solving when a choice can be made between problem solving or reporting on compliance afterward. Compliance review is thus often regarded as the "last resort" after problem solving has failed. On this point, the report states:

> In terms of the evolution of external accountability within Multilateral Financial Institutions, the ombudsman role is the most innovative of the CAO's three roles ... Generally speaking, the focus of the ombudsman role is on what is going to happen in the future, rather than what has happened in the past. Instead of finding fault, the ombudsman's aim is to identify problems, recommend practical remedial actions, and address systemic issues that have contributed to problems ... A key difference between the ombudsman function and many of the external accountability mechanisms is that our work does not necessarily end with the publication of a report ... The CAO can remain engaged if its role adds value and the parties request its participation. In some circumstances, the issues raised in the complaint may form the basis for a compliance audit or may be the subject of advice to IFC or MIGA management, in which case, the complainant is informed of how any remaining issues will be addressed.[19]

With this statement, the CAO implicitly criticizes the functioning of the Inspection Panel, which officially has no mandate to use problem-solving methods. The Inspection Panel is supposed to investigate whether management is or was in compliance with the World Bank's policies during the design and implementation of bank-financed projects.[20] Nevertheless, as described in chapter 3, while "investigating" the eligibility of a request, the Inspection Panel has on occasion taken on a problem-solving role. Efforts to solve problems during the eligibility phase were always welcomed by all parties involved.

By comparison, the CAO has three roles, including a problem-solving role. However, with three roles bundled within one function, there is the risk of confusion between the roles, as the CAO acknowledges:

> The advisory role continues to be the role that confuses internal and external stakeholders. The CAO's terms of reference allow it to provide an independent channel of advice to the president and senior management. However, that advice cannot detract from, nor pose a conflict of interest with, the ombudsman role, in particular, or with the compliance role. By drawing lessons to be learned and projecting them back into the

institution, the advisory role can reinforce the effectiveness of IFC and
MIGA. In 2002, the president clarified to IFC and MIGA that formal
advice would stem from complaints to the ombudsman and from compliance audits and would address process and policy issues in a broader
context than an individual context.[21]

The confusion arose with the original scope of the advisory role. In the
first Operational Guidelines, this role was described as: "Providing a source
of independent advice to the President and the management of IFC and
MIGA. The CAO will provide advice both in relation to particular projects
and in relation to broader environmental and social policies, guidelines,
procedures, resources and systems (the Advisory role)."[22] Four years later
the revised Operational Guidelines described the advisory role as: "Providing a source of independent advice to the President and the management
of IFC and MIGA. The CAO will provide advice in relation to broader environmental and social policies, guidelines, procedures, strategic issues,
trends, and systemic issues."[23] Here, the phrase "particular projects" was
dropped. The difference from the original description is further explained: "The CAO will not give project-specific advice. Any prior involvement in a project (irrespective of the nature of the involvement) has the
potential to undermine the CAO as a wholly impartial and independent
ombudsman or compliance auditor. Therefore, the CAO will refrain from
attending project briefings or other project-related meetings. Requests for
project-specific advice will also be routinely declined, as will informal conversations about specific projects."[24] The difference between the two formulations gives the impression that internal and external confusion and
difficulties had arisen. I consider wise the conclusion that the CAO should
no longer advise on specific projects. Otherwise, it could be understood
that project-specific advice is part of the ombudsman function.
So the CAO recognized the risk of a conflict of interest between the advisory role and the other two roles. In those first years I could not find a
similar statement on a possible conflict of interest between the first two
roles – the ombudsman role and the compliance role – although I believe
that such a risk exists. Those experts involved in a problem-solving or mediation procedure should not also be involved in a compliance review investigation if the mediation fails. So whether the CAO's internal procedures
include a "Chinese wall" (a legal expression used to denote a total separation of functions or roles in a process) between staff members involved in
the first phase, or role, and staff members involved in the second phase, or
role, was not clear in 2004.
In the revised guidelines of 2007 the three roles are separated within the
CAO: "All participants in a CAO Ombudsman process, in particular IFC/
MIGA staff and the sponsor, need to feel confident that their open and
frank participation in collaborative processes will not compromise their
position if a compliance audit is subsequently undertaken. Therefore, in

cases where the CAO Ombudsman transfers a complaint to CAO Compliance, confidential information received under the CAO Ombudsman role will not be shared with the CAO Compliance role, unless explicit permission to do so is provided by the relevant party/parties."[25] After the arrival of a complaint, the CAO will first screen a case to determine whether it is eligible. If it is eligible, the CAO will assess whether the case is "amenable"[26] to resolution (mediation role) or whether, instead, it "merits an audit"[27] (the compliance role). Unlike the Inspection Panel, following an audit, the CAO is formally mandated to further monitor the process and assess whether "compliance is reached."[28] Interestingly, during the process of complaint resolution, the CAO can offer "training and/or expertise to assist the stakeholders in this process"[29] of dialogue and negotiation. As far as I know, the IFC's CAO is the first accountability mechanism to offer support to complainants – similar to what in Canada is called "participation funding" (see chapter 6).

At the time, the NGOs also had problems understanding the roles and independence of the CAO. On the one hand, they criticized the CAO for taking a stand in favour of the IFC; on the other hand, they criticized the IFC for its "unsatisfactory response"[30] to the CAO's findings. The following statement was made by the Bretton Woods Project, an NGO initiative:

> In its recently published annual report for 2004–2005, the Compliance Advisor ombudsman (CAO) received 14 complaints. Experience with high-profile and often contentious projects in Guatemala, DRC [Democratic Republic of Congo], Brazil, India, Kazakhstan and Georgia, as well as the IFC safeguard policy review reveal that despite the CAO's best efforts to seek "rapid resolution of complaints and ensure public accountability of IFC and MIGA," it is powerless to stop them from acting with impunity. These institutions have ridden roughshod over the CAO's efforts by ignoring recommendations, contradicting findings and submitting inadequate or dismissive responses. On the other hand, questions regarding the CAO's role have also been raised by affected communities and civil society groups, many of whom have been dissatisfied with the way in which it has dealt with their complaints. It has been criticized for failing to take claims seriously enough; for coming down in favour of the IFC and/or the company; and for not going far enough in its recommendations, despite its own clear findings to the contrary.[31]

This statement might be based on a misconception about the *independent role* of the CAO, who will sometimes disagree with the requesters and sometimes disagree with the IFC and MIGA.

Notwithstanding the NGO criticism, the CAO has made some remarkable critical comments about the work of the IFC, especially on human rights issues, as is clear from the following examples:

In 2003, the CAO conducted a gap analyses with respect to some basic human rights instruments as well as the existing Safeguard Policies, which include some explicit and implicit references to human rights. The CAO also produced internal case studies on how three IFC projects might have been approached differently if human rights filters were to have been applied at the outset.[32]

In the summer of 2005 President Paul Wolfowitz asked the CAO to do an audit (compliance review) of MIGA's due diligence in a copper-silver mine project in the Democratic Republic of Congo. The following findings were published by the CAO:

> CAO found that MIGA adequately followed its underwriting and risk management due diligence, but that these core business processes did not address whether the project might either influence the dynamics of conflict or whether security provision for the project could indirectly lead to adverse impacts on the local community. While MIGA's initial adherence to its Environmental and Social Review Procedures (ESRPs) was adequate, CAO considers that its follow-through on some social aspects was weak. CAO found that weaknesses in the ESRP due diligence, and on conflict and security issues specifically, echo a number of concerns that were the subject of recommendations by CAO in its 2002 review of MIGA's ESRPs. Regarding security and human rights, CAO found that MIGA did not fully understand the implications for its client of implementing the Voluntary Principles on Security and Human Rights (as required by the Management Response to the Extractive Industries Review), nor did it assess whether its client had the capacity to properly implement them.[33]

The firm stand taken on human rights is remarkable given the difficulty that the World Bank's management has in raising issues of human rights as a result of the bank's Articles of Agreement, which do not allow interference in national politics (see chapters 2 and 6). The CAO's experience and expertise in training and assisting stakeholders in the process of negotiations and mediation should be of enormous value for other accountability mechanisms. A remaining question is how the staff will be able to create a "Chinese wall" between the two different roles within a single institution.

THE IMF: INDEPENDENT EVALUATION OFFICE

The International Monetary Fund has an "almost global membership"[34] of 185 countries. According to the IMF, "The Fund seeks to promote economic stability and prevent crises; to help resolve crises when they occur; and to promote growth and alleviate poverty. It employs three main functions – surveillance, technical assistance, and lending – to meet these objectives."[35] Since both the IMF and the World Bank were created at the same time at Bretton Woods in 1945 (see chapter 2), both institutions, although in principal two different institutions, have a close relationship. The headquarters of the two institutions are neighbours in Washington, DC, with a corridor between the two buildings below street level, and some of the executive directors of the World Bank are at the same time executive directors of the IMF. The division of work between the two is described by the IMF as follows: "Each institution must focus on its areas of expertise. Thus, World Bank staff takes the lead in advising on the social policies involved in poverty reduction, including the necessary diagnostic work. The IMF advises governments in the areas of its traditional mandate, including promoting prudent macroeconomic policies. In areas where the World Bank and the IMF both have expertise – such as fiscal management, budget execution, budget transparency, and tax and customs administration – they coordinate closely."[36]

The IMF has no accountability mechanism; instead, it has established an Independent Evaluation Office (IEO), decided upon by the board in April 2001 and established in the summer of the same year. According to a background paper presented to the board of the IMF, "the motivation to develop the role of independent evaluation at the fund stemmed from a desire to enhance the Fund's internal learning culture, foster a more broadly-based understanding of its mandate, and bolster the credibility of its work outside the institution."[37] The managing director of the IEO assists the board "in providing governance and oversight of the Fund."[38] The board appoints the director. As an evaluation function, the IEO differs from an accountability mechanism and thus is not the subject of this study. Nevertheless, the IEO is not a "pure" evaluation function inside the institution. The main purpose of this evaluation function is described as follows:

The IEO's overarching mission is to improve the IMF's effectiveness by:

- Enhancing the learning culture of the IMF and enabling it to better absorb lessons for improvements in its future work.
- Helping build the IMF's external credibility by undertaking objective evaluations in a transparent manner.
- Providing independent feedback to the Executive Board in its governance and oversight responsibilities over the IMF.
- Promoting greater understanding of the work of the IMF.[39]

In discussions about the role of the IEO compared to the other accountability mechanisms, especially the Inspection Panel of the World Bank, some experts from the IMF expressed the view that it would not make sense to create the same for the IMF. It was felt that the IMF does not execute projects such as those undertaken by the World Bank. Others disagreed, saying that the economic measures of the IMF could also have negative impacts on the lives of people in the countries concerned. On the website of the Bretton Woods Project, the following is mentioned about the first days of establishing the function:

> It looks likely that the unit will be independent from the staff and management and report to the board, with a core staff and contracted experts for specific projects. Staff wants the new unit to be limited to ex-post evaluations rather than carrying out on-going assessment of programmes. They argue that the Bank's Operations Evaluation Department has too much influence in the Bank. Executive Directors have mixed opinions with some arguing that the Policy Development and Review Department already has a systematic evaluation function, although admitting that staff can be biased, whilst others want the unit to be able to carry out on-going evaluations. Thomas Bernes, the Canadian ED [executive director] who heads the Board's Evaluation Committee, said that "most of the Board appreciates the need for a broad mandate."
>
> NGOs are calling for the unit to be fully transparent and French NGOs, led by Agir Ici, are calling for an appeals mechanism to hear the complaints of people affected by IMF policies. It should enable people affected by adjustment programmes to file lawsuits against policies that violate their fundamental rights or when their environment is threatened, and subsequently to obtain reparations. To be effective such a mechanism should be supported by an independent evaluation unit and impact assessments carried out prior to implementation of adjustment programmes.[40]

Also, the following interesting paragraph on consultation is mentioned in the background paper on the mandate: "In carrying out its mandate, [IEO] will be free to consult with whomever and whichever groups it deems necessary, both within and outside the fund."[41] So with the IMF paper, expectations arose that civil society would be listened to. The board finally reached a decision: "[T]he Executive Board should undertake an independent external evaluation of [IEO] within 3 years of its launching."[42] This all gives at least the impression that the IEO is more than just an internal evaluation function. The paragraph on consultation with the outside world has since then been reiterated – for example, in the revised "Terms of Reference" of 16 November 2004.[43]

In August 2001, a year after the decision to establish the IEO, Angela Wood of the Bretton Woods Project wrote a letter to the IEO about the proposed procedures and topics for evaluation, which she signed on behalf of a group of experts and other NGOs. From this document, it is clear that the NGOs want to play a role:

> It is equally important that civil society's views are considered, where appropriate, during evaluation. It will be necessary for the [IEO] to draw

up clear guidelines as to when and how stakeholders will participate in the evaluations ... In the interest of equity and independence we believe that it is essential that civil society and other external stakeholders as well as IMF staff and the Board should have the opportunity to formally and publicly submit their comments on [IEO] Reports ... It is essential that the [IEO] staff include experts in social and environmental issues as well as macro-economic issues. We are concerned that to date we have only seen notice of job vacancies for economists. The added value of the [IEO] is that it should be able to analyse IMF programmes and operations from perspectives other than those commonly held by economists.[44]

Remarkably, the NGO experts make a positive observation about the IEO concerning its relations with the IMF legal office, which at the same time is a negative observation about the Inspection Panel's relations with the legal counsel of the World Bank (see also chapters 3 and 7): "The [IEO] is not dependent on the opinions of the IMF legal office when legal issues arise relating to such issues as the powers of the [IEO] and the interpretation of its procedures arise. The role that the General Counsel plays in the Inspection Panel process in the World Bank has been a serious problem for the Inspection Panel."[45] Two months after the Bretton Woods Project wrote its letter to the IMF, the IEO said of its independence:

The IEO, fully independent from the IMF's management and staff, operates at arms' length from the Executive Board. This independence is strengthened by the following safeguards:

- The Director of the IEO is appointed by the Executive Board for a period of four years, renewable for a further three years. He [*sic!*] may not be appointed to the IMF staff at the end of his term.
- The Director of the IEO is solely responsible for the selection of IEO personnel (including external consultants) on terms and conditions set by the Executive Board with a view to ensuring that the IEO is staffed with independent and highly qualified personnel. When the office is fully staffed, a majority of its personnel will come from outside the IMF. In addition, IEO staff report exclusively to the Director of the IEO, not to IMF management.[46]

On 18 November 2005 a team of experts conducting an evaluation of the IEO announced on the IMF website that they "welcome input from all interested parties between November 18, 2005 and January 2006." This undertaking by the IMF is promising for those who believe that the international institutions should be more transparent and accountable for their acts. I do not know how many NGOs, individuals, or other stakeholders reacted. On the outcome, the IEO reports: "During the Board discussion of the report, IMF Executive Directors agreed that the IEO had served the IMF well and had earned strong support across a broad range of stakeholders, and that the IMF continued to need an independent evaluation office to contribute to the institution's learning culture and facilitate oversight and governance by the Board."[47]

In the meantime the IEO has published a substantial number of evaluation reports with a focus mainly on macroeconomic subjects such as an evaluation of the advice contained in the IMF's Exchange Rate Policy, the IMF's multilateral surveillance, technical assistance provided by the IMF, the role of the IMF in Argentina, or for example, evaluation of the IMF's approach to capital account liberalization. In a press release about the latter report, a rather striking finding was mentioned:

> Against the background of highly volatile international capital flows and the associated financial instability experienced by a number of major emerging market economies in recent years, the role of the IMF in capital account liberalization has been a topic of major controversy. The IMF's role is particularly controversial because capital account liberalization is an area where there is little professional consensus. Moreover, although *current* account liberalization is among the IMF's official purposes outlined in its Articles of Agreement, the IMF has no explicit mandate to promote capital account liberalization. Nevertheless, the IMF has given greater attention to capital account issues in recent decades, in light of the increasing importance of international capital flows for member countries macroeconomic management.[48]

THE ASIAN DEVELOPMENT BANK

In December 1995, not that long after the Inspection Panel was created at the World Bank, the Asian Development Bank also established an independent inspection function. The structure and development of this function at the ADB – referred to since 29 May 2003 as the Accountability Mechanism – makes it the best accountability mechanism to compare with the bank's Inspection Panel. At first glance, the ADB's independent inspection function and the Inspection Panel do not appear to differ much. The ADB's general approach is like that of the World Bank, being mainly demand-driven, and according to the ADB its objective is "to improve the quality and transparency of the Bank's operations, as well as its accountability."[49] There are two stages in the ADB's process, the eligibility stage and an investigation/inspection stage, with timeframes almost comparable to those of the World Bank. Similar to the procedure at the World Bank, the executive directors of the ADB can also file a request.

The same is true of the ADB's eligibility criteria: there is not much difference from the criteria of the World Bank. In the case of the ADB a request for inspection must also assert that "(a) the bank has failed, in formulating, processing or implementing a project, to follow its operational policies or procedures; (b) this failure has had or is likely to have a direct and material adverse effect on the requester's rights and interest; and (c) this failure was brought to the attention of the bank's Management, which failed within a period of 45 days to demonstrate that the Bank had followed, or was taking adequate steps to follow, its operational policies and procedures."[50] The factors that render a request beyond the scope of the policy are also almost identical to those of the World Bank.[51]

The difference was to be found in the institutional and procedural aspects of the ADB's mechanism. Until May 2003, the ADB did not have an independent inspection body akin to the Inspection Panel at the World Bank. Instead, the ADB had an Inspection Committee:

> Under the policy, a new standing committee of the Board, the Inspection Committee (the Committee), has been established to review requests for inspection and recommend to the Board whether an inspection is warranted. If the Board authorizes an inspection, the Committee will select a Panel of independent experts from an approved roster to conduct the inspection and to report its findings to the Committee. Based on the Panel's report and Management's response to that report, the Committee will make recommendations to the Board. The committee comprises six members of the Board, including four regional members (at least three of whom must be from borrowing member countries) and two non-regional members ... A roster of independent outside experts (the Roster), nominated by the President and approved by the Board, assist the Committee and the Board in implementing the Policy ... These experts remain on the Roster for five-year, non-renewable terms. Roster members must not have been employed by the Bank within two years preceding their appointment, and will be precluded from employment by the Bank for five years following the completion of their term.[52]

Requesters first have to send a written complaint to the ADB president, and management is tasked with responding to the complaint. If the requesters are still not satisfied, they can write to the Inspection Committee. In addition, according to the procedures: "(d) The Committee will ask Management to respond in writing to the request (except in cases considered clearly frivolous or clearly ineligible by the Committee); (e) the Committee will recommend to the Board whether an inspection is warranted, and the Board will take a decision on this recommendation; (f) if the Board authorizes an inspection, the Committee will select a panel of experts from the Roster to inspect the project and make a report to the Committee; (g) Management will respond in writing to the panel's report; and (h) the Committee will make a recommendation to the Board on the panel's report, and the Board will take a decision on this recommendation."[53]

Without going into a detailed description of the procedures of the first mechanism installed at the ADB in 1994, it is worthwhile to notice that the role of the experts on the roster cannot be compared to the role and mandate of the World Bank's Inspection Panel. The ADB's mechanism is not yet as independent as the Inspection Panel, and it does not comprise a permanent panel since the experts are chosen from a roster on a case-by-case basis. In the ADB's mechanism, it is the committee, composed of six board members, that finally sends a report to the entire board and decides on the steps to be taken by the panel.

First Case at the ADB

Only on 10 July 2001 did the board of the ADB first approve an inspection. This occurred for a project in Thailand after the internal process, in which management was initially asked to respond, was not satisfactory to the requesters. A panel of three members chosen from the roster was set up. The ADB received the request in April of the same year. The members of the panel were immediately confronted with difficulties in putting together a report. One of the three members of the panel reported on the experience of this panel during a conference in Washington, DC, organized by the College of Law at American University in cooperation with the Inspection Panel of the World Bank.[54]

Wiert Wiertsema describes what happened:

> Once the Panel was established, it was agreed that it would meet with the BIC [Bank Inspection Committee] on August 27 and 28 to discuss the draft Terms of Reference of the Panel and to finalize its work plan and timetable[55] ... It was the intention to start the investigations with meetings with the Requesters and other stakeholders in Thailand, in order to obtain a good understanding of the concerns raised ... [I]n accordance with the provisions of paragraph 52 of ADB's Inspection Procedures, the BIC had requested consent of the Government of Thailand for a site visit of the Panel. Unfortunately, only on September 6, the BIC received a response from the Government of Thailand containing several conditions ... including the requirement that the ADB would accept liability for any loss or damages claimed by the contractors as a result of the Panel's visit. Due to this the Panel could not travel to Thailand ... It discussed with the BIC the serious consequences of the ensuing unequal access to the different stakeholders in this inspection.[56]

According to Wiertsema, the committee tried again "to obtain consent to a visit of the site. Unfortunately, by October 10 another response from the Government of Thailand was received, reaffirming the conditions that prevented the Panel from visiting the country."[57] The panel was thus "forced" to work on the basis of the reports available. They then reversed the situation by inviting the requesters to come to Manila instead of visiting them at the project site, which was declined immediately by the requesters. Both the committee and the panel members knew that this was a precarious situation that could undermine the spirit of the mechanism. In a sort of last attempt, "the chairperson of the BIC decided to throw in all his weight by undertaking a mission to Bangkok to discuss the lifting of the conditions imposed on the proposed visit of the Panel. Anticipating and actually trusting that the visit of Mr. Lockhart would result in a breakthrough, the Panel decided to commence interviews with ADB staff on November 2. On November 8, the Panel was briefed by the BIC that regrettably and despite the mission, the Government of Thailand maintained its original position."[58]

The three panel members decided to suspend any further formal interviews. And regarding the requirements of the government of Thailand, Wiertsema states: "The conditions imposed undermined the effectiveness and soundness of the inspection system, and ran counter to the basic spirit and objective for the establishment of such a system. The Panel felt that if the matter would not be dealt with seriously, it would create cynicism and cause harm to the efforts so far made by the Bank to have greater openness and participation of the people who are affected by Bank financed activities."[59] The committee then asked the three panel members to prepare an interim report and informed them that "The Committee will request the panel to resume the inspection at a convenient time. However, if the situation does not change within a reasonable time frame, the Committee will request the Panel to submit its final report." This request was indeed eventually made, and the committee told the complainants that the panel's report "would not be disclosed."[60]

This all was a great disappointment to the first ADB panel. A final report was submitted along with a separate memorandum to the committee. In the memorandum several suggestions for future improvements of the mechanism were submitted. Most of these suggestions related to poor procedures and access to documentation, the prohibition against visiting the project site, the lack of transparency, and most of all the process's lack of independence. The dramatic experience of the first three panel members undoubtedly drew heavy criticism from the outside world. A newsletter of Friends of the Earth International stated: "The first ever investigation of the ADB Inspection Panel ended in a complete failure when last month the Panel decided to suspend its inspection into the Samut Prakarn Wastewater Facility ... Thai authorities also prohibited panel members to visit the project site 'For fear of civil disturbances.' It is likely that the Board Inspection Committee will have to conclude the inspection process and ask the Panel to finalize the report. If so, the first ADB inspection case ever will have concluded without a field visit, thus setting a discouraging precedent for the ADB's Inspection Mechanism."[61]

Clearly, the project was politically sensitive. Walden Bello[62] writes:

> Notes taken by a participant at the most recent meeting of the ADB
> board on March 25 that were made available to the author reveals an in-
> stitution that is deeply shaken and split by the report of an independent
> Inspection Panel on the project, which is located in Samut Prakarn prov-
> ince. Foremost among the critics during the board meeting was, not un-
> expectedly, Alternate Director Ram Binid Bhattarai, who represents a
> group of countries that includes Thailand. Bhattarai attacked both the
> Inspection Panel and the BIC for "disregard of the Thai authorities and
> lack of respect for the sovereign rights of Thailand." For Bhattarai, it was
> the BIC and Inspection Panel that were at fault for "politicizing the
> event," with "premature releases of information to the press and wel-
> coming flags in the Klong Dan community" ...
>   Bhattarai's comments were, however, mild compared to those of
> Director Zhao Xiaoyu representing China, who began by saying that
> while the report might strike some as "a nice piece of steak, to me it is a
> lousy dish that is overcooked." Asking what the bank had gotten after
> spending nearly $2 million on the inspection process, Zhao answered:
> "We have produced a pile of groundless damaging paper. The Bank's
> credibility is undermined, the staff demoralized, the Thai government is
> fed up, and a good environmental project is unduly held up for two
> years" ... The effect on ADB, he predicted, would be like the impact on
> the World Bank of the full-scale inspection done on the bank's contro-
> versial Western Poverty Project in China.[63]

According to Bello, Zhao was supported by a group of countries that included India, Bangladesh, the Philippines, and Pakistan. Board members
supporting the BIC report "were perhaps not as inflammatory in their comments but they were equally firm in their views. C. Alexander Severens,
speaking for the United States, faulted the Thai government for obstructing
a site visit, a move that eroded the credibility of the inspection process."[64]

Around the same time, a group of eleven NGOs from the US, Pakistan, Sri
Lanka, Japan, the Philippines, Cambodia, and Australia published a substantive report with recommendations to the ADB for revising its inspection
policy. The system, they argued, has many shortcomings, notably its lack of a
permanent inspection panel, which causes "logistical and substantial problems as follows: Although three or more members have been selected for an
Inspection Panel, their availability is not guaranteed as members usually
have full time jobs and other commitments ... During the set up of the
Samut Prakarn Panel, the candidates that were first identified from the
roster turned down the assignment due to time conflicts, conflicts of interests, and unwillingness to agree not to work for the bank for a certain
period of time after serving on the Panel."[65] They note that the lack of an

independent secretariat creates a potential conflict of interest since the ADB Secretariat's "primary role is administrative assistance to the Bank Management." The same could be the case for the Inspection Committee, as the NGOs observe: "Their function on the Board Inspection Committee puts Board members in the position of approving loans on the one hand and making decisions on inspection cases on the other hand, making conflicts of interests likely to occur."[66] Finally, the eleven NGOs criticize the ADB mechanism's lack of transparency: "The current Inspection Policy does not require the Bank to inform the public or provide updates on the status of Inspections and important events regarding Inspection cases."[67] In the course of 2002 the ADB received similar comments from other NGOs.

Consultation

According to the ADB, in 1998 a process had already begun to review the original system: "At the time of approval of the ADB Inspection Function, the Board stipulated a review within 2 years from its approval of the initial roster of experts as panel members; the review would assess the operations of the Board Inspection Committee (BIC) and related inspection procedures, and review the Inspection Function's application to ADB's private sector operations."[68] The first review did not result in much change since the ADB had "limited experience with the inspection process, and few conclusions could be drawn regarding the existing system. Only two requests, both regarding the Korangi Wastewater Management Project in Pakistan, had been filed by then, and BIC had deemed them both ineligible. Support for strong accountability mechanisms at ADB and other MDBs has continued throughout the past decade. In 2000, ADB's donors recommended a strengthened and more independent inspection function, and that it should also have oversight of private sector projects."[69] The impression is given that the problems of the ADB inspection function in Thailand accelerated the process.

The ADB began a public consultation to review its inspection function in the summer of 2002. An issue paper and drafts were posted on the ADB website for comments. The bank then held two rounds of public consultations in June and August 2002 in the cities of ten different ADB member countries. The first round was held in Tokyo, Manila, Frankfurt, Ottawa, and Washington, DC, and the second round in Phnomk Penh, Katmandu, Beijing, and Sydney. Between the first and the second rounds, a special session was held in Karachi.[70] Two independent consultants were contracted: David Hunter and Lori Udall.[71] Both of these remarkable individuals were key figures in the establishment of the Inspection Panel at the World Bank (see chapter 3 and the interview with David Hunter in appendix 3). In the autumn, internal consultations were held, followed by an informal seminar of the ADB's board.

During the consultations four options circulated:

Option A: Maintain the existing Inspection Function with improvements in the system such as strengthening the secretariat and streamlining the procedures; B: Establish an independent Inspection Panel based on the World Bank panel with improvements, including an independent secretariat, an annual budget, and at least one full-time chairperson of the panel; C: Adopt a problem-solving approach, perhaps similar to the ombudsman's role in IFC/MIGA's CAO office; D: Establsih a two-step approach with both a consultation and compliance review mechanism. This approach would (a) facilitate solving the problems of affected people at an early stage through consultation or some other form of dispute resolution; and (b) conduct a compliance review of those claims at the request of the claimants, irrespective of the problem, that raise potential policy violations.[72]

Many NGOs commented on the draft proposals. A recommendation from Friends of the Earth Japan, the Japan Center for Sustainable Environment, and Society Watch Japan includes a list of concrete steps to be taken:

- An "Ombudsperson mechanism" should be established. The mechanism will address the concerns of project-affected people;
- The Board Inspection Committee should be abolished;
- An independent permanent Inspection Panel should be established;
- The Inspection Panel and Ombudsperson mechanism will work independently, and requesters should be able to choose which mechanism they want to file their claim;
- The Inspection Panel should have its own Secretariat which is independent from the Management;
- Inspection process should not be lengthy or complicated. The complaint to the Management is unnecessary;
- If a request for inspection is not clearly ineligible, the Panel should conduct an initial investigation including a site visit;
- The 95% rule should be abolished;
- Requests for inspection/ombudsperson in local languages should be allowed;
- The loan agreement and other policies should include clauses to avoid backlashes against requesters. Requesters should be able to file a request anonymously;
- Every Panel's decision should be disclosed, including notification of the receipt, initial investigation, final report and monitoring report;
- It is necessary to monitor the implementation of the Board approved remedies. Management should report periodically to the Board

and the Inspection Panel/Ombudsperson regarding the progress of implementation of the Board approved remedies;

- Both Inspection and Ombudsperson policies should be applied to private sector operations.[73]

The Compliance Review Panel

The public-consultation process finally led to the creation of a new accountability mechanism to replace the previous inspection function. This new mechanism was approved by the ADB's board on 29 May 2003. The final report states: "The combined results of both internal and external consultations indicated, at the minimum, broad support for a compliance review panel that is an improved version of the WB [World Bank] panel. The term 'compliance review' has been used, during the review, as well as in the earlier draft working papers, the final working paper, and this paper, instead of 'inspection,' to avoid any negative associations in the use of the term 'inspection.'"[74]

So the term "inspection" disappeared from the name of the ADB's compliance mechanism and thus far remains in use only for the mechanism in place at the World Bank. As described in chapter 3, the term's use by the World Bank is perceived very negatively. Suresh Nanwani, who is senior counsel in the ADB's General Counsel Office, has said about the panel and the name: "In the US judicial system it is much easier to have such systems. For us in Asia it is somewhat different to disclose information. In general people shy away from direct confrontation. Inspection we are not accustomed to. It is difficult. It requires a whole lot of internationalization for both staff and countries. But as a public institution, we have to move in that direction. Otherwise, we cannot satisfy all the donor countries that want to know how their taxpayers' money is spent."[75]

The old system was supplanted by the creation of two separate but complementary independent functions: a consultation phase with a special project facilitator (SPF) and a compliance review phase with a Compliance Review Panel (CRP). Each function has its own procedures. It is remarkable how much of the newly adopted system can be traced back to the recommendations of the Japanese group of NGOs. A complainant's first access to the ADB is the office of the special project facilitator: "The SPF will be a special appointee at the equivalent level of director general appointed by the President, after consultation with the Board. The SPF will report directly to the President. As the SPF will be independent of the OD [Operational Department] and have full control of the consultation phase, he/she will enhance the credibility of ADB in facilitating the resolution of problems in projects in which it is a principal interested party."[76] This should be regarded as a logic step. The parties involved should first try to solve perceived problems before beginning a more complex complaint procedure.

There is a remarkable note in the report about the scope of the consultation phase, which is described as "broader than the current Inspection Function or the proposed compliance review phase. The consultation phase is outcome-driven, focusing not on the identification and allocation of blame, but on finding ways to address the problem of the project-affected people in ADB-assisted projects."[77] With this note, the ADB distances itself somewhat from the World Bank Inspection Panel, which officially does not have a problem-solving mandate. In more recent years, as was my experience, the World Bank Inspection Panel has recognized the importance of a problem-solving phase and has taken up this role, although without a mandate to do so and without set procedures.[78]

The SPF of the ADB has been given a well-described role, namely "to assist project-affected people with specific problems caused by ADB-assisted projects." He or she may employ all kinds of methods, such as: "consensus-based methods with the consent and participation of all parties concerned, e.g., consultative dialogue, good offices, or mediation ... The SPF may suggest different approaches, including convening meetings with various stakeholders, organizing and facilitating consultation processes, or engaging in a fact-finding review of the situation."[79] Clearly, the ADB has put its efforts into the creation of a strong consultation phase and, by doing so, has shown that it has more confidence in a positive approach than in a rather legalistic approach that bears the risk of demoralizing the people involved.

On the matter of who can file a request, the ADB has adopted essentially the same procedures as the World Bank. Complaints to the ADB may be filed "only by (i) any group of two or more people (such as an organization, association, society, or other grouping of individuals) in a borrowing country where the ADB-assisted project is located or in a member country adjacent to the borrowing country; (ii) a local representative of the affected group; or (iii) a non-local representative, in exceptional cases where local representation cannot be found and the SPF agrees."[80] This is almost exactly the same wording used in the World Bank's resolution. But there is one remarkable difference between the ADB's compliance mechanism and those in place at all the other MFIs. As Eisuke Suzuki and Suresh Nanwani note: "ADB's Inspection Function, however, not only allowed affected parties residing 'in the borrowing member country in which the relevant Bank project is being or will be implemented' to file a request, but extended the right to those 'in a member country adjacent to such borrowing member country.' ADB is the only MDB that allows affected people in a neighboring country to file a complaint."[81]

Other similarities between the ADB's process and that of the World Bank can be found in the procedures for the complainants, who are expected to file a complaint in writing, preferably in English or in any of the ADB member countries' languages. As well, the complainants' names are to be kept confidential if requested, although it is not clear who within the ADB is responsible for keeping the names confidential: the special project facilitator or management? In the case of the World Bank, responsibility for confidentiality remains with the Inspection Panel, which seems the most reasonable arrangement.

An interesting note is contained in the paragraph describing which complainants will be excluded. Here again, we see similarities to the procedures of the World Bank. For instance, cases about procurement and fraud are not within the mandate of the ADB's compliance mechanism. As well, the ADB will not accept "frivolous" cases. But the ADB notably adds that it is also not acceptable if a case is "generated to gain competitive advantage."[82] With this added stipulation, the ADB expresses its understanding of the risk that a complaint procedure could be used for purposes other than to protect the people in a project area from possible harm. Complainants could attempt to use the compliance mechanism for political and/or marketing purposes.

The consultation process includes eight steps (figure 4.1): (1) filing the complaint, (2) registering and acknowledging the complaint, (3) determining eligibility, (4) review and assessment, (5) a decision by the complainant either to continue the consultation process or to file a request for a compliance review, (6) comments by the Operational Department and the complainant on the SPF's findings, followed by recommendations from the SPF, (7) implementing a course of action, and (8) terminating the consultation process.[83]

By adopting the consultation process as such, the ADB chose a rather open procedure with a high degree of democratic norms, as evidenced by the options in the process for the complainants as well as by the following descriptions of the different steps to be taken:

> If the complaint is accepted, the SPF will undertake a review to determine how best to address the issues raised in it. The review will normally include site visits, interviews, and meetings with the complainant and the EA/DMC [executing agency/developing member country] government or the PPS [private project sponsor], as well as any other people the SPF believes would be useful.[84]
>
> [I]mplementing the consultation process requires the consent of every party involved, including ADB, the complainant, and the EA/DMC government or the PPS. If consent does not exist, then the options available for dialogue and consultation will be necessarily reduced. If the consultation process is working, all parties will continue with the process until an agreement is reached.[85]

For this latter stage, step 7, there seems to be no time limit, which means that the SPF could take the time necessary to implement a serious consultation process. The ADB recognizes that the process will not necessarily always succeed: "In some circumstances, the consultation process may end with no resolution. The SPF may, for example, determine that no further

Figure 4.1
Consultation process of the Asian Development Bank's compliance mechanism

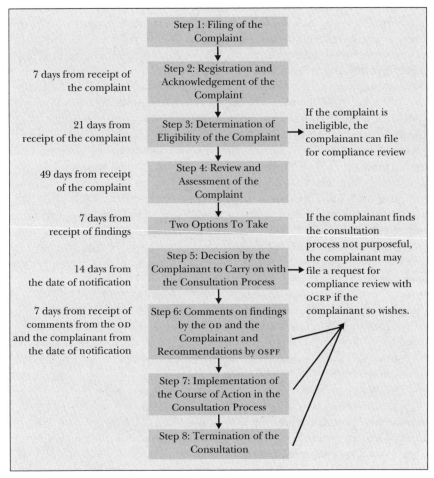

Source: Asian Development Bank, http://www.adb.org.

consultation will be purposeful. In such circumstances the SPF will submit a report to the President summarizing the complaint, the steps to try to resolve the issues raised in the complaint, and a recommendation. The final report incorporating the President's decision on the recommendation will be furnished to the complainant, the EA/DMC government or the PPS, and the Board for information."[86]

The degree of transparency is also high, as the report notes:

The SPF's operations at all stages of the consultation phase will be as transparent as possible, subject to this paragraph, and consistent with relevant ADB policies and procedures and the need to ensure that any dialogue and consultation process is given the maximum opportunity for success.[87]

Any remedial actions that are adopted as a result of the consultation process will reflect an agreement among the relevant parties, subject to ADB's procedures. The range of potential remedies is quite broad. Remedial actions, if any, will be specified in a written agreement or series of agreements made by the relevant stakeholders. Remedial actions involving a major change in the project will require approval by Management or the Board according to ADB's procedures.[88]

Finally, the SPF will also have the task of monitoring the implementation of agreements resulting from the consultation process.

The tasks given to the special project facilitator and the options at his or her disposal for coming to a solution and/or for advising on what measures should be taken to satisfy the complainants demonstrate that the ADB puts most of its efforts and confidence in a process that is intended to conclude with positive solutions. Still, if all the above described efforts fail, the complainants have the right to go to the Compliance Review Panel.

The Compliance Review Phase

The second step is the compliance review phase, for which a Compliance Review Panel with three members has been established.[89] Again, there are similarities to the structure of the World Bank Inspection Panel. The CRP has a full-time chair and two part-time members, appointed by the board on the recommendation of the president. The same people who can ask for a consultation process can also request that the Compliance Review Panel do an investigation if the complainants are not satisfied with the proposed mediation procedures or in case the parties cannot come to an agreement (see figure 4.1 above). Those who can file a complaint are: "(i) any group of two or more people (such as an organization, association, society, or other grouping of individuals) in a borrowing country where an ADB-assisted project is located or in a member country adjacent to the borrowing country[!]; (ii) a local representative of the affected group; (iii) a non-local representative, in exceptional cases where local representation cannot be found and CRP agrees; or (iv) any one or more Board members of the Board of Directors."[90] The description of those who can file a claim is again similar to the description in the World Bank's resolution establishing the Inspection Panel, with one exception: in the case of the World Bank, it is not possible to file a claim from an adjacent country.

As with the World Bank, the independent Compliance Review Panel reports directly to the board of the ADB or to the board's Compliance Review Committee, which is comprised of six board members and has an oversight function. The functioning of this committee, which has taken over the role of the former Bank Inspection Committee, reminds me of the Committee on Development Effectiveness (CODE), which is comprised of executive directors and board members of the World Bank. The Compliance Review Panel faces the same limitations as the World Bank Inspection Panel regarding the determination of harm. Harm can be deduced only from the activities executed by the ADB. Similar to the members of the Inspection Panel, the three panel members at the ADB are appointed for five years and for only one term.

At both institutions the geographical background of panel members is also taken into account. In the case of the World Bank, until 2007 two of the appointed members were selected from candidates from the so-called Group I countries, those that supply loans or donations to the World Bank. The practice was to select one from Europe and one from North America. The third member was selected from the Group II countries, those that borrow from the World Bank. The practice of appointing two members from donor countries was given up in the summer of 2007 with the appointment of Mr Roberto Lenton from Argentina. The panel now has two members from borrowing countries (Group II) and one from a donor country (Group I). At the ADB the arrangement is somewhat different: "Two panel members will be from regional countries, with at least one from a DMC."[91] The ADB's choice here makes sense given that it operates in a specific region, whereas the World Bank operates on more than one continent. Finally, the criteria for selecting panel members are quite similar at both institutions (see appendix 1).

Comparison of the CRP and the World Bank Inspection Panel

At first glance, the procedures for the CRP are similar to those of the World Bank Inspection Panel. A request must first be deemed eligible on the basis of identical requirements. For example, the requester has to specify that it "is, or is likely to be, directly affected materially and adversely by the ADB-assisted project."[92] The requester has to present a description of the harm or expected harm and credible evidence that this "material harm is, or will be, the result of an act or omission of ADB's failure to follow its operational policies and procedures."[93] The CRP is presumed not to investigate the borrowing country. And the panel cannot deal with requests related to activities for which the ADB has no responsibility. In the case of the World Bank, the requester is asked to show that it first tried to communicate its concerns to bank management in an effort to solve the problems before filing a claim. In the case of the ADB, the requester has to show that it first addressed the complaint to the special project facilitator. After a complaint is declared eligible, the CRP is expected to conduct a "thorough and objective review of policy compliance."[94] The CRP is expected to engage during the compliance review "with all stakeholders, including management and staff, the requester, the EA/DMC [executing agency/developing member country] government or the PPS [private project sponsor], and the Board member representing the country concerned, in a thorough understanding of the issues."[95] This all is very similar to the processes at the World Bank.

The differences in the processes of the World Bank and the ADB are as follows:

- The Compliance Review Panel must issue a draft report to both management and the requester for comments. The purpose of this is not further mentioned. One can assume that it is intended to give both management and the requester an opportunity to change factual misconceptions or to add information. The World Bank Inspection Panel, as far as I am aware, has never issued a *draft* report to management or to the requester. This internal procedure at the World Bank has given rise to much discussion since on several occasions management has asked for a draft in order to correct facts. In the years that I was a member of the panel, the argument against doing so was that if a draft was delivered to management, the requester should have the same right to see the draft and comment on it. This I still consider a fair judgment: both should see a draft or neither! And if issued to both, the draft should lead only to comments of a factual nature. Finally, at the ADB, it is the independent CRP that should decide whether the comments delivered in response to a draft report are factual or interpretations, the latter of which are never to be accepted.

- The Compliance Review Panel's mandate includes *postcompliance review and monitoring.* Complaints can still be lodged after the completion of an ADB project as long as a project-completion report has not yet been issued.[96] The issuing of a completion report at the ADB normally occurs one to two years after the project is physically completed and in operation.[97] In the case of the World Bank, a request can be filed only up to the point when 95 per cent of the project budget has been spent. At the ADB requesters have more opportunities to file a request – for example, in circumstances where the negative effects of a project become evident only after completion. In certain situations, this could be the case for projects with environmental and social impacts.

Although the ADB has established two different and separate compliance review functions, it is still criticized. A respondent to a survey about the accountability mechanisms used by the various institutions (see chapter 7) said:

[S]uch a mediation mechanism should be independent from management, unlike the case of the ADB, where the SPF is to report to the president. Also I would recommend that the two functions are independent from each other, so that requesters/local communities can call on both functions at the same time. Again, this is unlike the ADB, where complainants are required to go first to the SPF, while the CRP can be called upon only after the process with the SPF is exhausted. In my view a problem-solving/mediation mechanism should also be instrumental in advising management on how to implement recommendations from a compliance review process. It is very important that both functions are integrated into bank operations and procedures as a learning mechanism. The "costs" of accountability mechanisms should be identified as investments in strengthening and eventually improving bank operations (similar to training, etc.).

Having created two mechanisms that are independent of each other – an ombudsman function, or facilitator, and an accountability mechanism – the ADB is the first multilateral financial institution to have adopted both functions for the entire institution. In doing so, the ADB recognized the importance of the two phases. The first phase allows the bank to show its more "human face" by focusing most of its efforts on trying to solve problems before making them an issue for a quasi-legal judgment. The ADB process is more open and gives the requester a position equal to that of management. Moreover, a request is still admissible for a short time after completion of a project. For these reasons, I consider the ADB model a vanguard among the accountability mechanisms.

After adoption of the revised mechanism in 2003, the CRP received twelve cases: five were determined eligible and seven were not.

THE INTER-AMERICAN DEVELOPMENT BANK

The Inter-American Development Bank (IADB) was founded in 1959 with a focus on promoting sustainable economic and social development in Latin America and the Caribbean by providing financing and technical assistance. According to the bank's website, it was originally conceived as a partnership between nineteen Latin American countries and the United States, which is by far the largest donor to the IADB. Over time, the bank has expanded its membership, adding several English-speaking Caribbean countries, Surinam, and Canada between the late 1960s and 1980 and sixteen European states, Israel, Japan, and the Republic of Korea between 1976 and 2005.[98] With its governors, Board of Executive Directors, member countries organized in constituencies, and policies, the IADB is structured in the same way as the other multilateral financial institutions. In 1994, shortly after the World Bank established the Inspection Panel, the IADB also established an independent investigation mechanism. Although this mechanism shares similarities with the mandate and procedures of the Inspection Panel, there are differences. The similarities include: (1) the same sort of eligibility criteria, such as no procurement cases; (2) specification that a complaint will not be eligible if 95 per cent of the project budget has already been disbursed; (3) the definition of an affected party as a community of persons, such as an organization, association, society, or other grouping of individuals in the territory of a borrower; and (4) stipulation that former requests will again be eligible for consideration only if "substantial new evidence or circumstances not known at the time of the prior request are introduced."[99] Nonetheless, the differences are substantial. First, the IADB works with a roster of experts whose composition is ad hoc: there are fifteen individuals from at least ten different nations. Second, members of the roster may be employed by the bank two years following the termination of their position as an expert of the mechanism.[100]

On 3 February 2005 the IADB released a draft consultation and compliance review policy entitled "Proposal for Enhancement to the Independent Investigation Mechanism: Draft Consultation and Compliance Review Policy." The bank then invited those interested to comment. I was asked by officials of the IADB to comment on the draft policy. The following description of the proposed IADB mechanism is based on what I wrote for the IADB.[101] The draft policy is the revision of an earlier and rather different mechanism established in 1994 and amended in 2001. The proposed mechanism reflects the demand of both civil society and governments for accountability and follows the experience of other multilateral financial institutions, such as the World Bank. In proposing this new structure, the IADB recognized this demand, for which I praised the bank in my commentary. My remarks concerned (1) general issues, (2) progressive steps in the structure compared to other mechanisms, and (3) questions and mandate issues that needed to be addressed. I have tried here for the most part to follow the order of my original text.

General Comments

The proposed mechanism is well developed, as evidenced by detailed descriptions of the structure of the mechanism and the mandate of the different stakeholders. It is also clear that those drafting the proposal studied other accountability mechanisms, particularly the World Bank Inspection Panel.

The addition of a "consultation phase" to the IADB's mechanism is a bold step and fits perfectly with the concept that people should first try to solve their problems and discuss them before the problems are submitted to the IADB's Compliance Review Panel, this being the last step to be taken and only if necessary. Article B, paragraph 8, of the draft proposal states: "The Mechanism process is not a legal proceeding but is an internal function of the Bank related to the accountability of the institution and the quality and effectiveness of its projects." However, the split between the consultation phase and the compliance review phase gives the impression that the latter is a kind of arbitration. While this in itself is not wrong, the compliance review phase should be considered only semi-judicial since the reporting of the IADB's panel contains findings, not conclusions and measures, which is also the case with the World Bank Inspection Panel's

.reports. The findings of the IADB's panel, together with the proposed measures of management, finally lead to a decision by the Board of Directors.
Thus the final decisions stay in the hands of the executive directors, and as
a consequence, the compliance review phase can never be regarded as a legal proceeding.[102] Nonetheless, the semi-judicial character of the review
phase can help to clarify the structure and mandate of the mechanism, especially the division of responsibilities, reporting, and independence.

As described in the draft proposal, the two phases are clearly different in
structure and should be so in practice. The first phase is one of bringing
parties together and of creating trust and open communication. Every
party is taken seriously, including those who lack the education to go
through a consultation process. This phase comprises the negotiations
between the stakeholders on the process to be followed and, finally, the
process of moderation itself. With the likelihood that poor people will be
involved in future cases, it is advisable for the IADB to consider creating a
special fund or budget for so-called "participation funding." Canadian
expertise with the phenomena of participation funding might be very
helpful.[103] Negotiations between governments, a multilateral financial institution, and local communities entail a difficult and sensitive process.
Here, the IADB should seek the support of experts.

In the draft proposal, the consultation phase is clearly defined as the responsibility of the appointed executive secretary, a member of the IADB's
staff. That responsibility for the first phase is put into the hands of a staff
member is understandable since the first phase is a problem-solving phase
involving the heart of the organization itself. The strong responsibilities of
the executive secretary are recorded in part 2, Articles E to H, paragraphs
56 to 73. Paragraph 58, for example, mentions that the executive secretary
will "recommend a process," and this is followed by different articles sum-
ming up all the options in the process. Paragraph 60 states that "The entire process of assessing the Request and making a recommendation on
how to proceed should be completed by the Executive Secretary"; paragraph 65 adds that "The procedure is established on a case-by-case basis by
the Executive Secretary in consultation with the essential parties"; and
paragraph 68 indicates that the final report to the president, supported by
"quantitative evidence," is entirely the responsibility of the executive secretary. Consequently, his or her role is clear in this first important phase.

The appointment of an executive secretary who has knowledge of and
experience with social community work could work very well for the IADB
and for the people in the field.

Risk of Conflict of Interest

The second phase should be a new and different component. Unfortunately, in the draft proposal it is unclear where the responsibility of
the executive secretary ends and where the responsibility for the IADB's

Compliance Review Panel begins. Part II, Article D, paragraph 84, of the draft proposal states that during the second phase the executive secretary is to give "support" to the chairperson of the Compliance Review Panel. However, paragraph 85 indicates that the chairperson will review the decision of the executive secretary. In both paragraphs concerning the procedure, it is evident that the positions of the executive secretary and chairperson are to a certain extent interwoven. The executive secretary, responsible for the first phase, is an advisor to the panel in the second phase. Furthermore, the executive secretary is responsible for the daily running of the office and has to assist the panel in its work during the second phase. These two latter roles of the executive secretary suggest the risk that his or her work will be part of the "investigation" conducted by the IADB's Compliance Review Panel.

Why is it important to draw a clear line? The proposed structure could place the executive secretary in a situation of conflict of interest. Take the following scenario. In the first phase both the executive secretary and his or her staff as well as the contracted outside experts go through a lengthy process of moderation. They work hard and try to bring parties together, to create understanding, and to come up with a solution to the problems. The executive secretary and the office staff become committed players in the process. Nevertheless, it fails. The dossier then goes to the IADB's Compliance Review Panel. In such a situation it is almost inhuman to expect the executive secretary to be impartial when advising the panel in the next phase. A conflict between the two phases may thus be built-in, becoming inevitable.

A clear split between the two phases has been made by the Asian Development Bank, and I assume that this is so for the abovementioned reason. For the same reason, I advised the Inter-American Development Bank to consider a clearer split of responsibilities between the mechanism's two functions.

Progressive Steps

There are a lot of progressive elements to be found in the IADB's proposed procedures. Several steps reflect elements missing in other mechanisms.

For example, in describing the many functions of the executive secretary, part 1, Article D, paragraph 14, refers to "a record of lessons learned in the Mechanism process." If maintained in an analytical way, such a record will provide the bank with information for future reference about where things go wrong in projects. Evidence of the systemic reoccurrence of harm and problems can be found in many of the investigation reports of the World Bank Inspection Panel. However, as far as I know, no system has yet been developed at the World Bank to systematically record this information.

Another bold step taken by the IADB was the creation of a Public Registry (see part I, Article E, paragraph 30) with an ongoing processing function. This measure answers the demand for transparency. The same can be said about the provision that information and reasons be given to a requester in the event that deadlines will not be met (see part I, Article G, paragraph 32). The more openness the better!

Part II, Article C, paragraph 41, contains another noteworthy feature of the draft proposal, namely a query to requesters about what they "would like to see as a result of the Consultation Phase." The question here is about how requesters would like the consultation phase to work. On the one hand, this phase will create trust among the requesters since it shows that they are taken seriously by providing them with the opportunity to express their wishes. On the other hand, this phase might encourage the requesters to ask for too much based on an assumption that they have to negotiate and will never in fact obtain everything they initially demand. From the very beginning of the process, this latter situation could block negotiations. This could be an important consideration that needs further evaluation.

Part II, Article K, paragraph 73, of the draft proposal is about monitoring implementation of the negotiated actions. This is a strong tool. After all, given that a lot of effort will be expended arriving at solutions to the problems, it makes sense to monitor whether the outcome of the process is implemented properly. This provision is not yet to be found in any of the accountability mechanisms at the other multilateral financial institutions.

A very wise proposal is to be found in part V, paragraph 123, which makes it clear that the IADB considers its accountability mechanism to be an ongoing process of learning within the institution. The office and the chairperson of the IADB's Compliance Review Panel have to conduct an evaluation, review the mechanism's effectiveness, and submit suggestions for improvements to the mechanism policy. I advised the IADB to make sure that the office of the panel is allotted a proper budget and given a clear work description so that it can fulfil this important task. Also, this work has to be done in an analytical way and may be partly coordinated with the collection of data on "lessons learned" (see Article D, paragraph 14, cited above).

Questions and Remarks on Structure and Mandate Issues

There are several issues that are not addressed in the draft proposal or that give rise to further questions and critical commentary.

For instance, there is no reference to the subject of outreach. The question is how people in the member countries where IADB-financed projects are implemented are to know about their right to express their concerns and ask for a problem-solving process or for a report from the IADB's Compliance Review Panel. In the case of the World Bank, a provision in the resolution establishing the Inspection Panel states that management should inform the public about its right to file a complaint with the panel. Of course, this is not a task that those who are entirely involved in the daily work of the projects can be expected to fulfil. Put simply, the provision requires management to inform the people that they can go to the World Bank's headquarters and file a request for a compliance review if they do not agree with the project on which these same managers are working. This is as it should be. But the IADB could also choose to organize an outreach campaign itself from Washington, DC.

It will take time to create a climate in which management understands its role in the IADB's new mechanism for ensuring transparency and the involvement of affected people. It will be helpful to organize training for managers, especially for the country directors, so that they can begin to see that democratic processes are not easy and that what they think is right can be judged by others differently. Nevertheless, at the end of the day management will see the richness of the process. Most important is that all parties, including the executive directors, the executive secretary, and the staff of the Compliance Review Panel, adhere to the notion that the mechanism is part of an ongoing learning process. The process does not exist specifically to "blame and shame" any person but to help the organization and those who benefit from it to learn by doing so that corrections can be made along the way.

Part I, Article B, paragraph 20, is about the division of tasks between the full-time chairperson and the two on-call panel members. In the IADB's compliance review phase it is evident that the final report will be the work and opinion of these three members. For this reason it is crucial that all three members can base their opinion on equal access to information. To guarantee this, it is important to create an in-house information system so that the two on-call panel members are regularly informed about what in general is happening at the IADB, important mail addressed to the panel is received by the chairperson, and important meetings take place, including regular meetings between the three members. This is critical since the on-call members are not supposed to live in Washington and may have less familiarity with the agenda of the panel. Proper communication between the members is even more important if the first chairperson is to chair the panel for three years with a possible extension of another two years (see part I, Article D, paragraph 29). Communication skills should therefore be one of the key assets of anyone selected to chair the panel.

Part I, Article F, paragraph 31, refers to a specific situation where coverage under the mechanism is excluded, namely when "ninety-five percent of the proceeds have been disbursed." This limitation, although understandable from a technical point of view, seems a missed opportunity. The Asian Development Bank takes a different approach in that people can still file a case up to two years after full disbursement of the project loan.

Remaining Questions

Part II, Article C, paragraph 44, refers to the option for requesters to present new evidence. But then it is stated: "However, such submission will be considered a new Request and start the Mechanism process again from the time the revised Request is received." I wonder whether this isn't an unnecessary complication of the process. An option would be to specify a time period up to when additional information or evidence can be submitted. This can be determined by the stakeholders themselves taking part in the process. As long as information can be submitted, it is evident that this should be handed out to all parties so that they are given an equal opportunity to react to it. But again, drawing a line should be a matter for the parties involved.

Article C, paragraph 46, refers to the confidentiality of the names of the requesters. But the text does not make clear who will keep the names confidential. At the World Bank, after consulting the president, the Inspection Panel created the opportunity for requesters to keep their names confidential, the only provision being that the panel in turn must respect this choice. The reason for allowing confidentiality is that in some countries the requesters do not trust the local personnel of the bank office or do not trust management. Such difficult circumstances are probably rare but should not be excluded. I thus strongly advised the IADB to consider a similar provision.

In Article H, paragraph 104, one finds a rather pedantic text asking the IADB's panel to "keep in mind the fact that any policy or norm, no matter how carefully crafted, may contain aspects that are ambiguous, and subject to differing interpretations. If the Panel concludes that the Management of the Bank has made a reasonable, good faith interpretation of the Bank's Operational Policy, the Panel should give consideration to this fact before finding a violation of an Operational Policy." This text seems superfluous given the documented selection criteria in part 1, Article D, paragraph 17. The criteria for selecting panel members are "integrity, independence from the Bank's Management and ability to deal thoroughly, fairly and impartially with the requests brought to them." I recommended removing Article H, paragraph 104, from part 3.

Part 3, Article G, paragraph 100, is about attachments to the Compliance Review Panel's report. The proposal is to create the opportunity for borrowers/recipients to record their views and include them as an annex in the panel's final report. Recording the views of borrowers and any other stakeholders should be a normal part of the work of the IADB's panel. The views of certain stakeholders should not be given separate space in an annex but should be reflected in the report itself, just as are the views of other stakeholders. The final report of the Compliance Review Panel should present its findings without any intermingling of the views of other parties. Of course, there is nothing stopping the stakeholders from printing and publishing their own views and positions. The nature of a Compliance Review Panel or any other accountability mechanism is its independence.

Last but not least, part 3, Article I, paragraph 111, proposes giving management the right to disagree with the findings and/or recommendations of the panel.[104] Two things should be said about this.

First, the provision creates the erroneous impression that if the panel has a dispute with management about a project and its implementation, the panel becomes powerless. It is crucial that everyone at the IADB – the executive directors, management, and national authorities – understands the Compliance Review Panel's position when a case arises. One cannot emphasize strongly enough that it is not the panel members whose view of projects is inherently different from that of management. The problems submitted to the panel are based on a conflict between management and the requesters, not on a disagreement between management and the panel. The panel is a "last resort," a body from which the stakeholders who disagree with management can receive an independent opinion. The panel is a tool created by and for the executive directors. For these reasons the World Bank Inspection Panel does not accept a written report from management disputing the panel's findings. In the case of the World Bank, management is expected to deliver a report explaining the actions that it proposes, if any, as an answer to the panel's findings of noncompliance.

Second, one can still understand management's need to give its opinion. I mentioned before that although the IADB's Compliance Review Panel is not a legal mechanism, comparison with a legal system could still help to put the structure in perspective. Indeed, one could compare the panel's preparation of its reports with the work done in a judicial system and similarly compare management's response to these reports with the reply by rejoinder in a judicial system. In a judicial system there are always at least two parties in a dispute or conflict. This is also the case for requests filed with the IADB's panel or with the compliance mechanisms of the other multilateral financial institutions. The other party, namely the requesters, should have the same rights as management. The dilemma and danger is that this might open a "Pandora's box." Distributing the final report to the requesters for a reaction definitely creates the risk that the report will be published by the media before the executive directors have had a chance to decide on it. I suggested that the panel submit its final draft of a report to management for verification of facts, such as statistics and data. The panel would then decide whether the given information is factual or a matter of interpretation, with the facts accepted by the panel being included in the report.

At present, it has not yet been decided what the IADB's final compliance mechanism will be. The process of creating a mechanism began at the beginning of 2005. Many other experts have also reacted to the draft proposal. Since then, there has been only "deafening silence" from the bank. I have been informed that civil society is asking the IADB if and when it will take a decision. That about three years have passed raises the question of whether there has been any resistance inside the IADB against the original initiative. Some outside the bank argue that the bank could wait for a crisis with its involvement in major infrastructural projects, most likely within the context of the Initiative for the Integration of the Regional Infrastructure of South America (IIRSA). This "Initiative for the integration of regional infrastructure and physical integration of the continent was founded in 2000 by the heads of state of 12 South American countries and has since developed a portfolio for 348 infrastructure projects requiring a total investment of $38 billion in transportation, energy and communications."[105] One can predict that not all of these projects will be implemented without problems and without harm to local citizens. The introduction of a consultation and compliance review policy would not only benefit local people who are harmed or could be harmed but also protect the IADB against a reputational crisis similar to that experienced by the World Bank during its involvement in the Narmada Dam Project in the 1980s. However, a new coordinator, Ana-Mita Betancourt, has been appointed, and the process for revising the mechanism is still open. With a new president and a new coordinator at the IADB, new consideration of its mechanism is possible.

THE EUROPEAN BANK FOR RECONSTRUCTION AND DEVELOPMENT

The European Bank for Reconstruction and Development (EBRD) was established in 1991 after the Soviet Union disintegrated. In the bank's original documents, the USSR was a shareholder. At the time of the fall of communism, I was a member of the European Parliament and well remember the discussions about the establishment of the EBRD. It was a remarkably fast decision, one in which the United States and Canada were involved. Operating in twenty-seven countries from central Europe to central Asia, the EBRD is jointly owned by sixty countries. It is also owned by the European Investment Bank and the European Community, represented by the European Commission on the Board of Directors. According to the bank's website, its mandate, in contrast with that of the other MFIs, is to invest "predominantly in the private sector." The website also states that "The mandate of the EBRD stipulates that it must only work in countries that are committed to democratic principles. Respect for the environment is part of the strong corporate governance attached to all EBRD investments."[106]

The Central Eastern Europe (CEE) Bankwatch Network, an umbrella organization of NGOs from several European countries that monitors the activities of international financial institutions (IFIs) in eastern Europe, closely follows the activities of the EBRD. In June 2001 the network published a document in which the EBRD was asked to establish an "appeals/ compliance mechanism."[107] This document states that "Through a well-designed appeals/compliance mechanism, the EBRD can become more transparent and accountable to the people of Eastern Europe and of EBRD member states. Establishing such a mechanism will help the EBRD to apply its own policies more effectively. Social and environmental issues will be considered more carefully, and as a result, more appropriate and successful projects will be financed."[108] The Bankwatch Network further argues that there are several reasons underlying the need for such a mechanism. First, "It has been a constant struggle for NGOs and the public to get access to detailed information about projects at any stage of development or implementation." Second, accountability is at stake both for the people of eastern Europe and for "the taxpayers of the member nations who fund the EBRD." Third, "Project Sponsor compliance with EBRD policies and procedures is not closely monitored by the EBRD. CEE Bankwatch Network is aware of many instances in which Project Sponsors and even EBRD itself have failed to comply with EBRD policies and procedures."[109] The demand for the establishment of a compliance mechanism at the EBRD has been ongoing, receiving mention in almost every CEE Bankwatch document since publication of the initial 2001 document.

The EBRD has taken the demand seriously and organized sessions with representatives of the NGO community and with private-sector investors at its headquarters in London and elsewhere. On 14 May 2002 in an executive session the Board of Directors "endorsed the principle of establishing a mechanism whereby local groups that may be directly and adversely affected by a Bank-financed project would be able to raise their complaints or grievances with an arm of the Bank that would be independent from project operations."[110] On 16 October of the same year the bank published on its website a draft proposal for an "independent recourse mechanism."

At the same time the bank made clear that "It is well established under international law that IFIs have special privileges and immunities designed to enable them to carry out their operational activities without interference from national laws and national courts. Like other IFIs, the EBRD is not regulated by any bodies other than those forming part of its governance structure. By and large, the EBRD is beyond the reach of administrative and judicial recourse mechanisms established under national legislation to the same extent as other IFIs, except where immunities are waived."[111] Thus the bank recognizes its immunities and consequently mentions its responsibilities:

> It is the exclusive duty and responsibility of the EBRD's governance bodies to regulate its activities through the adoption of policies, procedures and rules and to monitor the Bank's compliance with its regulatory framework. As administrators and officers of a public institution, they necessarily take account of the requirements and needs of the Bank's stakeholders when making decisions. Where their decisions concern EBRD's project operations, they consider the interests of the groups that are or might be affected by Bank-financed projects. However, in the current governance structure of the Bank, there is no formal mechanism that enables such groups to make their specific concerns known to the Bank's decision-makers. Until 1993, this was also the case in other IFIs. Since that year, starting with the World Bank, most IFIs have established

mechanisms designed to formalize the means of recourse of the groups affected by the projects that IFIs finance. Two different approaches have developed.[112]

With the latter, the EBRD refers to both the problem-solving function and the compliance review function.

The EBRD then states that "This mechanism is predicated on the idea that it may be most advantageous for all parties to resolve problems (without need to apportion blame or fault) early with the view to avoiding larger and more intractable problems at a later stage."[113] In a footnote the EBRD refers to the role of the International Finance Corporation's ombudsman. The EBRD then positions itself somewhat at a distance from the other mechanisms, particularly the World Bank Inspection Panel, in noting about the status of the mechanism:

> With a view to ensuring the independence of the mechanism, other IFIs have established permanent offices and/or panels to carry out the compliance review function and/or the problem-solving function. Such independence may however be ensured through other means of a less bureaucratic and costly nature, more suited to the institution's specific mandate, organisation and resources. The EBRD needs a mechanism that is adapted to its focus on project finance and private sector development. While protecting the affected parties' right to exercise recourse, the EBRD's accountability mechanism should not impair its delivery capacity, in all its project operations, whether for the public or private sector clients.[114]

Concerning the status of the mechanism, another rather striking note is made: "The EBRD's organisation also mandates that the allocation of powers among its Board of Governors, Board of Directors and President be maintained."[115] This gives the impression that the EBRD sees the mechanisms in the other institutions as interfering in the powers of the Board of Governors, Board of Directors, and president. On the one hand, the EBRD certainly recognizes the influence an accountability mechanism can have on the institution; on the other hand, it does not recognize that the World Bank Inspection Panel was created by and for the bank's Board of Directors, who at the time held the opinion that they were in need of an independent body that could do an independent investigation in their name, as I describe in chapters 2 and 3.

The EBRD's mechanism is called the Independent Recourse Mechanism (IRM). Its structure is such that the mechanism "would make full use of the EBRDs existing Office of the Chief Compliance Officer (CCO) as coordinator of its processes and initial assessor of complaints received from affected groups. The CCO is not involved in project operations and his [sic!][116] independence is further ensured through his direct reporting to the

President and access to the Chairman of the Board's Audit Committee."[117] "The cco reports directly to the President and is independent of the Banking departments, the Environment Department and other departments or units involved in project operations." This reporting directly to the president still caused some concern about the cco's independence. However, according to an official of the EBRD, "It is incorrect, I believe to say that the IRM lacks independence as it is managed by the President. When the IRM is involved in decisions concerning projects that have already gone to the Board, those complaints and the IRM's assessment of those complaints go directly to the Board of Directors for consideration. The President transmits the document to the Board as the Chair of the Board, but does not otherwise comment on its content."[118] The cco's other responsibilities include ensuring that the bank's processes follow the highest standards of integrity and conducting investigations into cases of alleged misconduct by Bank officials, employees or consultants.[119] And "The IRM also includes a problem-solving function to be used where complaints or grievances can also, or alternatively, benefit from problem-solving techniques to assist in trying to resolve the underlying issues. Those techniques may include independent fact-finding, mediation, conciliation, dialogue facilitation, investigation and reporting."[120]

The international NGO community was immediately disappointed with the proposed structure of the mechanism. One wrote: "Friends of the Earth International feels strongly that there should be a clear distinction between a problem-solving role on the one hand and inspection and compliance review function on the other. Experience has shown that although complementary, these functions are fundamentally different in nature, objective and results. We suggest that the EBRD establish two separate windows that function independently from each other and have their own staff."[121] Another critique of the mechanism by this NGO pointed out that "the lack of clear and established policies at the EBRD in other than environmental areas is of major concern. The EBRD should work towards establishing a suite of policy requirements to address critical social and economic issues, along the lines of the safeguard policies that have proven so important at the World Bank. These would include, among others, involuntary resettlement, forestry, indigenous peoples and project supervision. All of these are of great relevance to the EBRD's mission."[122]

The NGOs were not the only parties to criticize the proposed mechanism. Two former chairmen of the World Bank Inspection Panel, Richard Bissell and Jim MacNeill, wrote the following rather harsh letter to President Jean Lemierre of the EBRD:

Dear President Lemierre,

When you requested public comment on the draft proposal for an "independent recourse mechanism" on 16 October 2002, we read the text with great interest, hopeful that one of the most important European institutions of finance was now ready to consider seriously its responsibilities to be accountable, transparent, and fully sensitive to the impacts of its financial activities on intended beneficiaries. As former Chairs of the World Bank Inspection Panel, we understand well the stakes involved, for the EBRD as an institution, for the Board, and for you as President.

We remember clearly the source of the mandate to the EBRD to undertake this initiative – the meeting of the G-8 in July 2000, when the global leadership called upon all the multilateral development banks to achieve "greater transparency, public participation and accountability, particularly including release of all country strategies and evaluation reports and increased effectiveness and accessibility of independent Inspection Panels in all institutions."

We were concerned when the Economic Summit of 2001, held in Canada, came and went with no word from the EBRD. Surprisingly, the G-7 finance ministers were able to congratulate the IMF, not considered the most reformable of institutions, on its progress in establishing an independent Evaluation Office. The Ministers went on to reiterate their call to the EBRD and other RDBs [reconstruction and development banks] to "establish or improve existing mechanisms, fully independent from staff responsible for project preparation, to ensure compliance of project proposals with policies and procedures prior to submission to the Board. We look forward to an assessment of the measures taken so far and further proposals being presented by the World Bank and by the RDBs by Spring 2002; strengthen or establish inspection mechanisms reporting directly to the Board; adopt a more open policy on information disclosure by making draft and final key policy and strategy documents available to the public." With the arrival of 2002, nevertheless, our hopes remained that the EBRD would demonstrate its willingness to join the rest of the international financial community in a clear commitment to accountability. That hope, unfortunately, has been dashed by the current draft.

The EBRD has chosen to make a proposal that fails almost all tests proposed by the world's financial leaders, and reflecting little from the experiences of other financial institutions. The EBRD would be best served by withdrawing the current proposal and starting with a fresh draft, rather than tinkering with a proposal certain to fail and frustrate all stakeholders, internal and external. This may seem to be a harsh judgment, but in matters of international accountability, institutions rise and fall with their credibility, and our interest in strengthening the EBRD leads us to be very clear in stating our view of what is missing from the proposal of 16 October.

1 The mechanism fails the test of independence. This is an internal mechanism, managed by the President. The experience of

other mechanisms has been that the perception and reality of independence is a *sine qua non.*

2 The mechanism covers only the EBRD's environmental policy and procedures. While the drafters may say that there are no other policies for the mechanism to oversee, that situation in itself should be a warning sign to the Board that there is too little oversight at a policy level. At least the *de minimus* roster of policies present in other multilateral banks should be developed at the EBRD and placed under jurisdiction of a viable accountability mechanism.

3 The release of information regarding issues at the mechanism is both conditional and vague. The value of transparency has been demonstrated time and again at other financial institutions as a means of enhancing public trust in the bank and its inspection mechanisms. There is good reason for the G-8 to have placed "greater transparency" at the top of their criteria for inspection mechanisms in 2000. People kept in the dark have a right to be suspicious.

4 The people appointed to the mechanism must have visible autonomy and effectiveness. The Chief Compliance Officer is a staff member, with multiple other duties, and the use of a lengthy roster for expertise has been shown to be a disservice elsewhere to both the claimants and to the bank. A roster's members have little incentive to become well-versed in the strategies and workings of the bank, and are thus unable to take the bank's real interests into account, and also carry little knowledge over from claim to claim, making the process less effective for claimants. Appointed panels with a limited number of members, even if part-time, are able to meet accountability needs much more effectively than a long roster of specialized professionals.

5 The tone of the proposal is that the mechanism will be far more focused on "problem-solving" than on "compliance." It makes sense for any institution to have a problem-solving ombudsman, but it should not be confused with the call of the G-8 for independent Inspection Panels. The litmus test for an effective ombudsman is far simpler. The existence of such an office would not obviate the need identified by the economic summits for a truly independent, transparent, and accountable inspection mechanism.[123]

This letter received the attention of a member of the European Parliament, Elly Plooij-van Gorsel, who tabled a written question to the European Commission asking for its reaction to the letter.[124] The commission answered only that it was aware of the consultations between management and the board of the EBRD on the creation of an accountability mechanism and that the question of the respected parliamentarian would be brought to the attention of the EBRD.

The comments of the different stakeholders were processed by management. In April 2004, a year later, the board of the EBRD approved the Rules of Procedure of the Independent Recourse Mechanism.[125] The latter document contains further details on the procedures of the compliance review and problem-solving functions and on the position of the CCO. A comparison of the two documents approved by the board in April 2003 and April 2004 does not reveal major differences. However, the document of 2004 is more detailed. In the second document the following is noted about the problem-solving function: "Terms of appointment of Problem-solving Facilitators. When performing IRM functions, Problem-solving Facilitators appointed from outside the Bank shall serve in their individual, personal capacity ... Problem-solving Facilitators shall be required to act impartially and independently and shall not participate in a Problem-solving Initiative in which they have or had a personal interest or significant involvement in any capacity, unless specifically authorized by the President."[126]

In response to the concern raised about the independence of the chief compliance officer, the bank decided that the CCO can declare a complaint eligible or ineligible only in concert with an independent expert from outside. For the EBRD, this structure is probably preferable to the structure of some of the other MFIs where members of the mechanisms, despite being outsiders who know nothing about the bank from the inside, are the final arbiters. The criticism from outsiders that the bank limits itself "only" to an environmental policy is refuted by experts at the bank, who point out that the environmental policies include several social dimensions.

The EBRD's procedures are similar to those of the World Bank with regard to who may file a complaint and the eligibility criteria of a complaint. As in the case of the Inspection Panel, an "affected group,"[127] defined as two or more people, may file a complaint, which may be submitted in their native language. The complainant may also be an "Authorised Representative." However, a limitation is apparent in the reference to "evidence that there is no adequate or appropriate representation in the local community."[128] As well, a complaint will be eligible only if "the Registered Complaint is from an affected Group and there is *prima facie* evidence that the project has, or is likely to have, a direct adverse and material effect on such group's common interest" and if "the Affected Group has initiated good faith efforts to resolve the issue with the Bank and other Relevant Parties and there is no reasonable prospect of resolving the issue through the continuation of such efforts."[129] Furthermore, as in the case of the World Bank, the complainants may ask for confidentiality respecting their identities.[130] There is a somewhat similar timeframe for the mechanism to investigate whether a complaint is eligible: twenty-five business days.

Nevertheless, differences between the IRM and the World Bank Inspection Panel prevail. One can conclude that the EBRD, in contrast with the World Bank and the Asian Development Bank, has chosen a mechanism that interweaves the problem-solving function and the compliance review function. The description of the cco's position shows some similarities with the director's position at the African Development Bank (see below). Since the EBRD mechanism was put in place, it has received eleven complaints, seven of which were declared ineligible.[131]

Procedures of the EBRD Mechanism

In June 2007 the NGO CEE Bankwatch Network published a report on how the EBRD mechanism has been functioning. Clearly, this NGO is rather disappointed with the results so far:

> A number of affected communities and NGOs have sought redress through the IRM in cases where they have found fault with EBRD operations and wished to have these wrongdoings addressed. While the nature of these complaints has varied, the results are inevitably the same: of all eleven cases submitted to the IRM, only four have been "registered" and so far the IRM has neither found fault with the EBRD's actions nor has it recommended any type of compensation for peoples and communities harmed by EBRD projects. As a result of these fruitless interactions, civil society has learned a number of lessons from its dealings with the IRM. Notably, the IRM does not pass judgment on ineffective EBRD policies and strategies; it does not encourage active engagement from all parts of civil society; it does not safeguard against the rights of workers in EBRD-financed projects; and it does not have power over the actions of the EBRD's clients.[132]

CEE Bankwatch might have been too early with its judgment. Shortly before the publication of its report, on 19 April 2007, a complaint was registered concerning the Vlorë Generation Project in Albania. In addition, on 6 July 2007 another complaint arrived from Georgia and was registered. The latter complaint was declared "eligible for further processing towards a possible problem-solving initiative but not warranting a compliance review."[133]

According to the cco:

> The complaint, submitted by members or supporters of the Civic Alliance for the Protection of the Vlorë Bay, relates to the construction of the Vlorë TPP [Thermal Power Generation Project] by *Korporata Elektroeergjetike Shqiptare* (KESH), an Albanian state-owned power utility company, on Treport Beach. The affected Group claims that the construction of this project on this "historic beach" will adversely impact the environment as well as the tourism and fishing activities of the region and consequently the livelihoods OF ITS MEMBERS. The group alleges non-compliance by the Bank with its Environment Policy pertaining to, *inter alia*, the precautionary approach to the management and

sustainable use of natural biodiversity resources, as well as meaningful public consultation. Alongside the EBRD, the Vlorë TPP has obtained funding from the World Bank and the EIB.[134]

In conformity with the procedures, the CCO appointed one of the IRM experts to do an eligibility assessment. This expert's report, which was "concluded in September 2007, contained a recommendation that the complaint be held eligible and warranting a compliance review, the first of its kind since the inception of the IRM, without prejudice to the ability of the CCO to recommend a problem solving initiative as well."[135] So the has IRM reached a new phase. Interestingly, in this case both the EBRD's Independent Recourse Mechanism and the World Bank Inspection Panel are involved.

Whether the IRM is finally weaker than the mechanisms at the other MFIs is in question. I still regard the ERDB's emphasis on problem solving as a choice for a more positive approach. Nevertheless, the mix of problem solving and compliance review still bears a risk of a conflict of interest, as I explain above in the case of the IADB's proposed mechanism and as I show below in the case of the African Development Bank.

THE EUROPEAN INVESTMENT BANK[136]

The European Investment Bank (EIB), the world's largest international public lending institution, with a portfolio greater than that of the World Bank,[137] consists of the EIB and the European Investment Fund:

> The 27 Member States of the European Union [EU] are the sharehold-
> ers of the EIB and they collectively determine the Bank's policies and ap-
> prove investments. Each Member State's share in the Bank's capital is
> based on its economic weight within the European Union. In the con-
> text of EU enlargement, the provisions of the EIB's Statute have modi-
> fied the Bank's capital shares and governance ... Fostering economic and
> social cohesion in the less favoured regions of the EU is the prime task
> assigned to the Bank by the Treaty establishing the European Commu-
> nity, and continues to be a core lending objective of the Bank.[138]

On the environment, the EIB has adopted a strong policy:

> The EIB takes a proactive approach to lending for the environment,
> guided by European Union environmental policies, some of the strictest
> and best developed in the World. In its activities, as an EU body, the Bank
> works closely with other EU institutions. The EIB finances projects that
> help directly to improve and protect the environment. When financing
> other kinds of investment, the Bank supports action that minimizes
> any adverse environmental impacts. By applying EU environmental

policies as its benchmark, the Bank's approach to safeguarding the environment is at least equivalent to international good practice, such as the "Equator Principles" (2003) ... The Bank subscribes to these principles when operating outside the EU.[139]

The EIB does not have an independent accountability mechanism that is similar or equal to those of the other financial institutions discussed above. Consequently, the EIB is often criticized by the NGO community. In January 2000 the NGO CEE Bankwatch Network launched a campaign to reform the EIB. The CEE Bankwatch policy coordinator, Jozsef Feiler, said: "The EIB is a public institution backed by public money and is supposed to support and follow EU policies, but in practice it has been allowed to decide for itself which policies to follow and which to ignore."[140] Soon afterward, members of the European Parliament asked the bank to establish an accountability mechanism similar to the other systems.[141] In 2002 the EIB asked the EU's fifteen member states,[142] which owned the bank at the time, for a substantial increase in its capital. Thirty NGOs from all over Europe asked the governments of these member states to link their replenishments to reforms, such as access to bank information, environmental standards, and more transparency in the bank's mandate for development outside the EU.

So far, the EIB has not received as much attention as, for example, the World Bank. Lawyers in the EIB's legal department are of the opinion that from a "constitutional point of view," the bank's position differs from that of the other development banks: "the Bank's remit and the basic principles governing its operations are embodied in various articles of the Treaty establishing the European Union and in it is the Bank's Statute, which is part of the treaty."[143] Thus the EIB is considered part of the EU framework and is guided by EU policies. According to the lawyers whom I consulted, the differences between the EIB and the World Bank are:

- The World Bank, for the most part, writes its own rules and policies, whereas the EIB is subject to the legislating bodies of the European Union, namely the Council of the European Union, the European Commission (drafting), and the European Parliament. People in the EU do not complain to the financers of a project but to a company or the government that has received a loan.
- European Union citizens do have direct access to the legal systems and national courts concerning these projects.
- Furthermore, these people can go to the European Court of Justice, which has direct jurisdiction over such matters.
- European Union law applies to the lenders of the EIB.
- European Union citizens, noncitizens residing in a member state, and legal persons (such as NGOs) with a registered office in a member state have the opportunity to file a complaint with the European

ombudsman,[144] who represents people affected by projects financed by the EIB and the European Development Fund (EDF).

- The European ombudsman has the right to open an inquiry into possible maladministration on his or her own initiative if he or she is of the opinion that a project financed by the EU needs an investigation (including cases outside the EU).

In May 2005 I chaired a workshop on accountability mechanisms for financial institutions during a World Bank conference in Amsterdam. The observations made above on the EIB's position concerning accountability were discussed. Luigi La Marca, of the EIB's legal department, announced the establishment of a Compliance Office at the EIB. About the mandate and the independence of the function, La Marca wrote:

Apart from the name of the newly appointed Chief Compliance Officer (CCO), Mr. Konstantin Andreopoulos, there is not much to say at this stage about its scope of activity and functioning. In particular, the issue of dealing with complaints, which I mentioned among the possible institutional alternatives to the establishment of a full Recourse Mechanism similar to those existing in other major IFIs, like the Investigation Panel of the World Bank, is not yet really decided. The complaint system at the EIB is presently substantially a two-level mechanism: (i) the possibility of filing complaints which are dealt by or under the authority of the Secretary General (SG) by virtue of the Code of Good Administrative Behavior and (ii) the possibility of recourse to the ombudsman, normally after the complaint with the SG has not given the results wished by the complainant. I do not think that the creation of the CCO will really modify this system, apart from the possibility to give the CCO the competence to deal with complaints instead of the SG. This aspect is still to be decided.[145]

When CEE Bankwatch requested information about the EIB's complaints mechanism, the response from the bank's information officer was rather similar.[146] The EIB's Compliance Office will not deal with complaints from the public; rather, the bank's complaints mechanism for the public is delineated in its Code of Good Administrative Behavior.

Nevertheless, the EIB began to change its language, which previously had always given the bank the appearance of a closed bastion in the friendly little town of Luxembourg, far away from places such as Washington, DC, where NGOs are used to demonstrating and where the media like to follow these demonstrations and actions. Nearly unnoticed, the EIB simultaneously started a revision of its Public Disclosure Policy in June 2004. Between May 2005 and January 2006 a solid process of consultation took place, including meetings with NGOs, with members of the European Parliament, and with members of the public. On 7 March 2006 the EIB published its newly drafted policy on the bank's website, followed on 12 April by the publication of the Public Disclosure Policy, as approved by the Board of Directors.[147]

A few aspects of the EIB's new disclosure policy are worth noting. With regard to transparency, the EIB states: "As an EU body, the EIB is committed to achieving the highest possible level of transparency in all its activities. The Public Disclosure Policy forms a crucial reference for implementing its transparency policy."[148] Concerning the disclosure of information, the bank points out that "The disclosure policy also operates within a framework established at an EU level covering human rights, democracy, and rule of law in countries and regions in which the Bank operates. On environmental issues it is guided by EU law and regulations, including those for assessing the impact of projects it supports, to help meet the challenges of achieving sustainable development. In its financing operations, the Bank recognizes the rights, interests and responsibilities of stakeholders to achieve sustainable outcomes."[149] And "the EIB's policy towards the formal process commonly known as 'Environmental Impact Assessment' (EIA) is summarized in its Environmental Statement (2004). The Bank requires that all projects, irrespective of location, comply with the requirements (principles and practices) of the European Union's EIA Directive (85/337, amended by 97/11 and 2003/35), in terms of the requirements for and scope and form of a formal EIA."[150] Moreover, "The Public Disclosure Policy's general principles apply to the EIB Group as a whole, which consists of the EIB and the European Investment Fund (EIF). The EIF is the Group's venture capital and small and medium sized enterprise guarantee vehicle. Specific rules on public access to EIF documents are drawn up and published separately."[151]

In the new Public Disclosure Policy,[152] substantial progress appears to have been made concerning transparency for the public, clear references to human rights and EIAs, and an appeal mechanism. Paragraph 5 states: "The Public Disclosure Policy is one of the policies and codes that have been drawn up to cover all aspects of EIB activities. Of particular relevance, when considering the Disclosure Policy, are the policies covering transparency, environmental and social issues, corporate responsibility, and governance, including those for anti-corruption and fraud. They can all be found at the EIB website." What accountability in practice means for the EIB is stated in paragraph 6: "The EIB is a body of the European Union. Its statute defines the Bank's role, scope of activities and governance structures and is a Protocol attached to the Treaty of Rome establishing the European Community. The Statute establishes the EU Member States as the EIB's shareholders. The Member States nominate members for the Bank's principal decision-making bodies: the Board of Governors, Board of Directors and the Management Committee. Through the governments of the EU Member States, the Bank is accountable to the citizens of the Union." Paragraph 7 adds: "The Bank has an extensive control and accounting structure with an independent Audit Committee appointed by and reporting directly to the Board of Governors, as well as international external auditors, and the internal audit and evaluation functions under its Inspector General. The EIB Group's Chief Compliance Officer ensures the internal observance of the Bank's statutory provisions, applicable rules, Codes of Conduct and professional standards, to prevent risks that might arise through failures by the Bank, its decision-making bodies or members of staff, in the discharge of their obligations." The latter is an internal mechanism intended to avoid risks.

However, an accountability mechanism comparable to the other MFI mechanisms was not included. Rather, under the title "Provisions for appeal," paragraph 106 notes the following options:

> In accordance with Article 195 of the EC [European Community] Treaty, EU [European Union] citizens or any natural or legal person residing or having its registered office in a EU Member State can also refer their appeal to the European Ombudsman. The Ombudsman has been set up to examine appeals about mal-administration in the activities of EU institutions and bodies and reports to the European Parliament. The actions of the Bank shall also be subject to judicial appeal before the Court of Justice of the EC in accordance with the relevant provisions of the EC Treaty, in particular Article 237.

Paragraph 107 adds:

> For cases where citizens or residents from non-EU countries wish to appeal against non-disclosure of EIB information, and whose cases are not being handled by the European ombudsman, appeal can be made to the Bank's Inspector General. In carrying out this task, the Inspector General acts independently from the Management of the Bank. His reports are sent to the independent EIB Audit Committee, at the same time as they are sent to Management.

In a footnote the following notable remark is made: "As set out in the Bank's 'Statement on Governance,' the Inspector General provides an independent recourse mechanism for investigating complaints that the European ombudsman considers to be outside his remit." The investigations will, according to an EIB official with whom I spoke, *mutatis mutandis*, follow those of the EU ombudsman.

In short, the procedures are as follows. Non-EU citizens can initially lodge a claim or request with the secretary general of the EIB in the event of problems. This first step is necessary so that an attempt can be made early in the process to solve the problems people have. The secretary general will carry out his or her own investigations. In doing this job, the secretary general and his or her staff are in no way restricted from going into the field and talking to the people. The first step is somewhat comparable to the eligibility criteria of the World Bank Inspection Panel. The Inspection Panel will not accept a claim if the requesters have not first tried to solve the problems with bank management. If the outcome of the secretary general's conclusions and the proposed actions do not satisfy the people in the project area, they can initiate a second step by lodging a claim with the European ombudsman. The ombudsman has the opportunity to do an investigation on his or her own initiative and in doing so to "by-pass" the rule that only EU citizens and residents can lodge a claim with the EU ombudsman. If the ombudsman feels that he or she cannot deal with the case (e.g., if it is outside EU law), the affected people can then take a third step by bringing their case to the EIB's inspector general. The inspector general operates independently of management and reports to the independent audit committee, whose members are appointed by and report directly to the governors of the bank. So, in effect, there exists an appeals mechanism. The difference from the accountability mechanisms of the other MFIs is in the three-step approach. Experience will show whether this process is more complicated and less result-oriented than the accountability mechanisms of the other MFIs.

During the EIB's long process of revising its Public Disclosure Policy (see above), CEE Bankwatch organized a conference on "the right to appeal," which was held on 30 November 2006. Officials from the EIB, the European Commission, the European Parliament, the European Ombudsman Office, and the World Bank, several experts from the NGO sector, and two former members of the World Bank Inspection Panel (Richard Bissell and myself) discussed the options for the EIB. The EIB officials confirmed the institution's different position due to its place within the European structure: "We do not think the EIB needs a similar mechanism such as the World Bank Inspection Panel ... The EIB is different from the World Bank and is part of the democracy of Europe, which means it operates within the EU institutional and legal framework. The Board of Governors have the lead and are the ones that can delegate since the EIB is not under the Parliament nor the Council. In a way it is like a national bank owned by a government." Moreover, the EIB has its recourse mechanism, as discussed above. Most of the EIB officials present at the conference are convinced that the EIB does better than the other MFIs. One EIB official said: "The World Bank discriminates since only two people can file a claim. With us a single person is recognized."

Another issue that was mentioned several times by NGO speakers is that the office of the European ombudsman is overloaded with work but has too little funding to take up all cases. As a consequence, if a case is accepted by the ombudsman, it can take a year before a report is published. Nevertheless, the secretary general of the European ombudsman's office said that he expected all cases received from outside the EU (except of course those deemed frivolous and those subject to future resource constraints) to be accepted by the ombudsman. Furthermore, the secretary general expressed the view that the ombudsman is willing to take a case after people have shown that they first tried, without success, to solve the problems with the EIB. The expending involvement of the ombudsman with the EIB has been welcomed by the European Parliament. In 2007 the Parliament adopted the 2006 annual report of the European ombudsman's activities, as outlined in the following paragraphs:

> 19. Warmly welcomes the declaration of the European Ombudsman of his intention to deal with the lending activities of the European Investment Bank (EIB) outside the EU using his powers of own inquiry, and notes that the Ombudsman will need to evaluate and ensure the internal capacity to deal with complaints in that regard;
> 20. Invites the Ombudsman to consider concluding a Memorandum of Understanding with the EIB on the modalities of the cooperation between the institutions as regards the exercise of the Ombudsman's powers to investigate complaints concerning instances of maladministration in the activities of the EIB, and takes the view that the EIB would be best placed to actively inform citizens affected by projects financed by the Bank of the possibility of complaining to the Ombudsman, including when these are third-country nationals resident outside the EU;[153]

As I was finalizing this book, the EIB was working on a memorandum of understanding together with the European ombudsman in order to clarify a division of tasks and roles between the EIB and the ombudsman.[154]

The differences between the EIB's mechanism and those of the other MFIs are evident. Although progress has been made at the EIB, the issue of an accessible accountability mechanism will depend on the outcomes of the first cases addressed using the recourse mechanism under the inspector general. This may never occur if the European ombudsman handles all cases and the outcomes satisfy the complainants. What is the timeframe for the procedures to be followed by people who want to lodge a claim? The recourse mechanism has not yet been used since so far no requests have reached that stage. How it will finally work can be answered only after the mechanism has been employed.

THE AARHUS CONVENTION COMPLIANCE COMMITTEE

Since May 2005 the EIB, as an institution of the European Community, has been party to the so-called Aarhus Convention.[155] The convention was adopted on 25 June 1998 in the Danish city of Aarhus, with the official title "Convention on Access to Information, Public Participation in Decision-Making and Access to Justice in Environmental Matters."[156] According to the European Commission, some of the particulars of the convention are as follows:

The Aarhus Convention establishes a number of rights of the public (individuals and their associations) with regard to the environment. The Parties to the Convention are required to make the necessary provisions so that the public authorities (at national, regional or local level) will contribute to these rights to become effective. The Convention provides for:

- the right of everyone to receive environmental information that is held by public authorities ... This can include information on the state of the environment, but also on policies or measures taken, or on the state of human health and safety where this can be affected by the state of the environment. Applicants are entitled to obtain this information within one month of the request and without having to say why they require it. In addition, public authorities are obliged, under the Convention, to actively disseminate environmental information in their possession;
- the right to participate in environmental decision-making. Arrangements are to be made by public authorities to enable the public affected and environmental non-governmental organizations to comment on, for example, proposals for projects affecting the environment, or plans and programmes relating to the environment, these comments to be taken into due account in decision making, and information to be provided on the final decisions and the reasons for it;
- the right to review procedures to challenge public decisions that have been made without respecting the two aforementioned rights or environmental law in general.[157]

Following the convention's adoption, an Aarhus clearinghouse was established. According to the United Nations Economic Commission for Europe (UNECE), the clearinghouse also contains "information relevant to the implementation of principle 10 of the Rio Declaration[158] at the global, regional and national levels around the world. The Clearinghouse supports the function of the Aarhus Convention's compliance review mechanism. It assists the Compliance Committee of the Convention with access to national implementing legislation and practices."[159] In October 2002 the first compliance committee was elected. According to the UNECE, the committee may "be triggered in four ways":

(1) a Party may make a submission about compliance by another Party, (2) a Party may make a submission concerning its own compliance (3) the secretariat may make a referral to the Committee and (4) members of the public may make communications concerning a Party's compliance with the convention. In addition, the Committee may examine compliance issues on its own initiative and make

recommendations; prepare reports on compliance with or implementation of the provisions of the Convention at the request of the
Meeting of the Parties; and monitor, assess and facilitate the implementation of and compliance with the reporting requirements under article
10, paragraph 2, of the Convention.[160]

On 27 April 2005 the Aarhus compliance committee received a "communication" – called a "request" in the case of most other accountability
mechanisms – from Alliance for the Protection of the Vlorë Bay, an
Albanian NGO. This communication concerned the Vlorë Thermal Power
Generation Project in Albania (mentioned above): "The communication
alleged that the Party concerned had failed to notify the public properly
and in a timely manner and to consult the public concerned in the decision-making on planning of an industrial park comprising, inter alia, oil
and gas pipelines, installations for the storage of petroleum, three thermal power plants and a refinery near the lagoon of Narta, on a site of
560 ha inside the protected National Park."[161] Here, the party concerned
is the Albanian government. According to the Aarhus compliance committee, the Albanian government responded as follows:

(a) The Government had not made a decision on the development of
the proposed industrial park as a whole; (b) A decision-making process
for the establishment of a thermal electric power station (TES) was
under way, but no decision on an environmental permit had been taken;
(c) The public had been provided with timely and adequate access to
information about construction of the thermal electric power station;
(d) The government had never received any request for information on
the project from the communicant; (e) The public had the possibility to
participate in the decision-making process for the TES, as three public
meetings had been organized at different stages of the process (i.e. feasibility study, scoping and environmental impact assessment), with participation of local citizens and NGOs; (f) Since the government had not
made any final decisions yet on the projects, there was nothing to
be challenged through the courts or other appeal bodies in Albania by
the communicant.[162]

The compliance committee further describes its subsequent correspondence with both the Albanian government and the "communicant." It notes
the communicant's concern "that there had been only pro forma public participation in the TES project ... The communicant further alleged that there
had been no public information or public participation with respect to the
decision-making processes concerning the proposed Albanian-Macedonia-
Bulgaria Oil (AMBO) pipeline."[163] The compliance committee goes on to
state that the government did not answer all the questions raised by the

committee and, more specifically, that "it failed to answer a number of other questions, including on public notification and participation procedures in the decision-making process for the industrial energy park."[164] The government, according to the committee, argues that it has decided only "about its location."[165] But the committee further notes that a decision on the industrial and energy park was taken by the prime minister at the time, who then instructed "various Ministries" to carry out the decision immediately.[166] Not surprisingly, the Aarhus compliance committee finally published a rather critical report about the role of the Albanian government.

But communications (mediation?) continue between the Aarhus compliance committee, the Albanian government, and the Alliance for the Protection of the Vlorë Bay. Clearly, so much more than "only" an electric power station is at stake.

Of further note with respect to this case are the Aarhus compliance committee's comments on the work of the three MFIs that, to some degree, have been involved in the project: the World Bank, the EBRD, and the EIB. According to the committee, the World Bank stated "it was not and had never been involved in the development of the industrial park project, but that it had consistently advised the Government of Albania that the development of any facility planned for such a park should be subject to an appropriate environmental assessment."[167] The communicant, we are told, reacted by stating "that even if the World Bank was not directly involved in the industrial park, it was aware of the other components that were envisaged for the industrial park as well as the intention to expand the TES."[168] Although not entirely clear from the committee's report, the same was the case for the other two MFIs: neither the EBRD nor the EIB was involved in financing the industrial park.

Having taken note of this information, the Aarhus compliance committee gives the three banks a remarkable compliment:

(a) Notes with appreciation the constructive contribution of the relevant IFIs, and in particular the World Bank and EBRD, to its process of review of compliance in connection with this communication which was very useful; (b) Is mindful of the fact that the involvement of these institutions in the TES project has probably stimulated a gradual increase in the application of the public participation and consultation procedures to the decision-making process by national authorities; (c) Also notes with appreciation the interest expressed by both the World Bank and the EBRD to support a structured approach to the implementation of the Convention in Albania.[169]

A stronger compliment for the World Bank I have never noticed before.

The head of Corporate Responsibility Policies at the EIB has confirmed the EIB's limited role in the project:

- The involvement of the EIB in this project was relatively small compared to the other IFIs;
- In 2006, we have received a complaint through our internal mechanism (Complaints Office) about this project;
- We have been invited by the Aarhus Convention committee to comment on their draft report;
- We have received the conclusions report to the attention of the Albanian authorities and inviting the IFIs involved to help;
- Like the World Bank and the EBRD, we have not yet taken any initiative in this respect;
- In every respect, and since the beginning, we have been in close contact with both the World Bank and EBRD in order to coordinate for a common position on this matter.[170]

The case in Albania is perhaps most remarkable for involving several MFIs and their accountability mechanisms as well as the rather new Aarhus compliance committee. This trend toward the involvement of more than one mechanism seems to be expanding. The independent review mechanism of the African Development Bank is involved in the so-called Bujagali Project in Uganda, along with the Inspection Panel of the World Bank. It is probably time for some harmony in rules and procedures between the mechanisms.

THE AFRICAN DEVELOPMENT BANK

The African Development Bank (AfDB) began to move toward governance reforms in 1995. In an internal document concerning the establishment of an inspection function, the bank noted: "the genesis of the proposal for the establishment of the Inspection Function lies in governance reforms that commenced in 1995 and that culminated in the adoption in 1999 of a new Vision, a Policy on Good Governance and the approval in June 2001 of a new organization structure of the services of the Bank as part of the operationalization of the Bank Group's new Vision."[171] The bank had been asked by some of its member countries to establish an inspection function and, "In response, the Legal Department prepared in 2001 a Concept Paper on the Establishment of an Inspection Committee for consideration by the Bank's Senior Management."[172]

Professor Daniel Bradlow[173] was asked by management of the AfDB to study the different accountability mechanisms in the other MFIs and to come up with draft terms of reference.[174] His study was delivered in the fall of 2003 as an internal memorandum to the bank's Board of Directors and was discussed at an informal meeting of the board on 4 December 2003. In his study Bradlow compares the different mechanisms and working procedures at the various MFIs, such as the "very expensive"[175] structure of the World Bank Inspection Panel, the earlier mechanisms of the ADB and the

IADB, and the EBRD's more "virtual panel,"[176] with its combined problem-solving and compliance review mechanism. Finally, he recommends the adoption of such an independent combined mechanism.[177]

Similar to the other MFIs, the AfDB involved interested stakeholders in the review process and published Bradlow's study, together with management's initial proposals, on the bank's website, inviting NGOs to comment on the proposed mechanism. Notably, the AfDB "wrote to five (5) regional umbrella non-governmental organizations located on the African continent notifying them of the Study, attaching hard copies of the documents posted on the Bank Group's website and inviting them to submit their comments. These regional NGOs were also requested to confirm that they would be willing to serve as lead coordinators within the areas of operation for seminars and workshops to educate local communities on the workings of the mechanism once it becomes operational."[178] The bank then found that only one regional umbrella NGO was willing "to act as a facilitator for the envisioned outreach exercise."[179] Also, very few comments were received, even though the initial period for comments was extended.[180] This was a regrettable outcome given that the AfDB's invitation demonstrated the bank's openness and readiness to work with the NGO community.

Finally, in the summer of 2004, a resolution was tabled and adopted by the Board of Governors that created an inspection function for the African Development Bank Group.[181] Article I, part A, of the resolution notes: "The CRMU [Compliance Review and Mediation Unit] has been established for the purpose of providing people adversely affected by a project financed by the Bank, the Fund, the Nigeria Trust Fund and other Special Funds administered by the Bank (collectively the 'Bank Group') with an independent mechanism through which they can request the Bank Group to comply with all its own policies and procedures." The AfDB mechanism is most similar to the proposed structure of the Inter-American Development Bank (see above). At both institutions a director with a strong mandate is responsible for the compliance review mechanism and for the mediation, or problem-solving, unit.

The involvement of this director in the two functions seems rather complicated because in executing the two tasks he or she runs the risk of a conflict of interest. After the Boards of Directors approved the establishment of the mechanism in 2004, they "referred the IRM [Independent Review Mechanism] Operating Rules and Procedures to the Committee on Operations and Development Effectiveness (CODE) to verify conformity between the Rules and the Establishment Resolution. The CODE confirmed the conformity between the IRM Rules and Procedures and the Establishment Resolution on July 2006, and the Boards of Directors thereafter approved on 28 July 2006 the IRM Operating Rules and Procedures on a no objection basis."[182] Article IV, paragraph 20, states: "If a request contains a bona fide allegation of harm arising from a Bank Group financed operation, and it appears to contain sufficient required information, the Director shall make a determination on whether the Request should either be: (i) registered for problem-solving exercise; and/or (ii) considered further for a compliance review." Then Article VI, paragraph 36, notes: "The objective of a problem-solving exercise is to restore an effective dialogue between the Requesters and any interested persons with a view to resolving the issue or issues underlying a request, without seeking to attribute blame or fault to any such party. A problem-solving exercise may be conducted only if the Request has been declared eligible in accordance with paragraph 20, but irrespective of whether a compliance review is conducted." Article IV, paragraph 43, adds: "Where at the conclusion of a problem-solving exercise, whether or not successful, the Director determines, as provided in paragraph 44 below, that a compliance review is warranted, the Director may include in the Problem-Solving Report a recommendation that the project undergo a compliance review." Finally, Article VII, paragraph 51, states: "The experts on the Panel shall each have one (1) vote and decisions of the Panel shall be taken by simple majority. The Director shall participate in all aspects of a compliance review undertaken by a Panel but shall have a vote only in the event of a deadlock in a Panel's deliberations." The latter paragraph shows clearly that the director, who has a strong mandate and decision-making powers respecting the problem-solving function, also has a crucial voice in the compliance review function. Thus, if the problem-solving function in which the director is active does not succeed, the director still has a vote in the compliance review phase. In the latter arrangement, contrary to the functioning of most other accountability mechanisms and contrary to the standard applied in most court systems, the usual involvement of independent members has been abandoned.

In the AFDB model the ruling authority resides with the director. Article IV, paragraph 19, notes: "When the CRMU receives a Request, the Director, on the basis of the information contained in the Request, shall, within fourteen (14) days of receipt of the Request, conduct a preliminary review to determine if the Request contains a *bona fide* allegation of harm arising from a Bank Group-financed operation and thereafter either register the Request, or ask for additional information or find the Request outside the CRMU's mandate."[183] And in Article IV, paragraph 25, we read: "If the Director finds that the matter is without doubt manifestly outside the CRMU's mandate, he or she shall notify the Requesters of his or her refusal to register the Request and of the reasons therefore."[184] Secondly, Article IV, paragraphs 34 and 35 describe how and when the director determines whether a request may be handled through a problem-solving exercise.[185] Subsequent paragraphs in Article IV describe what kind of problem-solving techniques the director may use, what the time frame is for a report on a problem-solving exercise, and if such an exercise is successful what types of solutions may be agreed upon by the requesters.[186] So determination of the eligibility and the problem-solving function is entirely within the mandate of the director, not within the mandate of the inspection function, as is the case with the World Bank Inspection Panel.

Article VI, paragraph 43, states that at the end of the problem-solving exercise, "whether or not successful, the Director" may determine "that a compliance review is warranted, [and] the Director may include in the Problem-Solving Report a recommendation that the project undergo a compliance review."[187] So in case a problem is not successfully resolved by the director, management, and the requesters, the request may become a subject for compliance. On his judgment, the director can also immediately recommend that a request be subjected to a compliance review rather than to a problem-solving exercise. However, Article VII, paragraph 48, explains that if the director does not recommend a compliance review when the requesters have asked for one, "the Request shall be referred to the Chairperson of the Roster who shall determine the eligibility or otherwise of the Request for compliance review within twenty-one (21) days after the Directors determination."[188] In the latter article, we find a first role for a member of the inspection function, namely the chairperson.

Article VII, paragraph 45, states: "The compliance review recommendation shall include draft Terms of Reference which shall set out the scope and time frame for the compliance review and shall provide an estimate of the budget and a description of additional resources required to complete the review and shall identify two experts from the Roster (one of whom shall chair the Panel) who shall constitute, together with the Director, a Panel to conduct the compliance review."[189] During the compilation of the report, the two members of the inspection mechanism have a vote. Article VII, paragraph 51, further notes: "The Director shall participate in all aspects of a compliance review undertaken by a Panel but shall have a vote only in the event of a deadlock in a Panel's deliberations."[190]

So the only way that the Compliance Review Panel can reach a finding independently of the view of the director is if the two panel-review experts agree.

Another difference between the AfDB's mechanism and the World Bank Inspection Panel is the option that the Compliance Review and Mediation Unit (CRMU) has to investigate a project until it is completed. Bradlow's memorandum to the Board of Directors states: "A project will be deemed to be completed 12 months after physical completion of the project or 12 months after final disbursement under the loan or grant agreement or the date of cancellation of the disbursement amount."[191] Like the ADB, the AfDB allows recourse to its mechanism after a project's physical completion, giving the mechanism in the latter case a broader mandate than that of the World Bank Inspection Panel. Moreover, the CRMU can "monitor the implementation of recommendations that it makes."[192]

During preparations to establish the AfDB, a remarkable piece of advice was offered to the board that appears to indicate an overly cautious approach arising from a concern about the possible effects on the organization of such a mechanism: "Finally, the establishment of the mechanism as proposed would not adversely affect the status, immunities and privileges of the Bank Group. The mechanism would neither perform judicial functions nor be an internal dispute settlement mechanism like the Administrative Tribunal. Rather it would be an internal administrative body whose raison d'être is to safeguard the Bank Group's immunities and privileges by making its operations more accountable to its member states and State participants."[193] There appears to be no explicit acknowledgment of the importance of making the operations accountable in such a way that the poor benefit from the process. However, there are also similarities between the AfDB's mechanism and the Inspection Panel: a minimum of two people can lodge a claim; their case can be filed by foreign representatives in exceptional circumstances; cases concerning procurement or corruption are ineligible; and last but not least, the findings and recommendations, as in the case of the World Bank, must be disclosed.

In the summer of 2005 Per Eldar Sovik was appointed director of the AfDB's mechanism. Soon after, in the autumn, the bank went ahead by starting a procedure to select three members for its roster of experts. Establishing its mechanism somewhat after most of the other multilateral financial institutions has been an advantage for the AfDB given the dialectics of progress. It is also encouraging to find that a special requirement containing the phrase "lessons learnt" is included in the description of the experts' role. This emphasis shows that the AfDB has chosen a positive approach instead of the somewhat legalistic approach seen with some of the other mechanisms.

In April 2007 the AfDB's Board of Directors appointed three experts, of whom I am one. The other two are Dr Madiodio Niasse, a Senegalese national, and Professor Daniel Bradlow, who as mentioned above, advised the bank on the terms of reference for its mechanism.

A first request arrived in the summer of 2007 concerning the Bujagali Hydropower Project/Bujagali Interconnection Project in Uganda, a project intended to develop Uganda's abundant hydrological resources as a means to produce the most inexpensive power for domestic use and export to neighbouring countries. The director declared the case eligible and recommended a compliance review to the board, which was accepted in September 2007. The World Bank Inspection Panel has received two requests concerning this same project.

THE JAPAN BANK FOR INTERNATIONAL COOPERATION

In October 2003 an interesting new mechanism, referred to as the Objection Procedures, was established by the Japan Bank for International Cooperation (JBIC) following a wide consultation procedure that included academics, industry circles, ministries of the Japanese government, and

NGOs.[194] The bank's Study Group on Environmental Guidelines began its work in October 2000 and held its last meeting on 25 July 2001. The minutes of the study group, composed of many senior experts from academic and government institutions, have been made public via the Internet.[195] According to the study group, its members spent "a considerable amount of time examining the possibility of incorporating procedures and standards established by the World Bank Group."[196] The study group realized that the operations of the JBIC are rather different from those of the World Bank, which in the early preparation stages often works with governments and provides generous support.[197]

The Objection Procedures mention the provision for a so-called "Examiner for Environmental Guidelines ... that is under direct control of the Governor and is independent of the Bank's departments responsible for individual lending or investment projects."[198] The description of the examiner's mandate and of the procedures to file a request show some similarities to the other mechanisms, such as: independence, time schedules stipulating when the mechanism must report, the ability of the examiner "freely to access the information necessary for his/her activities,"[199] and the option for the examiner to encourage dialogue between the parties concerned.[200] In addition, objections can be submitted in any official language of the recipient countries,[201] and requesters may ask that their names be kept confidential.

The difference between the JBIC's mechanism and those of the other MFIs is to be found in its reporting procedures. After finalizing his or her report, the examiner must immediately send it to the parties concerned so that they then may "submit to the Examiner their opinions on the contents of the report. The Examiner shall pay due respect to such opinions and if he/she deems that the opinions contain matters useful for the monitoring of the project in question, may transfer the opinions to the Operational Department."[202] The options that the JBIC has chosen for its examiner are in conformity with my own preference, as described above in my discussion of the model used by the Inter-American Development Bank and in chapter 6. As long as the examiner is free to decide whether the given opinions are relevant or not, his or her independence will remain. Even more important, the examiner "can make recommendations regarding measures that JBIC should take based on its findings."[203] This latter option is not (yet) part of the mandate of the World Bank Inspection Panel.

There is also a drawback inherent to the examiner's defined role. According to Ms Ikuko Matsumoto, of Friends of the Earth Japan, "Unlike the Inspection Panel, which addresses the problems of compliance, the examiner cannot address the problems of compliance with a wide range of policies and procedures, the scope of the Objections Procedure is limited to the guidelines, excluding other important policies and procedures such as [an] information disclosure policy, economic assessment of investment operations, or monitoring and evaluation."[204]

The process further includes the following: "Within one (1) month after the submission of the Examiner's report to the Governor, the Operational Department shall submit in writing to the Governor setting forth its opinions on the Examiner's report and, in the case that the Examiner concluded in the report that the guidelines have not been complied with by the Bank, measures to be taken from then on for the Bank's compliance with the Guidelines, as necessary."[205] It might be a matter of wording and the technicalities of translation, but in the case of the World Bank, management is not supposed to give an opinion on the panel's findings. Instead, management has to respond to the Inspection Panel's findings in a manner that describes proposed actions to mitigate, correct, and improve a situation that is found not to be in compliance with bank policies. Similar to the procedure at the World Bank is the provision at the JBIC that the reports of both the examiner and the Operational Department be published.

An interesting aspect of this process is the expectation that the examiner is to "take due care of the human rights and business interests of the Requester and other parties concerned, and not to behave in such a manner as to unduly injure the Requester and other parties concerned ... The examiner must listen to the opinions of the persons concerned in a well-balanced manner, and must conduct individual interviews in such a manner as not to diminish the people's trust in the Examiner's neutrality."[206] I have not found in any other policy establishing an accountability mechanism a similar reference to the sensitive nature of the working methods of a member of the mechanism. In response to my question in 2005 about how many cases have been received since the JBIC's mechanism for an objection procedure was established, the current examiner, Professor Kazuo Matsushita, stated: "fortunately, none so far."[207] As of the spring of 2007, the annual reports of the objections procedures mechanism show that so far no complaints have arrived.[208] In response to my question of why no requests have been received, Ms Naomi Kanzaki of Friends of the Earth Japan wrote: "In my view there are several reasons why no complaints were made so far. One of the reasons is that applicable projects are relatively new and not naturally limited. There are a lot of problematic projects which were ongoing before the Guidelines and Procedures were established. Another reason is that the complaint can be made only after JBIC [has] made a final decision to finance projects and indicated the results of its appraisal."[209]

5

Accountability for
the Private Financial Sector

The ever-expanding world of private-sector companies and private financial institutions is evolving. This development has become a source of concern for many. Who will control the activities of companies and the
financial sector? How will the environmental impacts of investments in major infrastructural projects be regulated? The wide-ranging impacts of
fraudulent bookkeeping and the downfall of companies – particularly
Enron, thousands of whose employees lost their jobs and pensions – has
spurred the US Congress to take action. On 23 January 2002 Congress adopted the so-called Sarbanes-Oxley Act. This Act is a strong answer to a
lack of regulation, making control of public companies possible. Today,
the Act, commonly called "Sox," is well known in law firms, in international accountancy firms, and inside the board rooms of large public companies, and US courts have already prosecuted managers for fraudulent
acts, putting some of them behind bars for years. The Sarbanes-Oxley Act
is all about accountability.[1]

Recently, these events have been followed by a serious crisis in the private-
bank sector. The crisis began in the summer of 2007, and where it will go is
not yet clear. An earlier crisis in 1974 led to the establishment of the Basel
Committee on Banking Supervision. The latest work of the committee was
the creation of Basel II (described below), which is a set of capital requirements that are more risk sensitive. Unfortunately, the implementation of
Basel II by national regulatory authorities came too late to have major impacts on the present crisis. Besides, Basel II does not contain clear requirements regarding environmental and social impacts, the major purpose of
the committee's work.

Within companies as well, one can find representative opinions of society.
People today are concerned about the stability of the financial sector and
about social and environmental changes in the world. These opinions and
concerns have also motivated some in the private sector to act. Amitai Etzioni
does not believe the traditional neoclassical assumption that people seek
only to maximize the utilities perceived as "the best means to serve their
goals" or that they decide as individuals in an era of radical individualism:

The neoclassical assumption that the market economy can be treated as a separate system, a system that is basically self-containing, and whose distinct attributes can be studied by the use of a perfect competition model, is replaced here with the assumption that the economy is a sub-system of a more encompassing society, polity, and culture. It is therefore assumed that the dynamics of the economy, including the extent to which it is competitive, cannot be studied without integrating social, political and cultural factors into one's paradigm. Moreover, social collectivities are to be viewed, not as aggregates of individuals, but as having structures of their own, structures that place individuals (and other sub-units) not according to their individual attributes, but which deeply affect their dealings with one another.[2]

So people depend on one another, and people do care. Accordingly, accountability is a universal concern today.

While in the 1980s and 1990s nongovernmental organizations (NGOs) focused attention on multilateral financial institutions (MFI), more recently their attention has begun to shift toward private-sector banks. At the same time, the private-sector companies and private banks have embraced the new trend of corporate social responsibility (CSR). According to Clive Crook, "most multinationals have a senior executive, often with a staff at his disposal, explicitly charged with developing and coordinating the CSR function."[3] Crook observes that CSR is everywhere: "There are executive education programmes in CSR, business school chairs in CSR, CSR professional organizations, CSR websites, CSR newsletters and much, much more."[4] The cry for CSR is so loud that many have started to wonder whether it is all about public relations – or, as some say, mostly cosmetic. A declaration of good intentions is no longer accepted as sufficient: there must be follow-up on the implementation of these intentions. For example, Oxfam-Novib, a Dutch NGO, created the Dutch CSR platform and stated that "Corporations are expected to do everything within their power to enable, promote and implement CSR practices throughout their chain of operation."[5]

In this chapter I first briefly describe the existing international supervision of private financial institutions by the so-called Basel Committee and mention some existing legislation related to the supervision of private banks. Subsequently, the recent history of the role of the International Finance Corporation (IFC) in the creation of environmental and social guidelines, or standards, for the private financial sector is reviewed. This is followed by a discussion of the rather new Equator Principles, a set of voluntary principles adopted by a rapidly increasing group of major private banks. I will examine and comment on the different reactions to these principles. The starting point is that private financial institutions, like the MFIs discussed in chapters 3 and 4, should be held accountable for their acts and thus should also establish an accountability mechanism.

BASEL II: SETTING REGULATIONS AND GUIDELINES

For much longer than the MFIs, private banks have been subject to non-binding regulations intended to secure their solvability. This section of the chapter first briefly describes the existing (international) process by which the Basel Committee on Banking Supervision (BCBS) sets regulations and guidelines and formulates legislation.

After the liquidation of a German bank in 1974, with cross-border jurisdictional implications, the G-10 countries[6] formed a standing committee under the auspices of the Bank for International Settlements (BIS) based in Basel,[7] called the Basel Committee on Banking Supervision.[8] The BIS and the Basel Committee are not identical. The BIS, which is the world's oldest international financial institution,[9] was established in 1930 to deal with reparation payments "imposed on Germany by the Treaty of Versailles following the First World War." From the end of the Second World War until the early 1970s, the BIS "focused on implementing and defending the Bretton Woods system."[10] The Secretariat of the Basel Committee is hosted by the BIS, but decisions are taken by the committee itself and approved by the central bank governors and heads of supervision of the G-10 countries.[11] The recommendations and set standards of the Basel Committee become binding only after being transformed into legislation by national states or, in the case of Europe, by the European Union. In the latter case, legislation must first be proposed by the European Commission and then adopted by both the European Counsel and the European Parliament.

In 1974, after the failure and liquidation of Germany's Bankhaus Herstatt and a serious disturbance in international currency and banking markets, the Basel Committee was originally established as the Committee on Banking Regulations and Supervisory Practices.[12]

About its role, the Basel Committee states:

> One important objective of the Committee's work has been to close gaps
> in international supervisory coverage in pursuit of two basic principles:
> that no foreign banking establishment should escape supervision;
> and that supervision should be adequate. In May 1983 the committee
> finalized a document entitled "Principles for the Supervision of Banks'
> Foreign Establishments," which sets down the principles for sharing su-
> pervisory responsibility for banks' foreign branches, subsidiaries, and
> joint ventures between host and parent (or home) supervisory authori-
> ties. This document is a revised version of a paper originally issued in
> 1975 that came to be known as the "Concordat."[13]

The committee further notes:

> The topic to which most of the Committee's time has been devoted
> in recent years is capital adequacy. In the early 1980s, the Committee

became concerned that the capital ratios of the main international banks were deteriorating just at the time that international risks, notably those vis-à-vis heavily-indebted countries, were growing. Backed by the Group of Ten Governors, the members of the Committee resolved to halt the erosion of capital standards in their banking systems and to work towards greater convergence in the measurement of capital adequacy. This resulted in the emergence of a broad consensus on a weighted approach to the measurement of risk, on and off the balance sheet.[14]

In July 1988 a capital-measurement system commonly referred to as the Basel Capital Accord, or Basel I, was adopted. Basel I was "limited to a rough-woven regulation of solvability requirements based on credit risks."[15] Basel II, released in June 2004,[16] is a revision of Basel I. Overtime, Basel I proved to be insufficient. Karl Cordewener, deputy secretary general of the Basel Committee, states: "The main reason for Basel II is we wanted to make capital requirements more risk-sensitive and follow banks best-practices."[17] Basel II's focus is on setting capital requirements for internationally active banks based on three pillars. The first pillar sets minimum capital requirements for credit and operational risks, the second deals with the banks' own assessments of risks and supervisory oversight, and the third treats information disclosure and market discipline.

For Basel II, three consultation rounds have been held: in June 1999, January 2001, and April 2003. Karl Cordewener remembers that during the first two rounds the issue was raised of whether Basel II should also include environmental and social risks for private banks in the risk-taking process. "We supervise banks with the focus on stability of the banking system. Our aim is always the improvement of risk management and to guarantee the risks are secured by the banks, for example when granting loans and engaging in project finance. The subject of environmental and social risks is important by itself and banks should pay due consideration. Designing a regulation with environmental or social policy purposes, however, was considered beyond our limited mandate."[18]

The Basel II document has one reference that, in the context of Cordewener's comments, is worth noticing. Paragraph 510, which treats banks that use an approach based on internal ratings, states that a collateral-management requirement should include the following:

- The types of CRE [commercial real estate] and RRE [residential real estate] collateral accepted by the bank and lending policies (advance rates) when this type of collateral is taken must be clearly documented.
- The bank must take steps to ensure that the property taken as collateral is adequately insured against damage or deterioration.
- The bank must monitor on an ongoing basis the extent of any permissible prior claims (e.g., tax) on the property.

- The bank must appropriately monitor the risk of environmental liability arising in respect of the collateral, such as the presence of toxic material on a property.

Nevertheless, the Basel Committee has no formal legislative authority. Its judgments and recommendations cannot be enforced for private banks, which is the mandate of legislative authorities such as institutions of the European Union,[19] the US Congress (House and Senate), or national parliaments. The committee formulates guidelines and recommendations that legislative authorities *can* adopt and translate into national (or European) legislation.

Implementation of Basel II

Basel II has been transformed into European legislation under the

Proposal for Directives of the European Parliament and of the Council re-casting Directive *2000/12/EC* of the European Parliament and of the Council relating to the taking-up and pursuit of the business of credit institutions and Council Directive *93/6/EEC* on the capital adequacy of investment firms and credit institutions [*COM(2004) 486* final]. By setting new capital requirement for banks and investment firms, this proposal aims to ensure the consistent application within the European Union of the new international framework for capital requirements that has been adopted by the Basel Committee on Banking Supervision ("Basel II"). It envisages replacing the existing approach by three different approaches: a simple approach, an intermediate approach and an advanced approach. Financial institutions may choose the approach that suits them best.[20]

This new EU directive, which will come into force in 2008, unfortunately does not contain anything resembling the reference to environmental risks in paragraph 510 of the Basel II document. The word "environment" cannot be found. Rather, the main subjects of the directive are the provisions for the banks' own funds (to safeguard capital requirements), solvency ratios of private financial institutions, and harmonization of the supervision of the EU's credit institutions. I asked Gerald Dillenburg, an expert of the European Commission,[21] why a provision for monitoring the risks of environmental liability was not included in the directive. He explained: "Two years ago we had a long discussion if we should include this. We finally concluded that it would be overly burdensome for banks to monitor such risks."[22] He then mentioned that the new EU directive has nothing to do with the responsible environmental behaviour of banks but shall ensure that a decrease in the value of collateral is immediately taken into account. Furthermore, he pointed out that the major task of prudential financial legislation is to protect depositors and to ensure the stability of the financial system. According to Dillenburg, the incorporation of provisions for environmental or social policy purposes would go beyond the objectives of this legislation. These issues should be dealt with elsewhere – for example, by the directorate dealing with the environment. He also said that during the negotiations neither the European Parliament nor the European Council[23] brought up this type of issue.

The implication here is that we in Europe are still not able to coherently integrate legislation from other sectors into the financial sector – such as requirements to carry out an environmental impact assessment before financing projects that might harm the environment in the project areas or harm the people living in the areas. Is coherent integration not an EU mission?

Basel II is not at all a matter of course for the US Congress, as became clear at a hearing of a House Financial Services subcommittee in the fall of 2005,

> when lawmakers from both parties gave a harsh assessment of the central banks' credibility and intentions ... Rep. Barney Frank of Massachusetts, the lead Democrat on the House Financial Services Committee, said the Fed had treated lawmakers like 'ignorant peasants' on Basel II, and vowed to stop the standard in its tracks ... The hearing provided ammunition to other federal regulators. The day after the hearing, Fed officials met with representatives of the Federal Deposit Insurance Corp., the office of the Comptroller of the Currency, and the Office of Thrift Supervision to set a timetable for implementing Basel II. All three agencies have been advocating a go-slow approach, while the Fed has been trying to keep implementation on track to parallel adoption in other countries ... House Financial Services Committee Chairman Michael G. Oxley and other panel leaders issued a press release praising the postponement.[24]

An important critique expressed by the Federal Deposit Insurance Corp. was that "the new standards would give the 20 largest banks a competitive advantage and the OCC [Office of the Comptroller of the Currency] complained that the new standard was becoming unbearably complex."[25] Even though the focus in the US debate was on the stability of the banking system, the House lost time and played "a lagging role in implementation of Basel II."[26] As chairman of the Basel Committee, the then president of the Federal Reserve Bank, William McDonough, had a leading role. Nevertheless, it took the Federal Reserve Board until November 2007 to approve Basel II, which did not take effect until 1 April 2008, long after the crisis in the banking sector had begun.

Still, Basel II's requirement that banks "must appropriately monitor the risk of environmental liability arising in respect of the collateral"[27] has been understood by some in the private banks. On environmental risks, Chris Bray, head of Environmental Risk Policy Management at Barclays, states: "Many banks like us have been integrating environmental issues into their credit risk management process for over a decade. A significant development is how this fits in with requirements related to Basel II. The sentiment proposed in the Accord clearly indicates that environmental risk issues are now positioned as mainstream business considerations for the sector."[28]

So the guidelines proposed by the Basel Committee are held in high esteem and regarded as standard-setting. Therefore, those "collateral requirements" in the Basel II document that refer to environmental liability are somewhat promising. After all, including the requirements stipulated in paragraph 510 in future legislation driven by standards of the private financial sector itself, such as the Equator Principles (see below), could make a major difference. Doing so would mark the beginning of a recognition that the private sector has to accept a certain responsibility when financing sensitive projects with negative impacts on the environment and living conditions of people in the project areas.

GUIDELINES FOR COMPLIANCE AND A COMPLIANCE FUNCTION IN THE PRIVATE FINANCIAL SECTOR

In 2005 the Basel Committee on Banking Supervision published an even more remarkable paper, entitled "Compliance and the Compliance Function in Banks." It is important to note that the Basel Committee has taken a stand on the issue of compliance and risk management. As will be clear from the following, the committee fully recognizes the impact of regulations and codes in the banking sector without specifically naming any of them. Finally, what seems the most important aspect of the paper is the committee's request that private "banks"[29] establish a *compliance function*. The proposed structure shares some quite remarkable similarities with the structure of the World Bank Inspection Panel and with the nature of the accountability mechanisms of some other multilateral financial institutions, as will become clear below. Although there is no proof, such similarities cannot be coincidental. The far-reaching effects of the step taken by the World Bank in 1993 when it created an accountability mechanism, initiated by civil society and the US Congress, are once again evident. One could of course argue that the Basel Committee's proposal merely reflects the demands of the present time, noting as well its differences from the other mechanisms, but the marked similarities remain. Under the proposed structure, the mandate of the compliance function is to a certain extent even stronger than that of the Inspection Panel. Whether the Basel Committee came to this point of view under pressure both from the G-8, which requested that financial institutions establish independent accountability mechanisms, and from the international NGO community (see below) is not explained by the committee and therefore not clear.

Comparison of the Basel Committee's Compliance Function
with the World Bank Inspection Panel

The committee calls its paper a "framework of principles."[30] The first principle mentions establishing a "permanent and effective compliance function," a point that is repeated in the fourth principle: "The bank's senior management is responsible for establishing a permanent and effective compliance function within the bank as part of the bank's compliance policy."[31] When the paper elaborates on the status and functions of the compliance function, the similarities are visible. The fifth principle, for example, stresses that the function should be independent, which is also a basic principle of the World Bank Inspection Panel and of the accountability mechanisms used by the other multilateral financial institutions. The paper subsequently notes that the compliance function "should have a formal status within the bank to give it the appropriate standing, authority and independence. This may be set out in the bank's compliance policy or in any other formal document."[32] This formal document could be compared to the World Bank's 1993 resolution establishing the Inspection Panel, in which almost the same wording is used (see appendix 1).

At the same time, the paper incorporates sound-practice guidelines intended to assist banks in designing, implementing, and operating an effective compliance function. Jaime Caruna, chairman of the Basel Committee and governor of the Bank of Spain, notes: "Compliance has emerged as a distinct branch of risk management within the banking system, and banking supervisors have recognized the need to communicate fundamental supervisory expectations in this important and sensitive area. The Committee believes that this paper will provide banks with essential tools to meet these expectations."[33]

In the paper's introduction, "compliance risk" is defined as "the risk of legal or regulatory sanctions, material financial loss, or loss to reputation a bank may suffer as a result of its failure to comply with laws, regulations, rules, related self-regulatory organisation standards, and codes of conduct applicable to its banking activities ... Compliance laws, rules and standards have various sources, including primary legislation, rules and standards issued by legislators and supervisors, market conventions, codes of practice promoted by industry associations, and internal codes of conduct applicable to the members of the bank."[34] The specific areas on which banks have to focus are described as typically including "areas such as the prevention of money laundering and terrorist financing, and may extend to tax laws that are relevant to structuring of banking products or customer advice. A bank that knowingly participates in transactions intended to be used by customers to avoid regulatory or financial reporting requirements, evade tax liabilities or facilitate illegal conduct will be exposing itself to significant compliance risk."[35]

The sixth principle mentions that the compliance function should have sufficient resources. On this point, the World Bank's 1993 resolution is silent, but it was my experience during the era of President Jim Wolfensohn that in practice the panel always got the necessary resources. The tenth principle refers to the provision that specific tasks of the compliance function "May be outsourced," but this remains "subject to oversight by the head of compliance."[36] The World Bank Inspection Panel has a budget to hire specialists when conducting investigations and missions that require answers to very specific questions. The paper also mentions that the compliance function should educate staff on compliance issues. This was also the practice during the years when I was a member of the Inspection Panel. How the compliance function is grouped is not clear. The paper states that "there should be a group compliance officer or head of compliance with overall responsibility for coordinating the management of the bank's compliance risk."[37]

Rather different is the indication that the compliance function, despite its clear and frequently mentioned independence, is expected to have a close working relationship with management: "The concept of independence does not mean that the compliance function cannot work closely with management and staff in the various business units. Indeed, a co-operative working relationship between compliance function and business units should help to identify and manage compliance risks at an early stage."[38] It is further stated that "the head of Compliance may or may not be a member of senior management. If the head of compliance is a member of senior management, he or she should not have direct business line responsibilities. If the head of compliance is not a member of senior management, he or she should have a direct reporting line to a member of senior management who does not have direct business line responsibilities."[39] The source of this proposed relation with management is probably to be found in what the committee calls a principles-based approach.

On this matter, Professor Arnold Schilder, a member of the Basel Committee and chairman of the committee's Accounting Task Force, states: "When the Basel Committee issued a first draft of this paper in October 2003, it made a conscious choice to issue a principles-based rather than a prescriptive document."[40] In contrast, the World Bank Inspection Panel, as was my experience, has a more distant relationship with management. The panel is never involved in advising management to help to identify risks. As described in chapter 3, the World Bank Inspection Panel becomes involved only when a request for an investigation arrives and is declared eligible. The follow-up process has a rather legal nature. The Basel Committee's paper and Schilder's statement show that the committee had different intentions for the role of its compliance function: a less rule-driven and more flexible mechanism.

That the committee gave its compliance function staff a close working relationship with management does not mean that it did not foresee a risk

of conflict of interest. On the contrary, the paper states: "The independence of the head of compliance and any other staff having compliance responsibilities may be undermined if they are placed in a position where
there is a real or potential conflict between their compliance responsibilities and their other responsibilities. It is the preference of the Committee
that compliance function staff performs only compliance responsibilities."[41] So the head of the compliance function can never be placed in the
position of making a judgment about its own work.

The Basel Committee makes one rather striking observation concerning
the risk of a conflict of interest: "The independence of compliance function
staff may also be undermined if their remuneration is related to the financial performance of the business line for which they exercise compliance responsibilities. However, remuneration related to the financial performance
of the banks as a whole should generally be acceptable."[42] On different
grounds, the remuneration system of the World Bank Inspection Panel has
often been criticized. Only the chair of the panel has a full-time contract.
The remuneration for the other two members of the Inspection Panel is determined by the workload created by the requests lodged with the panel.
This seems the wrong approach, as it leaves the panel open to accusations of
trying to create a request. For this reason, as was my experience, the panel
always has to be very careful when talking to potential requesters.

Another difference from the Basel Committee's compliance function is
to be found in the reporting role of the World Bank Inspection Panel. The
panel reports only and directly to the executive directors of the bank. The
Basel Committee's proposed compliance function has a "formal reporting
obligation to senior Management."[43] Nevertheless, it has the "right of direct access to the board of directors or a committee of the board."[44] This
latter provision shows that the committee recognizes the importance of enabling the compliance function to protect its independence through direct
access to the board. This access is also described in the following: "The su-
pervisor of the bank and the board of directors should be informed when
the head of compliance takes up or leaves that position and, if the head of
compliance is leaving the position, the reasons for his or her departure."[45]
After all, if the head of the compliance office is leaving the function, it
could be because he or she does not agree with the way management has
identified or ignored a risk of noncompliance.

Also different from the mandate of the Inspection Panel is that the staff
of the Basel Committee's compliance function are accorded the right "to
conduct an investigation of possible breaches of the compliance policy and
to request assistance from specialists within the bank (e.g., legal or internal
audit) or engage outside specialists to perform this task if appropriate."[46]
So instead of a more restrictive, demand-driven accountability mechanism,
such as the World Bank Inspection Panel and the compliance review mechanisms of both the Asian Development Bank and the Inter-American
Development Bank,[47] the proposed compliance function for the private

banks will have a broader mandate. It can "carry out its own initiative in all departments of the bank in which compliance risk exists."[48]

Not mentioned in the Basel Committee's paper are the risks of financing projects that harm or could harm the environment or the living conditions of people in the project areas. Basel II's reference to appropriately monitoring the risk of environmental liability is not directly included in the committee's description of risks. Nevertheless, it is implicitly included with mention of the "self-regulatory organization standards," as noted above. Without a doubt, these standards should include the so-called Equator Principles, described below.

HISTORY OF THE INTERNATIONAL FINANCE CORPORATION

Outsiders look upon the World Bank as one institution. Nevertheless, the World Bank comprises a group of five institutions.[49] Among these, a remarkable institution less known by the general public is the International Finance Corporation (IFC). Just a few years after the Bretton Woods Conference in 1944 and the creation of the World Bank and the International Monetary Fund (IMF), a former US banker, Robert Garner, together with the president of the bank at the time, Eugene R. Black, and others, wanted to create a new separate private-sector investment arm affiliated with the World Bank to support private enterprises.[50] "This new multilateral entity, at first internally termed the International Development Corporation, would be owned by governments but act like a corporation and be equally comfortable interacting with the public and private sectors. It would lend money, take equity positions and provide the technical expertise in appraising private investment proposals in developing countries as the World Bank was doing for Public sector projects."[51]

The idea was mostly supported by US officials and received formal recognition for the first time in 1951 in a document prepared by the US Development Policy Advisory Board, headed by Nelson Rockefeller. After the 1952 presidential elections support for the idea decreased, but a modified proposal was taken up again two years later. The Articles of Agreement were finally drafted by the World Bank in 1955 and adopted by thirty-one member countries. The IFC officially came into existence in the summer of 1956.[52]

A first investment of US$2 million was made in 1957 with Siemens in Brazil.[53] In 1963 IFC membership reached 75, and in 1984 it was 125, with the IFC's capital doubling that year to US$1.3 billion. In 2002 membership was 175, with a committed portfolio of US$21.6 billion (including US$6.5 billion in syndicated loans) and projects in 75 countries.[54] On the mandate of the IFC, the World Bank states:

> IFC invests in sustainable private enterprises in developing countries without accepting government guarantees. This direct lending to

business is the fundamental contrast between IFC and the World Bank: under their Articles of Agreement, IBRD [International Bank for Reconstruction and Development] and IDA [International Development Association] can lend only to the Governments of member countries. IFC was founded specifically to address this limitation in World Bank lending. IFC provides equity, long-term loans, loan guarantees, risk management products, and advisory services to its clients. It is the largest multilateral source of loan and equity financing for private sector projects in developing countries.[55]

In a half-century the IFC has obtained firm footing in its promotion of economic development through the private sector. According to the World Bank Group's own publications, the IFC "invests in sustainable private enterprises in developing countries without accepting government guarantees ... IFC seeks to reach businesses in regions and countries that otherwise would have limited access to capital."[56]

In the context of this study, the key phrases in this IFC statement are "sustainable private enterprises" and "limited access." The first phrase refers to what the bank holds as one of its basic principles. The IFC's operations should by definition be sustainable. Whether "sustainable" for the IFC is the same thing as "sustainability" for those involved in the protection of the environment is questionable. "Sustainable" could also be interpreted as "robust and economically viable." The second phrase, "limited access," is a reference to the bank's mission to fight poverty and improve living standards for people in the developing world. Thus it is understood that the IFC operates in regions with limited access to capital. Although the IFC is a partner in the World Bank Group, in principle it functions as a private bank more than any other member in the group. In this sense one can argue that the IFC has two wings. On the one hand, it is a multilateral development organization; on the other hand, it operates in the private sector. This unique position gives the IFC a special responsibility and makes it the natural leader in the globalized world of private investment and in the operations of private banks. The IFC could be the means for international civil society to gain some control over the operations of private banks in order to guarantee that these operations are conducted in accordance with international standards or, in this case, World Bank standards. Nevertheless, with its given task, the IFC finds itself in the rather difficult position of having to determine which should come first: profitability or poverty reduction?

The IFC seems to be the institution within the World Bank Group whose role is the most responsive to current economic developments. Whereas the IBRD and IDA are a heritage of the post-Second World War period, the IFC conducts itself like a player on a chessboard that knows it has to compete with others. Meanwhile, the World Bank has taken note of its own diminishing general position and influence in the world economy. Under the heading "Assessing Development Effectiveness," the bank states: "In many countries the resource flows from the World Bank – and even official development assistance (ODA) flows more broadly – are not large enough for the money alone to make a major difference relative to the scale of the challenge. ODA totalled about $54 billion in 2000. This was only one-third as much as the private foreign direct investment flowing to developing countries, which in turn made up only about one-tenth of those countries' total investment of nearly $1.5 trillion."[57]

This shift away from investments by multilateral financial institutions and toward a much bigger role for private investment was also recognized by Christopher Swann in the *Financial Times* on the occasion of the sixtieth anniversary of both the World Bank and the IMF, the two Bretton Woods institutions, in the spring of 2004: "Although the IMF and World Bank have changed considerably since 1944, they have changed less than the global economy they oversee. Not only has the distribution of world economic power shifted substantially, making the distribution of power within the institutions seem anachronistic, the financial system has been transformed. The fixed exchange rates and capital controls that formed the basis of the financial systems of the late 1940s have long since been swept away and private capital flows have grown dramatically."[58]

At the same time, a clear recognition of the reduced power of the MFIs in general is still far from an accepted reality among the general public and the governments of the member countries of the institutions. An explanation for this lack of awareness might be found in their existing political powers, which derive from an era in which states were predominantly the actors in the international arena,[59] especially after the Second World War. Both the IMF and the World Bank are still accepted worldwide by most states and governments to be leading powers. Nevertheless, at the same time, the bank is losing ground given its diminishing lending portfolio.

World Bank lending to borrowers in East Asia and the Pacific in various sectors – such as economic management of public-sector governance, financial and private-sector development, human-urban and rural development, and environmental and natural-resource management – dropped from an average of US$5.516 billion per year between 1993 and 1997 to US$2.979 billion in the year 2000 and US$1.773 billion in 2002.[60] In a decade the World Bank lost two-thirds of its portfolio to the private banks. However, one has to note that so far the World Bank's involvement has differed from that of the private banks. For the middle-income countries, lending from the private sector and from the World Bank is no longer regarded as very different. These countries normally fall under the lending programs and interest rates of the IBRD, and the applicable interest rates are almost equal to the rates of the private banks.

Over the past decade, in response to this dramatic turn of events, where the private sector seems poised to take over the World Bank's role as leading lender, the bank has begun to use its funds to back commercial lending to the private sector. Hilary French states: "The IFC, which lends directly to private enterprises, is much smaller than the Bank itself. But on average each $1 the IFC lends is attached to $5 of private investment – a ratio that greatly expends this agency's influence. Given the World Bank's growing interest in private sector lending, the IFC is expected to expand in the years ahead."[61] Still, the figures show that the IFC has likewise been confronted with a diminishing portfolio in recent years as a result of strong competition from the private-sector banks. At the beginning of the 1980s the IFC already had to compete with other multilateral banks and private banks when it came to its market share and operations in the private sector. In 1980 the IFC had a market share of 75 to 80 per cent, in 1990 this was around 30 per cent, and today it is less than 10 per cent.[62] Its biggest competition today comes from the export credit agencies.

The IFC also Under Pressure

Not safeguarded against external criticism, the IFC came under scrutiny when it financed the Pangue/Ralco Hydroelectric Project in Chile, which the IFC had undertaken in December 1992 as a stand-alone project. The project consisted of a series of dams that would flood lands of the Mapuche communities south of the BíoBío River, communities that for centuries had struggled for their territories under the power of the Chilean state.[63] On this issue, Marcos Orellana, senior attorney at the Center for International Environmental Law (CIEL), states:

> The Pangue dam was chosen to be the first because its environmental impacts were believed to likely be less intense than those that will be caused by construction of the Ralco dam. The Pangue dam is an obvious "foot in the door" for the coming dams, as its engineering design required the creation of a huge reservoir upstream that could regulate downstream flows.
>
> The IFC contended that the project provided for an environmental impact assessment and ensured maintenance of a minimal ecological flow. Given the absence of environmental regulations in Chile at the time, the standards set by the IFC assumed great importance. Confusion over applicable environmental and social standards, and inability to manage conflictual relationships with client corporations, however, revealed the IFC's lack of capacity to design and oversee implementation of environmentally sensitive projects.[64]

A broad alliance of NGOs began to criticize the IFC for its involvement in the Pangue Dam Project. They "denounced non-compliance with applicable World Bank operational directives, such as those regarding the protection of wildlands, involuntary resettlement, indigenous peoples, and assessment of cumulative impacts."[65] A request for an investigation into the social and environmental aspects was lodged with the World Bank Inspection Panel in 1995 by a Chilean organization, the Grupo de Acción del BíoBío, supported by CIEL and hundreds of other NGOs. The panel declared the request inadmissible "because the Resolution that established the Inspection Panel restricts the Panel's mandate to the review of alleged violations of operational policies and procedures related to the design, approval, or implementation of projects financed by IBRD and IDA only."[66]

As a result, President Wolfensohn decided to allow an independent expert, Dr Jay Hair, president of the International Union for the Conservation of Nature (IUCN), to review the environmental and social aspects. The result of this investigation was the release of the Hair Report on 15 July 1997, with many critical findings concerning the IFC's approach to the project. According to Orellana, the findings of the review team were kept secret by the IFC, "which claimed that privileged commercial information belonging to its clients was involved."[67] An affected company had threatened to sue the IFC if it released the report. More than a year later "a heavily edited version" of the report was made public.[68]

The IFC disagreed with Hair's methodology and conclusions: it argued that the IFC was in compliance with five out of eight World Bank policies, disagreed that the board was not fully informed, and moreover, emphasized that the IFC's involvement in the project had resulted in an environmental impact assessment, which was publicly disclosed in Chile. The IFC accepted the following findings:

- IFC should have taken a more systematic approach to the analysis of environment and social impacts in the Pangue project.
- IFC should have waited for more complete information and analysis of the downstream impacts of the dam, before making certain key decisions to move forward with financing for the project.
- IFC should have handled the indigenous peoples issues more thoroughly and, in particular, assessed indirect impacts of the project on indigenous people.[69]

The experience with the Pangue Dam had far-reaching implications for the IFC. First, the IFC started with an internal process of institutional reform and increased its staff from two to eighty people responsible for "the environmental clearance process, the clarification and drafting of applicable environmental and social standards, and an initial effort towards the mainstreaming of environmental concerns in lending operations. More significantly, the Pangue dam provided impetus for the creation of an accountability mechanism within IFC known as the Office of the Compliance/Advisor Ombudsman (CAO)."[70] The IFC also decided "to condition the issuance of further loans on the adequate resolution of all outstanding environmental and social issues."[71]

The IFC and Its Relation to Private Banks

When in 1999 German national Peter Woicke was appointed the new executive vice president of the IFC, he posed a question to the institution: "What distinguishes us from other private banks? Is it with lower prices or with a different product?"[72] The difference is most probably found in the origin and nature of the World Bank. The bank and the IFC benefited from civil society's heavy criticism of their involvement in large infrastructure projects that caused harm to the environment and thousands of people living in the project areas.[73] Most notably, this exposure to criticism gave these institutions a head start in formulating policies and procedures to ensure environmental accountability.

Woicke immediately became one of the pioneers who advocated social and environmental standards. On human rights, still a nonissue at the bank, he has said:

> Human Rights can be regarded as behavioral and institutional norms expressed as injunctions and aspirations, as well as international legal requirements. Modern businesses, as capitalism has evolved, have slowly assimilated an ever-wider set of these norms, most often those directly related to their operations, such as limits on working hours, worker safety measures, sick leave, non-discrimination requirements, and so on. In some cases, these norms have been imposed by legislation. In other cases, norms have been adopted voluntary because of idiosyncratic aspirations, societal pressures, or changing political contexts. Sometimes businesses find that they can gain an economic advantage by adopting a new norm that redefines the prevailing rules in their market ... IFC, as a development institution, has witnessed these phenomena directly. In 1998, IFC adopted a comprehensive set of environmental and social safeguards for its project finance lending operations, primarily in response to external criticism. However, by late 2000, management of the corporation had come to the determination that the safeguards could provide an opportunity for market advantage and perhaps the preferred norm for project finance among major commercial banks.[74]

The notion that social and environmental standards also have a market value arose when the IFC became involved in the Chad-Cameroon Petroleum Development and Pipeline Project.[75] At the time, Herman Mulder,[76] senior executive vice president in charge of Group Risk Management at ABN-AMRO Bank, met with Woicke.[77] Mulder was impressed by the way that the World Bank and the IFC undertook their projects and by the high standards of their policies and procedures. ABN-AMRO Bank is a partner in the Chad-Cameroon project.[78] Mulder has said: "We, private banks, should come up with the same rules on the road as IFC. It should be global, credible, and comprehensive and tested in the market: a valid global benchmark."[79] According to Suellen Lazarus, who was then a senior advisor at the IFC, Peter Woicke "recognized the growing pressure on his bank and its clients, and had been impressed with the approach that IFC developed to manage environmental and social risk in the Chad-Cameroon pipeline project. He felt that his bank needed a method for evaluating environmental and social issues in the projects that it financed, but could not do it alone. Too often when he asked questions about environmental or social issues in individual projects, the answers were not good enough."[80]

Woicke and his staff formed a small working group and decided to organize an executive workshop in October 2002 in London.[81] Representatives of a still rather small group of major private banks came to the meeting. In addition to ABN-AMRO Bank, which hosted the meeting, Citigroup and Barclays took the lead.[82] At this closed meeting the decision was taken to start designing the principles "for categorization of projects according to IFC's procedures, [to be] followed with general application of IFC's environmental and social policies and guidelines."[83]

About this meeting, Lazarus says:

The objective was to consider the potential for enhanced cooperation, leadership and convergence within the international finance community on these issues. Little did we anticipate that this ambitious goal would be realized in such short order. Senior executives responsible for project finance and risk management were invited from a small group of the world's leading international banks. Banks were invited based on their role in the project finance market and to reflect geographic diversity and a broad range of coverage of industry sectors. Those institutions that had expressed strong commitment to a sustainable agenda were also included. In the end, nine banks accepted the invitation and, together with IFC, were represented at that meeting. The discussion ... progressed quickly. It moved from reluctance to take responsibility for environmental and social risks, to recognition that they were increasingly inescapable, to agreement that the banks cannot continue to expect others to handle these issues. War stories were shared, and the banks found greater commonality than they expected in facing these issues. Not fully knowing the consequences of investments was no longer good enough.[84]

Together with the IFC, four banks – ABN-AMRO, Barclays, Citigroup, and WestLB AG – formed a core working group to design "common standards and rules for engagement, particularly in the oil and gas industry."[85] The key players in the process were Christopher Beale (global head of Project and Structured Trade Finance, Citigroup), Richard Burrett (head of Sustainable Development Business Group, ABN-AMRO), Chris Bray (head of Environmental Risk Policy Management, Barclays), and Foster Deibert (head of Sustainability Management, WestLB). The group of four banks is often called the "gang of four." Soon afterward, they concluded that they could not deal with only the oil and gas industry: "It would be seen as unfair treatment within their institutions – and by their oil and gas clients – when there were also complicated issues in other industries, including power, mining, infrastructure and agribusiness."[86] They first referred to the "London Principles," which later became known as the "Greenwich Principles" since the meeting was taking place near Greenwich.

From Greenwich to Equator

A second meeting took place, again in London, in February 2003, this time hosted by Citigroup. At this meeting the name "Greenwich Principles" was dropped. Many of those involved explained to me that Greenwich could easily be changed into "green wash" and from "green wash" into "white wash."[87] In short, a wrong connotation was anticipated. Lazarus has noted that at the second meeting a few banks dropped out of the process and others came to participate, but she does not want to say which banks dropped out.[88] Some banks present expressed the fear that they would be undermined by those that did not subscribe. At the same time, Citigroup, which was convinced of the merit of the coming principles, was rather pushy about adopting them. They expressed a willingness to sign even if no one else did.[89] I presume that a first draft must have already circulated by then since Lazarus writes that the banks present "broadly supported" the principles but also "needed to consult internally, with clients and with civil society, to see how they would be received."[90] It is worth noting that the private sector decided to listen to civil society. Underlying this was the recognition that the private sector and civil society together form the rules and regulations of the world today and by doing so bypass traditional democratically elected institutions such as national parliaments.

In May 2003 the banks met again in Düsseldorf, Germany, at the headquarters of WestLB. The draft principles were further formulated. The IFC explained its categorization process and the environmental and social policies and procedures. Another change decided upon was that the principles would apply not only to emerging market projects but also to project finance globally. The IFC's offer to provide training for management further supported the banks in their considerations. The participants finally concluded in Germany "that the IFC/World Bank industry standards would be applied to all projects throughout the world, whereas for emerging markets, where regulatory frameworks were often not well developed, IFC's safeguard policies would also be applicable."[91] The final decision had to be taken at the different private banks' headquarters. The banks also organized several consultation meetings with the NGO community. These meetings were still held regularly between the Equator banks and the NGOs when both were involved in an ongoing review.[92]

Before the official announcement from the group of banks adopting the principles, the *Financial Times* published an article on the draft principles. The article mentioned that "to date, only ABN-AMRO, Barclays, Citibank, and WestLB are understood to have committed to the Equator Principles. These banks are involved in talks to bring other financial institutions on board. Tomorrow, representatives from the banks are expected at meetings in Amsterdam with other banks, NGOs and the IFC." A remarkable figure is mentioned in the article: "In 2001, ABN-AMRO, Barclays, Citibank and WestLB arranged more than $15 billion in project finance or 17.5% of the market occupied by the 20 largest arrangers, according to data from consultancy Dealogic."[93] On 4 June 2003 the first ten banks to adopt the Equator Principles announced their decision, and the principles were introduced.

It is obvious that the four leading banks had already experienced criticism from civil society for financing sensitive projects, as had most other financial institutions around the world, which were growing increasingly alert to the risk to their reputations of participating in controversial transactions. Often these projects and the activities of the NGO community were reported in the media.

When I interviewed Herman Mulder, he explained in laudatory terms what happened at ABN-AMRO in the years before the adoption of the Equator Principles:

HM: Now let me give you a bit of background on how it all came about and the questions you're asking: "was it Brent Spar, was it Chad-Cameroon?" I would say it was none of them or both of them. And I have to go back to 1998 when we had a wake-up call from Friends of the Earth on our involvement in the Grasberg Mine in Papua New Guinea. I was the youngest senior executive vice president. In fact, I was the one in my business career who brought this project to the bank, and then the first day I was head of risk of the bank, I was confronted with this complaint. What else could the board do but say, "well, you do it yourself." So we had a meeting with NGOs. They complained about our role in this project. They had about 5,000 signatures, which they presented at the conversation. It was the first time that an NGO was invited into the building. I mean those were the old days; you ignored them.

So what do you do when you receive those who are criticizing your policy? You say, "we will study it and come back to you," which we did not within three weeks but only two months thereafter. In that second meeting with Friends of the Earth we did three things: one is we admitted guilt. In other words, we were saying: "if we would have had the same project now we would not have participated in this project." Secondly, we prepared to exit the credit because we felt we should not be associated, based on the new analysis we had.

MVP: So you listened to them?

HM: We were listening and said, "we do not want to be associated with this project anymore because things are not as they should be." And thirdly we offered, on a confidential basis, to sit down with Friends of the Earth to review future mining projects. Because we recognized that they had knowledge we did not have ... My colleagues from Jakarta went there. That was also the reason why we said this is a legacy issue, we should not do it again. At that discussion the response of Friends of the Earth was, "we accept your admission of guilt. We don't want you to exit this project because we want you to exercise your influence with the sponsor of this project, Freeport ...

MVP: Very wise of them.

HM: Absolutely, that response triggered our responsibility. So don't sell the credit. And [fourthly], Friends of the Earth was not prepared to sit down with us on a confidential basis to review further projects. That also was an interesting comment, which we can't do because we have clients. So we did exercise some pressure. There was a judge – I don't know what here name was – a former judge who was appointed on behalf of Freeport who went in into the project and came also to some critical conclusions. Freeport did a few things better, but it never was fully resolved. This was our first wake-up call. The second wake-up call was that the Dutch banks were criticized for their role in APP, the paper and pulp industry in Indonesia ...

We started drafting the mining policy, with a similar approach. And also oil and gas policy, a similar approach, starting with the draft. And I got increasingly critical comments of my colleagues that we might be walking too far ahead of the flock. The financial sector is a typical laggard because we do not have a material direct environmental footprint. Indirectly yes, but not direct. In one particular case it really became an issue. It was when we were competing with an American bank in Venezuela on an oil project. They were prepared to wave the Tokajaku clause. And my Japanese is not good enough, but the Tokajaku clause basically requires borrowers to apply and set minimal standards for environmental issues.

I am chair of the Group Risk Committee, and we were not prepared to waive that. The other US bank was. So that's where we sat. I mean we are here competing on something which should not be part of the competition. Environmental and social and ethical issues should be something which for the leading professional banks should be the same. We compete on price, we compete on clauses, but not on standards. That was the trigger for me. So I could do two things: either we were going to compromise our standards – which we didn't – or we were going to do something else. That's where the breakfast meeting with Peter Woicke came, and I said, "well, Peter, you have an issue, you have standards. I'm competing."[94]

As mentioned above, in a press release of 4 June 2003 ten banks announced their adoption of the Equator Principles. Mulder told me that from the outset the "gang of four" banks – ABN-AMRO, Barclays, Citibank, and WestLB – did not want to announce the adoption of the principles before ten private banks were also ready to do so. Finally, ten private banks – with headquarters in Western Europe, the United States, and in one case, Australia – agreed. The collective press release stated:

> Ten leading banks from seven countries today announced the adoption of the "Equator Principles," a set of guidelines developed by the banks for managing social and environmental issues related to the financing of development projects. The banks will apply the principles globally and to projects' financings in all industry sectors, including mining, oil and gas, and forestry. The banks adopting the Equator Principles today are ABN-AMRO Bank, Barclays plc, Citigroup Inc., Crédit Lyonnais, Credit Suisse Group, HVB Group, Rabobank Group, the Royal Bank of Scotland, WestLB AG, and Westpac Banking Corporation.[95] Together, these banks underwrote approximately $14,5 billion of the loans in 2002, representing approximately 30% of the project loan syndication market globally in 2002, according to Dealogic. The Equator Principles are based on the policies and guidelines of the World Bank and International Finance Corporation (IFC). The banks received extensive advice and guidance from IFC, the private-sector investment arm of the World Bank, in drafting the Equator Principles. In implementing the Equator Principles, banks currently have or will put in place internal policies and processes consistent with the principles.[96]

The first ten banks to adopt the Equator Principles independently published their own press releases.[97] Although one can find similar sentiments of satisfaction in each of these press releases, some of the banks also point out that the principles coincide with practices that they already had in place. The press release from Credit Suisse First Boston, for example, noted that it was "the first financial institution to introduce an environmental management system certified under ISO 14000 in 1997."

Bernd Schanzenbaecher, director of Sustainability Affairs for Credit Suisse Group, has said: "We first did not know if we had to join the principles. Credit Suisse was already for a long time bound under the obligation to comply with Swiss environmental legislation (regulating issues related to contaminated sites) and integrate environmental risks in its loans and credits. Subsequently, environmental risks were integrated in Credit Suisse's business globally for delivering loans and financial services for financers of large projects. Finally, we also adopted the principles since it was in accordance with our common practice."[98] The Credit Suisse website states the following about sustainability:

All businesses are interconnected with their social environment on many different levels. A company's long-term business success is dependent on its ability to gain a comprehensive understanding of its responsibilities vis-à-vis its clients, shareholders and employees, as well as society and the environment.

At Credit Suisse Group, sustainable development means achieving economic success by addressing environmental, social and commercial expectations vis-à-vis the company and by reaching decisions that achieve a fair balance between society's needs today and in the future. Based on its commitments, the Group strives to actively take account of social and environmental issues in its business activities, thus contributing to long-term business success at various levels and creating added value for the company.

Several independent rating agencies and index providers have repeatedly rated Credit Suisse Group as one of the best in its industry in terms of sustainability, and it has subsequently been included in sustainability indexes such as the FTSE4 Good Index Series, the Dow Jones Sustainability World Index, and the Dow Jones STOXX Sustainability Index.[99]

Chris Lendrum, an executive director with Barclays, said in a press release from this institution: "At Barclays we take our social and environmental responsibilities seriously. We have long been aware of the sensitivities surrounding project financing and only lend when we are satisfied that environmental impacts are being managed in accordance with stringent environmental criteria. We have been pleased to work alongside other leading banks to adopt the Equator Principles which gives us the opportunity to further formalize our commitment."[100]

Citigroup is a major private bank in the group, with 200 million customer accounts in more then 100 countries. Citigroup's press release quotes the chairman and chief executive officer of Citigroup's Global Corporate and Investment Bank, Charles Prince: "The adoption of the Equator Principles signifies a major step forward by the financial sector to establish a standardized, common framework to address the environmental and social issues that arise from development projects. We are extremely proud to be part of this voluntary, private-sector initiative and we are confident that we will see more and more banks active in project finance adopt these principles in the coming months."[101]

THE EQUATOR PRINCIPLES

What are the principles? The Equator Principles I contain nine requirements, including three exhibits, applicable to the Equator banks themselves and to their clients. The first principles were revised three years later and called the Equator Principles II; these contain ten principles and four exhibits (see below and also appendix 2).

Both sets of principles are based mainly on the World Bank's and the IFC's policies and procedures. Here are the first nine principles of Equator 1, released in June 2004.[102]

Principle 1 states: "We have categorized the risk of a project in accordance with internal guidelines based upon the environmental and social screening criteria of the IFC as described in the attachment to these Principles (Exhibit I)."

Principle 2 specifies that it is the borrower's duty to carry out the environmental assessment (EA), but this assessment will be deemed legitimate only if it is "consistent with the outcome of our categorization process and addresses to our satisfaction key environmental and social issues identified during the categorization process."

Principle 3 notes what should be addressed in the EA:

(a) assessment of the baseline environmental and social conditions,
(b) requirements under host country laws and regulations, applicable international treaties and agreements,
(c) sustainable development and use of renewable natural resources,
(d) protection of human health, cultural properties, and biodiversity, including endangered species and sensitive ecosystems,
(e) use of dangerous substances,
(f) major hazards,
(g) occupational health,
(h) fire prevention and life safety,
(i) socioeconomic impacts,
(j) land acquisition and land use,
(k) involuntary resettlement,
(l) impacts on indigenous peoples and communities,
(m) cumulative impacts of existing projects,
(n) participation of affected parties in the design, review and implementation of the project,
(o) consideration of feasible environmentally and socially preferable alternatives,
(p) efficient production, delivery and use of energy, and
(q) pollution prevention and waste minimization, pollution controls (liquid effluents and air emissions) and solid and chemical waste management.

After this impressive list of "requirements," the principle further states that the EA has to address compliance with the "applicable host country laws, regulations and permits required by the project"; refer to the minimum standards applicable under the World Bank and IFC Pollution Prevention and Abatement Policy and in the case of middle-income countries refer to the World Bank Development Indicators Database; and finally take into account the applicable IFC Safeguard Policies.[103] Principle 3 concludes with a strong statement: "In each case, the EA will have addressed, to our satisfaction, the project's overall compliance with (or justified deviations from) the respective above-referenced Guidelines and Safeguard Policies."

Principle 4 notes that for all Category A projects, and as considered appropriate for Category B projects, the borrowers or third party experts have to prepare an environmental management plan (EMP) based on conclusions of the EA that addresses mitigation, action plans, monitoring, management of risk, and schedules.

Principle 5 provides that the borrower (or third party expert) consult "in a structured and culturally appropriate way with project affected groups, including indigenous peoples and local NGOs." It also is expected that "the EA or a summary thereof, has been made available to the public for a reasonable minimum period in local language and in a culturally appropriate manner." In the case of a Category A project, the EA and the EMP "will be subject to independent expert review."

Principle 6 notes: "The borrower has covenanted to: a) comply with the EMP in the construction and operation of the project, b) provide regular reports, prepared by in-house staff or third party experts, on compliance with the EMP and c) where applicable, decommission the facilities in accordance with an agreed Decommission Plan."

Principle 7 adds: "As necessary, lenders have appointed an independent environmental expert to provide additional monitoring and reporting services."

Principle 8 explains: "In circumstances that a borrower is not in compliance with its environmental and social covenants, such that any debt financing would be in default, we will engage the borrower in its efforts to seek solutions to bring it back into compliance with its covenants."

And principle 9 stipulates: "These principles apply to projects with a total capital cost of [US]$50 million or more."

Finally, the principles also contain in an exhibit "The World Bank and IFC Specific Guidelines," which explain that as of June 2003 two sets of guidelines were to be used: first, all the environmental guidelines contained in the 1998 World Bank Pollution Prevention and Abatement Handbook (PPAH); and second, a series of environmental, health, and safety guidelines written by IFC staff but not yet in the handbook. The exhibit notes that "When completed, these new guidelines will also be included in the Pollution Prevention and Abatement Handbook."[104]

In the revised Equator Principles II of July 2006, Exhibit II (discussed below) still contains the list of issues to be addressed in the social and environmental assessment documentation (see appendix 2):

a)   assessment of the baseline social and environmental conditions
b)   consideration of feasible environmentally and socially preferable
     alternatives
c)   requirements under host country laws and regulations, applicable
     international treaties and agreements

d) protection of human rights and community health, safety and security (including risks, impacts and management of project's use of security personnel)

e) protection of cultural property and heritage

f) protection and conservation of biodiversity, including endangered species and sensitive ecosystems in modified, natural and critical habitats, and identification of legally protected areas

g) sustainable management and use of renewable natural resources (including sustainable resource management through appropriate independent certification systems)

h) use and management of dangerous substances

i) major hazards assessment and management

j) labour issues (including the four core labour standards), and occupational health and safety

k) fire prevention and life safety

l) socio-economic impacts

m) land acquisition and involuntary resettlement

n) impacts on affected communities, and disadvantaged or vulnerable groups

o) impacts on indigenous peoples, and their unique cultural systems and values

p) cumulative impacts of existing projects, the proposed project, and anticipated future projects

q) consultation and participation of affected parties in the design, review and implementation of the project

r) efficient production, delivery and use of energy

s) pollution prevention and waste minimisation, pollution controls (liquid effluents and air emissions) and solid and chemical waste management

Since June 2003 the initiative of the ten banks has been followed by sixty other banks,[105] an export credit agency, and a Canadian life insurance company. The latter self-announced new "member" of the group raises a question: who can be a member? And what if some in the group do not implement the principles as seriously as the others? Can the group exclude them? The speed of the developments might also create risks. Do the members of the entire group fully agree with each other? Do they take the same position when involved in revising the World Bank and the IFC's policies? On this point, André Abadie, of ABN-AMRO Bank, said in 2006: "At the moment we are resisting because it is very difficult for us to peek over our neighbour's fence and make sure that what they're doing is appropriate. And each bank has its own client base, its own processes and strategies. It is very difficult for us to determine whether they are applying the Equator Principles effectively. And particularly as the organization grows, this may be an argument to try and come up with an organizational structure. At the end of next year you may have fifty organizations that have adopted the Equator Principles."[106] As more banks adopt the principles, Abadie's concerns become inceasingly valid (see also chapter 8).

An Industry Approach: Determining, Assessing,
and Managing Environmental and Social Risk

The Equator Principles are adopted by commercial banks of their own volition. The principles are not binding laws but a set of voluntary guidelines for managing environmental and social issues in project finance. Nevertheless, the principles could have far-reaching effects if implemented according to the policies. The preamble of the principles explains that the banks believe that adoption of and adherence to the principles "offers significant benefits to ourselves, our borrowers and local stakeholders."[107] And the banks stress that customers who do not adhere to the principles will not be provided loans.

These far-reaching effects are also recognized by the international law firm Freshfields Bruckhaus Deringer (FBD). In a report on the principles, FBD states: "The Equator Principles are a shining beacon for responsible banking. Their impact on the financial market generally and their success in redefining banking considerations has been far greater than anyone could have predicted ... For some commentators, however, the real test for the Equator Banks lies in ensuring that the Equator Banks apply the Equator Principles fully and consistently. Some stakeholders, including nongovernmental organizations (NGOs), point to the limitations of the Equator Principles and their inconsistent interpretation and implementation by the Equator Banks."[108]

Indeed, the NGOs were skeptical in the beginning about the sincerity of the private banks' promise to make a real effort, and in part their suspicions may still remain. In FBD's report, the following comments are made on this situation: "The Equator Banks are entitled to take pride in what they have achieved in a relatively short time. The NGOs may be disappointed by the lack of visible progress made by Equator Banks, but they should recognize that for the Equator Banks to have come so far in less than two years is for these banks as a group of competitors the equivalent of travelling at light speed."[109] Yet the report goes on to say that the banks have not reached this position "entirely of their own volition,"[110] and the writer of the report, Paul Watchman, notes that an important role has been played by Equator bank chairmen and chief executives, by sovereign states and multilateral lenders, and finally, also by members of the NGO community, notably Friends of the Earth and BankTrack.[111]

Watchman shows that the NGOs are ambivalent, being caught between enthusiasm for the principles and cynicism about the real intentions of the banks adopting the principles: "As might be expected, it is not difficult to find praise for the Equator Principles from the World Bank, the IFC or the Equator Banks as, in a sense, they have ownership of the Equator

Principles, having facilitated their developments, drafted or adopted them. It is reasonable, however, to ask if there are any other groups who believe the Equator Principles have delivered and continue to deliver very real benefits, or whether there is an unacceptable degree of self-congratulation on the part of the owners."[112] Finally, Watchman notes a conflict within the NGO community itself. Some, he argues, will go on criticizing the banks "as opponents of social and environmental progress,"[113] while others have become more open, such as BankTrack, which is closely following the implementation process and reporting about developments.[114]

The financial sector's concern with the subject of sustainable finance was not a new development. As noted above, various international initiatives and codes of conduct had already been adopted by some of the private banks.[115] One remarkable undertaking, mentioned in chapter 1, is the Global Reporting Initiative (GRI), established in 1997.[116] The GRI is a joint initiative of the United Nations Environment Programme (UNEP) and the Coalition for Environmentally Responsible Economies (CERES), an American NGO. CERES was founded in 1989 and is "the largest coalition of investors, environmental and public interest organizations in North America."[117] CERES is best known for the CERES Principles, a set of ten principles covering the major environmental concerns facing companies, including energy conservation, reduction and disposal of waste, and risk reduction. Companies endorsing the Principles must commit publicly to those Principles, address issues raised by the CERES network and other stakeholders and report annually on their progress in meeting the CERES Principles."[118] The goal of the GRI is to have private companies produce a yearly sustainability report about their operations. Together with representatives of the private sector, investors, NGOs, unions, and many other groups, the GRI developed a system of procedures for how and what to report. The system has been adopted by over 1,000 major companies around the globe, some of whom have also adopted the Equator Principles. Public reporting about the sustainability of operations is crucial. The difference with the Equator Principles is that the latter are formulated in a way that makes them much more enforceable: the Equator Principles are detailed about what exactly is to be done, or not, during the entire project cycle, whereas the CERES Principles and other undertakings, such as the UNEP Finance Initiative, are formulations about how to implement many wonderful intentions.

CIVIL SOCIETY DEMANDING ACCOUNTABILITY: THE COLLEVECCHIO DECLARATION

As mentioned earlier, the NGO community had begun to shift its attention toward private banks. A total of 102 NGOs met in Collevecchio, Italy, in 2002 to discuss their position regarding the private financial sector and to come up with a common declaration.[119] The overwhelming majority of the NGOs present were based either in North America (39 in the United States and 4 in Canada)[120] or in Europe (33 in the European Union and 7 in other European countries). By the time the Collevechio Declaration on Financial Institutions was ready for publication on 27 January 2003 and published in Davos, the private banks had already begun their own initiative with the formulation of the Equator Principles.[121] About the independence of the two initiatives, Suellen Lazarus has said: "At the time Collevecchio was developed, the banks were already developing their own principles. The NGOs were very surprised by it, and it knocked them off their seats. Here were banks ready to adopt these principles and no one was making them do it."[122] On this point, Johan Frijns, coordinator of BankTrack, has commented: "This is really nonsense; we were aware of this from the beginning, and besides some banks invited us to comment on their drafts."[123] So both the private banks and NGOs were working on a proper working concept for the private financial sector in the same period.

The declaration by the 102 NGOs contains six principles and immediate steps, preceded by an explanation or the background of the document:

> [I]n the current context of globalization, financial institutions (FIs) play key roles in channelling financial flows, creating financial markets and influencing international policies in ways that are too often unaccountable to citizens, and harmful to the environment, human rights, and social equity ... FIs have played a role in irresponsibly channelling money to unethical companies, corrupt governments, and egregious projects. In the Global South, FIs' increasing role in development finance has meant that FIs bear significant responsibility for international crises, and the crushing burden of developing country debt. However, most FIs do not accept responsibility for the environmental and social harm created by their transactions, even though they may be eager to take credit for the economic development and benefits derived from their services.[124]

The declaration further states that as a result of the pressure of the Bretton Woods institutions (i.e., the World Bank and the IMF), the financial markets in the South have been privatized and liberalized, making it easier for the FIs to "unfairly benefit from their power at the expense of communities and the environment."[125] Thus the NGOs started a campaign on the accountability and responsibility of FIs aimed at getting them to "promote the restoration and protection of the environment, and promote universal human rights and social justice."[126]

The six principles of the declaration and related steps are, in brief:

1 Commitment to Sustainability: (a) FIs should measure environmental and social impacts of their portfolio; (b) should create objectives, strategies, timetables, and performance indicators to increase the sustainability profile of their portfolio; (c) should foster sustainability through a

shift of their business to proactively sustainable practices that improve environmental and social conditions, such as the reduction of the carbon footprint of their portfolios in favour of investment in renewables; (d) should make sure staff are trained and capacity is built to ensure sustainable objectives.

2 Commitment to "Do No Harm": (a) FIs should create transaction-based procedures that screen and categorize potential deals on the basis of environmental and social sensitivity; (b) should adopt internationally recognized, sector-specific, best practice standards[127] that could justify the refusal of a transaction.

3 Commitment to Responsibility: (a) FIs should bear full responsibility for the impacts of the transactions and not help to engineer country bail-out packages that aggravate the debt burden and should bear responsibility for the environmental and social costs created by their transactions; (b) FIs should recognize that the ability of countries to service external debt depends on the maintenance of social and ecological systems and should refrain from lobbying against innovative debt-relief calls.

4 Commitment to Accountability: (a) FIs can advance accountability by consulting civil society groups when creating sustainability policies, objectives, procedures, and standards and have public consultations with affected communities and respect their right to say "no" to a transaction; (b) FIs must also support regulatory efforts that increase the rights of stakeholders to have a more influential voice in the governance of FIs and their transactions.

5 Commitment to Transparency: FIs should publish annual sustainability reports according to international formats, including the sustainability profile of the portfolio, a breakdown of core business activities by sector and region, and the implementation of the FI's sustainability policies and procedures.

6 Commitment to Sustainable Markets and Governance: (a) FIs must recognize government's market frameworks and should work to make markets capable of fostering sustainability by supporting public policy as well as regulatory or market mechanisms that foster the internalization of social and environmental externalities; (b) should avoid inappropriate use of tax havens or currency speculation creating instability and should strive to make financial decisions based on long-term horizons and reward clients that do the same.[128]

The declaration can be considered a call for action or also a set of principles proposed by the NGO community, which, like the banks, is a strong and well-organized group – as the Collevechio Declaration attests. This relation between the NGO community and private banks seems to be rather new. In the past, the standard reaction of NGOs was one of distrust concerning the private banks' intentions in adopting the principles. I often heard the expression "it's just a public-relations matter for the private banks."

So the NGOs started to follow all the activities of the Equator banks. As had been the case when the NGO community was monitoring the World Bank's creation of the Inspection Panel,[129] its members were very well informed and knew how to find out what went on internally with the private banks, being aware of when the group of Equator banks met. The Collevechio Declaration was the community's first reaction and just the beginning. Soon, some of these NGOs had also undertaken the creation of BankTrack,[130] an umbrella organization comprised of an international group of well-established NGOs – such as the Bank Information Center (BIC), the World Wildlife Fund (WWF), Amigos da Terra, and Friends of the Earth – that "track" the operations of the private financial sector. To a certain extent, the rather new work of BankTrack can be compared to what the BIC did in the first place with the World Bank and also with the other multilateral financial institutions. BankTrack is based in Utrecht, the Netherlands, and the BIC is based in Washington, DC. According to Frijns, not all NGOs want to be identified just as NGOs since there are major differences between one NGO and another. BankTrack, he says, represents just fourteen NGOs.[131]

No U-Turn Allowed for Private Banks

The first document produced and widely circulated by the newly established BankTrack was "No U-Turn Allowed." In the introduction Bank-Track states:

> The EPs [Equator Principles] as a springboard: they must be the starting
> point of a much wider process, extending such principles not only to
> project finance but to all bank activities, whether they act as a financial
> advisor, underwriter, arranger, manager etc. Existing critical loopholes
> in the EPs, resulting from the use of vague and non-binding language,
> must also be addressed. Artificial thresholds such as EPs only being appli-
> cable to projects with a total capital cost of $50 million or more must be
> done away with ... In this ambitious process, good intentions alone are
> not sufficient. The EPs, as a voluntary set of principles, will be meaning-
> less unless independent monitoring and compliance mechanisms
> are put in place. Signatories cannot expect to receive much public credit
> without accountability procedures that ensure that banks practice what
> they preach on the ground. For the same public to be able to judge what
> is going on, it is crucial that EP banks are committed to transparency
> and openness in their operations.[132]

BankTrack has also come up with an additional set of demands, inspired by practical and procedural provisions, mainly focused on having the banks create a set of strict internal procedures leading to proper implementation of the Equator Principles. The organization is not yet convinced that the Equator Principles meet a high standard, so it has requested that the banks identify "existing environmental and social policies, procedures and standards and screen them for possible incompatibility with EPs commitments."[133] It has also called for new procedures: "Banks should create formal due diligence procedures for researching environmental and social risks of project finance transactions as early as possible in the project cycle."[134]

BankTrack also requests that the banks "identify personnel and create governance/accountability systems for implementing EPs. All project finance staff should be responsible for implementing the EPs, while a senior manager or team should take the lead on implementation and reporting to the Board ... Compliance with EPs and superior environmental and social performance should be fully integrated into performance evaluations and bonuses."[135] This latter demand is most likely based on the experience of NGOs with the World Bank system of incentives. At the World Bank, management is rewarded mainly on the basis of the amount and size of the loans issued, a system that has long been criticized because, under time pressure, proper environmental and social assessments could be compromised. Under the heading "Implementation and Integration," BankTrack further demands training programs for staff, mechanisms to regularly monitor borrower compliance, formal processes for addressing borrower noncompliance, and board-approved annual goals and action plans that will continually improve implementation of the Equator Principles.[136]

Regarding loan covenants, BankTrack demands more precise restrictions and rules: "Whenever possible an implementation program for specific covenants should be attached in the legal agreement. Such programs specify the steps to be taken in executing the project, those responsible for the action, and the timing or phasing of steps ... In cases of massive breach of the Environmental Management Plan or host country laws and regulations, or in cases of any substantive claim by affected or local people of socially unacceptable misbehavior, loans should be cancelled ... [and] borrowers [should] release EAs before project appraisal, not just during a 'reasonable timeframe.'"[137] The NGOs rightly note that "transparency is vital to promote accountability and demonstrate banks' good faith."[138]

Besides the obvious general information that should normally be available, BankTrack also demands that rather far-reaching information be released, such as details about "projects not financed due to lack of compliance with EPs ... Banks should describe the internal guidelines they have adopted as a result of EP commitment, and explain any deviations from the IFC environmental and social safeguard policies and/or Pollution Prevention and Abatement Handbook ... describe how implementation of EPs relates to the institution's systems of implementing general policies (e.g., anti-money laundering) and managing credit risk ... [and describe] how consultants are selected, what instructions are given to them with regards to EPs and whether these involve site visits."[139]

Whether private banks will be able to meet these latter demands, given the private nature of their transactions, is questionable.

Finally, BankTrack makes a statement concerning accountability, the main subject of this study:

> A critical shortcoming of the current EPs is the lack of independent accountability mechanisms. The EPs put most of the social and environmental responsibilities on the borrower, without any way for affected communities to have recourse to the bank in cases where bank standards are not being met or implemented. Equator Banks suggested that they could police themselves by observing in co-financing deals how lead banks suggested the due diligence, procedures, and standards required of the EPs. However, mere observation of each other is a wholly inadequate system of accountability. Banks must be accountable not only to themselves, but also to the public and those communities that are affected by their transactions. BankTrack therefore urges Equator Banks to create a joint "independent accountability mechanism" (IAM), to ensure the implementation and continuous improvement of the Equator Principles and to provide project affected communities a mechanism for recourse.[140]

BankTrack further says that besides an independent accountability mechanism, there should also be provision for a recourse mechanism: an ombudsman. It then notes that the private banks do not "need to start from scratch with their IAM. There now exists over a decade of experience with the various accountability mechanisms of the World Bank Group, the Asian and Inter-American Development Banks and several Export Credit Agencies."[141]

Since releasing its "No U-Turn Allowed" document, BankTrack has twice published anniversary assessments of the Equator Principles – in June 2004 and June 2005 – in which it ranks the Equator banks on the implementation status of the principles. The 2004 assessment stated that a year after the launch of the principles, "it is still difficult to measure how the principles are being implemented by endorsing banks, and whether they are making a difference to the environment and communities. The promise of the Equator Principles – that clients will ultimately design and implement more environmentally and socially benign projects, spurring more sustainable development – still holds some hope ... Attempts to analyze EP implementation from an institutional perspective (e.g., changes that individual banks have made in their daily operations) reveal that lack of transparency undermines the ability of the public to evaluate the EP's overall effectiveness."[142] This report again demands that the banks establish an independent accountability mechanism and that "Equator banks exclude projects which fail to meet their environmental and social standards."[143] It also criticizes those Equator banks that tried to persuade the World Bank not to give up its financing of extractive industries.[144]

The 2005 assessment states that that many Equator banks reacted to the 2004 document with the argument "that one year – or less in case they signed on later – was not enough to test Principles and invites allegations of 'Greenwash.'"[145] On project implementation, the 2005 document states:

A closer look at the disclosure efforts of the individual banks shows a mixed picture. Many of the banks that have chosen to report seem to have improved over the last year. However, the vast majority (80%) of Equator Banks is providing limited or no disclosure. Among the more transparent banks, few have risen to the higher level of reporting proposed by BankTrack and the ethical investing community ... Given the poor rates and quality of public reporting by EP banks, it is difficult to ascertain the state of EP implementation generally among the banks. The quality and extent of implementation seems to vary greatly. For example, at least four banks do not have environmental management systems designed to manage environmental/social risks.[146]

It is remarkable that, ten years after the initial pressure on the World Bank and other multilateral financial institutions to address the need for transparency, the private financial institutions are again being asked to create independent accountability mechanisms. This subject was put before the participants of my survey on accountability for the financial sector. The results are discussed in chapter 7.

Why Private Banks Adopted the Equator Principles

The creation of the Equator Principles did not escape the notice of lawyers from the very beginning. A document containing the results of a survey on the principles, published by the international law firm Freshfields Bruckhaus Deringer, reports on the history of the principles, the role of NGOs, the considerations of private banks when choosing whether to adopt the principles, and project assessment. This was the first study to treat private banks' opinions on the principles. In this document, the group that adopted the principles is called the "club." It is noted that the first group "did not want to create an elite of banks or an exclusive club, but wanted to attract 'as broad a church as possible.' Rather than setting a high barrier for entry and making sure that only banks (such as the founding four Equator Banks and other international banks such as HSBC) that are able to achieve the highest standards of social and environmental responsibility are admitted, they opted for a policy of actively encouraging participation by banks with less developed social and environmental policies and procedures."[147]

Nevertheless, the law firm examined the banks' reasons for either adopting the principles or not. According to its survey, the reasons for doing so were many: "Reputation; business as usual; high-level commitment;

stakeholders and NGO activism; protection of market share; level playing field; industry standard; virtuous circle; sustainable development and financial risk rating."[148]

The first reason, "reputation," turned out to be an important factor. "During the survey, banks and sponsors returned repeatedly to the value and importance of reputation, the need to protect a good reputation and the difficulty in regaining a good reputation, if tarnished."[149] The survey results suggest two different ways that a bank's reputation can be placed at risk: (1) as a result of its internal decision-making process regarding which projects to finance and (2) as a result of "the vulnerability of the reputation of the bank to what the bank's customer or clients do, such as what project sponsors do in areas which are out of control of the bank."[150] The difficulty that banks face when attempting to regain a good reputation is shown in a statement by Chris Lendrum, group vice chairman at Barclays, about a student boycott of Barclays during Apartheid in South Africa: "Even today we are dogged by the perceptions about South Africa."[151] Finally, it is noted that some Equator banks, contrary to what the NGOs expected, have declined to implement advisory mandates or have resigned from such mandates when sponsors have demonstrated an unwillingness to comply with the principles.[152]

On the third reason, "high-level commitment," the report notes that at several Equator banks adopting the principles was a top-down initiative.[153] This commitment from the top encourages respect for the principles among everyone in the bank who is in charge of project finance. Those staff members who do not adhere to the principles risk career limitations.

On the fifth reason, "protection of market share," the report states:

Some Equator Banks have adopted the Equator Principles in order to differentiate themselves from their competitors or to protect or increase their market share. These banks believe that, in future, an increasing number of mature sponsors will choose an Equator Bank because the increased due diligence required by the Equator Principles is likely to mean that the project will attract less adverse criticism from stakeholders (including local governments or sovereign states), [and that] political risk will be diminished ... In some cases, the sponsor does not really need to finance a project but by borrowing money from such bodies, they obtain a greater degree of protection against political risk.[154]

The researcher goes even further, noting that although "there is no hard evidence yet," signs are that "major sponsors show a preference" for the Equator banks.[155] The report mentions that "there is a growing belief among Equator Banks that a virtuous circle is beginning to develop where sponsors, aware of the stringent requirements of the Equator Principles, are bringing more robustly assessed projects to the Equator Banks."[156] In other words, the Equator Principles are beginning to show their far-reaching effects. Nevertheless, some non-Equator banks have already adopted "more rigorous social and environment assessment practices."[157] The researcher regards this development as a risk, stating that if the non-Equator banks go further with their standards, they will undermine the Equator Principles and thus "place a cancer at the very heart" of them.[158] Without a doubt, subsequent developments will have to be closely followed by the founders of the principles (see chapter 8 for my comments and recommendations).

Additional warnings are given not to be too optimistic at present. With some projects, Equator banks "become involved too late in the development of a project to influence fundamentals, such as the route of pipelines, roads or railways or the site selection of dams or airports. Where this is the case, it may be argued that the Equator Principles become window dressing or, at best, a device for dealing with political risk as the project can no longer in reality be subject to the rigours of a robust and objective social and environmental assessment in line with the requirements of the Equator Principles."[159] And similar problems are mentioned for projects that were planned before adoption of the principles.[160] In light of the need for due diligence, banks are made aware of the risks that they take when financing projects that will be underway for years: "The ability of lenders to alter the shape or direction of a project thereafter generally will be limited. Nevertheless, due diligence must be taken extremely seriously in light of the requirements of the Equator Principles and the potential lender liabilities."[161]

Reasons for Non-Equator Banks to Disengage

In contrast to the many reasons for adopting the principles, fewer reasons are mentioned for not doing so: "scepticism; necessary internal systems not in place; similar procedures already in place; increase market share; fear of contagion; and review of Safeguard Policies."[162] The researcher notes that a number of major banks did not adopt, "such as Lloyds TSB (which is widely recognized to be among those banks with the most advanced environmental credit risk assessment systems and procedures),[163] Deutsche Bank, Bank of Scotland, Société Générale and BNP Paribas (the last three are recognised as having leading project finance practices)."[164] It is then observed that the refusal of these banks to adopt the Equator Principles does not automatically mean "a lack of concern on their part about environmental or human rights issues."[165] Rather, other reasons for not adopting the principles are in play, such as a suspicion that doing so is a matter more of public relations than of accountability, skepticism "about the true value"[166] of the principles, questions about the capacity of the Equator banks to implement them, the high costs of implementation, and fears about where this all "would all end."[167] Regarding the many Japanese banks involved in the project-finance market, the researcher assumes that these banks follow the strong guidelines of the Japan Bank for International Cooperation (JBIC), but the report also questions what the Japanese banks do when the JBIC is not involved. Finally, there is a reference to a perceived NGO focus on the Equator banks, which is seen as leaving the non-Equator banks in the shadows.

With reference to the non-Equator banks, it is worth noting the exceptional position of the ASN Bank,[168] a Dutch-based bank established in May 1960 by the Dutch workers' unions and an insurance company. This bank has explicitly stated that it sees no need to adopt the principles since environmental and social investments are the core of its business. In July 2003 a spokesman of the ASN Bank, Jeroen Jansen, made the following rather remarkable public announcement:

> On the basis of a full sustainability analysis, the ASN Bank terminates, starting immediately, its investments in the European Investment Bank (EIB) and the World Bank. Our major objection is a lack of a sustainable policy at the EIB and the negative effects of World Bank projects on the environment and the local population. The existing investment in the EIB will be sold. With our decision not to invest in the EIB and the World Bank, we want to give a signal that those prominent global financial institutions absolutely do not meet the sustainable principles that financial institutions are expected to implement.[169]

The ASN Bank gives the following reasons for its decision regarding the EIB: "The ASN Bank reproaches the EIB for its lack of transparency, environmental expertise, its own environmental policy and criteria, and social indicators necessary to map impacts on the local population. The EIB does not grant inspection in their project financing and fails to control the impacts. Besides, the EIB lacks sustainable reporting and did not sign onto the United Nations Environmental Program. For a large financial institution like the EIB, we think it is incredible that they lack their own environmental policy, environmental expertise, and an assessment mechanism."[170]

About the World Bank, the ASN Bank states:

> The World Bank differs positively from the EIB concerning transparency, environmental criteria, social policies, and human rights [sic!]. Moreover, the World Bank provides more information on project financing and has at its disposal its own accountability mechanism. However, the shoe pinches when the World Bank has to put in practice its own policies and procedures. Large projects in oil and transport in Africa, Asia, and Eastern Europe cause fundamental problems with a huge scope. Unintended effects of World Bank-financed projects are corruption, environmental degradation, and forced resettlement, despite the criteria and the independent supervisory organ. The dimension of the projects reinforces the problems in an absolute manner, and because of that we rule the World Bank out for investments.[171]

In 2005 I received a background note on the ASN decision:

The WB's mission (to fight poverty) aims at promoting global sustainable development ... According to the WB's official statement, there can be no reduction in poverty without growth, and there can be no growth without private-sector-led investment, which in turn requires states and civil society to play a maximum facilitating role. According to critics, the problem with this program is the social cost of the adjustment: costs are born primarily by the most vulnerable members in society, while the wealth of the few in power increases significantly. Part of the criticism is open to interpretation or reflects a fundamental (anti-globalization) point of view. However, the examples that were analyzed show large negative social, environmental, and economic (often irreversible) effects on developing countries. These negative effects seem to be larger than the benefits. The large number of cases gives reason to believe that the negative effects are structural and not only incidental.[172]

This rather radical position cannot simply be ignored. The ASN Bank, although still a rather limited national bank, grew from 197,000 private accounts in 2003 to 318,000 in 2006.[173] Consumers are attracted by the bank's position on the Equator Principles and want to be assured that their money is invested in socially and environmentally sustainable projects. I further comment on this in chapter 8. I wonder whether the ASN Bank's decision has been noted at the headquarters of either the World Bank in Washington, DC, or the EIB in Luxembourg.

It is not only private banks that have adopted the Equator Principles. The Danish export credit agency Eksport Kredit Fonden (EKF) and the Canadian insurance and financial management company Manulife Finan-cial have also done so. In a sense, they are somewhat "strange ducks" in the group. Vinco David, of Atradius Dutch State Business, a major export credit agency,[174] says that his firm did not adopt the principles because "We insure credit risks related to export transactions. These transactions are reassured with the Dutch state. The social and environmental review of all our transactions (including project finance) meets the OECD Common Approaches.[175] We cover the banks. In case of project-finance transactions, such as major oil and gas projects, the banks adhere normally already to the Equator Principles. In our experience, we see even more stringent re-quirements in the OECD Common Approaches than in the Equator Princi-ples and adhere to these more stringent standards."[176]

Shortly afterward, a group of export credit agencies (ECAs) exchanged information with experts from the Equator Principles financial institutions (EPFIs) responsible for implementing the principles. It became clear that the standards of the banks that adopted the Equator Principles and the standards adopted by export credit agencies such as Atradius were not that different. Indeed, any differences were a matter more of language than of substance. Subsequently, the ECAs and EPFIs harmonized their standards.

However, the ECAs still tend to go further and to be more explicit in their implementation of universal standards. On 12 June 2007 the OECD Working Party on Export Credits and Credit Guarantees adopted and published the "Revised Council Recommendations on Common Approaches on the Environment and Officially Supported Export Credits."[177] Besides clear objectives – such as ensuring coherence between policies; fostering transparency, predictability, and responsibility; and preventing and/or mitigating adverse environmental impacts – and besides an extensive annex with examples of projects that should be classified as category A, the "Common Approaches" document "demands" compliance not just with the IFC standards but also with the Equator Principles. Paragraph 5 of "Annex III: Reporting Template for Category A and Category B Projects" states:

Environmental Standards/benchmarks applied:
i)   Compliance with Host Country Standards
ii) International Standards against which the project was benchmarked

- World Bank Safeguard Policies
- IFC Performance Standards
- Regional Development Bank [e.g., ADB, AfDB]
- Standards of the European Union
- Other internationally recognised sector-specific or issue-specific standards that are not addressed by the World Bank Group [e.g., ILO standards].

So the ECAs adopted a broader variety of standards than the EPFIs.

According to the report published on the Equator Principles by the international law firm Freshfields Bruckhaus Deringer, the IFC has "the key to future success of the Equator Principles."[178] As mentioned before, during the writing of this report, the IFC revised its safeguard policies (already renamed "Performance Standards") through a consultation process with the Equator banks and the NGO community.[179] The report also refers to a fear on the part of non-Equator banks, Equator banks, and NGOs that the new standards may be "vague, aspirational" and end up "altering the Equator Principles accordingly."[180] There is also an expressed fear that the new standards could give some Equator banks reason to withdraw from the principles or to "implement ... at different levels, thus undermining the object of a level playing field."[181] The same fear can be heard in the NGO community.[182] However, the report states that the fears of some have probably been superseded since four banks adopted the principles in the first half of 2005.[183] Since this study does not discuss the different policies, procedures, and revision processes of the institutions, except their human rights policies, I do not further elaborate on these matters.

On the scope of the Equator Principles, the report by Freshfields Bruckhaus Deringer refers to criticisms expressed mainly by the NGO community, namely the restriction of the Equator Principles to project finance and the US$50 million threshold. Concerning the first restriction, the report explains why project finance was chosen, noting that repayments depend on good project performance and that banks therefore have more enforcement powers with the loan documentation (including loan covenants) than with other types of lending transactions.[184] The report then notes that some of the Equator banks "have adopted an 'Equator-Lite' approach to other forms of lending or have applied policies which are more stringent than the Equator Principles to some activities."[185] Some other Equator banks, such as J.P. Morgan Chase, have gone even further than the principles by "adopting an environmental policy which incorporates an environmental management system that includes planning, training, implementation, measurement, reporting and review, and that will apply to new business and existing business that comes up for renewal or extension after 1 September 2005."[186] Besides the latter argument, other arguments are mentioned, notably that "the limitation was seen by a number of Equator Banks as a milestone rather than a final destination."[187]

The second limitation, the US$50 million threshold, seems to have created more discussion among the banks. Some banks expressed fear that asking their borrowers to fulfil the exercise of implementing all the Equator Principles (policies and procedures) for projects starting at $10 million, instead of at the higher $50 million threshold, would put a disproportionate burden on those financing the smaller projects. In other cases, such as that of ABN-AMRO Bank, the threshold was dropped "from its mining policy on the basis that it was difficult to justify this restriction to NGOs (amongst others)."[188] The report's researchers are rather outspoken on the $50 million threshold, noting: "It could be argued that, if the Equator Banks do not want to form part of the bottom end of the project finance market, they should either formally withdraw from it or do away with the financial threshold to remove the risk of potential social and environmental abuses."[189] In November 2005, after the report was published and presented at a meeting of the UNEP Finance Initiative in New York, the Equator banks decided to drop the $50 million threshold and to bring the matter to the respective authorities in the Equator banks for a final decision.[190]

THE PRINCIPLES: SOFT LAW OR HARD LAW?

Since the principles are entirely voluntary and participating lenders do not have to sign onto the principles, a violation of any of the Equator Principles would not raise any question of liability unless the substantial content of a violated principle was similar to that of local laws. The Equator Principles primarily provide an internal framework for a commercial bank to conduct its business. At least, this is the view often expressed by officials of the banks adopting the principles. Whether the apparent voluntary basis could change in the future remains to be seen. After all, accepting the principles as soft law is only one step away from accepting them as hard law. But this step is not yet in sight. Not yet.

Judge Christopher Weeramantry, a former vice president of the International Court of Justice, wrote the foreword to a recent publication reflecting the work of the Centre for International Sustainable Development Law (CISDL). Weeramantry describes briefly how soft law generally changes into hard law and comments on the actual situation regarding sustainable development laws:

> Sustainable development is one of the most vibrant current topics in the development of domestic and international law. It is also one of the least developed topics in international law, legal jurisprudence and scholarship ... There is a belief on the part of many that the concept of sustainable development is simply "soft" law. Some may say that this concept is only aspirational. However, I believe that sustainable development is a substantive area of the law in a very real sense. Courts and countries must endeavour to administer and implement sustainable development law, just as is done with other "hard" and established rules ... International law arises initially from the realm of aspirations. All of its principles are formulations of aspirations, gradually hardened into concrete law. For instance, the Universal Declaration of Human Rights began with the formulation of a series of aspirations. But as time advanced, these aspirations became firmer, crystallized, and became part of accepted international law. These were infused into domestic law, becoming hard law subject to judicial settlement and enforcement.[191]

Almost the same thing is stated by Edith Brown-Weiss,[192] who also comments on the increasingly powerful role of civil society in the international system:

> The negotiation of and compliance with both binding and nonbinding legal instruments takes place in an international system that is rapidly changing. These changes have important implications for international law ... The emerging international system consists of networks of states, international organizations, nonstate actors and millions of individuals. While sovereign states continue to be central actors, they have decreasing freedom to act unilaterally. Nonstate actors are performing increasingly complex tasks that formerly might have been the exclusive prerogative of states ... For purpose of "soft law" the most important characteristic of the merging systems is that there are many new relevant international, national, and local actors in addition to states. The 1997/98 Yearbook of International Organizations recorded 6,115 intergovernmental organizations and 40,306 nongovernmental organizations, for

a total of 46,421 international organizations. There are also other relevant actors: multinational corporations, subunits of national governments, ad hoc transnational associations, ethnic minorities, and illicit enterprises. The new transnational elites are interested in securing particular results and may have extensive resources to devote to the tasks.[193]

Yet the international community is still at the beginning of recognizing a legal basis underlying business principles and codes of conduct, says Carolyn Deere in the CISDL publication:

> First, the legal community has much work to do, to systematically incorporate the root causes of natural resource degradation into international legal research. Economic policies and dynamics are key drivers impacting both the pace of natural resource use and the effectiveness of laws. The world's macro-economic policies – on trade, investment, exchange rate, interest rates, developing country debt – have a critical influence on prices and incentives for natural resources ... Where countries find themselves under intense pressure for debt servicing, the urge to generate foreign exchange through natural resource extraction drives overexploitation ... Finally, many laws reinforce rather than address the disconnection between economic, social and environmental dynamics and laws relevant to sustainable development ... An integrated approach is needed, which actually considers and responds to intersecting issues.[194]

Deere also reminds the reader of the Johannesburg Plan of Implementation,[195] which asks the financial sector to incorporate sustainable development into its decision-making processes. Deere notes that the legal community does not have to wait in order "to fill vital gaps of analyses and action." She mentions diverse areas, asking: how can we "improve the effectiveness and feasibility of initiatives to hold companies (from the North and the South) legally liable, including in their home countries and abroad, for investment decisions and natural resources? – How can legal principles and guidelines be used to regulate the role of multinational corporations in international treaty-making processes with respect to the management and use of natural resources? – What are the options for an improved international regulatory framework for corporations?"[196]

Although the international community emphasizes the need for private banks to accept liability for the projects they finance, this requirement has not yet been accepted by the banks adopting the Equator Principles. The disclaimer of liability is recorded in the principles themselves. Stephen Kass and Jean McCarroll note: "The Equator Principles expressly declare that they 'do not create any rights in, or liability to, any person, public or private.' Thus, although borrowers will be bound by the environmental and social covenants that lenders put into the loan documents for covered projects, lenders themselves are not contractually bound to adhere to the principles or to enforce them against their borrowers in any meaningful fashion."[197] Kass and McCarroll thereupon make a remarkable observation. They note that according to the principles, a project has to be categorized as an A, B, or C. As mentioned above, a project is categorized as an A if it is likely to have "significant adverse social or environmental impacts that are diverse, irreversible or unprecedented."[198] Then they state that categorizing a project as a C "is the functional equivalent of issuing a 'finding of no significant impact' under the National Environmental Policy Act or a 'negative declaration' under the New York State Environmental Quality Review Act and, while U.S. and New York State laws permit affected groups to challenge in court the adequacy of the record on which such a declaration is based, there is no parallel right under the Equator Principles. Similarly, while affected groups may comment publicly on an assessment or a management plan, there is no legal right under the Equator Principles to challenge an assessment or a management plan that is perfunctory or otherwise deficient."[199]

Kass and McCarroll also comment on the beauty and the weakness of the principles at the same time: "The Equator Principles allow for an independent environmental expert to provide ongoing monitoring of a project where appropriate, but do not mandate it. In addition, although the principles require the environmental assessment to be made public, there is no similar requirement for the management plan or for continued public disclosures regarding the project's compliance."[200] They continue with the example of the Baku-Tbilisi-Ceyhan (BTC) pipeline project,[201] which is opposed by many NGOs, without necessarily endorsing the criticism of the NGO community: "Whatever one thinks of the merits of these contentions, the BTC project is a useful case study in how the Equator Principles have worked in practice. It may also offer some guidance as to their application in the future in the related issues of enforcement, public accountability and transparency ... the Equator Principles are voluntary ... any obligation with respect to any institution or entity, public or private, is specifically disclaimed. The BTC project has not given the world any reason to think that this will change in the near future."[202]

Finally, Kass and McCarroll offer a rather remarkable observation by unravelling the obligations of the different stakeholders in the process and the avenues for enforcement: "The documents underlying the BTC project, however, do include the environmental covenants that the Equator Principles require, and these covenants are thus binding obligations of the energy companies promoting the project, enforceable by the lending banks if not by others."[203] This comment is rather striking and, if correct, perhaps the beginnings of a description of how to enforce the principles. The comment reminds me of a note I received from Maurizio Ragazzi, of the legal department at the World Bank, quoting Oscar Schachter, one of the masters of international law: "Law is eminently a practical subject and its practitioners generally have little interest in theory. However, a purely technocratic approach to international law has its perils, even for the practitioner. In a non-hierarchical system, lacking a supreme authority, a claim of legal force ultimately rests on the underlying postulates of the system."

The report on the Equator Principles by Freshfields Bruckhaus Deringer also makes several remarkable references to the liability of private banks involved in projects with serious problems such as pollution or contamination:

> Banks should consider whether they wish to be in the position of having the right to force the borrower to remedy pollution or contamination. If banks do wish to have such a right and fail to exercise it, then potential liability for 'knowingly permitting' could arise. The more information that banks require or possess about pollution, contamination, environmental harm or damage, the greater their potential exposure to liability for knowingly permitting, where they have a right and not necessarily a duty to act but fail to do so ... There may also be similar or analogous liability triggers, such as shadow directorship, principal/agency relationships, complicity in the acts or omissions leading to the pollution or failure to act to protect against or prevent pollution or complicity in human rights abuses.[204]

After these alarming messages, the report softens its position somewhat with the remark: "There are a number of general reasons why banks are not usually held liable for knowingly permitting pollution or human rights abuses."[205]

Nevertheless, twenty-five pages later, under the subheading "Lender Liability," the report is even more outspoken on liability:

> Even outside the realm of international law, taking all of the potential liability difficulties together, it may be that the Equator Principles bring banks and their officers and directors within categories of legal liability, including criminal liability. This is because they receive information regarding environmental performance or legal non-compliance as part of the ongoing monitoring of the contribution or operations of a project required by the Equator Principles. Therefore, conditions precedent where a bank may be seen as "signing off" that a standard reached is acceptable or covenants in loan documentation and management or the monitoring of documentation need to be carefully handled by the bank in order to guard against such risks.[206]

The following example of a risk is noteworthy. In the *Economist*, a journalist described the dramatic illegal logging in Indonesia using data from the World Food and Agriculture Organization (FAO) and the World Bank. Indonesia is losing 2 million hectares of forest a year, and in the past fifteen years one-quarter of its total forest cover has disappeared. Only around one-third of this loss is estimated to be from legal logging. Legal logging brings in an income from royalties of US\$6.5 billion, so it is clear that Indonesia loses enormously from illegal logging. The money generated from unlawful forestry creates an illegal world in which the low-paid judges and police, who should exercise control, can become corrupt. Moreover, when those involved deposit black money earned in the illegal business, private banks play a role. Accepting money derived from illegal activities is a risk: "Under 'know your customer' rules now in force in America and other jurisdictions, banks can be prosecuted if they do not make a reasonable effort to establish the uses and source of the funds they handle. Institutions that provide letters of credit for the export of illegal logs, for example, or finance palm plantations on illegally cleared land, might find themselves liable to prosecution."[207]

Hilary French presents commercial banks in a much more positive light concerning the enforcement of borrowers' compliance with environmental requirements: "Commercial banks, for instance, require exhaustive studies of possible risks before making loans, a process known as 'due diligence.' Increasingly, banks are viewing environmental issues as an important consideration in this process ... In the wake of recent U.S. court cases, they worry that a hazardous waste dump will be discovered on a property that they lent money for, and that they will be held liable. They also fear that violations of environmental laws will lead to large financial penalties that will undermine a borrower's creditworthiness."[208] French further refers to Bradford Gentry of Yale University, who has expressed the view that the international commercial banks "are very effective enforcers of local and international environmental requirements"[209] when they want to be.

Some argue that transforming the Equator Principles into law will finally kill the intentions of the principles. Hans Ludo van Mierlo, chief of Public Affairs at the Dutch Banking Association, says:

> Companies that are already convinced (mission, structure, and culture) to adhere to sustainable policies and consider the consequences of their acts for people, planet, and profit, have the lead ... In dialogue with other precocious stakeholders they will create guidelines. By doing so, they create for themselves and a small group of fellow supporters a super class. This self-declared super status is at the same time a public promise that can work positively both internally in the culture and externally with its image and selection of clients. By changing the norm of this super class into a declaration of 'generally binding,' all élan [fervour] of a process of further investments into sustainability is taken from it. No longer will there be a premium on idealism and the courage to carefully open up new horizons. No bonus in the form of personal satisfaction, a better image for the company, and an extra for clients that can be guided along the road of sustainability. Legislation and a declaration of generally binding will take away the motor from

growing maturity. Everybody will immediately go back to the lowest level obliged: end of creativity, vitality, and progress.[210]

Whether by adopting the principles the banks have opened a "Pandora's box" remains in question. There seems to be no option for return.

The First Equator Principles Compliance Complaint

On 9 December 2005 the Equator bank ING received a first compliance complaint regarding its consideration of a loan for pulp and paper production projects in Uruguay.[211] The projects are located "on the River Uruguay forming the natural waterway border between Argentina and Uruguay ... and involve nearly US$2 billion of foreign direct investment (FDI), the largest single FDI in Uruguayan history ... The industry will produce 1.5 million tons of pulp, utilizing 4 million tons of wood per year ... The plants are expected to employ 3000 workers during construction and 300 low-paying long-term wage workers in a region that is extremely rich in natural resources and heavily reliant on tourism and fisheries for local livelihoods."[212] The complaint, issued by the Center for Human Rights and Environment (CEDHA) in Argentina, was initially lodged with the International Finance Corporation, which had been asked to invest in the project, with the project sponsors, Botnia (Finland) and ENCE (Spain), and finally with ING.

CEDHA represents "nearly 40.000 affected stakeholders, including local. communities and civil society organizations in both Uruguay and Argentina."[213] In the complaint, CEDHA notes that the Government of Uruguay has supported eucalyptus tree plantations for the European pulp and paper industry "for over a decade."[214] The complaint further states that "The decision to transfer processing technology from Europe to Uruguay coincides with tightening of European legislation and phasing out second-rate technology by 2007."[215]

The complaint explains that in the spring of 2005, shortly before the project was presented to the executive directors of the World Bank, "strong opposition" was expressed "largely from stakeholder communities in Argentina who were ignored in the consultation process and then proceeded to file the complaint to the CAO [compliance advisor ombudsman]."[216] According to the requesters, the complaint lodged with the IFC ombudsman is based on violations of the IFC's operational policies (OPs) for projects on international waterways, for environmental assessment, and for disclosure of information. It is noted that in a rather critical report the CAO expressed "serious concern for the rights and expected impacts on local stakeholders which were not properly consulted, and explicitly recognizes not only the deficient nature of the Environmental Impact Assessment as well as the 'questionable' nature of IFC's due diligence in complying with policy, but also the legitimate and coherent position of the claimants in the case."[217]

The CAO's preliminary assessment report has been well received by the complainants, who state that it "transmits to the IFC the same concerns expressed by local community stakeholder groups both in Uruguay and Argentina."[218] By contrast, there seems to be (so far) no trust in a new stakeholder consultation process launched by the IFC. In the meantime, "numerous other legal recourse mechanisms are being considered or have been already utilized by stakeholders to seek redress."[219] CEDHA notes that the Argentine government "threatened Uruguay that it would file a complaint to the International Court of Justice in the Hague (the dispute resolution mechanism established by the Rio Uruguay Treaty for violations of the treaty), if adequate social and environmental assessments of impacts to Argentine stakeholders were not considered (as mandated by the treaty), and if Uruguay did not seek explicit approval of the projects by Argentina."[220] The complainants further examine other legal options. As a result of the complaint process, further consideration of the project by the board of the World Bank was suspended "until the CAO finishes its audit, and until concerns over the expected accumulative social and environmental impacts, as well as impacts to the local tourist industry in Argentina and Uruguay, are thoroughly considered and mitigated."[221] The requesters showed how sensitive the project was in terms of its cross-border political implications.

Finally, with references to ING's "Moral, ethical and professional obligation to uphold its commitments to the Equator Principles," CEDHA notes "enormous risks with ING involvement in these projects in terms of legal process."[222] ING is asked "to cease any and all considerations of financing to Botnia and/or ENCE initiating all and any necessary investigations, considerations and assessments of the violations presented."[223] According to CEDHA, the projects violate the following principles:

- Principle 1: "The corresponding environmental and social screening and assessment criteria mandated by IFC categorization of the project as Category A is clearly deficient."[224]
- Principle 2: "The EIA [environmental impact assessment] is not consistent with the outcome of the Equator Principles' categorization process and does not address the most sensitive social and environmental concerns expressed by stakeholders."[225]
- Principle 3: "CAO has identified many deficiencies within the EA [environmental assessment] reports, and found that many subjects are not properly addressed."[226]
- Principle 4: "The borrowers have not prepared an Environmental Management Plan (EMP), and thus have not addressed issues concerning mitigation, action plans, monitoring, management of risk and schedules."[227]
- Principle 5: "During the EA process, no consultation occurred between the proponents and directly affected community and particularly Argentine stakeholders, as well as deficient and inadequate consultation with Uruguayan stakeholders ... Currently a cumulative impact

assessment (CIS) is being conducted by the same illegitimate and discredited consulting group, while an ill-devised stakeholder engagement is generating great resistance and concern amongst local stakeholders."[228]

What is clear from the complaint is that the NGO community is exerting pressure on the Equator banks to adhere to the principles. According to Jorge Daniel Taillant of CEDHA, ING announced that it would not finance the pulp and paper mills if Argentina did not agree to invest.[229] According to a press release issued by BankTrack on 13 April 2006: "The ING Group announced in an April 12 letter that its participation in the 1.7 billion USD controversial paper mill project of Finnish company Botnia in Uruguay 'is no longer under consideration.'"[230] The NGO community had scored a major triumph. Nevertheless, Uruguay went ahead with implementation of the project, which started operations in November 2007. As a result, tensions between Argentina and Uruguay have increased, and even the king of Spain failed in his attempt to mediate the conflict. Ever since, heavy protest has resounded.[231]

In January 2006 BankTrack published a study, together with the World Wildlife Fund (WWF), that reports "a growing commitment to sustainable banking within the international banking sector. However, the study also highlights the need for the sector to adopt more transparent financing policies in order to advance sustainability while reducing exposure to risk."[232] The study, entitled "Shaping the Future of Sustainable Finance: Moving the Banking Sector from Promises to Performance," ranks "the financing policies of 39 international banks across 13 issue areas, from climate change to human rights. The study also benchmarked the banks' policies against international norms, and found that banks are failing to uphold environmental and social standards developed by UN agencies and other international bodies"[233]

BankTrack and the WWF developed a scoring system for evaluating the banks' policies. Equator banks could earn points on the policies that apply to the banking sector. A zero is given when there is "No publicly available policy addressing the subject." A one is earned for a "Vaguely worded or 'inspirational' policy with no clear commitments." A two is earned if there are "Some clear commitments, but no part of the policy meets relevant international standards." A three is given if "Some parts of the policy meet international standards, but other parts are either absent, vague or below relevant international standards." And finally, a four can be earned if "all, or nearly all, of the policy meets or is in line with relevant international standards."[234] BankTrack and the WWF then created a "grade conversion scale." The "average numerical grades can be translated into a letter grade according to the following scale: 0.00–0.50 E, 0.51 to 0.75 D-, 0.76 to 1.25 D, 1.26 to 1.50 D+, 1.51 to 1.75 C-, 1.76 to 2.25 C, 2.26 to 2.50 C+, 2.51 to 2.75 B-, 2.76 to 3.25 B, 3.26 to 3.50 B+, 3.51 to 3.75 A-, 3.76 to 4.00 A."[235] According to the study, only two of the thirty-nine Equator banks that the

organizations ranked earned a D+: ABN-AMRO Bank and HSBC Group. All
the other banks scored lower. The two organizations note that implementation of the policies was impossible to assess since "little information is available about their [the banks'] systems or practices for implementations."[236]

Equator Principles II

The Equator Principles (EPs) were developed in the spring of 2003. Three
years later, the Equator banks met to discuss the revision of the principles.
According to the banks, recent developments in the project-finance industry
had triggered the need for a revision: "The revisions to the existing EPs
are being undertaken to 1) reflect implementation learning from the past
2½) years, 2) incorporate comments from various stakeholders received
during this period, and 3) ensure incorporation of, and consistency with,
the IFC Performance Standards. IFC's Board approved the IFC Performance
Standards, which take the place of the previous IFC Safeguard Policies, on
February 21, 2006."[237]

Unlike the original principles, the Equator Principles II are applicable to
all new project financings with total capital costs of over US$10 million (pre-
viously over US$50 million), making them applicable to even more projects.
Also, it is noted that the Equator banks are committed to making their clients aware of the Equator Principles. This new statement implies that the
Equator banks must partly take responsibility for ensuring that the principles are applied during projects, instead of primarily screening potential
projects in order to determine whether they are Equator Principle-proof.

Another major change is the introduction of a social and environmental
assessment (SEA) mechanism, whereas previously this was called an environmental assessment. This change can possibly be attributed to revision
of the IFC's policies. Under the new principles, social impacts clearly also
have to be taken into account. It is interesting to note that Exhibit II of
the principles, which provides an "Illustrative List of Potential Social and
Environmental Issues to Be Addressed in the Social and Environmental Assessment Documentation," no longer specifies only "occupational health
and safety" but also "labour issues (including the four core labour standards)."[238] (One of the four labour standards is a prohibition against child
labour.) This can be considered a reference to human rights.

Under the Equator Principles II, the project sponsor (borrower) also
has to ensure continuous consultation, disclosure, and community engagement, as well as the existence of appropriate procedures in order to
receive and address concerns or grievances about social and environmental issues by individuals or groups from among project-affected communities. Also new is the requirement that the Equator banks must periodically
issue a public report on their implementation processes and experience.
This can be considered an effort to ensure that all Equator banks operate
according to the principles. The enforcement of more transparency could

indeed tackle the free-rider problem, and it definitely enhances the impact of the Equator Principles II on project financing.

On 26 April 2006 BankTrack published a first reaction to the draft Equator Principles II. A rather strong statement is made at the outset of the document: "While the draft EP II does offer some improvements, the overall approach is based on establishing the lowest common denominator and allowing some of the least committed institutions to hold the standards back."[239] Moreover, BankTrack regrets that the Equator Principles financial institutions (EPFIs) did not use the momentum to address the weaknesses in the principles and in the IFC's new Performance Standards. BankTrack and other NGOs had informed the EPFIs in October 2005 about a weakening of previous policies, "particularly around protections for displaced persons and minimum more vague consultation requirements for communities."[240] Nevertheless, BankTrack notes some improvements: "The most obvious improvement in the EP II draft is the expansion of the scope of the Principles to include the expansion or upgrades of an existing project with significant social and environmental effects and project finance advisory services."[241] BankTrack welcomes recognition of grievance mechanisms for affected people and lowering the threshold at which the principles become applicable to projects from US$50 million to US$10 million.

At the same time, BankTrack expresses its discontent that other financial services provided by the EPFIs are not included, namely corporate loans and debt and security underwriting. BankTrack again mentions the lack of accountability mechanisms to ensure that the principles are integrated into the banks' operations, the lack of transparency, and the lack of coordination between the EPFIs. Finally, the report concludes that the "most significant failure in the EP II draft is the decision to ignore its most serious critiques: the lack of consistent and rigorous implementation of the Principles."[242] BankTrack is awaiting a decision that to date ABN-AMRO Bank has not yet taken about the financing of Shell Oil's highly criticized Sakhalin II project. A decision on the latter will have been taken by the time this study is published.

A question remains to be answered that so far the NGOs, the IFC, and the EPFIs have not yet posed. What if an IFC project in which an EPFI is involved is guaranteed with money provided by the International Development Association (IDA) or the International Bank for Reconstruction and Development (IBRD), both of which are members of the World Bank Group, and a request for an investigation later arrives at the World Bank Inspection Panel? What policies would then have priority in the judgment to be made: the policies of IDA and the IBRD or the IFC's new safeguard standards?

Equator-Proof

A weakness in the system of the Equator Principles is the lack of a clear structure or rules for those adopting the principles. The individual private financial institutions have not yet created an official structure among themselves, other than having regular meetings and running a website.[243] At one of the regular meetings held by the Equator banks, it was mentioned that one of their biggest challenges is to get the banks to act and speak as one group. Nevertheless, some in the group are afraid of the risk of antitrust and competition accusations.[244] The meetings are closed, and no minutes are produced. However, since June 2003 several meetings have been held with the NGO community.

What internal steps the EPFIs have taken is hard to survey. If information about the implementation of the principles exists, it is not public. As a group, the EPFIs formally do not have a form of organization or consultative structure. However, managers responsible for the internal implementation and acceptance of the principles within the EPFIs meet about once a year with each other. In addition, meetings with the IFC, export credit agencies, clients, and BankTrack take place from time to time, and the EPFIs have rotating coordinating roles. There is also regular consultation between the experts of the EPFIs. According to Leonie Schreve of the Office of Environmental Social Risk Management at ING Bank, who filled one of the coordinating roles for a period, the EPFIs are cautious about officially organizing themselves as a group: "We have to be careful not to breach antitrust laws when putting down too many rules or procedures amongst the EPFIs or adopting minutes of those that meet. The group of EPFIs remains a group of individual competitive banks which only agree upon adhering to certain environmental and social standards for project finance. Nevertheless, there is a general consensus that some governance should be in place."[245]

In the spring of 2007 confusion arose about which banks are EPFIs. On its website, BankTrack states:

> Confusion at the EP Secretariat highlights grave flaws in implementation. The Equator Principles Secretariat is unaware just exactly which banks have adopted the Equator Principles. Minzuho Bank, an Equator Principle Financial Institution since October 2003 and now hosting the EP Secretariat, has no knowledge of the latest two banks that claim to have signed up to the principles. Respected Buenos Aires-based business website INFOBAE informs that Banco Galicia of Argentina became a signatory to the EPs on March 19. The Buenos Aires-based news service reveals Banco Galicia will adhere to the Equator Principles, making it the first Equator Principle Financial Institution from Argentina and the first from Latin America's Southern cone.[246]

A similar story about Sweden's Nordea Bank is mentioned. BankTrack confronted what it calls the Equator Principles Secretariat with the conflicting information and received confirmation that the two banks "have not signed on to the Equator Principles."[247] When asked about this confusion,

Schreve said: "The website notes a brief description a bank should publicly commit itself to the principles and take the necessary implementation steps. During the writing of this study the procedures were redrafted since these, as appears from this situation, are not clear enough. A form has to be filled in by the financial institution allowing the coordination to mention the institution on the site of the Equator Principles."[248]

Nonetheless, more is happening then one can see from the outside. Schreve briefly describes the procedures that are followed by ING:

> In the past, the commercial and risk management departments in the bank dealt with environmental and social risks, but it was not embedded in the general risk assessment. Therefore, an Environmental Social Risk Team with Risk Management has been established, which has implemented specific policies and procedures to manage environmental and social risks (amongst other Equator Principles) in the overall risk assessment of all Wholesale Banking products and services. We advise if a proposed project is Equator-proof. It has to be an early reporting. First the in-house environmental and social experts study the project outlines. They consider it "no-go" or "go." "Go" means that a project has the ability to comply, though full compliance has not yet been established or evidenced. "No-go" refers to projects that are unable or unwilling to comply. Then independent impact assessment experts analyze the proposed project, followed by advice of the Environmental Social Risk Team to the commercial department and the approval authorities. The advice is binding and can only be overruled by the Executive Board. For all A and B projects, clients have to report periodically to us about the implementation of all necessary steps as recorded in the principles. If it is an A project, an independent consultant is involved. In case we are not satisfied, the commercial department then will start a dialogue with the project sponsor to demand to do all that is necessary to re-establish compliance. It took the bank some years to reach this stage. Now we can say we make a better deal by negotiating with our clients.[249]

Thus a group of EPFIs are the frontrunners. "Some EPFIs," says Schreve, "have more significant project finance portfolios and have therefore built up extensive experience. As a result of EP II, EPFIs now really need to evidence what implementation steps have been taken and how many projects were reviewed. See principle 10 about recording and implementation. That is rather strong." On the complaint of the NGOs that EPFIs do not have an independent accountability mechanism, Schreve makes a remarkable statement: "Governance has to come. It is a subject we discuss, and I foresee that there will be agreement to install a certain amount of governance rules."[250]

As a business standard, will the Equator Principles survive down the road? On 6 July 2006, the day the Equator Principles II were made public, the new vice president of the IFC, Lars Thunell, said: "In 2004, net private capital flows to developing countries increased to $300 billion – that is, four times the amount of governmental development aid provided to these countries. Private sector investment, rather than aid, is now the driving force for development. With more and more financial institutions taking on board environmental and social issues, responsible banking stands to be a leader in sustainable development."[251] The question is whether the Equator Principles are powerful enough to set the standard.

Chinese Investors

Despite the consistent pressure of the NGO community and the positive intentions of the EPFIs, the Equator Principles could still be undermined by the fast-increasing flows of foreign direct investment from new large investors such as Chinese banks. This is at least the fear of many in the finance world. China has become *the* major investor in Africa, putting billions of dollars into mainly infrastructural projects, such oil exploration and road construction. As some say, the Chinese are everywhere and today in some countries are the major donor. Former World Bank president Paul Wolfowitz warned in October 2006 that "big Chinese banks do not respect the principles."[252] Wolfowitz is not the only one to have levelled this accusation at Chinese banks. Recently, the *Financial Times* referred to statements made by the president of the European Investment Bank, Mr Philippe Maystadt: "The competition of the Chinese banks is clear ... They don't bother about social or human rights conditions ... The international finance community needs to consider this problem," and "We have to think about the degree of conditionality we want to impose."[253] The *Financial Times* goes on to explain that, together with the other development banks, Maystadt wants to develop a common approach "and to avoid what he called 'excessive' conditions."[254] In the reference here to "excessive" conditions, one can detect the pullback position of a financer. That such a statement comes from a member of the European Investment Bank is not surprising since the EIB has never been a frontrunner on this subject.

A remarkably positive story about Chinese investment practices has been distributed by Oxfam America,[255] which cites an article published in a Peruvian daily paper entitled "Nativos agradecen a petrolera" (Natives thank the oil company). The article reports how pressure by the Chinese oil company SAPET forced the Peruvian government to approve the withdrawal of an oil concession that allowed for extraction operations on land reserved for the protection of isolated indigenous peoples.

The latter story perhaps reveals that not all Chinese actors are reluctant. And maybe it also shows that some "Western" actors, or financial institutions, derive comfort from criticizing Chinese activities. Could these activities be a helpful excuse for them not to comply with the standards? The real challenge is how to convince new players involved in foreign direct investment, such as Chinese banks, to comply while trying to find consensus of opinion.

Are the Chinese indeed as unscrupulous as portrayed? At a conference organized by the European Centre for Development Policy Management in December 2006 in Maastricht,[256] a group of African experts and officials of African governments reported that today Africans face a much more respectful and, most of all, equal dialogue with the Chinese compared to what they usually experience with European and US officials. Others expressed concern about the interventions in natural habitats that take place without serious assessments, which could harm future African generations. Clearly, the environment is no longer a subject discussed only in European and North American forums.

In June 2007 the European Union (EU) sent a first official EU delegation to Beijing to discuss the possibilities for cooperation between the EU and China concerning Africa.[257] China and the EU agreed on the overall assessment of Africa's political and economic situation and concluded that there was a lot of common ground on most issues discussed. However, no Chinese bank has yet adopted the Equator Principles. Subsequently, at the end of June 2007, the European Commission organized a conference in Brussels on *Partners in Competition? The EU, Africa and China.*

CONCLUDING REMARKS

Although much remains to be done, the Equator Principles are in any event a groundbreaking phenomenon, as many have argued. In the final analysis, the risk of liability might make both Equator banks and non-Equator banks even more proactive and rigorous in their demands on the owners of projects. According to the preamble to the principles, the banks "recognise that our role as financiers affords us opportunities to promote responsible environmental stewardship and socially responsible development,"[258] which proves again that the private sector today is the vanguard in creating rules and regulations in response to globalization (see chapter 1). That private banks are ready to assess the broader scope of their financed projects (see paragraphs 1 and 3 of the principles) could be rather consequential, as was my experience with projects at the World Bank.[259]

The abovementioned figures and developments show a shift of power from multilateral financial institutions to the private financial sector. Maurice Strong,[260] secretary general of the 1992 UN Conference on Environment and Development, the so-called Earth Summit, has said about the World Bank and the Equator Principles: "The World Bank is on the decline. The lending function was far less relevant. They are expensive and their overhead was very high. In the past, poor countries could not borrow from the private sector. Now the private sector is taking over. And how do we assure this will go well? If it does not start now, it will be a missed opportunity. The time horizon is long anyway. Many projects that are in process now, fifteen years from now could be a source of embarrassment to the companies."[261]

It is also important to note that the nature of multilateral financial institutions is somewhat different from that of private banks. (This issue is considered in depth in chapter 7, which provides the results of an international survey on the accountability mechanisms of both MFIs and private banks.) Nevertheless, in the Basel Committee's compliance report,[262] in the Collevecchio Declaration, and in other NGO documents, the Equator banks are called upon to install an independent accountability mechanism similar to that of the MFIs. In the report issued by Freshfields Bruckhaus Deringer,[263] the question is raised about the role of an ombudsman. It will be hard for private banks to ignore civil society's demands for compliance.

The EP participating banks need to organize themselves into a more effective consociation not only to police their ranks for promotion of the Equator Principles but also to ensure that the EP participating banks are responsible for their conduct in the application of the principles. This means the EP participating banks must be subject to an independent appraisal for compliance. Finally, an effort has to be undertaken to make the Equator Principles a global benchmark. The potential for this to happen is supported by the fact that the group of banks adopting the principles continues to increase: by January 2008, fifty-eight banks had adopted the principles.

6

The Daily Work
of an Accountability Mechanism

If you seek to be appreciated and loved, this is the wrong post.
Nobody will ever be satisfied by the panel reporting: neither management nor the requesters.

This was the first warning I received after being appointed a member of the
World Bank Inspection Panel. The work of the panel is still pioneering and
groundbreaking. During the five years that I sat on the panel, it was confronted with all kinds of dilemmas: strong opposition to the panel's mandate, attempts to undermine the mechanism, the need for the panel and its
staff to anchor its independent position within the institution, and hindrances arising from the limits of the mandate. My personal experiences
formed the basis of a survey about the mandate and structure of such mechanisms. Before looking at the results of this survey in chapter 7, I want to
give an overview of the complex subjects with which the Inspection Panel
can be confronted, but this overview is certainly not complete. Today, the
members of the panel are likely to be confronted with new questions.

The most striking realization that I came to while a member of the panel
is that there is a lack of liability when society wants to hold the World Bank
(and other international organizations) responsible for its actions. Human
rights violations in project areas required the panel to face this limitation
on holding the bank accountable. Nevertheless, the existence of the Inspection Panel has raised hopes. In the first part of this chapter, the bank's
position on human rights is considered. In the second part, other issues
are taken up related to the position of the mechanism within the institutions that form the background for the survey.

The field in which the Inspection Panel operates cannot be properly described without first indicating what other experts have written about the
World Bank and its operations, the Inspection Panel, or other accountability mechanisms. Those that have studied the panel's status, mainly lawyers
specialized in international law, portray the panel as a new entity in the
arena of international law. They give great value to the impact of the panel's

reports, which are seen as an initial form of international jurisprudence, and thus consider the panel to be a step toward further development of international law.

THE INSPECTION PANEL, HUMAN RIGHTS, AND CHANGING INTERNATIONAL LAW

The mandate of the World Bank Inspection Panel is restricted to the bank's Articles of Agreement,[1] as discussed in chapter 2. The term "human rights" does not appear in the Articles of Agreement. Thus the bank officially faces difficulties addressing human rights violations, which, according to the bank, are supposed to be national internal matters.[2] Nevertheless, there are World Bank policy statements that do contain the term "human rights." The first such statement was the Indigenous Peoples Policy.[3] In 2003 the compliance advisor ombudsman (CAO) of the International Finance Corporation (IFC) took up the issue of human rights,[4] and the IFC adopted a human-rights-related policy on child labour that remarkably does not exist for the other members in the World Bank Group, namely the International Development Association (IDA) and the International Bank for Reconstruction and Development (IBRD). In contrast to the World Bank and the other multilateral financial institutions (MFIs),[5] one can find two occurrences of the term "human rights" in the introduction to Article 1 of the "Agreement Establishing the European Bank for Reconstruction and Development" (EBRD).[6] Another example of a government body adopting a policy on human rights is the export credit agency Export Development Canada, which in 2002 established the position of compliance officer, with a mandate "to review and help resolve issues concerning transparency and disclosure, environmental reviews, human rights and business ethics."[7] Yet the "mother" of the organizations, the World Bank, lags far behind. Writing about the scope of the panel's mandate and its limitations, Ibrahim Shihata,[8] general counsel at the World Bank from 1983 to 1998, states:

> The Panel's substantive jurisdiction is limited no doubt to matters
> that are attributed to the Bank and for which the Bank can take correc-
> tive measures. Giving the Panel an unrestricted right to further investi-
> gate whether the actions of Bank borrowers are consistent with all
> international agreements on human rights and the environment with-
> out any limitation, as advocated by certain NGOs [nongovernmental
> organizations] and authors, would give the Panel the role of a guardian
> and enforcer of international agreements concluded outside the Bank
> and a judge of whether they have been violated by the states parties
> to them.[9]

Shihata is no doubt against a "policing role" for the Inspection Panel. In his view, the panel should certainly be mandated to investigate human rights issues (and environmental issues) as long as they are covered by the bank's own policies and raised by affected parties. This is where he draws a line, as human rights violations taking place in borrowing countries in the context of a bank-financed project are not within the mandate of the bank and thus not within the mandate of the panel. By taking this position, Shihata defends the view that as an international organization the World Bank cannot be held responsible for such violations. With all due respect for the masterpiece that he left to the bank with the publication of his study of the Inspection Panel, I consider his view legalistic and conservative. I regret that I can no longer discuss the matter with him since he has passed away.

Two of his former colleagues from the Asian Development Bank – Eisuke Suzuki, a former deputy general counsel and former director general of the Operations Evaluation Department, and Suresh Nanwani,[10] a former senior counsel – today draw a different conclusion, making reference to the work of the International Law Commission of the United Nations.[11] The following introduction to a recent trail-blazing article by the two lawyers about the responsibility of international organizations and their accountability mechanisms is important to note:

> While the United Nations General Assembly adopted the Articles on Responsibility of States for Internationally Wrongful Acts prepared by the International Law Commission (ILC) in December 2001,[12] only recently did the ILC decide to include the topic of "responsibility of international organizations" in its long-term work program.[13] Although the International Law Association (ILA) has been considering the accountability of international organizations through its Committee on the Accountability of International Organizations, established in May 1996, the timing of the ILC's decision to include the topic was related to the completion of its state responsibility project in 2001. Article 57 of the Articles on Responsibility of States for Internationally Wrongful Acts provides: "These articles are without prejudice to any question of the responsibility under international law of an international organization, or of any state for the conduct of an international organization." The key element in the conception of state responsibility developed under the ILC's project was, in the words of James Crawford, "the abandonment of an exclusively synallagmatic conception of responsibility," i.e., the responsibility of one state to another state.[14]

With their reference to the work of the International Law Commission and to articles adopted by the UN, Suzuki and Nanwani expose the position of international organizations, which have always considered themselves immune on the grounds that international law is a matter of a state versus a state. But as Suzuki and Nanwani note, this is no longer the case: "The legal personality of international organizations could no longer be seen as a

démarche for member states to avoid joint and several responsibility for
their conduct. It would be 'fantastic' to assume that international organizations 'are authorized to violate the principles they were established to
serve' and it would 'be perverse, even destructive, to postulate a community expectation that IOs [international organizations] need not conform
to the principles of public order.' It is now clear that the legal character of
international organizations entails a responsibility for their conduct."[15]

In other words, Suzuki and Nanwani contest the position of Shihata and
others by saying that states, and with them the international organizations,
cannot hide themselves when the international organizations that they have
established violate the rules and principles: the international organizations
are accountable for their behaviour. Suzuki and Nanwani further describe
the increasing arena of international law. More and more parties are demanding a position in the arena. "As international organizations expand
their roles and activities in an ever-increasing number of areas of international life, there is a corresponding expansion of responsibility for their interactions with an equally increasing number of other nonstate entities like
individuals, groups of individuals, transnational corporations, nongovernmental organizations, minorities, and indigenous peoples. These nonstate
entities are also claiming 'their particular legal position[s] within the ambit
of international law.'"[16] International organizations "must, therefore, also
be deemed subject to a commensurately expanded reach of general or cus-
tomary international law," and the rights and duties of any of these organizations "must depend upon its purposes and functions as specified or implied
in its constituent documents and developed in practice."[17]
Suzuki and Nanwani then observe:

> One of the most tangible results of these developments is the establish-
> ment of inspection functions or accountability mechanisms for multi-
> lateral development banks (MDBs), allowing third parties to file
> complaints regarding violations of a bank's internal policies and
> procedural requirements in designing, processing, or implementing
> MDB-assisted projects ...[18]

> The establishment of the World Bank's Inspection Panel in late 1993
> was an extraordinary development that further underpinned the trans-
> parency and accountability of MDBs. Never before had any entity inde-
> pendent of the governing organs of an international organization
> existed to hear and investigate complaints filed by private individuals
> and groups affected by the organization.[19]

Despite their enthusiasm, Suzuki and Nanwani still see many weaknesses
in the different systems:

> However remarkable this development in demanding accountability of
> MDBs may be, banks still consider accountability mechanisms as internal
> governance tools for enhancing the operational effectiveness and

discipline of the organization. As such, the question of accountability remains, strictly speaking, within the purview of the organization's internal law ...[20]

Thus far, MDBs have more or less patterned their accountability mechanisms after the basic procedural requirements established by the World Bank Inspection Panel. The absence of access to effective remedies stemming from an MDBs immunity from local jurisdiction is the essential reason for the establishment of the accountability mechanism as an internal mechanism, independent of local jurisdictions in which MDBs remain immune.[21]

So the MDBs are not bound by national laws and are rarely bound by international treaty law. Another criticism made by Suzuki and Nanwani is that "The basis for the review is limited only to a failure of the MDB to follow its operational policies and procedures. This limitation formally resonates with the principle of non-interference with the domestic affairs of other states. The Inspection Panel or accountability mechanism of any of the MDBs does not have the competence to investigate the borrower's accountability."[22]

As mentioned in chapter 3, some of the World Bank's executive directors expressed their view that the Inspection Panel's mandate should also cover the actions of the national authorities implementing the projects. This position was not supported by the Group II (i.e., recipient) countries. Suzuki and Nanwani also describe the remaining "Structural limitations for private third party's overall access to international fora."[23] Access to the systems is still dependent on governments that will not allow claims filed by individual citizens "against other states to go forward without retaining a right of control and veto."[24] So although the accountability mechanisms could be the beginning of making the international organizations accountable for their actions, there is still a long way to go.

One of the most recent senior vice presidents and general counsels of the World Bank, Roberto Dañino,[25] has expressed personal views showing that he understands the position of those criticizing the bank for its restricted Articles of Agreement and its inability to deal with human rights. Speaking at a conference in New York on 1 March 2004,[26] Dañino reminded those present that the bank is primarily a financial institution. Moreover, he said, "The Articles provide that only economic considerations of economy and efficiency shall be relevant to the decisions of the Bank and its officers, and these must be weighed impartially."[27] Then Dañino raised an interesting question similar to one the Inspection Panel had posed earlier in the case of the Chad-Cameroon oil pipeline (see below):[28] "What then constitute economic considerations for these purposes?"[29] He provides the following answer:

In making decisions about the investment of limited public resources available, the Bank – like its private sector equivalents – needs to evaluate the wisdom of its proposed investment. And, these must include the "investment climate" in the recipient country. The Bank has already accepted the fact that issues of governance are relevant for purposes of the economic analysis but, in my view, it goes further than this – it is now widely recognized that there are a host of political and institutional factors which may affect economic growth. Research has shown that substantial violations of political and civil rights are related to lower economic growth. Similarly, it has long been recognized in the Bank that political considerations can have direct economic effects.[30]

Dañino then goes yet a step further. With reference to those who believe that only economic rights, not political rights, are relevant, he says: "In my view there is no stark distinction between economic and political considerations: there is an interconnection among economic, social and cultural rights on the one hand, and political rights on the other."[31] Indeed, it is generally accepted at the political level that "all human rights are universal, indivisible, interdependent and interrelated. Also from a financial point of view I believe the Bank cannot and should not make a distinction between different types of human rights. It needs to take all these considerations into account. In all cases, however, Bank decision making must treat these considerations impartially, treating similarly situated countries equally."[32] Finally, Dañino concludes:

Within both these constraints there is still a great deal of latitude. Insofar as human rights constitute a valid consideration for the investment process they are properly within the scope of issues which the World Bank must consider when it makes its economic decisions. And this consideration should include all human rights: those classified as economic, social and cultural, as well as those classified as civil and political. Moreover it stands to reason that we must address the potential economic consequences of human rights situations, and consider the risk ex ante, not only ex post facto.[33]

THE WORLD BANK, THE IMF, AND HUMAN RIGHTS

What responsibilities the World Bank and the International Monetary Fund (IMF) have under international human rights law has also been studied by Mac Darrow, who outlines what conditionality means in the operations of the bank. On the IMF, Darrow states:

In basic terms "conditionality" is a portmanteau word that encompasses all the policies that the Fund wishes a member to follow so that it can resolve its problem consistently with the Articles. Certain of its features and underlying assumptions have already been referred to in passing. While a subject of equal practical relevance to the financial assistance activities of both the Bank and Fund, the legal doctrine purporting to regulate the exercise of conditionality at the Fund is quite specific and relatively well developed, and accordingly warrants separate analyses here.[34]

On the legal basis for conditionality Darrow writes:

> The term "conditionality" was not intentionally included in the original Articles, nor in subsequent amendments. Neither did the original Articles contain any explicit statement that the Fund had to adopt policies on the use of its resources. However a series of early Executive Board decisions and Annual Report references put the matter beyond doubt. The view that the Fund could prevent any proposed uses of Fund resources that it considered improper prevailed in a decision of 10 March 1948,[35] a decision representing "a thorough-going adoption of the United States view that drawing rights were to be conditional."[36]

According to Darrow, it took until 1968 for the fund to include a first amendment with clear language requiring that the fund have policies on the use of its resources.[37] Darrow also refers to the IMF's assumption that human rights are a social issue that should be dealt with by the World Bank. He notes a division of labour between the two institutions: the bank is in charge of long-term development and social issues, and the IMF is in charge of the macroeconomic developments. Darrow sees this as alarming, criticizing the arrangement for ignoring human rights: "The systematic characterisation of human rights as 'social' concerns is itself alarming, ignoring human rights' very obvious 'economic' aspects, and consigning them by this definition to macro-economic irrelevance."[38] Thereupon, Darrow notes a move by the IMF toward internal acceptance of human rights. He mentions a set of instructions on confidential standards issued by the managing director's office in 1988 that suggest IMF country missions should take into consideration the possible socio-economic consequences of adjustment programs.[39]

On the question of who dictates the policy-development process at the World Bank, Darrow says that although opinions differ, it is the legal department and more specifically the general counsel's office that play an important role in operational and internal accountability structures.[40] He further states:

> The Bank's overall record in practice tends to show incremental and opportunistic mandate expansion, belying internal logic or anything close to systematic legal regulation. Anecdotal accounts suggest that the key officials in the legal area have not infrequently been taken by surprise on major policy developments, such as selective forays by the Bank into areas such as criminal law reform, and prior to that, Bank President Wolfensohn's declared intention to tackle corruption.

Such developments have on occasion been followed up by ex-post-facto, and occasionally slightly tortured, "economic effects" justifications.[41]

Darrow mentions the contrast in a subsequent reference to a letter from former bank president Jim Wolfensohn to former president of Indonesia Bacharuddin Jusuf Habibie, in which Wolfensohn is "effectively threatening human rights-based conditionality."[42] So a certain schizothymia has entered the World Bank. Introducing various rules and regulations is favoured but not in relation to human rights, except in cases when doing so would be to the bank's advantage.

Darrow makes clear how much conditionality has been imposed on the "clients" of the World Bank and the IMF in a "one-way" direction, placing the World Bank above the parties.

CAN THE ARTICLES OF AGREEMENT BE CHANGED?

According to Andrés Rigo Sureda, it has never been easy to change the Articles of Agreement:

> The Articles of Agreement of the Bank were written in the 1940s. From the beginning, the Bank had been expected "at all times to adapt itself to the changing needs of the world, if only to ensure its continued relevance," but the requirements for amending the Articles are very strict. Amendments must be approved by the Board of Governors.[43] In addition they must be accepted by a qualified majority of at least sixty percent of members of the Bank with at least eighty-five percent of the total voting power.[44] Not surprisingly, the Articles have been amended only twice. As a result, the burden of adapting the Bank to the changing needs of its member countries has rested on the process of interpretation. Formal interpretation of the Articles is the competence of the Board of the Executive Directors and requires only a simple majority of those voting. A number of formal interpretations were made at the beginning but increasingly have become so rare that their number has decreased to only one in thirty-five years.[45]

Rigo Sureda further concludes that in due course the process of informal interpretation has prevailed. He then refers to former general counsel Ibrahim Shihata, who provided management and the board "the opportunity to discuss the issues and concur on a sound legal framework within which to proceed, without resorting to a formal interpretation. This allowed for further adaptation in a subtle and flexible way."[46]

Thus, so far, the World Bank and the IMF have *formally* stayed out of the discussion by appealing to the Articles of Agreement. Nevertheless, daily events at the bank have shown some early moves toward changing this approach. In its turn, the Inspection Panel has also contributed to the process of change by exceeding its mandate and ignoring the Articles of Agreement when it reports on human rights violations discovered by the panel in the context of a bank project.

THE CHAD-CAMEROON CASE AND LIABILITY

The issue of human rights and liability was raised in the case of the Chad-Cameroon oil pipeline.[47] In 1988 the Government of Chad reached an agreement with a consortium comprised of three multinational oil companies to explore 4.8 million hectares in three oil fields in the south of Chad.[48] Cameroon became involved since the oil would be transported via a pipeline of 900 miles through its territory. In Chad the oil field operations would be the responsibility of ESSO Exploration and Production Chad Inc., while the Chad Oil Transportation Company S.A. (TOTCO) was established to handle the transportation of the oil. In TOTCO there is equity participation by the state of Chad and the oil consortium. In Cameroon a similar system was created, with the Cameroon Oil Transportation Company S.A. (COTCO) deriving its equity from the participation of the oil consortium and the Republic of Cameroon. The parties involved asked the World Bank for an International Development Association (IDA) loan in the case of Chad and wanted the World Bank to participate in a set of additional projects, such as capacity building, control over oil income expenditures, and so on.[49]

Before the World Bank approved its loans, a symposium was held in the Netherlands, organized by the Netherlands Committee and the International Union for the Conservation of Nature (NC-IUCN) and financed by the Dutch government.[50] The topic and question was who would bear the liability if in the future environmental damage occurred due to the Chad-Cameroon pipeline:

> Given the serious environmental risks involved in this project, one of the main conditions should be the establishment of a legal framework covering the issue of liability for environmental damage. For all actors involved, it should be clear from the start what acts may trigger liability. A sufficient framework regulating liability for environmental damage of the project parties, whether public or private, may very well contribute to the prevention of environmental damage. On the one hand the scheme of liability with regard to environmental damage provides for the legal responsibility of someone who has violated a binding legal norm by damaging the environment as well as for the obligation to remedy the damage, while at the other hand it is a means of protecting the local communities from damage to their environment.[51]

At the symposium, which I attended as an observer,[52] experts discussed the loopholes in national legal instruments and the absence, or at least the lack, of clarity of a legal structure on which to rely in case of future environmental damage. The Chadian lawyer Deoukoubou Christophe stated: "It should be underlined from the start that, with regard to the environmental protection and related responsibilities, the Chadian national legal system lacks suitable legal instruments. However, there are some national laws on which a person's responsibility for environmental damage may be based, irrespective of that person being an individual or a legal entity. In addition, the responsibility for environmental damage of the consortium and that of TOTCO may also be based on the TOTCO Convention of Establishment, which binds them to the state of Chad."[53] He spoke about excessive delays in the adoption of laws, the lack of transparency of national legislation, the "government's sincere willingness to apply them,"[54] and the fact that people hardly know about the laws. He added: "it must be stressed that Chad does not have appropriate legal instruments to govern an oil project of such large scale, involving major impacts on nature and the environment."[55] But what is more, by referring to Article 21.5 of the convention adopted by the parties involved in the project,[56] he made clear that "The Convention prevails over the laws of the Republic of Chad in the event of contradiction and incompatibilities between them."[57]

Another expert at the symposium, Saman Zia-Zarifi,[58] was even more pessimistic about the opportunities that local people have to claim their rights:

> Based on the information available currently, this paper concludes that there is effectively very little legal recourse for any individuals in Chad or Cameroon whose person or property may be damaged by the activity of these companies. As set out in more detail below, these Multinational Corporations (MCNs) can operate with impunity as a result of a number of systematic, structural and material shortcomings in the law as it applies to the transboundary activity of corporations. The domestic legal system of Chad and Cameroon, which would ordinarily (and ideally) adjudicate any claims against the private companies operating the pipeline, suffer from a variety of shortcomings that prevent them from adequately monitoring the activity of MCNs in their jurisdictions. Furthermore, the complicated legal structure of the MCNs' involvement in the pipeline project shields them from liability in Chad or Cameroon. Finally, the tremendous asymmetry of resources in favor of the MCNs allows them to effectively resist, and at worse, bully into submission, the local judiciary.[59]

After the symposium, on 11 April 2000, the organizers sent a letter to the president and executive directors of the World Bank indicating the different obstacles discussed during the symposium, such as "the lack of predictability and liability as a result of non-applicability of national laws, the non-applicability of international treaties, wide powers of the consortium to act as an official state organ: violating the rule of law, the lack of predictability and liability as a result of ambiguous articles, absence of the right to an effective remedy through a fair and public hearing by an independent and impartial court and the lack of appropriate enforcement mechanisms."[60]

The symposium's organizers then advised the World Bank:

> As stated above, current legal methods do not adequately account for the range and influence of the activities of multinational corporations. International law does not apply to legal persons, while the host states in the developing world often lack the power or political will and the legal means to effectively control these powerful companies ... In the absence of any meaningful legal accountability for the companies involved in the pipeline project, the only source of normative regulation for the behavior of the companies involved comes from the World Bank's Guidelines. Application of these Guidelines, though not of direct legal force, should be conditional for participation by the World Bank. The availability of these Guidelines, and the oversight performed by the Bank, its member states, and various NGOs on compliance with these guidelines, are at the moment the best means to enforcing a minimum of accountability of the oil companies involved in World Bank funded projects.[61]

In other words, the involvement of the World Bank through its guidelines and controlling mechanism was for the participants the only available guarantee that these guidelines (i.e., policies and procedures) would be met.

The World Bank responded to the issues that the symposium organizers raised in their letter. On the lack of predictability and liability as a result of the nonapplicability of national laws, the bank said: "It is undisputed in international business that the parties to an international agreement enjoy the freedom to choose the applicable law governing their business-related relationships."[62] Reading this, one could say that the operations of the private sector or transnational corporations enjoy total freedom of choice. However, this might be too simple a conclusion given the bank's further comments:

> The International Law Institute mentioned expressly, in its 1979 Resolution, that "contracts between a State and a foreign private person shall be subjected to the rules of law chosen by the parties," and that the rules of law chosen in accordance with the preceding provisions shall govern the incidence of contractual liability between the parties, in particular those raised by the State's exercise of its sovereign powers in violation of any of its commitments towards the contracting partner" ... This is the case of the two "Conventions d'etablissement" concerning TOTCO and COTCO. Article 30 of the COTCO Convention expresses this principle of freedom of choice of the governing law and defines the applicable law.[63]

This statement makes clear that one needs to consult lawyers to understand, if possible, which laws will be applicable when an incident arises. It
is also clear that local people will need the support of lawyers with experience in international law. This will by no means be possible to afford for
most, if not all, people in Third World countries, let alone the involved
states themselves. So I would like to stress that the World Bank and other
MFIs and also Equator banks should take measures to guarantee that
proper budgets are made available for local people and their representatives in cases of incidents through appropriate arrangements on an international level, paid from the project budget (see the discussion of
"participant funding" below).

During the discussions on the Chad-Cameroon oil pipeline, the Bhopal
incident was often put forward as an example. In December 1984, a
Union Carbide plant in Bhopal, India, began leaking 27 tons of the
deadly gas methyl isocyanate. The six safety systems to avoid such leaks
were not operational. Half a million people were exposed to the gas.
Thousands of people died immediately, while ten thousand died in the af-
termath. According to the Bhopal Medical Appeal the region is still suffer-
ing. In 1999 it was revealed that local groundwater and well water near
the site contains mercury levels "between 20.000 and 6 million times
those expected." In the case of Bhopal, it was almost impossible for the local people to claim their right to receive compensation: "It took until
1989 that Union Carbide, in a partial settlement with the Indian government, agreed to pay out some $470 million in compensation. The victims
weren't consulted in the settlement discussions, and many felt cheated by
their compensation $300–$500 or about five years worth of medical expenses. Today, those who were awarded compensation are hardly better
off than those who weren't."[64] Union Carbide later expressed its discontent with the way the compensation was handled but claimed that it was
the responsibility of the authorities in India to pay out the compensation.
In 1991 the local government of Bhopal brought criminal charges against
Union Carbide's CEO at the time of the disaster. So far, the case has not
come to court. The Bhopal disaster makes clear that local people will be
the victims and losers if a state and a transnational corporation are involved in serious incidents. Undoubtedly, there will be increased pressure
from the world community on financial institutions and governments to
carry out social impact assessments. Most of this pressure can be expected
in the natural resource sectors, such as agriculture, mining, energy, road
construction, forestry, fishing, and tourism.[65]

REQUEST FROM CHAD LODGED
WITH THE INSPECTION PANEL

The Inspection Panel received a request for inspection on 22 March 2001
from Ngarlejy Yorongar,[66] a member of Chad's National Assembly, who

acted on behalf of more than 100 residents in the vicinity of the three oil fields in the project area in southern Chad. The panel investigated,[67] and in the "Executive Summary" of the final report, we wrote the following general note about the project:

> The Chad-Cameroon Oil Pipeline Project (hereinafter referred to as the Pipeline Project or the Project) is the largest energy infrastructure development on the African continent. Estimated at US$3.7 billion, it is being funded largely by private industry (Exxon Mobil, Petronas, and Chevron). It involves the drilling of 300 oil wells in the oilfields in the Doba region of Southern Chad and the construction of a 1,100 km long export pipeline through Cameroon to an offshore loading facility. With petroleum reserves estimated at 225,000 barrels per day, the Project is expected to yield approximately US$2 billion in revenues to Chad over a 28-year operation period. The World Bank and the International Finance Corporation (IFC) are participating in the project by providing US$39.5 million and US$100 million respectively.[68]

While investigating the situation on the ground in Chad, the panel refused to ignore serious human rights violations, which were included in the final report. Thanks to the perceptivity of a representative of a Chadian NGO representing the people in the field, we were directed to the right area and villages where the pipeline was crossing the fields.[69] Without her, we might not have arrived in a village where the panel heard stories from the entire community about what had happened to them. Many of the families had lost their crops as a result of the ongoing construction. The people told us that when the officials came to see them and negotiate about compensation, they came with the army. To understand the impact of such an act, one has to know that the southern part of the country where the pipeline was constructed had just gone through a long civil war that pitted the Christians in the south against the Islamic peoples from the north. At the time of the civil war, President Deby of Chad was a a colonel in the army of the previous president. During the war many people in the south lost their lives. Fear of the army still existed. Bringing in soldiers in such a situation was interpreted by the panel as a strong form of intimidation. The panel reported the following findings:[70]

> The Panel has also examined several reports addressing governance and human rights situations in the country, and the extensive exchange of correspondence between Bank Management and NGOs in Chad and abroad. The Panel also takes note of the fact that on more than one occasion when political repression in Chad seemed severe, the Bank's President personally intervened to help free local opposition leaders, including the representative of the Requesters, Mr. Yorongar, who was reported as being subjected to torture.[71]

Nevertheless, the panel also noted:

> The Panel appreciates the fact that the frequently imprecise concepts
> of "governance" and "human rights" acquire special significance in the
> context of the Bank's mandate and operations. Nonetheless, the Panel
> takes issue with Management's narrow view, and draws attention in this
> connection to the United Nations Universal Declaration of Human
> Rights adopted in December 1948,[72] three years after the Bank's
> Articles of Agreement cited above entered into effect. On the fiftieth
> anniversary of this Declaration, the Bank wrote: "The World Bank be-
> lieves that creating the conditions for the attainment of human rights is
> a central and irreducible goal of development. By placing the dignity of
> every human being – especially the poorest – at the very foundation of
> its approach to development, the Bank helps people in every part of the
> world build lives of purpose and hope. And while the Bank has always
> taken measures to ensure that human rights are fully respected in
> connection with the projects it supports, it has been less forthcoming
> about articulating its role in promoting human rights within the coun-
> tries in which it operates.[73]

And finally (on this, see also chapter 2):

> As for Human Rights, Management states in its Response to the Panel
> that "the Bank is concerned about violations of human rights in Chad as
> elsewhere while respecting the Bank's Articles of Agreement which re-
> quire the Bank to focus on economic considerations and not on political
> or other non-economic influences as the basis for its decisions. In evalu-
> ating the economic aspects of any project, human Rights issues may be
> relevant to the Bank's work if they may have a significant direct eco-
> nomic effect on the project. Having carefully considered all aspects of
> this issue, Management's conclusion is that the Project can achieve its
> developmental objectives." In other words, according to the Manage-
> ment Response, if human rights issues have "significant direct economic
> effects" on a Bank financed project, they become a matter of concern to
> the Bank.[74] Otherwise they don't. In this case, Management feels that
> the project "can achieve its development objectives," so human rights
> issues are of no direct concern.[75]

Based on the panel's statement of its findings, one can understand its
dissatisfaction with the bank's refusal to take up the issue of human rights
violations in the borrowing countries. This statement may have attracted
the attention of Roberto Dañino (see above), who later made a similar
statement.

Sadly enough, recent developments in Chad now demonstrate even
more the necessity of (legal) support for local people in project areas.
The Inspection Panel expressed its concern over the capacity of the country

to implement the projects under the loan agreement, based on the following findings, noted in paragraph 13:

> A key objective of the Capacity Building Project, and a major rationale
> for the Bank's involvement in the Project, was to develop and strengthen
> the institutional capabilities of the government to a level where it could
> manage the petroleum sector in [an] environmentally and socially
> sound manner. This included increasing the Government's capacity to
> the point where it could begin to monitor the project effectively before
> the revenues start to flow. This objective has not been achieved and
> raises questions about the Project's ability to realize several of its social
> objectives ... The Panel recognized the lack of human and institutional
> capacity at the national level to manage and monitor projects of this
> magnitude and complexity.[76]

The Government of Chad, supported by the Chadian National Assembly,
recently breached the contract with the World Bank when it disregarded
the Petroleum Revenue Management Law by adopting amendments to the
law. According to a World Bank press release:

> [This legislation, which was] adopted by the National Assembly and passed
> into law by the President of the Republic of Chad in 1999, was a deciding
> factor in the World Bank Group's support for the Chad-Cameroon Oil
> Pipeline Project, which represented a unique opportunity for Chad to use
> its oil revenues to finance desperately needed poverty reduction. As part of
> the loan agreement with the World bank, the Government of Chad specifi-
> cally undertook not to amend or waive any provisions of the law in ways
> that would "materially and adversely affect" the revenue management
> program established under the law. The law directed the bulk of direct
> revenue to the Government from the Chad Cameroon Pipeline Project to
> agreed-to "priority sectors," such as health, education and rural develop-
> ment, that are linked to improved living standards and poverty reduction.
> The law also created a Future Generations Fund, to ensure there would be
> some benefits to the population once the oil reserves are exhausted.[77]

The bank further expresses its realistic fear that the amendments will
broaden the definition of priority sectors and include other sectors such as
territorial administration and security. This would allow the transfer of
US$36 million from the Future Generation Fund plus the reallocation of
royalties and dividends to nonpriority sectors. According to the bank, this
will "substantially weaken the poverty focus."[78] In this press release, the
bank announced its suspension of disbursements to Chad.[79] In September
2008 the World Bank finally withdrew from the project.

Even more alarming is the possible transfer of money to military spending. Chad has become part of the crisis in Sudan. The Sudanese government is trying to overturn the Government of Chad and unseat President

Idriss Deby.[80] The risk that Chad will fall back into a civil war is serious. If at the end of the day the oil revenues are used for military activities, one may wonder what kind of development has been created by a project involving the World Bank, which entered Chad just when the country was trying to recover from a civil war.

INSPECTION PANEL REPORTING

Another subject often debated concerns publication of the panel's reports and what these reports can contain. In the questionnaire for the international survey that I conducted on the various accountability mechanisms, I state: "The reports, with their findings from the Inspection Panel, are finally made public exactly as they were written by the Panel members. It is the release of the findings to the public domain that constitutes the strength of the work of such mechanisms." Independent publication of the panel's findings could make the difference for people who are trying to protect their rights. In the case of the World Bank Inspection Panel, I have often noticed that publication of reports can have a substantial effect.

In my experience, two things can happen in the reporting process. In a regular case,[81] the panel finalizes its report and sends this to the secretaries of the bank's Board of Directors and to management. Management then has six weeks to write its report, which sets out how to mitigate or change those elements of the project that, according to the panel's findings, are not in compliance with the policies of the institution. At this point, the report remains confidential. After six weeks the executive directors table the two reports at a board meeting and, together with the panel and management, discuss what should be done. Finally, the decision of the board, along with both reports, is made public. So the public has the opportunity to examine the decisions of the board within the context of the panel's report. The executive directors are aware that civil society and the media will follow their decisions closely in sensitive cases. Thus they will take decisions that do not contradict the findings of the Inspection Panel too markedly. This is where the influence of the panel is to be found.

The second thing that can happen in the reporting process, which should not surprise the readers of this study, is that down the road the panel can be confronted with attempts from inside the bank to change its textual findings. One such incident was so clear that it created a weighty discussion among panel members about whether, in response, they should resign their "seats" on the panel. Finally, nobody drove home the point by doing so. When the panel explained that it did not want any interference in its final work, its position was defended by a group of executive directors who understood the role of the panel. As a consequence, the panel's insistence on noninterference was accepted by management. Over and over again the panel had to explain that it is not the panel, but the complainant, that has a conflict with management. The panel is supposed to be above the other parties.

Informing the public about the failures of an institution is something rarely executed. Henry McCandless, a consultant on accountability with a background in the Office of the Auditor General of Canada, is rather adamant when describing the intentions and practices of authorities when informing the public:

> The range of authorities' intentions across the planet that call for publicly-challenged equity statements is huge, but if the statements were required, those affected by the intentions would soon learn how to figure out the basic fairness trade-offs and what's missing from the statements. As George Washington said, citizens will make sensible decisions if they are reasonably informed. What has been missing in benefit-cost assessments that governments claim they [are] already producing is the information we need on the "who" questions: who benefits and who pays – and for how long.
>
> Considering obvious examples in the use of natural resources, what would a rigorous publicly-challenged equity statement have explained to the several million citizens of Toronto about the development plans to wall off their downtown lake waterfront with condominiums? What would it have explained to British Columbians about the Bamberton land proposal on lower Vancouver Island, or clear-cut logging? What would it have explained to Prince Edward Islanders or Skye residents about the bridge proposals? Or to the Dutch, about freight railway tracks across The Netherlands from Rotterdam into Germany, or the Australians for their car racing track in parkland? Or the merits of an intended huge dam in China or India?[82]

If McCandless were writing his book today, he could add to his list, for example, a reference to the streamlining of the Mississippi, the occupation of natural water reservoirs for industrial purposes, and the information on the risks of these interventions that was given to the citizens of New Orleans.

Exceptions to the rule of publication arise, for instance, in the case of a mediation process involving proprietary information, when one can understand that such information should not be made public. But what if the information relates to the actions and profits of a private company developing an infrastructural project that could concern the lives of thousands or millions of people, as mentioned by McCandless? And what to do with information related to national security? Who will determine whether information is dangerous to national security? In the case of certain states, I would not leave this decision in the hands of governing regimes. It is evident that large infrastructural projects involving the lives of many people or changes in social systems such as health care need proper procedures and norms. It is obvious that new norms should be developed regarding what can be published, which authorities can make this decision and with what mandate, and which procedures are available. In the development of such norms, the highest degree of transparency is a must if we want to rely on and trust our democracies.

INDEPENDENCE OF THE INSPECTION PANEL

From the start, the independence of the Inspection Panel has been studied and criticized but remains of vital importance. A panel that has no independence has no meaning. The resolution establishing the panel states that "Members of the Panel shall be elected on the basis of their ability to deal thoroughly and fairly with the requests brought to them, their integrity and their independence from the Bank's Management, and their exposure to developmental issues and to living conditions in developing countries."[83] The members of the panel often have to explain their status of neutrality. In almost every lecture or workshop they attend, the question is raised of how independent the members can be. The doubt or disbelief expressed is certainly caused by the fact that the members receive an income paid by the World Bank, the institution that they are supposed to independently "control" or investigate. The answer to such related questions is that the guarantee of the panel's independence is laid down in the resolution establishing the panel, which prescribes that after their term with the panel is over, members can never again work for the World Bank. In addition, the resolution prescribes that former employees of the bank, whether staff, management, or board members, can be appointed a member of the Inspection Panel only after they have been absent from the bank for at least two years. By creating these rules, the bank's Board of Directors wanted to guarantee the mechanism's independence from management. The members of the panel appointed so far have never been previous employees of the World Bank. Whether two years will create enough distance is in question. Some experts who participated in the survey discussed in chapter 7 have expressed the view that two years is not enough, and others feel that no one should be appointed who has worked for the institution before.

The resolution stipulates a term of five years for each member and adds that "no member may serve for more than one term."[84] The underlying principle is that panel members should have no future bank function. The belief is that exclusion from future work at the bank will make members more independent.[85] Nevertheless, after five years in service, members presumably have a lot of knowledge. Thus despite the need for independence, there is also an argument that strong knowledge and experience are being lost too soon. The possibility of a member serving a second term, as is common in leading functions in the United Nations, is under discussion. The independence of the panel members should also extend to hired experts who advise the panel. The panel has had to learn this through experience.[86]

WEAKENING OF THE SAFEGUARD POLICIES

Over the years both the World Bank and the other MFIs have developed important policies of which, without doubt, the Environmental Impact Assessment Policy and the Indigenous Peoples Policy have been the most influential.[87] The importance of other safeguard policies also cannot be underestimated, among them Natural Habitats, Forests, Pest Management, Cultural Property, Involuntary Resettlement, Safety of Dams, Disputed Areas, and International Waterways.[88]

The safeguard policies and procedures of the World Bank Group and the other MFIs and the business principles of the private sector are for the most part not explicitly covered by the survey questionnaire,[89] which deals mainly with the different structures of accountability mechanisms. The development of the policies of the different bank institutions and their "legal implications" would be a study in itself. The exception I made was for the existence or non-existence of human rights policies since their absence affects the overall credibility of the entire institution (see chapter 7).

Policies and principles are constantly under discussion and regularly revised. At present, the IFC, for example, is in the middle of a process, together with the Equator banks and civil society, to "update" its policies.[90] Nevertheless, some issues concerning the policies must be raised since they are related to the functioning or mandate of the mechanisms. The following practical or managerial subjects related to the policies were presented in the questionnaire.

Often the question is raised of whether the Inspection Panel should be involved in the reassessments of safeguard policies. During my years at the bank, I was involved in discussions about the revision of both the Forests Policy[91] and the Indigenous Peoples Policy[92] on an informal basis. Legal advisors to the panel consider the involvement of panel members to be a conflict of interest. The view expressed is that the panel is there to investigate whether bank projects have been conducted according to the bank's policies. Although one can very well understand the more legalistic approach of this view, it is regrettable that the experiences of the members of the panel both at the bank and in the field investigating compliance with bank policies are not taken into account when policies are amended by the board. This situation derives from the rule that a judge does not make the law but only enforces it. The discussion in itself is an indication of further steps toward making the accountability mechanisms within the MFIs, such as the Inspection Panel, more judicial.

Each time the policies are revised, the process of revision is followed closely from outside the World Bank by the NGO community and, in the case of IFC policies, also by the Equator banks. On this point, Shannon Lawrence of Environmental Defense notes:

In principle, the World Bank's safeguard policies, as they are called, are important tools to protect communities and the environment. By

ensuring environmental assessment standards, consultation with affected communities, information disclosure, compensation and livelihood restoration, the protection of biodiversity, and other goals, the
safeguard policies help to reduce the negative impacts of development
projects and promote positive outcomes. The safeguard policies were
designed to guarantee certain standards of social and environmental
protection in World Bank projects, even if these protections are not
provided under national law. Recognition of the power imbalances
within countries, through which communities' rights are often sub-
verted, was an important factor in the development of the safeguard
policies ... Despite the importance of the safeguard policies and their
achievements, the World Bank's policy framework has come under increasing pressure since the late 1990s. The Bank failed to comprehen-
sively implement and to consistently update its safeguard policies based
on the latest best practice standards and the findings of multi-stakeholder reviews. Elements of Bank Management and some member governments have disingenuously argued that the policies cost too much,
and have charged them with slowing or reducing Bank lending.[93]

Some critical observers of the Inspection Panel go a step further, saying
that the policies of the World Bank have been compromised by the bank as
a result of panel reporting.[94] In Washington, DC, one can listen to the view
expressed regularly that some of the stronger bank policies, such as the
Indigenous Peoples Policy, are being weakened as a result of critical reporting by the panel on policy violations. With this critique, the NGO community
has conveyed its conviction that the panel's reports have a strong influence.
No doubt there is an influence on the bank, as has often been expressed by
management itself, by the board, and by the president. Yet this has sometimes led to derisive reactions within the panel's internal circles. One such
remark was: "It is one or the other: you believe in strong policies without
any control on enforcement or you want the control." So the final query of
the questionnaire was whether the MFIs and transnational corporations
(TNCs) take steps to weaken their principles in response to strong judgments made by the members of accountability mechanisms.

"USE OF COUNTRY SYSTEMS"

Lately, there have been proposals from management to transform the process that guarantees the use of the safeguard policies in World Bank projects. Today, the bank is in competition with private-sector banks that
operate in the same market, and in the past decade it has lost part of its
market to the private banks.[95] In particular, middle-income countries can
borrow from the private sector at almost the same interest rates and conditions. Questions have been raised about the bank's many procedures, policies, and principles. Why go through such a lengthy process, particularly if

it is also costly? Besides, many countries feel they have already put in place enough systems, institutions, and national legislation to guarantee the equivalence of their own policies and standards with those of the World Bank. This process was accelerated by the entry of the twelve eastern European states into the European Union. These twelve countries, six of them borrowing countries,[96] had to adopt the European environmental and social legislation before entering the union.[97]

One effect of the so-called "use of country systems" is clear: the bank will "make use of the country's national, sub-national, or sectoral implementing institutions and applicable rules, laws, regulations, policies, and procedures for the activity being supported by the Bank."[98] The idea is that the costs for the borrowing countries will be substantially reduced since they do not need to create parallel structures to the systems they already have in place. Inside and outside the bank the question of what this new approach will mean for the role of the Inspection Panel has been raised and intensely discussed. The conclusion has been that the role of the panel has not changed. The "use of country systems" will be in place only in countries that have national legislation equal to the policies and safeguards of the World Bank. In case of minor gaps, management has to make sure these are filled with supplementary policies.

Thus, when a request is submitted to the panel by a country that is using its own systems, the panel "could, with regard to the issues raised, examine Management's assessment of the equivalence of the relevant Bank policies and procedures with the country system."[99] In practice, this means that the panel has to make a "judgment" about the judgment of management when declaring a country's systems equal to the policies and safeguards of the bank. With Ibrahim Shihata's earlier concern in mind, one can raise the question of whether this makes the panel more of a "policing body." If so, the mandate of the panel would be rather different from what it was before. Former president Jim Wolfensohn wrote in 1998 about the panel that "By giving private citizens – and especially the poor – a new means of access to the Bank, it has empowered and given voice to those we most need to hear."[100]

ACCESS TO THE INSPECTION PANEL

Another crucial subject for the optimal functioning of the mechanism is its accessibility by affected people. The panel has often been asked how people in remote areas confronted with the execution of World Bank projects in their living area can even know about the Inspection Panel, let alone the procedures to file a claim. International NGOs likewise point out this problem, which they see as contributing to an unlevel playing field. While reporting on the procedures of the Asian Development Bank (ADB), a group of eleven NGOs have stated the following about this issue: "The ADB's requirements for an eligible Inspection Request are based on

the assumption that the ADB is working with project-targeted counter-
parts that are (a) well informed about ADB policies and procedures and
(b) have the resources and technical knowledge equivalent to the ADB.
The legalistic language of the Inspection Policy and the requirements for
filing an Inspection reveal the ADB's lack of awareness of the cultural and
resource differences between itself as an international institution and the
project-targeted local communities."[101]

The resolution establishing the Inspection Panel states the following
about outreach: "Management will make significant efforts to make the Inspection Panel better known in borrowing countries, but will not provide
technical assistance or funding to potential requesters."[102] As far as I have
observed, management has hardly shown any effort over the past decade to
make the panel known in the borrowing countries, especially in the most
remote areas where access to the panel could be of critical importance. It
might be too much to ask that management inform the bank's clients
about how and where they can file a complaint against the projects that
management designs and implements. On the other hand, management
should be trained to understand that access to the panel is an essential
right for vulnerable people who are harmed or could be harmed.

The subject of languages has also been an issue since the beginning of
the accountability mechanisms. The question is whether people have the
right to lodge a claim in their own native language. The ADB has received
criticism because its Inspection Policy requires complainants to make their
requests in English even though English is the official language of only a
small group of countries. The abovementioned group of eleven NGOs commented on this: "Even in countries where English is the official language,
local people usually speak their own languages and cannot be expected to
conduct correspondence in English as required by the Policy or to understand the ADB policies, which also only exist in English. The ADB's requirement to file inspection Requests in English stands in opposition to the
World Bank's Inspection Policy, which accepts Requests in all languages
and expects the Bank Management to translate their responses to the language spoken by the Requesters."[103]

The most encouraging and fascinating proposal concerning access of
the poor to an accountability mechanism is to be found in Canada. As a
member of the Inspection Panel, I took part in a round table discussion in
Canada at McGill University in Montreal. Canadian and World Bank experts discussed different topics and exchanged information with a main focus on environmental impact assessments. During the session, Husain
Sadar, a Canadian expert, referred to the Canadian Environmental Assessment Act, which contains a provision for "participant funding." Article 58
of the Act states: "(1.1) For the purposes of this Act, the Minister shall establish a participant funding program to facilitate the participation of the
public in comprehensive studies, mediations and assessments by review
panels established under either subsection 33(1) or 40(2)." Canada

appears to be unique in what it offers to its citizens. Thus, in the case of large projects such as energy plants and pipelines, Canada sets aside a portion of the budget to support the participation of those in the vicinity of the project who might be affected.[104] People may use the budget for legal advice, to organize information sessions, to train complainants on how to operate in hearings, and so on. A democracy is optimal when a government sets aside a budget for those who want to oppose the acts of the same government. A somewhat similar opportunity is offered by the IFC's ombudsman (the CAO), who offers training support for people who take part in a mediation process (see chapter 4).

RELATIONS BETWEEN THE INSPECTION PANEL AND MANAGEMENT

Over the years, the relationship between the Inspection Panel and management has had its ups and downs. But more recently, it has entered somewhat calmer waters. Managers had to get used to the panel becoming involved in its projects at a certain stage, depending on when a request for an investigation arrived. This involvement was certainly felt to be inconvenient. In the early years an expression circulated in the bank among management: "Are you panel-proof?" Nevertheless, the cry in the outside world for an independent accountability mechanism was received at the bank. These days there is full acceptance of the existence of the mechanism, but this does not automatically mean that the outcomes of the panel's work are easily accepted.

In the daily relations between the Inspection Panel and management there are several recurring issues. As mentioned earlier, the panel has had to press hard to gain access to all the relevant internal documents related to a project. This can concern even internal e-mail conversations about a project. For management, this was not an easy issue. Internal protests were expressed. One day, President Wolfensohn asked whether we wanted to see e-mails to grandmothers. So the panel had to explain that today official communications are often in the form of e-mails. The panel finally convinced management that e-mails about projects could lend insight into the way that projects and decisions were developed.

Relevant internal documents could also contain proprietary information – for example, in cases where the private sector is involved. Members of the Inspection Panel and their staff are subject to the same requirements of confidentiality as the bank staff. In certain cases they may even have to sign a specific confidentiality agreement in order to get access to information provided to third parties under such conditions. This is no different from requirements in the private sector. The panel has always respected this rule and, for this reason, has insisted that it be able to see such contracts.

On several occasions bank management raised the question of whether it could view the final draft version of a panel report to verify factual details. The argument was that factual errors in data could be avoided. The question was heavily debated. Given the independence of the mechanism, one can fully understand the hesitation or unwillingness to grant management's request. The panel's Administrative Procedures state: "Recommendations and findings of the Panel shall be strictly impartial: only facts relevant to the Request or investigation under consideration shall be relevant to their decisions. Consideration of political factors shall be strictly prohibited."[105]

An argument in favour is that real facts, such as figures and data, could be interpreted wrongly. If such errors were then communicated to the panel, it could decide whether to accept the information as pure fact or to treat it as interpretative. So the final say was to remain with the panel. Those who were against granting management's request argued that doing so would open the door to involving management, whose members are an object of panel investigations. Another strong argument against delivering the final draft of panel reports to management is that the requesters are not given the same opportunity to see draft reports. Creating this opportunity for the requesters was felt to be a risk, as the draft reports might be leaked before the board could take a final decision.

Another issue affecting the panel's relations with management concerns the position of the general counsel (GC), head of the legal department at the World Bank. The GC is an advisor to both management and the Board of Directors. As a result, he or she is also an advisor to the Inspection Panel. The structure stems from the US legal system. Those educated in Roman law (the system in most European countries) regard this structure as producing a conflict of interest. When this was discussed at the time of the panel's establishment, the then general counsel, the late Ibrahim Shihata, disagreed with the view that a conflict of interest existed:

> The request of some NGOs that the Board should have a legal counsel to advice on Panel matters, separate from the Bank's General Counsel, was not granted. It was recalled that the General Counsel is the Counsel of the Bank as a whole, not one organ of it. He or she provides legal advice to both the President and the Board on all matters, and neither the President nor the Board has a role in the formulation of his or her views. This position allowed the General Counsel to issue statements to the Bank's underwriters and external auditors without either of them questioning his statements. In any event, the General Counsel was not involved in the preparation of Management's response to the Requests for Inspection, and there was no scope, therefore, for the "conflict of interest."[106]

Thus the argument that there existed a conflict of interest was not accepted.

It is nevertheless clear that the general counsel is deeply involved in bank matters. The GC signs the Statutory Committee Report, which informs the board that the loan and project submitted for approval complies with the bank's legal requirements. This report is of interest to the borrower and the other members of the institution. The legal department approves all loans, amendments, and other project documents before they go to the board for verification that they are in compliance with all applicable policies and procedures.

RELATIONS BETWEEN THE INSPECTION PANEL AND THE PRESIDENT

The president of the World Bank is president not only of the board but also of management and staff. When communicating with the president, one has to be clear about the capacity in which he or she is functioning. In the years that I was a member of the Inspection Panel, the panel always had easy access to President Jim Wolfensohn. If difficulties arose, it was a matter of him, rather than the panel, being placed in a dilemma: he had to decide whether to support management in its resistance to the panel's findings or to accept the findings of an independent panel working on behalf of the board of the bank. And difficulties indeed arose on several occasions. I will never forget the irritations between Wolfensohn and Jim MacNeill, chairman of the panel, about bank projects and panel findings. If future living conditions of thousands of people in a project area were at stake, Jim MacNeill could fight for their rights, reminding the president and his staff about the bank's rule that after a project's completion people in project areas must always find themselves in a situation at least equal to or better than their circumstances before the project was undertaken. People should never be worse off. The president, in turn, sometimes had to defend a project on the grounds that the resulting economic development would bring long-term benefits to a whole nation. In these discussions it was often pointed out that today's developed countries also went through difficult times during which people lost their land and jobs, such as when coalmines were closed. At the end of the day, the panel's findings were always accepted by President Wolfensohn.

Before tabling a report at a board meeting, the panel always had a meeting with the president. In fact, if Wolfensohn himself was chairing a board meeting at which a panel report was tabled, the panel's message had its best chance of being brought fully to light. In accordance with the bank's internal rules,[107] when the president is absent, board meetings are chaired by one of the bank's managing directors. In such cases, the panel automatically finds itself in a different position. One cannot expect an official of management to be as independent as the president. A senior manager, who bears a responsibility for the project placed on the table, will tend to defend management. The president is normally aware of his or her double function and should be able to distinguish between these two roles. I never understood why the board members, who had established the Inspection

Panel as *their* mechanism to investigate difficult projects on *their* behalf, never decided to designate one of the executive directors to chair a meeting in which a panel report was tabled.

In the past, the accountability mechanism of the Asian Development Bank had to report first to the president. Under the first revision of the resolution, the mechanism now reports directly to the board and to the president as chairman of the board. At the Inter-American Development Bank the structure of the relationship is still the same as the ADB's previous situation: investigation reports go to the president for approval before they are sent to the entire board. At the European Bank for Reconstruction and Development, the Office of the Chief Compliance Officer sends the report of an assessment either to the president or directly to the board.[108]

As mentioned in the introduction of this chapter, the subjects described above formed the basis of an international survey. The results of the survey are recorded in the next chapter.

Results of an International Survey

This chapter details the outcomes of a questionnaire-based survey on accountability mechanisms. A selected focus group of international experts (see appendix 4) responded to the survey.

Participation in the survey was limited to those who created the mechanisms, managers in the institutions confronted with investigations, members of staff of the mechanisms, or representatives of nongovernmental organizations (NGOs) that closely follow the multilateral financial institutions (MFIs). In any event, those who are well informed about the phenomenon of accountability mechanisms constitute a rather small group of people from around the globe. These individuals formed the basis for the creation of the focus group that received the survey. In the introduction to this book, the criteria for selecting the focus group are described. Originally, I planned to study both transnational corporations (TNCs) and the private financial sector. In the course of the study, I limited myself to the financial sector. In the questions posed by the survey, TNCs are still visible.

The questions raised and the responses that were received are grouped here in twelve sections. Each section is introduced with background information related to the questions grouped within it. When necessary, background information is presented for a specific question.

In some cases I will comment on the nature of the responses either directly or at the end of a section (under the subheading "Lessons Learned"). The responses to forty of the survey's forty-seven questions have been processed: the remaining questions either overlapped or were irrelevant. In most cases the tabulated responses are presented as rounded percentages. In general the participants responded to most questions, leaving a question unanswered only in rare cases. If a question was clearly not answered by a substantive group, I make note of this. It has to be mentioned that in some cases the experts were not easy to place in one group or another – for example, a respondent who used to work for an MFI but is now an independent consultant. A total of seventy-four specialists, or experts,[1] responded to the survey. In the few cases where one questionnaire was answered by two or more respondents, the answers were still treated as those of a single respondent. The four different groups of respondents were:

Group 1: twenty-four experts working for MFIS

Group 2: thirteen experts working for different transnational corporations, many of them private banks

Group 3: fifteen users of the accountability mechanisms: representatives of NGOS

Group 4: twenty-two independent experts from different parts of the world

ACCOUNTABILITY MECHANISMS: A RESPONSE TO THE FAST GROWTH OF CROSS-BORDER FINANCIAL TRANSACTIONS

The first two questions of the survey were related to the need for the creation of accountability mechanisms in general for MFIS and TNCS. Cross-border financial transactions have increased significantly in recent decades.[2] Foreign direct investment capital inflows in developing countries have surged by 40 per cent to US$233 billion. The role of large TNCS in the world economy continues to grow, which is reflected in foreign direct investment and in the operations of foreign affiliates.[3] Resource flows from the World Bank are only one-third as much as the private foreign direct investment flowing to developing countries.[4] These questions were followed by four questions concerning the independence of the mechanisms, a difference in their structure for MFIS and the private sector, and the need to always make the mechanisms' reports public.

Question 1

Amid globalization and rapidly growing international financial transactions, an urgent need arose for the existence or creation of "accountability mechanisms" within multilateral financial institutions.

The most important outcome was that in general all groups agreed that there is a need for accountability mechanisms for both the MFIS and the private sector. When asked about such a need, the MFIS, the NGOS, and the experts from the private sector overwhelmingly agreed, at 100%. Among the experts working with or for the MFIS themselves, 83% agreed, while among the group of independent researchers, the total was 70%.

The following statements were offered:

• One expert made this statement about the clear need for MFIS to have accountability mechanisms: "Certainly some constituencies thought it was urgent, but there was also a school of thought that the banks should remain 'banks,' and not be accountable to the public except through the government shareholders. In effect, it was a crisis for governance of the banks, given the strong views in both directions."

- An expert well informed about the World Bank said: "I am not sure if I would agree with the statement that an 'urgent need arose.' The World Bank's Inspection Panel arose after a very long and protracted campaign by advocacy NGOs. The U.S. Government was instrumental in pushing for the Inspection Panel's creation. It was a number of years before other MFIs instituted their own accountability mechanisms with EBRD [European Bank for Reconstruction and Development] only instituting in 2004."
- Other experts wrote: "Until then there was practically no accountability for IFIs [international financial institutions] in spite of the lofty goals of their stated operational policies."
- "The growing negative social and environmental impacts of development were a major influence too."
- "There is a definite need to ensure accountability. As the role of MFIs is to assist poverty alleviation and development, there exists a need to ensure that there is consistency of approach and that these goals are appropriately met. As MFIs operate in a public arena and are funded by taxpayers' money, it is essential that they be accountable and transparent."

Many reactions also referred to the lack of options for bringing the MFIs under any court system. One lawyer for an MFI stated, "MFIs should have a Panel system to be reviewed by judicial experts since MFIs are not under the court system of any country." Others said that there should also be strong domestic courts that can address the actions of governments that now fail to appropriately carry out their mandates. Another issue mentioned by several experts from the different groups was that accountability mechanisms have always existed and were not necessarily created as a consequence of globalization or of an increasing number of international financial transactions. Globalization perhaps increased the urgency.

Question 2

There is also the need to create accountability mechanisms within TNCs and private banks.

On the question about the need for such mechanisms for the private sector, the four groups confirmed their positions as indicated in their responses to question 1. Again, the NGOs were most convinced, at 93%. Interestingly, 92% of the experts from the private sector themselves agreed, followed closely by the experts from the MFIs, at 91%. This time the independent experts, at 81%, seemed to be more convinced about the need for the mechanisms in the private sector.

Remarkably, the experts from the MFIs saw a greater need for the private sector to have accountability mechanisms. When asked about the institutions for which they work, 83% agreed, but when asked about the private sector, the figure rose to 91%. The opposite view was held by the experts from the private sector, 100% of whom agreed concerning the MFIs while reporting only 92.3% agreement for their own sector. It is understandable that the respondents tended to be more hesitant when contemplating mechanisms for their own work places. One MFI expert expressed the point this way: "These institutions need an Accountability Mechanism as much as the MFIS, if not more, for the simple reason that they are profit driven. Pursuit of profit can sometimes blur social concerns." Another MFI expert was rather harsh in his assessment of the private banks: "This development is less clear. For most TNCs and private banks, the management is looking for protection from civil society, rather than true accountability."

Statements made by respondents from the private sector revealed somewhat different sentiments than those implied by the summary data. One private-sector expert wrote:

> Specific accountability mechanisms for commercial private banks/
> financial institutions would be highly inappropriate. Private commercial
> banks do not implement projects on the ground. They are also not ac-
> countable to "affected communities" like a publicly-funded MFI (e.g.,
> World Bank, IFC [International Finance Corporation], EBRD, ADB
> [Asian Development Bank]). They are accountable to their sharehold-
> ers. Of course, private banks must act within their own good citizenship
> standards and seek to finance transactions that meet high standards. But
> the difference is, private banks do not interact with affected communi-
> ties. This is the project developer's role. Private commercial banks
> ensure that the project developer is adhering to certain environmental
> and social standards (e.g., Equator Principles or some other standard) and
> then ensure that the project sponsor is meeting its environmental
> and social obligations through third-party review and monitoring.

Another expert from the private sector agreed with the latter statement, writing: "Accountability amongst TNCs and private banks differs from MFIs, as the private sector has a primary responsibility to its shareholders and a secondary responsibility to other stakeholders. However, the interests of all stakeholders need to be taken into account, and the private sector increasingly understands the risks of limited transparency and accountability."

One of the independent experts made the following remark: "I doubt that this is a 'necessity,' rather a response to a widespread social pressure." Almost all the other comments from the independent experts strongly supported the need for accountability mechanisms:

- "I agree [with the statement in question 2], voluntary action is not sufficient, and the only effective instruments at the moment are accountability Rules and Stock Exchange Rules. Parmalat's collapse shows these are
  insufficient."
- "There is absolutely a need for such mechanisms that work mainly cross-
  border and that may become 'untouchable' – in this, there should be no
  difference for Multilateral Organizations and TNCs. For the latter, these

count even more: Multilateral Organizations have representatives of all countries in the Board to represent their interest."

This latter statement interestingly raises the issue of democratic control, which is lacking in the private sector. Another expert defended the private nature of the private sector, saying: "I think that they should have such mechanisms, that it would be good for them if they did, but I think that it is an issue for TNCS and private banks."

An NGO expert referred to the subject of law: "I wonder whether real accountability can be generated internally in such entities or whether we should ensure they are subject to the law of the countries they operate in as well as to international law."

Question 3

Accountability should be the same for MFIS, TNCS, private banks, and export credit agencies (ECAS).

On the question of whether accountability should be the same for MFIS and the private sector, the respondents were at odds about the differences between multilateral organizations and the private sector. The standard deviation was high. A strong majority of the NGO experts agreed (73%), as did a small majority of the officials from the MFIS (52%), while a majority of the private-sector experts disagreed (61%). The independent experts were almost equally divided.

All the experts seem to have agreed on the importance of accountability. But between the groups, there was no clear basis for the difference of opinion on whether accountability should be standardized:

- One expert from the private sector argued: "Standardized market transparency in a global environment is essential."
- An NGO expert wrote: "I think that this question is too vague. Given the very different structure and function of these institutions, the structure and function of accountability mechanisms should be different. That is not to say that accountability should be considered different at each of the institutions; merely that the way in which that accountability is reached might have to be different."
- One MFI specialist stated: "Different stakeholders/different objectives. So the accountability mechanisms should also differ."
- Almost the same wording was chosen by another NGO expert: "The principle is the same, the modalities different."
- An independent expert said: "The different bodies serve different functions and stakeholders. Consequently the type and extent of accountability must be different if it is to be meaningful."
- Another independent expert wrote: "Recognizing considerable differences in the nature of mandate, corporate structure, operational procedures and management styles, it may not be possible or even desirable

to adopt the same Accountability Mechanisms for each and every financial institution/organization." Several more comments contained the same message.

In their own ways, many expressed that public entities should be more accountable than the private sector since they rely on public money or tax money:

- One expert from an MFI wrote: "With public ownership, the level of Accountability is probably the highest for MFIs and Export Credit Agencies."
- Another said: "I can understand the point that allocation of public money merits more probity than the use of private funds. If a corporation wants to waste its own money, and causes no harm (to society or environment) in the process, should it be prevented from doing so? The phrase 'the same' is too strong in the question unless explained or qualified." This specialist went further, adding: "MFIs require the highest accountability, since their multilateral nature often provides them immunity from any national or international law."

As mentioned above, many respondents referred to the fact that people have the option to turn to local courts when private-sector projects are in violation of standards, even though most also mentioned poor and inefficient local legislation and regulatory mechanisms. One MFI expert wrote that it is too costly for private business to have an accountability mechanism and said that private banks will be able to utilize the existing systems of MFIs and export credit agencies when they examine loans to megaprojects. Nevertheless, just like the other three groups, the majority of MFI experts were in favour of accountability mechanisms.

The majority of experts from the private sector believed that there was a need for the creation of accountability mechanisms for their own sector. Nevertheless, most private-sector respondents maintained that in their sector the system should be different:

- "There are very different roles, responsibilities, and stakeholders for MFIs, TNCs, private banks, and ECAs."
- "The mandates, audiences, and stakeholders of each differ. The more public an organization, the more it is expected to be accountable, as its mandate is primarily linked to serving the public good."
- Another private-sector respondent made almost the same comment but went further, saying: "Accountability amongst TNCs and private banks differs from MFIs, as the private sector has a primary responsibility to its shareholders and a secondary responsibility to other stakeholders. However, the interests of all stakeholders need to be taken into account, and the private sector increasingly understands the risks of limited transparency and accountability."

- One private-sector expert offered another view: "TNCs and private banks are already under legal accountability systems for financial control, such as National Banks, SOX [Sarbanes-Oxley Act] and Basel II.[5] This is out of the scope of our expertise. The impact of their transactions on developing countries and sustainable development is lacking an accountability system."

LESSONS LEARNED

Overall, it is clear that many in the private sector themselves believe in the necessity of accountability mechanisms. The representatives of the NGOs gave a high level of credence to the idea that the private sector is in need of accountability mechanisms but maintained that these should have their own unique structure. The immunity of the MFIs against liability for adverse project outcomes is definitely a hindrance for people who are harmed by a project financed by one of the MFIs, as has been argued before. That the liability of the MFIs would be clearer in the case of cross-border projects financed by private commercial banks is just as doubtful.

The notion that accountability and also liability in the private sector are covered by national legal procedures was somewhat pertinent for certain respondents. Within a robust democracy with strong environmental and social laws, and where people have substantial access to complaints procedures and financial support to file their claims in courts, it might in "normal" circumstances be right to rely on the legal system and the provisions delivered by the state to protect citizens' rights. Nevertheless, incidents like the deadly gas leak in Bhopal indicate the difficulties that the poor can encounter while defending their rights. The financial power of companies able to hire "an army" of lawyers is overwhelming. In the case of activities of a TNC operating outside its "homeland," it is even more difficult. I conclude that at present the need to create independent accountability mechanisms both at the MFIs and in private financial institutions seems irrefutable.

Question 4

The level of an institution's accountability is related to the level of independence of its mechanism.

Almost all the experts endorsed the importance of independence. Among private-sector experts only two individuals disagreed, while the majority agreed. Not surprisingly, the NGO experts overwhelmingly agreed, at 100%. For members of the MFI group, the total was about the same; with one exception they all agreed. Among the independent experts, two had no opinion and the rest agreed.

The statements from the MFI experts were strong:

- "Conditio sine qua non."
- "In order to be objective you need to be independent."

- "The greater the independence the greater degree to which the mechanism can seek to hold actors accountable, though it is not just the level but also the remedies available."
- Another made a remarkable statement on the issue of independence: "But in an inverse relationship. Greater accountability does not necessarily result from greater independence."
- "There may be alternatives if the mechanism's emphasis is on resolution of disputes."

The few comments made by the private-sector experts were somewhat different. As one could expect, they showed a greater understanding of the private sector's different position. One said: "In theory, yes, but in practice, and as it applies to banks, less so. Independent assessment of bank's activities would be cumbersome, and the model should be that the bank undertakes to be transparent and accountable, and this is audited by public opinion." I agree with this remark on transparency; nevertheless, I wonder how the public can hold a bank accountable if there are no rules and structures concerning how to assess the bank's conduct. In a way, one of the independent experts raised this issue, saying: "Partially, independence is no guarantee, as independent bodies have no means of ensuring access to 100% of documents. Even last week there were press reports of large-scale shredding of documents by the UK government."

One private-sector expert saw determining the level of "independence" as a tricky matter and went on to say: "An Accountability Mechanism, to be effective, can NOT be just FAULT FINDING as [with] the World Bank Inspection Panel. For it to be effective, an ombudsman-like role/function that seeks to find solutions to problems is more effective. This can still be a highly independent function and not report directly to 'project management' (e.g., reporting to a project sponsor CEO). The key here, again, is full independence to report/disclose on recommendations and findings."

LESSONS LEARNED

I agree with the latter comment. If an institution establishes only an accountability mechanism or compliance review panel without a problem-solving function, it runs the risk of creating a highly judicial system that will deal mostly with the question of guilt and liability.

On the independence issue, I want to note that as long as the insiders of an institution are in the position of overseeing their own conduct – as has long been the case in many organizations and companies and as is often still the case – outsiders will not trust the outcomes of the investigations or the results of any control mechanism. It is human nature to defend errors when they are an effect of one's own activities. It is the same nature that makes outsiders uncomfortable with the outcomes. This has long been known, so it is surprising that it took so much time before independence became an issue at the different organizations. During my time in the European Parliament, we discussed the independence of the the European Commission's evaluations of European development projects. It was considered very normal for officials, responsible for the design and implementation of projects, to evaluate their own activities.[6] With further globalization and the fast growth of cross-border investments, the issue has become of paramount importance, as shown in chapter 1.

Question 5

There is a significant difference between accountability functions for private banks and for multilateral financial institutions.

The views expressed on this point were somewhat in line with the responses given to the question posed earlier about accountability being the same for MFIs and private-sector institutions. On the distinction between accountability functions used by private banks and by MFIs, the respondents were more convinced than before. The MFI experts themselves agreed most strongly (87%), followed by the NGO experts (85%). Likewise, 72% of the private-sector experts agreed. The independent experts diverged somewhat from the others: only 50% agreed, 28% had no opinion, and 21% disagreed.

Thus the summary of responses showed a high majority reconfirming their earlier expressed opinion that there is a significant difference between the functions used by private banks and MFIs. The written comments overwhelmingly referred to the different nature of the institutions. Statements from the MFI experts included:

- "This is an important topic and well worth discussing in greater depth. The private and public entities have different definitions for the term, in my view."
- "I don't know of any private banks with an accountability mechanism. But they would have to be different since they have different forms of governance, objectives, founding statutes, etc."
- Another MFI expert referred again to the different legal positions of MFIs and private banks, saying: "Due to their multilateral nature, MFIs have an inherent immunity status that private banks do not have. Accountability functions of MFIs therefore do have an inherent legal dimension, and are for complainants in fact the last resort for redressing efforts. Accountability functions of private banks would have more a complaint function. They provide these institutions with a facility to learn from mistakes reported by complainants. In case of non-redress,

complainants can in this case still file civil and/or criminal court cases. Such an option does not exist for MFIS."

This view from an MFI expert was also echoed in a strong statement by an NGO expert:

- "Sure there is a difference between accountability functions, but at the end of the day, the public has a right to sue private institutions, while they cannot sue the World Bank. So accountability 'mechanisms' will be different if you factor in legal rather than quasi-legal processes. I would argue that those who have experience with arbitration mechanisms that involve the private sector, those who have experience with class action lawsuits and suing corporations for their environmental and social impacts, as well as those who have experience with accountability mechanisms in the public sector should put their heads together and analyze what the differences are, whether those differences imply seriously different approaches, and how citizens can gain greater standing in all cases."

I can only agree with this perspective: further study is necessary.

A more fundamental concern, mentioned mostly by MFI experts, was whether there should be a difference:

- "Why should these be different accountability functions? Moreover, it makes matters unnecessarily complicated."
- "There is a significant difference but there need not be, although due consideration must be given to ownership structure and mandate differences. It is inevitable that the use of public funds by an international organization will attract higher levels of scrutiny and accountability."
- "There certainly are differences ... but the accountability mechanisms of private banks draw inspiration from those of MFIS."

This latter view may be near the truth. Again, an MFI expert suggested that the subject warranted further study. I can only agree.

LESSONS LEARNED

The comments made about the immunity status of the MFIS, particularly the conclusion that the accountability mechanisms of the MFIS "therefore do have an inherent legal dimension," are important to notice (see chapter 6). Yet it is evident that accountability as a concept should not be different for MFIS and private-sector financial institutions. The distinction could, but not necessarily should, be found in what one MFI respondent referred to as "ownership structure and mandate differences." Indeed, because the MFIS operate with tax money, it is clear that civil society has the right to ask them to be accountable. TNCs are owned by shareholders, and private financial institutions are owned both by shareholders and by depositors who entrust their private capital to the banks. Those who own shares in TNCs, such as private share holders and pension-fund holders, could demand that TNCs be held accountable. In the case of private banks, this demand could also be made by those who have accounts at the institutions. However, there is more: the scale of the private financial institutions and their influence today in the globalized world make them equally, if not more, responsible for the developments and changes the world is experiencing. As stressed in chapter 1, we need new structures of control since the influence of nation-states is diminishing as a result of globalization. What these structures should look like is the urgent question.

Even though civil society is losing ground, it still believes that it can control the world locally, regionally, and nationally via democratically elected bodies, such as parliaments, or via their representatives in the international organizations created by nation-states. Today, the private-sector financial institutions are the driving force. Thus they have an obligation to open up to the world society. To do this, they must create an accountability mechanism (see chapter 5 and the recommendations of the Bank for International Settlements). What format and structure it should have needs further study. But its creation could begin with an initiative of the group of banks that adopted the Equator Principles. As a group, they could establish a mechanism that in its working procedures would be somewhat similar to the mechanisms of the MFIs. With the success of the Equator Principles, there would be good momentum behind such an initiative.

Finally, accountability without transparency is not accountability. Conversely, transparency without openness or final publication of accountability reports is not transparency. These concepts are interrelated, a view that leads to the following question.

Question 6

The reports of the accountability mechanisms must always be made public.

Not surprisingly, on the issue of public reporting, there was overwhelming agreement among NGO experts (100%) and strong agreement among MFI experts (87%), private-sector experts (85%), and independent researchers (81%). The reactions to the question were crystal clear, as illustrated by the following comments:

Respondents working for an MFI:
- "Globalization, involvement of the general public requires transparency and disclosure."
- "If not open to the public, the mechanisms themselves jeopardize its reason d'être."
- "The only guarantee for full independent accountability is maximum transparency to the public."

- "Unless they contain information protected by intellectual property rights or could be deemed as dangerous to national security."
- "I guess there may be cases where secrecy might be positive but it's hard to imagine a specific case. I would not exclude that possibility though."
- "Absolutely, but some provisions should be made to protect individuals and proprietary information."

Respondents working for the private sector:
- "This is the key ingredient to an effective accountability mechanism: full disclosure and public reporting."
- "However, carefulness should be taken into account."

Respondents working for the NGO sector:
- "If there is some specific difficulty to disclose information on business confidentiality, only this confidential information could be deleted. But if that information is really important to judge public interest, the information should be disclosed."
- "Only if and when they become public do the accountability procedures reach their end."
- One respondent referred to the processes and roles of accountability mechanisms that give good reason for not making reports public. Even if the mechanisms are independent and fair, in the case of arbitration or mediation processes they should allow for the privacy of the parties involved. The respondent said: "Findings of fact should always be public, but if the parties to an agreement have been able to resolve a conflict to the satisfaction of claimants, and the claimants do not feel it is in their interest to disclose terms of the agreement, then there should be some accommodation." The respondent finally remarks that "public disclosure or transparency is not the same or 'equal' to accountability or problem-solving."

Independent experts:
- "Not necessarily. It depends on the structure of the organization and to whom the organization is accountable. It may be that 'naming and shaming' is not the most effective sanction for a private institution."

LESSONS LEARNED

It is clear from the statements that probably all the experts adhere to a high norm of maximum transparency and public reporting. I assume that most, if not all, of them know the sensitivity and importance of informing the public properly and at the right time. Nevertheless, many of them pointed out the exceptions that could or should be made. The following exceptions were mentioned as grounds for not disclosing information: (1) circumstances when parties involved agree not to disclose the outcome of a mediation process, (2) proprietary information, (3) information protected by intellectual property rights, and (4) information that could be deemed dangerous to national security. It is unlikely that anyone would object to these exceptions. The risk is in the interpretations. Who will declare information relevant to national security – the security committee of a democratically elected parliament or a minister under control of this parliament? Certain choices made in a democracy must be accepted. But not all states in the world have highly democratic systems.

What remains is the overwhelming agreement that reports finally have to be made public. Indeed, accountability and transparency go together.

AN ACCOUNTABILITY MECHANISM AND A PROBLEM-SOLVING FUNCTION

The World Bank has two different mechanisms, or functions, concerned with accountability (see chapters 2 and 3). The resolution that created the Inspection Panel gives the panel a mandate to investigate projects financed by the International Development Association (IDA) and the International Bank for Reconstruction and Development (IBRD), which together are still responsible for the main part of bank operations. The panel has no jurisdiction over projects undertaken by the International Finance Corporation (IFC) unless a request for investigation of an IFC project also financed by IDA/IBRD is presented to the panel.[7] The function of mediation is not introduced in the resolution, which determines the Inspection Panel's mandate.[8]

At a later date, the IFC, the third party in the World Bank Group, created the position of compliance advisor ombudsman (CAO). The CAO has three functions. First, there is a compliance role, which mandates the CAO "to independently assess whether IFC and MIGA [the Multilateral Investment Guarantee Agency] have complied with their safeguard policies, guidelines and procedures." The second role, the advisory role, tasks the CAO with providing "independent, timely and objective advice to the President of the World Bank Group and management of IFC and MIGA." The CAO's primary role is that of ombudsman, which requires that he or she "provide an accessible and effective mechanism for handling complaints"[9] and thereby "help resolve issues raised about the Social and Environmental projects and improve outcomes on the ground."[10] While the World Bank Inspection Panel reports directly to the bank's executive directors on violations in a quasi-judicial way, the work of the IFC's ombudsman can be seen as mediation or problem solving. The ombudsman reports to IFC management and regularly to the president.[11] As described in chapter 4, the CAO's different roles within the IFC caused confusion at the beginning among the stakeholders because it contains the risk of a conflict of interest.

Question 7

MFIs should have clearly separated and defined compliance functions: both a problem-solving/mediation mechanism and, as a last resort, an accountability mechanism, such as the Inspection Panel, that finally can come to a "judgment."

The need for a certain split between the two functions was well understood among the senior experts from the four focus groups. An overwhelming majority reacted positively to the notion of separating the two functions. The private-sector experts (100%) and the NGO experts (93%) agreed most strongly. Somewhat less coherence was found within the other two groups, with agreement among independent experts standing at 84% and among MFI experts at 75%.

These percentages suggest a perspective that is somewhat different from that indicated in the written comments:

- Some MFI experts shared the view that "the ombudsman function is relevant. However, what counts most is an independent investigation body like the Inspection Panel. The mix of functions within IFC/CAO is *not* helpful: tasks should be separated."
- Other MFI experts saw separation as an organizational matter to be addressed within the institutions: "Mediation [i.e., problem-solving] and inspection functions are both required but can be contained in one mechanism assuming that the mechanism has an appropriate constitution/terms of reference."
- One MFI expert commented on the situation at the Asian Development Bank (ADB), where the two functions are split: "However, such a mediation mechanism should be independent from Management, unlike the case of the ADB, where the SPF [special project facilitator] is to report to the President. Also I would recommend that the two functions are independent from each other, so that requesters/local communities can call on both functions at the same time. Again, this is unlike the ADB, where complainants are required to go first to the SPF, while the CRP [Compliance Review Panel] can be called upon only after the process with the SPF is exhausted. A problem-solving/mediation mechanism should also be instrumental in advising Management on how to implement recommendations from a compliance review process. It is very important that both functions are integrated into bank operations and procedures as a learning mechanism."
- There were two comments from the private sector, one of which referred to the World Bank Inspection Panel: "It has not been as effective as it could have been because it is a fully 'fault finding' mechanism. IFCs ombudsman mechanism is more solution-oriented and mediation driven ... Problem solving and mediation is in my opinion part of the business units, where Accountability comes under Supervision and/or Audit."
- One NGO expert made the following suggestion: "There is some risk that the mediation mechanism could be used as a further means of delay in meting out justice if the monitored body is not pursuing it in good faith. To counter this risk, an appropriate time limit for reaching resolution should be defined in advance, after which affected individuals/groups/ NGOs could proceed to the Panel/adjudication mechanism."

Many comments on this question also came from the independent researchers, such as:

- "It should be made possible to the IP [inspection panel] to by-pass the ombudsman procedure if necessary."
- "Here could well be other models as well."
- "It is as yet unclear what types of actions are being covered by the 'accountability mechanisms' being addressed in the questionnaire."
- "Needless to say that having more than ONE entity leads to more confusion, dilution of focus and bureaucratic rivalries and competitions. Depending upon the complexity/severity of a particular issue or issues, the Panel can then recommend specific way(s) to resolve it. Moreover, the Panel can identify a particular party, say the host country, the World Bank or an independent mediator etc. most suited to resolve certain issue(s). Such arrangements may have more credibility."

Question 8

Private banks (notably, the Equator banks) and TNCs should also have both a mediation function and an independent accountability mechanism.

In response to the question of whether private banks and TNCs should also have both functions, again a majority of all the groups agreed, but this time the experts' opinions differed to some extent. The highest majority was found among the NGO experts, of whom 92% agreed, a figure that does not differ much from their answer to the previous question concerning the MFIs. As described in chapter 5, the private financial institutions are under pressure to follow the MFIs in establishing an independent accountability mechanism modelled on the World Bank Inspection Panel. So the high percentage of the NGO community supporting this is not surprising.

The private-sector experts, who had been remarkably supportive of having both mechanisms at the MFIs, were less convinced when asked about their own sector, showing diversity in their reactions. Yet a majority agreed, at 61%. Without a doubt, the question was new when it was raised, and at this time the NGO community had started to put pressure on the private financial sector to establish an accountability mechanism. By contrast, the MFI experts, at 77%, showed greater agreement when asked about the private sector. The independent experts, at 60%, showed hesitation comparable to that seen among those from the private sector.

From the written comments, I cannot find a general trend that distinguishes one group of experts from another. Throughout all groups, four different types of comment arose. First, there were comments expressing *strong agreement*:

- "Yes, an Independent Investigation function is most important."
- "It would be to the benefit of all parties involved, especially if the mediation function works properly."

- "They should also have timeframes within which they should submit their findings/reports to avoid undue delays (if any)."

Second, there were comments expressing *strong disagreement*:

- "Private businesses are able to utilize existing systems such as courts and external auditors. In addition, it is too costly for private business to have an accountability mechanism."
- "It may be more appropriate that TNCs and private banks should emphasize the mediation function."
- "I disagree strongly, although I think it is a good idea, because I think it is difficult to prescribe such a mechanism to private banks."

Third, there were comments expressing *conditional agreement*:

- "Both mediation and accountability are certainly needed both for banks and TNCs. But whether those two mechanisms need to be *inside* the TNCs and banks is not clear. There may be a case for independent but mandatory mediation and accountability functions. In view of this caveat: +2."
- "Private Banks and TNCs should have these functions. However, how to secure the independence of the mechanism is really the key for these functions."
- "Voluntary sector initiatives are often very effective but need independent verification. The GRI [Global Reporting Initiative] offers an accountability system for private banks and TNCs on sustainability reporting and performance."

Fourth, there were comments expressing the view that there should be *only a mediation function*:

- "As private banks and TNCs are not immune under international law, accountability mechanisms should be situated in the national political sphere (i.e., courts), not separate. A mediation function should be required."

Some respondents raised interesting questions, such as: "If more than one bank is financing any one project, how would several accountability mechanisms work together?" Another asked: "To whom is such an organism accountable. For the World Bank this is the Board, for the private banks too?"

LESSONS LEARNED

While the two functions – one for problem solving and one for compliance/accountability review – are both recognized by most, it is obvious that a common idea about how to segregate the two functions does not yet exist. It is remarkable that no one mentioned the risk of a conflict of interest when one entity has to deliver both functions. The only comment that was somewhat related to this issue was the one that mentioned the need for an appropriate "constitution/terms of reference."

The two mechanisms – the compliance advisor ombudsman for the IFC and the Inspection Panel for IDA, the IBRD, and (in certain cases, as described above) the IFC – have not yet found an optimal balance, the exception being the arrangement at the Asian Development Bank.

This lack of balance could be resolved by introducing both an ombudsman function and a fully separate accountability mechanism for an entire institution. As described in chapter 4, two separate functions that are independent from one another have been implemented by the Asian Development Bank. The European Bank for Reconstruction and Development and the African Development Bank have also established independent review mechanisms that combine the mediation/problem-solving function with the compliance/inspection function. On this, the World Bank, which provides the role model for the other MFIS, is lagging behind.

In any case, it is clear that many questions for the private sector still remain to be answered. From the responses, one can conclude that the experts tend to be a little more doubtful about the need for the mechanisms with respect to their own sectors. Nevertheless, there is a majority view that both functions – a problem-solving mechanism and a compliance review/ accountability mechanism – are necessary for MFIS and private banks as well as for TNCS. This finding is a strong outcome of the study.

MANDATE OF AN ACCOUNTABILITY MECHANISM

The mandates of the different accountability mechanisms are constantly debated at the institutions that have such mechanisms. The basis of the World Bank Inspection Panel's mandate is related to the operational policies and procedures set by the bank,[12] such as those concerning environmental impact assessment, involuntary resettlement, and indigenous peoples. Its main task or mandate is to investigate whether management has violated these policies while designing and implementing a bank-financed project once a request for such an investigation has been submitted to the panel. The panel investigates, for example, whether the rules and procedures, assessments, screening, identification of adverse impacts, monitoring and implementation, categorization of the project, action plans to cover mitigation, and time schedules according to the policies are met. Along these lines, the panel has been valued as an important tool for affected people who want their complaints to be heard.

The panel is a demand-driven mechanism and cannot carry out an investigation if no request is received. The panel cannot investigate a project if 95 per cent of the project budget has already been spent, and the panel cannot monitor whether and how the actions agreed to by management as a result of a panel investigation are implemented. Yet in 2003, for the first time, the executive directors of the World Bank asked the panel to observe on the ground whether the agreed-upon mitigating measures were being implemented by management.[13]

Other mechanisms, such as the new Independent Review Mechanism of the African Development Bank, provide for a monitoring function as a result of lessons learned. The function is to be performed by the director of the Compliance Review and Mediation Unit. The complaints mechanism of the Japan Bank for International Cooperation (JBIC) also has a monitoring function. In this section, three questions are raised about a mechanism's mandate as it relates to the monitoring function.

Question 9

It is counterproductive to first carry out a full investigation without the power to monitor whether the necessary mitigation actions are implemented.

The majority of all four groups of experts agreed that it is counterproductive if an accountability mechanism does not have a mandate to determine whether the mitigation actions recommended following an investigation are implemented. Interestingly, the MFI experts, who have the most experience with the work of the mechanisms, agreed most strongly, at 73%. They were followed by the private-sector experts, at 66%. What is remarkable is that almost one-third of the private-sector experts did not provide written comments in response to this question. The majority of NGO experts (60%) agreed. Finally, the independent experts were the most divided among themselves, with only 57% in agreement. What could have caused this is not clear. Possibly the question (formulated as a statement) was too provocative. In a different wording the question was repeated later on (see below).

Among the few within the MFI group who slightly disagreed, the comments included:

- "The effectiveness of the mechanism would be greatly enhanced if authority to monitor is also provided."
- "It is at least sub-optimal."
- Another took the position that monitoring should be done only on the basis of a new request: "If there is a clear mechanism to monitor agreed implementation of mitigating actions, no role of a Panel is required. Only if there is a demonstration of neglect by management, the Panel should have a role based on an additional request."
- One asked whether the monitoring should be carried out by the panel or by a body outside the bank: "A full investigation, eventually released to stakeholders, is a powerful landmark on its own, with or without monitoring. Clearly, investigation plus monitoring would be more effective. Where the necessary monitoring function should best reside is not clear; inside the IP [inspection panel], or outside the IP in the WB [World Bank], or even outside the WB? All three sites have different merits."

Among the private-sector experts, almost no comments were made – in contrast to the NGO experts:

- "At least citizens affected get findings of fact. While I agree that it's wrongheaded for the Bank to deny the Panel the oversight function to ensure that mitigation and action plans are put in place, it is not counterproductive, but rather insufficient, for a full investigation to be carried out without having the power to do follow-up monitoring."
- "Maybe not counterproductive but certainly not effective. Lack of monitoring function is a 'Break in the chain' of accountability."

One NGO expert who disagreed said that it should be the role of the NGOs themselves to monitor whether mitigation takes place. This comment is almost similar to the previously mentioned comment made by the MFI expert who said that there could be an additional request.

Among the independent experts, there was one strong statement:

- In my opinion, this is the most serious weakness in most if not all Environmental Impact Assessment related legislation, which has so far been promulgated by many countries, including Canada. The principal question which needs to be asked: Why conduct costly and lengthy assessments or inspections without giving at least equal weight/importance to comprehensive follow-ups of all the resultant conclusions and recommendations?

Question 10

After an investigation has been completed by an accountability mechanism and after the executive directors and board of the institution have taken a decision concerning mitigating actions, the mechanism should have the opportunity to follow up, review, monitor, and report on implementation of such actions.

So, in a slightly different formulation, the question about follow-up monitoring[14] was asked again. The majority in all four groups overwhelmingly agreed. Both the independent experts and the NGO representatives showed 100% agreement, followed by the private-sector respondents (92%) and the MFI experts (82%).

Among the independent experts, few comments were expressed:

- "Otherwise there is no proof of reaction."
- "Without this, commitment to put matters right can be questioned. There could be, however, serious financial implications for such an unlimited mandate."

Despite all the harmony or conformity concerning the need for follow-up monitoring, some experts argued that it should not be done by the accountability mechanism itself:

- "Accountability may be demonstrated in a number of ways, including having the organization report out on its activities either to its governing body or publicly. It seems as though it would be simple for the mechanism that conducted the investigation to circle back and check up on what the institution has done. This can improve the policies, practices, and methodologies of the institution as well as improve the project itself."

One MFI specialist said that there must be a follow-up but saw a need to clarify who would conduct the follow-up and when. By comparison, others were clear about who should be responsible. In almost similar wording, two MFI experts said that follow-up should be done by the board of the institution itself:

- "This would substantially enhance the credibility of an accountability mechanism, though obviously the final responsibility for the mitigation itself ought to remain with the Executive Directors or Board."

On this question, an NGO specialist was the only one who referred to the Operations Evaluation Department (OED), the evaluation department of the World Bank:

- "This sounds desirable, but may put a large burden on a small mechanism such as the Inspection Panel. Couldn't there be a division of labor with the OED at the World Bank?"

POST-MONITORING

A rather different way of monitoring is post-monitoring. It should not be confused with the process of monitoring whether a bank implements the recommended mitigating actions after an investigation has been completed. The Inspection Panel does not have a mandate to do post-compliance monitoring. This means that in cases where complaints are filed after the closing date of the loan and where more than 95 per cent has been disbursed, the panel is prohibited from accepting a request. This restriction has been criticized from outside the World Bank. The Asian Development Bank, after its first revision of the mandate and procedures of its accountability mechanism, decided to grant requesters the opportunity to file a claim in the post-implementation phase, the maximum time span being two years. The logic behind a revision of the rule is that harm can also appear after a project has been implemented, especially environmental effects.

Question 11

Accountability mechanisms should have the opportunity to investigate projects after completion for a period of at least two years.

It is rather striking and convincing that again an overwhelming majority agreed with the necessity of post-monitoring. Again, the NGO experts and the independent experts strongly agreed, at 100%, followed by the MFI experts (87%) and the private-sector experts (85%).

One MFI expert was rather outspoken:

- "Yes, especially because not only the construction but also the operation and even its maintenance (or lack thereof) may cause harm to people and the environment."
- However, another MFI expert was not convinced: "It should depend on the nature of the Accountability Mechanism, but in general the lending decision is in question, not its implementation."
- Another MFI expert said: "While the investigation period to the implementation period may create a gap, the question is what leverage the Bank has to resolve problems after its funds have been fully disbursed? The Bank's ability to influence changes may be very limited at that point."
- A private-sector expert likewise stated: "What recourse is available after the project has been completed? Seems pointless."

Some raised the question again of whether post-monitoring should be a function for the accountability mechanism or for an operations evaluation department. One MFI expert pointed out that it could lead to a duplication of functions and overlapping mandates.

Others had difficulties with the word "investigation." One private-sector respondent noted: "Agree, but 'investigation' is the wrong approach and implies a 'policing' mentality. There should be a solution-oriented approach to ensure that issues are being resolved on the ground in an effective and timely manner." Nevertheless, most of the MFI experts were more convinced that post-monitoring is necessary:

- "This is necessary for the benefit of lessons learned and the need for a 360-degree cycle."
- "It should be up to the function to decide in what cases ex-post investigations will be approved. The function should decide on a case-by-case basis."
- "Many environmental and social impacts accrue or become realized well after the project is operating, such as accumulation of wastes. 'Completion' in World Bank Group jargon is far too early."

Finally, one independent expert noted:

- "Without such provisions, any Environmental Impact Assessment exercise and/or inspection, no matter how comprehensive it may be, cannot achieve its intended goals and objectives."

In all groups, many expressed the view that the two-year period is arbitrary. One MFI expert stated that the period should be "At least 10 years." Others asked "Why two years?" Among the group of independent experts, the following comments were made:

- "Maybe even longer, the (unexpected) side-effects of projects and programs may even occur much later than after 2 years."
- "In some projects the period could appear to be quite short. Big-scale investment in water management shows an impact on the environment in a later stage."

LESSONS LEARNED
The study clearly shows that a high majority agree with the need for a follow-up role. It is also clear that further study is necessary to clarify who should do it and when. I would not exclude the accountability mechanisms since their members know from previous compliance investigations what has gone wrong. Moreover, since they are part of the discussion leading to further mitigation plans, they know what should be expected in the field. In a manner similar to their earlier reporting on compliance, they can report back to the board on implementation of the mitigation action plans.

HUMAN RIGHTS INCLUDED IN THE POLICIES AND MANDATE

As is clear from chapters 2 and 6, the World Bank is officially still bound by its Articles of Agreement, which do not allow the bank to interfere in national politics. For this reason the bank has always taken the position that it officially could *not* act when human rights were abused in project areas. In the past decade this position has come under fire. Former president Jim Wolfensohn, Roberto Dañino (the general counsel, who has left the bank), members of the Inspection Panel, and many specialists inside and outside the bank are definitely among those who have tried to put human rights on the bank's agenda. The trend is going in the direction of accepting human rights as a condition of project compliance. These developments led to the following three questions.

Question 12

Human rights should be reflected in the policies of the international financial institutions (IFIs) given the existence of the Universal Declaration of Human Rights (UDHR), signed by most of the countries in the world.[15]

Confirmation of the trend was clear. Not surprisingly, the NGO experts overwhelmingly agreed, at 100%. Remarkably, the private-sector experts showed similar conviction, recording 100% agreement, while 95% of the independent experts agreed. The exception was to be found among the MFI experts themselves. A majority agreed, at 68%, but notably, 22.7% did not have an opinion and 9% disagreed.

The reasons for some hesitation among the MFI experts, the group that provided the most comments, could have their origin in the experience of the experts with such a sensitive subject as human rights in the course of negotiating with governments on loans, projects, and conditionality. In the background, there is always the pressure inside the bank(s) to respect the Articles of Agreement. Several reasons were mentioned:

- The UDHR "is not a multilateral treaty but a set of principles."
- "It is a political statement instead of a legal question. It is a wasp's nest. Besides, if you take into consideration the present and traditional role of the United States in the IFIs, you run the risk of arbitrary rules."
- "The UDHR is too general and the UN body responsible for safeguarding Human Rights, the Human Rights Commission, is politicized."
- "It is not clear that the IFIs would be able to develop a capacity to make a difference in this arena. On the other hand, if a government has such practices consistently in violation of global human rights standards; there should be no lending program at all to that country."
- "Emphasize 'reflected,' as it is otherwise too difficult to get consensus as to what they specifically include."

Two other MFI experts found the question too vague and inconsistent since I did not go further with questions related to social and environmental agreements and covenants:

- "The elements of Human Rights should be broken down in operational terms (see the good practice set by IFC's child and forced labor policies),[16] not stated in general terms."

Another referred to the difficulties that some officials in the World Bank experienced while trying to introduce human rights and, more specifically, to Peter Woicke,[17] who:

- "was open and persistent that he was pushing hard for a formal Human Rights Policy and so published and repeated widely. Peter was not kept on as expected. Without an influential champion as Peter was, it looks as if human rights policy is re-dying in the World Bank Group at the moment."

The private-sector experts did not provide any comments. And among the independent experts, some had problems answering the question:

- "My response would depend on precisely how 'human rights' were covered by IFC policy. At the one extreme could be the situation that IFC policy states that there will be no lending to countries that violate human rights. The problem will be who judges this? At the other extreme there could be mention of human rights but expressed so vaguely as to be meaningless – as happens today in many African countries. So I find it impossible to answer meaningfully."

- "The human rights double standard should be removed, although this would require: (1) recognition of the international human rights obligations borne by the Bank directly, viz. respecting the human rights treaty obligations of its members (Shihata's opinions are dated on this, but opinion within the Legal Department now seems divided); and (2) getting revised OPS [operational policies] through the executive board, a highly challenging task."

Nevertheless, some independent experts expressed strong agreement:

- "I cannot agree more on the principle."
- "It should be a pre-requisite to World Bank aid."
- "How can the World Bank claim to have an effective, meaningful and credible 'INVOLUNTARY RESETTLEMENT POLICY' if it does not comply with the Universal Declaration of Human Rights?"

Among the NGO experts there was a remarkable observation that the European Bank for Reconstruction and Development, "which recognized the importance of Human Rights in its operations based on permanent violations in Turkmenistan, officially announced that it will not finance the Turkmen government. This happened one week after President Wolfensohn visited the country and promised investment in the private sector." Another NGO comment clearly expressed what many others tried to say:

- "The World Bank, as an institution that is at least nominally part of the UN system and the community of nations that are party to international treaties and conventions, should have to uphold international law, not claim exemptions from it. While I don't think that the Bank should be an "enforcer" of international law, since they have neither the respect nor experience necessary to do so, they should be accountable to international law. They should be held to those standards. I would suggest that those who are concerned about how international law has been flouted by the World Bank, and for that matter how international law is systematically undermined by international trade agreements, should begin to think about structures that can be put in place to enhance and enforce human rights and environmental laws."

Question 13

Investigating human rights violations has to be part of the mandate of the accountability mechanisms of IFIs.

The responses to this question were almost the same as for the previous question on policies: an overwhelming majority strongly agreed that human rights should be part of the mandate. The NGO representatives most strongly agreed, at 100%, and provided the fewest comments. They were followed by the private-sector experts (92%) and the independent experts (90%). Within the group of MFI experts, there was again a range of views: 69.5% agreed, 17% disagreed, and 13% did not have an opinion.

The written comments again contained different messages. A comment of many was that policies on human rights first have to exist before an accountability mechanism can investigate reported violations related to a project in a project area. Otherwise, the question could be understood to imply that the accountability mechanisms could investigate any human rights violations, including those with no relation to planned or implemented projects. This possibility, of course, is not part of the background to the question. But even though most understood this to be the case, some wondered whether human rights should even be part of the mandate of an accountability mechanism. A few experts from across the MFI, private-sector, and independent-expert groups clearly stated that human rights violations should be the province of other organizations:

- "We need to improve the international court system."
- "A development bank is not the primary institution for addressing such issues."

Nevertheless, the message was that with human rights reflected in the policies of the institutions, an accountability mechanism should be mandated to investigate human rights issues if people in a project area claim that there have been violations as a result of an MFI project.

THE PRIVATE SECTOR TAKES THE LEAD
At the end of this section of the survey, I included a provocative statement to the effect that some transnational corporations and private banks have already included human rights in their business principles. The example of Shell, which trains its personnel on human rights issues, was mentioned. I was interested in determining whether the respondents recognized a development within the private sector, which has moved faster to include human rights in its mandates than have most of the multilateral organizations, such as the World Bank. Indeed, it is the private sector that has taken the lead on this issue.

Question 14

It is true that some transnational corporations and private banks have in some cases already included human rights standards in their list of standards or business principles.

Not surprisingly, the private-sector experts themselves were most convinced, at 83%. Among the other groups, a majority also agreed: 76% of the independent experts, 72% of the MFI experts, and 67% of the NGO experts. Although some doubt was expressed by the NGO experts, it is remarkable that a majority agreed, as it shows the NGO sector's faith in the private sector.

The respondents' comments were few and sometimes cynical, but a few recognized this development in the private sector and mentioned names of companies.[18] One comment from the NGO sector was very specific in mentioning ABN-AMRO Bank:[19]

- "ABN-AMRO does not finance companies without an explicit policy and practice of respecting human rights or indigenous rights related to forest extraction or plantation development management."

Yet most believed that such policies are a matter more of public relations (PR) than of actual implementation and monitoring. An MFI expert wrote:

- "The issue is how TNCs and private banks make such nice PR statements. The independent monitoring thereof remains an issue of concern. Regarding Shell operations in Nigeria, there the NGOs get to talk to 'Public Affairs' personnel only." Little comment was made by the private-sector experts. One wrote: "True, some but not all." Another mentioned several companies: "Rabobank, HBOS, Westpac, Shell and signatories to the UN Global Compact initiative, although the implementation level is considered to be limited."

LESSONS LEARNED

Numerous questions were raised: about specific policies on human rights, about who will judge whether these policies have been violated, about whether human rights issues should be left to other bodies in the UN system, and about whether the MFIs can keep away from a "wasp's nest." Despite a certain hesitance and the awareness that many of these questions have to be answered, the overall message was still that the majority seeks reflection of human rights concerns in the policies of the multilateral financial institutions.

POSITION OF MEMBERS
OF ACCOUNTABILITY MECHANISMS

Members of the World Bank Inspection Panel often have to explain their status of neutrality, which is crucial to ensuring their credentials and authority. The guarantee of independence is laid out in the resolution establishing the panel,[20] which prescribes that after a single five-year term with the panel, members can never work for the World Bank again. Moreover, anyone who has worked at the bank can be appointed as a member of the Inspection Panel only after they have been absent from the bank for at least two years. Another issue related to the position of the members is whether they should have the opportunity to be appointed for a second term. Some argue that by limiting members to a single term, the institutions are losing strong knowledge and experience too soon. Exceptional is the view that a panel member's work should be considered a profession. In this section, three questions are raised concerning the position of members of the mechanisms.

Question 15

Former members of management and former executive directors of an institution can be appointed only if they have been absent from the institution for at least two years.

The majority of all groups agreed that an such appointment should be preceded by a two-year absence: 87% of the NGO experts, 78% of the MFI experts, 69% of the private-sector experts, and 60% of the independent experts. Among the independent experts 10% had no opinion, so remarkably, 30% disagreed.

It is not easy to interpret the meaning of these responses, particularly the levels of disagreement, since in their comments many stated that they disagreed on the grounds that the two-year period is too short. There was no comment pleading for less than two years or even for deleting this restriction. Only a few experts saw the past experience of former employees of the institutions as an advantage. One MFI expert wrote:

- "Former staff also understand the Bank's policies and procedures and its decision making process."
- This comment was immediately followed by reference to a dilemma that many mentioned: "It is possible that hiring just out of a bank appointment can give rise to conflict of interest, but it is also possible that you are missing very good candidates here and that through the screening process conflicts of interest can be avoided."
- One private-sector expert stated: "I see value in having the knowledge and understanding of the business fresh in people's minds. One can often be the best critic of one's own work when asked to look at it from another perspective."

This latter comment was not made by anyone else. Most comments from among the MFI experts indicated that the period of absence from an institution should be at least five or ten years, while some others in this group shared the view of the respondent who said, "I don't think they should be eligible."

The question of whether former employees should be appointed to an accountability mechanism at all is broadly present in the comments made by the experts of the other three groups:

- "Why not hire independent external members with no previous connection with the bank?"
- "Perhaps it is not wise to include at all former members of Management or Board."
- "They should not judge their own decisions."
- "They should not be considered at all."

Question 16

A member of an accountability mechanism should be appointed for only one term.

The question concerning whether members should serve one or two terms caused a lot of discussion. Among the respondents, there was less consensus compared to many of the other questions. The MFI, private-sector, and independent experts were all divided among themselves, so no distinct way of thinking was evident within any one group versus another. It was clear that the experts in the field of accountability mechanisms do not yet have a common opinion on the issue.

The MFI experts were the most divided: 39% agreed, 39% disagreed, and 22% did not have an opinion. And we see almost the same response from the private-sector experts: 38% agreed and 38% disagreed. The independent experts were also divided: 42% agreed and 58% disagreed. Only among the NGO experts, at 57%, can we find a small majority who somewhat supported the question as stated.

There were three categories of comments. First, there were the few who did not elaborate on whether panel members should serve one or two terms but instead came up with other suggestions, such as the importance of not rotating the members at the same time.[21] One mentioned a possible compromise of six to seven years.

Second, approximately one-third of those who made a comment expressed a strong belief that it should be no more than one term:

- "No, independence is crucial. Also a five-year term serves that purpose."
- "For only one term, as it is with the Inspection Panel, and ineligible for further work within the Bank."
- "There is an argument to be made that experience is important and should be utilized, [but] panel members are a mixed bag. Some of them should not be given a second term. If the possibility exists, then it could mean ten years of bad judgment. We cannot assume that all panel members are always going to be intelligent, impartial and have integrity. This is particularly important given the way that the Panel members are appointed. I think one term is enough."

Third, the majority made comments expressing agreement with the option of more than one term. Many of them saw allowing only one term as a waste of experience:

- "Two terms might allow more continuity. Institutions and projects are complex."
- "Regular replacement for its own sake increases costs."
- "A person may apply for a second term (not more), but apply to the vacancy like all others. Those who decide then will take into consideration the risks of a second term (probably the chance to be re-elected will decrease for that reason)."

Question 17

Working for an accountability mechanism is a profession.

The last question in this section concerned the issue of whether the work of panel members can be recognized as a profession. Again, there was a range of answers within the groups. The only group to express majority disagreement was the independent experts, at 47%, with 35% agreeing and 18% expressing no opinion. In the other three groups, a small majority agreed: 59% of the MFI experts, 58% of the private-sector experts, and 54% of the NGO experts. Again there were various views.

Of the twenty-four written comments, only three expressed a positive view, and even then these respondents favoured slightly altering the idea; one MFI expert wrote: "Yes, being independent (also in perception of people), being fair and having outreach within as well as outside the Bank is a special profession." Ten of the comments did not express either a "yes" or a "no" but instead detailed what the respondents considered necessary to fulfil the function properly. Some mentioned a range of talents and skills, and one MFI expert said: "It may develop into a specialty within a profession (lawyers, engineers, financial experts, etc.)."

The remaining eleven comments were rather negative about the idea of making this task a profession:

- A private-sector expert wrote: "Disagree. The Panel shall be comprised of individuals fully articulate in issues related to environment, society and economics in emerging markets."
- An NGO representative stated: "I kind of like the idea that Panel members are drawn from a field of candidates that have long-term experiences in development, policy, politics, environmental protection, advocacy, and that have technical/legal expertise. The fact that they have to leave the position and not become a permanent fixture gives them greater ability to use their judgment to assess the facts of a case and have the integrity to stand by their findings. Someone who assumes a long-term staff position could easily fall into a pattern of wanting to move a particular agenda, or carve out a career, and be less candid, honest, and strong. There may be a

way to claim the best experience from "retired" panel members by creating an association that can review, evaluate, critique and work to improve accountability and enforcement. But I would not want to see a professional cadre established, unless the entire structure and intent of these mechanisms is completely rethought."

The following comments were brief and to the point:

- "More of an occupation than a profession."
- "Only a lawyer would argue that case. Next, he/she would insist that a legal degree is a necessary precondition to membership in a Panel."

So altogether there was a predominantly negative feeling about the idea of turning this task into a profession. More emphasis was placed on independence, knowledge, impartiality, and outstanding experience in development, in politics, in environmental protection, and in social justice.

LESSONS LEARNED

The responses indicate that the two-year waiting period is not enough, that a period of five or more years is considered a minimum (although still open to doubts), and that it is preferable to appoint individuals who have had no history with an institution at all. So a clear majority advocates strong independence.

On the subject of whether panel members should serve one or more terms, there is no common view. The outcome somewhat surprised me. I had expected the majority to defend one term as the best guarantee of independence.

I doubt that the work of the members of accountability mechanisms should be regarded as a specific profession. What is clear to me is that those appointed should have rich experience in the field of development and impact assessments, in international organizations, and in the international (political) arena. Making the work of panel members a profession could undermine the profound sincerity of the function. It is not just a job; it is a highly regarded task that comes with a huge responsibility.

POLICIES, PROCEDURES, AND PRINCIPLES

The safeguard policies and procedures of the World Bank Group and the other MFIs and the business principles[22] of the private sector did not form the basis of the questionnaire. The exception I obviously had to make was with regard to human rights policies since I took the position that their absence affects the credibility of the entire institutions (see the responses to questions 12 to 14 above). Over the years the World Bank and the other MFIs have developed important policies, of which, without doubt, the Environmental Impact Assessment Policy and the Indigenous Peoples Policy have been the most influential.[23] The other important safeguard policies also cannot be underestimated: Natural Habitats, Forests, Pest Management, Cultural Property, Involuntary Resettlement, Safety of Dams, Disputed Areas, and International Waterways.[24] Policies and principles are constantly under discussion and regularly revised. The development of the policies of the different institutions and their "legal implications" is a study in itself.

Nevertheless, some issues concerning the policies cannot be ignored since they are related to the operations or mandates of the mechanisms. The following practical or managerial subjects related to the policies were presented in the questionnaire: the importance of training management and staff on the policies, the meaning of the policies (i.e., guidelines vs legal instruments), the involvement of the accountability mechanisms in the reform process of the policies, the possible effects of the so-called "use of country systems" for the World Bank Inspection Panel, and the weakening of the policies.

Training for the Policies

For management, working with policies is primarily a matter of implementation. During my five years as a member of the Inspection Panel, I recognized a difference in the level of awareness about the content or, even more, the value of the policies among bank staff. Some defended the policies as a valuable tool of the bank and its development goals; others looked upon them as technical rules that simply had to be implemented. One respondent expressed another common view concerning the policies: "The problem is that if the safeguard policies are regarded simply as an obstacle, and not as an essential part of sustainable development, if they come into the picture late in the project cycle and they are viewed by the project team more as waste of time and scarce budgetary recourses, then the problems start." So one's judgment of the policies depends heavily on training and on an understanding of the value of the safeguards.

Question 18

Staff of the institutions working with the policies should regularly be trained on the importance, values, and procedures of the policies.

The majority of all groups overwhelmingly agreed, with 100% of the MFI, private-sector, and independent experts in favour. Only among the NGO experts was there any disagreement, with 7% opposed. The written comments in all groups showed the same tendency. Words such as "self-evident," "critical," and "fundamental" were often used:

- An NGO expert wrote: "Without proper training, policies and guidelines will not be implemented."

Two key comments were made by experts of two different MFIS:

- "but the question is not very strong. Of course, training is needed. More importantly, seasoned professionals need to be hired. The increasing frequency of 'average generalists' being responsible for safeguard policies is striking to the Inspection Panel. As is the converse, the decreasing frequency of thoroughly experienced professional social and environmental experts."
- "Part of such training should include a full appreciation of the work of the Accountability Mechanism."

Given the strong consensus among the respondents, citation of further comments on the training of staff is not necessary.[25]

POLICIES AND PRINCIPLES AS A "LEGAL" INSTRUMENT

In the case of the World Bank, concern was sometimes expressed that the panel was too legalistic in its approach and that the policies were never intended to be a legal instrument for enforcement. Some felt that the policies themselves leave room for judgment. A member of the bank's staff stated: "It is all about constraints, opportunities, and trade-offs. The Panel in its review of compliance does not fully appreciate the combination of a judgment and a trade-off." This statement shows how much sensitivity there is when the Inspection Panel has to examine whether project activities are in compliance with the World Bank's policies and procedures.

Question 19

Policies and business principles are, in the first place, not written as legal instruments.

While a majority of all groups agreed, there was also a minority in all groups but one who disagreed. The private-sector experts agreed most strongly, at 72%, followed by the independent experts, at 61%. Of the MFI experts, 59% agreed. The largest minority to disagree was found among the NGO experts: 58% agreed and 42% disagreed.

In the comments from the NGO experts, I perceived a desire that the policies be legally binding. Some said this directly:

- "In the long run, policies and principles should have a binding character."
- "Generally agree, but policies for IFIs tend to substitute for legal instruments because MFIs have immunity and do not consider themselves as parties to international conventions. Not the same with TNCs."
- "We have seen 'trade offs,' letting a borrower water down or modify policy implementation in return for a more efficient implementation of the

project's aims. The judgment for this is made by some review group from outside. But the policy modification has meant that protections given to communities or to environment have been watered down, and these policies in some cases had been their main protection. In this sense, policies should have legal binding power. If not, the stronger party (the Bank, the Borrower) will insist on them when suited, and will let them go when not suited to them."

Among the private-sector experts, only one respondent provided a comment:
- "But they need to be seen as integral to the manner in which the organization undertakes its business."

Not surprisingly, the MFI experts were divided in their many comments. Although a small majority agreed (59%), their statements gave another impression. Some of the experts were of the opinion that the situation concerning the legal nature of the mechanisms changed as a consequence of the establishment of the Inspection Panel. One placed this perceived development in a historic context:

- "Originally of course, they were not really designed primarily as legal instruments. They were said to be mandatory, but as there was no compliance mechanism, the legal question did not arise. As soon as a compliance mechanism started to function, legalistic questions arose. The policies have to be complied within reasonably legal terms, where significant."

Other MFI experts wrote:

- "They tend to be written as legal documents."
- "Agree upon Principles and Policies, with accompanying methods for variances, should be binding on staff, otherwise there is institutional chaos."
- "Policies and business principles are quasi-legal instruments given that they are binding and enforceable."

The foregoing statements I interpret as expressing the view that the policies are (more or less) "legally" binding. Nevertheless, some of the MFI experts tended to reject the legality of the instruments:

- "Fully agree (they are not legal instruments). This is a major explaining factor in the implementation difficulties of the present policies."
- "Policies and Principles should never be written as or argued to be legal instruments. Policies should be living documents that are amended as things change and as things are learned."

The comments from the independent experts were also diverse:

- "Generally this is true. But it depends on the institution and the intent of the policy and/or principle. I am familiar with policies on gender equality having greater force than formal country law."
- "Legal instruments can very well include lists of guidelines and statement of principles. Creating very volatile wishy-washy texts may lead to a lot of uncertainty and ultimately non-compliance." "However such principles CAN be written as legal instruments – i.e., legal norms. But I hasten to add that there will invariably need to be a hierarchy within such norms. Some norms will be more important and overriding than others. But this is a matter for discussion I believe."

LESSONS LEARNED

Generally, I found in many reactions strong support for the view that the policies have to be understood at present as close to binding "legal" instruments, but I also noted some warnings that the policies should not make the processes too legalistic. A few participants referred to the difficulty this creates during normal daily duties. Nevertheless, those who supported the view that the policies should be treated as binding rightly pointed out that they are society's only means to make the MFIS (or IFIS) accountable for their actions. Nevertheless, I understand the dilemma that if policies are used only to "blame and shame," instead of being part of a learning process, they will finally fail to fulfil their original purpose. But having said this, I want to be explicit on my position that full implementation of the policies, or performance standards,[26] is absolutely necessary and should not hold up a learning process.

The Inspection Panel has been asked why it was not involved in the design or reform of the policies. This formed the basis for the next, rather provocative, question.

Question 20

Members of accountability mechanisms should have the formal opportunity to be involved in the process of reforming policies.

Notably, the responses within all groups ranged from "agree" to "disagree." Yet there was a difference between the NGO experts, of whom a clear majority agreed (73%), and the private-sector experts, of whom a majority disagreed (54%). To some extent, the independent experts, at 60%, concurred with those in the NGO group. Among the MFI experts, there was an almost equal split between those who agreed (43%) and those who disagreed (39%), while 17% had no opinion.

The four comments made by private-sector experts all clearly indicated opposition to the idea, with one expressing the need to "Avoid conflict of interest impacting their independence."

Eighteen comments were made by the MFI experts, six of whom expressed strong opposition to the option of involvement, as in the statement:

- "Policy (rule) makers and Panels should be separated as judges and law makers are separated."
- Another wrote: "I disagree. This would be blurring the responsibilities. It is for the policy makers to take into account the recommendations of the accountability mechanisms."

Most of the other comments from the MFI group did not express direct opposition, and almost all stated a preference for allowing members of accountability mechanisms only an advising role, without final say on policy changes. One said:

- "The decision on revision of policies should neither be the role of the Panel nor of Management: it 'should be the Board's function.'"

Almost all the independent experts who provided a comment expressed disagreement with any (formal) involvement of the members of accountability mechanisms in policy reform. One commented:

- "If you want the Inspection Panel to become a more independent and authorative body, you should not mix it up with policy making."

Among the three comments made by NGO experts, two conformed with the views expressed by the other groups. Nevertheless, the statistical outcome for this question indicated that, in contrast to the other groups, the NGO experts were the most positive about the suggestion.

To sum up, among the non-NGO groups, there was strong disagreement with the idea of allowing the members of accountability mechanisms formal involvement in the revision or design of policies. Respondents expressed the view that, at the very most, the members of the mechanisms should have an informal role that permits them to make only policy recommendations.

Each time the policies are revised, the process of revision is followed closely outside the World Bank by the NGO community and in the case of IFC policies also by the Equator banks. As described in chapter 6, the World Bank has been accused of weakening or watering down its policies after the Inspection Panel wrote some rather critical reports on certain bank projects, the most obvious of which was the report on the China Western Poverty Reduction Project.[27]

Question 21

IFIs and TNCs weaken their principles as a result of strong judgments of noncompliance made by accountability mechanisms.

Only among the NGO experts did a clear majority agree with this statement, at 78%. Among the other three groups, the independent experts indicated the highest level of disagreement (53%), followed by the private-sector experts (50%) and the MFI experts (47%). Remarkably, among the MFI and independent experts, many did not have an opinion or perhaps did not want to answer the question: of the seventy-one respondents, fifteen did not fill in the numeric part of the question, and only one of them was from the NGO group. Among the private-sector experts, 25% had no opinion, and among the MFI experts this figure was 32%. So, except for among the NGO group, there was more disbelief than belief that principles are weakened as a result of the work of the accountability mechanisms.

Comments from the NGO experts included:

- "We do have the strong impression that Inspection Panel criticism of failure to reach policy standards has led to efforts to lower those policy standards. If you can't score goals, change the position of the goalposts! We have seen this with rehabilitation from displacement – before, the policy was strong about full rehabilitation, but subsequent 'reviews' have watered it down a lot, because implementation was not measuring up to policy statements."
- "Agree for IFIS, not sure for TNCs. Bank staff tries to 'panel-proof' their projects."
- "TNCs usually lack accountability mechanisms, so this impact does not yet occur."

One independent expert argued the opposite:

- "The contrary is true: it increases their credibility to outsiders and it keeps managers on their toes to avoid problems arising that weaken the image of the MFIs."
- Another said: "It can work both ways."

Still, some of the MFI experts said that there is some truth in the statement:

- "Yes, I feel that is so. The Inspection Panel and all accountability mechanisms must struggle against such tendencies. Weakening the law is inadmissible wherever just because compliance is fostered."
- "This is an important issue and bears watching. I believe one could make an argument to say there has been weakening, but probably needs more time before any conclusion can be made."

Even though the majority of respondents indicated their disbelief that policies are weakened because of the activities of accountability mechanisms, some doubts were expressed. An MFI expert familiar with one of the mechanisms said:

- "Without an independent assessment of its implementation or external enforcement, the policies, strong or weak, will be largely ignored, as they were in the Bank prior to 1994."

That the NGO experts expressed such conviction that the weakening of policies is taking place – a conviction also found among some of the MFI experts – raises the question of whether the NGO group sees the situation from a different perspective. Perhaps this is because they are more often in the field than many of the others – a question that remains to be answered.

The background to the last question in this section is illustrated by a discussion I recall hearing in the offices of the Inspection Panel. At a certain time, the NGO community turned somewhat against the panel, claiming that the panel's reporting had led to a weakening of the bank's policies (as indicated above). A panel staff member rightly responded with the question: "What do they want: good policies without a mechanism that will assure they are implemented? That does not make sense."

Question 22

The adoption of strict policies is more important than an independent assessment of their implementation or external enforcement.

An overwhelming majority in all groups rejected the idea that the policies themselves should be considered more important than the mechanisms that control their enforcement. Confronted with this provocative statement, only 8% of the NGO experts, 8% of the private-sector experts, and 5% of the independent experts agreed. There was some difference between the latter three groups and the group of MFI experts, 19% of whom agreed.

Overall, one can again conclude that the accountability mechanisms are accepted and seen as a necessity for policy enforcement. Most of the comments referred to the situation at the MFIs. Very little was said about the private sector. One respondent remarked that the TNCs still lack accountability mechanisms, which makes it difficult to evaluate policy implementation.

"USE OF COUNTRY SYSTEMS"

Chapter 6 discussed the mandate of the World Bank Inspection Panel after bank management proposed the introduction of the so-called "use of country systems," which means that by agreement between a government and the World Bank,[28] the bank's policies may be replaced by national policies that the two parties agree are similar to the bank's policies. The rationale behind this was that most of the middle-income countries now have national legislation that in principle is similar or equal to the different World Bank policies. These countries want to be recognized for the policy improvements they have made. At the World Bank, management showed concern that if the bank ignored these improvements, the middle-income countries could easily borrow from the private capital market – a trend that had already been visible for some years. Nevertheless, the question was raised of what this means for the Inspection Panel when a request arrives related to an approved project. The NGO community expressed its concern over the mandate of the Inspection Panel. Two questions related to this issue were included in the survey.

Question 23

A new approach, the "use of country systems," has to be understood in the light of the market in which both the World Bank and private banks operate.

The question is rather open to multiple interpretations, which perhaps explains why it was not answered by a proportion of each of the four groups of respondents.[29] Nevertheless, the majority from all groups agreed.

Not surprisingly, the private-sector experts indicated the highest level of agreement (86%), followed by the MFI experts (74%), the independent experts (62%), and the NGO experts (50%). Among the NGO experts, 33.3% had no opinion and 17% disagreed. The comments from the latter three groups were numerous and diverse, whereas only one private-sector expert made a comment:

- "The goal of continuing improvement and best practice must be kept in mind, but naturally balanced with the realities of the specific country."

One MFI expert noted the different official position of the World Bank compared with the private banks:

- "According to the Articles of Agreement of both IBRD and IDA they are lenders of last resort (i.e., when there is no reasonable financing available for the country or project) so they should NOT be competing with private banks."

The other comments from the MFI experts were somewhat different:

- One group viewed the "use of country systems" that are in line with bank policies as a positive development, with one expert writing: "Yes, absolutely, but it is a contribution to a greater harmonization good."
- Another went further, commenting on what it means for the position of the Inspection Panel (see also question 24): "My understanding of 'use of country systems' is to improve the governance of the recipient countries and to save the administration cost and time of the recipient countries. In fact under 'use of country systems' the Panel may have some problems on what to investigate; however, the super goal of development is not good investigation by panel but alleviation of poverty through good governance."

- Another group of MFI experts was not convinced that the "use of country systems" is a positive development, with one stating: "'Understood,' perhaps, but not agreed with. It's a cop out by the Bank."
- Another sharing this view added: "The new use of country systems approach, as currently designed, is part of the generic weakening of all safeguards. The logic is clear, if a country has adequate standards and if they are proven to be effectively implemented, then country standards could supplant safeguards. But the new approach is not based on that fundamental premise."

The independent experts also offered divergent comments:

- One saw the "use of country systems" as clearly fundamental: "The 'country systems policy' also has a large element of National Capacity Building built in to it. Building country capacity may well be the most important aspect of the 'country system policy."
- Another independent expert was not convinced that the countries will implement their systems (as some of the MFI experts also suggested): "A country may have excellent laws on its books but what counts is the systematic and effective implementation of the laws."

The NGO experts mainly expressed the same reservations about the intention and capacity of the countries to implement their own adequate systems. One noted the competition between the World Bank and private banks, and others referred to the effects and nature of the standards or policies:

- "Some NGO experts are negative about the suggestion that the World Bank also operates on a World Market."
- "WB should not care about market share, but about its development mandate."
- "If development is to be seen as a market, the Bank can scrap its motto of 'alleviation of poverty'!"
- "What worries me in all of this is that there are no consistent standards that can be relevant to whichever financial institution, company, or government agency is involved in financing and developing a project. While I don't believe in a cookie cutter approach to development, there should be some fundamental standards and principles to apply in all cases. The point should, again, be about getting the best development impact, causing the least trauma for citizens, and actually raising living standards, improving environmental quality, and expanding democratic spaces for citizens. The market should not be the only determinant to how, or which, policies are applied."

The effects of the "use of country systems" on the mandate of the Inspection Panel, a concern expressed by many NGO experts, formed the basis of the next question.

Question 24

The work of the World Bank Inspection Panel will not change as a result of the "use of country systems." The panel can still investigate projects on the basis of the bank's policies. The only additional task of the panel, with regard to the issues raised, is to examine management's assessment of the equivalence between relevant bank policies or procedures and a borrowing nation's "country system."

When asked to comment on the effects of the "use of country systems," a majority of the MFI, private-sector, and independent experts expressed agreement with the statement. This was not the case with the NGO experts, who mostly disagreed or did not have an opinion, thus confirming the protests of the NGOs at the time that the "use of country systems" was introduced. Again, this question was not answered by all of the respondents.[30]

Those respondents most convinced that there will be no change in the work of the Inspection Panel were from the private-sector and MFI groups, both of which recorded 75% agreement. A slightly smaller majority of the independent experts also agreed (62%). Among the NGO experts, 46% disagreed, a substantial 31% had no opinion, and only 23% agreed.

The comments from the MFI experts went in all kinds of directions:

- Some saw an additional task for the Inspection Panel: "IP work will change in the sense that an extra instrument/check will be added to the IP's 'tool box.'"
- One MFI expert expressed disagreement with any role for the panel in case of the "use of country systems": "This is not the Panel's job. The Panel's job is to assess compliance."
- Another expert was concerned about the role of the panel: "I am concerned with the new country approach. That should change as the priority. The role of the IP should keep up with changing circumstances."

The comments from the NGO experts showed a concern about the possible undermining of both the Inspection Panel and the safeguard policies:

- "I have the strong feeling that Panel's work will be undermined."
- "Equivalency of country systems will not be assessed based on full safeguards, but based on brief synthesis."
- "Disagree. 1. The Bank's General Counsel has stated that the Panel cannot make qualitative judgments about a country's national systems. The Panel will not be able to adequately assess Management's determination of equivalence without reviewing the quality of country systems. 2. Point of reference for Panel will no longer be full Safeguard Policies but weakened Statement of objectives and principles."

The independent experts offered different and equally valuable views, with some expressing the opinion that the World Bank should more or less stick to its safeguard policies:

- "If the statement means that WB policies should now only be assessed according to country systems: as WB money is a loan, accountability should certainly be assessed against country policies. As the WB's added value to commercial banks is 'development,' WB's policies should certainly remain a benchmark. This way both should be additional. Problems could arise when WB and country policies appear to conflict – but this kind of difference should have appeared and been solved in an early phase of the negotiations on the project and loan. If they appear during IP activities, you have a problem. Probably best solved by following country rules – it is a loan, so it is 'their' money; if this doesn't work out, it will become lawyer's work to find the solution for that specific case."
- "Never allow management to escape from its own policies."

Other independent experts saw that an impact on the work of the panel is inevitable:

- "The Panel's mandate will have to change to allow it to hold Bank staff accountable to those country equivalent systems that the bank has deemed to be equivalent to the Bank's own safeguards. This is going to require a lot of additional investigation and study for each case the Panel has to investigate. One finally is asking the relevant question: 'What options if any does the Panel have in case such equivalence is NOT there?'"

LESSONS LEARNED

The idea that the "use of country systems" is intended "to improve the governance of the recipient countries," as one respondent wrote, sounds to me somewhat arrogant. More positive was the comment that "building capacity may well be the most important aspect of the 'country systems.'" I find formulating a judgment on this subject to be a dilemma. On the one hand, the development cooperation community should recognize and support the progress made by countries that have seriously "invested" in their development. On the other hand, I understand the clear concern about the impact of the "use of country systems" on the work and mandate of the Inspection Panel and the risk that the policies will be undermined. This concern seems well founded.

PROCEDURES TO BE FOLLOWED
BY REQUESTERS FILING A CLAIM

The resolution establishing the Inspection Panel lays down the steps to be taken by people who feel they have been or could be harmed by a project in their area financed by the World Bank. Paragraph 16 of the resolution reads: "Requests for Inspection shall be in writing and shall state all relevant facts, including, in the case of a request by an affected party, the harm suffered by or threatened to such party or parties by the alleged action or omission of the bank. All requests shall explain the steps already taken to deal with the issue, as well as the nature of the alleged actions or omissions and shall specify the actions taken to bring the issue to the attention of Management, and Management's response to such action."[31] In other words, a file can be delivered to the Inspection Panel only after efforts have been made by the requesters to solve the problems in the area in the first place. A claim will be accepted only if local or regional attempts to address problems have been unsuccessful and the conflict remains unresolved. The steps to be taken imply that requesters have sufficient knowledge of how to follow all the procedures to file a claim. In the daily practice of the Inspection Panel, regular explanations have to be given about how to file a claim. The following four questions related to the position of the requesters were raised in this section of the survey.

Question 25

Filing a claim with the Inspection Panel will be extremely difficult for vulnerable people who do not understand the legal and technical implications.

In general, an overwhelming majority of three of the four groups agreed with this statement. The NGO experts were the most convinced (100%), followed by the independent experts (95%), and the private-sector experts (91%). The NGO experts work with people in the field who are eligible to file a claim, and often it is the NGOs themselves that represent the poor when a claim is filed. Somewhat different was the position of the MFI experts, of whom a much smaller majority agreed (58%). This difference is important to notice since the MFI experts have years of experience with the system of accountability mechanisms.

One MFI respondent rightly indicated that the wording "will be" in the statement implies that filing a claim is not difficult at present: "This is already the case. It is not going to be something new as implied by the statement." The question was formulated after the earlier question on the introduction of the "use of country systems," and this might have influenced the answers, as shown in the percentages. The earlier question concerned whether it will be more difficult than it is at present to file a claim with the introduction of the "use of country systems" (see previous section).

The written comments gave a somewhat different picture than the percentages. No group presented a distinct view. In all groups there was some cynicism:

• One NGO respondent made a somewhat contradictory comment: "Intimidating process, but the Panel's forms are quite clear and simplified."

- Some independent experts showed their reservations about the bank's intentions to be accessible to the poor: "As no doubt the World Bank intends."
- Another independent expert wrote: "Filing claim procedures must be made easier so that grieved parties and especially vulnerable groups are treated in a fair and just fashion. By putting such a heavy burden on individuals or parties who may be exposed to real or perceived risk, the Bank is making the process more tilted towards its own benefit."
- An NGO expert noted that the poor have to be supported "by other stakeholders, who should have the right to file complaints with or on behalf of them ... We were only able to do it because of guidance from two overseas NGOs, and we were only able to contact them because we had at hand a centre that could handle the e-mail communications."
- The role of the NGOs was also recognized by MFI experts: "Many private organizations are offering their services to help the vulnerable people. It is an issue, but not a major one."
- Another MFI expert wrote: "The Panel has made every effort to make this process as simple as possible and has published brochures that contain suggested Request forms in 14 languages. Also the Panel's operating procedures state that a request may be filled in any language. But yes, filing any type of request is very difficult for poor, uneducated people."

Respondents also noted the importance of outreach so that people know that they have the right to file a claim:

- One MFI expert stated: "The establishment of an inspection mechanism should normally be accompanied by outreaches to potentially affected persons."
- One comment from the independent experts was rather comprehensive about how to reach the people and inform them of their rights: "It is almost certain that these people do not have the information that an Inspection Panel does exist, that it is possible to start a procedure against World Bank projects. If they have this information, it is not certain that they will apply against a mighty powerful institution, because for them it seems to be steered from a long distance, not controlled by anyone, autonomously working. What would later be the personal consequences/ implications when you start such a process? What would be the financial consequences (support by lawyers and technicians, labour-time lost, travel expenses, etc.)? How to reach them? Invite them, and provide them with information on the IP."

Finally, one statement by a private-sector expert was remarkable since it conveyed the assumption that the NGOs are not impartial:

- "The concern here, also, is that advocacy NGOs drive the process on behalf of vulnerable people. One way to get around this is to ensure vulnerable people are represented by an impartial third party who is recognized by all stakeholders as fair and who is representing the needs and rights of the vulnerable groups (rather than taking an advocacy role)."

The second question in this section was about whether it is acceptable for the members of an accountability mechanism to provide guidance to potential requesters. As is clear from the different responses, this is a somewhat sensitive issue.

Question 26

Support from the staff of accountability mechanisms or providing a certain form of guidance to potential requesters is acceptable.

Here, we see in the percentages agreement with the statement within all groups but to varying degrees. The most convinced were again the NGO respondents (93%), followed by the MFI experts (82.6%), the private-sector experts (60%), and the independent experts (56%).

Many of the written comments offered views that were rather different from those suggested by the percentages. Within the MFI group, there were statements in support of the idea (1) that panel staff should be able to help the requesters, (2) that support can be given if it concerns only technical guidance, and (3) that a guidance role for panel staff is clearly a conflict of interest. The comments were as follows:

- Some MFI experts expressed the view that the requesters should get guidance: "It is not necessary for requesters to know all the legal details for filing a claim. The staff of the accountability mechanism can put the requesters' claims in the necessary legal frame."
- Other MFI respondents mentioned the need for restrictions: "Staff should be allowed to assist potential requesters as long as they give objective info. Prevent becoming part of the request. Alternatively, Bank staff and others should also assist requesters."
- Some MFI experts totally disagreed: "No, there would be no verifiable limits to this 'interventionism.'"
- And, finally, a very clear and relevant statement showed the dilemma: "No judge can orient a claimant to file a claim to be judged by him/her."

In their statements the private-sector experts all either held back on expressing full agreement or disagreed outright:

- The most positive response was: "Purely to ensure that the feedback is direct, focused and relevant."
- Another wrote: "Not by members of inspectional panel that will decide on the claim, but colleagues, assistants or independent departments of the MFI – Representatives of NGOs could assist the requesters."

- One expert mentioned another option: "This support should be given, but most likely through local authorities to whom the first complaints will be raised by the people involved." (This expert did not mention whether this is also possible in countries where human rights are violated.)

Not surprisingly, the NGO respondents saw a role for themselves in the process:

- "I prefer support by NGOs, who may seek technical advice by mechanism."
- Others described the need to support the poor who want to file a claim: "It is possible that a community at the grassroots will require basic information – a request will need to follow some sort of format, will require some supporting evidence, whatever else is needed. This information will need to be explained. How this can be given is not so easy – even e-mail communications are not always available."
- Some still saw a role for the staff of accountability mechanisms like the Inspection Panel: "Staff could support the requesters in formulation of the complaint in legal terms, and it could be the transparent process (like letter to Panel, response of the staff how the complaint should look with explanations of legal terms included in redrafted complaint, and verification of requester."

Almost all the independent experts emphasized that support for the poor in the process of filing a claim is necessary but should not be executed by the staff of the accountability mechanism that will deal with the request. Some comments were:

- "Support should be given by institutions independent of the accountability mechanism or the bank."
- "If there is a special member of staff responsible for 'public liaison' and helping requesters to file claims: and provided this staff member did not take part in any investigation that they have helped lodge, this could be feasible. If the staff members who help formulate a request then later adjudicated the request there will be a conflict of interest. The statement does not make clear the role of the staff involved."

Two of the independent experts referred to the options offered by project sponsors to file a claim and make a principal statement:

- One mentioned the situation in Canada: "In the Canadian EIA [environmental impact assessment] Process there is a provision called 'Participants Funding' program for the interveners. In line with established criteria, the federal Government of Canada provides financial assistance to selected individuals/groups to enable them hire professionals and technical experts to assist them to prepare their case properly. Perhaps, the Inspection Panel and/or the World Bank should consider looking at the Canadian model or some other such practices for designing its own 'Participant Funding' mechanism."

- In line with the Canadian legislation, the other respondent formulated how financial support for requesters should be built in: "It is not the staff of accountability mechanisms; it should be reserved from the beginning in the finance proposal. If not disbursed after the period of time in which claims are acceptable, the money to formulate a claim shall be reimbursed. Only in this case it is imaginable that requests can be made and approved."

The operating procedures of the World Bank Inspection Panel state that a request may be filed in any language. This fact formed the basis for the next question.

Question 27

Accountability mechanisms should accept claims (hand) written in native languages.

Again, an overwhelming majority of all respondents agreed, with the NGO and private-sector groups both standing at 100%, followed by the MFI experts (91%) and the independent experts (75%).

The written comments differed considerably from the numeric indicators. The percentages suggested a cohesive opinion among the respondents, whereas the comments from all groups noted rules and practical obstacles that mitigate against accepting "any" language. The MFI officials stated:

- "The official languages of the country should be accepted."
- "Requesters should invest something in the process."
- "In the case of the African Continent there are over 700 native languages, this requirement could impose an onerous burden on the mechanism and cause delays."

The only comment on this question from the private sector group was positive about "any" language but not about the suggestion that handwritten requests should also be acceptable:

- "Of course, hand written however is something different."

Some NGO experts also wondered whether a request can be written in "any" language:

- "No complaint can be in any language. Responses also have to be translated."

- "A practical framework would have to be made here. Maybe it could be in national or nationally recognized languages. We have many local tribal languages here, we would not say it should be written in them, but it could be one of the 16 national languages officially recognized."
- "They have to fully understand Bank's policy to send claim, yet it still helps to write the claims in their own language."

The independent experts generally offered two kinds of comments. Some fully supported the statement and suggested improvements:

- "Under the Canadian EIA Process, proponents are required to submit environmental impact statements (EISs) in both official languages (English and French). If and when such process involves Canada's aboriginal people, the proponents are often required to prepare an 'Executive Summary' of the EIS in the aboriginal language. In addition, native language interpreters may be hired during public meetings to assist the elders to present their views/comments in their own respective native tongues."
- One respondent went even further: "If the question would have been in 'English only' I would agree; however, most native languages – indigenous languages – are not written languages. If you would suggest that a claim can be recorded in a tape recorder and as such acceptable I would say 'strongly agree.'"
- "If it is possible to have an independent translation afterwards – of course. Thresholds should be as low as possible. If thresholds are high, what's the raison d'être of installing an Inspection Panel?"

The comments of other independent experts were related more to what the effects of accepting a request in a native language are for the administration:

- "Oh dear! This will make life difficult for the accountability mechanism! But it is for them to decide on whether they have the necessary logistical support to treat effectively such hand-written claims in a native language."
- "I have no problem with it. But in an increasing global world possibly the opinion should be limited to one or other of the official languages of the United Nations."
- One comment echoed the MFI expert who stated that the requesters also have to invest in the process: "Mildly disagree, as there needs to be some onus on claimants to make an effort."

A final question related to the procedures to be followed by requesters was raised.

Question 28

People have the right to file a claim with their names known only to the accountability mechanism.

Again, a strong majority of all respondents agreed: 100% of the NGO experts, 96% of the MFI experts, 89% of the independent experts, and 69% of the private-sector experts.

Although very few comments were made, with none coming from either the NGO or private-sector groups, those offered were rather strong. The MFI experts wrote:

- "The point of an accountability mechanism should be to get the issues resolved, not endanger lives."
- "Yes, provided the names can be examined in private and secure proceedings by Bank Management."
- "But this should be verified and accepted by the Panel in order to avoid misuse of the tool."

Comments from the independent experts included:

- "Essential in countries that deny people their basic human rights."
- "Indeed, I strongly agree. See the consequences of people who made corruption known in the EU. The person who rings the bell should be protected always!"
- "As with any potential whistleblower."

LESSONS LEARNED

The position of the requesters in the process should be an issue of constant care. Many respondents expressed this understanding in their comments. As one respondent observed, the process is rather "intimidating" for poor people living in remote areas far away from Washington, DC. Therefore, the NGOs play an important role in translating the procedures and representing the poor. Whether the staff of an accountability mechanism should support the requesters in the process of filing a claim should be pondered very cautiously. The extent to which support can be given depends first on clear, simple, and transparent procedures. If the procedures to be followed in a specific case are not clear, adequate explanations about the technicalities could be given. This should be the limit. I agree with the statement that "No judge can orient a claimant to file a claim to be judged by him/her." Access to the mechanism is fundamental. The suggestion to adopt a system similar to the Canadian environmental impact assessment, which contains the option of funding for participants, is valuable. For me, the optimal level of democracy is realized when a government or an institution delivers funding to affected people in order to help them to defend their rights, even if their activities go against the proposals of the ruling parties.

Canada has to be praised for adopting such legislation, and many governments and institutions can learn from this initiative.

RELATIONS BETWEEN THE ACCOUNTABILITY MECHANISM AND THE EXECUTIVE DIRECTORS

Chapter 3 explains how, why, and when the World Bank's executive directors decided to establish the bank's independent Inspection Panel, which was officially installed by the board. The panel reports directly to the president and the executive directors. Over time, the history of the board's role in the panel's inception has tended to be forgotten. If this history is lost, there is a risk that the independence and the value of an "open door" for the poor outside the bank will be weakened. Good relations between the panel and the board are of crucial importance if the independence and strength of the mechanism are to remain secure.

The five questions in this section of the survey were related to the relationship between the board and the mechanism based on my five years of experience at the World Bank.

The first question is about the opportunity that the resolution establishing the panel missed by not including a clear paragraph explaining who will select and appoint new panel members. Recently, the Human Resources Department has organized and mainly handled the process of selecting new members. Two executive directors representing their colleagues on the board – the managing director and the general counsel – have formed the selection committee. It is not clear whether the entire board has had access to the long list of candidates. Settling on a short list is a crucial operation.

The NGO community has also demanded a role in selecting the members of the mechanisms. The second question in this section is about a possible role for the NGO community. Other questions refer to regular meetings between executive directors and the accountability mechanism. A final question concerns the executive directors' opportunity to ask or instruct the mechanism to do an investigation.

Question 29

The executive directors of the board of IFIs should have a leading role in the process of selecting the members of an accountability mechanism, including access to the list of candidates and to all information about them.

The majority of all experts agreed, with the MFI experts remarkably recording the highest figure (92%), followed by the private-sector experts (70%), the NGO experts (64%), and the independent experts (63%).

The comments offered were diverse across all groups – although almost no comments were made by the private-sector experts – and no typical opinion distinguished one group from another. Approximately four different comments were to be found.

First, a few respondents did not really see the necessity or practical possibility of fully involving the entire board:

- One MFI expert wrote: "I would agree that those selecting candidates should have access to the list and information for all candidates. However, practically speaking, Boards are not set up with the necessary infrastructure to actually run the process of finding candidates and I do not see a need to establish such a parallel infrastructure."

Second, some respondents stressed the importance of full independence:

- A private-sector expert stated: "I could agree to this given the fact the mechanism is absolutely independent."
- One independent expert did not favour a leading role for the board: "Not an independent process. They should have a role, but not the leading role."

The latter comment shows a desire for the process to be fully independent. Which independent entity should organize and lead the process is not mentioned.

Third, many respondents expressed agreement with the statement:

- An MFI specialist wrote: "The only way of ensuring that the best and most independent candidates are selected."
- Among the NGO experts, the same view was expressed: "Board staff – not management – should run process and select candidates."
- An independent expert stated: "The board is fully responsible, including selection of members. I can imagine, however, a procedure that is open for others to come up with names, but selection itself should be done by the board."

Among those who agreed that the board should have the final decision, some suggested that the process can be delegated to a committee. Most of them stated that all members of the board should still have access to the information on all candidates:

- An independent expert said: "In an ideal world all Directors should be involved – to be operational it will be the Committee with 2 Directors representing them. This Committee should have the long-list. The others should have insight on request."
- Another added: "It is normal that any Board member can have access to any and all of the committee's papers and candidate details should they so desire. It seems strange that this is not the case for the Bank's Board and candidates for the Inspection Panel."

- One MFI specialist wrote about the World Bank Group's process: "This is the case in the WBG: Code Chairman leads the Selection Panel on the basis of Terms of Reference, approved by the Board." (Whether the other board members should have access to the lists of candidates only on request is not clear from this comment.)

Fourth, some respondents went further in their commentary on how the process should be conducted:

- One MFI expert wrote: "If NOT already done so, the Bank needs to establish a clearly defined 'PANEL MEMBERSHIP ELIGIBILITY CRITERIA' and a detailed account of the selection process used to appoint panel members. This document should be available to the general public."
- Two comments, among them the following view expressed by an independent expert, mentioned difficulties in the process: "There is also presumably power of the Executive Board to delegate such functions. Experience in human rights accountability processes shows how the merit principle can be compromised where selection is carried out by political bodies. This may not be such a problem for large memberships acting collegially (e.g., human rights treaty bodies), but uneven membership would cause serious problems for a 3-member Panel."
- Finally, one NGO expert showed discontent with the present process at the World Bank: "However, other factors to consider include who makes the final decision and who else participates. I think the Board should be involved, or a committee of the board, but there are so many interests that Board members have and that they bring to the selection process. I have always thought that the selection process was unsatisfactory – the human resources department of the Bank doesn't understand what the Panel is and what types of candidates should be considered; the involvement of NGOs has been uneven and arbitrary, and the power dynamics inside the Bank are complicated and cause conflicts. The President should be advised by the board, but should also get independent advice from many sources."[32]

The next question was about some role, if any, for NGOs in selecting the members of an accountability mechanism. During my years at the World Bank, and during my time outside the bank in discussion with the NGO community, a role for civil society in the selection process was regularly mentioned.

Question 30

The NGOs are free to express their thoughts about the profiles of the potential members of an accountability mechanism such as the Inspection Panel but have no say about possible candidates.

The majority of all groups agreed with the statement: 85% of the private-sector experts, 74% of the MFI experts, 72% of the independent experts, and 62% of the NGO experts. However, the respondents' comments gave a somewhat different picture: those who agreed and those who disagreed were equally divided. Many commented on the procedures or asked "which NGOs?" Some said it is finally boards that decide who to appoint after having listened to the opinions coming from outside the banks.

One MFI expert correctly pointed out that the statement is actually two questions in one:

- "Two questions. Therefore, can't answer. Agree with the first part, not the second." So this respondent disagreed with the proposal that the NGOs should not have *a final say.*
- A comment from an independent expert with the same opinion was short and clear: "They should have a say."
- An MFI specialist wrote: "NGOs should be free to express their thoughts and have a say about possible candidates."
- And an NGO expert stated: "Only if it is shared with NGOs; not sure if it is (at ADB, NGOs were encouraged to identify potential candidates but there was no formal NGO role during writing or final selection). Lists should be shared. World Bank does not do this." No respondent in favour of a role for the NGO community described a clearer picture of how this could be organized.

Some referred to the need to have clear procedures and criteria:

- An MFI specialist commented: "Civil society should have a role and not be excluded. Agree on generic criteria for selection of IP members first, before individuals come into the process."
- One independent expert asked whether "consultation rounds" could be held.
- An MFI expert wondered which NGOs could be involved: "Which NGOs? This could easily get completely out of hand. More details as to what are required in order to make a meaningful judgment on this statement."
- An NGO expert interestingly commented: "Possible candidates should be scrutinized by the public. It means there should be prior information and discussion about the views of the candidates. However I am really against a situation that the World Bank NGO Working Group or a D.C.-based NGO will say yes or no about possible candidates."
- The relevant question in this latter comment was partly answered by another independent expert: "As long as it is clear that the NGO is not a political party in disguise!"
- An MFI expert also formulated an answer to the question: "Which NGOs? If international advocacy NGOs, it then creates a conflict of interest. They should be free to nominate candidates but should not be formally part of process."

The view that the NGOs are free to express their thoughts was broadly supported.

The other half of the group was of the opinion that this does not mean NGOs should have a say:

- An independent expert commented: "Freedom of speech issue here. They may have no INFLUENCE but can say what they want, surely?"
- A private-sector expert wrote: "They should be involved in giving input as any other stakeholder, but NGOs should not have preferential treatment or 'veto' rights."
- One independent expert did not see a role for the NGOs at all: "This should be retained. Otherwise it will be difficult to expand buy-in to results/outcomes of the Panel's activities."
- Finally, one MFI expert made a remarkable observation: "If the selection process becomes too open and names start floating around you may risk losing interesting applications."

Question 31

Regular meetings between the executive directors, their alternates, and members of the accountability mechanisms are crucial to ensuring the efficiency of the mechanisms within the IFIs.

The outcome of the numeric responses to this question suggested that regular meetings between these parties are a matter of course: 100% of the private-sector experts agreed, followed by 88% of the MFI experts, 87% of the NGO experts, and 79% of the independent experts. Again, however, the comments gave a totally different picture. Only three reactions were mainly positive, while all the others noted that meetings between the mechanism and the board should not be too frequent and referred to the need for a certain distance in order to preserve the mechanism's independence. None of the private-sector respondents provided a comment on this question.

Two independent experts fully supported the statement:

- "Seems logic."
- "Such interaction is needed to keep both parties informed and to keep them in accord."
- And one MFI expert stated: "Of course, communication and transparency are crucial, especially when one is in favour of the principle of Corporate Social Responsibility!"

In all the other comments, questions were raised about "how regular" the meetings should be and about the mechanism's independence. Comments from the MFI experts included:

- "Regular meetings are not required. A periodic, formal reporting process will suffice."
- "I would say 'periodic,' not 'regular.'"

Similar statements were made by members of the other groups.

Some experts again referred to the need for rules and procedures to clarify the matter:

- "As noted earlier, the document containing 'Operational Procedures of the Inspection Panel' should define the nature of such relationships and dealings so that the general public is fully aware of it."

Many experts from both the MFI and independent groups went further, hammering home the need to protect the mechanism's independence:

- "As long as the independence of the members is respected and no indications are given to them of how to deal with specific Requests."
- "Such meetings must not compromise or be perceived as compromising the independence of members of the inspection mechanism."

One independent expert maintained that any decision on meetings between the board and the mechanism's members should be made by the mechansim:

- "The Panel should only meet the Directors when the Panel, and no one else, deems it fit to do so. Otherwise the independence of the Panel may be undermined."

The resolution establishing the World Bank Inspection Panel contains the following text: "In view of the institutional responsibilities of Executive Directors in the observance by the Bank of its operational policies and procedures, an Executive Director may in special cases of serious alleged violations of such policies and procedures ask the Panel for an investigation, subject to the requirements of paranumeric percentages 13 and 14 below. The Executive Directors, acting as a Board, may at any time instruct the Panel to conduct an investigation."[33] The subsections referred to here provide the option both for an individual executive director (in special cases) and for the executive directors (acting as a board) to ask the Inspection Panel for an investigation. In its history, the panel has received only one such request from the Board of Directors.[34]

Question 32

It is important that the executive directors of IFIs have the opportunity to instruct their problem-solving mechanisms and accountability/compliance mechanisms to intervene when problems occur in the field.

The outcome of the numeric responses to this question again indicated strong majority agreement: 91% of the private-sector experts, 81% of the independent experts, 80% of the NGO experts, and 75% of the MFI experts. In the first of these two groups, nobody disagreed. And although a majority of the MFI experts indicated agreement, a remarkably high minority (25%) disagreed.

As with the other questions in this section, concerns emerged in the comments. Hesitation about the (existing) option for board members to ask the World Bank Inspection Panel to conduct an investigation was clearly expressed by the MFI experts:

- "Such requests may lead to conflicts in the Board and polarize or cause division in the Board."
- "I would say 'No' since I have a problem with the word 'instruct.'"[35]
- "This would be contrary to all established Rules of Procedure and allow Executive Directors an opportunity to 'interfere' and promote vested interests."

One comment from an MFI expert referred to the fact that so far there has been only one case in which the board has exercised the option:

- "This approach has yielded very few requests." The only comment made by an expert of the private sector was: "Only if there is hard evidence of non-compliance."

The independent experts made a few comments of a different nature:

- "I think it would be better to make the good functioning of accountability/compliance mechanisms a responsibility of one of the Executive Directors."
- "The Panel should receive instructions from the Directors as a Board. Otherwise, there will be a direct bearing on the Panel's independence."
- "Should be dismissed if they do not."
- "Seems common sense that this should be the case. What is worrying is that the Board has not referred more problematic cases to the IP for an opinion. Possibly this is something that the IP needs to raise with the Board."

LESSONS LEARNED

It is evident that the boards of the IFIs, including the World Bank, should have the lead in selecting the members of the accountability mechanisms, as is the case for the Inspection Panel. This implies that the board should be informed of all candidates who either apply or are nominated for a position on the mechanism. I understand the desire to create a detailed account of a newly designed selection process, which is not easy to develop since privacy issues could easily be at stake. Outside stakeholders, such as

NGOs, should at the beginning of the process be given the opportunity to exchange their views about the selection process and about the criteria used for the selection.

That the World Bank's board has only once "instructed" the Inspection Panel to investigate a project is a matter of fact. This opportunity, which has existed since the panel was first established, is surprisingly not welcomed by many. Those who commented on the matter expressed the fear that it could lead to conflicts and jeopardize a mechanism's independence. I am not convinced of this danger. The Inspection Panel is a mechanism of and for the board, which could make much more use of it while ensuring the panel's independence at the same time. When the board "instructed" the panel to investigate a project in China, it finally accepted the panel's rather critical report, although I have to admit that the board did not emerge from the process undivided. Some board members heavily criticized the panel, while others praised it for its work. Ever since, the panel has always defended its China report.

How often an accountability mechanism can meet with the board should depend on the workload and on questions raised by the panel or the board. One respondent's comment that a mechanism "should remain at a certain distance from the Executive Directors in order to protect its independence" has its merits. Meetings between an accountability mechanism and the board of an institution are important. Nevertheless, these meetings must never lead to an infringement on the independence of the mechanism.

RELATIONS BETWEEN THE ACCOUNTABILITY MECHANISM AND MANAGEMENT

As described in chapter 6, relations between an accountability mechanism and management are rather atypical. This section contains several questions about this relationship. The first question is about the sensitivity of the relationship. Other questions concern the mechanism's access to information, management's influence on the mechanism's reporting, and the specific relationship between the mechanism and the institution's general counsel.

Question 33

Given the role of an accountability mechanism, it is normal for the relationship between management, panel members, and staff to be sensitive.

Not surprisingly, the MFI experts agreed with this statement most strongly, at 92%, followed by the NGO respondents (85%), the independent experts (80%), and a much smaller majority of the private-sector experts (55%). The extensive written comments showed the experience that many have had with such mechanisms, but the NGO respondents provided no written statements.

The most striking statement was made by one of the MFI experts:

- "If the relationship isn't somewhat tense, the Panel probably isn't doing its job."

Other comments from the MFI group were milder:

- "This is the reality. However, I consider it important that the members of the Accountability Mechanism and its staff stress that the focus on policy compliance primarily addresses issues of process. Individual roles of Bank staff and Management should not be the focus of compliance review. In addition I consider it essential that the potential of an Accountability Mechanism as a learning tool is stressed as well."
- "Yes, both parties need to play their respective parts without blurring the roles."
- Another noted that it takes time for such a mechanism to be accepted within an institution: "One should monitor for a number of years the acceptance of the work of the Panel."

A private-sector expert tried to find a solution to the sensitive nature of the relationship by referring to the Dutch "poldermodel," which requires all involved parties to talk and negotiate as long as necessary to reach a common agreement.

The following four statements by independent experts are self-explanatory:

- "It would be strange if there wasn't sensitivity. No 'tension' would be indicative that the Panel was either being ignored or was held in low esteem."
- "Indeed, subject to certain preconditions, a degree of tension can be taken as a positive indicator of the Panel's impact."
- "This is bound to happen. Auditors in any institution are viewed with scepticism."
- "This is a structural problem facing all institutions with accountability mechanisms, and one I have yet to see satisfactorily resolved."

Other statements noted the capacity and readiness of the institutions to accept the nature of the mechanisms and in principle to respect their findings:

- "It really depends upon the way the World Bank and Management understands the nature and scope of the ROLE of the Inspection Panel."

In the daily relations between management and the Inspection Panel, there are several recurring issues. Constantly, the panel has had to press hard to receive all relevant internal documents in order to execute its work properly. The following two questions are related to a mechanism's access to information.

Question 34

All relevant documents, including e-mails, will be delivered to the accountability mechanism when requested.

Not surprisingly, a strong majority of the NGO experts (93%) agreed, followed by an awe-inspiring majority of the MFI experts (92%), by the independent experts (89%), and by the private-sector experts (70%). It is remarkable that the MFI experts agreed so unanimously since many of them have been confronted with difficult investigations and with demands from members of the mechanisms to deliver documents showing the decisions taken at certain moments during the implementation of projects. Most of the written comments were made by the MFI and independent experts.

Some of the comments differed from the numeric outcome. A few MFI experts did express their agreement in writing:

- "Crucial for fact finding!"
- And somewhat cynically: "In an ideal world this would be obvious."

But more MFI experts suggested that this could be done only within a structure of rules:

- "Subject only to specific provisions of the rules of Procedure of the Accountability Mechanism."
- "Panels' authority to access info data should be clearly defined."
- "Protection of confidentiality/sensitivity of certain documents must however be assured by the Panel."

One MFI expert with a lot of experience with the World Bank Inspection Panel wrote:

- "This is an invasion of staff deliberations, and is appropriate for a criminal or corruption investigation where there is criminal wrongdoing. Review should be limited to official and draft Bank documents and interviews and field investigations. There is already too little right to privacy and the Panel is not that type of investigative body."

The private-sector experts offered only two comments:

- "Agree – but, again, this invokes the 'policing' mentality."
- "Define 'relevant.'"

The only comment made by an NGO respondent was:

- "Depends on what is 'all relevant': a certain level of confidentiality is acceptable."

The independent experts were more or less divided:

- "Otherwise no point in having the Panel."
- "It should come as close as possible to Court's rules – so, the same principles as in legal affairs should be applied."
- "There is nothing special about e-mail. It is merely the 21st century form of written communication. Defining what is 'relevant' and what constitutes 'invasion of privacy' is more important. Guidelines in this regard should be formulated."

A substantial number of independent experts asked what documents are relevant:

- "It depends what criteria is used and who exactly decides what document is relevant and what is NOT. In making such requests one must be mindful of the commercial, security and other interests of the Bank as well as time and expenses involved in making such documents available to the Panel."

Other independent experts noted the downside of allowing access to e-mails:

- "What about privacy?"
- "E-mails are used for all kinds of simple thoughts, non-issues etc., like bi-lateral conversations, brainstorms etc. To use these e-mails would give them too much a formal status, and may lead to different communication patterns that may block creativity."
- "There's a need to be realistic. The administrative burden for both the Accountability Mechanism and the Management that this involves should be borne in mind, for some projects; because e-mail is so easy, a great many e-mails may have been exchanged and rather frequently. Not all of these will be very important, most probably will not be. It will therefore be a burden for both the Management to keep a well-filed dossier of e-mails and for the Accountability Mechanism to sift through the e-mails for important material. Furthermore, such a rule would give an incentive to use the telephone much more."

Those who commented on the sensitivity of proprietary information anticipated the next question, which treats this issue directly.

Question 35

Members of an accountability mechanism should have access to proprietary information when necessary with the condition of confidentiality.

A majority of the respondents in all groups fully agreed: 100% of the MFI experts, 93% of the NGO experts (exceptionally, 7% disagreed), 90% of the independent experts, and 77% of the private-sector experts (a comparatively smaller majority). In responding to the previous question, a number of experts expressed concerns with the implications of allowing access to e-mail; this time the respondents' comments mainly reinforced the numeric outcome.

One MFI expert noted the difference between the two questions:

• "Agree. This is different from staff e-mails."

Other comments from the MFI experts included:

• "Otherwise they cannot complete a relevant investigation."
• "The mechanism should have access to all relevant information. The issue of confidentiality is paramount and must be honored."
• "The final report should also take into account this principle."

Similar comments were made by private-sector experts:

• "Agree. However, confidentiality agreements must be signed."
• "They should have access to all information that will enable them to undertake their function responsibly."

The independent experts partly agreed, offering similar comments:

• "They can't do their job properly without this information."
• "Yes, provided that this is agreed to by the Bank and is mentioned in the membership eligibility criteria also."

By comparison, some independent experts expressed doubts about whether the World Bank Inspection Panel can gain access to such information:

• "True, but unlikely to be respected by the management responsible for handling the proprietary information except under duress."
• "If relation with the case can clearly be demonstrated/proved – only what if this does not happen? Who should judge if IP's request for a certain type of information is not accepted? The IP is an internal instrument, and if the Board denies access to the information ..."

One independent expert made a statement about private enterprises:

- "The problem with this question is that enterprises are entitled to keep lots of information secret and this makes control on their activities extremely difficult. If we see enterprises as social mechanisms, and not only economic entities, then there is reason to oblige to be open on many crucial questions: environment, social, cultural etc."

The NGO experts did not offer many comments, but one remarkably stated:

- "They should have the possibility to publicize the information, unless it would be on financial information that can be confidential. Information on social, environmental and HR [human resources] issues should not be confidential."

On several occasions World Bank management has raised the question of whether management can view the final draft version of a panel report in order to verify factual details. The argument has been that factual errors in data could thus be avoided. Given the independence of the mechanism, one can fully understand the panel's hesitation or unwillingness to do so. The panel's Administrative Procedures state: "Recommendations and findings of the Panel shall be strictly impartial: only facts relevant to the Request or investigation under consideration shall be relevant to their decisions. Consideration of political factors shall be strictly prohibited."[36]

An argument in favour of granting management access to draft reports is that the panel could misinterpret real facts, such as percentages and other data. If such errors were then communicated to the panel, it could decide whether to treat the information as pure facts or to accept management's clarification of the data. So the final say would remain with the panel. Those opposed argue that it would open the door to the involvement of management, whose members are an object of investigations. Another argument against delivering draft reports to management is that the requesters do not have the same access. It is felt that creating this opportunity for the requesters would be a risk. The next question is about whether management should have access to an accountability mechanism's draft reports.

Question 36

Management should not have access to a mechanism's report before finalization: it is against the notion of independence and should be avoided at all times.

As is clear from the numeric outcome, there was much diversity of opinion among the respondents. Only the NGO experts recorded 100% agreement.

The only other clear majority was found among the MFI experts, at 63%, followed by a small majority of independent experts (53%) and by a minority of private-sector experts (38%). Of the four groups, the private-sector respondents were most divided, with 46% disagreeing and 15% offering no opinion.

Almost all of the comments made by the NGO experts referred to the position of the requesters and made the same point:

- "Not unless the claimants also have an opportunity to see a draft, and can comment on the findings. There ought to be equal access to the process from the claimants, who, once their claim is filed, are often left out of any serious communication, have no right to comment on drafts, or to respond, or to have a say in determining the remedies."

The reference here to equal access for the requesters was echoed by many in the other three groups. Comments from the MFI experts included:

- "Otherwise, civil society should have the same opportunity for reasons of fairness and efficiency. In any event, the final outcome would not be a Panel independent document but the result of 'negotiations' with the other party or parties."
- "If the requesters do not have this right, why should management get it? The risk of an in-crowd situation is foreseen."

One independent expert was entirely against the idea that management should see draft reports:

- "I don't think that this is acceptable. Good accountability mechanisms need to be transparent and delivering a judgment about management or a project without giving the opportunity to demonstrate that the judgment is excessively harsh is unfair."

Others in this group had fewer problems:

- "As long as independence is strictly preserved, I feel sharing drafts for factual checking serves both IP and management, as well as producing a more effective final report. If sharing drafts weakens independence, then no sharing."

One MFI expert noted the situation at the Asian Development Bank:

- "Under the ADB system, both Management and the requesters will have a possibility to make comments on the draft final report of the Panel. The Panel will decide whether to adjust/incorporate/change their report. These comments will be annexed to the final report."

Similar wording was found in comments offered by the independent experts:

- "Independent people in a mechanism will remain independent even if they are sitting on management's lap. It seems reasonable to get feedback on a draft report first, judge the new information, and adapt a report if the Mechanism-people feel this would be appropriate."
- "Eventually only the 'factual' part could be sent on."

One MFI specialist wrote:

- "The Inspection Panel is an accountability mechanism for the World Bank. It is not designed to be an extra-legal authority. It is important that the work be correct and objective. Sharing with management can promote trust and objectivity if managed in the correct way. Management should not have editorial control but the ability to check the facts and make sure that all issues have been considered. Management should not have ability to slow the process down."

Finally, a comment by one private-sector expert was short and clear:

- "Necessary to check the facts, but not the conclusions."

The last question to be raised about the relations between an accountability mechanism and management concerns a mechanism's relationship with the general counsel. Since the establishment of the World Bank Inspection Panel, the bank's general counsel has been the legal advisor both for management (and the president) and for the panel. Given the sensitivity of the panel's work, many have argued that it should be advised by an independent legal counsel.

Question 37

The relationship between an accountability mechanism and the general counsel of an institution should at all times be impartial.

A high majority in all groups agreed: 100% of the NGO experts, 92% of the private-sector experts, 86% of the MFI experts, and 83% of the independent experts.

The private-sector experts offered no comments. With only a few exceptions, all the respondents from the other three groups stressed the importance of impartial or independent legal advice. The following examples are representative of the comments from the MFI specialists:

- "If by 'impartial' you mean independent, I agree. For the reasons that you have above, I find it very difficult for the General Counsel to be

really impartial on operational matters. He himself or his/her department is totally involved in the project's decision making."

- "To say that it should be 'impartial' sounds like motherhood. No one
would argue the reverse. The question is whether the General Counsel
of the Board (and Management) should also be the Counsel of Panel, as
he now is. The answer is 'no.' An independent mechanism should have
access to its own exclusive Counsel."
- "If it is not impartial, IP needs its own impartial legal advice."

One MFI expert had a somewhat different view:

- "Depends on the role that General Counsel plays. If the Inspection Panel
needs legal advice, they should be able to go to law firms to get it."

The few comments from the NGO experts were of the same nature:

- "The same counsel should not represent the Bank and the Inspection
Panel because of the potential conflicts of interest you note above."
- "Of course there is clear conflict of interests that we noticed in practice."

The independent experts echoed these sentiments:

- "Indeed – they should avoid becoming 'partie et juge.'"
- "If this were not the case it would be rather odd."

One independent expert made an extraordinary observation:

- "The General Counsel, being a lawyer, is always guided by his Code of
Ethics and namely the principle that he should give independent and
impartial advice to his client. It appears that the General Counsel has
several clients. Firstly the Bank, secondly the Board, thirdly the Management and fourthly the Panel. But this should not necessarily mean that
the advice of the General Counsel is dependent on who is asking for
such advice. But be that as it may. The Panel being an accounting mechanism should perhaps be independent of the General Counsel also in
the same way as advisers to a Central Reserve Bank for example cannot
be advisers to the commercial banks also. A regulatory authority in the
same breath has to be independent from the regulated bodies. The
Panel should perhaps therefore have within itself an expert trained in
the legal field to assist in the work of the Panel."

LESSONS LEARNED
That the relationship between an accountability mechanism and management is by nature sensitive should surprise no one. I quite agree with the

statement: "If the relationship isn't somewhat tense, the Panel probably isn't doing its job." An accountability mechanism is a new component within an institution comparable to a transplanted kidney in the body, which will initially show signs of rejection. The kidney is essential to the body's cleaning functions, but the body first has to get used to it and then has to accept and welcome the new component. From day one, I have repeatedly stated in meetings with management that the World Bank should be proud to have installed the Inspection Panel within the institution. Yet how to deal with this very exceptional and necessary function is a matter of style and experience.

The presence of a mechanism undoubtedly means that it is given access to information needed to fulfil its task, including internal documents and e-mails. Access to proprietary information is not felt to be a problem. The members of the Inspection Panel and other mechanisms are bound by the same confidentiality rules as management. Access to conversational letters, including e-mails that are part of project files, seems to be a different matter. That privacy could be at stake is evident. It is up to the members of an accountability mechanism to exercise prudence in arguing with management and to choose between what is truly essential for an investigation and what is not. Access to information should never lead to a witch hunt. In case of conflict over access, it is necessary that the panel rely on its own legal counsel.

Whether management should have access to an accountability mechanism's preliminary reports in order to verify facts and other numeric data is another issue. Shortly after I became a member of the Inspection Panel, I expressed a positive attitude about the idea. What would argue against it? After all, it could be good to have an extra check on data. In any event, the panel members would finally decide among themselves what to regard as facts and what as interpretations. Clearly, one downside is that giving management the right to verify the factual content of draft reports would constitute preferential treatment vis-à-vis the requesters. This goes against any logic for the creation of an accountability mechanism as the first "open door" for people in the project areas. So access should also be given to them. However, that would create another dilemma. If a preliminary report went out to too many people involved before it was finalized, it could easily be leaked to the press, giving the outside world access to draft findings before the board of the institution had access and before a report was finalized. The most compelling case against allowing both management and requesters to see draft reports is the risk that the process would lead to a pandemonium of arguments between the independent mechanism, management, and the requesters, thus undermining the process and finally the mechanism itself. So the best option is probably to retain the rule that a report is to be delivered to management and the board only after it has been finalized.

Whether the general counsel of an institution should also advise the members of an accountability mechanism – as is currently the case at the World Bank – is a matter on which many of the survey respondents expressed disagreement. For a long time, many have argued that the World Bank should appoint an independent legal advisor to the Inspection Panel. As one respondent wrote about the World Bank, the department of the general counsel "is totally involved in the project's decision making." Therefore, the same person cannot be an independent advisor to the Inspection Panel. However, also valid is the argument made by one respondent that because the general counsel is guided by a code of ethics, he or she can be expected to give independent and impartial advice to all parties. Nevertheless, the same respondent finally recommended that an independent legal advisor should be available to a mechanism, similar to a legal advisor of a Central Reserve Bank. This option is a valuable one that needs further study.

STAFF OF THE ACCOUNTABILITY MECHANISMS

Just as the independence of an accountability mechanism is important, also important is the independence of the staff of such mechanisms. This is even more the case when staff are appointed from an institution's regular staff, as has mainly happened with the members of the World Bank Inspection Panel. The following question on this topic was asked.

Question 38

The staff of an accountability mechanism should clearly show that they understand the importance of the independence of the mechanism.

This question about the independence of the members of a mechanism seems so obvious that it was probably perceived as being beyond debate. Indeed, the NGO, MFI, and independent experts all strongly agreed, at 100%. Only the private-sector experts recorded a lower majority, at 92%, but within this group 8% had no opinion.

There were few comments. These reflected the numeric outcomes and came mainly from the MFI and independent experts. Comments from the former group included:

- "Not only show that they understand but, more importantly, behave at all times in line with the importance and independence of their role."
- "The independence of staff of the accountability mechanism enhances its credibility and gives confidence to a requester about its impartiality."
- "In order to give IP staff members a possibility of career within the WBG special arrangements with HR department should be made, comparable to OECD-staff."
- "I would add a 'fire-wall' agreement."

Two specialists asked how to guarantee the independence of panel members:

- An MFI specialist wrote: "Yes, but how?"
- An NGO respondent wrote: "With an oath or what?"

The three independent experts who made comments all offered suggestions:

- "The important thing is that the staff ARE TRULY INDEPENDENT of the parent institution and not that they show that they understand this. If they are found not to be independent they should be dismissed forthwith."
- "The Inspection Panel in close consultation with the World Bank Management needs to develop clear terms of reference for engaging/hiring such experts. Outside experts hired in support of the work of the federally appointed panels under the Canadian Assessment and Review Process were given a copy of their terms of reference."
- "Confer Independence rules for UK auditors. Failure to sign them is a disciplinary offence, even for a junior secretary."

Question 39

The independence of experts contracted during investigations must be ensured.

Here, we see numeric outcomes quite similar to those for the previous question about the independence of mechanism staff. Both the NGO and private-sector experts recorded 100% agreement, followed by the MFI experts (96%) and the independent experts (95%).

Not many comments were made. Again, there were those who asked "how" the independence of contracted experts can be ensured. For example, an NGO respondent wrote:

- "In principle yes but how?"

Some referred to instructions and to contracts with the consultants, as in these comments from independent experts:

- "Independent of what? The project under investigation? The task manager? The host country? All can be cause of concern. All consultants should have to declare that they have no conflict of interest in cases with which they are involved."
- "All such issues need to be clearly stated and properly dealt with in the terms of reference or employment conditions agreed to jointly by the Bank and the Inspection Panel."

An MFI specialist disagreed with the latter comment when it comes to a bank's involvement in the contracts:

- "The Panel probably needs explicit instructions for independent outside experts it may contract. Obviously such contracting should not involve any bank department."

One MFI expert had a different view on independence:

- "Objectivity should be ensured. Independence is not the primary consideration."

Two MFI specialists referred to the status of hired consultants:

- "Only means of giving credibility to Panel's reports."
- "However, the final responsibility of any investigation rests with the Panel."

Two specialists made remarkable notes about the position of the consultants:

- In reference to the situation at the World Bank, one MFI specialist stated: "It seems that the same experts are contracted on a regular basis. In order to expand the knowledge basis to find fresh views and to prevent prominence of an expert, the Inspection Panel should make sure that there is sufficient rotation of experts."
- An independent expert wrote: "Use more than one expert for each area of focus. Do not pay them a fee, only expenses."

LESSONS LEARNED

The numeric outcomes and the comments on the independence of the staff of an accountability mechanism were clear. The overwhelming majority agreed with the importance of independence. There is no need for any further comment on this. The same goes for the consultants hired by the mechanism. The independent expert who suggested that the consultants should be paid only for their expenses raised an important issue that was not dealt with in the questionnaire in general: the costs of an accountability mechanism. I do not think that consultants hired by the mechanism should work on such a basis. Experts doing a good job need recognition through proper payment. The point about rotation of experts has more merit. As there is rotation of the members of the mechanisms, this should also be the case for the consultants they hire.

STATE OF AFFAIRS, FUTURE DEVELOPMENTS, AND OPTIONS

It was inescapable to ask the respondents what the accountability mechanisms will look like down the road. The existing mechanisms are epoch-making institutions, as all the respondents know. The World Bank Inspection Panel is recognized by many as the pioneer. Other MFIs have followed the bank's lead. Senior management in the private financial sector is well aware of the outside demand that it also establish independent accountability mechanisms. The first step is the hardest and raises questions about what structure a new mechanism will have and about what similar mechanisms exist.[37] So a final, general question was raised.

Question 40

What will the state of accountability mechanisms be ten years from now?

Fifty-six respondents took the time to reflect on the question. Together, their responses provide a rich source from which we can form an impression of what accountability mechanisms will or should look like in the years to come. An overwhelming majority of the experts were convinced that the mechanisms will further grow and develop. No specific view distinguished one group from another. Only two respondents thought that *the situation will not change*:

- An MFI expert wrote: "Unchanged."
- A private-sector respondent said: "Should be somewhat similar to what we have today."

A number of comments expressed *optimism about the future*. Such comments from the MFI experts included:

- "I believe if present trends continue, accountability mechanisms will have profound influence on the conduct of doing business in IFIs."
- "Probably more robust than they are now. The process of global democratization should ensure that development."
- "They will be functional, professionalized organs given the globalization and dwindling natural resources."
- "The basic structure may not be changed. I hope the operation of accountability mechanisms improve gradually year by year."

The following comments were made by the independent experts:

- "They will grow in scope, outreach and importance."
- "I think that these kinds of mechanisms will develop further under pressure of the governmental requirements of Corporate Social Responsibility. Of course there a lot of cultural differences in the world. But in view of the increase of globalization and (global) resembling mechanism of rationalization, these kinds of mechanisms will converge."

One NGO expert wrote:

- "Stronger, because of high levels of information through the Internet, satellites, etc. It becomes increasingly difficult for an IFI to hide away from what it is financing."

Some experts expressed the expectation that *the scope of the mechanisms will increase*:

- An independent expert wrote: "More widespread. Better recognized. Developing in to a recognized field of expertise in its own right."
- An MFI expert enthused: "I believe it will be very different; great strides have been made over the past 3 years."
- A private-sector expert said: "No doubt that there will be more focus on accountability as the environmental issues and human rights will be higher on the agenda in the future. Implementation of protocols and principles will be more common and thus the need for accounting will grow accordingly. There will however be a lesser number of institutions which will not comply with the rules and regulations; it will simply not be accepted anymore by the society. If this makes life easier for accounting mechanisms is however doubtful."
- Another MFI respondent speculated: "Perhaps one common one for MFIs, one for the Equator institutions, one for the bilateral donors etc."
- One NGO representative explained: "Reinforcing accountability mechanisms is not an isolated issue or task. It means the reinforcement of some other issues, which constitute the basis of this wanted reinforcement. Human Rights – the stepping stone of all development concerns – may they be economic, financial, political, social, etc. The Panel should definitely have an extended mandate. It's too limited what it can do, since investigations can't go further than questioning the Operational Policies and Procedures set by the Bank ... Even if some other violations are found, they remain out of consideration. And even if questions related to indigenous peoples, resettlement and environmental disasters are all about human rights, they are not seen as such – weakening the importance of such questions."

In this vein, a few commented on accountability specifically within the private financial sector:

- An MFI expert wrote: "There will be many more Accountability mechanisms, in the private as well as in the public sectors. Civil society organizations will also be subject to audits and controls and their own accountability will be more emphasized."
- Another MFI expert stated: "Mandatory for private sector and multilateral banks."

- An NGO respondent said: "Hopefully more effective than it is now, particularly with regard to the private sector arms of IFIs."

Some experts reflected on *the mediation, or problem-solving, function*, speculating that it will become more important than compliance review:

- One MFI expert wrote: "Accountability Mechanisms would exist 10 years from now although their nature may be different. The tendency is to establish mechanisms that combine problem solving with compliance functions. I would surmise that in the future greater emphasis would be placed on the problem-solving function."
- An NGO expert concurred: "Greater emphasis on problem solving; stronger acceptance within institutions and within governments; less contentious or controversial; more involved in follow-up on implementation of remedial actions; more able to engage with claimants and local people in a more meaningful way."
- An independent expert stated: "Hopefully by that time the members are able (apart from being able to apply the 'rules') to identify the dilemmas which at this stage are not being recognized and (more so) resolve them into a win-win solution. This will build a natural bridge between the ombudsman and his/her mediation approach (which by its nature has identifying a win-win as its natural goal) and the compliance approach of the Panel."

Other respondents showed *concern that the mechanisms will be undermined.* Such comments from the MFI experts included:

- "I am afraid that Accountability Mechanisms will still be very much fragile: tolerated rather than fully endorsed by and institutionally embedded in IFIs. Currently the political will is largely absent with the big powers in the world to support multilateral models of economic cooperation. Similarly there is also not much of political sensitivity to the interests of project-affected communities. Dominant thinking remains market and competition oriented, rather than a focus on cooperation and solidarity. Accountability Mechanisms only will become stronger if political will is invested in IFIs to improve their accountability to the common good."
- "I think that in the coming years the Accountability Mechanisms will go through difficult times as part 2 and part 1 countries questions their efficacy and think of them more as obstacles than contributors to sustainable development. 10 years from now, however, I think that like a pendulum they will be back in full force and respectability."

One NGO respondent was very pessimistic:

- "We suspect that there is growing resistance to accountability Mechanisms. MFIs and banks will look for risk-free investments, and maximum returns often means short-cutting on social and environmental standards. This is precisely the area where accountability mechanisms will be at work, and this will not be taken easily by MFIs. This is all in a context of worldwide capital demanding for itself freedom from restrictions, either from State or from accountability mechanisms. Hence, all the more reason to demand now strong accountability mechanisms."

One MFI expert mentioned what is necessary to *prevent a downgrading of the mechanisms*:

- "If safeguard weakening is allowed to continue, if the Inspection Panel itself is weakened or constrained in any way, if World Bank Group staff gets the message that safeguard compliance is not as important as other factors, the accountability mechanism will suffer, and development effectiveness will suffer. And so: If safeguards are revised commensurate with need, and if they are kept current, if the IP is nurtured, if hiring more effective social and environmental professionals is strengthened, if managers have compulsory and meaningful training, the accountability mechanism will contribute strongly to improved development effectiveness."

A few respondents offered *critical notes*:

- An MFI expert simply stated: "Hopefully more result-oriented."
- One independent expert had a rather limited scope for the mechanisms in mind: "Accountability Mechanisms will only check marginally, since the idea of accountability and objectivity is internalized to such an extent that no one would dare trying only to push a limited agenda forward."
- Another MFI respondent foresaw other problems: "There will be more of them but they will be more efficient. Between now and ten years there will be growing concern about the cost/benefits of accountability mechanisms."
- One independent expert anticipated the mechanisms developing in different directions: "Two possibilities. One is that they will be weaker because they will not take steps to incorporate regional and national details/difference. They will also have stepped back from the difficult challenge of engaging with stakeholders throughout their activities. They might also have become more active to Management. In short, the answer is fully endogenous to the Accountability Mechanisms themselves."

This latter view should be noted by all present and future members of accountability mechanisms, including myself. We shoulder a substantial responsibility.

Two private-sector experts made almost identical, and rather remarkable, comments on *the role of civil society* in shaping the accountability mechanisms:

- "Accountability will be defined by stakeholders, not by the institutions."
- "Increased independence, multi-stakeholder partnerships."

With major experience in the field of international law and/or legal issues related to financial institutions, many of the respondents offered *differing legal perspectives*:

- One MFI expert wrote: "It will develop into a special arbitration mechanism whereby private individuals will seek damages or compensation for MDBs [multilateral development banks]."
- This view was echoed by an NGO expert: "Accountability mechanisms are crucial. However, they should not be limited to mechanisms related to the institution, but also include legal mechanisms."
- Another MFI expert expressed the opposite view, suggesting that the countries themselves can handle future cases: "It may adjust because of stronger concerns that the mechanism violates national sovereignty in some cases. It may also migrate toward more mediation. Hopefully, borrowers will have stronger court systems to address these concerns ten years from now."

Concern was also expressed that *the mechanisms are too procedural*:

- One MFI specialist wrote: "My hope is the mechanisms by the time are not more formalized as they are already today."
- An independent expert stated: "If too procedural and demanding a path is taken by Accountability Mechanisms, they could paralyze an organization. In that case, they are likely to be downgraded. If they can do their job in a proportionate manner, they could enhance the reputation of their institution and therefore their own status. At all times, however, they will be under pressure to relax their standards."
- One independent expert, while speculating about what the future may hold, made a remarkable note about there being too many mechanisms: "Hopefully more independent. Respect for professionalism. There is a danger of a multitude of inspection mechanisms in the world. This raises serious issues of uniformity of approach or at least of coordination and coherence."

One independent expert speculated that *the IFIs will need to adapt*:

- "I suspect that all Bretton Woods institutions will change markedly in the next few years. The UN is a shambles (too much administration, not enough action), and the IMF and WB will be under increasing pressure to reform so as to compete on equal terms with private-sector lenders – they are not unique, and the EU and many international governments will also have to adapt. The cause is the need for public institutions to be properly accountable, and accountability includes objective scrutiny."

Finally, one independent expert placed *the future of the mechanisms on the shoulders of panel members*, giving them a major personal responsibility:

- "It will be an inspiration. It will certainly work if the best minds form part of it. Humans make institutions and not the reverse. An independent mechanism will come to light only and only if people with independent minds are appointed thereon. I hasten to add that there is a danger that the Mechanism will gather so much momentum and independence that it will be a victim of its own independence and may develop an 'institutional arrogance' if such independence is not self-contained."

CONCLUDING REMARKS

The wealth of wisdom expressed in the respondents' comments does not make it simple to add concluding remarks without incurring the risks of misinterpretation, of not mentioning the remarkable words of some respondents, and of being too brief about what was said. Nevertheless, here is an attempt.

On the one hand, I share the overwhelming optimism that accountability mechanisms will be broadly accepted, be more robust, improve gradually, and finally grow both in the world of multilateral financial institutions and in the private financial sector. I also share the hope that there will be "a lesser number of institutions which will not comply with the rules and regulations" – which, as was noted, "will simply not be accepted anymore by the society." Those who share this optimism are probably also of the opinion that the existing accountability mechanisms are the only "control" that we now have over MFIs and that we may soon have over private banks (private investments), which can no longer be directly regulated by national elected institutions. Accountability mechanisms are all we have. And it is an absolute necessity that they be further harmonized.

On the other hand, I share the concern that the mechanisms may become too procedural and legalistic. I fully understand the warning from the expert who noted the "danger of a multitude of inspection mechanisms in the world." I understand the comment that the mechanisms could "violate national sovereignty" and the hope that national institutions will soon have "stronger court systems to address these concerns."

I am not certain whether this hope is realistic in a globalized world. And as long as we are not sure that national authorities can and will defend the rights of the poor confronted with the negative impacts of internationally financed projects, we must at least have accountability mechanisms such as the Inspection Panel. Whether ten years from now such mechanisms will finally prove to be the best answer is a question that needs further study and debate. And as the last respondent quoted above wisely noted: "It will certainly work if the best minds form part of it. Humans make institutions and not the reverse. An independent mechanism will come to light only and only if people with independent minds are appointed thereon.

8

A Swan Song
and a Major New Development:
Conclusions and Recommendations
for Future Mechanisms

My experience as a member of the World Bank Inspection Panel was unique. It created the opportunity to look back over the past decade – and to anticipate the developments ahead of us. We definitely live in a rapidly changing world, for better or worse. In chapter 1, I described the phenomenal increase in foreign direct investments (FDIs), and I asked who is controlling these private and multilateral investments and what their implications are for millions of people. Today, we face a loophole; people harmed by projects financed by the multilateral financial institutions (MFIs) cannot take any of the MFIs to court because when the MFIs were created they were granted immunity. Those who are aware of the loophole – most of all members of international nongovernmental organizations (NGOs) supported by lawyers specialized in international law – no longer accept MFI immunity, which was based on articles of agreement established long ago in a world that was very different from today. The old structure of international law concerns the responsibilities of one state to another. And, as explained by some contemporary experts in international law, we have to abandon this concept so that MFIs can be held accountable.

I therefore agree with Eisuke Suzuki and Suresh Nanwani, who state: "The legal personality of international organizations could no longer be seen as a démarche for member states to avoid joint and several responsibility for their conduct. It would be 'fantastic' to assume that international organizations 'are authorized to violate the principles they were established to serve' and it would 'be perverse, even destructive, to postulate a community expectation that International Organizations need not conform to the principles of public order.' It is now clear that the legal character of international organizations entails a responsibility for their conduct."[1]

And it is not only the accountability of the MFIs that is in question. The world community has little at hand to control private-sector foreign direct investments since the old governing systems do not respond to the new structures of the globalized economy. Earlier attempts to address the problem failed, notably the effort to ratify the Multilateral Agreement on Investment (MAI).

The new world society still needs a new system of co-regulation and legal mechanisms, one based not on the traditional international legal systems that govern relations between states but on new international law. This goes beyond the scope of my study but nonetheless needs to be resolved. In this study I have addressed the first steps toward a new era of balanced governing systems that are appropriate to the new global economy, namely the accountability mechanisms of financial institutions. What these should look like is a major question that must soon be answered. In this chapter I consider what should still be done to improve the structures and mandates of the MFIs' existing accountability mechanisms in such a way that they are able to fulfil their purpose. The international community has already driven the MFIs in the right direction, pressing them to establish the mechanisms over the past decade. Concerning the private sector, the demands for accountability arose more recently, and although the Equator Principles are a very promising development, they nonetheless are not accompanied by an accountability mechanism. The challenge for the private sector is to take up its responsibility, given its lead role in the global economy, and together with society stakeholders to formulate structures through which we can hold private-sector institutions accountable. In the old days governments were the leading factors in society, so society had a means to hold governments accountable. If we conclude that today the private sector is taking over the role of governments, the need for a new system of co-regulation is that much greater. We need to fill this gap in our democratic society before it further undermines democracy itself.

I have looked only at the mechanisms that the world currently has in place to hold the financial institutions directly accountable, namely those that have been adopted by the the multilateral financial institutions. Establishment of these mechanisms was among the first signals of a changing era in the field of international law. This study shows that many involved in the financial world believe we need accountability mechanisms to control foreign direct investments both from the MFIs and from the private financial sector. The mechanisms will not necessarily be the same for the MFIs and the private financial institutions. There are different stakeholders and audiences, mandates and roles, and most of all ownership structures. It is clear that the MFIs operate with public funds. The MFIs' accountability mechanisms have an international legal dimension, and they are often the only means by which people affected by MFI projects can address their problems.

As discussed in chapter 1, the scale of the private financial institutions and their influence today in the globalized world make them equally, if not more, responsible for rapid development, whether sustainable or nonsustainable. They can be held accountable by shareholders and by those who have deposit accounts at their banks. People who are harmed by projects financed by private financial institutions have the opportunity – at least in democratic countries – to rely on national court systems. Yet it is questionable whether these courts will be either willing or able to defend the rights of the poor in connection with projects involving transnational corporations. The case of Bhopal (see chapter 6) shows that national laws are never equal to international contracts and that local people will be the victims and losers if a weak state and a transnational corporation are involved in serious incidents.

On accountability, Henry McCandless writes: "We like to believe, regardless of the evidence, that people in authority will do the right thing. Or, if we don't think they will, we expect that someone will deal with it."[2] McCandless is right to issue such a warning. We have to be constantly alert and follow what is happening. Unlike Sebastian Mallaby, who in his book about Jim Wolfensohn accuses both the Inspection Panel and the NGO community of exaggerating some of the effects of the operations of the World Bank,[3] I am of the opinion that today the world needs citizens, citizen groups, and NGOs eager to follow closely what the institutions are doing. I agree with Mallaby only on the point that members of the NGO community should also be held accountable. Who are they and whom do they represent? These are relevant questions that constantly have to be answered. Finally, it is important to note that accountability goes with transparency, which cannot exist without access to information.

Thus the only way for civil society to hold the MFIs responsible is to lodge claims with the accountability mechanisms that are in place today at most MFIs. I agree with the many lawyers specialized in international law who maintain that the establishment of the World Bank Inspection Panel was an extraordinary development and a first means to make the MFIs liable for their acts by allowing nonstate actors to lodge a request for an investigation in cases of violations of a bank's internal policies and procedural requirements for designing, processing, and implementing projects. The World Bank Inspection Panel has been the pioneer and is still the role model for the accountability mechanisms that exist at the other MFIs. The experts in international law and the NGO representatives – in fact, a small group at the time – who were able to convince the US Congress and the European Parliament to put pressure on the World Bank to create the Inspection Panel did a historic and remarkable job. Never before had private individuals or communities or other nonstate actors possessed the right to hold international institutions accountable for their operations. Led by Congressman Barney Frank, the group forced the World Bank to establish the Inspection Panel. The impact of the group's work may have greater implications than its members probably anticipated at the time. Nevertheless, there is a long way to go. The mandates of such mechanisms need further improvement.

The MFIs still base their actions on the World Bank's old Articles of Agreement, including Article IV, section 10: "Political Activity Prohibited."

The bank will not formally intervene in cases of human rights violations or accept its own responsibility in such cases. The issue of human rights has shown that together the World Bank and the Inspection Panel are in an equivocal situation: on the one hand, the Inspection Panel has instituted recourse for people who are harmed by bank projects; on the other hand, the bank officially refuses to deal with human rights. International lawyers are right to state that the bank can no longer hide behind the articles of agreement when involved in projects where human rights are violated. I am proud that during my term, my two colleagues and I went beyond our mandate and refused to restrain ourselves when reporting on human rights violations in connection with the Chad-Cameroon Oil Pipeline Project. We did the right thing in reporting our findings.

Those who criticize the Inspection Panel for having too much of a "policing role" argue that it was an omission for the World Bank not to have created two separate mechanisms with clearly defined responsibilities: a problem-solving mechanism and a compliance review mechanism. The mandate of the Inspection Panel, the compliance review mechanism, does not extend to all members in the World Bank Group but applies only to the International Bank for Reconstruction and Development (IBRD) and the International Development Association (IDA) – as well as to the International Finance Corporation (IFC) when one of its projects is financed or guaranteed with money from the IBRD or IDA. And the IFC has only an ombudsman role. This lack of balance should be resolved by introducing both the "ombudsman function" and a fully separate "accountability mechanism" for the entire institution. If problems occur, the institution should first try to solve them via a problem-solving mechanism instead of an immediate investigation. Other MFIs, such as the Asian Development Bank (ADB) and the European Bank for Reconstruction and Development (EBRD), have introduced both roles. In this regard, the World Bank, which provides the role model for the other MFIs, is lagging behind. Today, the accountability mechanism of the Asian Development Bank is a model for the World Bank rather than the other way around.

The panel should not become a purely legal mechanism, a risk that arose with the introduction of the so-called "use of country systems." If in future cases the panel has to decide whether bank management correctly declared the national policies of a borrowing country equal to the policies of the bank, it will be required to make a judgment regarding the national laws of the country concerned based on a comparison of its national laws and procedures with the World Bank's policies and procedures. This, to me, means that the panel could become a sort of "supranational court." Many experts with experience with the panel expressed the view to me that the World Bank's policies have to be understood as nearly binding "legal" instruments. And this is the dilemma: on the one hand, one wants to have clear procedures and standards to which one can hold the institution accountable; on the other hand, the mechanism should not become a mere "blame and shame" instrument. The findings of the Inspection Panel and the other mechanisms should contribute to a process of learning. I also recommend that the panel not only hire lawyers as members of its permanent staff but also diversify by hiring experts from disciplines such as social and environmental science. Yet we have to demand full implementation of the policies or performance standards and not allow any weakening of these policies. Too much is at stake for future generations.

The Inspection Panel has not yet found its optimal structure and mandate. The main restriction on the panel is that it is not permitted to investigate the role of national authorities responsible for the realization of a project. Since the panel can not investigate implementation failures for which national or local authorities are responsible, the panel has no other option than to report on possible failures by management to supervise the project properly. This position contains an enormous obstacle to reporting the real failures and could lead to unfairness in judgments made when everybody knows that the problems on the ground are the result of poor local or national implementation of the project.

Also lacking in the panel's mandate are two different monitoring roles. First, the panel is not allowed to determine whether the mitigating actions that the board adopts based on panel findings are implemented. However, on one occasion the panel was asked by the board to further monitor the developments in the case of Yacyretá, so a change of the mandate might be underway. Second, also missing is the option of post-monitoring by the panel so that it can investigate projects after 95 per cent of the project budget has been spent. It doesn't make sense to have a cut-off before completion. On the contrary, only after full implementation and the start of operations can it be guaranteed that no harm has been done to people and the environment. The World Bank should follow other MFIs, the ADB, and the EBRD in allowing investigations for at least one year after completion.

I tend to disagree with the suggestion made by some that the work of a member of an accountability mechanism is a profession. Making it a profession might turn panel members into technical auditors. To hold an institution such as the World Bank accountable for its acts is more than that. The resolution establishing the panel states that the panel shall consist of three members to be appointed by the board for nonrenewable periods of five years.[4] Members are to be "selected on the basis of their ability to deal thoroughly and fairly with the requests brought to them, their integrity and their independence from the Bank's Management, and their exposure to developmental issues and to living conditions in developing countries."[5] This first description of what is expected of members of the mechanism is still valid and should not be changed, although such a broad description or definition runs the risk of misinterpretations. On the basis of my experience, I can see the following competences and experiences as necessary for candidates for the post: international experience and sensitivity to different cultures, inside knowledge of the international political arena, the ability to empathize both with the requesters in the field and management, the skill to work in a team and to understand the different working cultures of experts from different continents of the world, an ability to communicate, and finally, the talent to listen carefully and to make balanced and reasoned final judgments.

I disagree with the idea that former members of a financial institution should be permitted to become members of the same institution's accountability mechanism if they have been absent from the institution for two years. It might seem tempting to accept someone with a good reputation who also has institutional experience, but independence is such a crucial factor that the mechanism should never be placed in a position where it has to make a judgment on a project in which a member of the panel has been involved in the past. Whether a former manager could be a member of an accountability mechanism at another MFI is something else. As well, limiting panel members service to a single term seems the best guarantee of independence. From the start, the Inspection Panel's independence has been studied and criticized, but it remains of vital importance. A panel without independence has no meaning.

The follow-up question that should be raised is who is to select candidates and appoint the members of the mechanisms. This is all the more important since, as mentioned before, the accountability mechanisms of the MFIs are the only tools society has at present to control the institutions. The members should definitely be neither appointed nor selected by management. The selection process needs further study and revision. At present, management has far too large a role in the process, which I consider very unhealthy. The board should consider installing a selection committee on which members of the board themselves would sit, along with carefully selected members of civil society organizations and representatives from the acting panel. An option could also be to appoint to the selection committee a member of the international group of parliamentarians who follow the World Bank closely. It should be a more open process in which candidates can be nominated not only by governments but also by civil society groups. The final decision would still rest with the board.

It is of crucial importance that any accountability mechanism have a good relationship with the board of the institution. During my years as a member of the Inspection Panel, the panel regularly had to explain that it was not the panel that had a conflict with management. The panel is supposed to be above the parties. A conflict or disagreement that exists and leads to a request for an investigation is a conflict between the requesters and management, not between management and the panel.

To do their work properly, it is crucial that the accountability mechanisms have access to all relevant documents, including internal documents. This could include access to e-mails as long as these e-mails contain information concerning the project under investigation. Members of the mechanisms have to adhere to the same rules of confidentiality as the staff of the institutions. Of course, such access should not lead to witch hunting.

Another matter to which attention should be drawn is a position taken by the European Investment Bank (EIB). Until the very recent adoption of a new Disclosure Policy in 2006, the EIB did not explicitly provide the opportunity for non-European Union citizens harmed by EIB projects to have their complaints investigated. The bank was a somewhat invisible and closed institution. At present, either citizens or a single citizen can file a complaint (the EIB does not exclude complaints from single citizens as the other MFIs do). Complaints are initially filed with the Office of the Secretary General and then, if the response is not satisfactory, with the European ombudsman. If the ombudsman is of the opinion that he or she is not authorized or able to take up the case, there is finally the option to involve the inspector general of the EIB, who operates independently. The difference from the other MFIs is that this three-step approach could be a more expedient process. However, there is no practical experience as yet with this method.

And last but not least, the position of the requesters in the process should be a matter of constant concern and care. The MFIs should seriously consider designing a system of participation funding such as is used in Canada. The first accountability mechanism to offer "training and/or expertise to assist the stakeholders" in the dialogue and negotiation process is the IFC ombudsman (see chapter 4). For most poor people, gaining access to the mechanisms is too big a step. It should be made possible for the poor to rely on a budget from which they can cover expenses for necessary consultation as well as for training on how to lodge a claim and on how to play a role in a hearing. There should be a sufficient budget with clear criteria for making it accessible to the poor. In a democracy the ruling authorities should be fully prepared to finance nonviolent action by less advantaged citizens when they protest or ask to be involved. In cases of intimidating circumstances, requesters should have the right to keep their names confidential and known only to the members of the accountability mechanism in charge of verification.

So far so good.

Over the past decade, the accountability mechanisms of the MFIs have matured. The mandates and procedures are not perfect, but we can find some hope that society will be able to hold the institutions accountable. Nevertheless, I doubt whether attention to the MFIs should be our main priority. The position of the MFIs in the mainstream of foreign direct investments (FDIs) is diminishing dramatically. Global official development assistance (ODA) is like the stream of water from a kitchen tap. If we fix our attention only on the tap, we shall miss the swelling river in the garden where water is already rising above the river banks. The FDI of the private sector is far larger than that of the MFIs. And these private investments no longer come from Europe, North America, Japan, or Australia alone. China has become a major investor in Africa and other parts of the world (including the Unites States). It appears that the MFIs of today are singing a swan song. Their time is running out. They are bureaucratic institutions designed for the past. The only institution within the World Bank Group that is somewhat prepared for the new era is the International Finance Corporation, whose members deal with the private sector.

Amid all these rapid changes, a rather remarkable phenomenon has appeared on the horizon. The middle-income countries are bypassing the World Bank, the IMF, and other MFIs to become clients of private banks. The reason, as many believe, is that private financial institutions work much faster and are less bureaucratic. Besides, the interest rates for the middle-income countries are the same at the World Bank as in the private sector. So why go to the World Bank for a loan if it can be obtained with fewer complications elsewhere? Yet, at the same time, a major group of private banks have adopted the Equator Principles and by doing so they have agreed that they will work with the same policies and standards as the IFC and the World Bank when financing projects in countries where the World Bank and other MFIs operate as well. I find this a fascinating phenomenon: the middle-income countries are trying to avoid complicated rules by switching over to private banks, while those private banks, which perceive them as new clients, are going in the other direction by adopting the same procedures and standards as the IFC and the World Bank.

What is the background for such a remarkable development? Of course, institutions in the private financial sector are confident that avoiding serious harm in the projects they finance will protect them against liability that might come to the fore some day. But there is more. An increasing group of senior and middle management, those who have leading positions and could change the working methods of the private enterprises, have resurrected the old historic principle that each merchant cares for people. Indeed, some believe that it is time for a change and that the private sector also has to accept its responsibilities. And some have done so, leading to the creation of the Equator Principles. The banks that adopted them, for which they have to be praised, took a major step. The Equator Principles could have far-reaching effects – comparable to the effects of environmental treaties such as the Kyoto Protocol – if the principles are implemented.

For some, the creation of such principles is just a matter of public relations. Others argue that by adopting the Equator Principles, the private financial institutions have made themselves vulnerable to liability. This might be the case and could be helpful in assuring the implementation of the principles. But again, we should protect these novel principles against cynicism that could undermine and weaken or even kill the spirit in which they were conceived. The banks that adopted them definitely need time to define their new role of stewardship. And the principles have to spread farther over the globe as an accepted standard. However, time is passing, and after five years there should be some proof of the positive influence of the principles and more openness about the working of the grievance mechanisms that management should establish, according to principle 6, in cases where a project is classified as belonging to Category A. There is a real threat that the principles will be undermined. Fear of competition with Chinese banks should therefore not lead to watering down the principles, as some bankers suggest. On the contrary, those bankers should try to persuade private equity funds and private banks from China – as well as from Russia, India, and any other country that has not yet recognized these developments – that it is time to adopt the principles themselves.

Last but not least, in the near future it will be crucial to create a mechanism that will hold the private financial institutions accountable for the effects of what they finance. This is a matter of choice. Some request for investments should not be granted. The financial institutions are not just innocent spectators on the sidelines of the playing field when making choices. Most foreign direct investments today come from private financial institutions. This factor in itself is sufficient reason for private financial institutions to be held accountable for the choices they make.

It is appropriate to mention here that there are several different options for the mechanisms that the Equator Principles financial institutions could establish. What form the mechanisms should take will have to be decided by the institutions themselves. Otherwise, the day may soon come when shareholders demand such mechanisms. In anticipation of this demand, the institutions could make use of the experience gained by MFIs over the past decade, as detailed in this study. If the MFIs are ready to take this last step, they will bring about a major change in the world that will go far beyond the immediate effects (large and small) of foreign direct investments.

If there is one positive side to the present financial crisis, it is the cry for more control over the private financial institutions. The fact that their investments in major infrastructural projects can bring about damage to the environment and living conditions has been ignored by most governments for too long. Governments did not have the courage to act, but now is an unprecedented opportunity for the international community to insist that the private banks acknowledge and accept the importance of oversight through independent accountability mechanisms.

Resolution Establishing
the World Bank Inspection Panel

22 September 1993

International Bank for Reconstruction and Development
International Development Association
Resolution No. IBRD-93-10
Resolution No. IDA-93-6
"The World Bank Inspection Panel"

The Executive Directors:
Hereby resolve:

1 There is established an independent Inspection Panel (hereinafter called the Panel), which shall have the powers and shall function as stated in this resolution.

COMPOSITION OF THE PANEL

2 The Panel shall consist of three members of different nationalities from Bank member countries. The President, after consultation with the Executive Directors, shall nominate the members of the Panel to be appointed by the Executive Directors.

3 The first members of the Panel shall be appointed as follows: one for three years, one for four years, and one for five years. Each vacancy thereafter shall be filled for a period of five years, provided that no member may serve for more than one term. The term of appointment of each member of the Panel shall be subject to the continuity of the inspection function established by this Resolution.

4 Members of the Panel shall be selected on the basis of their ability to deal thoroughly and fairly with the requests brought to them, their integrity and their independence from the Bank's Management, and their exposure to developmental issues and to living conditions in developing countries. Knowledge and experience of the Bank's operations will also be desirable.

5 Executive Directors, Alternates, Advisors and staff members of the Bank Group may not serve on the Panel until two years have elapsed since the end of their service in the Bank Group. For purposes of this Resolution, the term "staff" shall mean all persons holding Bank Group appointments as defined in Staff Rule 4.01 including persons holding consultant and local consultant appointments.

6 A Panel member shall be disqualified from participation in the hearing and investigation of any request related to a matter in which he/she has a personal interest or had significant involvement in any capacity.

7 The Panel member initially appointed for five years shall be the first Chairperson of the Panel, and shall hold such office for one year. Thereafter, the members of the Panel shall elect a Chairperson for a period of one year.

8 Members of the Panel may be removed from office only by decision of the Executive Directors, for cause.

9 With the exception of the Chairperson, who shall work on a full-time basis at Bank headquarters, members of the Panel shall be expected to work on a full-time basis only when their workload justifies such an arrangement, as will be decided by the Executive Directors on the recommendation of the Panel.

10 In the performance of their functions, members of the Panel shall be officials of the Bank enjoying the privileges and immunities accorded to Bank officials, and shall be subject to the requirements of the Bank's Articles of Agreement concerning their exclusive loyalty to the Bank and to the obligations of subparagraphs (c) and (d) of paragraph 3.1 and paragraph 3.2 of the Principles of Staff Employment concerning their conduct as officials of the Bank. Once they begin to work on a full-time basis, they shall receive remuneration at a level to be determined by the Executive Directors upon a recommendation of the President, plus normal benefits available to Bank fixed-term staff. Prior to that time, they shall be remunerated on a *per diem* basis and shall be reimbursed for their expenses on the same basis as the members of the Bank's Administrative Tribunal. Members of the Panel may not be employed by the Bank Group, following the end of their service on the Panel.

11 The President, after consultation with the Executive Directors, shall assign a staff member to the Panel as Executive Secretary, who need not act on a full-time basis until the workload so justifies. The Panel shall be given such budgetary resources as shall be sufficient to carry out its activities.

POWERS OF THE PANEL

12 The Panel shall receive requests for inspection presented to it by an affected party in the territory of the borrower which is not a single individual (i.e., a community of persons such as an organization, association, society or other grouping of individuals), or by the local representative

of such party or by another representative in the exceptional cases where the party submitting the request contends that appropriate representation is not locally available and the Executive Directors so agree at the time they consider the request for inspection. Any such representative shall present to the Panel written evidence that he is acting as agent of the party on behalf of which the request is made. The affected party must demonstrate that its rights or interests have been or are likely to be directly affected by an action or omission of the Bank as a result of a failure of the Bank to follow its operational policies and procedures with respect to the design, appraisal and/or implementation of a project financed by the Bank (including situations where the Bank is alleged to have failed in its follow-up on the borrower's obligations under loan agreements with respect to such policies and procedures) provided in all cases that such failure has had, or threatens to have, a material adverse effect. In view of the institutional responsibilities of Executive Directors in the observance by the Bank of its operational policies and procedures, an Executive Director may in special cases of serious alleged violations of such policies and procedures ask the Panel for an investigation, subject to the requirements of paragraphs 13 and 14 below. The Executive Directors, acting as a Board, may at any time instruct the Panel to conduct an investigation. For purposes of this Resolution, "operational policies and procedures" consist of the Bank's Operational Policies, Bank Procedures and Operational Directives, and similar documents issued before these series were started, and does not include Guidelines and Best Practices and similar documents or statements.

13 The Panel shall satisfy itself before a request for inspection is heard that the subject matter of the request has been dealt with by the Management of the Bank and Management has failed to demonstrate that it has followed, or is taking adequate steps to follow, the Bank's policies and procedures. The Panel shall also satisfy itself that the alleged violation of the Bank's policies and procedures is of a serious character.

14 In considering requests under paragraph 12 above, the following requests shall not be heard by the Panel:

(a) Complaints with respect to actions which are the responsibility of other parties, such as a borrower, or potential borrower, and which do not involve any action or omission on the part of the Bank.

(b) Complaints against procurement decisions by Bank borrowers from suppliers of goods and services financed or expected to be financed by the Bank under a loan agreement, or from losing tenderers for the supply of any such goods and services, which will continue to be addressed by staff under existing procedures.

(c) Requests filed after the Closing Date of the loan financing the project with respect to which the request is filed or after the loan financing the project has been substantially disbursed. This will be deemed to be the case when at least ninety five percent of the loan proceeds have been disbursed.

(d) Requests related to a particular matter or matters over which the Panel has already made its recommendation upon having received a prior request, unless justified by new evidence or circumstances not known at the time of the prior request.

15 The Panel shall seek the advice of the Bank's Legal Department on matters related to the Bank's rights and obligations with respect to the request under consideration.

PROCEDURES

16 Requests for inspection shall be in writing and shall state all relevant facts, including, in the case of a request by an affected party, the harm suffered by or threatened to such party or parties by the alleged action or omission of the Bank. All requests shall explain the steps already taken to deal with the issue, as well as the nature of the alleged actions or omissions and shall specify the actions taken to bring the issue to the attention of Management, and Management's response to such action.

17 The Chairperson of the Panel shall inform the Executive Directors and the President of the Bank promptly upon receiving a request for inspection.

18 Within 21 days of being notified of a request for inspection, the Management of the Bank shall provide the Panel with evidence that it has complied, or intends to comply, with the Bank's relevant policies and procedures.

19 Within 21 days of receiving the response of the Management as provided in the preceding paragraph, the Panel shall determine whether the request meets the eligibility criteria set out in paragraphs 12 to 14 above and shall make a recommendation to the Executive Directors as to whether the matter should be investigated. The recommendation of the Panel shall be circulated to the Executive Directors for decision within the normal distribution period. In case the request was initiated by an affected party, such party shall be informed of the decision of the Executive Directors within two weeks of the date of such decision.

20 If a decision is made by the Executive Directors to investigate the request, the Chairperson of the Panel shall designate one or more of the Panel's members (Inspectors) who shall have primary responsibility for conducting the inspection. The Inspector(s) shall report his/her (their) findings to the Panel within a period to be determined by the Panel taking into account the nature of each request.

21 In the discharge of their functions, the members of the Panel shall have access to all staff who may contribute information and to all pertinent Bank records and shall consult as needed with the Director General, Operations Evaluation Department and the Internal Auditor. The borrower and the Executive Director representing the borrowing

(or guaranteeing) country shall be consulted on the subject matter both before the Panel's recommendation on whether to proceed with the investigation and during the investigation. Inspection in the territory of such country shall be carried out with its prior consent.

22 The Panel shall submit its report to the Executive Directors and the President. The report of the Panel shall consider all relevant facts, and shall conclude with the Panel's findings on whether the Bank has complied with all relevant Bank policies and procedures.

23 Within six weeks from receiving the Panel's findings, Management will submit to the Executive Directors for their consideration a report indicating its recommendations in response to such findings. The findings of the Panel and the actions completed during project preparation also will be discussed in the Staff Appraisal Report when the project is submitted to the Executive Directors for financing. In all cases of a request made by an affected party, the Bank shall, within two weeks of the Executive Directors' consideration of the matter, inform such party of the results of the investigation and the action taken in its respect, if any.

DECISIONS OF THE PANEL

24 All decisions of the Panel on procedural matters, its recommendations to the Executive Directors on whether to proceed with the investigation of a request, and its reports pursuant to paragraph 22, shall be reached by consensus and, in the absence of a consensus, the majority and minority views shall be stated.

REPORTS

25 After the Executive Directors have considered a request for an inspection as set out in paragraph 19, the Bank shall make such request publicly available together with the recommendation of the Panel on whether to proceed with the inspection and the decision of the Executive Directors in this respect. The Bank shall make publicly available the report submitted by the Panel pursuant to paragraph 22 and the Bank's response thereon within two weeks after consideration by the Executive Directors of the report.

26 In addition to the material referred to in paragraph 25, the Panel shall furnish an annual report to the President and the Executive Directors concerning its activities. The annual report shall be published by the Bank.

REVIEW

27 The Executive Directors shall review the experience of the inspection function established by this Resolution after two years from the date of the appointment of the first members of the Panel.

APPLICATION TO IDA PROJECTS

28 In this resolution, references to the Bank and to loans include references to the Association and to development credits.

The Equator Principles II, July 2006: A financial industry benchmark for determining, assessing and managing social and environmental risk in project financing[1]

PREAMBLE

Project financing, a method of funding in which the lender looks primarily to the revenues generated by a single project both as the source of repayment and as security for the exposure, plays an important role in financing development throughout the world.[2] Project financiers may encounter social and environmental issues that are both complex and challenging, particularly with respect to projects in the emerging markets. The Equator Principles Financial Institutions (EPFIs) have consequently adopted these Principles in order to ensure that the projects we finance are developed in a manner that is socially responsible and reflect sound environmental management practices. By doing so, negative impacts on project-affected

---

1 For the Equator Principles I, see http://www.banktrack.org/doc/File/policies%20and%20processes/Equator%20Princ.

2 *Project finance* is "a method of funding in which the lender looks primarily to the revenues generated by a single project, both as the source of repayment and as security for the exposure. This type of financing is usually for large, complex and expensive installations that might include, for example, power plants, chemical processing plants, mines, transportation infrastructure, environment, and telecommunications infrastructure. Project finance may take the form of financing of the construction of a new capital installation, or refinancing of an existing installation, with or without improvements. In such transactions, the lender is usually paid solely or almost exclusively out of the money generated by the contracts for the facility's output, such as the electricity sold by a power plant. The borrower is usually an SPE (Special Purpose Entity) that is not permitted to perform any function other than developing, owning, and operating the installation. The consequence is that repayment depends primarily on the project's cash flow and on the collateral value of the project's assets." *Source:* Basel Committee on Banking Supervision, *International Convergence of Capital Measurement and Capital Standards ("Basel II")*, November 2005, http://www.bis.org/publ/bcbs118.pdf.

ecosystems and communities should be avoided where possible, and if these impacts are unavoidable, they should be reduced, mitigated and/or compensated for appropriately. We believe that adoption of and adherence to these Principles offers significant benefits to ourselves, our borrowers and local stakeholders through our borrowers' engagement with locally affected communities. We therefore recognise that our role as financiers affords us opportunities to promote responsible environmental stewardship and socially responsible development. As such, EPFIs will consider reviewing these Principles from time-to-time based on implementation experience, and in order to reflect ongoing learning and emerging good practice.

These Principles are intended to serve as a common baseline and framework for the implementation by each EPFI of its own internal social and environmental policies, procedures and standards related to its project financing activities. We will not provide loans to projects where the borrower will not or is unable to comply with our respective social and environmental policies and procedures that implement the Equator Principles.

SCOPE

The Principles apply to all new project financings globally with total project capital costs of US$10 million or more, and across all industry sectors. In addition, while the Principles are not intended to be applied retroactively, we will apply them to all project financings covering expansion or upgrade of an existing facility where changes in scale or scope may create significant environmental and/or social impacts, or significantly change the nature or degree of an existing impact.

The Principles also extend to project finance advisory activities. In these cases, EPFIs commit to make the client aware of the content, application and benefits of applying the Principles to the anticipated project, and request that the client communicate to the EPFI its intention to adhere to the requirements of the Principles when subsequently seeking financing.

STATEMENT OF PRINCIPLES

EPFIs will only provide loans to projects that conform to Principles 1–9 below:

Principle 1: Review and Categorisation

When a project is proposed for financing, the EPFI will, as part of its internal social and environmental review and due diligence, categorise such project based on the magnitude of its potential impacts and risks in accordance with the environmental and social screening criteria of the International Finance Corporation (IFC) (Exhibit I).

Principle 2: Social and Environmental Assessment

For each project assessed as being either Category A or Category B, the borrower has conducted a Social and Environmental Assessment ("Assessment") process[3] to address, as appropriate and to the EPFI's satisfaction, the relevant social and environmental impacts and risks of the proposed project (which may include, if relevant, the illustrative list of issues as found in Exhibit II). The Assessment should also propose mitigation and management measures relevant and appropriate to the nature and scale of the proposed project.

Principle 3: Applicable Social and Environmental Standards

For projects located in non-OECD countries, and those located in OECD countries not designated as High-Income, as defined by the World Bank Development Indicators Database, the Assessment will refer to the then applicable IFC Performance Standards (Exhibit III) and the then applicable Industry Specific EHS Guidelines ("EHS Guidelines") (Exhibit IV). The Assessment will establish to a participating EPFI's satisfaction the project's overall compliance with, or justified deviation from, the respective Performance Standards and EHS Guidelines.

The regulatory, permitting and public comment process requirements in High-Income OECD Countries, as defined by the World Bank Development Indicators Database, generally meet or exceed the requirements of the IFC Performance Standards (Exhibit III) and EHS Guidelines (Exhibit IV). Consequently, to avoid duplication and streamline EPFI's review of these projects, successful completion of an Assessment (or its equivalent) process under and in compliance with local or national law in High-Income OECD Countries is considered to be an acceptable substitute for the IFC Performance Standards, EHS Guidelines and further requirements as detailed in Principles 4, 5 and 6 below. For these projects, however, the EPFI still categorises and reviews the project in accordance with Principles 1 and 2 above.

---

3 Social and Environmental Assessment is a process that determines the social and environmental impacts and risks (including labour, health, and safety) of a proposed project in its area of influence. For the purposes of Equator Principles compliance, this will be an adequate, accurate and objective evaluation and presentation of the issues, whether prepared by the borrower, consultants or external experts. Depending on the nature and scale of the project, the assessment document may comprise a full-scale social and environmental impact assessment, a limited or focused environmental or social assessment (e.g. audit), or straight-forward application of environmental siting, pollution standards, design criteria, or construction standards. One or more specialised studies may also need to be undertaken.

The Assessment process in both cases should address compliance with relevant host country laws, regulations and permits that pertain to social and environmental matters.

Principle 4: Action Plan and Management System

For all Category A and Category B projects located in non-OECD countries, and those located in OECD countries not designated as High-Income, as defined by the World Bank Development Indicators Database, the borrower has prepared an Action Plan (AP)[4] which addresses the relevant findings, and draws on the conclusions of the Assessment. The AP will describe and prioritise the actions needed to implement mitigation measures, corrective actions and monitoring measures necessary to manage the impacts and risks identified in the Assessment. Borrowers will build on, maintain or establish a Social and Environmental Management System that addresses the management of these impacts, risks, and corrective actions required to comply with applicable host country social and environmental laws and regulations, and requirements of the applicable Performance Standards and EHS Guidelines, as defined in the AP.

For projects located in High-Income OECD countries, EPFIs may require development of an Action Plan based on relevant permitting and regulatory requirements, and as defined by host-country law.

Principle 5: Consultation and Disclosure

For all Category A and, as appropriate, Category B projects located in non-OECD countries, and those located in OECD countries not designated as High-Income, as defined by the World Bank Development Indicators Database, the government, borrower or third party expert has consulted with project affected communities in a structured and culturally appropriate manner.[5] For projects with significant adverse impacts on affected

---

4 The Action Plan may range from a brief description of routine mitigation measures to a series of documents (e.g., resettlement action plan, indigenous peoples plan, emergency preparedness and response plan, decommissioning plan, etc). The level of detail and complexity of the Action Plan and the priority of the identified measures and actions will be commensurate with the project's potential impacts and risks. Consistent with Performance Standard 1, the internal Social and Environmental Management System will incorporate the following elements: (i) Social and Environmental Assessment; (ii) management program; (iii) organisational capacity; (iv) training; (v) community engagement; (vi) monitoring; and (vii) reporting.

5 Affected communities are communities of the local population within the project's area of influence who are likely to be adversely affected by the project. Where such consultation needs to be undertaken in a structured manner, EPFIs may require the preparation of a Public Consultation and Disclosure Plan (PCDP).

communities, the process will ensure their free, prior and informed consultation and facilitate their informed participation as a means to establish, to the satisfaction of the EPFI, whether a project has adequately incorporated affected communities' concerns.[6]

In order to accomplish this, the Assessment documentation and AP, or non-technical summaries thereof, will be made available to the public by the borrower for a reasonable minimum period in the relevant local language and in a culturally appropriate manner. The borrower will take account of and document the process and results of the consultation, including any actions agreed resulting from the consultation. For projects with adverse social or environmental impacts, disclosure should occur early in the Assessment process and in any event before the project construction commences, and on an ongoing basis.

Principle 6: Grievance Mechanism

For all Category A and, as appropriate, Category B projects located in non-OECD countries, and those located in OECD countries not designated as High-Income, as defined by the World Bank Development Indicators Database, to ensure that consultation, disclosure and community engagement continues throughout construction and operation of the project, the borrower will, scaled to the risks and adverse impacts of the project, establish a grievance mechanism as part of the management system. This will allow the borrower to receive and facilitate resolution of concerns and grievances about the project's social and environmental performance raised by individuals or groups from among project-affected communities. The borrower will inform the affected communities about the mechanism in the course of its community engagement process and ensure that the mechanism addresses concerns promptly and transparently, in a culturally appropriate manner, and is readily accessible to all segments of the affected communities.

---

6 Consultation should be "free" (free of external manipulation, interference or coercion, and intimidation), "prior" (timely disclosure of information) and "informed" (relevant, understandable and accessible information), and apply to the entire project process and not to the early stages of the project alone. The borrower will tailor its consultation process to the language preferences of the affected communities, their decision-making processes, and the needs of disadvantaged or vulnerable groups. Consultation with Indigenous Peoples must conform to specific and detailed requirements as found in Performance Standard 7. Furthermore, the special rights of Indigenous Peoples as recognised by host-country legislation will need to be addressed.

Principle 7: Independent Review

For all Category A projects and, as appropriate, for Category B projects, an independent social or environmental expert not directly associated with the borrower will review the Assessment, AP and consultation process documentation in order to assist EPFI's due diligence, and assess Equator Principles compliance.

Principle 8: Covenants

An important strength of the Principles is the incorporation of covenants linked to compliance. For Category A and B projects, the borrower will covenant in financing documentation:

a) to comply with all relevant host country social and environmental laws, regulations and permits in all material respects;
b) to comply with the AP (where applicable) during the construction and operation of the project in all material respects;
c) to provide periodic reports in a format agreed with EPFIs (with the frequency of these reports proportionate to the severity of impacts, or as required by law, but not less than annually), prepared by in-house staff or third party experts, that i) document compliance with the AP (where applicable), and ii) provide representation of compliance with relevant local, state and host country social and environmental laws, regulations and permits; and
d) to decommission the facilities, where applicable and appropriate, in accordance with an agreed decommissioning plan.

Where a borrower is not in compliance with its social and environmental covenants, EPFIs will work with the borrower to bring it back into compliance to the extent feasible, and if the borrower fails to re-establish compliance within an agreed grace period, EPFIs reserve the right to exercise remedies, as they consider appropriate.

Principle 9: Independent Monitoring and Reporting

To ensure ongoing monitoring and reporting over the life of the loan, EPFIs will, for all Category A projects, and as appropriate, for Category B projects, require appointment of an independent environmental and/or social expert, or require that the borrower retain qualified and experienced external experts to verify its monitoring information which would be shared with EPFIs.

Principle 10: EPFI Reporting

Each EPFI adopting the Equator Principles commits to report publicly at least annually about its Equator Principles implementation processes and experience, taking into account appropriate confidentiality considerations.[7]

DISCLAIMER

The adopting EPFIs view these Principles as a financial industry benchmark for developing individual, internal social and environmental policies, procedures and practices. As with all internal policies, these Principles do not create any rights in, or liability to, any person, public or private. Institutions are adopting and implementing these Principles voluntarily and independently, without reliance on or recourse to IFC or the World Bank.

EXHIBIT I: CATEGORISATION OF PROJECTS

As part of their review of a project's expected social and environmental impacts, EPFIs use a system of social and environmental categorisation, based on IFC's environmental and social screening criteria, to reflect the magnitude of impacts understood as a result of assessment. These categories are:

- Category A – Projects with potential significant adverse social or environmental impacts that are diverse, irreversible or unprecedented;
- Category B – Projects with potential limited adverse social or environmental impacts that are few in number, generally site-specific, largely reversible and readily addressed through mitigation measures; and
- Category C – Projects with minimal or no social or environmental impacts.

EXHIBIT II: ILLUSTRATIVE LIST OF POTENTIAL SOCIAL AND ENVIRONMENTAL ISSUES TO BE ADDRESSED IN THE SOCIAL AND ENVIRONMENTAL ASSESSMENT DOCUMENTATION

In the context of the business of the project, the Assessment Documentation will address, where applicable, the following issues:

a) assessment of the baseline social and environmental conditions
b) consideration of feasible environmentally and socially preferable alternatives

---

7 Such reporting should at a minimum include the number of transactions screened by each EPFI, including the categorisation accorded to transactions (and may include a breakdown by sector or region), and information regarding implementation.

c) requirements under host country laws and regulations, applicable international treaties and agreements

d) protection of human rights and community health, safety and security (including risks, impacts and management of project's use of security personnel)

e) protection of cultural property and heritage

f) protection and conservation of biodiversity, including endangered species and sensitive ecosystems in modified, natural and critical habitats, and identification of legally protected areas

g) sustainable management and use of renewable natural resources (including sustainable resource management through appropriate independent certification systems)

h) use and management of dangerous substances

i) major hazards assessment and management

j) labour issues (including the four core labour standards), and occupational health and safety

k) fire prevention and life safety

l) socio-economic impacts

m) land acquisition and involuntary resettlement

n) impacts on affected communities, and disadvantaged or vulnerable groups

o) impacts on indigenous peoples, and their unique cultural systems and values

p) cumulative impacts of existing projects, the proposed project, and anticipated future projects

q) consultation and participation of affected parties in the design, review and implementation of the project

r) efficient production, delivery and use of energy

s) pollution prevention and waste minimisation, pollution controls (liquid effluents and air emissions) and solid and chemical waste management

Note: The above list is for illustrative purposes only. The Social and Environmental Assessment process of each project may or may not identify all issues noted above, or be relevant to every project.

EXHIBIT III: IFC PERFORMANCE STANDARDS ON SOCIAL AND ENVIRONMENTAL SUSTAINABILITY

As of April 30, 2006, the following list of IFC Performance Standards were applicable:

- Performance Standard 1: Social & Environmental Assessment and Management System
- Performance Standard 2: Labor and Working Conditions

- Performance Standard 3: Pollution Prevention and Abatement
- Performance Standard 4: Community Health, Safety and Security
- Performance Standard 5: Land Acquisition and Involuntary Resettlement
- Performance Standard 6: Biodiversity Conservation and
- Sustainable Natural Resource Management
- Performance Standard 7: Indigenous Peoples
- Performance Standard 8: Cultural Heritage

Note: The IFC has developed a set of Guidance Notes to accompany each Performance Standard. While not formally adopting the Guidance Notes, EPFIs or borrowers may use the Guidance Notes as useful points of reference when seeking further guidance on or interpretation of the Performance Standards. The IFC Performance Standards, Guidance Notes and Industry Sector EHS Guidelines can be found at www.ifc.org/enviro.

EXHIBIT IV: INDUSTRY-SPECIFIC ENVIRONMENTAL, HEALTH AND SAFETY (EHS) GUIDELINES

EPFIs will utilise the appropriate environmental, health and safety (EHS) guidelines used by IFC which are now in place, and as may be amended from time-to-time.

IFC is using two complementary sets of EHS Guidelines available at the IFC website (www.ifc.org/enviro). These sets consist of all the environmental guidelines contained in Part III of the World Bank's Pollution Prevention and Abatement Handbook (PPAH) which went into official use on July 1, 1998 and a series of environmental, health and safety guidelines published on the IFC website between 1991 and 2003. Ultimately new guidelines, incorporating the concepts of cleaner production and environmental management systems, will be written to replace this series of industry sector, PPAH and IFC guidelines.

Where no sector specific guideline exists for a particular project then the PPAH's General Environmental Guidelines and the IFC Occupational Health and Safety Guidelines (2003) are applied, with modifications as necessary to suit the project.[8]

The table below lists both the World Bank Guidelines and the IFC Guidelines as of March 1, 2006.

---

8 Exception (the following are World Bank Guidelines not contained in the PPAH and currently in use): Mining and Milling – Underground; Mining and Milling – Open Pit.

Table A2.1
Industry specific EHS guidelines

World Bank guidelines (PPAH)	IFC guidelines
1 Aluminum Manufacturing	1 Airports
2 Base Metal and Iron Ore Mining	2 Ceramic Tile Manufacturing
3 Breweries	3 Construction Materials Plants
4 Cement Manufacturing	4 Electric Power Transmission and
5 Chlor-Alkali Plants	Distribution
6 Coal Mining and Production	5 Fish Processing
7 Coke Manufacturing	6 Food and Beverage Processing
8 Copper Smelting	7 Forestry Operations: Logging
9 Dairy Industry	8 Gas Terminal Systems
10 Dye Manufacturing	9 Geothermal Projects
11 Electronics Manufacturing	10 Hazardous Materials Management
12 Electroplating Industry	11 Health Care
13 Foundries	12 Life and Fire Safety
14 Fruit and Vegetable Processing	13 Occupational Health and Safety
15 General Environmental Guidelines	14 Office Buildings
16 Glass Manufacturing	15 Offshore Oil and Gas
17 Industrial Estates	16 Polychlorinated Biphenyls (PCBs)
18 Iron and Steel Manufacturing	17 Pesticide Handling and Application
19 Lead and Zinc Smelting	18 Plantations
20 Meat Processing and Rendering	19 Port and Harbor Facilities
21 Mini Steel Mills	20 Rail Transit Systems
22 Mixed Fertilizer Plants	21 Roads and Highways
23 Monitoring	22 Telecommunications
24 Nickel Smelting and Refining	23 Tourism and Hospitality Development
25 Nitrogenous Fertilizer Plants	24 Waste Management Facilities
26 Oil and Gas Development (Onshore)	25 Wastewater Reuse
27 Pesticides Formulation	26 Wildland Management
28 Pesticides Manufacturing	27 Wind Energy Conversion Systems
29 Petrochemicals Manufacturing	28 Wood Products Industries
30 Petroleum Refining	
31 Pharmaceutical Manufacturing	
32 Phosphate Fertilizer Plants	
33 Printing Industry	
34 Pulp and Paper Mills	
35 Sugar Manufacturing	
36 Tanning and Leather Finishing	
37 Textiles Industry	
38 Thermal Power Guidelines for New Plants	
39 Thermal Power Rehabilitation of Existing Plants	
40 Vegetable Oil Processing	
41 Wood Preserving Industry	

Background Interviews

CONGRESSMAN BARNEY FRANK OF MASSACHUSETTS,
LEAD DEMOCRAT ON THE HOUSE FINANCIAL
SERVICES COMMITTEE[1]

They said, "You can't do that." I said, "Yes we can."

I met with Mr Frank in his office at Capitol Hill. He spoke passionately about the time he was involved in the creation of the Inspection Panel. I thanked Mr Frank for giving me the opportunity to talk to him and explained that he is considered one of the founding fathers of the World Bank Inspection Panel, a phenomenon whose history has to be written down. Luck was not with me. Back home it appeared that my tape recorder had not recorded anything of my discussion with Mr Frank. Nevertheless, he allowed me to interview him again by telephone from the Netherlands.

MVP: What happened in the days of the initiation of the Inspection Panel? Who came to see you, and what did they ask you as chairman of the House-Financial Services Committee? When did you get involved?

BF: I do not remember who came to see me. I had working for me this woman, Dr Sydney Key, an economist from the Federal Reserve, who is a very good economist. And she was the one who was in touch with the people from the NGOs, and I believe they did not ask us.

MVP: That is important to know. Did you first demand the bank to install a special independent investigation committee [Morse Commission] to investigate Narmada in India? Was this later followed up with a demand for the independent Inspection Panel?

BF: The Morse Commission on Narmada had already happened by the time I got involved. I don't know what the timing is, but I didn't take over here until 1993. I am pretty sure the Morse Commission was before that, and I was not involved in the Morse Commission. But the Morse Commission was an example for us on how something like this could work. And as I remember we were talking essentially about sort of institutionalizing that. Not having it have to be an ad hoc thing each time. So they came to me and asked me to make the syndication. I mean the bank needed us to "ok" the money, and ...

MVP: You mean the normal US contributions to the bank?

BF: Yes, every three years we vote money. The three-years tranche they call it, and I had two demands before I would vote the money. That and much more release of information. So the Inspection Panel and more release of information: the country reports on the projects.

MVP: Your demands have led to the publication of the country reports. That also was an improvement. Did you organize one or two hearings?

BF: That was at the same time. And I did more than two hearings, I believe. I think we had several hearings. As to the structure and mandate. I think that was kind of frankly negotiated by the NGOs and the bank.

MVP: Was the structure and mandate of the Inspection Panel formulated by you and the committee? Do you remember David Hunter, Professor Hunter from the US University who was involved in the creation of the structure of the Inspection Panel?

BF: No, I don't remember the names. But the structure and the mandate I can tell you ... the structure was that it had to be independent, and the mandate was to be able to listen to critics of the program of a particular project both governmental and nongovernmental from within the country independently, because one of the big things we had to resist [was that] the bank as an institution could not and would not listen to people in a particular country other than the government. And an important part of the Inspection Panel was precisely to give nongovernmental people, citizens or organizations, from the affected country someone to talk to. That was explicit that the governments of the countries where the projects were happening could not veto the communications from their own residents. In other words, before that the only people that the bank could talk to in a country where they were planning a project were the governments. And we said: "No you have to have citizens, not governments, to talk to the bank through the Inspection Panel."

MVP: So it was the opening up to the real people?

BF: Yes, as far as the discussions, yes.

MVP: Did you have any discussion with management or the president of the World Bank? And if so, how did they react?

BF: I worked very closely with ... There was a former congressman named Matthew McHugh, a very good man. He was the assistant to the president of the bank at the time. And I talked to him, and they said to me: "Look, you can't order us to do anything." I said: "I agree, and you can't order me to pass the bill with the money." So it was a kind of step-by-step operation. And in fact, at the time I said: "We are not going to vote the whole three years. We are going to vote it one at a time." They said, "You can't do that." I said, "Yes we can."

MVP: Was Treasury in favour or did you put some "pressure" on them, and if so, how?

BF: So we did talk to them and basically make clear that yes they could refuse to appoint the panel and make the country reports available. And I could pop the bill. So that's the way it worked. And Treasury was reluctant. Treasury was on the same side as the bank, and they just had to go along. Larry Summers was the guy at Treasury that we had to deal with who came from the bank. So we just told Treasury: "It is hard ... money for the World Bank is never popular in Congress." It was hard enough for them to get the money with me supporting it. If I opposed it, they would have no chance of getting the money. That is the role of the chairman of the subcommittee.

MVP: Why is this not popular?

BF: Because it is seen as giving money to foreigners. People never like to do that. And secondly, in the case of the bank, they were cross-fired from both the left and the right if you remember. So that was the problem.

MVP: Did you talk to the president of the bank?

BF: I had some conversations with the president, but my dealings with the bank were through McHugh. In fact, I think that it is a model that others should follow, and I have advocated that. In fact, President Iglesias, at the Inter-American Development Bank, had me speak there and I have argued for that model to be followed. I think that everyone agrees it works very well.

MVP: First time we met, you said a lot about the necessity of accountability mechanisms in general at the present time. You gave me examples of how people should have access to information on what governments and companies do. People should be more involved in the decisions that affect them. You strongly supported the idea of openness and accountability in general. Can you say again a bit more about that?

BF: Well, what I touched on. You have people working with each other; you need to have a channel for independent criticism to be heard. Not to have an ability to say no and to veto it, but to be heard. And that is what this kind of a panel does.

MVP: As you might know, the other multilateral financial institutions have followed the World Bank by installing their own accountability mechanisms.

In the private sector one can notice similar developments – for example, in the financial sector. So do we need a similar system in the private sector and for example in the private-bank sector?

BF: I am not an expert in the private sector.

MVP: Ok, but you could imagine it might be helpful?

BF: You are pushing me into areas I haven't thought about, I might say.

MVP: Ok, well Barney, I thank you a lot, and when it is finished you will get it, and I might give you the first book.

BF: I'd be delighted. Looking forward to it, thank you.

JIM WOLFENSOHN, PRESIDENT OF THE WORLD BANK (1995–2005)

If you do not think that the Western China Poverty Project was a political investigation, you are probably crazy.

On 9 April 2005 I met with Jim Wolfensohn during a long lunch in his personal dining room in the headquarters of the World Bank in Washington, DC. It was one of his last weeks as president of the World Bank. The book *The World's Banker: The Story of Failed States, Financial Crises and the Wealth and Poverty of Nations*, by Sebastian Mallaby, a columnist with the *Washington Post*, had just been published. In a way, this book presented a caricature of Wolfensohn. I told Jim that how one perceives the book depends on what one wants to understand. For me, it is the story of how he gave a human face to the bank and opened its doors to civil society. We talked about the Inspection Panel and its relations with the board. I asked him what kind of bank it was when he arrived and about the role of the board? The interview below reproduces parts of what we discussed.

MVP: What bank did you find when you came?

JW: I think that the first thing is that, until I came, the board had less information and less involvement by a significant margin than it would have liked. Management ran the bank. The board was a necessary element in the approval process. To a degree it was much less engaged than it is today. It got much less information. There was considerably less disclosure of problems. And what I believe I have started, although I do not get much credit for it, is to treat the board as a board and say "management must notify the board of everything it knows so that the board can participate as a board and take responsibility." And we should engage them much more. So increasingly in the last ten years, and sometimes I wonder whether I did the right thing, we have given the board more and more information, earlier and earlier. And the result of that is that the board has been more empowered, and has taken on more responsibility. It wasn't just looking at OED [Organization Evaluation Department] reports years later. They wanted to be much more involved during the process and be more a board of directors to which issues could be referred.

If there hadn't been I think that move to empowering the board, an Inspection Panel would have been a very unlikely addition. Because the Inspection Panel needed as a prerequisite an informed board that was up to date and engaged on the issues. But once you had a more informed board there was almost a need for an Inspection Panel. Because they needed an arm that would be able to follow through the issues which they were interested in [and that] could report to them directly on each problem. And do the thing which board members just couldn't do, which is travel out to the field, talk to NGOs, receive complaints, and ensure that management would do what it had promised to do. The objective of the Inspection Panel is not to look for right or wrong. It is to look whether management is conducting itself in the way that it has promised.

MVP: Don't you think the Inspection Panel was the result of demands from the US Congress and lobbying from an international alliance of NGOs, already in the days of your predecessor?

JW: There has always been a request, but I may be wrong, although you have people always asking for accountability. It is the "cat's cry" and it is still the "cat's cry" today. The request for oversight by the board has been there for years. The point that I make is that the effectiveness of oversight was assisted by the board having greater access to an involvement in the management process. I think the effectiveness of a panel was greatly increased because of a greater knowledge of the board. And what Barney Frank and others had been looking for was greater responsibility of management to the board and the Congress, or to the congressional bodies. That predated me as a reflection of the frustration of the board that it wasn't getting information and that they were not able to pass information through to Congress.

Congress was getting frustrated, and so they pressed for some sort of body that could look into the complaints, and there were many, about the bank. It was at the time that the NGOs were at the height of their criticism of the bank. You had the meetings of the bank in Madrid, where people were hanging banners from the ceilings. A huge critical wave of the bank went to Congress, which is why Barney Frank and others said, "We got to get these people under control and therefore we need some instrument." But there is a difference in having an instrument and having an effective instrument. And what I think we did in the '90s when I came in was to give the panel some teeth and give the board some teeth because of the greater involvement and greater information in what was going on. I did not seek to give the board greater information because there was a panel. I did it because I was used to have a board better informed. But the advantage of having a better informed vehicle of the panel was something that made it work. So the only point I am trying to make is that to make the panel effective on paper you needed to have a new relationship between management and the board.

MVP: Jim, you fully endorse the crucial function of the Inspection Panel. Nevertheless, the panel sometimes had the feeling we had to explain to the board "we are a mechanism created by you and for you," which was not always clear.

JW: Well, I think that one of the problems with the board is that it changes all the time. And in a couple of years I do not think the board, if you should ask board members ... that at this moment in time the board does not look at the panel as a tremendously active and current instrument of the board practice. I think that the panel at this moment is probably underutilized. Put it this way, I do not know personally what the panel is doing. I have little knowledge personally whether they have three cases or thirty-three cases. I don't meet much with them. They do not seek my advice ... So maybe they talk to the board but they are not talking to me. What I know is that my hope of using the Inspection Panel as an instrument of mine as well as chairman of the board has never been fulfilled. I know much more about what is happening in IFC on inspection than I do in relation to the bank. Because when things come up at IFC, a group comes and talks to me about it. Just this morning I met on a case in Bolivia. I have, from time to time, meetings with our leading friend from Papua New Guinea, Meg Taylor. They more or less keep me informed with what is going on.

Relations between Management and the Inspection Panel

MVP: Would you still defend the mechanism?

JW: I think it is a very good mechanism and it is an evolving mechanism. I think the principle that you could have – that interested parties can come to [the panel], have the agreements looked at it in a public way, from a group that is independent of management – is an extremely important and commendable tool. Extremely important. But if you are going to get the benefit from it, it shouldn't be just to come up with the verdict guilty or not guilty. It should be something which is a part of the process.

MVP: Is it becoming too legalistic?

JW: Yes. But how can it become part of a process? Management never sees the panel. If the panel is so into itself, than I don't see it. I never sit down and talk to them unless it is on some crisis matter. You can say it is my fault for not calling them, but I do not believe it is. I will tell the next president that he needs to sit down with the lady who runs it and talk about how he can utilize the panel in a better way than I had been able to. Because I think it is something that is very useful. In the last seven weeks of my term, it is too late for me to do it. And I have seen no evidence of anyone being interested in doing it from the panel side.

MVP: The panel has to keep its independence?

JW: Oh I am sure. But if the chairman wants to do that, that's fine. Maybe the chair talks a lot to the dean of the board. But I am chairman of the board, and I would have thought, personally, that they would have reached out to me. And they haven't and that is fine with me but it does remove, in my opinion, the temptation of the panel to do other things than just responding to complaints. You can not build bridges with an episodic or occasional drink party. What you need to do is to have a consistent platform over the years. A consistent series of this you are constructing to build relationships. It is not a question of waking up one morning and saying: "I want to build a relationship with the board." I was one of your biggest defenders of the panel. So I am not against the panel. I have in fact tried to establish the panel. The thing that is interesting to me is having been in that position, and I should say it could easily be my fault.

MVP: Officially, there is CODE [Committee on Development Effectiveness], with which the panel regularly exchanges information with the board. I know for a fact we established a formal relation with the board.

JW: Yes, but if you do that ... maybe you do that. I am sure you do. But there is no informal meeting with management advisory.

The Mandate of the Inspection Panel

MVP: I'd like to go back to the mandate of the panel. Why was IFC not included? As you know, the panel only can investigate a project of IFC if IDA or IBRD money is involved. What, for example, was the case with the Bujugali project in Uganda.

JW: Well, I have never been in great religion with the idea that it shouldn't. IFC should be part or not part of the Inspection Panel. But the IFC people think that they need a speedier and a more personal process because they are competing with other institutions in the private sector. And if they told the clients that they're going to have two years or longer in the process with the Inspection Panel because they are subject to it, I think that the probability is that they will lose business. It is not that they are against having looked at it, but they want to have it looked at in a less formalistic way.

MVP: IFC has a problem-solving mechanism: the ombudsman. They first try to solve it before it is an accountability issue. The Asian Development Bank first had a weak sort of Compliance Review Panel. They changed it into two separate mechanisms. So a problem-solving, or ombudsman, function and a compliance-review mechanism. In this bank there is a problem-solving mechanism in IFC and an Accountability Mechanism for IDA and IBRD. Shouldn't both functions separately exist for IBRD, IDA and IFC?

JW: I do not know why it was not done, but it probably should be done. In all other aspects we now moved to the problem solving in terms of the personnel disputes, in terms of things inside the bank. There is always a resort first to problem solving. And I think that should be the case here too. For me, it would be an improvement. So I would personally favour a sort of ombudsman type approach on projects before one gets to the complaint mechanism, which is basically the panel.

MvP: Both functions in one?

JW: No. But I think if you are having a problem-solving mechanism it should be a problem-solving mechanism which is not just designed to determine whether we followed the rule of law, the letter of what we should have done to comply with article whatever it is or rule x. If there is a legitimate problem which is arising, there ought to be a better mechanism here for taking that and dealing with it. Now, the way that it is done at the moment is that vice presidents get these problems. And NGOs ride in and we then try and deal with them. But it is at least arguable that it would be better if you had someone who was constantly looking at these things and who could take a task in terms of looking at them. I think there is a strong case for that.

MvP: Correct me if I am wrong. I regular noticed a certain US culture in the bank and in the panel that is more used to look rather legalistic when judging on projects and problems. The US style is judging to the letter of the law instead of the principle of the law, the more European style.

JW: Well, I think that the desire was to keep the panel out of the substance. And to leave the decision making to the bank and to make sure that we had fulfilled our responsibility. That we did in fact notify at due time. And that we appeared to section 3 and that we gave them x number of times and we did whatever it was we had to do. That is the function of the panel. The panel is not to say whether we did right or wrong. The panel was to look at whether we adhered to the rules.

MvP: I was told there have been attempts in the past by some executive directors when the panel was created to give it the right to investigate also on the operations of national authorities because of the Articles of Agreement certain Group II[2] countries were opposed to it.[3]

China Case

JW: But if you take the Western China project, it got down to the issues of whether we did or did not meet the letter of the law. In terms of counting the rodents or looking at the grains of sand or doing what we had to do.

The real issue was whether we were disadvantaging the Tibetans. And whether in fact it was Tibet, and whether people were less well off or better off. And that was the case that was being "cried." So we were trying the case but on the wrong basis. The thing that I was legally concerned about was: how are we dealing fairly with the people that are affected, and what are the ramifications of doing that in terms of the impact on the Tibetan culture?

The people were not the least bit interested in whether or not we gave a 120 days notice or whatever time schedule. They were concerned about the political aspects of the project. And you in the panel are not supposed to be involved in the political aspects. But in fact MacNeill, Jim, was deeply moved from the NGO point of views about the politics. It didn't come out as that but it was very clear that the case that the panel was trying was not the case that the public was trying. What they were concerned about was to block the project – that was what the Tibetans wanted. For us, we took a somewhat different view. We thought this people would be a hell of a lot better off physically, emotionally, and in terms of the sustenance. Because we had done 1,300 projects like this. The debate really was about the politics: Was this in the Tibetan areas and were we ...?

MVP: We didn't say a word about political sensitivities and questions. We kept politics outside the door.

JW: You didn't say a word but it was on the base of what you were looking at. It was couched in the framework of had you done proper due diligence, have you seen ...?

MVP: We looked at the policies, as is the mandate.

JW: Anyway, what you succeeded in doing was that the bank didn't do the project. There was no subsequent possibility of anybody looking whether anything was done right or wrong.

MVP: You might remember that the China case was so far the only case for the Inspection Panel lodged by the board itself. We have been made the messengers of what management and the board had made a mess itself. People tend to forget that.

JW: I don't think the panel did anything wrong. I am just saying that in terms of what the panel should be looking at is that in my opinion the panel was armed to do a certain investigation. It was quite obviously caught up in politics from the very beginning. I am not making any judgment. But the whole thing was politicized right from the beginning.

MVP: Do you remember the press releases published after our report came out? Your own government praised the panel into heaven and the Chinese government wishing us in hell asked: Who are those three people who can judge a project that hundreds of Chinese experts have worked on for years?

JW: The Chinese said we screwed them, and then they pulled the project. And the result of it was that nobody gained.

MVP: Do you know if the project goes on? We never heard of it.

JW: I know that within two weeks,[4] the NGOs called us to ask what was happening. And we said to them, "How the hell do we know?! They just pushed us out."

MVP: They were asking you?

JW: Asking the region.[5]

MVP: I want again to go back to the panel mandate. The ADB said, "The mandate the Inspection Panel of the World Bank has, doesn't make sense if it is not allowing an investigation after 95% of the budget has been spent." They say it doesn't make sense because harm can come out half a year or two years later. Environmental outcomes show sometimes much later. So they draw the line two years after completion of the project. Don't you think this should be the case in the World Bank as well?

JW: I have never thought about it to be honest. It makes a lot less sense trying to get it before the damage is done ...

Human Rights and the World Bank

MVP: Article 4 in the Articles of Agreement says, "Political Activity Prohibited." I was reading the book of Sebastian Mallaby. The panel and its previous chair MacNeill were attacked. Mallaby never heard both sides, which is a mortal sin for a journalist. He based his view on the panel on what he was told by an expert once hired by the panel and who chose the side of management, which became very problematic for our independence, a basic rule for the panel. In the case of the Comprehensive Development Framework, Mallaby accused you of screwing up things or something like that. He then criticizes you of breaking with apolitical traditions. Isn't that the world upside down? Are the previous structural adjustment loans with all its rules enforced on the countries, no political interventions?

JW: I always thought that the suggestion that we be nonpolitical is complete nonsense. I think everything is political. It is the nature of the institution. If you get involved in food or education projects, or a housing project, or an environmental project, every one of those things has political implications. If you do not think that the Western China Poverty Project was a political investigation, you are probably crazy.

MVP: How about Chad-Cameroon?

JW: Also political.

MVP: Human Rights are not mentioned in the Articles of Agreement. Officially prohibited ... under the same article.

JW: Well, in fact it may be officially prohibited. But what we are doing every day of the week is seeking to realize the undertaking [of the] bill of human rights.

MVP: Did you call President Idriss Deby of Chad when he used the first $40 million of the project to buy weapons?

JW: I called him up and told him the project was off, unless they completely and absolutely paid back the money, and as far we were concerned everything was over. So they paid us back. When he put the leader of the opposition in jail, I called him up and told him the same thing. He was released the next day. If that is not politics, I don't know what is.

Well, [Ibrahim] Shihata[6] told me that I could not go into corruption because it was political. And I said, "it is political but what if I simply say that it is economic and social?" So I redefined it, and a year later everybody was talking about it. I see that article as something that I do not understand. What I do understand is that it is in the narrow political sense of arguing for the conservatives against the liberals or the Labor Party that we should stay out of party politics. I think we probably should. But even there, if the party politics is a dictator against democracy we'll come up and say we want democracy. That is pretty political.

MVP: As you say, everything is political. The panel again decided not to be part of any political process after it received a request for an investigation from Chad that was lodged by Mr Yorongar, who at the time was running for presidency. We did not want to become a tool in an election campaign and for that we delayed the investigation until the elections were over.

JW: He was put in jail.

MVP: You think we could have avoided that if we had taken the case earlier?

JW: No.

MVP: We then met with him in Paris, after you got him out of prison. He showed us his torture and what happened to his body and ...

JW: I bet he was beaten up, wasn't he?

MVP: It was bad.

JW: Chad is not a very nice place.

MVP: Could you still defend this project?

JW: Chad-Cameroon? I am 100 per cent convinced that it is a good project. I think you have to start with the facts: that we are dealing with a world were everything is not Holland or the United States, and where you have one-fifth of the world including most of the people in Chad who have nothing. You can criticize countries for lack of capacity, lack of governance, lack of a legal and judicial system, lack of a financial system that works and broadly very poor capacities. Now 400 million people in the world live in states that don't function at all. Chad-Cameroon are not like middle income countries, according to our recognition. They are extremely badly performing countries. The world today is looking to judge everything and reward everything to those countries that have good capacity, good legal systems, good everything, and they are then matched on the bases of 15 out of 20 yardsticks which they meet, and then you can get money from the Millennium Goals Challenge Account, you can get money from various sources, from the Canadians and this one and that ... from the Dutch.

Thus everybody is selecting the good countries through running a deal in the top 18 countries or the top 30 countries. There are 140 of these countries, to which Chad and Lao PDR [Peoples Democratic Republic][7] belong. Now what do you do with those countries? Are we going to sit around for ten years and say "we are ready to deal with you," when you are the person that has no support, puts in an honest legal system, puts in impeccable accounting system, puts in impeccable environmental systems? When you know and I know that there are ten people running the country and probably five of them are corrupt and the country has to grow up? It took a generation in Holland and several generations here.

And my position is, absolutely clearly, that if you can define the project in a way that can make advances in transparency, can put them to the test of meeting those standards and grow as they go, that is the only thing you can do because in the case of Chad they have no income other than from this project. In the case of Lao PDR their only asset is power and order. Do you want to wait ten years with the expectation at home that you will be able to train people without a job for them to go to, and then hold them in Chad? When they get their training they are offered a job in Paris or they are offered a job somewhere else. You are not going to keep them. The only way which you can keep this people in the countries is that you have a viable project going ahead. You make some mistakes going forward. Otherwise, you agree with the panel and everybody else that you shouldn't have done this, you shouldn't have done that then you never do anything.

MVP: I agree with your vision and explanation of the situation. But do not forget that in the case of Chad, the panel was in line with what you are saying. We went into the strengths and the weaknesses without writing off the project. Still, we later on were informed about the difficulties in the region and people from the region warning about the deterioration of the local situation that could cause another conflict.[8]

JW: There is that risk. Except that it has not happened. The money has gone to Paris, it has gone into an absolutely transparent box, the box is very clear we know what money is going in and what money is going out. It is public. It is on the front page of the newspaper. You have people on it who are from the government, and you have an independent group that is reviewing it every three months. It is not just the banks. The International Review Panel, they come to my office. They say: "so far so good." And if the man, the person, or the chair wants to get his hands on the money, he has got to talk to us because it is transparent. Let me put another proposition to you. If you didn't do that, and you said it is all too difficult, you wouldn't do the project.

MVP: Well, you don't have to convince me. I understood the dilemma but found it wise the bank got involved. It meant a certain guarantee and transparency. As far as I am correct, this was also the position of my colleagues, but that is up to them.

JW: Lao Peoples Democratic Republic, six years ago, I flew there. You had to take a helicopter to fly out in the field to meet the natives, to spend the night in the field with the electricity experts. And I would say that these experts were making the best possible effort they can to do alleviation of poverty, to deal with indigenous people. The bureaucrats from the Electricité de France were there and cultural experts and everything else. I don't think the French would have this interest if we weren't there. EDF [European Development Fund] is now really trying to take this on, and I can tell you. And I can literally tell you that it is lively ahead of everything we have ever done before. Is it perfect? Probably not. Should they spend twice as much? Probably. But it is in the air as a contractual section, and they do have to deal with indigenous people and so on, and it is hugely different from everything we have ever done in Lao ever before. But it is better to have us in there insisting on this, or let the Libyans or somebody else do the project, then none of this would be done.

Weakening World Bank Policies

MVP: Why is the World Bank always under attack and not the other development banks?

JW: Because it is the most visible, and secondly I would say the attack is much less today than it was ten years ago. Ten years ago you used to have attacks with the people attacking us being offshore and pumping in shells and never talk to them. Today the attacks are always joined with dialogue. That is a huge difference. I don't mind, and it is important to be under review and possibly under attack. You got to be able to have the dialogue, and the big change in the last ten years is that today although there are attacks there is also instantly dialogue. And there is a light use change ... in fact, as I am leaving. I am surprised and thrilled to know that the NGO community in general is giving me a dinner. And people from all over the world are coming to say thank you. I also have been offered to chair two NGOs.

MVP: Experts from the NGO society say that because of the panel, the policies of the bank are weakened. Do you believe that is true?

JW: I do not see any connection. I do not think there is the slightest consideration given to the will of the Inspection Panel, which is going to look for an optimal. You'd better speak to Shengman [Zhang],[9] but I don't think, as far as I know, there has ever been that consideration. I never heard it once. It would really amaze me if Jim Adams or Shengman thought any time about the panel. They think about doing what is right, pragmatic.

MVP: The new issue is the so-called "use of country systems," meaning that projects financed by the bank no longer have to be in compliance with the policies and procedures of the bank. Instead, they have to comply with their own national laws and regulations that management finds to be equal to the bank's policies. Question is what does it mean when a request is lodged to the panel? The NGOs say it means that the policies are undermined.

JW: We get criticized if we try to impose World Bank conditions. It is called conditionality, it is called unreasonableness, and the NGOs, the very same NGOs, will criticize us like hell for what they call conditionality, without ever knowing or defining. There was conditionality that was associated with the so-called Washington Consensus, which for most people means charging fees for schools, privatizing water companies, and opening capital markets before they are ready to be opened, and freeing up trade so that rich countries can sell to them. And that is a complete parody of what happened or what's intended. But for most people, that is conditionality. And the fact that that does not exist or there are utterly different elements in the conditions no one ever debates. There is in terms of the bank now a very clear approach, which is that they are not preconditions. They are not preconditions in regard to privatization; they are not preconditions in the case of capital markets ...

MVP: What about environmental impact assessments?

JW: There is a precondition on the environmental impact assessments, and sometimes that puts people off. But with the exception of the environmental impact, which we think affects the whole of the world, as well as the local people, the opening of national markets is now clearly on a case-by-case basis. Now, what we are seeking to move to is not to weaken the approach we would have to the country. We have the desire to meet certain standards. But what we are trying to do is to build those standards within the country policies. Or if the country is doing it in a different way, lean over backwards to accept the way the country is doing it and then make sure that they do it. We want to build capacity and ownership in those countries. And what we would prefer would be to have the people work through the country ownership and country capacities because it then works for us and for a lot of donors. And we have managed to get a couple of these through the board, and we are trying.

Too Legalistic

MVP: Let's say one of the loans in such a project is leading to a request to the Inspection Panel. What then would be the role of the Inspection Panel? In the summer of 2004 there was a discussion with the board and management. A statement was made by the chair of the Inspection Panel, Ms Brown-Weiss, and by General Counsel Mr Dañino saying that nothing was going to change for the Inspection Panel. Here is my case: A group of people in Mexico come forward saying: this project harms, and it is under the use of country systems. The role of the panel then is to make a judgment if management did the right thing in declaring the policies of the country, Mexico, equal to the World Bank policies. Doesn't that make the panel at least look into national legislation, making it a sort of "supra-national court"?

JW: Well, I am sure that it is different, and I haven't looked at the issue to be honest with you. When I came to look at the question on Mexico and national systems, so far as I can recuperate there was no mention of the panel. It certainly did not feature in anything that I said on that day. So I do not know the answer on that. If we accept national systems, if we make the country being upset, they should then see whether they adhere to national systems. And if we have weakened what the bank would otherwise have done, then I presume it is the panel that says to us, "by accepting the national system, you weaken the conditions that would have been applied by the bank."

MVP: That means that they have to make a judgment on both, let's say, bank's legislation and on national legislation ...

JW: Well, I think that is exactly right. Well, national process, not politics, national process.

PROFESSOR DAVID HUNTER: INCEPTION OF THE INSPECTION PANEL

The bank didn't want the panel.

Professor Hunter, of American University, Washington, DC, was one of the driving forces behind the creation of the World Bank Inspection Panel. I had already met with him in the office of the Center for International Environmental Law (CIEL) in the summer of 2003, not far from the White House. At the time of the interview, he was acting director of the centre. The corridors and offices were piled with documents. On the wall still hung a Narmada poster. He was full of information and spoke quickly and directly. I asked him to explain what the setting was in the days of the establishment of the Inspection Panel. Did it begin in

Washington, DC? Was the Narmada Dam a drop in the bucket, or was it the main reason for demanding accountability?

DH: I think there were a number of things that were happening, Narmada was one of them, and other controversial cases as well. There was Polonoroeste, the Brazilian rain forest case, involving the original proposal to punch a road through the Brazilian Amazon. In the beginning of the early '80s, for the first time, civil society was starting to engage with the bank generally. And they were primarily environmental activists, primarily in the US and Europe. The people that were working on it were also primarily lawyers or policy activists, so they put the discussion into a policy framework in a push for policies. Whatever ...

MVP: There where no policies at the time?

DH: Well, the first external environmental policy was 1981 or something like that; previously, the bank had Operational Manual Statements that were relatively internal and not always considered mandatory. But then the five major environmental groups got alerted to the World Bank partly because of Narmada, and also I think it was one of the major dams in Thailand and Planaflora, the rain forest in Brazil. Five groups in Washington started to look at the World Bank activities. They were: Friends of the Earth, Environmental Defense Fund, Sierra Club, the Natural Resources Defense Council [NRDC] and the National Wildlife Federation.

MVP: Sierra Club, what's that?

DH: It is actually one of the largest groups in the US, it is mostly domestic and has a huge membership group, and it does a lot of lobbying in Congress and at the state level ... These five were Washington based groups, and they had different connections to these projects on the ground and some partner organizations in Europe, particularly in Germany [Urgewald] and Switzerland [Bern Declaration]. But to be honest the connections on the ground were not yet that great. The global movement was starting. I am speaking of the early 1980s. They were hearing concerns and started to distrust the viewpoints being provided by the bank. And they were surprised to find out that things like environmental assessment, which we were taking for granted domestically, were not being routinely done. Whether there was a policy or not, it quickly got revised thereafter.

Soon thereafter the discussion concerning indigenous people began. The forestry policy was a major debate and was put into a policy framework. Then as time went on, and I jump ahead a little bit in to the very early '90s, Narmada became the major international controversial case. So at that point policies were in place, but we started to question whether they have been complied with. And then Lori Udall and some other activist came up with an idea. Actually Lori decided to have an independent fact-finding mission go ... and so she created a mission.

MVP: She came to see me in the European Parliament asking if I could table a resolution on the subject.

DH: She asked me to go and be part of the team and kind of put it into a framework of law. I never could go. She wanted human rights lawyers to go. One of my colleagues at the Center for International Environmental Law, Chris World, went and wrote a report in light of what they saw as human rights norms.

MVP: That was besides the Morse Commission?

DH: Before Morse or during the same time, because Morse took time to go. I'm not sure about the timing, but it was one model and I think that that may have given the motivation for the Morse Commission because these fact finders were coming back and they were saying things ... well ... and they were pretty good reports. So Lori and others pushed, I was only marginally involved; at that time other groups were more involved. Lori knows the history. They asked the bank and through this external pressure from US and European donors the Morse Commission was created ...

MVP: How did they do that, by writing letters?

DH: I'm only guessing because I wasn't actively involved in the creation of the Morse Commission. But I assume that they were the same techniques that we used during that period for the creation of the Inspection Panel that took place a bit later. It was essentially a combination of hearings that the congress and some European Parliaments held on specific cases, including on Narmada. People came to speak about Narmada. There was pressure from Treasury. There was some reaction in European capitals as well, particularly Germany and Switzerland. That was really the beginning.

So it was some kind of mutual dialogue, and Lori would be able to identify which IDA discussions it was because she was more engaged in that. It was often tied to the IDA replenishments. So I don't know exactly what the political engagement was for Morse. But there was this huge drumbeat about Narmada, and I think that the bank understood that an independent evaluation could maybe help them. At the same time, there was a guy named Eric Christianson at NRDC who wrote an article on an independent appeals commission for the World Bank policies. That was the first writing on it.

The two things were going somewhat parallel, and they came together after Morse. Then the European Bank for Reconstruction and Development [EBRD] was created. It is kind of funny. I worked for the Centre for International Environmental Law and was not involved in banks until 1990. Then we got a grant to work on the newly formed EBRD. It was a new bank and it was Europe. There was some hope that this bank would be more progressive on our issues. CIEL picked up and wrote an article about the EBRD proposing an independent appeals commission and even drafting a set of procedures for it. It was published in some obscure journal;

nobody ever read it. And that was written by Durwood Zaelke, who is the founder of CIEL, and Chris Wold. Personally, I happened to be living in Prague and ended up introducing them around and helping them out and that's how I came to CIEL. About a year later, the Morse Commission is over, we're now at IDA 9 – I think the one in 1992 or 1991. The Morse Commission came out with its report. It was quite devastating about Narmada, and it has also shown us the power of these independent commissions. At the time, Lori Udall and some others were working on the Hill in Congress.

She was at the Environmental Defense Fund (now Environmental Defense) and lobbied the Congress. By that time her father and her uncle were both retired from politics, but now her brother and cousin are both in the Congress. Lori and Chad Dobson, who ran the Bank Information Center, he actually is in some ways the chess master in all of this stuff, in the policies and everything, lobbied Barney Frank. His history will be interesting for you to get. Lori needed something to ask for. Barney was very interested in what was going to be the fallout, so there were two things that we were going to ask the Congress to make noise about with respect to replenishment. One was a renewed information policy, a revitalized access to information policy, and the other was an appeals mechanism to improve compliance with environmental and social policies ...

MVP: During the lobby in the Congress you asked for what?

DH: We asked the House Banking Committee or maybe it was Foreign Relations ... The chairman of the banking committee was Barney Frank, who was concerned about human rights and environmental issues around the bank, and he said: "well, what do you want?" Lori and others said: "we want an information policy and an accountability mechanism." And he said: "fine." He called up Treasury, and he said that's what we are gonna have to have ...

MVP: What just a few people can do together ...

DH: It is very interesting, one of the early things is the testimony that Lori Udall gave to the Congress calling for this.

MVP: What year was that, 1991?

DH: Probably 1992, it happened pretty fast. What happened then was Lori called me and said, "Do you have some ideas about these mechanisms?" We were working on it together, and I said, "Yes, I do, I have some articles written out. I'll send them over to you." I remember because it was so funny, because it taught me a different lesson. About two or three weeks later, the deadline was getting there, and Congressman Frank wanted to see something and people wanted to see some text.

And others here and in Europe ... and we needed to get something on paper. Lori was doing the first draft, she was having trouble and I said:

"Lori, the first draft is already done as an appendix to one of those articles I sent you. Because back when Durwood and Chris wrote that article and I helped write that – I just edited it – we did the draft procedures, you can start with those." So she called me back fifteen minutes later, and she said: "You're right, those are great." And I said: "Why didn't you read it?" She said: "Well, it's a law review." And what it taught me is that most of the activist community never reads academic literature. And it is true, we are too busy, we don't read the academic press, we don't have enough time. It really taught me a lesson about the fact that those two groups don't communicate. Lori was sitting on essentially what she needed and didn't know it because she didn't have time to read academic literature. I said: "I'll come over." So I went over to her office and with the electronic version of that draft. And we sat in her office and made a draft that then was attached to her testimony – I think we labelled it a "draft appeals mechanism" – and we sent it to the Treasury Department. And Treasury probably ... We don't know what happens internally; what we do know is that at some point the legal department of the bank came with a proposal. That wasn't adequate, but wasn't bad. Treasury called us and sat down with us ... this happened several times. And said, "what do you think about this?" We critiqued it.

MvP: During what presidency was this?

DH: This was Bush I, and Pat Coady was the American executive director.

MvP: It's quite open, I'm surprised.

DH: Well, Chad Dobson has very good relationships, and we had very good relationships with Treasury. The money for the bank was held up by a Democratic Congress, and Pat was totally supportive of it. It must have been the summer of 1993. Actually I gave you two early dates. All of that happened in the fall of '92 and beginning of 1993. And I remember going down to Treasury, at least twice, including the last time when we said we could live with the draft procedures. This is what the bank history doesn't suggest ... and in some ways we never talked about it ...

MvP: So Treasury gave directions to the World Bank what to do.

DH: Absolutely, of course ...

MvP: Yes of course, but the Americans are not the only owners of the bank that have opinions ...

DH: Well, they weren't on this either. In the meantime, in June and July, Peter Bosshard was getting at the other side of the ocean on this. Both German and Swiss groups were supporting this effort. It is remarkable because it is civil society driving this. The bank was told by the largest borrowers what to do. And Treasury was working with other borrowers to tell the bank that they had to come up with a proposal on accountability mechanisms. And I assume Treasury sent our ideas over to the bank. Because there were some similarities between our ideas and what they came up with – three members and things like that. The name was different, but clearly the structure was like ours.

Two other things were going on independently, completely independently. Or one other thing is completely independent. Danny Bradlow meanwhile had spoken to the Canadian Parliament about an ombudsman. And when Lori and I were drafting procedures we got his testimony to the Parliament. Though we were coming up with what we called an Independent Appeals Commission – that was our name for it. And we decided we liked that better than an ombudsman model. So we told Treasury ... and Danny was pushing the ombudsman. We brought Danny in – I think he met with Treasury. We decided we didn't like the ombudsman: it was too soft, too flexible. We wanted something to hold them accountable because we're lawyers, and it would work. So we rejected the ombudsman, but it was an important thing because Danny was an outside independent, having spoken about the need for accountability, and he had already spoken to the Canadian Parliament before the US ever got there, so there was an ally there already."

MVP: Did Danny Bradlow take up your view and change his position?

DH: He never totally changed his position. But at that point we had nothing. So he was supportive of any accountability mechanism. And because we were far more politically active, Danny would write something occasionally, but he wasn't out there lobbying. He supported us. He would occasionally say, "I still like the ombudsman idea." But has always been a supporter of the panel because the basic concept of accountability was what he cared most about. And he has never really cared that his ombudsman idea was modified, although we do now have experience with that model at the IFC. This was early; it must have been in the fall or early '93. Then Peter Bosshard in Switzerland came with the Bern Declaration. That is the only other thing that I remember. I do know there was lobbying going on by the German groups ...

MVP: And in the European Parliament it was me ...

DH: So there was a lot going on in Europe. But one thing I can specifically remember, because I was part of it, is that Lori, Peter and I wrote an article together, not an article but a paper, on the panel.

MVP: The three of you wrote an article?

DH: I think it was just a white paper, and we circulated it along all the policymakers, but in particular we did it for the Swiss Parliament – it was translated into German or French. And then I went over, and Peter and I held meetings with Swiss parliamentarians, partly in English, partly in German. My German isn't very good, that's why I remember. And then there was a press hearing, and there was NGO networking meetings, and the Swiss ED [executive director], who was quite supportive as well. And Eveline Herfkens, the Dutch ED, was quite supportive. We did many meetings with all the EDs here in DC as well. And we had activists from Europe calling in. And then, finally it got to a point. Of course, there were things we didn't like about it, but we said to Treasury and Barney: "This is good enough." We could live with it. Two drafts came out of it, as I recall it. There was one draft that had to go back because it wasn't independent enough, so it had to go back to the bank, presumably the general counsel, for more work. And I think there were a couple of fights over the provision whether the panel members could work for the bank again. That was one of the last ones. Which is interesting because it still comes up to be very important ... you know, for me, it may be the most important provision for maintaining independence of the mechanism. It was interesting – when I applied I had four different phone calls asking me, four different times, specifically asking me, you're only forty-one years old, and you know you will never be able to work for the World Bank Group again? They kept calling me back so I could confirm again.

MVP: From the bank?

DH: Human Resources, when I applied to be on the panel. Because they couldn't believe that somebody that young would be willing to forego ever working for the bank again.

MVP: There is more in life than working for the World Bank.

DH: That's right, but I'm not sure people who work for the bank realize this. It has also shown that they had probably gone down the road a lot with previous applicants, before they realized the job precluded future work at the bank ... and people were not focused enough on it, early on. I think it is an important provision. Anyhow, I think it is an important provision and the net result is that the panel was created. And I don't want to suggest that the process was entirely US orientated – it's just that was my perspective. I think the initial ideas came out the way I said, and then civil society from Europe and other countries helped to spread it. I mean Lori Udall and I and Peter Bosshard spread the concept as being part of the global IDA demands. Both the information policy and the accountability mechanism became European demands as well. I can't remember it exactly. Before we said it to Congressman Frank it was probably discussed with the Europeans as well – that's the way we operated. So my role was pretty narrow; I was basically the lawyer on the procedures. Lori is a lawyer too. She is the one that made it happen politically and Chad Dobson.

MVP: So you're talking about Chad Dobson, Lori Udall, yourself, Peter Bosschard, Danny Bradlow, Heffa Schuking in Germany, and Christianson, with this article on the Independent Appeals Committee ...

DH: The bank didn't want the panel. There was no support internally from the bank, other than from the Board of Directors. And there was broad support at the donor level. But I don't recall. Chad and Lori might. I don't recall any support from senior management for it. From my impression, we were in a constant struggle to make sure it was independent from the general counsel's office from the very beginning, while the general counsel was drafting the resolution. So it wasn't aggressive in style but it was definitely something that was imposed upon the bank by the donors – partly in light of the findings of the Morse Commission. There is no doubt in my mind that there was limited to no support in management. Now, that history got rewritten after it was created by Shihata's book.

MVP: You think that's something missing in the book of Shihata?

DH: He claimed it because he was the internal draftsman. And he claimed it for a very political reason. His book came out very early, very fast. He wanted the panel to be like ICSID, the International Center for Settlement of International Disputes. Where the general counsel of the World Bank sits and oversees that. He expected that he would be able to control the panel. And I think he thought it would run out of the general counsel's office. Even though the structure of it did not end up being that way, but that was because there was a very strong fight for independence. I don't remember what the issues were, but it had to do with the fact that it was presented to the board and not to the president. All issues of independence. I don't have all the details on this, but after the panel was created there was a dispute over it – I tried to find the letters recently, and Lori may have them – at some point early around Arun in Nepal, which was the first claim. The general counsel made a legal claim by interpreting the resolution that created the panel. I give Lori full credit for this; I was willing to let it slide, and Lori called me and said we can't let this slide. It was a minor issue but she was absolutely right.

MVP: What was the issue?

DH: I can't remember but the point was that the general counsel shouldn't have the ability to control the panel's interpretation of things. So Lori and I wrote a letter that went to President Wolfensohn and the general counsel, claiming that there was a conflict of interest for the general counsel doing this. The general counsel – Ibrahim Shihata – went ballistic over the fact that civil society representatives were questioning whether there was conflict of interest, and he claimed questions of integrity. We did not question his integrity: we were questioning the structural questions of the general counsel's role in providing advice to the board, the bank, and the panel in the context of a panel claim ... He asked for a meeting, we granted it to him. We walked in.

The opening line from the general counsel of the World Bank was: "Do you know how rare it is for someone in my position to meet with people

like you?" Lori and I looked at each other, kind of shocked ... but it got
more congenial after he found out we were both serious lawyers ... this
mattered to him, he kind of backed off. We ended up having ... well, it
never was a good relationship because there was always this tension, but we
at least had a respectful one after that low point of starting. And we actually
would have periodic lunches where he would call and I remember him two
years later saying ... I don't know why NGOs dislike me so much. And I said
it's not that we dislike you personally ... you know when things get in the legal department we can't participate, and its just that you exercise control
over the institution. So it got to be fine but that was a very important conflict in which civil society weighed pretty heavily and won through the
Board of Directors.

PAUL ARLMAN, DUTCH MEMBER, BOARD OF DIRECTORS, WORLD BANK GROUP, 1986–1990

> We gave an economic approach to something we all acknowledged:
> a social disaster in India.

We met in the Hague, in Mr Arlman's residence, built at the end of the nine-
teenth century. He was full of anecdotes from his period in Washington, DC.
A good pot of coffee and a serene atmosphere in the house created the
right spirit for our intensive discussion.

MVP: I understand you were very involved in the discussions that led eventually to the establishment of the panel? When did it all start?

PA: It started for me in 1988 or 1987. We received disturbing messages
from the activists in India: from Mehdi Patkar. These messages were picked
up by the international environmental movement in an activist format.
The spokesman and organizer was Wouter Veening. Wouter, who was accompanied by five to ten people from all kinds of environmental organizations, had the idea to talk to the executive directors about those dams.
Bank staff did not welcome this initiative; however, I picked it up. In this
group, the Canadian and the American offices were also present, from neither office the executive director but the advisor – the French, English,
and German. So the core of the EU was there. Scandinavia was also present.
I chaired it; usually we met in my office, very informally. No official reports
were made. Bank staff was also heard.

In a certain way, we were acting like the panel as we were having bank
staff involved and were asking questions like, "What do you think about
this?" and "What do you know about that?"

There it appeared, after we heard Patkar and the environmental activists' story, that bank staff partly did not know it themselves. Bank management did not appreciate our finding out about cases that had been

decided upon or discussed with India. The role of the bank in India, IDA, has always been one of direct bargaining with India itself. Bank management did not attend. They preferred not to discuss it. I always, and I also found this in old notes, we always invited the Indian executive director. He never attended and also did not contact us. But he was always informed. I informed him beforehand – excellent information – when the group would meet. If there were reports made, he would receive these undoubtedly. Therefore, it had to be held in the open. However, it was simultaneously very clear that we had rather different opinions about that, and the bank could not continue in this fashion. That continued for two or three years. Then [November 1990], I passed it on to Eveline Herfkens, and she approached this from a more social angle than an environmental one.

MvP: Is that a sensitive subject, bargaining with India?

PA: Yes, India negotiated about almost everything. One time, in a board discussion on a water project in India, things were said about pricing that I found worrisome. When I made an appointment with staff, seven different experts came by to discuss water pricing in India. It appeared that there was no rational pricing. From an economic perspective that was for us an argument to say: "Those Narmada Dams have been wrongly designed." The issue was not that one should or should not build a dam. When you are building a dam, and you do not set up a suitable compensation for those who are damaged and without economically pricing of water and electricity produced, then something is wrong. We gave an economic approach to something we all acknowledged: a social disaster in India.

The NGOs had a lot of local, really grassroots information. Hereafter, Patkar visited at least twice. Bank staff was always present during these visits and they often didn't like this. Bank management didn't show up; they preferred not to discuss it. We always invited the Indian director's office. He never showed up and didn't contact us. But I always informed him beforehand. He no doubt received reports if they were made, so that was a high level of transparency. At the same time it was clear that we had very different opinions on this subject and that the bank couldn't continue working this way. This went on for two, three years. Eveline Herfkens took over in November 1990. She approached the issues even from a more social perspective, rather than the environmental perspective.

MvP: Obviously, both aspects were present in the Narmada Dam case.

PA: Yes, of course, and the numbers of people involved were huge.

MvP: Two hundred thousand persons?

PA: Oh, easily.

MvP: There were no arrangements for compensation?

PA: There were absolutely none that we were aware of. This was entirely India's policy. At the time the issue was discussed at a higher level when the Indians said, "we will throw the bank out of the project." The bank eventually left the project.

MvP: That also occurred after the panel's report on China. The difference is that the decision was made in Peking; they would continue the project without the bank.

PA: And of course, that also occurred in the similar way in China.

MvP: Who took the initiative to establish an Inspection Panel according to you? I know that the US Congress got involved after the Morse Commission.

PA: No, we didn't do this. During my time, I can't remember us saying: "This has got to have institutional consequences within the bank." Let me state it as follows: I can't remember that we ever spoke about it in the sense that "the decision making in the bank isn't good enough." It did create room for the bank to listen more to NGOs. As a result, the late president Conable created even more room for them.

Conable, a decent Republican, was a man who was very open to other views. He mostly agreed with environmental argumentation. For this I can say: hats off for Conable! The Bush Sr administration was absolutely not interested, but Conable was.

Let me personally refer to the current "water-pricing regime" in the western states in the US ... They built enormous dams and provide water on the basis of fifty-year-term contracts against very enjoyable prices. They grow cotton in areas that can not deal with it, unless it is heavily subsidized.

MvP: Who pays the price for this, also the people that lost their land?

PA: No, at the cost of the US taxpayer. The benefits go, via low electricity prices and dominantly low water prices, to already wealthy farming ventures in California. At the time we didn't say "there has to be a different way of decision making within the bank." The panel is of course a different way of decision making.

MvP: You used your influence in the Narmada Dam case. That might have affected the bank and management to listen more to NGOs. What other institutional issues can you recall? And when did you leave?

PA: I left on November 1, 1990. Clearly, the establishment of the panel started hereafter. After the Inspection Panel was founded, I received a thank you note from my successor, Eveline Herfkens, for starting the process. She continued it. I do not know where or when the institutional decision-making issues were discussed. This happened when I was already gone.

MvP: I understand that after the Morse Commission's report, the US Congress put pressure on the bank and demanded to create a permanent independent accountability mechanism.

PA: That might very well have been the case because all the big US environmental organizations were involved and intensely lobbied Congress. Congress felt that the bank should listen to the US opinion.

I recall that we felt hardly supported by the Operations Evaluation Department [OED]. OED wrote thick reports that were rarely taken into account by the board. The board's mistake. As I recall it, the board has never pointed out systemic faults like those that were made in Narmada. Moreover, OED operates and operated after, and not previous to, board decision making. A link between OED and the Inspection Panel would of course not be too bad. I was present during the establishment of OED, around 1974 to 1975. McNamara was president. It was decided that Operations Evaluation should report simultaneously to the board and to the president.

MvP: Where did you see resistance in those days? Who weren't pleased with what you did? Can you elaborate more on that?

PA: By way of example, I recall that the bank came up with a program for Haiti. I knew little about Haiti, but I had just read a long article in the *New Yorker*. I said in the board, "The staff's story about Haiti is beautiful, but it seems totally different from what others see as the reality." Staff's stories were always too optimistic.

MvP: What did they say?

PA: Bank staff's attitude was always optimistic. Even on a country like the Zaire of Mobuto. They brought to the board the continuation of a Gecamines project – on which I had voted against when a similar proposal was sent to the EIB board, of which I was a member from 1981 to 1986 – and in the discussion it became clear that the situation, and especially the nonconformity with bank policies of the country, had not changed in twenty years. So I proposed the board would decide not to devote any more resources to Zaire as the government of that country had no interest in development anyhow. Six colleagues expressed support for my view after the meeting, but none voted with me. Some few years later the bank stopped lending to Zaire entirely. Incidentally, with an IDA project like that the proceeds would be lent at soft terms to the government, and the difference with the much harder onlending terms to Gecamines would end up in government coffers anyhow.

Bank senior management counted among them some who coveted the theory that "the board is like mushrooms: you feed them shit and keep them in the dark." This was also clear in the management's initial refusal to give board members access to the bank's databases. This has of course changed very much in later years.

MvP: The ultimate say in the bank's business is with ...?

PA: On issues that the Americans find of importance, they tended – and tend still – to try to force through their views. They pressure the president and the staff, sometimes heavily. Some are better in resisting than others. Conable, who had close ties with Bush Sr, was an independent man, but he too had to pick his fights carefully.

MVP: The twenty-five EU countries[10] pay more for the bank than the US. Did Europeans try to get a joint grip in your time?

PA: The answer is rather no, we didn't. That's not for want of trying but nearly always one of the larger EU countries; part of the American dominated G-7 found a reason to agree on substance but that in this or that specific case, they just had to give it to the Americans. Directors from Germany, France, and the UK got instructions from their capitals; directors for a more cosmopolitan constituency like we, did not. And again, the Americans are good at playing the Europeans against each other.

MVP: An accountability mechanism like the panel is to be applauded, and praise to the US for insisting to set this up. But it should remain virtually independent and not fall victim to the legalisms of our time. The gradual introduction of country agreements under which management are to judge national legal systems against bank policies would make that difficult. This might even impede access to the panel.

PA: I agree that there is that danger: also in Europe there are areas where informal forms of intermediation show much more success and effectiveness. Do not forget that legalisation also means that power shifts to that party that can more easily afford expensive lawyers. The more rules one has, the more they can get under or through them.

HERMAN MULDER, SENIOR EXECUTIVE VICE PRESIDENT, GROUP RISK MANAGEMENT, AND ANDRÉ ABADIE, HEAD OF SUSTAINABLE BUSINESS ADVISORY, ABN-AMRO BANK

We compete on price, we compete on clauses, but not on standards.

On the twelfth floor of one of the most visible modern buildings of the financial suburb of Amsterdam, the so-called "Zuid-as" (South-Axis), one can find the office of Herman Mulder. Mulder is the senior executive vice president of Group Risk Management at ABN-AMRO Bank, a private institution with over 110,000 employees in more than sixty countries. ABN-AMRO is one of the largest non-American banks operating on the US market. Mulder is known as one of the founding fathers of the Equator Principles, which today have been adopted by sixty-one major private banks. He spoke with passion about the changing role of corporations and the financial sector. During our interview on 8 July 2004, we were later joined by André Abadie, the head of the Sustainable Business Advisory at ABN-AMRO Bank.[11]

History of the Equator Principles

MvP: Why has ABN-AMRO adopted the Equator Principles? What was the turning point? Was it the Brent Spar or was it the involvement of the bank in the Chad-Cameroon oil pipeline?

HM: With IFC we had a joint cause. It was also Peter Woickc[12] who immediately recognized the opportunity to take the initiative to meet with project finance banks to say, "can we raise the bar?" Now let me give you a bit of background on how it all came about and the questions you're asking: "was it Brent Spar, was it Chad-Cameroon?" I would say it was none of them or both of them. And I have to go back to 1998 when we had a wake-up call from Friends of the Earth on our involvement in the Grasberg Mine in Papua New Guinea. I was the youngest senior executive vice president. In fact, I was the one in my business career who brought this project to the bank, and then the first day I was head of risk of the bank, I was confronted with this complaint. What else could the board do but say, "well, you do it yourself." So we had a meeting with NGOs. They complained about our role in this project. They had about 5,000 signatures, which they presented at the conversation. It was the first time that an NGO was invited into the building. I mean those were the old days; you ignored them.

So what do you do when you receive those who are criticizing your policy? You say, "we will study it and come back to you," which we did not within three weeks but only two months thereafter. In that second meeting with Friends of the Earth we did three things: one is we admitted guilt. In other words, we were saying: "if we would have had the same project now we would not have participated in this project." Secondly, we prepared to exit the credit because we felt we should not be associated, based on the new analysis we had.

MvP: So you listened to them?

HM: We were listening and said, "we do not want to be associated with this project anymore because things are not as they should be." And thirdly we offered, on a confidential basis, to sit down with Friends of the Earth to review future mining projects. Because we recognized that they had knowledge we did not have ... My colleagues from Jakarta went there. That was also the reason why we said this is a legacy issue, we should not do it again. At that discussion the response of Friends of the Earth was, "we accept your admission of guilt. We don't want you to exit this project because we want you to exercise your influence with the sponsor of this project, Freeport ...

MvP: Very wise of them.

HM: Absolutely, that response triggered our responsibility. So don't sell the credit. And [fourthly], Friends of the Earth was not prepared to sit down with us on a confidential basis to review further projects. That also was an interesting comment, which we can't do because we have clients. So we did exercise some pressure. There was a judge – I don't know what here name was – a former judge who was appointed on behalf of Freeport who went in into the project and came also to some critical conclusions. Freeport did a few things better, but it never was fully resolved. This was our first wake-up call. The second wake-up call was that the Dutch banks were criticized for their role in APP, the paper and pulp industry in Indonesia.

We said, rather than responding to incident by incident or to pressure from outside, let us draft a policy for this very vulnerable area for this forestry-related business. We consulted with the leading clients we have in the sector. That allowed us to draft a fairly high-standard policy. Subsequently, we spoke to the NGOs and said, "this would be the policy, what's your feeling about it?" We approved the policy including the comments of the NGOs and put it on the web. And we rolled it out. So we went to the laggards in the sector, including our clients and said, "well, where are you?" So that was groundbreaking that forestry policy. It was not the intention but it got a lot of publicity. Like the Equator Principles also got much bigger than I thought it would be.

MvP: Are you surprised about that?

HM: Wait, there was more. We started drafting the mining policy, with a similar approach. And also oil and gas policy, a similar approach, starting with the draft. And I got increasingly critical comments of my colleagues that we might be walking too far ahead of the flock. The financial sector is a typical laggard because we do not have a material direct environmental footprint. Indirectly yes, but not direct. In one particular case it really became an issue. It was when we were competing with an American bank in Venezuela on an oil project. They were prepared to wave the Tokajaku clause. And my Japanese is not good enough, but the Tokajaku clause basically requires borrowers to apply and set minimal standards for environmental issues.

I am chair of the Group Risk Committee, and we were not prepared to waive that. The other US bank was. So that's where we sat. I mean we are here competing on something which should not be part of the competition. Environmental and social and ethical issues should be something which for the leading professional banks should be the same. We compete on price, we compete on clauses, but not on standards. That was the trigger for me. So I could do two things: either we were going to compromise our standards – which we didn't – or we were going to do something else. That's where the breakfast meeting with Peter Woicke came, and I said, "well, Peter, you have an issue, you have standards. I'm competing."

MvP: Did you already work with the IFC policies?

HM: Yes, we made a general reference to the safeguard guidelines, but we never kind of delved into it saying, "what does it really mean?" I mean really study what we were agreeing. It also was not included in the documentation.

It didn't have teeth. Then we said, "what can we do? You have an issue here, I have an issue." That's what we called "the London meeting," and Peter Woicke and Suellen Lazarus were there with the other ten banks. It was a name-and-shame meeting. The OCP [Crude Oil Pipeline Project],[13] in which WestLB AG was involved, was mentioned. We declined that before. That was another initiative in my organization that I declined something, as we did in Ecuador for environmental reasons. Citibank had Camisea as a major issue, in Peru, that's another mine. At least we were with the ten project-finance banks sitting together. We mentioned Papua New Guinea and also gave a presentation of Chad-Cameroon. We felt at that point in time very proud of what at least the menu, the theory, of [what] Chad-Cameroon would look like. So we had this meeting the full day in London and then the so-called "gang of four" was created.

By the way, twenty of them, half the group, were bankers. None of them worked for corporate communications, those people who defend the bank against criticism from outside. No, the ones who were there were either from the business or risk management, which in itself was very interesting. That was, I think, the beginning of the winning. If it had been corporate communication, it would be green-wash. In London the "gang of four" was created: one from us, ABN-AMRO, one from Citigroup Inc., one from Barclays plc, and one from WestLB AG. They drafted in eight months the Equator Principles.

The Equator Principles and ABN-AMRO Bank

MVP: Was it a decision of the executive board?

HM: It doesn't necessarily have to be the highest authority in the bank. The highest authority in the bank is the Group Risk Committee/Holding, of which my boss, Tom de Swaan, is the chairman, and I'm the co-chairman. It's us who decide. It is not only the policies, the drafting of it, but it is also the ensuring of the compliance with those policies.

MVP: Fascinating, the private sector is taking over the role of governments.

HM: I agree with you: the self-regulatory ability of the leading players. See for example the twenty-five member countries of the EU: even Norway, Switzerland, and Turkey, Rumania, Bulgaria are affected and even bound to whatever is happening in Brussels, so you don't have to be a member of the EU to be influenced to the rules. That is true for the Equator Principles as well. We have now twenty-one banks,[14] one export credit agency.

[André Abadie, head of the Sustainable Business Advisory, arrives and is introduced by Herman Mulder.]

HM: André came three years ago. He is now the head of the department drafting the policies, monitoring the compliance, and has contact with IFC for environment, for the extractive industries, for Equator I follow-up, the redefinition of the safeguard guidelines, and for Equator II.

MvP: Are the principles a quality mark that can be recognized by the outside world?

HM: No, it's basically a minimum standard. But it is not something which I would say some banks are further ahead in applying the minimal standards than other ones. It is not an agreement amongst the banks to consult with each other on this issue. It is a very loose conglomerate of banks without a structure. It is a minimum standard which we commit to. Banks individually may deviate and even improve it.

MvP: Some banks go further, but it is never less?

AA: Yes ... The thing that it does suggest, if you want to talk about a quality mark, is that if a transaction has been approved by an Equator bank, you at least know that it has been through a rigorous due diligence process, which is the fundamental starting point. What's becoming more and more important is [that] due diligence is one thing but the ongoing monitoring is something we are going to be increasingly required to do. We can discuss this in the context of Chad-Cameroon in a moment.

MvP: Are the principles an internal mechanism to be used to measure a safe partner?

AA: If you have a syndicate of banks in a transaction, such as – let's take BTC [Baku-Tbilisi-Ceyhan pipeline project],[15] for example – three of the four lead arranging banks were Equator banks.

MvP: Three out of four?

AA: Three out of the four lead arranging banks were Equator banks: Citigroup, Mizuho Corporate Bank, ABN-AMRO, which was the three. The one that was not was BNP [Paribas]. Now, as a result, we would ensure that the due diligence and the project structuring are at a level that is acceptable as far as the Equator Principles are concerned. Therefore, any syndicate banks that come into the syndicate are by default investing in a project that has already been through that process. So by default they have to accept the Equator Principles as a minimum standard. Conversely, if we were in a situation where – let's reverse the tables and let's say there were three non-Equator banks and one Equator bank – we would insist that the project meets with the Equator Principles. If the other three banks say, "well we aren't bound by them, this is the project, take it or leave it." Then it is up to us to exercise our right and say, "well, we leave it at that stage." Or we insist that "no, if you want us to market to a general syndicate of banks, understand that, apart from us, if you are going to find other banks – 70 per cent or 80 per cent of those would be Equator banks." They will require that the Equator Principles will have been assessed.

MvP: So, in fact, you are controlling the market already?

AA: It is de facto becoming the standard.

HM: When we convened that meeting in London, we were looking at the lead table of project financers. In other words, those who were in charge of the agenda. If you have the top ten banks, then you have basically the architects of all project finance here in the world involved.

MvP: How much of it is risk assessment?

AA: Well, I would say almost all of it. But as much as risk assessment it is risk management. It is prudent business selection. For us, when we look at a project, it is not just about the Equator Principles: you are also looking at the client and the other sponsors that are involved. For instance, if you look at Camisea – Camisea in Peru is a category A project. Shell initially was the lead sponsor. They elected to pull out of the transaction for a number of reasons not necessarily just environmental. The project has gone ahead with second- and third-tier operators – I won't name who they are – but that's one of the reasons we decided we don't want to be involved in this. Had Shell remained in the project, we may have looked at it. Because even though you are talking about a category A, high-impact project ...

MvP: Shell stepped out?

AA: Shell stepped out. You remember that you are talking about a high-class, quality sponsor who can make sure that they will manage, mitigate and improve whatever may be: they can manage the situation properly. So for us, yes it is about risk assessment. But it is also about doing the right business ultimately. And it is about making sure that we also can convert the potential rough diamonds, or the dogs, into good projects at the end of the day. So there is also business rationale behind making sure that you do your risk assessment and risk investigation appropriately.

Banks That Have Not Adopted the Equator Principles

MvP: So far with the partners of the principles, more then 80 per cent of the market for private-sector projects is covered. What banks so far are still outside and why?

AA: Depending on whether you consider Dexia a Belgian or French Bank, only one French bank has adopted. The two or three reasons that I've been given are that legally and culturally it is very difficult for them to tell a client what they should and shouldn't do. Because apparently you are getting to undue influence. This is the explanation that Calyon [the merger between Crédit Agricole and Crédit Lyonnais] has given us as to why BNP and Societe Generale haven't adopted. Another reason is that the French banks find it very difficult to delineate between what is project financing and what is nonproject financing. Their fear is that by adopting the Equator Principles they will have to apply the Equator Principles to a large portion of their business. At the moment, project financing is about 10 per cent of our business. So the Equator Principles, strictly speaking, applies to a very small subset of our business. However, we are going further and stretching it over and applying to other parts of business.

But for a French bank, they see that spill-over effect as potentially larger. So they're having conceptual difficulties with the application. The Japanese banks – apart from Mizuho Corporate Bank – have said that they don't need the Equator Principles because any project financing they do would involve JBIC. JBIC themselves have the equivalent to the World Bank standards. So they would be duplicating everything. We understand that they are changing ...

MVP: With Suellen Lazarus of IFC, I discussed the southern banks from the oil countries, Arabic banks – Saudi Arabia. She said: "Those banks are usually state-owned, and they will never accept or adopt this because it then is a sort of statement as if the national legislation is not correct. They apply to the national legislation."[16] That was her explanation. She mentioned one southern bank considering. I think it is Brazil probably ...[17]

HM: They would be the first one to join. I wouldn't be surprised. Brazilians are very sensitive to environmental issues, so ...

AA: I myself have spoken to four South African banks, and I got lukewarm responses from that. They're thinking. They're in a process ...

MVP: What about Russian or Chinese [banks]?

AA: That's a good question.

HM: It is interesting the way we prepared our oil and gas paper with the Russian companies. I mean there is receptivity there on the client side, not on the bank side. And they are following anyhow. But some of the Russian oil companies are definitely prepared to raise that bar towards the BP [British Petroleum]/Shell level, whatever they can do. It will take them years and years, but nevertheless.

MVP: And India and China?

AA: This gets into the question whose responsibility is it ultimately to go out there and try ...

MVP: What is the right answer to the criticism the banks have adopted the principles for public-relations reasons?

HM: Well, let me give on that point just one simple sentence. We are in it, and it is not just the Equator Principles, but it is much broader. We are a sustainable bank not because we must, because there is pressure, but because we want to be.

AA: And I think the point that Herman mentioned earlier is that if you look at who it was within those banks: it was the business people. So you had immediate buy-in and immediate traction. If it was going to be corporate communications who parachuted this on top of the rest of us, then there may be cause for that criticism. But as you can see ...

The Equator Principles and Shareholder Value

MVP: To what extent do the Equator Principles maximize shareholder value?

HM: It is long-term. I believe a bank who has an ambition to be a leader in sustainable development over time will be a preferred employer, a preferred investment, and a preferred partner. And there are an increasing number of examples: in the public, in the private sector, in the energy sector where companies who are leading the issue have a better shot at the right business.

AA: And to add to that: through the efficient and effective application of the policies over time, your portfolio should migrate to a quadrant of the industry sector where there is less risk. Ultimately, less risk will turn into better results.

MVP: Are the principles also a market for the ABN-AMRO, which is a training market for other banks?

AA: I think it is interesting. In fact, I had this discussion this morning, with a colleague of mine saying that it could be increasing opportunities for us to do risk assessment for other major emerging market banks where they don't have risk assessment in place, where they can learn from us. Not just environmental and social, but I'm talking about a broad range of risk projects and issues. So I don't think that it receives much management attention in terms of a strategic priority, but I can see that there would be opportunities ultimately. And the question is: is that something we would like to focus on as a bank?

HM: You may further elaborate on the Basel II Capital Framework. There is a new regulatory environment being created for in practice all banks worldwide. We have been one of the leading participants in the drafting. We have now started to assist central banks and selected commercial banks worldwide to help them coming into the Basel world, and Basel is not just a technical exercise – Basel is also something which requires companies and banks to define their values, their business principles, their governance structure, and sustainable development is part of that.

MVP: Are you going to train, for example, with a training kit?

HM: Yes, because they will be our partners in Indonesia or China. We don't want to be associated with the wrong partner. So there is a self-interest there too.

MVP: One day you won't need IFC anymore.

HM: Well, I disagree with that. I mean they may have gone down from whatever percentage, either 50 per cent to 5 per cent. I think the presence of IFC adds qualitatively significantly to the integrity of the entire project, not just of the banks but also of the local authorities, also of the sponsors. I mean if we've gone into extractive industries – yes, you can see big money and big oil work together and they have now become responsible, so what is the need for IFC? Yes, we need IFC or the World Bank definitely. They make it sure that the integrity of what we created, is the proof in the pudding, the eating thereafter is going to be monitored by IFC, and they will only monitor effectively in vulnerable areas. If you sit at the table.

MVP: I asked Lazarus: "Do you see IFC in a monitoring role?" And she said: "No, we're not there to monitor."[18]

HM: Well, if you are monitoring, then you are in charge.

MVP: Isn't there the liability question? I understand IFC refuses to take any liability of the acts of the Equator banks. They said, "it is wonderful that the Equator Banks accept the policies and principles of IFC and the World Bank." They welcome that very much. But they don't want to be responsible or liable for it, and that I can understand from a legal point of view.

HM: I'm firmly convinced that IFC, but it is also true for EBRD as well as for ADB, must be there in a participative role, which means that their liability does not go behind their technical participation in the project. But their political presence ...

MVP: Politics is a "no" word in the World Bank.

HM: It is extremely important. Talk about Chad-Cameroon and other places: the local government has to comply with its part of the deal as well. So IFC or one of the other IFIs has been at the table, and if IMF for instance is involved in the monitoring of the resource allocation – I mean all the issues – we will need them.

MVP: Interesting what you are saying: you still give them a role.

HM: It is the entire integrity of all the stakeholders in the project. It's banks, it is foreign sponsors, it is the central host government.

Implementation of the Equator Principles and Internal Organization

MVP: How does ABN-AMRO implement the principles? Is there an implementation plan? I understand you trained over 5,000 members of staffing in the sixty countries you are operating in.

HM: We have handled 5,000 colleagues, as you say. We have about 3,000 passionate about this who believe there is a value to be created. And the others are ...

MvP: ... not involved?

HM: No, who are eternal cynics. Who do not care less. And we have about 100,000 who are indifferent or undecided. So it is not just Equator. It goes further than that: it goes to the heart of the bank.

MvP: How are you going to train the people that need to know the policies and change their attitudes?

HM: I call them the young Turks, with them.

MvP: The "young Turks," who are they?

HM: The young staff in their mid-twenties or thirties.

MvP: Committed still?

HM: It is their bank tomorrow. It is a very competitive environment in which we are operating. So the question is: "how do we make a difference as an employer and as a business partner for clients?" This is one of the areas of development. We have a Young Bankers Association, we have a community clearly stimulated by us, also in the board and at my level to say, "well, come on, show us the way. You take charge." It is not just top-down.

MvP: Those young people ... they have to make their business and their career. In the World Bank one of the obstacles is the ranking of the people. It is the incentive system; their career is depending on how much money has been put into projects. Time works against them. And assessments take time. Is that the same for the ABN-AMRO?

HM: Here André comes in. I mean, the board and I can excite the young Turks. André is the one who is dealing with the bishops in the organization who may be the obstacles, who are setting the bonuses.

MvP: What does that mean?

HM" We have a carrot and a stick, and we have a vision.

MvP: Okay, if it is only the carrot, it is dangerous. But you need all three.

AA: Increasingly, I'm seeing that our role used to be, well, a little bit of carrot as well, but primarily the stick, by focusing purely on the principles and any policies. What we need to do is focus on the operational procedural aspect, which is translation of business principles into policies, including the Equator Principles, and turning those into something that, in practice on a daily basis, can be understood. Give them assessment criteria; give them tools and assistance so that they know. When I get a project on my desk, I know what questions I have to ask. I know what it is I should be looking for. So we are equipping the professionals within the project-finance arena with the necessary tools.

MvP: Do they have the policies on their desk?

AA: They have got access to the policies through the intranet [Internet] site. Certainly, the leading project-finance professionals have got summaries of the policies, so they know "these are the standard issues I need to look for." We are developing a tool right now with the IFC that we roll out in the fourth quarter, which will assist in the categorization and the assessment of projects. So we are certainly equipping the forces, if you will, with what it is they need to do. At the same time though, you can give people the best equipment, but you got to make sure that intellectually they buy into this as well. So there has got to be training that goes on ...

HM: And I would like to make a compliment. I think that Glen Armstrong and Suellen Lazarus and many more in the IFC have helped us a great deal.

MvP: So how many people did you train?

AA: Seventy-five people. The total project finance world is in the bank I believe one hundred. Seventy-five is not only project financing, but it was fifty of them project financing. But then it was also risk people, it was client coverage, it was credit people. The idea was those were the trainers; those were the ones that would disseminate the information further down. The tool we are currently developing is going to be rolled out to all the practitioners. Primarily, it is the people who need to work with it. But on our website there is information ...

MvP: How independent of the investment officer or banker is the control/judgment on the implementation of the policies made?

HM: As in most of the banks, we are the independent risk function. So I do not have a personal responsibility. Risk is independent from the business.

MvP: Risk assessment?

HM: Risk approval.

MvP: Risk approval – okay, how many experts do you have in a complicated project to do the assessment? The World Bank Inspection Panel has a budget for it. For example, with the Chad-Cameroon pipeline, we were in need of oil specialists from universities; we had one from Canada who knows how thick a pipeline has to be to in order to have zero risks for leakages – that kind of expertise.

AA: But by default on all category A projects, the banks will have an independent consultant to advise on all environmental and social issues. On selected category B's we will have that: for example, I'm just looking at a project in Saudi Arabia which is a category B project, and there we have hired an independent consultant to look at certain issues. So there certainly is a certain flexibility for us to do that. In terms of who is paying for the expertise: we share it between ourselves and the client. But I'm not necessarily saying that's the standard form. Traditionally, we would expect that when looking at a project, the client would already have prepared a lot of information, so there wouldn't necessarily be the need to have an independent consultant. But certainly, if we ourselves require over and above what the client has prepared, then we need to be prepared to pay that ...

HM: We're facing the issue here in this context that as we proceed and progress we need to have more in-house capability.

Chad-Cameroon and ABN-AMRO

MVP: During the Chad-Cameroon oil pipeline investigation of the panel, the name of ABN-AMRO circulated. Although it has to be clear that was no part of our investigation. Procurement is not part of our mandate. That's why we never came on your doorstep. We were looking at Exxon, of course, the whole process, indigenous peoples, the environmental impact assessment, social impacts, information consultation, etc. I must say I was impressed by the role of Exxon. Still, it is rather risky. Chad is still in deep troubles, politically. You are in the middle of that since, if I am correct, you are in charge of the oil money?

HM: Well, we have shared interest with IFC. We have proclaimed Chad-Cameroon as, until BTC came, the model. And the model will become five years from now a legacy issue because in the meantime we have raised our bar. But right now it is the model. So we have a shared interest with Exxon Mobil and IFC and with the Equator banks involved to make sure it is going to be implemented as planned. And that required tough discussions, also with Exxon.

MVP: Also with them?

HM: Absolutely. And we are a natural partner.

MVP: The problem is probably not with Exxon but with the Governments of Chad and Cameroon.

HM: The local government should not have a probability to renege on its obligation because they have the sense that maybe one of the others sponsors would have a different opinion. We have to draw one line and make sure that Chad and Cameroon will comply with every syllable of the agreement and comply with the spirit ...

MVP: Don't you have concerns about what is happening on the spot?

HM: I just want to be sure that it is done what has to be done. At this point I have no concern, but we have to look after ourselves there. You've been there?

MVP: Yes, I've been there. What I found the most sad to observe is a society living 500 years backwards from the Western world. Suddenly, the modern world runs in. Roads are broadened, trucks come in with truck drivers and prostitution. HIV/AIDS is introduced, and money starts to flow in the society. I don't know if you have ever seen our investigation report? I always will remember the answer of a teacher I asked if the lives of the children changed with the project. It was just a check, a mechanism of checking what's happening to the society when the project machinery comes in. I asked what happened to the children and what changed in their lives.

He said: "In no time a lot, in a bad way. Before there was of course money circulation: but very small money. Suddenly, there was huge money circulation, and the children suddenly understood that their parents were poor. They lost respect for the parents." It made those children vulnerable even more than they were already. A run to cities, where they end up as street children. It is so much an interruption in the society. True, the government will earn some money, and they might do something with it in the region, but in the same time ... Is this development?

HM: Is that what the World Bank calls striking about it?

MVP: A good question. The World Bank's main aim is poverty alleviation. One can say that is what they do at one hand, but on the other hand we see that certain groups become even more vulnerable. We found and reported, for example, that the HIV/AIDS issue was ignored. The bank didn't have a program on the spot. They should have anticipated that if you bring in truck drivers and oil men, those that dig the pipe in the ground, the risk is extremely high HIV/AIDS is introduced with the project.

HM: If it is left to the industry, probably it would not get the attention that it should. Here is another reason why we talk about the role of IFC and the World Bank. It is so essential for these types of projects in vulnerable areas, recognizing that no project is complete or perfect. Even if there is full compliance, there are unexpected issues which will be raised. Then there needs to be someone who is going to force us, whether it's the host government, or sponsor, or the banks who say, "well, this is a new issue: HIV. We have to do something about it."

MVP: On Chad, there is still concern. See the southern region, where 300 oil wells are drilled. At the particular moment while creating the stations, the wells and the pipeline, the project provided work for the local people. The local economy grew. Nevertheless, the food prices went up as a result of a sudden increase of the demand from the constructers in the region. That's what the NGOs had warned. The question is: what will happen five or ten years down the road? Will there still be jobs? That's why in the project a special budget was contracted for the south. ABN-AMRO is one of the lead arrangers of the project financing. So that's where you come in. Are you controlling?

HM: It is IMF who is managing it. IMF is monitoring it.

MvP: IMF? It makes sense if you say the state budget, okay. So they control if the state is fulfilling the contract? I do not think they also control the developments on the regional labour market. You know the story of the acting president? The former colonel fighting the south in the earlier civil war, who is now the president of Chad, we all know he took $40 million of the bank budget to buy weapons, and now, as I understand, he made his brother in charge of project implementation. In the bank they were furious.

HM: It is a tough question we are facing. I mean, with the benefit of hindsight, maybe it was better if Saddam Hussein would have stayed.

MvP: That's something.

HM: I mean, not taking sides, but there is always another side to the truth.

MvP: With the principles and the IFC policies, where do you see ABN-AMRO operate?

AA: All sectors.

MvP: Are the principles stated in the contract? The World Bank does it, but do you?

HM: We are not making references to the Equator Principles per se because they are not law. They're a guideline, a code of conduct, so to speak. The coverage and the clause of the contracts will refer to the principles underlying the Equator Principles, so to speak.

AA: If you would refer to the mechanism, you would require an environmental management plan.

MvP: Where is the contract made, in Amsterdam or in the national bank office? Singapore, Malaysia?

HM: All of these projects come from Amsterdam.

Legal Implications of the Equator Principles

MvP: Is your legal department involved in all of this?

AA: Yes, certainly, from an upfront perspective. They verified that there wasn't going to be any legal liability issue in the bank adopting. One particular issue that the American bank Citigroup primarily at the time was concerned about was whether there could be joint liability. If one bank in the US had to finance a project by implication just because you adopted the Equator Principles would that make all of us liable?

MvP: What was the answer?

AA: That is one of the reasons why there is no such thing as a signatory to the Equator Principles. We have all adopted them, but nobody has actually signed anything. So there is no legal agreement. There is not a piece of paper binding twenty-five institutions to the principles. It is a voluntary adoption and it's up to each bank individually ...

MVP: You make press releases together, but you don't sign together one document?

AA: Which will come to one of your next questions ... there is no actual governance.

MVP: If something in a project goes wrong, where is the liability then?

AA: Well, liability – if you are talking about legal liability – one gets into the whole lender liability debate which is a lot bigger than where the Equator Principles come into play. That is a derivation upon our control: do we as a financial institution actually operate a facility? I think that's a much broader topic – I think just in terms of liability, or let us say responsibility. I think what is probably a more appropriate question is: "provided we [i.e., have we] showed you process that we have assisted a project responsibly and we believe that it is best practice, or good enough practice if you will, at the time?" Then that's as much as we need to point towards. Anything can go wrong in a project. I mean if you look at BTC at the moment, there is proof that, despite the fact that we all applied significant due diligence[19] in assessing the project, there are issues that come up you can't prevent. But what's important for us is at least to be able to reflect and say, "look, this is the new standard. We knew what we were getting ourselves into up-front, these are the mechanisms we have in place to make sure that these issues are monitored, managed, and improved effectively on an ongoing basis." So there has got to be continual due diligence, if you want, as much as [possible] up front.

MVP: There is also international law. The principles could be considered as soft law. Soft law can be changed into hard law, what can be enforced. Do you expect that to happen with the Equator Principles?

AA: I think you are already seeing that the Equator Principles is de facto a compliance standard. So it is moving from soft I guess into harder law. If it ever becomes *de jure*, the reference standard, it remains to be seen. But I think the question that needs to be answered is again, given that no one has actually been signing the Equator Principles, they haven't been codified into international law, then you ...?

MVP: After I gave a lecture on the Equator Principles, I received an e-mail of Bob Wessels, a Dutch law professor, who wrote he had never heard of the Equator Principles. He said indeed it first is soft law, but at the long run, looking at US, UK, Dutch law, it could be hard law. He said: "even soft law can already be binding if it is not followed because it is a promise to the public."[20]

HM: Maartje, you are going precisely to [know] why we have every ambition to be on these issues a leader because I'd rather draft that law myself then. And that's what BP and Shell are also basically doing in their work. I mean by taking the lead, they put the pressure on their competitors.

AA: That comes back to self-governance. To us, self-governance is more important than compliance.

M: So there is a liability, or a responsibility, as André says.

Relations of Equator Banks with the IFC

MvP: That's quite a statement. Is there anything else to be said about legal implications?

HM: Many, many compliments to IFC. And I just want to say this is where IFC can really add value – maybe fifty years from now they will be redundant, but not yet. If we all are saints then we do the training ourselves without peers and ...

MvP: But for the moment it is still necessary?

HM: The next then years I think we really need IFC. And the other IFIs as well.

MvP: That means that you still believe in an international mechanism or institution formed by national states. It is a group of states which constituted the World Bank and its partners, including IFC. At the same time the factor state, in my opinion, is losing out at the moment.

HM: Yes, but where we're not losing out, and therefore I think there is a future for IFC and or any of the IFIs. In this conglomerate world: IFC, World Bank, EBRD – they should be standard bearers.

MvP: Okay, you are still in line with what I am saying. But I'm sorry, I was a politician. What is still for the Dutch government? Where are their powers? Can national governments and parliaments still control? And even the EU is in question. The giant cross-border financial transactions at activities at present time can not be controlled by them. That is why the Equator Principles are so interesting.

HM: And because of that IFC has the ability with their constituency in the governance. What we did in Equator was not drafting something new. What we said is we are going to adhere to what is there already. There was an article on Peter Woicke following the Equator Principles saying he now feels "the heat of the Equator banks in his neck." He needs to go further and that's why we drafted our own internal safeguard guidelines discussing human rights issues. We are catching up with him. IFC has the ability to further raise the bar. Still a lot has to be done on a worldwide basis to raise the bar even further. It's a journey.

HM: Just on that Salim report, that is the key question.

AA: Are you familiar with the Salim report?

MVP: Of course.

AA: We decided, coincidentally at an Equator meeting in Washington, that it was time for the private-sector banks to be heard as well on the Extractive Industries Review. We certainly weren't involved in the initial assessment. And given a number of reasons, primarily given the fact that we are bankers to the extractive industries and in addition as Equator banks, we are a significant stakeholder in any change of the policies. We believe it was certainly our right to have our voice heard.

HM: Just, extractive industries. Are we ... top what? Top 5, top 4? We have a significant interest as ABN-AMRO.[21]

AA: We are certainly in the top 5. So we certainly thought that it was in our interest if we say, "look we have a view on this issue, which we like to share." We think we have a voice which needs to be heard because this impacts our clients, our business. And in addition, and this is actually something that we told some of your former colleagues at the Dutch government, we – ABN-AMRO and Citibank primarily – given our experience in both Chad-Cameroon and BTC, have first-hand experience of the senior role that the World Bank and IFC and other multilaterals can play in ensuring that projects of that nature can become the blueprint for development which can be implemented and managed appropriately and responsibly. And so we do see the value of having the World Bank Group continue to have involvement in extractive industries.

I know that there has been some suggestion that the Equator Principles can quite easily step into the shoes of the multilaterals. The reality is we cannot. We don't have the political authority, we certainly don't have the staff and capability, recourses, or experience or expertise to be able to overnight step into the shoes and say: "fine, we're here; we can do a Chad-Cam." We would be lying to ourselves if we'd believe we could. So we fundamentally see the role the World Bank needs to play on a continuing basis in extractive industries. And as banks, that voice and that opinion needs to be heard. So we put that across.

This is a very important sector to us. In terms of our role in the renewable sector, we certainly applaud the World Bank Group's announcement that [they] want to increase their investment by, I think, 20 per cent over the next five years in the renewable industry. We certainly would like to have an involvement in that. Within the World Bank management response, there is also the call for the establishment of a body, if you will, of interested stakeholders to decide together what should be the future of extractive industries. We certainly are committed and would like to be a partner.

HM: Including NGOs.

AA: Including NGOs ... academics, NGOs, big business, multilaterals, Equator banks, whoever ...

MvP: You said you are making new policies. Not existing ones. And the $50 million limit for the principles. Are you going below that?

AA: Yes.

MvP: Is there any limit?

AA: Well, there is an economic limit. I mean given the amount of cost that goes into setting up project financing. It does become a trade-off between what is economically viable and what is practical. We, certainly on many projects, have dropped the bar completely. Because we see that a lot of money projects currently are at the $30–35, $40–45 million market. And the impacts are exactly the same as anything above $50 million.

MvP: It was a figure at a certain moment?

AA: Well, it is primarily because materially less than 1 per cent of project financing is under $50 million. It so happens that of that list of 1 per cent, a large part of them are mining projects. So we said, certainly for the mining sector, let's drop that bar, we as ABN-AMRO. I'm not sure what the other banks are doing. I'm sure that they're considering it, as we are applying the Equator Principles below that. But we certainly have. In addition, we stretched the Equator Principles to apply to nonproject financing. The impacts nonetheless are exactly the same as in project financing.

HM: There is an interesting point what André is mentioning. Because the naive hope we have, although it's not so naïve, I think, is that by a number of banks having approved or have promised to adhere to the Equator Principles, that it will have a ripple effect on the rest of the organization. And that is helping us in competing with those banks and other banks in nonproject-finance business. Because undoubted there will be the passionate in Citi or Bank America, saying: "Hey, this is project finance, now does it apply to equity, does it apply to client business, nonproject-finance business?" So by having this on the table it raises the bar gradually within the other institutions.

MvP: It is spreading ...

HM: It's spreading.

AA: If you look at our hydroelectric dam business, I can't think of one transaction that is currently on the books that is a project financing. So by definition the Equator Principles do not apply to any hydroelectric dam financing. But we currently are developing a policy, and my starting point is to say: "it doesn't matter what kind of transaction, the Equator Principles should be used, just because of the impacts that hydroelectric development has."

HM: And we will make sure that our colleagues know that we have such a policy.

MVP: And that can be taken over. Is that something that you freely will circulate?

HM: No, they're synopses because we don't want the public to check out our policies in depth.

MVP: No?

HM: No, otherwise you get a legal drafting conversation with NGOs. We want to have our freedom, but we are going to put the synopsis of the policies on our web.

Structure of the Group of Equator Banks

MVP: Is there an organizational chart of the group of Equator banks?

AA: At the moment we are resisting because it is very difficult for us to peek over our neighbour's fence and make sure that what they're doing is appropriate. And each bank has its own client base, its own processes and strategies. It is very difficult for us to determine whether they are applying the Equator Principles effectively. And particularly as the organization grows, this may be an argument to try and come up with an organizational structure. At the end of next year you may have fifty organizations that have adopted the Equator Principles.

It is going to be very difficult for us to police on a global basis. So we certainly have left it up to each bank individually to say, "look, it is up to you to implement, to train, and to report on what it is that you're doing," the consistency if you will, which is what NGOs are looking for. Consistency is ultimately what they want, and accountability. And to a large degree if you leave that to the project-finance market forces, where you do have project-finance banks cooperating together and working together on projects to make sure that when there is a syndication, everyone is applying exactly the same standard. We all finance the same projects. Then the market will take care of a lot of that consistency itself. That is the fundamental belief. Clearly, we have a bilateral project where one bank is involved in a single project, how can we necessarily make sure that a bank has applied the Equator Principles? Is it our responsibility to look at that?

MVP: Don't you think that if one bank of the group is not performing in the way it should in your eyes, it is also having its backlash on you?

AA: It could ultimately. And we fully accept that. I mean how we deal with that going forward is something that needs to be discussed.

MVP: Do you accept as a group a new member?

AA: It is up to anyone. If someone writes in and says we commit to ...

MVP: You cannot say "no"?

AA: No, if anyone writes in ... if Postbank writes in and says, "we commit to, complied with the Equator Principles," that would be strange because I don't think that they do in project financing. But ultimately, if someone commits to adhere to the principles, than they're a welcome member. There is no secret handshake, it is no secret club. It is open for all.

HM: But we do have regular gatherings with the Equator banks.

AA: Yes, we certainly do, and with IFC. IFC has held training sessions, one day workshops and that is again where you try to ensure that there is consistency. But everyone knows we are all singing from the same "song sheet," if you will. And the Equator Principles are very transparent. We all know exactly what it is we should be complying with. It is very open to everyone what the bar should be.

MvP: You cannot expel a member, as you cannot say "no" to someone entering.

AA: Again, we haven't been faced with that. I can honestly think of one bank in particular that has never showed up for meetings, and we don't know what it is doing and doesn't answer phone calls. But does that mean they're not doing anything?

MvP: You have one like that?

AA: Yes, but I'm not going to mention who they are. Maybe they don't have a project-finance focus right now and maybe they adopted it because in the future they would like to start focusing on project financing. So again, each bank has got its own story.

Relations of Equator Banks with NGOs

MvP: You mentioned your relations with NGOs. So what relation is it? And what is your opinion about the Collevecchio Declaration?

AA: Well, it depends on how you define accountability. Should we apply the standards and prove to the NGOs that we have applied them, and we tick all the necessary boxes? Does it mean that again, it comes into the next phase in which increasingly we're going to be responsible for the monitoring and ongoing assessment, so continued due diligence? That's the reason why I'm saying it depends on how you define it because we ourselves and the NGOs disagree on the definition of accountability. What came out of the meeting last week in London that we had with the NGOs is that we are going to establish a working group.

Six representative banks from the Equator Principles and several NGOs are going to sit down for the next six months and start agreeing on: What is transparency? What is accountability? What are we talking about? Let's make sure we're first speaking the same language. And then start working towards: How do we achieve that? So that makes you comfortable with what it is we are doing. And we say to the NGOs: "if you're saying that you want to have more a role in project assessment and ongoing monitoring, then you yourselves NGOs will need to be accountable. So let's just be very clear what our relationship is going to be." So the doors are open for dialogue on the subject of ...

HM: Engagement.

AA: Engagement.

MVP: And the Collevecchio Declaration, is it an issue?

AA: Look, I mean, clearly that there are some very good suggestions in there. The difficult one for us is this whole third-party validation of our business. You know ultimately each organization has its own strategy, risk processes. To bring in an NGO to determine whether a transaction is appropriate or not doesn't take into account what our strategy is, doesn't take into account the business rationale. So it is really difficult to say: "well, you can eavesdrop on our decision-making process." Because there is a lot more that goes on behind that.

MVP: I do understand that NGOs, like in BTC, are involved. Is that so?

AA: Yes, and they continue to be. On a lot of projects you have local-interest NGOs and community groups who are involved in the monitoring, hired by the client, ultimately. Well, I mean, in BTC it is certainly part of the monitoring, which we would expect on a going-forward basis. I expect that any project sponsor where there are complex issues that need to be managed, that they would involve the local communities. Whether it is through employment, whether it is through monitoring capabilities, and whatever it may be. Even in nonproject financing, we looked at Indonesia recently, we insisted that the client have special development programs in plants, and they have involved, I think, something like fourteen local NGOs on this oil refining to make sure that a lot of these issues are covered.

MVP: My God, and do they disagree?

AA: They do, they have different interests. But the interesting thing here is, you take a look at BTC pipeline and you have the majority of the local NGOs who are supporting the project. They see on the first hand the development opportunities. And you have a lot of the international NGOs that have an issue with the project. I know one international NGO in particular who has been invited to monitor and to become involved, and they haven't done anything. In fact, the local NGOs in Georgia have accused them of sitting there for thirteen years, talking, talking, talking, and not delivering anything. So you have got a situation there where it is all very well for you to have a voice and to say something, but ultimately if you're that concerned about making sure that a project like BTC is appropriately managed and operated, then put your money where your mouth is. Get down and get your hands dirty. And not all the NGOs are willing to do that.

MVP: Civil society is increasingly demanding accountability mechanisms being introduced in the private sector, including the financial sector. What is your answer to that?

HM: Public and private sectors even more today need to earn "trust" from their stakeholders, including civil society, how they use the funds, capital, made available to them. Because of their prominence, multinational corporations have a special duty to apply their own, high voluntary standards in their areas of influence. It is part of their accountability as well as in their interest that independent "verification" occurs from time to time. Such "verification" must be professional and also multifaceted – i.e., not limited to compliance only, but also include a broader social, economic, environmental impact analysis.

SHAWN MILLER, CITIGROUP

The accountability mechanism should be at the project level.

I have known Shawn Miller since the time we both worked in Washington, DC. I talked to him on the phone. He was in New York, where we works for Citigroup. I was at my desk in Amsterdam.

He recalled the annual meeting of the World Bank and the International Monetary Fund that was held in Prague. At the time, he was with the International Finance Corporation. Mr Miller and I and some of our colleagues met outside the meeting venue. We were surrounded by the riot police trying to protect the conference area where the meeting took place. On the other side of the fences were thousands of demonstrators, mostly youngsters. On their banners were texts such as "The world is not for sale" and "The World Bank and IMF destroy our future." In a sense they were just asking for a better world. Nothing was wrong with that. Among them, some extremists made it difficult and at moments dangerous. One rock from the street flew over our heads and hit another delegate behind us.

MVP: Weren't you there when we were making pictures on that bridge when we were in Prague for the annual meeting of the World Bank and IMF?

SM: Yes, I was IFC's NGO liaison for a couple of years. And then, well I started at IFC back in late 1995, and just left them last July. So I was there about nine years. After the NGO work I went back to the environment department and did project due diligence from the social aspects. I worked on Bujagali, and then the past two and a half years I was working on the BTC [Baku-Tbilisi-Ceyhan] pipeline and other projects in the extractives sector. So I certainly was exposed to NGOs, the Inspection Panel, accountability mechanisms, and those types of issues.

MVP: So you are now at an Equator bank. These banks and IFC are meeting together once in a while. I hear about it, I never have been in. Last week there was one in Switzerland.

SM: Yes, I am Citigroup's environmental and social risk management director. I was in Zurich for the NGO meeting with the Equator banks. We had a full set of meetings with the NGOs, BankTrack, and others. I think it went pretty well. IFC was not in attendance.

We felt that this was an opportunity to have direct dialogue with NGOs, and it went well. Obviously, we talked about the draft IFC performance standards and things like that. I know NGOs have raised the issue of accountability mechanisms in a previous meeting, which I did not participate in. But it really wasn't raised in this meeting. I think that most Equator banks would have a very tough time with that concept right now just because it is so new.

MVP: Exactly, well that is what I found talking to some of them. I was in the headquarters of one Equator bank last week, and they still have to train their people. They don't even understand, in my feeling, what they've signed. I am surprised about it and the consequences are absolutely not considered enough yet.

SM: I think that was one of the frustrations that the NGOs expressed, was that there is a very large degree of ... Well, most banks have obviously different approaches to environmental and social risk management. All of the Equator banks noted to the NGOs something to the effect: "Look we work for different institutions, we are competitors, and we approach things from our own institutional perspectives and priorities. However, we do coordinate generally on certain things, but we can't have a unified position on everything.

MVP: Why did Citigroup join the Equator Principles? Did they have already something that went in that direction before?

SM: You mean why did we join the Equator Principles? Yes, Citigroup did have certain environmental initiatives prior to adopting the Equator Principles. There was an Environmental Affairs unit for a number of years. But there was not a specific environmental and social risk management structure or approach in the corporate and investment bank. Pamela Flaherty, who is a senior vice president on environmental issues and global community relations, leads the Environmental Affairs unit. She reports to the CEO and sits right next to Bob Rubin and has very senior access. Pam has directed these issues for a number of years for Citigroup, but earlier it was more of a reactive approach. Pam and Chris Beale were very involved in helping advance the Equator Principles. Citigroup, ABN-AMRO, and other banks realized that there needed to be a better standard, or "framework," for all of the competitors to work from. So essentially the original four approached IFC and said, "We want to understand what is your process, what is your approach, policies and all of that," and then it just kind of evolved from there.

MvP: At what level was this decision in the bank taken to join the principles? Was it in the Board of Executives or in the Supervisory Board?

SM: The CEO, back then, two years ago it was Sandy Weill. Now it is Chuck Prince. But it has support from the top, from the CEO level.

MvP: Yes, but not as far as the supervisory Board?

SM: There is a committee on the board called the Public Affairs Committee, and certain board members are on that, and I do believe that they discussed that with that committee. We also have an Environmental and Social Policy Review Committee that includes a number of senior management representatives.

MvP: Who is then responsible since then? Is it you?

SM: There is shared responsibility for implementation. I am the director of environmental and social risk management, so I am in charge of Equator Principles implementation, training, etc., on a global basis. I am also in charge of looking at specific project deals that come through our Project Finance unit. So, yes, I am leading in the investment bank the environmental and social risk management policy and the Equator Principles. But then we have people like Pamela Flaherty that leads us at the corporate level. She engages with the NGOs, all of that. But yes, it is a shared responsibility.

MvP: Since you have the experience of both working for a MFI and working for a private bank, can you say something about the distinction between MFIs and private banks, concerning the accountability mechanisms?

SM: Yes, I feel very strongly that the institutions, which are commercial banks, are very, very different from International Financial Institutions like IFC or EBRD. I think the inspection mechanisms that have been set up in those institutions are very, very appropriate. I think that I could argue as to the effectiveness of the Inspection Panel versus maybe another form that is more solution-oriented, such as the IFC CAO [compliance advisor ombudsman]. But I think that having accountability mechanisms is fully appropriate for those public institutions because obviously they are taxpayer-supported.

MvP: That's an issue, the taxpayer-supported. That is why it is different?

SM: Oh, I wouldn't say that's the sole reason, but obviously IFIs also have a development mandate. If taxpayers are supporting these IFIs, public monies are being used. Then there should be a greater level of transparency and a greater level of accountability.

MvP: But in your case, in the private bank, it is customers ...

SM: So, for private banks, the key stakeholders are shareholders, employees, and customers. Right? We do not receive subsidies or money from the taxpayers. So first and foremost you know we need to look at customers, employees, and shareholders and really look at their interests. That doesn't mean that we are not concerned with people on the ground that are being affected by our financing, absolutely not. I feel very strongly that if our money is being used for a project on the ground, there needs to be a certain degree of standards and compliance that are being met for those projects. And I think that that's why the Equator Principles are there: because there are certain standards that need to be applied. In terms of, say, an inspection mechanism, I feel strongly that that's not appropriate for a commercial entity or a bank.

MVP: What would you organize for it then?

SM: So the accountability mechanism – or grievance mechanism – should be at the project level, so local people have access to a grievance process. The project sponsors are the ones on the ground and are applying the IFC policies or applying the Equator Principles to their projects. For category A projects, we ensure that the project sponsor is meeting and reporting to lenders on their compliance with the environmental management plan.

MVP: But if they don't, what do you do?

SM: Well, if they don't, then we've got certain legal remedies that we could invoke, up to calling a loan default. Now, I would be honest and say that that is probably a rare case. There are certain things like "Cure Periods," and if there were a real problem on the ground we would try to work with the client to come to ensure that they are coming into compliance and finding a solution.

MVP: Do you need something else, a sort of moderator or whatever names you give it?

SM: I think if you are reading the Equator Principles closely it does say that if a client is not meeting its obligations under Equator and under what essentially is in the environmental management plan, then each financial institution will undertake a process to bring the client back into compliance. So there would be a discussion and probably even a negotiation to say, "Look, this issue is not being properly managed. You are not complying with it, and you have, whatever, three or four, five, six months to come back into compliance." Now, if the client is not willing to come back into compliance and not willing to engage appropriately, then we could say, "Sorry, you're not complying with the environmental management plan, you are not complying with the covenants that are outlined in the long documentation, so we can call a default on the loan." So that is really the final remedy. So if there was a syndicate of banks, if that was happening, I am sure that the syndicate would be working in concert with one another rather than just tell one bank to talk to the project sponsor and ensure they are coming back into compliance.

MvP: That is almost the same wording as I heard from one of your colleagues, one of the other Equator banks. And mostly the big projects are always in a syndicate. A syndicate seems more or less the practice in big projects.

SM: Yes, I would say in every category. You probably have other syndicate members and at least one other major bank that is probably a signatory to Equator, and they would be looking at these issues the same as Citigroup would be.

MvP: A statement has been made by a former member of the Inspection Panel saying that the work done by those panels is a job of specialists. How do you see that?

SM: I am not quite sure if you have to have a professional ombudsperson or professional inspection person to undertake some of this work. I think that the advantage that the Inspection Panel has had is that you have had people with very diverse and different backgrounds involved in the process. I think that the key to these kinds of processes is to have people that have a very good knowledge and experience on the ground working either with communities, environmental management, in development, and understand development. It's key to have professionals who have some technical capacity in environment and sustainable development. I think that people can be trained in ombudsman-type roles. But the key is to really understand development and to understand how these projects are going to affect communities.

MvP: But if you make it a profession, it might be very technical people, and you're losing the idea behind it when it was set up.

SM: I see what you are saying.

MvP: The IFC projects coming in front of the panel have not always been easy. The panel was of the opinion that IFC should be part of the mandate of the panel.

SM: That's a debatable thing. But from IFC's perspective, I think that they feel very strongly that the Inspection Panel doesn't have jurisdiction over IFC projects, unless it is a joint project ...

MvP: Or a guarantee ...

SM: Exactly, say like Chad-Cameroon or Bujagali, they were joint projects and they were being financed both by the bank and IFC, and therefore the Inspection Panel could be involved. But I think that one of the problems when I talked to World Bank colleagues and also IFC officials: IFC has a very private-sector orientation, and business confidentiality is a really key thing.

MVP: But the Panel Members are under the same rules as any other manager of the World Bank, when it comes to confidentiality of proprietary information.

SM: Let me mention the policing mentality. I think part of the problem from my viewpoint is that the way the Inspection Panel was set up is very fault-finding. They can seize e-mail records and computers, and just the way the Inspection Panel has been set up caused concern for me. From my perspective, I feel that if there was less of a policing role, and much more of a problem-solving orientation, that that would have a greater impact on the borrower. I think that millions of dollars are spent on some of these investigations, and what is the real impact on the ground? So you have the Inspection Panel, then you have management and staff that are trying to implement recommendations, and there seems to be a huge disconnect. So in my perspective, I think that the Inspection Panel in some ways is trying to be a link to communities, but in other ways it may have an only limited role of influence.

MVP: Don't you think that it stems from the legalistic approach that was there from the beginning on?

SM: Yes, I do. Yes. They are very procedural-oriented.

MVP: I wonder if this is an effect that stems from the American legal system/ culture? Is it not different from the European style, or the Roman law, which is more principle-driven, while the American system is more rule-driven?

SM: I am not a lawyer, so I can't really comment, but that is a good point. I think that when [Ibrahim] Shihata was helping to set this up, he and the bank obviously wanted to ensure that there was a very defined procedure, and I think he had certainly a large influence on that. You were in the Inspection Panel, so you probably have a better idea on that.

MVP: Well, I think that my questions may make clear where I am coming from.

SM: Right, I can understand that.

MVP: Okay, can we go back to your own bank, Citigroup. What kind of training has been given in the Citigroup Bank?

SM: I just arrived here last July, so I have been here six or seven months. First of all, before I arrived Citigroup had a very significant risk-skills training program. This is not environmental or social risk but essential risk skills, medium risk skills. And in those risk training programs, which are a week long, there was already a two- or three-hour module for environmental-risk training. So this has been incorporated actually using a lot of the training that IFC had done for financial intermediaries. I think one person from

Citibank had attended that and kind of incorporated it into Citigroup's broader risk-skills training. So when I came on board last July, one of the key things I had to focus on as part of my job responsibility was to develop separate environmental and social risk-management training for our Corporate and Investment Bank. The focus was largely on the Equator Principles. So I included people obviously from our Project Finance unit, individuals from our unit that deals with official agencies like IFC and export credit agencies; it included risk officers who look at these transactions from a risk perspective, it included a couple of people from legal, a few public affairs officers, and key industry sector representatives. So I tried to get a broad swath of individuals from across our Corporate and Investment Bank.

MVP: How many people work for Citigroup?

SM: I think 270,000. So, anyway, that was a day-long training. And I hired Glen Armstrong of Sustainable Finance Ltd to help me devise and implement this training program. You probably know Glen. He and I devised a one-day training course for Corporate and Investment Bank employees. Glen and I presented the training jointly: he did half a day and I did half ...

MVP: If you spread it, or I would say those officials in the bank that have to deal with the big projects, the financing of that. You might have to train thousands of people.

SM: Yes, this has been the problem. Those first two we called pilot training programs. But I first of all had to focus on the project finance people who were implementing Equator and applying Equator. Obviously, I can't get thousands of people in these training programs, so I am looking at doing some web-based applications, maybe just doing a one- or two-hour type open training in an auditorium, etc.

MVP: It is rather impressive what is happening. Thank you very much for your insights.

SUELLEN LAZARUS, SENIOR ADVISOR TO THE VICE PRESIDENT OF OPERATIONS AT THE INTERNATIONAL FINANCE CORPORATION

While we are not officially part of the Equator Principles, we have a real stake in it: we are tied to its success.

On 4 May 2004, I met Suellen Lazarus in her IFC office in Washington, DC. We discussed the role of the IFC during the creation of the Equator Principles.

MVP: Who took the initiative to create the Equator Principles, or what was the cause to create them?

SL: It really has been Herman Mulder of the ABN-AMRO Bank coming to Peter Woicke. We just had finished the Chad-Cameroon pipeline. Mulder was very impressed with the kind of work IFC did on Chad-Cameroon, to make sure that local people share with benefits of the project. He said, "That is the kind of thing we could never do in our balance sheet – there is a lot of environmental risk, but we do not have adequate policies for managing it. When I ask questions about environmental issues to staff, I do not get the right answers. But if I indicate we should not proceed with projects because of environmental risk, staff note that our clients will just go to the bank next door and ABN-AMRO will lose the client and the project. So developing environmental policies is not something we can do alone. We need IFC to play a convening role. So would you do something?"

Some months later we organized a meeting in London at the ABN-AMRO headquarters with nine international banks that we invited; Herman and Peter both chaired it. We had a series of banks make presentations that day. ABN-AMRO about Chad-Cameroon, and other banks talked about what they have done well and where they have problems on environmental issues. And it was from that, in the course of the day, the banks started sharing their problems when approaching environmental issues, which was an amazing thing for banks to be candid about. They moved very quickly to agreeing that they needed to manage these issues better. And basically, there was consensus that a few of them should go away and come back with a plan.

MVP: What are the expectations of IFC? Will it be a crucial change of working with clients compared to the "era without the Equator Principles"?

SL: We lend $6 billion a year. It is not all project finance; we invest equity and make corporate loans as well. But let us assume we do $3.5 billion in project finance each year. The project-finance market globally is about $60 billion. We are doing 2 to 3 per cent of the project-finance market. In the past we could ensure that what we were doing for our own account was done responsibly from an environmental and social point of view. Suddenly, with the Equator Principles we are reaching 80 per cent of the project finance market from the perspective of facilitating these projects to be done in a very good environmental and social way. So to suddenly leverage ourselves, it brought a tremendous reconfirmation of our principles, our policies and procedures. It is the first real independent confirmation. To have others say, "This is the standard that has proven to be the best over time." At the same time it put the spotlight on us and put scrutiny on us in a way that we had not experienced before.

It poses questions: Could we do better? Are the policies and procedures clear enough? Are the banks doing it properly? And if they don't, how does that reflect on us? So even while we are not officially part of the Equator Principles (it is the banks who have done the Equator Principles), we have a real stake in it: we are tied to its success. Our reputation is tied to it.

MvP: Did IFC communicate with management of IDA and IBRD and the board of the World Bank during the preparations of the whole operation? If so, what was their position or advice? Did the board approve?

SL: When the Equator Principles were being drafted, we did let the World Bank staff in the environment department know what was going on. We invited them to the launching of the principles in June. One of the things we wanted to make sure was that there was no liability to IFC or to the World Bank for using our policies and procedures, and we asked that language to this effect be included in the principles.

We informed the board of the World Bank and IFC, since it was not a matter of approval for the board, but we were sure that they would be interested in it. Neither IFC nor the World Bank is a party to the Equator Principles. Our policies and procedures are in the public domain and others can use them. Nonetheless, we wanted to make sure there was no liability to IFC or the World Bank. It had to be clear that we could not be responsible for a project when we were not lending to it. We worked with the legal departments of both IFC and the World Bank to develop language to incorporate in the principles.

We did not want any bank to use our name in a way that we would potentially take on responsibility or reputation damage. Each Equator bank has sole responsibility for implementation.

MvP: You wrote an article under the heading "The Equator Principles: A Milestone or Just Good PR." You explain that during the preparation phase of the principles, client consultations and meetings with the NGO community were held in the US and Europe. What took place?

SL: We didn't organize these NGO meetings; it was several of the banks that did this. Citigroup played the key role in talking to NGOs in the US, and ABN-AMRO had meetings with NGOs in Europe in the spring of 2003. IFC and the banks met for the first time to discuss a unified approach to environmental issues in October 2002. The NGOs had developed the Collevecchio Declaration in January 2003.[22] The NGOs wanted the banks to adopt Collevecchio, but the banks were not aware of Collevecchio until after the Equator Principles were unveiled. At the time Collevecchio was developed, the banks were already developing their own principles. The NGOs were very surprised by it, and it knocked them off their seats. Here were banks ready to adopt these principles and no one was making them do it.

MvP: What exactly is it that the EP banks have adopted? Will they operate under the same conditions and structure as IFC itself? If not, what are the differences?

SL: It is up to each bank to develop an implementation plan for application of the Equator Principles within the bank. There are probably as many different implementation plans as there are banks. I think what distinguishes the banks from what IFC is doing is that the banks are all placing responsibility for Equator directly into their business line. So if I am a banker who is doing a project-finance deal, and my job is to do the due diligence on a project and take it to the credit committee to get approval, my job is also to look and determine if the project is Equator Principles compliant. So part of my due diligence, in addition to looking at the economics, the market, the margin, the financial return, is also to confirm Equator compliance.

The IFC model is that the investment department officer who is responsible for the project speaks to the Environment and Social Development Department staff that is responsible for reviewing the social and environmental issues of the project. The experts in this department categorize the project, determine what the issues are, talk to the sponsor, negotiate changes if needed, and then they approve. IFC is moving away from that model. We are now mainstreaming environmental and social responsibilities. So the investment officer will become responsible for environmental and social issues, using the environmental and social specialists as expert resources. The EP banks have gone to that model directly. So a banker is responsible for the Equator Principles from the beginning. His/her job in the credit committee is to stand up and say, "I promise that this project complies with the Equator Principles."

MVP: Where does he or she get the expertise necessary, like on biodiversity, to make a judgment on compliance?

SL: Just like in IFC, the officer running a project-finance deal is probably an MBA or maybe a lawyer, and he/she has to find the expertise. It could be within the bank, but few banks have the resources of IFC and the World Bank. So if it is a complicated issue, the bank will have to hire consultants to advise them. The sponsor will pay for it. It is a challenge for the banks to get good expertise; making sure that experts know what they are talking about; making sure the right questions are being asked. The banks, I believe will find that with the more difficult projects, the category A projects, and what we call "big" category B, they will need help. They may not need IFC, but they might want a partner, an institution that has capacity. And especially in social impact issues, if there is, for example, resettlement and if there are indigenous peoples, they need continuing expertise. The banks know that with projects such as the Chad-Cameroon pipeline or the BTC [Baku-Tbilisi-Ceyhan] project,[23] they needed IFC.

MVP: How will IFC monitor the developments? Did IFC anticipate on possible consequences for IFC, if the EP banks do not fulfil what they have agreed to do?

SL: It is not our job to monitor them. But we do have several roles related to Equator. One is to encourage more banks to adopt the Equator Principles. Another is to provide training so the banks get trained in our environmental and social policies and procedures. We are offering a couple of training models. We charge for them. At this point we have trained over 365 bankers. The next thing we are doing is developing a toolkit, which is an online program that helps identify project environmental and social risks. Finally, we give implementation support. It is our way of making sure that the banks get what they need when questions come up. We do it in two ways. We have workshops on topics that the banks need help with. It is clear that the social issues were very confusing to the banks, more than the environmental issues. We had a workshop on social issues and one on environmental loan covenants. All of this is generic. We are not talking project specific. When they call with specific questions, we try to help them understand the policies and procedures while avoiding issues of judgment.

What is nice about Equator, it created an informal network. And don't forget, these are competitors who are now working together on these important issues.

MVP: Are sanctions foreseen if one of the group does not follow the principles. And if so, what could that be? Exclusion?

SL: I do not know. Actually, that is a question you have to ask the banks. What they do is really with one another. When they are together they ask each other, "what are you doing to implement?" So if one is not implementing, the others put pressure on them to do so.

MVP: Did the EP banks and IFC together constitute a relation with a self-governing body and rules? If so, what structure and what internal rules have been chosen? What different options were on the table?

SL: Indeed, the group of Equator banks is rapidly growing bigger. Nevertheless, the banks wanted these principles to be independently and voluntary adopted by each bank. So they are making a commitment themselves. They are not making a commitment with or to the other banks. They are very careful not to create formal structures. It is an informal network. Four key banks, ABN-AMRO, Citigroup, Barclays, and WestLB, at the first meeting formed a sort of informal secretariat. Citigroup now maintains the website. The four banks do not make decisions on behalf of the others, but instead it is almost like a coordinating committee.

MVP: So a governing structure comes into being?

SL: Recently, eleven banks wrote a letter to Mr Wolfensohn[24] about the Extractive Industries Review. They each had to agree to the letter. But in order to organize anything, you cannot have twenty people doing it, somebody has to do it.

MVP: What about the other banks that did not sign the letter?

SL: Some of them don't work in extractive industries, Rabobank, for instance. Others did not want to go through the internal clearances to get such a letter signed. It varied. I do not think any bank disagreed with the content of the letter. BankTrack[25] has just written a letter to the banks, one letter to those that signed and one to those that didn't sign.

MVP: What could be the position of the shareholders in the adoption and working of the Equator Principles?

SL: The shareholders probably play some role for some of the banks in the adoption. Some of the banks have shareholder activism on environmental and social issues. I know that in some of those banks, shareholder resolutions and shareholder meetings on these issues were coming up. The Equator Principles were an important part of the response. The only thing some shareholders might argue about on the other side is that the job of management is to maximize shareholder value. It might be argued that the Equator Principles do not maximize shareholder value because you are spending time on environmental and social issues. But this is an outdated point of view. Much of the financial world has recognized that environmental and social issues are risks. The principles are a way of managing risks. So assuming you have corporate social responsibility, and if you are reducing risks, you are improving the business profit.

MVP: And then? Should it be clarified for the shareholders?

SL: It is finally up to the banks to determine how they report about the principles, because there is no monitoring agency. Nevertheless, you should expect the banks to do something transparently about implementing Equator, either in the annual report or in their sustainability report. Information about how many projects were category A and B, and if they were not in compliance.

MVP: In paragraph 9 of the Statement of Principles[26] is stated, "The adopting institutions view these principles as a framework for developing individual, internal practices and policies. As with all internal policies, these principles do not create any rights in, or liability to, any person, public or private. Banks are adopting and implementing these principles voluntary and independently, without reliance on or recourse to IFC or the World Bank." So the banks consider their act nonbinding to anything or anyone. Question is how did IFC or the legal department of the bank judge on this?

SL: We asked the EP banks to incorporate language to ensure that there was no liability to IFC or the World Bank simply because they were using our policies. So the language you mention was our addition. The banks understood and agreed. The concern in the World Bank was by adopting the Equator Principles, are we taking on liability? Will somebody have legal recourse? There are two aspects of this. If the EP are not applied properly, we can have reputation damage. But that is not a legal risk. Some were worried concerning legal risk. The conclusion was that the legal risks probably decrease with the introduction of Equator. In the past, banks often said that they were using IFC/World Bank environmental policies and procedures. But if someone had asked them what those policies were, what steps they have gone through, they could not say, because no formal procedures were in place and they did not verify that these policies and procedures were being followed by borrowers. They could not show that they had done anything about it. Despite saying that they were doing something, they had no accountability for that. With Equator Principles, now they are going through a process and are clear about what that process is. The conclusion was it reduced liability for IFC/WB.

MVP: A highly esteemed Dutch lawyer, Prof. Dr Bob Wessels, who I informed about the Equator Principles and who then studied the website of the principles, wrote to me in an e-mail:

> The Equator Principles are new to me. It is a fascinating form of self-restriction, although further study might bring me to another indication of the nature of those principles. Again, fascinating for a lawyer, since the principles on the one hand seem to have a flexible content with a relatively weak status, a sort of 'soft law,' while on the other the commitment of a bank to those principles, in my opinion, legally has to be placed in the continuation/prolongation of the statutory objectives. Given the Dutch law, which will be not different from the UK or US law, one cannot act against those statutory objectives.[27]

The reaction of Mr Wessels could be crucial concerning the possible enforcement of the principles. If he is right with his first reaction, the principles then could have tremendous implications on the activities of EP banks and the rights of people that oppose the activities and actions financed by the banks.

SL: The borrower/project sponsor is responsible for project implementation, for meeting local and international standards. The Equator banks are lenders and often one lender among many. If someone wants to legally pursue them for an environmental breach, they can try. However, whether there are Equator Principles or not, pursuing a lender for environmental liability can happen. The banks have concluded that having the Equator Principles with processes and procedures puts them in a stronger place rather than a weaker position.

MVP: The EP Banks in the abovementioned paragraph 9 of the Statement of Principles state that they "do not create any rights in, or liability to, any person, public or private" and moreover that these principles are adopted and implemented voluntary and independently "without reliance on or recourse to IFC or the World Bank." In this light it is all the more remarkable that the banks on the basis of the same adopted principles think they have a say when it comes to World Bank policies and actions.

On 14 April of 2004, eleven of the EP banks[28] wrote to President
Wolfensohn referring to the release of the Extractive Industries Review
(EIR). The review, written by an international group of independent
experts composed by the World Bank, recommended the World Bank to
withdraw from investment in the extractive industries from the year 2008.

The eleven EP banks in return expressed to President Wolfensohn their
concern and drew his attention to the dangers of a withdrawal. Not only
that, they also sought the attention of Wolfensohn for the special relation
they have with the World Bank by saying:

> We consider ourselves to be important stakeholders of the World Bank
> Group (WBG) by virtue of our adoption of the WBG Safeguard Polices
> and Sector Guidelines through the Equator Principles, and through our
> role as co-financiers with the WBG of projects in the extractive industries
> and other sectors. The Banks which have adopted the Equator Principles
> collectively arranged $54 billion of project financing last year, and have
> become the largest stakeholder group which applies the Safeguard
> Policies and Sector Guidelines. They include Banks which are providers
> of financial services to some of the world's leading extractive industry
> companies and to public sector clients in the emerging markets, and
> which are firmly committed to continuing to be value-adding service
> providers to these clients ... We feel it necessary to draw your attention
> to the dangers of a withdrawal by the WBG from the financing of
> extractive industries.[29]

The above referenced letter of the eleven EP banks raises questions concerning the influence of the EP banks on the future of the World Bank policies. Isn't this just the other way around from what the principles were
supposed to do, namely to influence and urge the private sector to follow
the World Bank policies? This action is showing the opposite. The private
banks now urge the bank to take a step in line with the policies and actions
of the private banks.

SL: Yes, they have the right to try to influence the World Bank/IFC policies.
They have as much right as the NGOs or other key stakeholders. These
banks have to work with and live with these policies. Why shouldn't they
have the right? It is up to us to determine how much priority we give to
them. One of the NGOs said it was outrageous that the Equator banks are
lobbying us. Why is that outrageous? Isn't there freedom of speech?
Those banks are using the policies, and they need to know what it means
for their business.

Frankly, I do not think that the EP banks are inconsistent with the views
that IFC holds. They will not try to bring down our policies. Besides, IFC
has a leadership role. We want others to follow us. So it is not in our interest to downgrade the policies. We will consult with the EP banks just as we

consult with the NGOs and others. At the end of the day we will make our decision in a way we think that is best for us as a leader in the multilateral development world.

MVP: According to yourself in the abovementioned article, some banks who were involved in the preparation phase dropped out. To me it seems important to understand which banks dropped out of the process during or after the February 2003 meeting in London and before the principles were adopted in June that year. For what reasons?

SL: I will not tell you which banks dropped out. It is clear who the leading banks are in project finance. The Netherlands is almost covered, meaning most banks take part. Only FMO[30] does not take part yet. There are several reasons for banks not to take part. Some banks have other issues to deal with. Internally, there are too many other issues to focus on. Some banks say project finance is a small area in their business. If we do this for project finance, we have to do it for the rest of the bank. Others said, "wait a minute we are not ready for this yet." With some of the smaller banks, they did not want the scrutiny of the NGOs. They said, "we do our business the right way but we do not want to be on their list."

MVP: Did the different cultures in doing business, a European style and an American style play a role in the decision for some banks to drop out? Is the information correct that so far no Chinese or Arabic bank is interested in adopting the principles? And if so, is this a matter of cultural difference?

SL: Right now the principles are adopted in the Part I countries.[31] For the most part, that is where the major project finance is done. If a Chinese bank does not do project finance, there is no reason to adopt the principles. Nevertheless, there are some local banks that do project finance. And we would like to see them adopting it.

MVP: What about strong Arabic banks?

SL: They are government owned. Adopting the principles implies that they do not have good environmental and social policies. For them, that is a bit peculiar. So far there is no Brazilian,[32] Turkish, Indian or Chinese bank yet. One developing country bank is almost ready to come in.[33]

MVP: Could export credit agencies, of whom some have adopted strong social and environmental policies of their own and created an independent compliance mechanism, become a member of the group of EP banks? What relation does IFC have with the different export credit agencies (ECAs) since in a press release of the Equator Principles Secretariat is mentioned that those agencies have developed their own standards?[34]

SL: The export credit agencies adopted the "common approach" of the OECD. They can pick any principle – from IFC, EBRD, their home country, any standard. You do not know which one they will choose. It is a bit confusing and complicated. If you are a borrower getting financing from, for example, Citigroup and an ECA in a project, you have to work with the Equator Principles and whatever other standard the ECA utilizes. So far only the American Exim[35] has announced they will work with the Equator Principles if they deal with EP banks.

MVP: I was informed that some "non-Equator banks" are starting to announce to their clients that they are no part of the principles. As far as the information given to me is correct, those banks use the fact they do not take part as a marketing tool. Do you know of these developments?

SL: I also heard about this. Some EP banks worry about that. When talking to a client about the obligations related to Equator, another non-Equator bank may step into the deal. Generally, now the size of the group is strong enough. Most deals in the project-finance market are syndicated; four or five banks are involved. If you are the lead bank, putting together a syndicate and selling the deal to the bank market, you have to make it Equator compliant for maximum syndication success.

When we had a workshop on implementation in December 2003 in Amsterdam, one of the banks posed the question: Here is the scenario. You are one of ten banks in the deal with a total financing of $500 million. You are not the lead. You are taking a small participation of say $5 million. If the deal is not Equator compliant, what do you do? You have no influence. You will be not in the deal, all the Equator banks agree.

Relations between the IFC and the Secretariat of the Equator Banks

MVP: The EP banks have their own secretariat in the headquarters of Citigroup in New York. What is the working relation between IFC and this secretariat?

SL: It is not a formalized relationship. We coordinate and have regular contact. Citigroup manages the website and the process that a new bank goes through when announcing that they are adopting Equator. We alert each other when we learn that another bank is getting ready to adopt Equator.

MVP: Why was this secretariat established at the Citigroup and not in one of the other banks in Europe since the majority of the banks headquarters at the time was, and probably still is, in Europe? Why not, for example, in Amsterdam with the ABN-AMRO, one of the first banks together with IFC?

SL: The secretariat will rotate, I am sure. Citigroup had the capacity to get it up and running quickly when Equator was announced, so it was pragmatic to stick with them, but I am sure it will rotate to other banks over time ...

MVP: Are there any minutes made of the historical events, as one can see the different meetings: October 2002 hosted by IFC and ABN-AMRO in

London, February 2003 in London, May 2003 Düsseldorf, June 4 2003 Washington, December 2003 Amsterdam, May 2004 Rome?

SL: No, there are not minutes. Chatham House rules are used. Nothing is for attribution but the banks often post an announcement on their website following a meeting (www.equator-principles.com).

Internal Procedures and Consequences for the Equator Banks

MVP: Given the founding-father role of IFC in the creation of the principles, one can assume IFC has an opinion on how the banks should implement and live up to those principles. IFC personnel are involved in training sessions for staff of the EP banks. The question is what opinion IFC has concerning the structure those banks should have to implement the principles in the daily operations of the banks?

SL: It is up to the banks how internally to implement. We are not proposing. We, IFC, are not an adopting bank. We suggest, we encourage, we exchange views.

MVP: In your article you state that the principles in some banks were adopted and approved by senior management and in others by the Board of Directors. Given the state of the art of the principles or the expectations that run high, one expects that adopting of those principles is a matter of the Board of Directors of a bank.

SL: The most common model is that it is approved by the credit committee within a bank via a process with the finance staff. It depends on how the banks organize themselves.

MVP: So who in those banks should be responsible for the implementation of the principles? Is it the board, the legal department, management involved in environmental and social assessments and risk assessment, or others?

SL: In the first instance, implementation is the responsibility of the banker who is managing the project. Oversight for implementation is generally with the credit committees in a bank. There also may be a sustainability department that has some responsibility.

MVP: The NGO world is asking the EP banks to create like the World Bank and other development banks independent compliance mechanisms to assure that the principles are followed by the banks. What is the position of IFC in this?[36]

SL: Oversight by an independent compliance mechanism for the Equator Principles is unlikely to happen. The banks are not going to turn over oversight to an outside institution. I just don't see them doing it. Who is the right party to supervise them? They should be encouraged to self-report.

The ultimate accountability is with the borrower. We have to make sure they do what they say they will do. It is always a question of what is the responsibility of the financer and what of the borrower?

MVP: Isn't the risk in the gray zone between those two. And can the gray zone also be the excuse for both of them, the financer and the borrower, not having a responsibility?

SL: The project sponsor is on the ground implementing the project. The responsibility for what is done and not done has to ultimately be with them. Bankers can check, they can call defaults, but they cannot make the sponsor do something that they are unwilling to do.

MVP: What in the beginning was it that made the principles only applicable to emerging markets? And what was it that made it applicable to all project finance?

SL: It was in the emerging markets where banks faced problems, so initially the thought was that they would apply only to developing countries. At the meeting in Düsseldorf, one bank said that they do projects worldwide and perhaps there should be some consideration of applying Equator globally. The four coordinating banks talked about it and proposed that Equator is applied as follows:

(1) Categorization and OP [operational policy] 4.01: for all projects globally
(2) Industry standards: for all projects globally
(3) Safeguard policies to projects in developing countries (as defined by WB) only

MVP: In this regard also, why is there a limit of the use of the principles to projects of $50 million and above. What about smaller projects? What or who draw that line?

SL: Some banks wanted a $100 million limit and others wanted a $25 million. They agreed on $50 million.[37] The formal rule is $50 million, but a bank is free to apply Equator to smaller projects if they wish, and many are doing so.

Experts Who Contributed to the Study

The following experts contributed to this study. Their input was given in private and cannot be understood as any formal contribution from the institutions for which they work.

In alphabetical order:

DR SUSAN AARONSON: Senior fellow and director of Globalization Studies, Washington Center, Washington, DC; Kenan Institute of Private Enterprise; Kenan-Flagler Business School; University of North Carolina at Chapel Hill. United States.

ANDRÉ ABADIE: Head of Sustainable Business Advisory, Group Risk Management, ABN-AMRO Bank; involved in Equator II. The Netherlands.

EDUARDO ABBOTT: Former principal counsel, Operational Policy, World Bank Legal Department; appointed by the president and executive directors of the bank as the executive secretary of the World Bank Inspection Panel from the outset of its operations until December 2006. United States.

DR A.A. AKIN-OLUGBADE: General counsel of the African Development Bank Group. Tunisia.

PAUL ARLMAN: Executive director, European Investment Bank, 1981–1986; executive director, World Bank, 1986–1990; secretary general, Federation of European Financial Exchanges. The Netherlands.

PROF. EDWARD S. AYENSU: Member of the Inspection Panel from August 1998 to August 2003; acting chairman of the Inspection Panel from January 2002 to August 2003; chairman of the Council for Scientific and Industrial Research (CSIR). Ghana.

MANISH BAPNA: Executive director, Bank Information Center. United States.

RICHARD E. BISSELL: Member, Compliance Review Panel, Asian Development Bank; former chairman, World Bank Inspection Panel. United States.

DR PETER BOSSHARD: Policy director, International Rivers Network. United States.

LAURA CAMPBELL, LLM: Senior counsel, European Bank for Reconstruction and Development (EBRD). United Kingdom.

PETE CARKEEK: *Ethical Corporation* magazine. United Kingdom.

PAUL DE CLERCK: Coordinator, Corporate Campaign, Friends of the Earth International. The Netherlands.

DR TON DE WIT: Senior consultant, Nedworc. The Netherlands.

DR D. DE ZEEUW, IR.: Emeritus professor of environmental policy, Catholic University, Nijmegen; former president, Agricultural University, Wageningen; director of D. de Zeeuw Consultancy BV; former general director, Agricultural Research in the Netherlands; member of International Advisory Group, World Bank. The Netherlands.

DR WIM DUISENBERG: Former president, European Central Bank; former president, Dutch Central Bank; former minister of finance, the Netherlands; passed away in July 2005.

DR GERTRUDE EIGELSREITER-JASHARI: Lecturer, University for Applied Sciences, St Poelten, Austria; head of Association for Development Policy, St Poelten, Austria.

MIRANDA ENGELSHOVEN: Policymaker, Fair Trade (Dutch-based NGO). The Netherlands.

ALLARD G.A. EVERTS, IR.: Senior manager, Trompenaars Hampden-Turner. The Netherlands.

DR RICHARD FUGGLE: Professor of environmental studies, University of Cape Town, South Africa.

MANEESH GOBIN: Senior state counsel, Attorney General's Office, Mauritius.

DR J. GOEDEE: Lecturer in the Faculty of Social and Behavioral Sciences, University of Tilburg; implementation of change (banking) consultant. The Netherlands.

ROBERT GOODLAND, PHD: Served the World Bank Group from 1978 to 2001 as environmental advisor, contributing to many environmental and social policies; chief advisor of the Independent Extractive Industry Review of the World Bank Group's oil, gas, and mining portfolio, 2001–2004. United States.

FATHER TONY HERBERT: Director, Prerana Resource Centre, Hazaribag, India.

DR WILLIAM KENNEDY V: Executive director, Commission for Environmental Cooperation of North America, 2003–2006. Canada.

MANANA KOCHLADZE: CEE Bankwatch Network, regional coordinator for Caucasus; awarded the prestigious Goldman Prize, often referred to as the "Environmental Nobel Prize," on 19 April 2004. Georgia.

FRANS M. KRAGTEN: Director, Multilateral Development Banks and Government Relations, Rabobank International. The Netherlands.

LUIGI LA MARCA: Managerial adviser for European Union policies, Legal Department, European Investment Bank, Luxembourg.

FLORIS LAMBRECHTSEN, MBA: Advisor, KPMG Global Accountability Services. The Netherlands.

INGE LARDINOIS, MSC: Policy advisor, Ministry of Housing, Spatial Planning and the Environment, the Netherlands.

ALLISON C. LAWFORD, LLB, LLM: Corporate secretariat, Export Development Canada/Exportation et développement Canada.

SUELLEN LAZARUS: Senior adviser, ABN-AMRO Bank, Washington, DC, 1994–2005; senior advisor on the Equator Principles to the vice president of operations at the International Finance Corporation. United States.

DR MAC DARROW: Coordinator, OHCHR/UNDP Human Rights Strengthening (HURIST) Program, UN Office of the High Commissioner for Human Rights, Geneva, Switzerland.

JIM MACNEILL, OC: Member of the World Bank Inspection Panel, August 1997 to August 2002; acting chairman of the Inspection Panel, March 1998 to December 2001; director of environment, OECD, 1978–1984; secretary general, World Commission on Environment and Development (Brundtland Commission), 1984–1987, and lead author of its landmark "Our Common Future." Canada.

LEE MARLER: Deputy chief compliance officer, European Bank for Reconstruction and Development (EBRD). United Kingdom.

PROF. KAZUO MATSUSHITA: Examiner for Environmental Guidelines, Japan Bank for International Cooperation (JBIC); professor, Graduate School of Environmental Studies, Kyoto University. Japan.

DR JEAN-ROGER MERCIER: Former lead environmental specialist, Quality Assurance and Compliance Unit, Environmentally and Socially Sustainable Development, World Bank. United States.

SHAWN MILLER: Director, Environmental and Social Risk Management, Citigroup Corporate and Investment Bank; former social development staff member, Environment Department, International Finance Corporation (IFC); involved in Equator II. United States.

HANS MOISON: Director, Ernst and Young Accountants. The Netherlands.

HERMAN MULDER: Senior executive vice president, Group Risk Management, ABN-AMRO Bank. The Netherlands.

SURESH NANWANI: Associate secretary, Compliance Review Panel, Asian Development Bank. Philippines.

ALBERTO NINIO: Lead counsel, Environmentally and Socially Sustainable Development, World Bank; legal vice president, International Law Practice Group, World Bank. United States.

E.R. OUKO: Director, Internal Audit Department, African Development Bank. Tunis.

DR ELLY PLOOIJ-VAN GORSEL: Member of the European Parliament, 1994–2004; tabled written question in 2003 to the European Commission on an accountability mechanism for the European Investment Bank. The Netherlands.

REINIER P.W. PRIJTEN: Managing director, Bear Stearns, New York, United States.

ENERY QUINONES: Chief compliance officer, European Bank for Reconstruction and Development. United Kingdom.

DR FRANS-JOSEF RADERMACHER: FAW Research Institute for Applied Knowledge Processing, Ulm Germany; member of the Club of Rome. Germany.

DR HUSAIN M. SADAR: Adjunct professor, Department of Natural Resource Sciences, Faculty of Agricultural and Environmental Sciences, UNEP-McGill Environmental Impact Assessment Collaboration Center. Canada.

DR BERND SCHANZENBACHER: Office of the Chairman, Global Head Environmental Business Group, Credit Suisse Group. Switzerland.

HUUB SCHEELE, IR.: Programme officer for MFIs at Both ENDS (a Dutch-based NGO). The Netherlands.

RUTGER-JANSCHOEN: Managing director, SPAN Consultants. The Netherlands.

PROF. NICO J. SCHRIJVER: Chair of Public International Law, Leyden University, the Netherlands.

JOHN SHEEHY: Economist, UK Desk, European Commission. Belgium.

DR JOOST SMIERS: Professor of political science, Research Group Arts and Economics, Utrecht School of the Arts, the Netherlands.

EISUKE SUZUKI: Former director general, Operations Evaluations, and former deputy general counsel, Asian Development Bank; architect of the ADB's accountability mechanism. Philippines.

JURRIEN TOONEN, MD, MSC: Staff member, Health System Development, Royal Tropical Institute, the Netherlands.

KAY TREAKLE: Program officer, Environment Department, Reform of International Finance and Trade (grant-making area), Charles Stewart Mott Foundation. United States.

CONNIE VALKHOF: Account manager, Fair Trade (a Dutch-based NGO). The Netherlands.

LEEN VAN DER PLAS, RA: Chief auditor, ING Group Corporate Audit Services. The Netherlands.

IRENA VAN DER SLUIJS, MA: Policy advisor, Corporate Social Responsibility, Dutch Ministry of Economic Affairs. The Netherlands.

JAN PAUL VAN SOEST, IR.: Director, Sustainability Consulting. The Netherlands.

WOUTER VEENING: Director, Institute for Environmental Security, the Hague; deputy chairman, IUCN Commission on Environmental, Economic, and Social Policies. The Netherlands.

JACOB WASLANDER: Senior advisor to the executive director for the Netherlands, World Bank. United States.

DR WIERT P. WIERTSEMA: Senior policy advisor, Both ENDS; Member of the first Inspection Panel, Asian Development Bank, 2001. The Netherlands.

ALBERT WONG: Head of External Relations and Policy, Royal Dutch Shell plc. United Kingdom.

ROLF SELROD ZELIUS: Secretary, Asian Development Bank, Compliance Review Panel. Philippines.

Notes

INTRODUCTION

1 Alvaro Umaña Quesada, *The World Bank Inspection Panel,* vii.
2 The present members of the World Bank Inspection Panel did not fill in the questionnaire. My interpretation of their choice not to do so is that they want to remain neutral. Since they are members of the senior model, they would be the most "vulnerable" if they voiced their reactions. I respect their choice.
3 The Japan Bank for International Cooperation (JBIC) is one of the banks that set up an accountability mechanism (see chapter 4).
4 The Asian Development Bank did start its first inspection panel mechanism in 2001 and revised and adopted a new structure and mandate after its first experience in 2003 (see chapter 4).

CHAPTER ONE

1 W. Gavin Anderson, *Constitutional Rights after Globalization,* 18.
2 Ibid., 19.
3 Nico van den Oudenhoven and Rekha Wazir, *Newly Emerging Needs of Children,* 107.
4 Maartje van Putten, *The Future Has Begun,* television documentary on globalization, 50 min.
5 Michael Renner, *State of the World 2005,* 4.
6 Ibid.
7 Joost Oranje, "Zou de wetgever wel eens vonissen lezen?" (Do legislators ever read the sentences of the court?), interview with Judge Maarten Mastboom, *NRC-Handelsblad* (Rotterdam), 8 April 2006.
8 Renner, *State of the World 2005,* 5.
9 Maartje van Putten and Nicole Lucas, *"Made in Heaven,"* 113.
10 Manuel Castells, *The Information Age,* vol. 1, *The Rise of the Network Society,* 137.
11 Ibid., 102–3.
12 Ibid., 103.

13 Ibid.

14 United Nations Conference on Trade and Development, *World Investment Report 2005*, xix.

15 This is one of the reasons the World Bank adopted the so-called "use of country systems"; see chapter 6.

16 World Bank, *Annual Report 2002*, 50.

17 International Labor Organization (ILO), *A Fair Globalization*, 34.

18 Ibid., vii.

19 Ibid.

20 Ibid.

21 Ibid., 27.

22 Ibid., 119.

23 Thomas L. Friedman, *The Lexus and the Olive Tree*, 257.

24 Ibid.

25 Ibid., 168.

26 Ibid., 169.

27 Ibid.

28 Saskia Sassen, *Globalization and Its Discontents*, 199.

29 Ibid.

30 Ibid.

31 Ibid., 199–200.

32 Ibid., 201.

33 Wolfgang Kleinwächter, "Global Governance in the Information Age," 23.

34 Ibid., 44.

35 Ibid.

36 Ibid., 23.

37 Robert O. Keohane, "Global Governance and Democratic Accountability," 131.

38 ILO, *Fair Globalization*, 87.

39 Sheldon Leader, "Human Rights, Risks, and New Strategies for Global Investment," 658, 702, 703.

40 See http://siteresources.worldbank.org/ESSDNETWORK/Resources.

41 See http://www.worldbank.org; search for WBI, themes, governance, data, governance indicators.

42 Institute of Development Studies (IDS), "Making Accountability Count," 1.

43 Government of Manitoba, "Achieving Accountability," 3.

44 Ibid., 3.

45 Ibid., 4.

46 Ibid.

47 Ibid.

48 Richard Mulgan, "'Accountability,'" 555.

49 Ibid.

50 Ibid., 556.

51 Ibid.

52 Henry E. McCandless, *A Citizen's Guide to Public Accountability*.

53 Ibid., 22–3.

54 Ibid., 4, 5, 6.

55 Ibid., 82.

56 Ibid., 97.

57 Ibid., 130.

58 Jonathan Fox, "Civil Society and Political Accountability," 1.

59 Ibid.

60 Ibid.

61 ILO, *Fair Globalization*, 77.

62 In 2002 the same project was again lodged with the Inspection Panel with new information and facts.

63 Kay Treakle, "Accountability at the World Bank," 3.

64 See also Alvaro Umaña Quesada, *The World Bank Inspection Panel*.

65 See Treakle, "Accountability," 4.

66 Ibid., 2–3.

67 Ibid., 3–4.

68 The two countries signed a treaty establishing Yacyretá in 1973 and together established the Ente Binacional Yaciretá (EBY) as the legal authority to implement the project.

69 The Inspection Panel's difficulties having its mandate understood in its first years are described in chapter 3. The panel's recommendation to the board that the panel should do an investigation was first postponed, and after a lengthy and complicated process, the board mandated the panel not to do "an investigation" but instead to undertake "a review of the existing problems of the project." See Treakle, "Accountability," 62–3.

70 Treakle, "Accountability," 19.

71 See my discussion of McCandless above.

72 Treakle, "Accountability," 20.

73 Ibid.

74 Ibid., 20–4.

75 *The Economist* (London), 1 December 2005, http://www.economist.com/finance?PrinterFriendly.cfm?story_id=5257051.

76 Sylvester C.W. Eijffinger and Petra M. Geraats, "How Transparent Are Central Banks?" 3.

77 Ibid., 12.

78 McCandless, *Citizen's Guide*, 22–3.

79 In an e-mail of 19 April 2006, Professor Sylvester Eijffinger provided the following information on the background of the minutes: "As is standard, it concerns the minutes of the responsible Policy Board. In the case of the Federal Reserve System, it is the Federal Open Market Committee (FOMC), at the European Central Bank (ECB) it is the Governing Council, and at the Bank of England it is the Monetary Policy Committee (MPC)."

80 ILO, *Fair Globalization*, 125.

81 Robert O. Keohane and Joseph S. Nye Jr, "Redefining Accountability for Global Governance," 398.

82 Robert Dahl, quoted in ibid., 386.

83 Ibid., 386.

84 Ibid., 398.

85 Ibid., 399.

86 G8 Information Centre, http://www.g8.utoronto.ca/finance/fm010707.htm.

87 Paragraph 38 has six sections. Only two of these, related to accountability, are quoted.

88 G-8 Finance Ministers and Central Bank Governors, "G8 Finance Ministers' Meetings Strengthening the International Financial System and the Multilateral Development Banks."

89 Olivia McDonald, *Coming into the Light,* http://www.brettonwoodsproject.org.

90 Ibid.

91 Ibid.

92 I personally met only with the chairman of the group, Mr Bert Koenders, a member of the Dutch Parliament.

93 World Bank Inspection Panel, "A Staff Guide to the World Bank Inspection Panel."

94 Virginia Haufler, "Globalization and Industry Self-Regulation," 229.

95 Ibid., 230.

96 See http://www.OECD.org.

97 Unfortunately, I have not been able to study this relatively new complaint mechanism, added in 2000 in the OECD Principles of 1976. See Organization for Economic Cooperaton and Development (OECD), "OECD Principles of Corporate Governance."

98 OECD, "OECD Guidelines for Multinational Enterprises," 9.

99 Ibid., 32.

100 Dutch Ministry of Economic Affairs, internal memorandum, 2005.

101 OECD Watch, "Five Years On: A Review of the OECD Guidelines and National Contact Points."

102 Exxon Valdez Oil Spill Trustee Council, http://www.evostc.state.ak.us.

103 See http://www.CERES.org.

104 Ibid.

105 See http://www.globalreporting.org.

106 See http://www.unglobalcompact.org.

107 See http://www.iso.ch/iso/en/prods-services/otherpubs/iso14000/index.html.

108 See http://www.accountAbility.org.uk.

109 See http://www.sa-inrl.org/SA8000/SA8000.htm.

110 See http://www.cleanclothes.org/codes/ccccode.htm.

111 E-mail from Ken Maguire, 3 January 2006.

112 Ibid.

113 Ibid. Under the Equator Principles II, the bar has be lowered to US$10 million. See appendix 2.

114 E-mail from Ken Maguire, 3 January 2006.

115 "Managing Globalization," editorial, *Washington Post,* 19 February 2006, B06.

CHAPTER TWO

1 Bretton Woods is a resort in New Hampshire, where the IMF and the IBRD were negotiated.
2 International Bank for Reconstruction and Development (IBRD), *A Guide to the World Bank*, 151.
3 Allan Sproul, quoted in Edward S. Mason and Robert E. Asher, *The World Bank since Bretton Woods*, 33–4.
4 Edward Brown, quoted in ibid., 34.
5 Ibid.
6 Jonathan R. Pincus and Jeffrey A. Winters, *Reinventing the World Bank*, 1.
7 Ibid., 2–3.
8 International Bank for Reconstruction and Development (IBRD), "Articles of Agreement," Article I:
  The Purposes of the Bank are:
  (i) To assist in the reconstruction and development of territories of members by facilitating the investment of capital for productive purposes, including the restoration of economies destroyed or disrupted by war, the reconversion of productive facilities to peacetime needs and the encouragement of the development of productive facilities and resources in less developed countries.
  (ii) To promote private foreign investment by means of guarantees or participations in loans and other investments made by private investors; and when private capital is not available on reasonable terms, to supplement private investment by providing, on suitable conditions, finance for productive purposes out of its own capital, funds raised by it and its other resources.
  (iii) To promote the long-range balanced growth of international trade and the maintenance of equilibrium in balances of payments by encouraging international investment for the development of the productive resources of members, thereby assisting in raising productivity, the standard of living and conditions of labor in their territories.
  (iv) To arrange the loans made or guaranteed by it in relation to international loans through other channels so that the more useful and urgent projects, large and small alike, will be dealt with first.
  (v) To conduct its operations with due regard to the effect of international investment on business conditions in the territories of members and, in the immediate postwar years, to assist in bringing about a smooth transition from a wartime to a peacetime economy.
9 Article II, on membership in and capital of the bank, section 2, on authorized capital, subsection 2(a): "the authorized capital stock of the Bank shall be $10,000,000,000 in terms of United States dollars of the weight and fineness in effect on July 1, 1944. The capital stock shall be divided into 100,000 shares having a par value of $100,000 each, which shall be available for subscription only by members."

10 African Development Bank, http://www.afdb.org: "Callable capital is that portion of the subscribed capital stock subject to call only as and when required by the Bank to meet its obligations on borrowing of funds for inclusion in its ordinary capital resources or guarantees chargeable to such resources."

11 Bruce Rich, "A Cuckoo in the Nest," *Ecologist* 24, no. 1 (1994): 8, cited in Jean Hardy, "The History and Changing Objectives of the World Bank."

12 World Bank, "About Us," http://www.worldbank.org.

13 World Bank, *Annual Report 2004*, 19:

   Callable Capital:

   (iv) $151,775 million of IBRD's capital may, under the Articles, be called only when required to meet obligations of IBRD for funds borrowed or on loans guaranteed by it. This amount is thus not available for use by IBRD in making loans. Payment on any such call may be made, at the option of the particular member, either in gold, in U.S. dollars or in the currency required to discharge the obligations of IBRD for which the call is made.

   (v) $26,461 million of IBRD's capital is to be called only when required to meet obligations of IBRD for funds borrowed or on loans guaranteed by it, pursuant to resolutions of IBRD's Board of Governors (though such conditions are not required by the Articles). Total: $178,236 million. Equity used in Equity-to-Loans Ratio – Reported Basis $31,332 million. (in 2003: $30,027 million).

14 World Bank, "IBRD and IDA Financial Statements as of March 31 2006."

15 Hardy, "History and Changing Objectives."

16 IDA funds are mainly made available by Group I member countries.

17 At the start of 1999 it was known that later in the year China would become a middle-income country and thus be assigned to the World Bank's IBRD desk. In the spring of 1999 the bank was confronted with negative publicity since management had proposed that the board approve the China Western Poverty Reduction Project. Under the circumstances of China's change from an IDA to an IBRD institution, the impression was created that the project was "rushed through" so that it could still be financed under the IDA rules and procedures. The negative publicity about this very sensitive project – which saw the resettlement of 57,775 poor farmers from the Haidong Prefecture to Dulan County, a Mongol and Tibetan Autonomous Prefecture of Qinghai Province, an area inhabited by about 4,000 people – led to the only case in which the Inspection Panel was asked by the executive directors of the World Bank to do an investigation. See World Bank Inspection Panel, "China Western Poverty Reduction Project (Credit no. 3255-CHA and Loan no. 4501-CHA)," 6. See also World Bank Inspection Panel, "Requests for Inspection, Request 16, China Western Poverty Reduction Project (1999), Investigation Report."

18 I do not comment on Articles IV, VI, and VIII to XI since they are more technical and far from the subject of this study.

19 Article IV, on operations, contains the following sections: (1) Methods of Making or Facilitating Loans; (2) Availability and Transferability of Currencies; (3) Provision of Currencies for Direct Loans; (4) Payment Provisions for Direct

Loans, (5) Guarantees; (6) Special Reserve; (7) Methods of Meeting Liabilities of the Bank in Case of Defaults; (8) Miscellaneous Operations; (9) Warning to Be Placed on Securities; (10) Political Activity Prohibited.

20 This refers to member countries, also called donor countries (Group I) and borrowing countries (Group II).

21 Article IV, section 10: "The Bank and its officers shall not interfere in the political affairs of any member; nor shall they be influenced in their decisions by the political character of the member or members concerned. Only economic considerations shall be relevant to their decisions, and these considerations shall be weighed impartially in order to achieve the purposes stated in article 1."

22 Mason and Asher, *World Bank*, 235.

23 At the time Warren C. Baum was an associate director of Projects.

24 Warren C. Baum, referring to the IBRD's "Operational Memorandum 7.02," 22 August 1966, quoted in Mason and Asher, *World Bank*, 235.

25 Baum, quoted in ibid., 235–6.

26 Ricardo Faini and Enzo Grilli, "Who Runs the IFIs?" 4. Faini is from the University of Rome Tor Vergata and the Centre for Economic Policy Research, London. Grilli is from Johns Hopkins University, School of Advanced International Studies, Washington, DC.

27 World Bank Group Staff Association, "The Bank Group Is Always Navigating in Political Waters," 1.

28 The Staff Association refers to John Maynard Keynes (1883–1946), the world-famous economist on whose work generations of economists still rely.

29 John Maynard Keynes, quoted in World Bank Group Staff Association, "Bank Group," 1.

30 Ibid.

31 Ibid.

32 Alex Shakow was secretary of the World Bank in 2001.

33 Alex Shakow, quoted in World Bank Group Staff Association, "Bank Group," 1.

34 When I was a candidate for a position on the Inspection Panel, a personal friend, former congressman and Democrat Don Bonker, contacted the liaison, Matthew McHugh, also a former congressman, to find out the status of my candidacy.

35 World Bank Group Staff Association, "Bank Group," 1–2. Examples of political pressure from the US in this document include:
   • Peter Riddleberger, the World Bank's liaison to Capitol Hill in the late 1970s, recalls: "We were blasted by the U.S. Soybean Association because we were going to lend money to China for soybeans and to Malaysia for palm oil. We went to talk to them, to explain that China might be a huge market for U.S. soybeans. It took some work, but they turned around. The U.S. Soybean Association eventually even opened an office in Beijing" (1).
   • "By the time of Bank President A.W. Clausen, the U.S. share of IDA replenishment reached almost $1 billion. On the down side, this magnitude of funding provided for plenty of press coverage and gave congress members wonderful opportunities to grandstand to congressional districts" (1–2).

- "President McNamara forged a strong alliance with the U.S. Catholic Coalition, based on personal friendships, despite the fact that he spoke forcefully about the need for population control (the Roman Catholic Church strongly opposes any form of birth control besides abstinence)" (2).
- "After World War II ended, the Soviet Union began to court poor countries and offer aid to expand their sphere of influence. The U.S. strengthened foreign aid to counter this influence, often using the Bank as its means" (2).
- At other times, congress members proposed amendments to limit contributions if the Bank lent to countries where U.S. private property had been expropriated" (2).

36 Ibid., 2.

37 International Bank for Reconstruction and Development (IBRD), *Accountability at the World Bank*, 96.

38 See the question on this in chapter 7.

39 World Bank Inspection Panel, "Chad-Cameroon Petroleum Development and Pipeline Project (Loan 4558-CD); Management of the Petroleum Economy Project (Credit 3316-CD); and Petroleum Sector Management Capacity Building Project (Credit 3373-CD)," 82.

40 Ibid., 61, original emphasis.

41 Ibid.

42 N'Djaména is the capital of Chad.

43 Ibid.

44 IRBD, *Accountability at the World Bank*, 97–8, statement of the chairman of the Inspection Panel, E. Ayensu, 12 September 2002, Washington, DC:

Given the world-wide attention to the human rights situation in Chad ... and the fact that this was an issue raised in the Request for Inspection by a Requester who alleged that there were human rights violations in the country, and that he was tortured because of his opposition to the conduct of the project, the Panel was obliged to examine the situation of human rights and governance in the light of Bank policies. We are convinced that the approach taken in our report, which finds human rights implicitly embedded in various policies of the Bank, is within the boundaries of the Panel's jurisdiction. The Panel is pleased that by-and-large Bank Management agrees with the Panel's approach to this sensitive subject and has pledged to continue to monitor the developments in this area within the context of the applicable policies ...
The Panel believes that the human rights situation in Chad exemplifies the need for the Bank to be more forthcoming about articulating its role in promoting rights within the countries in which it operates ... [and] perhaps this case should lead ... to study [of] the wider ramifications of human rights violations as these relate to the overall success or failure of policy compliance in future Bank-financed projects.

45 J.G. Taillant, "Human Rights and the International Financial Institutions," n.p. Taillant refers to the International Covenant on Economic, Social and Cultural Rights that came into force in 1976.

46 Ibid.

47 Ibid.

48 Universal Declaration of Human Rights, "Preamble."

49 IRDB, *Guide to the World Bank*, 31.

50 Since 1995 the European Investment Bank has been closely followed by the Central Eastern Europe (CEE) Bank Watch Network, an international NGO with member organizations from ten countries from central eastern Europe and the Commonwealth of Independent States (CIS), which includes Russia, Kazakhstan, Ukraine, Uzbekistan, Georgia, Azerbaijan, Belarus, and Kyrgyzstan. The network monitors international financial institutions in the region. As stated on its website (http://www.bankwatch.org), the network's five main objectives are:

(1) To create public awareness about International Financial Institutions activities in Central and Eastern European countries and their social and environmental impacts.

(2) To promote public participation in the decision making process about policies and projects of International Financial Institutions, on the local, national and regional levels.

(3) To help non-governmental environmental organizations and citizen groups to monitor what the International Financial Institutions are doing in the Central and Eastern Europe.

(4) To change or stop environmentally and socially destructive policies and projects of International Financial Institutions in Central and Eastern Europe, and promote alternatives.

(5) To cooperate with environmental citizen organizations in stopping destructive activities of Transnational corporations and to limit their overall impacts on the environment in Central and Eastern Europe.

51 The Board of Governors is formed by representatives of all governments who are members of the World Bank. In many cases these representatives will be ministers of finance.

52 Article V, section 2(a): "All the powers of the Bank shall be vested in the Board of Governors consisting of one governor and one alternate appointed by each member in such manner as it may determine." Section 2(b): "The Board of Governors may delegate to the Executive Directors except the power to:

(i) Admit new members and determine the conditions of their admission;

(ii) Increase or decrease the capital stock;

(iii) Suspend a member;

(iv) Decide appeals from interpretations of this agreement given by the Executive Directors;

(v) Make arrangements to cooperate with other international organizations (other than informal arrangements of a temporary and administrative character);

(vi) Decide to suspend permanently the operations of the bank and to distribute its assets;

(vii) Determine the distribution of net income of the Bank."

53 These eight shareholders are the United States, Japan, Germany, France, the United Kingdom, China, the Russian Federation, and Saudi Arabia.

54 IBRD executive directors' voting status, Corporate Secretariat, 31 December 2007:

United States: 265,219 votes = 16.38%

Japan: 127,250 votes = 7.87%

Germany: 72,649 votes = 4.49%

France: 69,647 votes = 4.30%

United Kingdom: 69.647 votes = 4.30%

China: 45,049 votes = 2.78%

Russian Federation: 45,049 votes = 2.78%

Saudi Arabia: 45,045 votes = 2.78%

55 Switzerland became a member of MIGA in 1988.

56 World Bank document of Corporate Secretariat, 5 January 2004: "Constituency 18: Antigua and Barbuda, the Bahamas, Barbados, Belize, Canada, Dominica, Grenada, Guyana, Ireland, Jamaica, St Kitts and Nevis, St Vincent, and the Grenadines."

57 Andrés Rigo Sureda, "Informality and Effectiveness in the Operation of the International Bank for Reconstruction and Development," 566. Rigo Sureda, who was then a senior advisor on international financial matters for Fulbright and Jaworski LLP, explains that his views should not be attributed to the World Bank or to Fulbright and Jaworski LLP. See also Rigo Sureda's more detailed recent study, "The Law Applicable to the Activities of International Development Banks."

58 IBRD, "Articles of Agreement," Article V, section 4(a).

59 Rigo Sureda, "Informality and Effectiveness," 566, referring to Articles of Agreement, Article V, section 5(b).

60 Ibid., 567.

61 Ibid.

62 Ibid., 568.

63 Mason and Asher, World Bank, 87.

64 Eugene Robert Black was president of the World Bank from July 1949 until December 1962; see the archives of the World Bank at http://www.worldbank.org.

65 Jochen Kraske et al., Bankers with a Mission, 92.

66 Ibid., 112.

67 Ibid., 89.

68 "Second Report of the Ad Hoc Group Nr. R2007-0089," 14 May 2007, 30, paragraph 78. This is an internal and confidential report that circulated on the Internet in the spring of 2007.

69 Ibid., 39, paragraph 114.

70 At present, the World Bank has 186 member states.

71 Five agencies comprise the World Bank Group; see http://www.worldbank.org.

72 World Bank, http://www.worldbank.org.

73 Ibid.

74 Kraske et al., Bankers with a Mission, 115.

75 Mason and Asher, World Bank, 407.

76 Ibid., 128–35.

77 Ibid., 213.

78 Ibid., 257.
79 World Bank, "World Bank Group Historical Chronology," 212.
80 Kenneth Piddington, quoted in ibid., 207.
81 World Bank, "World Bank Group Historical Chronology," 210.
82 Barber Conable, speech at the bank's annual meeting, Washington, DC, July 1991, quoted in World Bank, "World Bank Group Historical Chronology," 221.
83 Mason and Asher, *World Bank*, 66.
84 Ibid.
85 Richard Scobey, sector manager for the Africa Regional Office, gave a presentation on 5 June 2000 in Washington, DC, at which I was present.
86 World Bank, *Annual Report 2006*, 66.
87 Ibid., 8.
88 Ibid., 11.
89 Ibid., 10.
90 Hardy, "History and Changing Objectives."
91 IBRD, *Guide to the World Bank*, 25.
92 Rigo Sureda, "Informality and Effectiveness," 568.
93 Mason and Asher, *World Bank*, 416–17.
94 I remember the wording quite well.
95 Kraske et al., *Bankers with a Mission*, 110. Kraske is referring to an interview with President Black (date and publication unknown).
96 Ibid.
97 International Development Association (IDA), "Articles of Agreement," Article V, section 1, on the use of resources and conditions of financing, has in total seven subsections, lettered "a" through "g."
98 Kraske et al., *Bankers with a Mission*, 110.
99 Countries in the same constituency as Spain are Costa Rica, El Salvador, Guatemala, Honduras, Mexico, and Nicaragua.
100 Together in the constituency with Portugal are Albania, Greece, Italy, Malta, San Marino, and East Timor.
101 The other members in the constituency of the Netherlands are Armenia, Bosnia and Herzegovina, Bulgaria, Croatia, Cyprus, Georgia, Israel, Macedonia, Moldova, Romania, and Ukraine.
102 See http://europa.eu/abc/european_countries/index_en.htm.
103 Member countries of the World Bank are divided between Group I countries (those that finance loans and donate for projects) and Group II countries (those that borrow for projects). According to the World Bank's *Annual Report 2003*, the following new EU countries were eligible in 2003 for bank funding: Czech Republic, Hungary, Estonia, Slovakia, Lithuania, and Latvia. At present, 19 of the the 25 EU countries are Group I countries, including the 15 former or "old" EU states. In January 2007 Bulgaria and Romania also entererred the EU.
104 World Bank, *Annual Report 2005*.
105 Portuguese EU Presidency, "Communiqué from the Presidency of the EU on the Conclusion of the Negotiations for the 15th Replenishment of the IDA, 2007–12–14."

106 The German executive director, Eckhard Deutscher, spoke to me about this. As a result, an e-mail was sent to a German member of the European Parliament, Ms Karin Junker. Whether this has led to any action is unknown.

107 When the G-10 changed into the G-7, the Netherlands, long considered to have a strong economy with international influence, lost its seat. The Netherlands is still part of the G-10.

108 The governing structure of the IMF is identical to that of the World Bank.

109 J. Gold, quoted in Rigo Sureda, "Informality and Effectiveness," 572.

110 Ibid., 573. See also Mason and Asher, *World Bank*, 213.

111 Aldo Caliari and Frank Schroeder, "Reform Proposals for the Governance Structure of the International Financial Institutions," 3.

112 Footnote in the original: "Since the Fund's inception, for example, the types of decisions requiring a qualified majority have risen from 9 to 53. Currently there are 18 categories of decisions susceptible of US veto. Among them are: the decisions on giving certain uses to fund resources, etc."

113 Caliari and Schroeder, "Reform Proposals," 3.

114 Ricardo and Grilli, "Who Runs the IFIs?" 4.

115 Ibid.

116 Ibid., 5.

117 World Bank Inspection Panel, "China Western Poverty Reduction Project (Credit no. 3255-CHA and Loan no. 4501-CHA)."

118 Robert Goodland, "Environmental and Social Lessons to Be Learned from the World Bank's Fiercest Controversy," 2.

119 See my interview with President Wolfensohn in appendix 3.

120 World Bank Group, "Mission Statement," http://www.worldbank.org:
   Our dream is a world free of poverty.
   To fight poverty with passion and professionalism for lasting results.
   To help people help themselves and their environment by providing resources, sharing knowledge, building capacity, and forging partnerships in the public and private sectors.
   To be an excellent institution able to attract, excite, and nurture diverse and committed staff with exceptional skills who know how to listen and learn.

   Our Principles
   Client centered, working in partnership, accountable for quality results, dedicated to financial integrity and cost-effectiveness, inspired and innovative.
   Our values
   Personal honesty, integrity, commitment; working together in teams – with openness and trust; empowering others and respecting differences; encouraging risk-taking and responsibility; enjoying our work and our families.

121 President Lewis T. Preston, who served from 1989 to 1994, was the successor of President Barber Conable.

122 Ibrahim Shihata, *The World Bank Inspection Panel*, 2nd ed., 2.

123 World Bank, "Effective Implementation."

124 Ibid., i.

125 Ibid., 9.

126 Ibid., 16.

127 Ibid.

128 Ibid., 22.

129 Shihata, *World Bank*, 2nd ed., 2.

130 World Bank, "From President to Executive Directors," 1.

131 As is clear from the report, an earlier draft had been sent to the executive directors.

132 Ibid., 22.

CHAPTER THREE

1 See appendix 3 for my interview with Congressman Barney Frank (Democrat), who was chairman of the House-Financial Services Committee at the time and asked the bank to release more information, such as making public the country reports.

2 Ibrahim Shihata, *The World Bank Inspection Panel*, 2nd ed., 5.

3 Footnote in the original: "Development Credit Agreement No. 1553-IN, and loan Agreement No. 2497-IN."

4 Ibid., 5.

5 As a member of the European Parliament, I wrote a letter to President Preston that was co-signed by eighteen other members of the European Parliament and tabled several resolutions in the European Parliament. See below in this chapter.

6 International Bank for Reconstruction and Development (IBRD), "Resolution No. IBRD-93-10 and Resolution No. IDA-93-6." For the entire text, see appendix 1.

7 INTACH, quoted in S. Santhi, *Sardar Sarovar Project*, "Preface."

8 See http://www.enceclopedia.com/html/N/Narmada.asp.

9 See http://www.democracynow.org/articlepl?sid=03/04/07/0413246.

10 Lori Udall, *The World Bank Inspection Panel*, 7.

11 I was a member of the European Parliament from 1989 to 1999, elected as a member of the Dutch Social Democrat Party.

12 "Resolution on the Disastrous Consequences of the Narmada Project in India," 185.

13 On 15 April 1991 the first draft resolution, prepared by myself and Mr Roger Barton, was tabled in the name of the Socialist Group in conformity with Article 64 of the Standing Orders of the European Parliament, No. B3-0635/91. Also tabled was a draft resolution by Ms Nel van Dijk in the name of the

European Green Party, No. B3-0656/91. In May a new draft resolution was tabled (same text) by myself, Barton, and Marijke van Hemeldonck, No. B3-0809/91. In July 1991 two remaining resolutions were tabled that to-gether formed the basis for the joint resolution: Doc. B3-1181/91, by myself and colleagues, on behalf of the Socialist Group; and Doc. B3-1210/91, by Mr Wilfried Telkämper, on behalf of the Green Party.

14 As a result of negotiations on speaking time, which was first divided between the political groups, my own group granted me one minute to speak.

15 Different figures circulated concerning the affected people. The figure of 1 mil-lion people refers to the entire project, which included much more then the Sardar Sarovar Dam.

16 *Debates of the European Parliament*, 9 July 1992, no. 3-420/251.

17 See World Bank, "World Bank Group Historical Chronology."

18 Udall, *World Bank Inspection Panel*, 8. See also the website of the Government of British Colombia: http://www.protocol.gov.bc/protocol/prgs/obc/2004/2004_TBerger.htm.

19 Udall, *World Bank Inspection Panel*, 8.

20 In the European Parliament the word "Committee" was used instead of "Commission."

21 "Resolution on the Narmada Dam (India)," 156.

22 See appendix 3 for the entire interview with Paul Arlman, executive director from the Netherlands, 1986–90.

23 Herfkens's name is misspelled.

24 Devesh Kapur, John P. Lewis, and Richard C. Webb, *The World Bank*, vol. 2, 699.

25 Ibid.

26 Ibid.

27 Ibid., 700.

28 See my interview with Professor David Hunter in appendix 3.

29 Professor Bradlow, director of the College of Law at American University in Washington, DC, is the author of several articles about the Inspection Panel. At the time, he addressed a US congressional oversight hearing and contributed his views on the structure of an Inspection Panel. Since 2007 Professor Bradlow has been a member of the Independent Review Mechanism of the African Development Bank.

30 Dana Clark is a former director of the International Financial Institutions Program at the Center for International Environmental Law (CIEL) in Washington, DC.

31 Kapur, Lewis, and Webb, *World Bank*, vol. 2, 700.

32 Ibid.

33 Ibid.

34 Ibid., 701.

35 IBRD, "Resolution No. IBRD-93-10 and Resolution No. IDA-93-6."

36 Udall, *World Bank Inspection Panel*, 9. There is an abundance of information on the Internet related to the Morse Commission report.

37 Bradford Morse et al., *Sardar Sarovar*, 53.

38 Udall, *World Bank Inspection Panel*, 9.
39 Ibid.
40 Kapur, Lewis, and Webb, *World Bank*, vol. 2, 702. See also Udall, *World Bank Inspection Panel*, 10.
41 Udall, *World Bank Inspection Panel*, 10.
42 Kapur, Lewis, and Webb, *World Bank*, vol. 2, 703.
43 Ibid., 705.
44 Ibid., 706.
45 E-mail from Lori Udall, 22 February 2006.
46 The NGO community was not alone on Capital Hill in lobbying for creation of the panel. Chad Dobson, a very effective, Washington-based lobbyist who was the founder and first director of the Bank Information Center (BIC), organized the so-called Tuesday Group, a monthly meeting of NGOs and Treasury officials. The meetings are facilitated by Dobson, whose focus is merely on the broader issue of transparency within the World Bank. Dobson has good access to Capitol Hill and direct access to the Democrat Barney Frank. Dobson, together with lawyers from the Centre for International Environmental Law, has earned the trust of Southern NGOs. Ms Greetje Lubbi, at the time the director of the Dutch NGO that financed BIC, said to me about this period: "In those days it still was very difficult to get information from the Bank on planned or ongoing projects. Dobson was very effective in getting information out of the Bank and shared it with the Southern partners. That was all rather new." And Ms Lubbi is right. Today, the bank makes much more documentation available to the public than it did ten years ago.
47 E-mail from Lori Udall, 22 February 2006.
48 The subcommittee met, pursuant to notice, in room 2128, Rayburn House Office Building.
49 A world Bank replenishment is an agreement between the donor countries (Group I) and the bank about each donor country's contribution to the bank over a period of three years. Given the usual three-year time span, replenishment fourteen could overlap with replenishment fifteen.
50 United States House of Representatives, "Authorizing Contributions to IDA, GEF and ADF," 1–2.
51 Ibid., 5.
52 Ibid., 5–6.
53 Ibid., 7–8.
54 Ibid., 9–10.
55 Udall, *World Bank Inspection Panel*, 13.
56 United States House of Representatives, "Authorizing Contributions," 45.
57 Ibid., 51.
58 Ibid.
59 Ibid.
60 E-mail from Lori Udall, 22 February 2006.
61 Ibid.

62 Ibid.

63 United States House of Representatives, "World Bank Disclosure Policy and Inspection Panel," 2.

64 Ibid.

65 Ibid., 4.

66 Ibid.

67 E-mail from Lori Udall, 22 February 2006.

68 United States House of Representatives, "World Bank Disclosure Policy," 14.

69 Ibid.

70 Congressional Record – House, September (1993), H 7166.

71 See my interview with Congressman Barney Frank in appendix 3.

72 Material submitted to the subcommittee and Chairman Frank also contained a proposal by Proffessor Daniel Bradlow of American University in Washington, DC, who proposed a World Bank ombudsman instead of an independent Inspection Panel.

73 The Wapenhans Report was an internal report that was leaked. It is referred to in many documents from the Centre for International Environmental Law and in the writings of Udall and others.

74 This concern is mentioned in several internal bank documents.

75 World Bank, "Operational Manual Statement 2.36."

76 Shihata, *World Bank*, 2nd ed., 41: "Before the Bank's reorganization in 1987, its operational policies were contained mainly in Operational Manual Statements (OMSs) and Operations Policy Notes (OPNs). These were both issued, under the authority of the President, by the then existing office of the Senior Vice President, Operations, in the form of general instructions, supplemented occasionally by Operational Circulars or less formal notes from the Senior Vice President, Operations. Following the 1987 reorganization, OMSs were gradually reflected in new documents called 'Operational Directives' or 'ODs,' some of which included changes from earlier OMSs and some of which were completely new."

77 World Bank, "Operational Directive 4.00."

78 Footnote in the original: "OD 4.00, Annex A (1989), replaced by OD 4.01 (1991), and ultimately replaced by OP [Operational Policy] 4.01 (1999)."

79 Footnote in the original: "OD 4.15 (1992)."

80 Footnote in the original: "OD 9.01 (1992). This draft OD was circulated to the Executive Directors and was later issued in the absence of a request for discussion."

81 The GEF was launched on 28 November 1990, jointly administered by the World Bank, the United Nations Development Programme (UNDP), and the United Nations Environment Programme (UNEP).

82 World Bank, "Operational Directive 4.01."

83 Ibid., 2.

84 In response to my question, raised on 15 January 2003, about whether the status of the Operational Directives had been changed, the executive secretary of the Inspection Panel, Eduardo Abbott, said:

ODs, which combine mandatory policy, bank procedures and good practice in a single document, are being converted into OPs [Operational Policies] and BPs [Bank Procedures] in an effort to simplify the policies and clarify their requirements. Over the years, in fact, various problems, arisen in projects' implementation, led many EDs [executive directors] to question whether the ODs were binding instruments. Some ODs were seen as too detailed and unclear in their boundaries and flexibility. As a result, in 1992 the Board decided to replace gradually the existing ODs with OPs and BPs, which are binding on the staff, and GPs, which are not binding. The conversion process is near completion, although it has to be noted that not all the Bank ODs have been converted.

85 World Bank, "Operational Manual Statement 4.01."

86 Shihata, *World Bank*, 2nd ed., 1.

87 E-mail from Lori Udall, 22 February 2006.

88 Internal World Bank information that I received.

89 Ibid.

90 Shihata, *World Bank*, 2nd ed., 1–2; the footnote to this passage reads: "Memorandum from the President, Operations Inspection Function: Objectives, Mandate and Operating Procedures for an Independent Inspection Panel (R93-122/2 para.2), September 10, 1993 (limited circulation)."

91 Ibid., 3.

92 Ibid., 3–4.

93 Footnote in the original: "For Example, in *Bushell v. Secretary of State for the Environment* [1981] A.C. 75, it was held by the House of Lords that government policy was not a subject for discussion at a local enquiry."

94 Footnote in the original: "The existence of a dispute need not necessarily be a prerequisite for a judicial enquiry according to a statement by A.L. Smith M.R. in Re *Carus-Wilson and Greene* (1886) 18 Q.B.D. 7: 'I do not see why there should not be an arbitration to settle matters, as to which, even if there was no actual dispute, there would probably be a dispute unless they were settled.'"

95 This refers to footnote 13 in paragraph 18 of the resolution.

96 Footnote in the original: "para. 21. Also paras. 6, 13 and 14, which refer to the Panel conducting hearings and not just investigations."

97 Footnote in the original: "The binding character lies in the fact that Bank Management is obliged to take certain specified actions following the Panel's findings. However, the particular actions to be taken pursuant to the Panel's findings will be subject to a report to the Executive Directors by the Bank Management, who cannot, however, depart from the Panel's findings. The Executive Director's approval is necessary to proceed with implementation of the Panel's findings."

98 V. Sk. Nathan Kathigamar, "The World Bank Inspection Panel, Court or Quango?" 138–9.

99 Chairman Jim MacNeill, Eddy Ayensu, and myself.

100 There was some cynicism in the question, which was asked shortly after the
    2000 US elections and the judgment by the US Supreme Court on the election
    results in Florida. This is the only time that the US Supreme Court has inter-
    vened in the business of a state, resulting in the final victory of President G.W.
    Bush.

101 Chatterjee wrote this article before the second revision of the resolution.

102 Charles Chatterjee, "IBRD Inspection Panel Procedures," 395.

103 Resolution No. IBRD-93-10.

104 Resolution No. IDA-93-6.

105 See appendix 1 for the entire resolution.

106 IBRD, "Resolution No. IBRD-93-10 and Resolution No. IDA-93-6," Article 3:
    "no member may serve for more than one term."

107 Shihata, *World Bank*, 2nd ed., 33.

108 IDA is within the mandate of the Inspection Panel. Two IFC projects – the
    Chad Petroleum Development and Pipeline Project and the Bujagali Project
    – have been investigated by the Inspection Panel since IDA got involved.

109 Footnote in the original: "Jay D. Hair et. al, *Pangue Hydroelectric Project: An Inde-
    pendent Review of the International Finance Corporation's Compliance with Applicable
    World Bank Group Environmental and Social Requirements*, April 4, 1997."

110 Lori Udall, "World Bank Inspection Panel," 7.

111 Mr De Jong left the bank shortly thereafter and was replaced by one of Presi-
    dent Wolfowitz's "cronies."

112 R. Goodland, "Environmental and Social Lessons to Be Learned from the
    World Bank's Fiercest Controversy," 2.

113 Jim Wolfensohn, "Foreword," in Alvaro Umaña Quesada, *The World Bank
    Inspection Panel*, vii.

114 See my interview with President Jim Wolfensohn in appendix 3.

115 Ernst-Günter Bröder is a former president of the European Investment Bank
    in Luxembourg, was a governor of the European Bank for Reconstruction and
    Development in London, and was a member of the special advisory group of
    the Asian Development Bank.

116 Alvaro Umaña Quesada was a professor and director of the Natural Resources
    Management Program at the Instituto Centroamericano de Administración
    de Empresas (INCAE), a Latin American graduate school of management.
    He was Costa Rica's first minister of natural resources and is a member of both
    the Rockefeller Foundation and the World Resources Institute.

117 Richard Bissell has been a senior official with the United States Agency for In-
    ternational Development (USAID) and a professor at several US universities.
    At present he is the executive director of the Policy Division at the National
    Academy of Sciences in Washington, DC, and a member of the accountability
    mechanism of the Asian Development Bank.

118 I was often told that Bröder's experience as president of the European Invest-
    ment Bank was enormously valuable during the establishment of the working
    procedures of the panel, and he was well respected throughout the bank. Bröder
    soon organized a meeting with the NGO community and also gained its respect.

119 IBRD, "Resolution No. IBRD-93-10 and Resolution No. IDA-93-6," Article 27.

120 See also Shihata, *World Bank*, 2nd ed., 155.

121 Ibid.

122 World Bank, "Practical Suggestions Based on Experience to Date," 2.

123 Shihata, *World Bank*, 2nd ed., 162–3.

124 World Bank, "Review of the Resolution Establishing the Inspection Panel: 1996 Clarification of Certain Aspects of the Resolution."

125 Group I countries are those that contribute to the bank, while Group II countries are those that borrow from the bank.

126 World Bank, "Practical Suggestions," 3. I was told that one executive director expressed his concern that "some borrowers might have perceived the panel as a sort of International Court of Justice."

127 Ibid.

128 Sebastian Mallaby, *The World's Banker*, 6.

129 Ibid., 277.

130 In its list of recommendations to the board, Oxfam UK in Ireland also mentions consultation with the president in exceptional circumstances.

131 Footnote in the original: "The issues listed in that paper included: form and composition of the Panel; the Panel's function; the role of the Board; extension of the Panel's function to private sector operations in IFC and MIGA; and disclosure issues."

132 Shihata, *World Bank*, 2nd ed., 156.

133 Ibid.

134 Oxfam United Kingdom (Ireland), *The World Bank Inspection Panel*.

135 Shihata, *World Bank*, 2nd ed., 156.

136 Ibid., 157–8.

137 Ibid., 158.

138 Ibid.

139 Today, the situation is the opposite, with the majority of private-sector experts believing that independent accountability mechanisms are necessary. See chapter 7.

140 Shihata, *World Bank*, 2nd ed., 158–9.

141 Information provided by Lori Udall.

142 This is an expression used by management.

143 Shihata, *World Bank*, 2nd ed., 165.

144 Ibid.

145 IBRD, "Resolution No. IBRD-93-10 and Resolution No. IDA-93-6," Article 19.

146 World Bank, "Review of the Resolution," 1–2.

147 Shihata, *World Bank*, 2nd ed., 169–70.

148 World Bank, "Review of the Resolution," 2.

149 Ibid.

150 Shihata, *World Bank*, 2nd ed., 166.

151 Ibid., 171.

152 Ibid.

153 Ibid., 167.

154　Ibid., 168.

155　Ibid.

156　Ibid.

157　Ibid., 168n28.

158　It is perhaps superfluous to mention that I was not a member of the panel in this period. All that is written above is based on what I was told and on what I could find in panel documents.

159　The panel is quoted in ibid., 175. See also Umaña Quesada, *World Bank.*

160　Shihata, *World Bank*, 2nd ed., 175.

161　Ibid., 175.

162　Ibid., 173–204.

163　Ibid., 176–83.

164　Ibid., 182.

165　Ibid.

166　See ibid., 184–6, and annex I-3, "Board Conclusions of the Second Review of the Panel's Experience – April 20, 1999." For the report, see World Bank, "The Report of the Working Group on the Second Review of the Inspection Panel."

167　Shihata, *World Bank*, 2nd ed., 187. Shihata adds that "The latter criteria were defined in the report to mean 'criteria other than the existence of *prima facie* evidence of the Bank's serious failure and the resulting material adverse effect."

168　Ibid., 188.

169　Ibid., 189. During investigations, this latter restriction has often been regarded as a hindrance by the panel when it has been confronted with compliance failures by the bank that the requesters previously did not not refer to in their requests. In some of these cases, the panel has found a way to report on the failures.

170　Ibid.

171　Ibid.

172　Ibid. This position was changed in 2004 when the board asked the panel to monitor the mitigation actions that management was supposed to take. The board decided on this change after the panel submitted to the board both its report on Yacyretá and an Action Plan intended to remedy the violations that the panel had discovered.

173　Ibid., 190.

174　Ibid., 190n61: "*The Wall Street Journal,* January 12, 1999, at A2 and A8. A similar story by the same writer, Michael Philips, appeared in *The Globe and Mail,* January 11, 1999, at B9."

175　These comments about the changes to the panel's mandate in 1999 were explained to me when I was subsequently appointed to the panel. When I arrived at the World Bank, the panel had just begun to work with its new enlarged mandate.

176　Umaña Quesada, *World Bank*, vii.

177　Lewis T. Preston, "Foreword," in Shihata, *World Bank*, 2nd ed., xiv.

178 See note 178.

179 A reference to World Bank, "Report of the Working Group," Article 14.

180 Shihata, *World Bank*, 2nd ed., 189, referring to World Bank, "Report of the Working Group," Article 16.

181 Ibid., again referring to Article 16.

182 Ibid., 187.

183 Ibid., 193.

184 The panel included a letter of preface with its report to the executive directors, "Paraguay/Argentina: Reform Project for the Water and Telecommunication Sectors, SEGBA V Power Distribution Project (Yacyretá)." This letter from the three members of the panel, Edith Brown-Weiss, Tongroj Onchan, and myself, stated: "This was one of the most controversial and complex projects reviewed by the Panel to date. The project is more then 20 years under implementation, thousands of people claim to be adversely affected, it is marred by allegations of corruption, and there is no satisfactory completion in sight."

185 Ibid., xxiii.

186 Shihata, *World Bank*, 2nd ed., 194.

187 Ibid. Shihata goes on to mention two academics in particular who wrote their own comments. On Daniel Bradlow, a professor of law at American University in Washington, DC, he writes:

> In his otherwise learned comments, he argued in particular that Management's response to a request for inspection should not include any factual record to support its answer on whether it has included any factual record to support its answer on whether it has complied or intends to comply with Bank policies and procedures. This, according to him, would best enable the Panel to freely establish the factual record regarding the allegations included in the request. Coming from a professor of law, this suggestion may be particularly troublesome. The fact that the party to which alleged violations are attributed may present its point of view in no way deprives the investigator from reaching his independent conclusion. Nor does the fact that Management knows more about the project deprive the Panel, which has access to all Bank files and all Bank staff, from ascertaining whether the information provided by Management is accurate. Any lawyer knows that unfairness does not result from the attempt by a party facing allegations of misconduct or abuse of powers to present its version of the factual record or that such a party may be in a better position to know the facts. Rather, unfairness results from depriving a party from defending its position according to the facts available to it. (195)

The other academic to whom Shihata refers is Professor Devesh Kapur, a coauthor with Lewis and Webb of the book *The World Bank*, which recounts the bank's history. Shihata writes:

> Unlike other commentators, Professor Kapur supported a "more restrictive regime for the Inspection Panel," which he saw as "adding further to the powers of the North, especially the U.S., vis-à-vis developing countries."

According to Kapur, "[t]he parallels between the Bank's Inspection Panel and the Independent Counsel statute in the U.S. are striking. Both were driven by good liberal intentions responding to real abuses (although in the Bank's case even the circumstances surrounding the birth of the Inspection Panel would not meet the smell test of governance it applies to its borrowers); both were hijacked to partisan political ends; both ended up causing damage; both need to be either laid to rest or severely modified, and both prove the adage that the best can be the enemy of the good. (196)

188 Ibid., 202.
189 Ibid., 202–3.
190 Ibid., 203.
191 Ibid., original emphasis.
192 World Bank, "The 1999 Clarifications of the Board's Second Review of the Inspection Panel," paragraph 2.
193 Ibid., paragraph 5.
194 Ibid., paragraph 6.
195 Ibid., paragraph 11.
196 Ibid., paragraph 13.
197 Dana Clark, Jonathan Fox, and Kay Treakle, eds, *Demanding Accountability*, 17.

CHAPTER FOUR

1 International Bank for Reconstruction and Development (IBRD), "Resolution No. IBRD-93-10 and Resolution No. IDA-93-6." See also chapter 3. For the entire text, see appendix 1.
2 See, for example, Eisuke Suzuki and Suresh Nanwani, "Responsibility of International Organizations," 219; and Kay Treakle, Jonathan Fox, and Dana Clark, "Lessons Learned," 247.
3 Suzuki and Nanwani, "Responsibility," 219.
4 Ibid.
5 The export credit agencies deserve more attention but are beyond the scope of this study.
6 Commission for Environmental Cooperation (CEC), "Bringing the Facts to Light: A Guide to Articles 14 and 15 of the North American Agreement on Environmental Cooperation," 1. This document further states:

When Canada, Mexico and the United States established the North American Free Trade Agreement (NAFTA), they also agreed on an environmental side accord, the North American Agreement on Environmental Cooperation (NAAEC). One of the principal aims of the NAAEC is the promotion of effective enforcement by the Parties of their domestic environmental legislation. Accordingly, the NAAEC provides, under Articles 14 and 15, a means by which anyone living in any of the three countries of North America may bring the facts to light concerning the enforcement of environmental legislation on the books of any of the three countries. Under Article 14, written assertions that a Party to the NAAEC is failing to enforce an environmental law effectively may be submitted by any person or nongovernmental organization to the Secretariat of the Commission for Environmental Cooperation (CEC), the institution established to steward the implementation of the NAAEC. (1)

7 Inter-American Development Bank (IADB), "Propsal for Enhancement to the Independent Investigation Mechanism."

8 Compliance advisor ombudsman (CAO), *Annual Report 2002–03*, 19.

9 CAO, *Annual Report 2006–07*, 46.

10 Ibid., 1.

11 Ibid., iv.

12 The first guidelines were published in April 2000, and the revised guidelines were published in May 2004. In this book the guidelines of 2000, 2004, and 2007 are used. See http://www.cao-omudsman.org.

13 CAO, "Operational Guidelines" (April 2007), 5.

14 Ibid.

15 Ibid.

16 Ibid.

17 Ibid.

18 CAO, *Annual Report 2004–05*, 5.

19 Ibid., 13.

20 The mandate of the World Bank Inspection Panel covers the IBRD and IDA, both of the World Bank Group. IFC is not part of the mandate unless an IFC project is also financed with IDA or IBRD money, as was the case with the Chad-Cameroon pipeline.

21 CAO, *Annual Report 2004–05*, 15.

22 CAO, "Operational Guidelines" (April 2000), 7.

23 CAO, "Operational Guidelines" (April 2004), 2.

24 Ibid., 36.

25 CAO, "Operational Guidelines" (2007), 18.

26 Ibid., 14.

27 Ibid.

28 Ibid.

29 Ibid., 17.

30 Bretton Woods Project, "Internal Accountability Creates 'Institutional Discomfort.'"

31 Ibid.

32 CAO, *Annual Report 2003–04*, 18.

33 See http://www.ifc.org.

34 See http://www.imf.org.

35 Ibid.

36 See "The IMF's Role at a Glance," at ibid.

37 International Monetary Fund (IMF), "Making the IMF's Independent Evaluation Office Operational."

38 Ibid.

39 See http://www.ieo-imf.org.

40 Bretton Woods Project, "IMF Agrees More Transparency."

41 IMF, "Making the IMF's Independent Evaluation Office Operational," 7.

42 Ibid., 8.

43 IMF, "Terms of Reference for the Independent Evaluation Office of the International Monetary Fund."

44 Angela Wood et al., "Letter from the Bretton Woods Project in Response to the IMF's Independent Evaluation Office Proposals."

45 Ibid.

46 See http://www.ieo-imf.org.

47 IMF, Independent Evaluation Office, *Annual Report 2007*, 8.

48 IMF, "IMF's Independent Evaluation Office Announces Release of Report on the IMF's Approach to Capital Account Liberalization," 1, original emphasis.

49 Asian Development Bank (ADB), "ADB's Inspection Policy." See also Ibrahim Shihata, *The World Bank Inspection Panel*, 2nd ed., annex III.

50 Ibid., 14–15.

51 Ibid.

52 Ibid., 12–13.

53 Ibid., 16–17.

54 The conference *Public Accessibility to International Financial Institutions: A Review of Existing Mechanisms and Interim Experiences*, 11 April 2003, Washington, DC.

55 Soon after this meeting in Manila, I had a meeting with Wiert Wiertsema in Amsterdam to exchange notes on our experiences with the working methods of the mechanisms and to discuss the necessary steps to be taken for a full investigation. Already at the time, it turned out to be very difficult for the three panel members to gain access to bank documents on the project.

56 Wiert Wiertsema, "The Asian Development Bank (ADB) Inspection of the Samut Prakarn Wastewatewr Management Project, Thailand," 2–3.

57 Ibid., 3.

58 Ibid.

59 Ibid.

60 Ibid., 4.

61 Friends of the Earth International, e-mail newsletter, received 24 January 2002, section 9, "Asian Development Bank."

62 Walden Bello is a professor of sociology and public administration at the University of the Philippines and executive director of the Bangkok-based research and advocacy organization Focus on the Global South.

63 Walden Bello, "Controversial report poisons ADB board-management ties," *Business World*, 11 April 2002.

64 Ibid.

65 Bank Information Center (BIC) et al., "Strengthening Public Accountability," 18–19. The co-authors of this document are the Coalition in Reforms for Efficient and Equitable Development (CREED), Pakistan; the Environmental Foundation, Sri Lanka; Gama Surakeema Savidhana, Sri Lanka; the International Rivers Network (IRN), United States; Mekong Watch, Japan; NGO Forum on the ADB, Philippines; Oxfam Mekong Initiative (OMI), Cambodia; the

Urban Resource Centre, Pakistan; the SUNGI Development Foundation, Pakistan; and Oxfam Community Aid Abroad, Australia.

66 Ibid., 20.

67 Ibid., 23.

68 ADB, "Review of the Inspection Function," iii.

69 Ibid.

70 Ibid., 49n8.

71 Ibid., 6.

72 Ibid., 49

73 ADB et al., "Recommendations to Inspection Policy Review of the Asian Development Bank," in ibid., 49n8. This document was prepared for submission at the ADB's Tokyo Consultation to Review the Inspection Function, 11 June 2002.

74 ADB, "Review of the Inspection Function," 8.

75 Interview with Suresh Nanwani and Eisuke Suzuki, April 2003, Washington, DC. Suzuki was director general of the Operations Evaluation Department at the ADB and architect of the ADB's mechanism.

76 ADB, "Review of the Inspection Function," 15.

77 Ibid., 18.

78 This was the case with the Indigenous Community Biodiversity Project of 2004 in Mexico.

79 Ibid., 16.

80 Ibid., 17.

81 Suzuki and Nanwani, "Responsibility," 209.

82 ADB, "Review of the Inspection Function," 18.

83 Ibid., 19, 20, 21.

84 Ibid., 19.

85 Ibid., 21.

86 Ibid.

87 Ibid.

88 Ibid., 22.

89 The present chairman is Augustinus Rumansare from Indonesia, the second member is Antonio la Viña, a Philippine national, and the third position is vacant as of January 2008. The previous two members were Vitus Fernando from Sri Lanka and Richard Bissell from the United States, who is a former member of the World Bank Inspection Panel.

90 Ibid., 25.

91 Ibid., 22.

92 Ibid., 25.

93 Ibid., 26.

94 Ibid., 24.

95 Ibid.

96 Ibid., 18.

97 Ibid., 18n15.

98 See www.iadb.org.

99 See http://www.iadb.org/aboutus/iii/independent_invest.cfm.

100 See IADB, "The IDB Independent Investigation Mechanism," 2–3. See also Shihata, *World Bank Inspection Panel,* 2nd ed., 495–500.

101 Search for "Compliance Review Mechanism" at http://www.iadb.org. My comments are published together with those of other experts. Note that my name is misspelled "Marrtje" van Putten.

102 IADB, "Propsal for Enhancement," 4.

103 Over the past decade Canada has developed special expertise in helping minorities and other affected people in areas with large infrastructural projects to come forward and express their problems and wishes. The Canadian Environmental Assessment Act stipulates that a very small portion of the total project budget (around 0.3%) is to be set aside for this purpose.

104 By comparison, the reports of the World Bank Inspection Panel are officially to contain no recommendations, only findings. In practice, some of these findings can be read as recommendations. This provision is related to the final decision, which is taken by the executive directors.

105 Search for "IIRSA" at http://www.iadb.org.

106 See http://www.ebrd.com.

107 CEE Bankwatch Network, "Empowering People: The Need for an EBRD Appeals/Compliance Mechanism."

108 Ibid., 3.

109 Ibid.

110 European Bank for Reconstruction and Development (EBRD), "Independent Recourse Mechanism," 1.

111 Ibid., 2.

112 Ibid.

113 Ibid., 2–3.

114 Ibid., 3.

115 Ibid.

116 In its later document, the bank corrected this error, changing "his" to "his/her."

117 Ibid., 4.

118 E-mail from Laura Campbell, counsel, General Counsel Office, EBRD, 1 June 2006.

119 EBRD, "Independent Recourse Mechanism," 12.

120 Ibid., 11.

121 Friends of the Earth International, "Comments on the Proposal for an Independent Recourse Mechanism at the EBRD."

122 Ibid., 1.

123 My thanks to Richard Bissell and Jim MacNeill for providing me with a copy of this letter.

124 See Written Question P-0439/03, at http://www.plooij.nl/engels/parlvr/082.htm. Note that the European Commission's answer to the question is only on the Dutch part of the website.

125 ERBD, "Independent Recourse Mechanism: Rules of Procedure."

126 Ibid., part 7, 23, paragraph 62.

127 Ibid., part 2, 4, paragraph 2.

128 Ibid., part 2, 6, paragraph 8.d.

129 Ibid., part 3, 9, paragraph 18.b and 18.c.

130 Ibid., part 4, 10, paragraph 21.

131 Search for "IRM" at http://www.ebrd.com.

132 CEE Bankwatch Network, "The Independent Recourse Mechanism," 2.

133 EBRD, Independent Recourse Mechanism (IRM), *Annual Report 2007*, 2–3.

134 Ibid., 3, original emphasis.

135 Ibid.

136 Parts of the text in this section on the EIB were originally presented at the World Bank's *ABCDE* conference, Amsterdam, 22–4 May 2005.

137 *Guardian* (London), 7 March 2004, http://politics.guardian.co.uk/eu/story/ 0,9061,1163631,00.html.

138 European Investment Bank (EIB), "2005 Corporate Responsibility Report."

139 EIB, "EIB Environmental Statement 2004," 1.

140 Jozsef Feiler, quoted in ibid.

141 Ieke van den Burg, "On the European Investment Bank Annual Report for 2001," 7, paragraph 20.

142 The EU then still comprised only fifteen member states.

143 EIB, "Eligibility Guidelines," 3.

144 For the competences of the European ombudsman, see http://www.euro-ombudsman.eu.int/glance/nl/default.htm.

145 E-mail from Luigi La Marca, spring 2005, soon after the World Bank conference.

146 Information provided by Bankwatch in the spring of 2005.

147 See http://www.eib.eu.int.

148 EIB, "The EIB Public Disclosure Policy," 6.

149 Ibid.

150 Ibid., 13.

151 Ibid.

152 EIB, "Public Disclosure Policy: Principles, Rules, and Procedures."

153 European Parliament Committee on Petitions, "On the Annual Report on the European Ombudsman's Activities in 2006," 8.

154 E-mail from Bram Schim van der Loef, Communication and Information Department, EIB, 12 December 2007.

155 According to Article 300(7) of the Treaty establishing the European Community (EC Treaty), international agreements concluded by the European Community are binding on the institutions of the community and on member states.

156 European Community, "The Aarhus Convention," 1.

157 Ibid.

158 United Nations Environment Programme (UNEP), "Rio Declaration on Environment and Development," Principle 10, states: "Environmental issues are best handled with participation of all concerned citizens, at the relevant level. At the national level, each individual shall have appropriate access to information concerning the environment that is held by public authorities,

including information on hazardous materials and activities in their communities, and the opportunity to participate in decision-making processes. States shall facilitate and encourage public awareness and participation by making information widely available. Effective access to judicial and administrative proceedings, including redress and remedy, shall be provided."

159 United Nations Economic Commission for Europe (UNECE), "About the Aarhus Clearinghouse."

160 UNECE, "Convention on Access to Information, Public Participation in Decision-making and Access to Justice in Environmental Matters."

161 UNECE Compliance Committee, "Findings and Recommendations with Regard to Compliance by Albania," 3.

162 Ibid., 3–4.

163 Ibid., 4.

164 Ibid., 5.

165 Ibid.

166 Ibid., 8.

167 Ibid., 6.

168 Ibid. This probably explains why the World Bank Inspection Panel also received a request for an investigation.

169 Ibid.

170 E-mail from Mr Felismino Alcarpe, head of Corporate Responsibility Policies, EIB, 6 February 2008.

171 African Development Fund (ADF), "ADF/BD/WP/2004/60: Bank Memorandum to the Board of Directors," 1.

172 Ibid.

173 Daniel Bradlow is a professor of law and director of the International Legal Studies Program at the College of Law, American University, Washington, DC.

174 Daniel Bradlow, "Study on an Inspection Function for the African Development Bank Group."

175 Ibid., 53.

176 Ibid.

177 Ibid.

178 ADF, "Bank Memorandum," 3.

179 Ibid.

180 Ibid.

181 African Development Bank (AfDB),
    "Resolution B/BD/2004/9-F/BD/2004/7."

182 E-mail from Per Sovik, director of the Compliance Review and Mediation Unit (CRMU), 23 January 2008.

183 AfDB, "Compliance Review and Mediation Unit of the Independent Review Mechanism, Operating Rules and Procedures," 6.

184 Ibid., 7.

185 Ibid., 9–10.

186 Ibid., 10.

187 Ibid., 11.

188 Ibid., 12.

189 Ibid.

190 Ibid., 13.

191 ADF, "Bank Memorandum," 7.

192 Ibid., annex IV, "Compliance Review and Mediation Unit of the Independent Review Mechanism, Operating Rules and Procedures," 2.

193 AfDB, "Bank Memorandum."

194 See Japan Bank for International Cooperation (JBIC), "Objection Procedures."

195 See JBIC, "Recommendations for the Japan Bank for International Cooperation's Environmental Guidelines," at http://www.s.g-egl-jbic.org.

196 Ibid., 5.

197 Ibid.

198 JBIC, "Objection Procedures," preamble, 1.

199 Ibid., 5.

200 Ibid.

201 Ikuko Matsumoto, "An NGO Evaluation of JBIC's Objections Procedure," 2.

202 JBIC, "Objection Procedures," 14.

203 Matsumoto, "NGO Evaluation," 2.

204 Ibid., 3. Matsumoto's references to monitoring and evaluation are not clear since the World Bank Inspection Panel does not (yet) have a formal mandate to monitor the implementation of necessary actions after findings of noncompliance. Evaluation is not part of the Inspection Panel's mandate but part of the bank's Operations Evaluation Department.

205 JBIC, "Objection Procedures," 14.

206 Ibid., 5–12.

207 E-mail from Kazuo Matsushita, 21 April 2006.

208 Search for "objection procedures" at http://www.jbic.org.

209 E-mail from Naomi Kanzaki, 23 January 2008.

CHAPTER FIVE

1 The contents of the Sarbanes-Oxley Act (2002) are: Title I, Public Company Accounting Oversight Board; Title II, Auditor Independence; Title III, Corporate Responsibility; Title IV, Enhanced Financial Disclosure; Title V, Analyst Conflict of Interest; Title VI, Commission Resources and Authority; Title VII, Studies and Reports; Title VIII, Corporate and Criminal Fraud Accountability; Title IX, White-Collar Crime Penalty Enhancements; Title X, Corporate Tax Returns; and Title XI, Corporate Fraud and Accountability.

2 Amitai Etzioni, *The Moral Dimension*, 4–5.

3 Clive Crook, "A Survey of Corporate Social Responsibility: The Good Company," *The Economist* (London), 22 January 2005, 3.

4 Ibid., 3–4.

5 Karolien Bais, "Corporate Social Responsibility," 23.

6 What today is the G-8 was then still the G-10, with actually eleven countries: Belgium, Canada, France, Germany, Italy, Japan, the Netherlands, Sweden, Switzerland, the United Kingdom, and the United States.

7 It is stated at the website of the Bank for International Settlements (http://www.bis.org; via the link to "Organisation and Governance"):

> The members of the Bank for International Settlements are the central banks or monetary authorities of Algeria, Argentina, Australia, Austria, Belgium, Bosnia and Herzegovina, Brazil, Bulgaria, Canada, Chile, China, Croatia, Czech Republic, Denmark, Estonia, Finland, France, Germany, Greece, the Hong Kong Special Administrative Region, Hungary, Iceland, India, Indonesia, Ireland, Israel, Italy, Japan, Korea, Latvia, Lithuania, Republic of Macedonia, Malaysia, Mexico, the Netherlands, New Zealand, Norway, Philippines, Poland, Portugal, Romania, Russia, Saudi Arabia, Singapore, Slovakia, Slovenia, South Africa, Spain, Sweden, Switzerland, Thailand, Turkey, the United Kingdom, and the United States, plus the European Central Bank.

> The legal status of the Yugoslav issue of the capital of the BIS is currently under review.

8 See http://www.riskglossary.com/articles/basel_committee.htm.

9 See http://www.bis.org/about/history.htm:

> The Bank for International Settlements (BIS) is an international organisation which fosters international monetary and financial cooperation and serves as a bank for central banks. The BIS fulfils this mandate by acting as:
> - a forum to promote discussion and facilitate decision-making processes among central banks and within the international financial community
> - a centre for economic and monetary research
> - a prime counterparty for central banks in their financial transactions
> - gent or trustee in connection with international financial operations
>
> The head office is in Basel, Switzerland, and there are two representative offices: in the Hong Kong Special Administrative Region of the People's Republic of China and in Mexico City. Established on 17 May 1930, the BIS is the world's oldest international financial organisation.

10 See http://www.bis.org/about/history.htm.

11 Conversation with Karl Cordewener, deputy secretary general of the Basel Committee on Banking Supervision, 15 November 2005, Basel.

12 See http://www.bis.org/about/history/htm. This was the original name of the committee, which was changed approximately fifteen years ago.

13 Basel Committee on Banking Supervision (BCBS), "History of the Basel Committee and Its Membership," 2.

14 Ibid.

15 Hans Moison, "Kredietrisico's onder Bazel II en IRFS," 5, my translation.

16 BCBS, "International Convergence of Capital Measurement and Capital Standards."

17 Conversation with Karl Cordewener, 15 November 2005, Basel.

18 Ibid.
19 EU legislation, in accordance with the so-called "Pillars," is adopted through a
    process involving the European Commission, the European Parliament, and
    the European Counsel, which issue a European Directive. This directive is fi-
    nally translated into national legislation. Supervision of the lgegislation's imple-
    mentation is the task of the national central banks.
20 See http://europa.eu.int/scadplus/leg/en/lvb/l24037.htm.
21 Gerald Dillenburg was seconded from the Deutsche Bundesbank and is work-
    ing for the European Commission as a principal advisor on capital adequacy.
22 Conversation with Gerald Dillenburg, 23 January 2006, Brussels.
23 The European Council is the authorizing body of the twenty-seven EU govern-
    ments.
24 Damian Paletta, "Backlash on Basel Hits Fed – What Now?" 19.
25 Ibid.
26 Richard J. Herring, "The Rocky Road to Implementation of Basel II in the
    United States," *Atlantic Economic Journal*, December 2007.
27 BCBS, "International Convergence," Article 9, paragraph 510, 108.
28 Chris Bray, quoted in Freshfields Bruckhaus Deringer, "Banking on Responsi-
    bility," 63.
29 BCBS, "Compliance and the Compliance Function in Banks," 8: "The
    expression 'bank' is used in this paper to refer generally to banks, banking
    groups, and to holding companies whose subsidiaries are predominantly
    banks."
30 Ibid., 9–15. The following ten principles are included:
    1   The bank's board of directors is responsible for overseeing the manage-
        ment of the bank's compliance risk. The board should approve the
        bank's compliance policy, including a formal document establishing a
        permanent and effective compliance function. At least once a year, the
        board or a committee of the board should assess the extent to which the
        bank is managing its compliance risk effectively.
    2   The bank's senior management is responsible for the effective manage-
        ment of the bank's compliance risk.
    3   The bank's senior management is responsible for establishing and com-
        municating a compliance policy, for ensuring that it is observed, and for
        reporting to the board of directors on the management of the bank's
        compliance risk.
    4   The bank's senior management is responsible for establishing a perma-
        nent and effective compliance function within the bank as part of the
        bank's compliance policy.
    5   Independence: The bank's compliance function should be independent.
    6   Resources: The bank's compliance function should have the resources to
        carry out its responsibilities effectively.
    7   Compliance function responsibilities: The responsibilities of the bank's
        compliance function should be to assist senior management in managing

effectively the compliance risk faced by the bank. Its specific responsibilities are set out below. If some of these responsibilities are carried out by staff in different departments, the allocation of responsibilities to each department should be clear.

8   Relationship with internal audit: The scope and breadth of the activities of the compliance function should be subject to periodic review by the internal audit function.

9   Cross-border issues: Banks should comply with applicable laws and regulations in all jurisdictions in which they conduct business, and the organisation and structure of the compliance function and its responsibilities should be consistent with local legal and regulatory requirements.

10   Outsourcing: Compliance should be regarded as a core risk management activity within the bank. Specific tasks of the compliance function may be outsourced, but they must remain subject to appropriate oversight by the head of compliance.

31 Ibid., 10.

32 Ibid., 11.

33 Jaime Caruna, quoted in Bank for International Settlements (BIS), "Basel Committee Issues Guidance on the Compliance Function in Banks," 1.

34 BCBS, "Compliance and the Compliance Function," 7.

35 Ibid.

36 Ibid., 15.

37 Ibid., 10.

38 Ibid., 10–11.

39 Ibid., 12.

40 Professor Arnold Schilder, quoted in BIS, "Basel Committee Issues Guidance," 1.

41 BCBS, "Compliance and the Compliance Function," 12.

42 Ibid., 12.

43 Ibid., 11.

44 Ibid.

45 Ibid., 12.

46 Ibid.

47 The Asian Development Bank calls its compliance review mechanism the Independent Inspection Function, and the Inter-American Development Bank calls its mechanism the Compliance Review Panel.

48 Ibid., 12.

49 The five institutions in the World Bank Group are the International Bank for Reconstruction and Development, the International Development Association, the Multilateral Investment Guarantee Agency, the International Center for the Settlement of Investment Disputes, and the International Finance Corporation.

50 Jonas Haralz, "IFCs 50th Anniversary: Documentary on IFC." For the history of the IFC, search "about ifc," then "history," and then "origins" at http://www.ifc.org.

51 Ibid., 2.

52 Ibid.

53 Ibid., 4.

54 See World Bank, *Annual Report 2002*, 9; and International Bank for Reconstruction and Development (IBRD), *A Guide to the World Bank*, 16.

55 IBRD, *Guide to the World Bank*, 16, 17, 18.

56 World Bank, *Annual Report 2002*, 9.

57 Ibid., 50.

58 Christopher Swann, "Bretton Woods Institutions, Sixty Years on, and Still Contentious," *Financial Times* (London), 29–30 May 2004.

59 In saying so, I do not take into account the operations of companies, such as the Dutch East Indian Company (Verenigde Oost Indische Companie), a trading firm already operating between the Far East and Europe in the sixteenth century.

60 World Bank, *Annual Report 2002*, 92.

61 Hilary F. French, "Assessing Private Capital Flows to Developing Countries," 161.

62 Figures provided by Joseph O'Keefe, spokesman of the IFC.

63 Marcos A. Orellana, "Indigenous Peoples, Energy, and Environmental Justice," 1–2.

64 Ibid., 3.

65 Ibid., 4.

66 Alvaro Umaña Quesada, *The World Bank Inspection Panel*, 9.

67 Orellana, "Indigenous Peoples," 4.

68 Ibid.

69 IFC, "Independent Review of the Chilean Pangue Hydroelectric Project."

70 Orellana, "Indigenous Peoples," 4–5.

71 Ibid., 4

72 According to Joseph O'Keefe, spokesman of the IFC.

73 See chapter 6.

74 Peter Woicke, "Putting Human Rights Principles into Development Practice through Finance," 328.

75 See chapter 6.

76 For my interview with Herman Mulder, see appendix 3.

77 According to several sources, Mulder and Woicke had a breakfast meeting that can be seen as the beginning of the Equator Principles.

78 ABN-AMRO Bank is one of the lead arrangers of financing for the Chad-Cameroon oil pipeline project.

79 Conversation with Herman Mulder, 8 July 2004, Amsterdam. See appendix 3.

80 Suellen Lazarus, "The Equator Principles," 2.

81 See Freshfields Bruckhaus Deringer, "Banking on Responsibility."

82 Conversation with Peter Woicke, 6–7 February 2006, New York.

83 Lazarus, "Equator Principles," 2.

84 Ibid.

85 Ibid.

86 Ibid.

87 Herman Mulder of ABN-AMRO Bank; Joseph O'Keefe, spokesman for the IFC; and Suellen Lazarus of the IFC.

88 For my interview with Suellen Lazarus, see appendix 3.

89 Conversation with Peter Woicke, 6–7 February 2006, New York.

90 Lazarus, "Equator Principles," 1.

91 See appendix 3.

92 The Equator Principles II were adopted in July 2006.

93 Demetri Sevastopulos, "Four banks adopt IFC agreement," *Financial Times* (London), 9 April 2003.

94 See appendix 3.

95 ABN-AMRO Bank is headquarted in Amsterdam, Barclays in London, Citigroup in New York, Crédit Lyonnais in Paris, Credit Suisse Group in Zurich, HVB Group in München, Rabobank Group in Utrecht, the Royal Bank of Scotland in Edinburgh, WestLB AG in Düsseldorf, and Westpac Banking Corporation in Sydney.

96 Equator Principles I, "Leading Banks Announce Adoption of Equator Principles."

97 For the press releases of the first ten banks to adopt the principles, see http://www.equator-principles.com.

98 Conversation with Bernd Schanzenbeacher, February 2004, Zurich. I visited with Schanzenbeacher and his team at the Credit Suisse Group headquarters.

99 See http://www.credit-suisse.com/sustainability.

100 For the press release from Barclays, see http://www.equator-principles.com.

101 For the press release from Citigroup, see http://www.equator-principles.com.

102 Equator Principles I, "Leading Banks Announce Adoption of Equator Principles."

103 Ibid., Exhibit II, "IFC Safeguard Policies: Environmental Assessment, Natural Habitats, Pest Management, Forestry, Safety of Dams, Indigenous Peoples, Involuntary Resettlement, Cultural Property, Child and Forced Labor, International Waterways." The IFC is the only member of the World Bank Group that has a policy on child and forced labour.

104 Ibid., Exhibit III, "The World Bank and IFC Specific Guidelines."

105 By the spring of 2006 forty-one financial institutions had adopted the first draft of the Equator Principles II. On 6 July 2006 these principles were revised, and on 28 July thirty-six financial institutions either adopted or readopted the Equator Principles in the form of Equator II. By 11 March 2008 sixty financial institutions had signed, including an African bank, and by (to come) the total was (to come).

106 See my interview with Herman Mulder and André Abadie in appendix 3.

107 See appendix 2.

108 Freshfields Bruckhaus Deringer, "Banking on Responsibility," 1–2.

109 Ibid., 6.

110 Ibid., 7.

111 On Banktrack, see http://www.banktrack.org: "BankTrack is a network of civil society organizations tracking the operations of the private financial sector and its effect on people and the planet. BankTrack aims to help create a

private financial sector strictly accountable to society at large whose operations contribute to creating healthy and just societies and preserve the ecological well being of the planet. The vision of BankTrack is further elaborated in the Collevecchio Declaration."

112 Freshfields Bruckhaus Deringer, "Banking on Responsibility," 33.

113 Ibid., 41.

114 See http://www.banktrack.org.

115 See World Bank, "Key Corporate Responsibility Codes, Principles and Standards."

116 See http://www.gri.org.

117 See http://www.ceres.org.

118 See http://www.ceres.org/our work/principles.htm.

119 The Collevecchio Declaration is signed by 39 NGOs from the United States, 9 from Italy, 4 from Canada, 4 from the United Kingdom, 4 from Australia, 3 from Czech Republic, 3 from Switzerland, 2 from the Netherlands, 2 from Germany, 2 from Lithuania, 2 from Indonesia, 2 from Bulgaria, 2 from Brazil, and 1 each from Norway, Armenia, Peru, Papua New Guinea, El Salvador, Pakistan, Thailand, Hungary, India, Jersey Islands (!), Denmark, Belgium, Nicaragua, Mauritius, Georgia, Uganda, Ghana, and Mexico. An additional 5 NGOs are listed without mention of any national affiliation.

120 One NGO, the Indigenous Environmental Network, is based in both the United States and Canada.

121 BankTrack, "The Collevecchio Declaration on Financial Institutions and Sustainability."

122 For my interview with Suellen Lazarus, see appendix 3.

123 E-mail from Johan Frijns, January 2006.

124 BankTrack, "Collevecchio Declaration," 1.

125 Ibid., 3.

126 Ibid.

127 A reference is made in ibid., 3, to the work of the World Commission on Dams and the Forest Stewardship Council. See also http://www.foe.org/camps/intl/declaration.html.

128 See BankTrack, "Collevecchio Declaration," 3.

129 On the inception of the World Bank Inspection Panel, see chapter 3.

130 See http://www.banktrack.org.

131 E-mail from Johan Frijns, January 2006. See also http://www.banktrack.org.

132 BankTrack, "No U-turn Allowed," 2.

133 Ibid., 3.

134 Ibid.

135 Ibid.

136 Ibid., 4.

137 Ibid., 5.

138 Ibid.

139 Ibid., 6.

140 Ibid., 7.

141 Ibid., 8.

142 BankTrack, "Principles, Profits or Just PR?" 44.
143 Ibid.
144 Ibid., 40.
145 BankTrack, "Unproven Equator Principles," 2–3.
146 Ibid., 5.
147 Freshfields Bruckhaus Deringer, "Banking on Responsibility," 51.
148 Ibid., 52.
149 Ibid.
150 Ibid.
151 Ibid.
152 Ibid, 53.
153 Ibid., 56.
154 Ibid., 59.
155 Ibid.
156 Ibid., 63.
157 Ibid., 63.
158 Ibid.
159 Ibid., 86.
160 Ibid., 87.
161 Ibid., 92.
162 Ibid.
163 Footnote in the original: "F&C Asset Management, *A benchmarking study: Environmental credit risk factors in the pan-European banking sector,* September 2002."
164 Ibid., 65–6.
165 Ibid., 92.
166 Ibid., 66.
167 Ibid., 68.
168 The ASN Bank has almost 260,000 clients. At present, it administers 3 billion Euros (saving accounts and investment accounts), and according to information provided by the bank's vice president, Jeroen Jansen, it is the largest sustainable investor.
169 ASN Bank, "ASN Bank Drops Investments in the European Investment Bank and in the World Bank," 1, my translation.
170 Ibid.
171 Ibid., 2.
172 Internal documentation of the ASN Bank, 2005.
173 Conversation with Jeroen Jansen, 19 December 2005, the Hague.
174 Atradius is a commericial company and the second largest credit ensurer in the world. Atradius Dutch State Business, a 100 per cent subsidiary of Atradius, functions as an export credit agency for the Dutch state. For more on Atradius, see www.atradius.com.
175 See Organization for Economic Cooperaton and Development (OECD), "Recommendation on Common Approaches on Environment and Officially Supported Export Credits."

176 Interview with Vinco David, December 2005, Amsterdam. Subsequent to this interview, representatives of Equator banks and export credit agencies met and, I was told, concluded that the standards of the export credit agencies and the Equator Principles have a lot in common.

177 OECD Trade and Agriculture Directorate Trade Committee, "Debt Sustainability and Responsible Lending," 9. The OECD Working Party on Export Credits and Credit Guarantees adopted and published the "Revised Council Recommendations on Common Approaches on the Environment and Officially Supported Export Credits."

178 Freshfields Bruckhaus Deringer, "Banking on Responsibility," 69.

179 The board of the World Bank approved the IFC's new Performance Standards on 21 February 2006.

180 Ibid.

181 Ibid.

182 I met with Johan Frijns, coordinator of BankTrack, and Peter Woicke, a former executive vice president of the IFC, on 27 November 2005 in Amsterdam. A prolonged debate ensued on whether changing the name from "Safeguard Policies" to "Performance Standards" would weaken the policies or whether the name change was just a matter of recognizing that the private sector would adopt "standards" but not "policies."

183 Since the report was published, even more banks have adopted the principles.

184 Freshfields Bruckhaus Deringer, "Banking on Responsibility," 70.

185 Ibid., 71.

186 Ibid., 119.

187 Ibid., 71.

188 Ibid., 73.

189 Ibid., 72.

190 In July 2006 it was decided that under Equator II the threshold would be lowered to US$10 million.

191 Christopher Weeramantry, "Foreword," in Marie-Claire Cordonier Segger and Ashfaq Khalfan, eds, *Sustainable Development Law: Principles, Practices, and Prospects*, ix.

192 Professor Edith Brown-Weiss of George Town University Law Centre was chair of the World Bank Inspection Panel from 2003 to 2007.

193 Edith Brown-Weiss, "Introduction," in Edith Brown-Weiss, ed., *International Compliance with Nonbinding Accords*, 1–2.

194 Carolyn Deere, "Sustainable International Natural Resources Law," 302–3.

195 The Johannesburg Plan of Implementation is the outcome of the World Summit on Sustainable Development, or the so-called "Rio + 10," held in Johannesburg from 26 August to 4 September 2002.

196 Deere, "Sustainable International," 306–7.

197 Stephen L. Kass and Jean M. McCarroll, "Environmental Law," under subhead "Open Issues."

198 See Equator Principles II, Exhibit I: Categorisation of Projects.

199 Kass and McCarroll, "Environmental Law," under subhead "Open Issues."

200 Ibid.

201 The BTC pipeline project is a US$3.6 billion project comprising 1,700 kilometres of crude oil pipeline from Baku in Azerbaijan, through Tbilisi in Georgia, to Ceyhan in Turkey. British Petrol, the IFC, and various Equator banks are involved in the project. See http://www.caspiandevelopmentandexport.com/ASP/PD_BTC.asp.

202 Kass and McCarroll, "Environmental Law," under subhead "The BTC Project."

203 Ibid.

204 Freshfields Bruckhaus Deringer, "Banking on Responsibility," 102.

205 Ibid.

206 Ibid., 127

207 "The Logging Trade, Down in the Woods," *The Economist* (London), 25–31 March 2006, 67–9.

208 French, "Assessing Private Capital," 163.

209 Bradford Gentry, quoted in ibid.

210 Conversation with Hans Ludo van Mierlo, December 2005, Ilpendam, the Netherlands.

211 Center for Human Rights and Environment (CEDHA), "Equator Principles Compliance Complaint, regarding Proposed Pulp Paper Mill Investment in Fray Bentos Uruquay."

212 Ibid., 2

213 Ibid.

214 Ibid., 3.

215 Ibid.

216 Ibid. On the role of the IFC's ombudsman, see chapter 4.

217 Ibid., 2.

218 Ibid., 6.

219 Ibid., 7.

220 Ibid., 8.

221 Ibid., 3.

222 Ibid., 2.

223 Ibid.

224 Ibid., 4.

225 Ibid.

226 Ibid., 5.

227 Ibid., 6.

228 Ibid.

229 CEDHA, press release, 29 December 2005.

230 BankTrack and World Wildlife Fund, "ING bank dumps divisive 1.7 billion paper mill project."

231 CEDHA, "Dramatic Weekend Unfolds as Uruguay Issues Operating Permit to Botnia"; CEDHA, "Pulp Mill CEO Erkki Varis Says He's Famous Thanks to Conflict and Favors Private Investment over Social Conflict."

232 BankTrack and World Wildlife Fund, "Banks Failing Environment and Social Standards," 1.

233 Ibid.

234 BankTrack and World Wildlife Fund, "Shaping the Future of Sustainable Finance," 4.

235 Ibid., 72.

236 Ibid., 6.

237 As orginally stated on the website for the Equator Principles, http://www.equator-principles.com.

238 The four core labour standards are prohibition against: child labour, forced labour, the right of free association and collective bargaining, and freedom from discrimination. See appendix 2.

239 BankTrack, "Equator Principles II," 3.

240 Ibid., 6.

241 Ibid., 4.

242 Ibid., 19.

243 The website of the Equator Principles, http://www.equator-principles.com, is edited by several Equator banks (EPFIs) that rotate the function. The first editing was done by Citigroup Bank in New York.

244 I was told of this in private by two different stakeholders.

245 Conversation with Leonie Schreve, 28 March 2006, Amsterdam.

246 BankTrack, "Who Has Adopted the Equator Principles?"

247 Information provided by Johan Frijns, coordinator of BankTrack.

248 Conversation with Leonie Schreve, 28 March 2006, Amsterdam.

249 Ibid.

250 Ibid.

251 Lars Thunell, quoted at http://www.ifc.org.

252 Paul Wolfowitz, quoted in Reuters press release, 23 October 2006.

253 President of the EIB Philippe Maystadt, quoted in George Parker and Alan Beattie, "EIB Accuses China of Unscrupulous Loans," *Financial Times* (London), 28 November 2006.

254 Ibid.

255 E-mail from Oxfam America to the Dutch-based NGO Bothends, copy received 10 October 2006.

256 European Centre for Development Policy Management (ECDPM), seminar on *The Cotonou Partnership Agreement: What Role in a Changing World?*, Maastricht, the Netherlands, 18–19 December 2006. As vice chair of the ECDPM, I took part in the conversations.

257 Information provided by officials from the Dutch Ministry of Foreign Affairs in the Hague.

258 See appendix 2.

259 For example, in the China Western Poverty Reduction Project, for which 57,775 Chinese people were going to be resettled in Qinghai Province, located in western China, the Inspection Panel found and reported the

following regarding the scope and impact of the project: "The documentation fails to situate the move-in area within a realistic regional context. A network of social, commercial and political interactions clearly exist in Dulan County and Xiangride Townshi, yet no assessment is made of how these linkages and interactions will be affected, for better or worse, by a Project that will completely change the economy and demography of the county." See World Bank Inspection Panel, "China Western Poverty Reduction Project (Credit no. 3255-CHA and Loan no. 4501-CHA)," xvi.

260 In addition to his role as secretary general of the 1992 Earth Summit, which gave a significant push to global economic and environmental regulation, Maurice Strong has since been a senior advisor to former UN secretary general Kofi Annan (during which he oversaw the most recent UN reforms), senior advisor to former World Bank president Jim Wolfensohn, chairman of the Earth Council, chairman of the World Resources Institute, co-chairman of the Council of the World Economic Forum, and a member of Toyota's International Advisory Board. See http://iresist.com/cbg/strong.html.

261 Conversation with Maurice Strong, 3 November 2005, Amsterdam.

262 BCBS, "Compliance and the Compliance Function."

263 Freshfields Bruckhaus Deringer, "Banking on Responsibility."

CHAPTER SIX

1 International Bank for Reconstruction and Development (IBRD), "Articles of Agreement."

2 See the discussion of Article 5 in chapter 2.

3 Article 1 of Operational Policy 4.10 on Indigenous Peoples (revised July 2005) reads:

> This policy (1) contributes to the Bank's (2) mission of poverty reduction and sustainable development by ensuring that the development process fully respects the dignity, human rights, economies, and cultures of Indigenous Peoples. For all projects that are proposed for Bank financing and affect Indigenous Peoples, (3) the Bank requires the borrower to engage in a process of free, prior, and informed consultation. (4) The Bank provides project financing only where free, prior, and informed consultation results in broad community support to the project by the affected Indigenous Peoples. (5) Such Bank-financed projects include measures to (a) avoid potentially adverse effects on the Indigenous Peoples' communities; or (b) when avoidance is not feasible, minimize, mitigate, or compensate for such effects. Bank-financed projects are also designed to ensure that the Indigenous Peoples receive social and economic benefits that are culturally appropriate and gender and intergenerationally inclusive.

In the previous Operational Directive 4.20 on Indigenous Peoples, adopted in September 1991, the term "human rights" did not appear before paragraph 6, which reads: "The Bank's broad objective towards indigenous people, as for all the people in its member countries, is to ensure that the development process fosters full respect for their dignity, human rights, and cultural uniqueness."

4 See compliance advisor ombudsman (CAO), *Annual Report 2003–04*, 18:

> In 2003, the CAO conducted a gap analyses with respect to some basic human rights instruments as well as the existing Safeguard Policies, which include some explicit and implicit references to human rights. The CAO also produced internal case studies on how three IFC projects might have been approached differently if a human rights filter were to have been applied at the outset.
>
> One tension facing the CAO is the extent to which it should be involved in providing such advice without prior guarantees of eventual disclosure. In this instance, the CAO took the unusual step of providing assurances to IFC that it would not release the information publicly unless IFC chose to do so. The decision was taken as the issues are critical to advancing the institution's sustainability agenda and have been an important contribution to the live debate about how best to reflect human rights concerns in IFC's revised Safeguard Policies.

5 The websites of the African Development Bank, the Inter-American Development Bank, the European Investment Bank, and the Japan Bank for International Cooperation do not mention human rights in their articles of agreement or mission statements.

6 European Bank for Reconstruction and Development (EBRD), "Agreement Establishing the European Bank for Reconstruction and Development," introduction to Article 1: "The contracting parties, Committed to the fundamental principles of multiparty democracy, the rule of law, respect for human rights and market economics ... Welcoming the intent of central and eastern European countries to further the practical implementation of multiparty democracy, strengthening democratic institutions, the rule of law and respect for human rights and their willingness to implement reforms in order to evolve towards market-oriented economies."

7 Export Development Canada (EDC), "2003 Annual Compliance Program Report," 4: "EDC's human rights initiative was the topic of discussion at an internal meeting held mid 2003. The meeting was convened in order to confer about EDC's current system for communicating human rights issues with DFAIT [Department of Foreign Affairs and International Trade] pursuant to the Memorandum of Understanding signed in 2002. The CO [compliance officer] advised that perhaps, if changes were to be made to this system, other government departments be included in the dialogue in order to ensure consistency of application of the government of Canada's practices in this regard."

8 Ibrahim Shihata is seen as one of the founding fathers of the Inspection Panel. The first edition of his book *The World Bank Inspection Panel* (1994) is internationally recognized as a standard reference work on the panel's compliance mechanism. This also applies to the second edition, *The Inspection Panel: In Practice* (2000). Unfortunately, he passed away in 2001. The panel has not always agreed with the statements in Shihata's books.

9 Shihata, *World Bank*, 2nd ed., 210.

10 Suresh Nanwani is presently the associate secretary of the Compliance Review Panel of the Asian Development Bank.

11 See http://www.un.org/law/ilc/ilcintro.htm: "The International Law Commission was established by the General Assembly in 1947 to promote the progressive development of international law and its codification. Most of the Commission's work involves the preparation of draft on topics of international law. Some topics are chosen by the Commission and others referred to it by the General Assembly or the Economic and Social Council."

12 Footnote in the original: "Responsibility of States for Internationally Wrongful Acts, G.A. Res. 83, U.N. GAOR; 56th Sess., Sup No. 10, U.N. Doc. A/Res/56/83 (Jan. 28, 2002). See generally The International Law Commission's Articles on State Responsibility: Introduction, Text and Commentaries (James Crawford ed., 2002)."

13 Footnote in the original: "U.N. Int'l L. Comm'n, Report of the International Law, Fifty-Second Session, U.N. GAOR, 55th Sess., Sup No. 10, at 292, U.N. Doc. A/55/10 (2000)."

14 Eisuke Suzuki and Suresh Nanwani, "Responsibility of International Organizations," 179.

15 Ibid.

16 Ibid., 180.

17 Ibid.

18 Ibid., 180–1.

19 Ibid., 187–8.

20 Ibid., 181.

21 Ibid., 206.

22 Ibid., 210.

23 Ibid., 200.

24 Ibid.

25 Roberto Dañino left the World Bank at the beginning of 2006.

26 Dañino spoke at a the conference *Human Rights and Development: Towards Mutual Reinforcement*, co-sponsored by the Ethical Globalization Initiative and the Center for Human Rights, New York University School of Law, New York, 1 March 2004. He stated emphatically that he was expressing his personal views. The conference lectures are published in Philip Alston and Mary Robinson, eds, *Human Rights and Development*.

27 Roberto Dañino, "The Legal Aspects of the World Bank's Work on Human Rights," 515.

28 Earlier, the Inspection Panel had made a similar statement in its report on Chad. See the section below entitled "Request from Chad Lodged with the Inspection Panel."

29 Dañino, "Legal Aspects," 515.

30 Ibid., 515–16.

31 Ibid., 517.

32 Ibid.

33 Ibid., 524.

34 Mac Darrow, *Between Light and shadow*, 45.

35 Footnote in the original: "'Decision No 284-4, 10 March 1948,' *Selected Decisions*, 8th (1976) at 35–36."

36 Ibid., 46–7.

37 Ibid., 47.

38 Ibid., 51.

39 See ibid., footnote: "E. Denters, *Law and Policy of IMF Conditionality*, 135–36 (1996). Denters intimated (at n. 38) that three members of IMF staff had confirmed this to him in interviews, but would not disclose copies of the written instructions themselves." At the World Bank it was often confirmed that the president made some senior managers responsible for closely following the human rights situation in sensitive projects such as the Chad-Cameroon pipeline and for presenting their findings to the president, who could act.

40 During my years at the World Bank, I noticed that it was not only the legal department that was involved in the policy and procedure making. On specific issues, such as the environment and the rights of indigenous peoples, to name two, it was obvious that bank specialists with experience in particular areas played a very important role. A good example is Dr Robert Goodland, who was the principal author of the World Bank's first Environmental Impact Assessment Policy and first Indigenous Peoples Policy.

41 Ibid., 122.

42 Ibid.

43 See IBRD, "Articles of Agreement," Article VIII.

44 See ibid., Article VIII, part A.

45 Andrés Rigo Sureda, "The World Bank and Institutional Innovations," 12.

46 Ibid., 13.

47 World Bank Inspection Panel, "Chad-Cameroon Petroleum Development and Pipeline Project (Loan 4558-CD); Management of the Petroleum Economy Project (Credit 3316-CD); and Petroleum Sector Management Capacity Building Project (Credit 3373-CD)." See also Sheldon Leader, "Human Rights, Risks, and New Strategies for Global Investment."

48 See http://www.worldbank.org: "The project intends to develop the oil fields at Doba in southern Chad (at a cost of US$1.5 billion) and construct a 1,070 km pipeline to offshore oil-loading facilities on Cameroon's Atlantic coast (US$2.2 billion). The sponsors are ExxonMobil of the U.S. (the operator, with 40% of the private equity), Petronas of Malaysia (35%), and Chevron-Texaco of the U.S. (25%). The project could result in nearly US$2 billion in revenues for Chad (averaging US$80 million per year) and US$500 million for Cameroon (averaging US$20 million per year) over the 25-year production period."

49 In the case of Chad, the World Bank financed the project via the International Development Association (IDA), and in the case of Cameroon it was both IDA and the International Bank for Reconstruction and Development (IBRD).

50 NC-IUCN symposium, *Liability for Environmental Damage and the Chad-Cameroon Oil Pipeline Project*, the Netherlands Institute of International Relations, the Hague, 25 February 2000.

51 Serge A. Bronkhorst, "Liability for Environmental Damage and the World Bank's Chad-Cameroon Oil and Pipeline Project," 9.

52 At the time, I was a member of the World Bank Inspection Panel, and it was realistic to assume that the panel might be involved at a later stage if a request for an inspection was submitted, as indeed happened.

53 Christophe Deoukoubou, "The Chad-Cameroon Oil and Pipeline Project," 25.

54 Ibid.

55 Ibid., 27.

56 "La Convention de Recherche, d'Exploitation et de Transport des Hydrocarbures."

57 Deoukoubou, "Chad-Cameroon," 28.

58 Saman Zia-Zarifi is a Senior Research Fellow in the Department of Public International Law at Erasmus University, Rotterdam.

59 Saman Zia-Zarifi, "The (Lack of) Responsibility of Multinational Oil Companies in the Proposed Chad-Cameroon Pipeline," 42.

60 Serge A. Bronkhorst, ed., *Liability for Environmental Damage and the World Bank's Chad-Cameroon Oil and Pipeline Project*, Annex II, 112–13.

61 Ibid., Annex II, 115.

62 Ibid., Annex III, 119.

63 Ibid.

64 See http://www.bhopal.org.

65 See A. Becker and Frank Vanclay, eds, *The International Handbook of Social Impact Assessment*.

66 A Human Rights Watch investigation in Chad at the beginning of 2008 has "determined that two opposition leaders whom the government says it is not holding were in fact seized by state security forces on February 3. Their arrests were part of a crackdown on political opponents in the capital N'Djamena following a coup attempt by Chadian rebels in early February. On February 21, the Chadian government stated that an official inquiry had been unable to locate Ibni Oumar Mahamat Saleh, spokesman for a coalition of opposition political parties, and Ngarlejy Yorongar" (see Human Rights Watch, "Chad: Account for 'Disappeared' Opposition Leaders, Two Missing Politicians Last Seen in Army Custody"). On 11 March 2008 I was informed by Reed Brody of Human Rights Watch in Brussels that Mr Yorongar was able to flee via Cameroon and arrived in Paris on 9 March.

67 During both the Chad and Cameroon cases, I was a member of the Inspection Panel and took full part in the investigations, meeting with the requesters in Chad and Cameroon as well as in Paris.

68 World Bank Inspection Panel, "Chad-Cameroon," ix.

69 The delegation travelled in the field in three cars. In the front car no one from the panel had a seat. This car, with a government driver, drove fast and directed the rest. I was in the second car and seated next to the NGO representative. She

tried to ask several times that we leave the main road and go into the field to meet with affected people in the villages. Only after my intervention explaining that it was up to the independent panel to decide where to go was the driver of the second car willing to give notice to the first driver that we were going to take another route.

70 The panel reports only findings, not conclusions. It is finally the Board of Directors that draws a conclusion on the basis of the reported panel findings and the reported answer of management to the findings.

71 World Bank Inspection Panel, "Chad-Cameroon," 61, paragraph 213.

72 Footnote in the original: "General Assembly Resolution 217 A (III) of 10 December 1948."

73 Ibid., 62, paragraph 214.

74 Footnote in the original: "Management Response, supra note 27, at § 151."

75 Ibid., 61, paragraph 212, original emphasis. Here, I take the opportunity to thank my colleagues for the moment we were able to show the courage needed to formulate a finding in such strong wording and to thank the staff of the panel who supported us in doing so.

76 Ibid., xi.

77 World Bank, "World Bank Suspends Disbursements to Chad."

78 Ibid.

79 See http://www.worldbank.org: "World Bank Statement on Chad – The WB Group President, in his December 8 statement, expressed serious concerns about a proposal from the Government of Chad to significantly alter the Petroleum Revenue Management Law. This law was a deciding factor in the WB Group's original support for the Chad-Cameroon Oil Pipeline. The government of Chad argues that the proposed changes are needed to boost revenue to its budget at a time of fiscal crisis. However in WB's view, the modifications alone will fail to provide a lasting solution to the recurring financial problems that Chad faces but would instead undermine the objectives of socio-economic development, poverty reduction, accountability and transparency that guided WB and international support for the Chad-Cameroon Pipeline project. The WB has proposed to the Chadian Government other measures to strengthen safeguards in the management of the country's public finances, while preserving the integrity of the oil revenue management system for the benefit of all Chadians. The WB Group is expecting to hear the Government's response to its proposals."

80 "Crisis in region Darfur dijt uit naar Tsjaad" (Crisis in Darfur region expands to Chad), NRC-Handelsblad (Rotterdam), 17 March 2006.

81 In a few cases, such as the panel's report on China, the report was leaked to the press before it went to the board. It is important to note that this never happened until after the report left the office of the panel and was handed out to the secretaries of the board.

82 Henry E. McCandless, A Citizen's Guide to Public Accountability, 130.

83 International Bank for Reconstruction and Development (IBRD), "Resolution No. IBRD-93-10 and Resolution No. IDA-93-6," 1. These combined resolutions

established the Inspection Panel on 22 September 1993. For the entire text, see appendix 1.

84 Ibid.

85 The previous Inspection Function at the Asian Development Bank permitted former members of the function to be re-employed by the ADB after a period of five years.

86 Once during an investigation I was unfortunately confronted with a problem regarding a consultant hired by the panel to advise us in Cameroon on the difficulties of the indigenous people living in the area where the oil pipeline crosses. I found it unacceptable that the consultant had also been an advisor to the oil company on how to compensate the people who had lost crops or land. In one meeting I was confronted with a strong "discussion" between the consultant and the requesters about their compensation. This I considered a conflict of interest, and I regretted that the panel had placed itself in such a situation.

87 The Environmental Impact Assessment Policy has been the policy most frequently tabled in the requests lodged with the panel, followed by the Indigenous Peoples Policy.

88 The policies and procedures of the World Bank, the IBRD, and IDA are available at http://www.worldbank.org/safeguards. They are also posted at http://www.inspectionpanel.org (search for "policies and procedures").

89 Most multilateral financial institutions use the word "policies," while in the private sector there is more diversity in the words used, among them "business principles" and "codes of conduct."

90 The IFC invited those interested to give comments on the draft revised safeguard policies, renamed "performance standards," via its website. The IFC's board adopted the new environmental and social performance standards on 21 February 2006.

91 The London-based NGO Forest Peoples Programme wrote a letter on the subject "Concerns about the Weakening of World Bank Safeguard Policies," dated 2 March 2001 and signed by NGO representatives from all over the world. The letter was also sent to Jim Wolfensohn (president), Ian Johnson (vice president, environment), Joanne Salop (managing director, operational policies), Maartje van Putten (member, Inspection Panel), Claire Short (minister for international development, UK), Eveline Herfkens (minister for development cooperation, the Netherlands), Maj-Inger Klingvall (minister for development cooperation, Sweden).

92 I have also been the "rapporteur" on the EU's Indigenous Peoples Policy.

93 Shannon Lawrence, "Retreat from the Safeguard Policies."

94 See, for example, Dana Clark, Jonathan Fox, and Kay Treakle, eds, *Demanding Accountability*.

95 This situation is in contradiction with the Articles of Agreement of the World Bank, which state that the bank will not finance a project if others can do it.

96 See World Bank, *Annual Report 2003*. In 2003 the following new EU countries were eligible for World Bank/EBRD funding: Czech Republic, Hungary, Estonia, Slovakia, Lithuania, and Latvia.

97 This legislation is the so-called "Acquis Communautaire," or "Community Patrimony."

98 On the consultation on the "use of country systems," see http://www.world-bank.org.

99 Edith Brown-Weiss (chairperson, Inspection Panel) and Roberto Dañino (general counsel, World Bank), "Joint Statement on the Use of Country Systems," 1.

100 Jim Wolfensohn, "Foreword," in Alvaro Umaña Quesada, *The World Bank Inspection Panel*, vii.

101 Bank Information Center (BIC) et al., "Strengthening Public Accountability," 21. The co-authors were: Coalition in Reforms for Efficient and Equitable Development (CREED), Pakistan; Environmental Foundation, Sri Lanka; Gama Surakeema Savidhana, Sri Lanka; Internationa Rivers Network (IRN), US; Mekong Watch, Japan; NGO Forum on the ADB, Philippines; Oxfam Mekong Initiative (OMI), Cambodia; Urban Resource Centre, Pakistan; SUNGI, Pakistan; and Oxfam Community Aid Abroad, Australia.

102 IBRD, "Resolution No. IBRD-93-10 and Resolution No. IDA-93-6."

103 BIC et al., "Strengthening Public Accountability," 22.

104 It was mentioned during the meeting that this is normally a small percentage of the total budgeted costs.

105 World Bank Inspection Panel, "Administrative Procedures," as amended by the panel on 10 July 1998.

106 Shihata, *World Bank*, 2nd ed., 171.

107 World Bank, "Board Procedures and Practices."

108 At the time of writing, it was not yet clear what kind of information is delivered directly to the board and what first goes to the president.

CHAPTER SEVEN

1 I refer to the survey participants alternately as respondents, experts, and specialists.

2 In the survey, I cited the *Economist* (London), 23 October 1999: "twenty years ago there was very little cross-border trade in bonds or shares. It now accounts for about $600 billion in bonds every day and $30 billion in equities." Moreover, on 7 October 1999 the *Economist* pointed out that "Derivative trading amounted to about $30 trillion a year in 1994 and $120 trillion in 2001 – or four times global GDP."

3 United Nations Conference on Trade and Development, *World Investment Report 2005*.

4 World Bank, *Annual Report 2002*.

5 See chapter 5.

6 At the beginning of the 1990s, I tabled a written question on this together with Maxime Verhagen, a member of the European Parliament for the Christian Democrats, who today is the minister of foreign affairs for the Netherlands.

7 Such was the case, for example, with the Chad-Cameroon Oil Pipeline Project (investigations were done separately in both countries) and with the Bujagali Energy Project in Uganda.

8 At the end of 1999 the Inspection Panel received a case in Argentina. The panel went to Argentina in the first eligibility phase. Supported by the World Bank's executive secretary, the chairman and I (as members of the panel) had to declare the case eligible or ineligible. Instead, we found out that the problems were based on a huge lack of communication between the stakeholders. Before we left the country with the team, the problems had been solved. In 2004 the panel received a case concerning a project in Mexico. On the spot, the chairman, two members of the bank staff, and myself were confronted with a conflict within the team of those implementing the project. Instead of declaring the case eligible, we advised the team to find a solution to the internal problem. The panel kept open the option for further investigations in case no solution was found. In those cases, the panel automatically found itself in a problem-solving role.

9 See http://www.ifc.org/cao.

10 Compliance advisor ombudsman (cao), "Operational Guidelines," 11.

11 A former president of the ifc, Peter Woicke, informed me that he had been in favour of direct reporting by the ombudsman to the board of the ifc.

12 See World Bank, "Operational Manual Statement 4.01":

Operational Policies (Ops) are short, focused statements that follow from the Bank's Articles of Agreement, the general conditions, and policies approved by the Board. Ops establish the parameters for the conduct of operations; they also describe the circumstances under which exceptions to policy are admissible and spell out who authorizes exceptions.

Bank Procedures (bps) explain how Bank staff carry out the policies set out in the Ops. They spell out the procedures and documentation required to ensure Bankwide consistency and quality.

Good Practices (gps) contain advice and guidance on policy implementation, for example, the history of the issue, the sectoral context, analytical framework, best practice examples.

Operational Directives (ods) contain a mixture of policies, procedures, and guidance. The ods are gradually being replaced by Ops/bps/gps, which present policies, procedures, and guidance separately.

Operational Memoranda (Op Memos) are interim instructions intended to elaborate on material in Ops/bps or ods. Once the instructions in Op Memos are incorporated into revision of the pertinent Ops/bps, the Op Memos are "retired."

Each of the above measures, except for Good Practices, is part of the Inspection Panel's mandate.

13 This occurred in the context of the Yacyretá Hydroelectric Dam, a project for the water and telecommunication sectors of Argentina and Paraguay, known as the Paraguay/Argentina Reform Project. It also occurred with the segba V Power Distribution Project, another joint undertaking of Argentina and Paraguay.

14 I prefer to call the monitoring of mitigation actions that derive from an earlier investigation follow-up monitoring. This is different from post-monitoring, which is monitoring of the effects of projects that have been implemented.

15 Of the 195 member countries of the World Bank, a large majority support the Universal Declaration of Human Rights, many of whose principles are already embodied in their constitutions, including countries with a wide diversity of cultures and religions.

16 The International Finance Corporation is the only member of the Word Bank Group to have introduced the subject of child labour.

17 Peter Woicke was executive vice president of the IFC and vice president of the World Bank Group until 2005.

18 The following companies are mentioned: British Petrol, Rabobank Group, HBOS, Westpac, and Shell.

19 ABN-AMRO Bank is one of the leading Equator banks.

20 International Bank for Reconstruction and Development (IBRD), "Resolution No. IBRD-93-10 and Resolution No. IDA-93-6." These combined resolutions established the Inspection Panel on 22 September 1993. For the entire text, see appendix 1.

21 Most MFIs have introduced the system of appointing members in different years, thus guaranteeing that those with knowledge and expertise do not "depart" at the same time.

22 Most multilateral financial institutions use the word "policies," while in the private sector there is more diversity in the words used, among them "business principles" and "codes of conduct."

23 The Environmental Impact Assessment Policy has been the policy most frequently tabled in the requests lodged with the panel, followed by the Indigenous Peoples Policy.

24 See World Bank, "Safeguard Policies."

25 Question 21 of the survey similarly raised the issue of training for management. This question generated a similar response and is not repeated in this study.

26 On 21 February 2006 the World Bank adopted the IFC's performance standards, thus replacing the IFC's policies with the IFC's performance standards.

27 World Bank Inspection Panel, "China Western Poverty Reduction Project (Credit no. 3255-CHA and Loan no. 4501-CHA)."

28 An agreement between a government and the World Bank is recorded in a so-called "project appraisal document" (PAD).

29 The question was answered by 19 of the 24 MFI experts, 7 of the 13 private-sector experts, 12 of the 15 NGO experts, and 13 of the 22 independent experts.

30 The question was answered by 20 of the 24 MFI experts, 8 of the 13 private-sector experts, 13 of the 15 NGO experts, and 13 of the 22 independent experts.

31 IBRD, "Resolution No. IBRD-93-10 and Resolution No. IDA-93-6."

32 Before I was appointed, President Wolfensohn informed himself of my background by speaking, for example, to a former president of the European Parliament.

33 IBRD, "Resolution No. IBRD-93-10 and Resolution No. IDA-93-6," paragraph 12.

34 This request concerned the China Western Poverty Reduction Project (credit no. 3255-CHA and loan no. 4501-CHA).

35 The word "instruct" is used in the resolution establishing the panel when referring to the board's option to instruct the panel to do an investigation.

36 World Bank Inspection Panel, "Administrative Procedures," as amended by the panel on 10 July 1998.

37 Another question about what internal procedures the mechanisms should use did not yield many new insights other than the necessity of regular face-to-face meetings and the importance of working on a consensus basis, with each member fully informed and fully participating in the writing of the report.

CHAPTER EIGHT

1 Eisuke Suzuki and Suresh Nanwani, "Responsibility of International Organizations," 3.

2 Henry E. McCandless, *A Citizen's Guide to Public Accountability*, 4.

3 See Sebastian Mallaby, *The World's Banker*.

4 International Bank for Reconstruction and Development (IBRD), "Resolution No. IBRD-93-10 and Resolution No. IDA-93-6," paragraphs 2 and 3. For the entire text see appendix 1.

5 Ibid., paragraph 4.

APPENDIX 3

1 For the position of the US Congress on Basel II, including Barney Frank's views, see Damian Paletta, "Backlash on Basel Hits Fed – What Now?"

2 Group I countries are those that contribute to the bank, while Group II countries are those that borrow from the bank.

3 This was told to me by a former US executive director who was with the World Bank during the establishment of the Inspection Panel.

4 I assume Wolfensohn means two weeks after the board meeting at which China announced that it would continue the project without the World Bank's involvement.

5 The "region" here refers to the vice president and management responsible for the project in China. It could also have been the offce of the World Bank in China.

6 Ibrahim Shihata was a former general counsel of the World Bank. He passed away in 2001.

7 The Lao Peoples Democratic Republic is still known by many people as Laos.

8 These warnings were prescient. Since 2007 the conflict in Sudan has expanded to Chad. According to specialists cited in several media sources, this is related to the oil wealth.

9 Shengman Zhang was a vice president and secretary of the World Bank at the time of this interview.

10 When Arlman was interviewed, the European Union consisted of twenty-five countries. On 1 January 2007 Balgaria and Romania entered the EU, bringing the total to twenty-seven.

11 The Sustainable Business Advisory is responsible for implementing approaches designed to facilitate more informed and responsible decision making within ABN-AMRO, taking into account triple-bottom-line issues relevant to each industry sector with which the bank engages.

12 From 1999 to 2005 Peter Woicke was executive vice president of the International Finance Corporation, the largest multilateral provider of loans and equity to the private sector in the emerging markets. See http://www.ifc.org.

13 The Crude Oil Pipeline traverses Ecuador, and the project has been heavily criticized by the NGO community.

14 At the time of this interview, there were twenty-one Equator banks. During the writing of this book, the total was already forty-one.

15 See http://www.caspiandevelopmentandexport.com/ASP/BTC.asp: "The Baku-Tbilisi-Ceyhan (BTC) project is a $3 billion investment to unlock a vast store of energy from the Caspian Sea by providing a new crude oil pipeline from Azerbaijan, through Georgia, to Turkey for onward delivery to world markets." See also www.bankwatch.org/issues/oilclima/baku-ceyhan/mbaku.html: "The Baku-Tbilisi-Ceyhan Export Oil Pipeline (BTC), a key component of US Energy Security strategy, is being financially backed by the International Finance Corporation, the European Bank for Reconstruction and Development, the American Export-Import Bank, the UK's Export Credit Guarantee Department, and a host of other export credit agencies."

16 For my interview with Suellen Lazarus, see below in this appendix.

17 On 12 August 2004 the Brazilian banks Banco Itaú and Banco Itaú adopted the Equator Principles.

18 For my interview with Suellen Lazarus, see below in this appendix.

19 See http://en.wikipedia.org/wiki/Due_diligence: "Due diligence (also known as due care) is the effort made by an ordinarily prudent or reasonable party to avoid harm to another party. Failure to make this effort is considered negligence. Quite often a contract will specify that a party is required to provide due diligence. A (US) example of a 'due diligence report' is a Phase I Environmental Site Assessment (ESA), which is performed to determine potential environmental conditions that may cause harm to the surrounding environment."

20 E-mail from Professor Bob Wessels, 11 September 2003, my translation from the Dutch. Wessels was responding to a lecture I presented at the annual bank conference of Ernst and Young in Utrecht, the Netherlands, 6 November 2003.

21 ABN-AMRO Bank is one of the major private banks with investments in the extractive industries.

22 Over a hundred NGOs signed the so-called Collevecchio Declaration in Davos Switzerland, 27 January 2003. The declaration calls upon financial institutions

to adopt six commitments: "1. Commitment to Sustainability. 2. Commitment to Do No Harm. 3. Commitment to Responsibility. 4. Commitment to Account-ability. 5. Commitment to Transparency. 6. Commitment to Sustainable Gover-nance." See BankTrack, "The Collevecchio Declaration on Financial Institutions and Sustainability."

23 See note 14 above. The BTC project is an undertaking of British Petroleum with involvement of the IFC.

24 Jim Wolfensohn was president of the World Bank from 1995 to 2005.

25 BankTrack is a network of civil society organizations with a focus on the activities of private banks based in Utrecht and set up in 2004. See www.banktrack.org.

26 Here, I am referring to Equator I. In Equator II, a similar statement is found in the "Disclaimer" that follows the principles. See appendix 2.

27 E-mail from Bob Wessels, 11 September 2003, originally in Dutch, my transla-tion. See note 20 above.

28 ABN-AMRO Bank, Bayerische Hypo-und Vereinsbank AG, Citigroup Inc., Crédit Lyonnais, Credit Suisse First Boston, Dexia, ING Group, KBC Bank, MCC S.A., Mizuho Corporate Bank Ltd, and Westpac Banking Corporation.

29 "Twelve Banks Speak out on the Extractive Industries Review."

30 Financierings Maatschappij Ontwikkelingslanden (FMO), based in the Hague, is a development bank originally owned by the state and privatized in the 1990s. In the fall of 2005 FMO also adopted the Equator Principles.

31 The member countries in the World Bank are divided into Group I and Group II countries. Group I are the donor countries. Group II are the recipient countries.

32 After I met with Lazarus, two Brazilian banks adopted the principles.

33 By the time of this book's publication, four Brazilian private banks had adopted the principles.

34 Equator Principles, press release, 5 August 2003.

35 American Exim is an export credit agency.

36 See BankTrack, "No U-turn Allowed."

37 In Equator II the bar has been dropped to US$10 million.

Websites

AccountAbility, http://www.accountAbility.org.uk.
African Development Bank, http://www.afdb.org.
African Development Bank Independent Review Mechanism, www.afdb.org/irm.
Asian Development Bank, http://www.adb.org.
Bank for International Settlements, http://www.bis.org.
Bank Information Center, http://www.bicusa.org.
BankTrack, http://www.banktrack.org.
Bankwatch Network, http://www.bankwatch.org.
Bhopal Medical Appeal, http://www.bhopal.org.
Bretton Woods Project, http://brettonwoodsproject.org.
Center for Human Rights and Environment, http://www.cedha.org.ar.
Clean Clothes Campaign, http://www.cleanclothes.org.
Compliance advisor ombudsman, http://www.ifc.org/cao.
Democracy Now, http://www.democracynow.org.
Enceclopedia.com, http://www.enceclopedia.com.
Equator Principles, http://www.equator-principles.com.
Europion Union, http://europa.eu.int.
European Bank for Reconstruction and Development, http://www.ebrd.com
European Bank for Reconstruction and Development, Independent Recourse
    Mechanism, http://wwwebrd.com/irm.
European Investment Bank, http://www.eib.eu.int.
European ombudsman, http://www.euro-ombudsman.eu.int.
Export Development Canada, http://www.edc.ca.
Find Law, http://www.findlaw.com.
Freshfields Bruckhaus Deringer, http://www.freshfields.com.
G-8 Information Centre, http://www.g8.utoronto.ca.
Global Reporting Initiative, http://www.globalreporting.org.
Inter-American Development Bank, http://www.iadb.org.
International Development Association, http://www.ida.org.
International Finance Corporation, http://www.ifc.org.
International Monetary Fund, http://www.imf.org.

International Organization for Standardization, http://www.iso.ch/iso.
Japan Bank for International Cooperation, http://www.jbic.go.jp.
Organization for Economic Cooperation and Development, http://www.oecd.org.
United Nations, http://www.un.org.
United Nations Global Compact, http://www.unglobalcompact.org.
Wikipedia, http://en.wikipedia.org/wiki.
WordNet, http://www.cogsci.princeton.edu.
World Bank Group, http://www.worldbank.org.
World Bank Inspection Panel, http://www.inspectionpanel.org.

Bibliography

African Development Bank (AfDB). "Bank Memorandum." Internal memo to the Board of Directors. 30 June 2004.

– "Compliance Review and Mediation Unit of the Independent Review Mechanism, Operating Rules and Procedures." http://www.afdb.org.

– "Resolution B/BD/2004/9–F/BD/2004/7." 30 June 2004. http://www.afdb.org.

African Development Fund (ADF). "ADF/BD/WP/2004/60: Bank Memorandum to the Board of Directors." 3 June 2004.

Alfredsson, Gudmundur, and Rolf Ring, eds. *The Inspection Panel of the World Bank: A Different Complaints Procedure.* The Hague: Martinus Nijhoff, 2001.

Alston, Philip, and Mary Robinson, eds. *Human Rights and Development: Towards Mutual Reinforcement.* New York: Oxford University Press, 2005.

Anderson, W. Gavin. *Constitutional Rights after Globalization.* Oregon: Oxford and Portland, 2005.

Asian Development Bank (ADB). "ADB's Inspection Policy: A Guidebook." October 1996. http://www.adb.org.

– "Review of the Inspection Function: Establishment of a New ADB Accountability Mechanism." ADB working paper. 29 May 2003. http://www.adb.org.

– et al. "Recommendations to Inspection Policy Review of the Asian development Bank," jointly prepared for submission at the ADB's Tokyo Consultation to Review the Inspection Function, 11 June 2002. In ADB, "Review of the Inspection Function: Establishment of a New ADB Accountability Mechanism," 49n8. ADB working paper. 29 May 2003. http://www.adb.org.

ASN Bank. "ASN Bank Drops Investments in the European Investment Bank and in the World Bank." Press release. 17 July 2003. http://www.asnbank.nl/.

Bais, Karolien. "Corporate Social Responsibility: Perspectives from the South." Leaflet. Centre for Research on Multinational Corporations (Amsterdam), January 2005.

Bank for International Settlements (BIS). "Basel Committee Issues Guidance on the Compliance Function in Banks." Press release. 29 April 2005. http://www.bis.org/press/p050429.htm.

Bank Information Center (BIC) et al. "Strengthening Public Accountability: Revised Recommendations to the Asian Development Bank (ADB) for Revising Its Inspection Policy." March 2002. http://www.bicusa.org/Legacy/Civil_ Society_ Recommendations-March_18_2002.pdf.

BankTrack. "The Collevecchio Declaration on Financial Institutions and Sustainability." 27 January 2003. http://www.banktrack.org.

– "Equator Principles II: NGO Comments on the Proposed Revision of the Equator Principles." 12 April 2006. http://www.banktrack.org.

– "No U-turn Allowed: NGO Recommendations to the Equator Banks: A Bank Track Analysis." January 2004. http://www.banktrack.org.

– "Principles, Profits or Just PR? Triple P Investments under the Equator Principles: An Anniversary Assessment." June 2004. http://www.banktrack.org.

– "Unproven Equator Principles: A BankTrack Statement." June 2005. http:// www.banktrack.org.

– "Who Has Adopted the Equator Principles?" Press release. 22 March 2007. http://www.banktrack.org.

– and World Wildlife Fund. "Banks Failing Environment and Social Standards." Press release 26 January 2006. http://www.wwf.org.uk/news/n_0000002270.asp.

– and World Wildlife Fund. "ING bank dumps divisive 1.7 billion paper mill project." Press release. 13 April 2006. http://www.banktrack.org/?id=55.

– and World Wildlife Fund. "Shaping the Future of Sustainable Finance: Moving the Banking Sector from Promises to Performance." 26 January 2006. http:// wwf.org.uk/shapingthefuture.

Basel Committee on Banking Supervision (BCBS). "Compliance and the Compliance Function in Banks." April 2005. http://www.bis.org/publ/bcbs113.htm.

– "History of the Basel Committee and Its Membership." January 2007. http:// www.bis.org/bcbs/history.htm.

– "International Convergence of Capital Measurement and Capital Standards: A Revised Framework." June 2004. http://www.bis.org/publ/bcbs107.htm.

– "Principles for the Supervision of Banks' Foreign Establishments." May 1983. http://www.bis.org/publ/bcbsc312.htm.

Becker, A., and Frank Vanclay, eds. *The International Handbook of Social Impact Assessment: Conceptual and Methodological Advances.* Cheltenham, UK: Edward Elgar, 2003.

Bello, Walden. "Controversial report poisons ADB board-management ties." *Business World*, 11 April 2002.

Boisson de Chazournes, Laurence. "Le Panel d'inspection de la Banque mondiale: À propos de la complexification de l'espace public." *Revue Générale de Droit International Public* 105 (2001): 145–62.

Bradlow, Daniel. "Study on an Inspection Function for the African Development Bank Group." 24 November 2003. http://www.bicusa.org/Legacy/adb_ inspection_function_study_report_24nov2003.pdf.

Bretton Woods Project. "IMF Agrees More Transparency." 14 June 2000. http:// brettonwoodsproject.org/art.shtml?x=15590.

- "Internal Accountability Creates 'Institutional Discomfort.'" 23 January 2006. Press release. http://www.brettonwoodsproject.org/article.shtml?cmd%5b126%5d=x-126-507739.

Bronkhorst, Serge A. "Liability for Environmental Damage and the World Bank's Chad-Cameroon Oil and Pipeline Project." In Serge A. Bronkhorst, ed., *Liability for Environmental Damage and the World Bank's Chad-Cameroon Oil and Pipeline Project,* 1–28. Selected papers from the Netherlands Committee and International Union for Conservation of Nature (NC-IUCN) symposium, held at the Netherlands Institute of International Relations (or Clingendael), the Hague, 25 February 2000. Amsterdam: Netherlands Committee for IUCN, 2000.

Brown-Weiss, Edith. "Introduction." In Edith Brown-Weiss, ed., *International Compliance with Nonbinding Accords,* 1–2. Washington, DC: American Society of International Law, 1997.

- and Roberto Dañino. "Joint Statement on the Use of Country Systems." 8 June 2004. http://www.worldbank.org.

Buss, Thomas. "Zwischen Immunität und Rechtsschutz: Das Inspection Panel innerhalb der Weltbankgruppe." *Recht der internationalen Wirtschaft* 5 (1998): 352–9.

Caliari, Aldo, and Frank Schroeder. "Reform Proposals for the Governance Structure of the International Financial Institutions." New Rules for Global Finance Briefing Paper no. 3. http://www.new-rules.org/docs/ifigovernancereform.pdf.

Castells, Manuel. *The Information Age: Economy, Society and Culture.* Vol. 1, *The Rise of the Network Society.* Oxford: Blackwell, 1996.

CEE Bankwatch Network. "Empowering People: The Need for an EBRD Appeals/ Compliance Mechanism." 20 June 2001. http://www.bankwatch.org/publications/ studies.shtml?x=167287.

- "The European Investment Bank: Accountable to Whom?" 31 January 2000. http://www.bankwatch.org/newsroom/release.shtml?x=156023.

- "The Independent Recourse Mechanism: Three Years on Questions Remain and Who Is It for – the EBRD or Those Affected by EBRD projects?" June 2007. http:// www.bankwatch.org/publications/document.shtml?x=2012925.

Center for Human Rights and Environment (CEDHA). "Dramatic Weekend Unfolds as Uruguay Issues Operating Permit to Botnia." Press release. 12 November 2007. http://www.cedha.org.ar/en/more_information/dramatic.php.

- "Equator Principles Compliance Complaint, regarding Proposed Pulp Paper Mill Investment in Fray Bentos Uruquay." Cordoba, Argentina, 18 May 2005. http:// www.cedha.org.ar/en/initiatives/paper_pulp_mills/complaint-letter-to-ing-eng.pdf.

- "Pulp Mill CEO Erkki Varis Says He's Famous Thanks to Conflict and Favors Private Investment over Social Conflict." Press release. 7 March 2008. http:// www.cedha.org.ar/en/more_information/pulp_mill_ceo.php.

Chatterjee, Charles. "IBRD Inspection Panel Procedures." *Journal of International Banking Law* 11 (1996): 392–6.

Circi, Mariarita. "The World Bank Inspection Panel: Is It Really Effective?" *Global Jurist Advances* 6, no. 3 (Berkeley Electronic Press, 2006): 1–29. http:// www.bepress.com/gj/advances/vol6/iss3/art10.

Clark, Dana. "The World Bank and Human Rights: The Need for Greater Accountability." *Harvard Human Rights Journal* 15 (2002): 205–26.

– Jonathan Fox, and Kay Treakle, eds. *Demanding Accountability: Civil-Society Claims and the World Bank Inspection Panel.* Lanham, MD: Rowman and Littlefield, 2003.

Commission for Environmental Cooperation (CEC). "Bringing the Facts to Light: A Guide to Articles 14 and 15 of the North American Agreement on Environmental Cooperation." 2000. http://www.cec.org/files/pdf/SEM/BringingFacts-Juno2_en.pdf.

Compliance advisor ombudsman (CAO). *Annual Report 2002–03.* 2003. www.ifc.org/cao.

– *Annual Report 2003–04.* 2004. www.ifc.org/cao.

– *Annual Report 2004–05.* 2005. www.ifc.org/cao.

– *Annual Report 2006–07.* 2007. www.ifc.org/cao.

– "Operational Guidelines." April 2000. www.ifc.org/cao.

– "Operational Guidelines." May 2004. www.ifc.org/cao.

– "Operational Guidelines." 2007. www.ifc.org/cao.

"Crisis in region Darfur dijt uit naar Tsjaad" [Crisis in Darfur region expands to Chad]. NRC-*Handelsblad* (Rotterdam), 17 March 2006

Crook, Clive. "A Survey of Corporate Social Responsibility: The Good Company." *The Economist* (London), 22 January 2005, 3.

Dañino, Roberto. "The Legal Aspects of the World Banks's Work on Human Rights: Some Preliminary Thoughts." In Philip Alston and Mary Robinson, eds, *Human Rights and Development: Towards Mutual Reinforcement,* 509–24. New York: Oxford University Press, 2005.

Darrow, Mac. *Between Light and Shadow: The World Bank, the International Monetary Fund and International Human Rights Law.* Oxford, UK, and Portland, OR: Hart, 2003.

Deere, Carolyn. "Sustainable International Natural Resources Law." In Marie-Claire Cordonier Segger and Ashfaq Khalfan, eds, *Sustainable Development Law, Principles, Practices, and Prospects,* 295–310. New York: Oxford University Press, 2004.

Deoukoubou, Christophe. "The Chad-Cameroon Oil and Pipeline Project: Liability for Environmental Damage under the National Laws of Chad." In Serge A. Bronkhorst, ed., *Liability for Environmental Damage and the World Bank's Chad-Cameroon Oil and Pipeline Project,* 24–9. Selected papers from the Netherlands Committee and International Union for Conservation of Nature (NC-IUCN) symposium, held at the Netherlands Institute of International Relations (or Clingendael), the Hague, 25 February 2000. Amsterdam: Netherlands Committee for IUCN, 2000.

Eijffinger, Sylvester C.W., and Petra M. Geraats. "How Transparent Are Central Banks?" *European Journal of Political Economy* 22 (2006): 1–21.

Equator Principles I. "Leading Banks Announce Adoption of Equator Principles." Press release. 4 June 2003. www.equator-principles.com/pr030604.shtml.

Equator Principles II. "The 'Equator Principles': A financial industry benchmark for determining, assessing and managing social and environmental risk in

project financing." July 2006. http://www.equator-principles.com/documents/
Equator_Principles.pdf.

Etzioni, Amitai. *The Moral Dimension: Toward a New Economics*. New York: Free Press,
1988.

European Bank for Reconstruction and Development (EBRD). "Agreement
Establishing the European Bank for Reconstruction and Development." Effective
28 March 1991. http://www.ebrd.com/pubs/insti/basics.pdf.

— "Independent Recourse Mechanism." Approved by the Board of Directors on
29 April 2003. http://www.ebrd.com/about/policies/irm/irm.pdf.

— "Independent Recourse Mechanism: Rules of Procedure." Approved by the
Board of Directors on 6 April 2004. http://www.ebrd.com/about/integrity/
irm/about/procedur.pdf.

— Independent Recourse Mechanism (IRM). *Annual Report 2007*. http://
www.ebrd.com/about/integrity/irm/about/report07.pdf.

European Community. "The Aarhus Convention." http://ec.europa.eu/environment/
aarhus/.

European Investment Bank (EIB). "2005 Corporate Responsibility Report." 24 July
2006. http://www.eib.org/about/publications/eib-2005–corporate-responsibility-
report.htm.

— "EIB Environmental Statement 2004." 5 May 2004. http://www.eib.org/
attachments/strategies/environmental_statement_en.pdf.

— "The EIB Public Disclosure Policy." 10 September 2007. http://www.eib.org/
about/news/eib-public-disclosure-policy.htm.

— "Eligibility Guidelines: Checking Consistency of Operations with EU Objectives." 24 June 2004. http://www.eib.org/about/publications/eib-eligibility-
guidelines.htm.

— "Public Disclosure Policy: Principles, Rules, and Procedures." 17 July 2007.
http://www.eib.org/about/publications/public-disclosure-policy.htm.

European Parliament Committee on Petitions. "On the Annual Report on the
European Ombudsman's Activities in 2006." Final report A6–0301/2007.

Export Development Canada (EDC). "2003 Annual Compliance Program Report."
http://www.edc.ca/english/compliance_guidelines.htm.

Faini, Ricardo, and Enzo Grilli. "Who Runs the IFIs?" Development Studies
Working Papers no. 191. October 2004. http://ideas.repec.org/p/cpr/ceprdp/
4666.html.

Forest Peoples Programme. "Concerns about the Weakening of World Bank
Safeguard Policies: Letter to the World Bank." 2 March 2001. http://www.
forestpeoples.org/documents/ifi_igo/wb_safegd_ngo_let_mar01_eng.shtml.

Fox, Jonathan. "Civil Society and Political Accountability: Propositions for
Discussion." Paper presented at the international conference *Institutions,
Accountability and Democratic Governance in Latin America*, the Helen Kellogg
Institute for International Studies, South Bend, Indiana, University of Notre
Dame, 8–9 May 2000.

— "The World Bank Inspection Panel: Lessons from the First Five Years." *Global
Governance* 6 (2000): 279–318.

French, Hilary F. "Assessing Private Capital Flows to Developing Countries." In Hilary F. French, ed., *State of the World 1998: A Worldwatch Institute Report on Progress toward a Sustainable Society,* 149–76. New York: Norton, 1998.

Freshfields Bruckhaus Deringer. "Banking on Responsibility: Part I of Freshfields Bruckhaus Deringer Equator Principles Survey 2005: The Banks." July 2005. http://www.freshfields.com/practice/environment/publications/pdfs/12057.pdf.

Friedman, Thomas L. *The Lexus and the Olive Tree: Understanding Globalization.* New York: Farrar, Straus Giroux, 2000.

Friends of the Earth International. "Comments on the Proposal for an Independent Recourse Mechanism at the EBRD." January 2003. http://www.foei.org/en/publications/financial/ebrd.html/?searchterm=Independent%20Recourse%20Mechanism.

G-8 Finance Ministers and Central Bank Governors. "G8 Finance Ministers' Meetings Strengthening the International Financial System and the Multilateral Development Banks." 7 July 2001. http://www.g8.utoronto.ca/finance/fmo10707.htm.

Goodland, R. "Environmental and Social Lessons to Be Learned from the World Bank's Fiercest Controversy." Paper presented to the World Bank Group, 18 September 2001.

Government of Manitoba. "Achieving Accountability." 1999. http://www.gov.mb.ca/health/rha/accounte.pdf.

Gowlland Gualtieri, Alix. "The Environmental Accountability of the World Bank to Non-State Actors: Insights from the Inspection Panel." *British Yearbook of International Law* 72 (2001): 213–53.

Handl, Günther. *Multilateral Development Banking: Environmental Principles and Concepts Reflecting General International Law and Public Policy.* The Hague: Kluwer Law International and Asian Development Bank, 2001.

Haralz, Jonas. "IFCs 50th Anniversary: Documentary on IFC." http:www.ifc.org/ifcext/50thanniversary.nsf/Content/IFCs_Origins.

Hardy, Jean. "The History and Changing Objectives of the World Bank." http://www.greenspirit.org.uk/resources/WorldBank.htm.

Haufler, Virginia. "Globalization and Industry Self-Regulation." In Miles Kahler and David Lake, eds, *Governance in a Global Economy,* 226–54. Princeton, NJ: Princeton University Press, 2003.

Human Rights Watch. "Chad: Account for 'Disappeared' Opposition Leaders, Two Missing Politicians Last Seen in Army Custody." Press release. 25 February 2008. http://www.hrw.org/doc/?t=africa.

Hunter, David, "Using the World Bank Inspection Panel to Defend the Interests of Project-Affected People." *Chicago Journal of International Law* 4 (2003): 201–11.

Institute of Development Studies (IDS). "Making Accountability Count." IDS policy briefing no. 33. November 2006. http://www.ids.ac.uk/ids/bookshop/briefs/PB33.pdf.

Inter-American Development Bank (IADB). "The IDB Independent Investigation Mechanism." 30 June 2000. http://idbdocs.iadb.org/wsdocs/getdocument.aspx?docnum=474362.

– "Propsal for Enhancement to the Independent Investigation Mechanism: Draft Consultation and Compliance Review Policy." 3 February 2005. http://idbdocs.iadb.org/wsdocs/getdocument.aspx?docnum=474362.

International Bank for Reconstruction and Development (IBRD). *Accountability at the World Bank: The Inspection Panel 10 Years On.* Washington DC: World Bank, 2003. http://siteresources.worldbank.org/EXTINSPECTIONPANEL/Resources/TenYear8_07.pdf.

– "Articles of Agreement." Amended 16 February 1989. http://siteresources.worldbank.org/EXTABOUTUS/Resources/ibrd-articlesofagreement.pdf.

– *A Guide to the World Bank.* Washington, DC: World Bank, 2003.

– "Resolution No. IBRD-93-10 and Resolution No. IDA-93-6." 22 September 1993. http://siteresources.worldbank.org/EXTINSPECTIONPANEL/Resources/ResolutionMarch2005.pdf.

– "Operational Memorandum 7.02." 22 August 1966.

International Development Association (IDA). "Articles of Agreement." Effective 24 September 1960. http://siteresources.worldbank.org/IDA/Resources/ida-articlesofagreement.pdf.

International Finance Corporation (IFC). "Independent Review of the Chilean Pangue Hydroelectric Project." 15 July 1997. http://www.ifc.org.

International Labor Organization (ILO). *A Fair Globalization: Creating Opportunities for All.* Switzerland: World Commission on the Social Dimension of Globalization, 2004.

International Monetary Fund (IMF). "Making the IMF's Independent Evaluation Office Operational: A Background Paper." 7 August 2000. http://www.imf.org/external/np/eval/evo/2000/Eng/evo.htm.

– "Terms of Reference for the Independent Evaluation Office of the International Monetary Fund." Revised 16 November 2004. http://www.ieo-imf.org/about/tor.pdf.

– Independent Evaluation Office (IEO). *Annual Report 2007.* August 2007. http://www.ieo-imf.org/pub/ar/pdf/2007Report.pdf.

– Independent Evaluation Office (IEO). "IMF's Independent Evaluation Office Announces Release of Report on the IMF's Approach to Capital Account Liberalization." IEO press release no. 05/02. 25 May 2005. http://www.imf.org/External/NP/ieo/2005/pr/eng/pro502.htm.

Japan Bank for International Cooperation (JBIC). "Objection Procedures." October 2003. http://www.jbic.go.jp/english/environ/pdf/objection.pdf.

– "Recommendations for the Japan Bank for International Cooperation's Environmental Guidelines." 9 September 2001. http://www.s.g-egl-jbic.org.

Kapur, Devesh, John P. Lewis, and Richard C. Webb. *The World Bank: Its First Half Century.* 2 vols. Washington, DC: Brookings Institution Press, 1997.

Kass, Stephen L., and Jean M. McCarroll. "Environmental Law: The Equator Principles: Lending with an Environmental String, Lender Commitments, Open Issues, the BTC Project, the Future." *New York Law Journal* 78 (23 April 2004).

Kathigamar, V. Sk. Nathan. "The World Bank Inspection Panel, Court or Quango?" *Journal of International Arbitratio* 12 (1995): 1–4.

Keohane, Robert O. "Global Governance and Democratic Accountability." In David Held and Mathias Koenig-Archibugi, eds, *Taming Globalization: Frontiers of Governance*, 130–59. Cambridge, UK: Polity Press and Blackwell, 2003.

– and Joseph S. Nye Jr. "Redefining Accountability for Global Governance: Political Authority in Transition." In Miles Kahler and David Lake, eds, *Governance in a Global Economy*, 386–411. Princeton, NJ: Princeton University Press, 2003.

Kleinwächter, Wolfgang. "Global Governance in the Information Age." *Development-SID* 46 (1 March 2003): 17–25.

Kraske, Jochen, et al. *Bankers with a Mission: The Presidents of the World Bank, 1946–1991*. New York: Oxford University Press, 1996.

"La Convention de Recherche, d'Exploitation et de Transport des Hydrocarbures." 19 December 1988. An agreement between the Government of Cameroon, the World Bank, and the oil companies involved in the Chad-Cameroon oil project.

Lawrence, Shannon. "Retreat from the Safeguard Policies: Recent Trends Undermining Social and Environmental Accountability at the World Bank." Environmental Defense, January 2005. http://www.environmentaldefense.org/article.cfm?ContentID=2464.

Lazarus, Suellen. "The Equator Principles: A Milestone or Just Good PR?" *Global Agenda* 2 (January 2004): http://www.equator-principles.com/ga1.shtml.

Leader, Sheldon. "Human Rights, Risks, and New Strategies for Global Investment." *Journal of International Economic Law* 9 (September 2006): 657–705.

"The Logging Trade, Down in the Woods." *The Economist* (London), 25–31 March 2006, 67–9.

Mallaby, Sebastian. *The World's Banker: A Story of Failed States, Financial Crises, and the Wealth and Poverty of Nations*. New York: Penguin, 2004.

"Managing Globalization." Editorial. *Washington Post*, 19 February 2006, B06.

Mason, Edward S., and Robert E. Asher. *The World Bank since Bretton Woods*. Washington, DC: Brookings Institution, 1973.

Matsumoto, Ikuko. "An NGO Evaluation of JBIC's Objections Procedure." Friends of the Earth Japan, 25 June 2004.

McCandless, Henry E. *A Citizen's Guide to Public Accountability: Changing the Relationship between Citizens and Authorities*. Victoria, BC: Trafford, 2002.

McDonald, Olivia. "Coming into the Light." Bretton Woods Project, April 2005. http://www.brettonwoodsproject.org.

Moison, Hans. "Kredietrisico's onder Bazel II en IRFS: Overeenkomsten en verschillen." *Eye on Finance*, October 2005, 5–16.

Morse, Bradford, et al. *Sardar Sarovar: The Report of the Independent Review*. Ottawa: The World Bank, Resource Futures International, 1992.

Mulgan, Richard. "'Accountability': An Ever-expanding Concept?" *Public Administration* 78, no. 3 (2000): 555–73.

Nurmukhametova, Elvira. "Problems in Connection with the Efficiency of the World Bank Inspection Panel." *Max Planck Yearbook of United Nations Law* 10 (2006): 397–421.

Orakhelashvili, Alexander. "The World Bank Inspection Panel in Context: Institutional Aspects of the Accountability of International Organizations." *International Organizations Law Review* 2 (2005): 57–102.

Oranje, Joost. "Zou de wetgever wel eens vonissen lezen?" [Do legislators ever read the sentences of the court?]. Interview with Judge Maarten Mastboom. *NRC-Handelsblad* (Rotterdam), 8 April 2006.

Orellana, Marcos A. "Indigenous Peoples, Energy, and Environmental Justice: The Pangue/Ralco Hydroelectric Project in Chili's Alto Bíobío." 21 July 2004. http://lic.law.ufl.edu/~hernandez/Trade/Orellan1.pdf.

Organization for Economic Cooperaton and Development (OECD). "OECD Guidelines for Multinational Enterprises." Revised 27 June 2000. www.oecd.org/document/28/0,2340,fr_2649_34889_2397532_1_1_1_1,00.html.

– "OECD Principles of Corporate Governance." 2004. http://www.oecd.org/dataoecd/32/18/31557724.pdf.

– "Recommendation on Common Approaches on Environment and Officially Supported Export Credits." 19 December 2003. http://www.oecd.org/dataoecd/26/33/21684464.pdf.

– "Debt Sustainability and Responsible Lending: 2007 Statement of Principles on Unproductive Expenditure." 19 July 2007. http://www.olis.oecd.org/olis/2007doc.nsf/7b20c1f93939d029c125685d005300b1/da291799450ca994c125731d0054fadc/$FILE/JT03230401.PDF.

– "Revised Council Recommendations on Common Approaches on the Environment and Officially Supported Export Credits." 12 June 2007. http://webdomino1.oecd.org/olis/2007doc.nsf/43bb6130e5e86e5fc12569fa005d004c/d4572f5ee6bc6d72c12572f800561d56/$FILE/JT03228987.PDF.

OECD Watch. "Five Years On: A Review of the OECD Guidelines and National Contact Points." 2005. http://www.oecdwatch.org/docs/OECD_Watch_5_years_on.pdf.

Oxfam United Kingdom (Ireland). *The World Bank Inspection Panel: Analysis and Recommendations for Review*. London: Oxfam UK, Policy Department, 1996.

Paletta, Damian. "Backlash on Basel Hits Fed – What Now?" *US Banker* 170 (2005): 19.

Parker, George, and Alan Beattie, "EIB Accuses China of Unscrupulous Loans." *Financial Times* (London), 28 November 2006.

Philips, Michael. Editorial. *Globe and Mail*, 11 January 1999, B9.

Pincus, Jonathan R., and Jeffrey A. Winters. *Reinventing the World Bank*. Ithaca, NY: Cornell University Press, 2002.

Portuguese EU Presidency. "Communiqué from the Presidency of the EU on the Conclusion of the Negotiations for the 15th Replenishment of the IDA, 2007-12-14." Press release. 14 December 2007. http://www.eu2007.pt/UE/vEN/Noticias_Documentos/20071214DA.htm.

Renner, Michael. *State of the World 2005: Redefining Global Security*. Washington, DC: World Watch Institute, 2005.

"Resolution on the Disastrous Consequences of the Narmada Project in India." *Official Journal of the European Communities*, no. C 240 (16 September 1991): http://europa.eu.int/eur-lex/lex/RECH_reference_pub.do.

"Resolution on the Narmada Dam (India)." *Official Journal of the European Communities*, no. C 241 (21 September 1992): http://Europa.eu.int/eur-lex/lex/JOIndex.do.

Ricarda Roos, Stefanie. "The World Bank Inspection Panel in the Seventh Year: An Analysis of Its Process, Mandate and Desirability with Special Reference to the China (Tibet) Case." *Max Planck Yearbook of United Nations Law* 5 (2001): 473–521.

Rich, Bruce. "A Cuckoo in the Nest: Fifty Years of Political Meddling by the World Bank." *The Ecologist* 24, no. 1 (1994): 8–13.

Rigo Sureda, Andrés. "Informality and Effectiveness in the Operation of the International Bank for Reconstruction and Development." *Journal of International Economic Law* 6 (2003): 565–96.

– "The Law Applicable to the Activities of International Development Banks." *Hague Academy of International Law Courses* 308 (2004): 9–252.

– "The World Bank and Institutional Innovations." In Edith Brown-Weiss, Andrés Rigo Sureda, and Laurence Boisson de Chazournes, eds, *The World Bank, International Financial Institutions, and the Development of International Law*, 11–21. Studies in Transnational Legal Policy no. 31. Washington, DC: American Society of International Law, 1999.

Santhi, S. *Sardar Sarovar Project: The issue of Developing River Narmada*. Thiruvanthapuram, Kerala, India: Indian National Trust for Art and Cultural Heritage (INTACH), 1994.

Sassen, Saskia. *Globalization and Its Discontents: Essays on the New Mobility of People and Money*. New York: New Press, 1998.

Schlemmer-Schulte, Sabine. "The World Bank Inspection Panel: Its Creation, Functioning, Case Record, and Its Two Reviews." *Zeitschrift für europarechtliche Studien* 1 (1998): 347–70.

Schlemmer-Schulte, Sabine. "Building an International Grievance System: The World Bank Inspection Panel – Selected Issues." In Jürgen Böhmer, ed., *Internationale Gemeinschaft und Menschenrechte: Festschrift für Georg Ress*, 249–84. Cologne: Heymann, 2005.

– "The World Bank Inspection Panel: A Model for Other International Organizations?" In Niels M. Blokker and Henry G. Schermers, eds, *Proliferation of International Organizations*, 483–548. The Hague: Kluwer Law International, 2001.

Sevastopulos, Demetri. "Four banks adopt IFC agreement." *Financial Times* (London), 9 April 2003.

Shihata, Ibrahim. *The World Bank Inspection Panel*. New York: Oxford University Press, 1994.

– *The World Bank Inspection Panel: In Practice*. 2nd ed. New York: Oxford University Press, 2000.

Suzuki, Eisuke, and Suresh Nanwani. "Responsibility of International Organizations: The Accountability Mechanisms of Multilateral Development Banks." *Michigan Journal of International Law* 27, no. 1 (Fall 2005): 177–225. http://www.forum-adb.org/PDF-Other/Suzuki%20&%20Nanwani%20article%20MJIL%2027-1.pdf.

Swann, Christopher. "Bretton Woods institutions, sixty years on, and still contentious." *Financial Times* (London), 29–30 May 2004.

Taillant, J.G. "Human Rights and the International Financial Institutions." Paper presented at the conference *Sustainable Justice 2002: Implementing International Sustainable Development Law*, Montreal, 13–15 June 2002.

Tremlett, Giles. "Conflicts at the heart of the EIB." *Guardian Unlimited* (London), 7 March 2004. http://politics.guardian.co.uk/eu/story/0,9061,1163631,00. html.

Treakle, Kay. "Accountability at the World Bank: What Does It Take? Lessons from the Yacyreta Hydroelectric Project Argentina/Paraguay." Washinton, DC: Bank Information Center, 1998. http://www.bicusa.org/en/Article.373.aspx.

– Jonathan Fox, and Dana Clark. "Lessons Learned." In Dana Clark, Jonathan Fox, and Kay Treakle, eds, *Demanding Accountability: Civil Society Claims and the World Bank Inspection Panel*, 247–78. Lanham, MD: Rowman and Littlefield, 2003.

"Twelve Banks Speak out on the Extractive Industries Review." Letter to President Wolfensohn of the World Bank. 5 May 2004. www.equator-principles.com.

Udall, Lori. "The International Narmada Campaign: A Case of Sustained Advocacy." In William Fischer, ed., *Toward Sustainable Development? Struggling over India's Narmada River*, 201–29. Armonk: M.E. Sharpe, 1995.

– "World Bank Inspection Panel." Contributing paper, World Commission on Dams. 2000. http://www.dams.org/docs/kbase/contrib/ins208.pdf.

– *The World Bank Inspection Panel: A Three Year Review*. Washington DC: Bank Information Center, 1997.

Umaña Quesada, Alvaro. *The World Bank Inspection Panel: The First Four Years, 1994–1998*. Washington, DC: IBRD/World Bank, 1998.

United Nations Conference on Trade and Development. *World Investment Report 2005: Transnational Corporations and the Internationalization of R&D*. New York and Geneva: United Nations, 2006.

United Nations Economic Commission for Europe (UNECE). "About the Aarhus Clearinghouse." http://aarhusclearinghouse.unece.org/about.cfm.

– "Convention on Access to Information, Public Participation in Decision-making and Access to Justice in Environmental Matters." http://www.unece.org/env/pp/compliance.htm.

United Nations Economic Commission for Europe Compliance Committee. "Findings and Recommendations with Regard to Compliance by Albania." 31 July 2007. http://www.unece.org/env/documents/2007/pp/ECE_MP.PP_C_1_2007_4_Add_1.pdf.

United Nations Environment Programme (UNEP). "Rio Declaration on Environment and Development." June 1992. http://www.unep.org/Documents.Multilingual/Default.asp?DocumentID=78&ArticleID=1163.

United States House of Representatives. "Authorizing contributions to IDA, GEF and ADF: Hearing before the subcommittee on International Development, Finance, Trade and Monetary Policy of the Committee on Banking, Finance and Urban Affairs." One hundred third Congress, first session, 5 May 1993. Washington, DC: Government Printing Office, 1994.

– "World Bank Disclosure Policy and Inspection Panel: Hearing before the subcommittee on International Development, Finance, Trade and Monetary Policy of the Committee on Banking, Finance and Urban Affairs." One hundred third Congress, second session, 21 June 1994. Washington, DC: Government Printing Office, 1995.

van den Burg, Ieke. "On the European Investment Bank Annual Report for 2001." Report of the European Parliament. 6 November 2002. http:// www.europarl.europa.eu/sides/getDoc.do?pubRef=-//EP//TEXT+REPORT+ A5–2002–0364+0+DOC+XML+V0//EN&language=EN.

van den Oudenhoven, Nico, and Rekha Wazir. *Newly Emerging Needs of Children: An Exploration.* Antwerp: Garant, 2006.

van Loo Marcel. "Sarbanes Oxley in Practice." Paper presented at the seminar *Eye on Banking,* Utrecht, the Netherlands, 3 November 2005.

van Putten, Maartje. *The Future Has Begun.* Documentary on globalization. 50 minutes. English, Spanish, and Dutch versions. IKON, 1990.

– and Nicole Lucas. *"'Made in Heaven': Vrouwen en de Veranderende Internationale Arbeidsverdeling"* [Women and the changing international division of labour]. Amsterdam: Evert Vermeer Foundation, 1985.

Wade, Robert. "Greening the Bank: The Struggle over the Environment, 1970–1995." In Devesh Kapur, John P. Lewis, and Richard C. Webb, eds, *The World Bank: Its First Half Century,* vol. 2, 611–734. Washington, DC: Brookings Institution, 1997.

Weeramantry, Christopher. "Foreword." In Marie-Claire Cordonier Segger and Ashfaq Khalfan, eds, *Sustainable Development Law: Principles, Practices, and Prospects,* ix–x. New York: Oxford University Press, 2004.

Wiertsema, Wiert. "The Asian Development Bank (ADB) Inspection of the Samut Prakarn Wastewater Management Project, Thailand." Paper presented at the conference *Public Accessibility to International Financial Institutions: A Review of Existing Mechanisms and Interim Experiences,* American University, Washington College of Law, Washington, DC, 11 April 2003.

Woicke, Peter. "Putting Human Rights Principles into Development Practice through Finance: The Experience of the International Finance Corporttion." Paper presented at the conference *Human Rights and Development: Towards Mutual Reinforcement,* co-sponsored by the Ethical Globalization Initiative and the Center for Human Rights, New York, University School of Law, 1 March 2004.

Wolfensohn, Jim. "Foreword." In Alvaro Quesada Umaña, *The World Bank Inspection Panel: The First Four Years, 1994–1998,* vii. Washington, DC: IBRD/World Bank, 1998.

Wood, Angela, et al. "Letter from the Bretton Woods Project in Response to the IMF's Independent Evaluation Office Proposals." Bretton Woods Project, UK, 22 August 2001. http://www.eurodad.org/articles/default.aspx?id=286&printfriendly=yes.

World Bank. *Annual Report 2002.* Washington, DC: World Bank, 2003.

– *Annual Report 2003.* Washington, DC: World Bank, 2004.

– *Annual Report 2004.* Washington, DC: World Bank, 2005.

– *Annual Report 2005.* Washington, DC: World Bank, 2006.

– *Annual Report 2006*. Washington, DC: World Bank, 2007.
– "Review of the Resolution Establishing the Inspection Panel: 1996 Clarification of Certain Aspects of the Resolution." February 1997. http://wblno018.worldbank.org/Institutional/Manuals/OpManual.nsf/8c800392c 8aa060e852570bb007fc744/001613891de31b448525672c007d081c?Open Document.
– "Board Procedures and Practices." Internal bank document.
– "Effective Implementation: Key to Development Impact." Internal bank document R92–195. 1 September 1992.
– "From President to Executive Directors: Portfolio Management: Next Steps – A Program of Actions." Internal bank document R93–125. 16 June 1993.
– "IBRD and IDA Financial Statements as of March 31 2006." Internal bank document.
– "Key Corporate Responsibility Codes, Principles and Standards." http://web.worldbank.org/WBSITE/EXTERNAL/WBI/WBIPROGRAMS/CGCSRLP/0,,contentMDK:20719568~pagePK:64156158~piPK:64152884~theSitePK:460861,00.html.
– "Mission Statement." http://www.worldbank.org/about/whatis/mission.htm.
– "The 1999 Clarifications of the Board's Second Review of the Inspection Panel." 20 April 1999. http://www.inspectionpanel.org.
– "Operational Directive 4.00." 1989.
– "Operational Directive 4.01." 1991. http://siteresources.worldbank.org/OPSMANUAL/Resources/210384–1091740411344/OD401AnnexD-EAProcedures-Internal.pdf.
– "Operational Manual Statement 2.36." May 1984. http://siteresources.worldbank.org/INTSAFEPOL/1142947–1116495579739/20507374/Update1 TheWorldBankAndEAApril1993.pdf.
– "Operational Manual Statement 4.01." January 1999. http://wblno018.worldbank.org/Institutional/Manuals/OpManual.nsf/toc2/9367A2 A9D9DAEED38525672C007D0972?OpenDocument.
– "Operational Policy 4.10 on Indigenous Peoples." Revised July 2005. http://wblno018.worldbank.org/Institutional/Manuals/OpManual.nsf/tocall/0F7D6 F3F04DD70398525672C007D08ED?OpenDocument.
– "Pollution Prevention and Abatement Handbook." July 1998. http://www.ifc.org/ifcext/enviro.nsf/Content/PPAH.
– "Practical Suggestions Based on Experience to Date." Document ISNP/95-3. 27 November 1995.
– "The Report of the Working Group on the Second Review of the Inspection Panel." Internal bank document. 9 December 1998.
– "Safeguard Policies." http://www.worldbank.org/safeguards.
– "World Bank Group Historical Chronology." Updated September 2005. http://siteresources.worldbank.org/EXTARCHIVES/Resources/WB_Historical_Chronology_1944_2005.pdf.
– "World Bank Suspends Disbursements to Chad." Press release no. 2006/232/AFR. 6 January 2006. http://web.worldbank.org.

World Bank Group Staff Association. "The Bank Group Is Always Navigating in Political Waters." *Newsletter*, October 2001.

World Bank Inspection Panel. "Administrative Procedures." Amended 10 July 1998.

– "Chad-Cameroon Petroleum Development and Pipeline Project (Loan No. 4558-CD); Petroleum Sector Management Capacity Building Project (Credit No. 3373-CD); Management of the Petroleum Economy Project (Credit No. 3316-CD)." 17 July 2002. http://siteresources.worldbank.org/EXTINSPECTIONPANEL/Resources/ChadInvestigationReporFinal.pdf.

– "China Western Poverty Reduction Project (Credit no. 3255-CHA and Loan no. 4501-CHA)." 28 April 2000. http://siteresources.worldbank.org/EXTINSPECTIONPANEL/Resources/CHINA-InvestigationReport.pdf.

– "Paraguay/Argentina: Reform Project for the Water and Telecommunication Sectors, SEGBA V Power Distribution Project (Yacyretá)." 1 March 2004. http://www.inspectionpanel.org.

– "Requests for Inspection, Request 16, China Western Poverty Reduction Project (1999), Investigation Report." 28 April 2000. http://siteresources.worldbank.org/EXTINSPECTIONPANEL/Resources/CHINA-InvestigationReport.pdf.

– "A Staff Guide to the World Bank Inspection Panel." Brochure. 2006. http://siteresources.worldbank.org/EXTINSPECTIONPANEL/Resources/StaffBrochure.PDF.

Zia-Zarifi, Saman. "The (Lack of) Responsibility of Multinational Oil Companies in the Proposed Chad-Cameroon Pipeline Project." In Serge A. Bronkhorst, ed., *Liability for Environmental Damage and the World Bank's Chad-Cameroon Oil and Pipeline Project*, 42–53. Selected papers from the Netherlands Committee and International Union for Conservation of Nature (NC-IUCN) symposium, held at the Netherlands Institute of International Relations (or Clingendael), the Hague, 25 February 2000. Amsterdam: Netherlands Committee for IUCN, 2000.

Index